ABOUT THE AUTHOR

Frances Meenan, B. Comm., MBS (NUI), Solicitor, has specialised in Irish employment law for the last number of years. She is a consultant and examiner in Labour Law for the Professional Course in the Law Society of Ireland. She has co-authored a textbook on Irish employment equality law, has edited a book of international conference papers and has published numerous articles on Irish and European employment law. She is in private practice in Dublin and has considerable experience of representing parties before the adjudicating bodies and the courts on employment matters.

WORKING WITHIN THE LAW

A Practical Guide for Employers and Employees

Second Edition

Frances Meenan

Foreword by
The Honourable Mr Justice Hugh Geoghegan

Oak Tree Press
Dublin

Oak Tree Press
Merrion Building
Lower Merrion Street
Dublin 2, Ireland
http://www.oaktreepress.com

A catalogue record of this book is
available from the British Library.

Second Edition
ISBN 1 86076 073 2

Printed in Britain by MPG Books, Bodmin, Cornwall

FOREWORD

I had the honour of writing the Foreword to the first edition of this book. Having opined that it would be immediately useful to both layman and lawyer, I looked forward "to the success of this book and to future editions of it in due course".

Happily, my prediction has come to pass. Frances Meenan's work has been much in demand and now a new edition is called for.

Employment law, like Family law, is dynamic. It is constantly changing and developing. My earlier words were written in May 1994. But as is clear from the author's introduction, many developments in terms of Statute Law, Case Law and European Community Law have occurred since then. Sexual harassment at work and indirect sex discrimination are two topics, taken at random, which are still in the process of legal development. The Employment Equality Act, 1998, when in force, could turn out to be a legal minefield.

I have little doubt that when another few years have passed, there will be a third edition. Some kind of statutory protection of the one-man sub-contractor in the building trade may well be in the offing. The conferring of work permits for the benefit of aliens pending the processing of their asylum applications may also require legislative intervention.

Working within the Law is not intended to be an academic textbook. It is intended to be intelligible to employers and employees but this does not mean that it is not of great value to practising lawyers, especially as a reference work.

In recent times, a special worry for school and hospital employers, in particular, is the sexual abuse allegation. The Protections for Persons Reporting Child Abuse Act, 1998, which came into force as recently as 23 January 1999, is fully explained in this second edition.

Without derogating from the value of any other part of this excellent book, a special word of commendation is appropriate for the section on unfair dismissal. This may well be the topic more than any other to which the interested employee will have recourse.

My earlier recommendation of Frances Meenan's book is heartily renewed in the light of this splendid second edition.

Hugh Geoghegan
Four Courts
Dublin
6 September 1999

For my Mother and
In memory of my Father

CONTENTS

SECTION ONE
RECRUITMENT AND THE CONTRACT OF EMPLOYMENT

SECTION TWO
TERMS AND CONDITIONS OF EMPLOYMENT

SECTION THREE
TERMINATION OF EMPLOYMENT

SECTION FOUR
INDUSTRIAL RELATIONS AND ADJUDICATING BODIES

ACKNOWLEDGEMENTS

My father would have been somewhat bemused that this book reached a second edition. Unhappily, he did not live to see it. A good father, gentleman, talented physician, gifted writer and historian, this is but a small tribute to his memory.

I am indebted to Mr Justice Hugh Geoghegan for so kindly agreeing to write the Foreword and for his kind words. I would also like to thanks so many other people for their assistance, including the Chairman and Staff of the Employment Appeals Tribunal, the Registrar of the Labour Court, the Director and Staff of the Equality Service, Keara Donnelly, BL, Patrick McCann, BL, Dr Eugene McCarthy, Helen Meenan, Solicitor, Jean Monnet Chair of EC Law, Kingston University, England, Charles Meenan, SC, Ruth O'Connor, Solicitor, Kevin O'Kelly of the European Foundation for the Improvement of Living and Working Conditions, Dr Albert Power, Solicitor.

Enormous gratitude is owed to Margaret Byrne of the Law Society Library and her staff who are always particularly helpful in providing sources of information, especially at very short notice. I would like to thank Brian O'Kane and Brian Langan of Oak Tree Press for all their editorial assistance in the preparation of this book and for their forbearance. Sheelagh El Harbi is deserving of my gratitude for her enormous assistance in the final preparation of the book.

Nobody can write a book in isolation without the constant encouragement of their family. I am particularly fortunate in family and I would particularly like to thank my mother, Charles, Anita, John and Helen for all their kindness and encouragement.

Finally, all responsibility lies with me.

TABLE OF CASES

TABLE OF STATUTES

STATUTORY INSTRUMENTS

EUROPEAN COMMUNITIES LEGISLATION

STATUTES OF THE PARLIAMENT OF THE UNITED KINGDOM

BILLS

INTRODUCTION

Over thirty years has now passed since the first major piece of Irish employment protection legislation, the Redundancy Payments Act, 1967, came into operation. The subsequent decade witnessed a major growth in other legislation, which was influenced by our membership of the European Community and also by an awareness of the increasing need for employment protection. During the 1970s, legislation was passed for statutory minimum notice, written terms and conditions of employment, statutory holidays and public holidays (amending earlier legislation), statutory provision on the manner of the payment of wages, equal pay and equal treatment for men and women at work, amendments to the redundancy legislation and provision for redress for unfair dismissal.

The impetus for change was sustained up to the mid-1980s, with provision for statutory maternity leave, guaranteed payments for employees in cases of employer insolvency, reduction in the hourly threshold for cover under certain protection legislation and a broadening of the scope of the trade disputes legislation. During the second half of the 1980s, there were no developments of substance. In contrast, the early 1990s was a period of immense change for both individual employment and industrial relations legislation, providing protection for regular part-time employees and new legislation and procedures in respect of the payment of wages. After many years of debate, the Edwardian Trade Disputes Act, 1906 (as amended by the Trade Disputes (Amendment) Act, 1982) was repealed, which led to the Industrial Relations Act, 1990. That latter Act also amends Ireland's industrial relations procedures as contained in the Industrial Relations Act, 1946 (as amended).

The year 1993 saw the coming into effect of the Unfair Dismissals (Amendment) Act on 1 October. Since the publication of the first edition of this book in June 1994, every year has witnessed major new legislation, in the main arising from European Community Directives: 1994 saw the Terms of Employment (Information) Act and the Maternity Protection Act; 1995, the Adoptive Leave Act; 1996, the Protection of Young Persons (Employment) Act, the Transnational Information and Consultation of Employees Act, and the Protection of Employment Order, 1996 (S.I. No. 370 of 1996), which provided for certain procedural requirements that an employer must follow in the event of collective redundancies; 1997, the Organisation of Working Time Act; 1998, the Employment Equality Act and the Parental Leave Act. Much of this legislation repeals and updates earlier legislation and brings EC/EU Directives into effect in Ireland.

The Minister for Justice, Equality and Law Reform originally announced that the Employment Equality Act, 1998, would come into operation on 1 September 1999; however, the date is now understood to be 18 October 1999. Hence, the current legislation had to be carried alongside the new legislation. More detail is provided on the new legislation, however.

The last five years has seen major legislative developments as well as key developments in case law on trade disputes, providing us with judicial interpretation of the Industrial Relations Act, 1990, and of course the rise in the number of applications to the courts in respect of the termination of the contract of employment. A period of consolidation and adjustment is needed so that both employer and employee are comfortable with the interpretation and application of all the new legislation. No doubt we will see interesting case law in respect of the employment equality legislation over the coming few years.

The purpose of this book is to encapsulate key employment law into a single text so that the reader will understand the contents of the legislation. Irish legislation has become increasingly complicated by the many different Acts with subsequent amendments, as well as by the fact that each group of Acts has different claims procedures. As an aid, the book contains various samples of statutory and non-statutory forms.

Working within the Law is for a universal audience — employers, employees, lawyers, industrial relations practitioners and students. To provide a total picture of the employment relationship, the book is divided into four sections: Recruitment and the Contract of Employment, Terms and Conditions of Employment, Termination of Employment, and Practice and Procedure. The first three sections set out the law and legislation and the final section explains in detail the practice and procedure under each piece of legislation

"The chief source of the law is the people" (Cicero, *De Legibus*); hence, it is my belief that the law, as it affects our working lives, should be demystified and made accessible to everybody.

I hope this book plays some part in that process.

Frances Meenan
August 1999

SECTION ONE

RECRUITMENT AND THE CONTRACT OF EMPLOYMENT

Chapter One

RECRUITMENT AND EQUALITY

At the time of going to press, the Employment Equality Act, 1998, was due to come into operation in mid-October 1999, thereby repealing the Anti-Discrimination (Pay) Act, 1974, and the Employment Equality Act, 1977. The new legislation re-enacts into Irish law the provisions of EC Directives 75/117/EEC and 76/207/EEC which provided for equal pay and equal treatment between men and women. The 1977 Act also provided for equal treatment on grounds of marital status.

As the Act should commence in mid-October 1999, the full provisions of the 1977 and 1974 Acts will not be referred to here. Instead, reference to the 1998 Act will be made, but it will be stated where the provisions are the same. Case law decided under the 1977 and 1974 Acts will be referred to where applicable under the 1998 Act.

The Employment Equality Act, 1998 provides for nine grounds of discrimination, to include gender, marital status, family status, sexual orientation, religion, age, disability, race and membership of the travelling community. Discrimination will be taken to have occurred where one person is treated less favourably than another is, has been or would be treated, on one of these grounds — where, for example, one person is a woman and the other is a man; they are of a different marital status; they are of different ages (i.e., between the ages of 18 and 65 — other than for vocational training) and so on. This is, of course, subject to various defences and exclusions. This Act will apply to employment generally (as well as to vocational training). Chapter 9 considers equality between women and men and Chapter 10 considers equality on other grounds where the various definitions are considered in more detail.

GENERAL PROVISIONS OF THE 1998 ACT

Section 8 of the 1998 Act provides that an employer shall not discriminate against an employee or a prospective employee and a provider of agency work shall not discriminate against an agency worker in relation to access to employment, conditions of employment, training or experience for or in relation to employment, promotion or regrading or classification of posts. All the discriminatory grounds shall apply to such discrimination.

There are certain exemptions in relation to the general provisions that are important in relation to access to employment. Section 6(3) of the Act provides that it shall not be deemed to be discrimination based on age where a person is treated more favourably or less favourably if the person is under 18 or over 65 years. Further, an employer may take positive measures to facilitate the integration into employment of persons over the age of 50, persons with a disability, or members of the travelling community. Further exclusions relate to employment in the Defence Forces, the Garda Síochána and in the prison service.

An employer shall be taken to discriminate against an employee or a prospective employee in relation to access to employment if the employer discriminates against the employee or prospective employee:

1. In any arrangements the employer makes for the purpose of deciding to whom employment should be offered; or

2. By specifying, in respect of one person or class of persons, entry requirements for employment which are not specified in respect of other persons or classes of person where the circumstances in which both persons (or classes of person) would be employed are not materially different.

An employer shall be taken to discriminate against an employee or prospective employee if, on any of the discriminatory grounds, the employer does not offer or afford to that employee or prospective employee the same terms of employment (other than remuneration and pension rights), the same working conditions and the same treatment in relation to overtime, shift work, short-time, transfers, lay-offs, redundancies, dismissals and disciplinary measures, as they offer or afford to another person or class of persons where the circumstances in which they would be employed are not materially different.

EQUAL TREATMENT

The 1998 Act provides that there cannot be less favourable treatment on the nine discriminatory grounds; this is known as direct discrimination. For example, a married woman cannot be asked during an interview about childminding arrangements, nor can a person be queried during an interview about their place of worship or whether they think they are too elderly for the job. Part III of the Act provides for specific provisions on equality between women and men. It provides for an equality clause relating to gender issues (see Chapter 9).

Indirect discrimination is more complex. Equality and the gender ground are considered first. Section 22(1) of the 1998 Act provides:

> Where a provision (whether in the nature of a requirement, practice or otherwise) which relates to any of the matters specified in paragraphs (a) to (e) of Section 8(1) [access to employment, etc.] or to membership of a regulatory body:
>
> (a)   applies to both A and B,
>
> (b)   is such that the proportion of persons who are disadvantaged by the provision is substantially higher in the case of those of the same sex as A than in the case of those of the same sex as B, and
>
> (c)   cannot be justified by objective factors unrelated to A's sex,
>
> then, for the purposes of this Act, A's employer or, as the case may be, the regulatory body, shall be regarded as discriminating against A on the gender ground contrary to section 8 or, as the case may require, section 13.

With this definition, the Act attempts to simplify the definition of indirect discrimination as compared with its definition in the 1977 Act. It should be noted that those described as "disadvantaged" in section 22(1)(b) are not only those disadvantaged by sex but also by reference to their marital status or family status (e.g., married women or single mothers).

In short, an employer cannot put a non-essential barrier to a job that would discriminate. Examples of indirect discrimination could be a requirement that a person had to be a member of a particular trade union (e.g. *Nathan* v *Bailey Gibson Ltd. and the Irish Print Union* [1996] ELR 114); or an upper age limit of 27 years, which would exclude many women from applying for the position because at that age they may still be at home rearing their families (although note age discrimination below).

The Supreme Court ruled in the case of *Nathan* v *Bailey Gibson Limited, the Irish Print Union* (see above) that indirect discrimination should now be considered within the light of the Equal Treatment Directive and ECJ case law. This has circumvented the strict provisions of the indirect discrimination provisions in the Employment Equality Act, 1977, and therefore it may be easier to bring claims in relation to discriminatory practices. It will still be applicable under the 1998 Act. In this specific case, Ms Nathan applied for a promotional position but it was custom and practice in the employment concerned that only a card-carrying member of the Irish Print Union could hold such a job. However the Union itself had strict rules before a union card was granted; namely, that the job must first be advertised and that there was no suitable (unemployed) IPU member applicant for the position. The company requested the IPU to issue such a card but this was refused. The Union and its unemployed members were practically all men — at the time there were 2,337 male and 283 female members — but it maintained that it did not discriminate. The Supreme Court concluded that section 2(c) of the 1977 Act referred to direct rather than indirect discrimination.

The Chief Justice (at p. 128) said:

> in such a case the worker is not required, in the first instance, to provide a causal connection between the practice complained of and the sex of the complainant. It is sufficient for him or her to show that the practice complained of bears significantly more heavily on members of the complainant sex than on members of the other sex. At that stage, the complainant has established a *prima facie* case of discrimination and the onus of proof shifts to the employer to show that the practice complained of is based on objectively verifiable factors which have no relation to the Plaintiff's [complainant's] sex.

In short, a prospective employee has to show that the practice complained of bears significantly more heavily on their own sex than on members of the other sex and then it is up to the employer to show otherwise. In *Conlan* v *University of Limerick and the Minister for Enterprise, Trade and Employment* ([1999] ELR 155) the principles of the *Nathan* case were followed and it was held that the requirements stipulated for a university position as Professor of Law were essential requirements. Such essential requirements were "a higher law degree", "several years' experience at a senior academic level" and "a leading published researcher in a specialist field of law". Dr Conlan complained that there was discrimination against women because there were very few women in such academic posts. However, the University fulfilled the onus of proof and it was concluded that these were essential requirements, which had no connection with the sex of the applicant.

Indirect discrimination in respect of the other grounds shall now be considered. Section 31(1) provides:

> Where a provision (whether in the nature of a requirement, practice or otherwise) relating to employment:
>
> (a) Applies to all the employees or prospective employees of a particular employer who include C and D or, as the case may be, to a particular class of those employees or prospective employees which includes C and D,
>
> (b) Operates to the disadvantage of C, as compared with D, in relation to any of the matters specified in paragraphs (a) to (e) of section 8(1),
>
> (c) In practice can be complied with by a substantially smaller proportion of the employees or prospective employees having the same relevant characteristic as C when compared with the employees or prospective employees having the same relevant characteristic as D, and
>
> (d) Cannot be justified as being reasonable in all the circumstances of the case,
>
> then, subject to subsections (4) and (5), for the purposes of this Act the employer shall be regarded as discriminating against C, contrary to section 8 [access to employment, etc.], on whichever of the discriminatory grounds gives rise to the relevant characteristics referred to in paragraph (c).

Again this definition is complicated. "C" and "D" are two employees, prospective employees or a class of employees/prospective employees. "C" and "D" can be compared with each other on the basis of age (i.e. they are of different ages), have different religious beliefs or one has a religious belief and the other has none, and so on. Hence, putting it simply, there cannot be any requirements or procedures which indirectly discriminate. Examples would be having an artificially high requirement for written or spoken English which is not required to carry out the job, which could lead to race discrimination; a non-essential requirement that people work on a Saturday, which could preclude from employment persons of the Jewish faith.

Regulatory bodies (trade unions, a professional or trade organisation or professional body which controls entry to, or the carrying on of a profession, vocation or occupation) shall not discriminate directly or indirectly in respect of membership or access to the profession or occupation (other than in respect of pension rights).

QUOTAS

Neither the 1977 Act nor the 1998 Act provide for rigid numerical quotas. The 1977 Act did provide that special training may be provided for in employment where a particular sex is under-represented in the previous year or to encourage members of the under-represented sex to take opportunities for doing such work, but this is quite significantly different to having quotas in employment.

In the case of *Kalanke* v *Freie Hansestadt Bremen* ([1995] IRLR 660), Mr Kalanke, a landscape designer, was denied the position of head of one of Bremen's "green area" departments. The female applicant, who was equally well qualified, was appointed to the position, as women were under-represented in such positions; the Land of Bremen had a regulation giving priority to women in such circumstances. The key question was whether this contravened Articles 2(1) and 4 of the Equal Treatment Directive (76/207/EEC). The Court considered that the Bremen law exceeded what was permitted by Article 2(4). In summary, the ECJ held that national rules that guarantee women absolute and unconditional priority for appointment and promotion go beyond promoting equal opportunities. This outlawed automatic quotas but it did leave an air of uncertainty, which *Marschall* (see below) has apparently cleared up.

Arising from *Kalanke*, the Commission issued a Communication for clarification of the meaning of Article 2(4), which is replaced by the following:

> This Directive shall be without prejudice to measures to promote equal opportunity for men and women, in particular by removing existing inequalities which affect the opportunities of the under-represented sex. . . . Possible measures shall include the giving of preference, as regards access to employment or promotion, to a member of the under-represented sex, provided that such measures do not preclude the assessment of the particular circumstances of an individual case.

The area of positive discrimination is worthy of note and particular reference is made to the European Court judgment in *Marschall* v *Land Nordrhein-Westfalen* ([1998] IRLR 39) in which a tenured teacher sought promotion in a comprehensive school. The civil service law of the Land of North-Rhine-Westphalia provided that:

> . . . where there are fewer women than men in the particular higher grade post in the career bracket, women are to be given priority for promotion in the event of equal suitability, competence and professional performance, unless reasons specific to an individual [male] candidate tilt the balance in his favour.

Mr Marschall was informed that since fewer women than men were employed in the relevant pay and career bracket, an equally qualified woman was to be appointed to the position. Mr Marschall challenged the decision in the Administrative Court, which observed that the regulation seemed to discriminate in favour of women and stayed the proceedings pending an Opinion from the European Court of Justice. The ECJ found that, because of deep-seated prejudice, men tend to be chosen for jobs ahead of women when they have equal qualifications. This arises from fears that women will interrupt their careers more often and that, owing to family and household duties, they will be less flexible in their working hours, or that they will be absent more from work because of childbirth, pregnancy or breastfeeding. The Court stated that the mere fact that a male and a female candidate are equally qualified does not mean they have the same chances. Accordingly, such a regulation may help to reduce actual instances of inequality as long as automatic priority over men is precluded. Therefore, as such a rule does not guarantee absolute and unconditional priority for women, it does not go beyond the limits of Article 2(4), unlike the rules at issue in the *Kalanke* case.

In summary, there may be "positive discrimination" as long as it is for the purposes of redressing an imbalance, there is no automatic preference or quota and the assessment of candidates is based on objective and fair criteria.

FORMS OF RECRUITMENT

When a vacancy occurs, the employer should draw up a job specification detailing the qualifications required for the position. All current employees, both male and female, should first be considered for the position, and the employer should explore the feasibility of various forms of work arrangement, such as job-sharing, part-time work or working from home, if appropriate. Each would make the position available to a greater number of employees, and provide for flexibility, if required.

Once the employer has decided what the job requirements are, the best and most equitable form of recruitment should be considered. Initially it may be through internal recruitment by advising staff of the vacancy on the company notice board and (if necessary) subsequent advertising in newspapers or through an employment agency. "Head-hunting" may be appropriate for certain vacancies; however, it may leave an employer open to allegations of discrimination.

No matter what recruitment method the employer uses, the most suitable person for the position must be found without resorting to any form of discrimination in the search.

Whilst not claims under the Employment Equality Act, 1977, the cases *of Gilheaney* v *The Revenue Commissioners* and *Meehan* v *The Revenue Commissioners* ([1998] 4 IR 150) (where the facts of both cases were similar) are worth noting, as the reasoning in these cases could possibly constitute "grounds other than sex", in the event of a similar set of circumstances happening again. In these cases, the applicants were civil servants at Executive Officer grade and employed as officers under the Civil Service Regulation Act, 1956. Mr Gilheany had applied for the position of press officer, which was also at the Higher Executive Officer grade, while Mr Meehan had applied for the position of training officer. Mr Gilheany was placed on a panel of successful candidates from which the position would be filled. When a vacancy arose, Mr Gilheany was the next person for promotion but a decision was taken not to fill the post from the panel but by way of lateral transfer of Dublin-based Higher Executive Officers. He therefore was not eligible. Mr Gilheany considered that this was invalid and sought a High Court order of *certiorari*, whereby he requested the High Court to quash this decision and issue a declaration that the Revenue Commissioners were obliged to appoint him to the position. Costello P refused the application on the basis (*inter alia*) that the applicant had no contractual right to the position and that he did not have an actionable "legitimate expectation" to the disputed promotion. Furthermore, the decision of the Revenue to fill the vacancy by way of lateral transfer rather than from the panel was reasonable in view of the Revenue's obligation under the government decentralisation programme and the inter-departmental promotion scheme.

ADVERTISING

Discriminatory advertising is prohibited, whether intentional or where such an intention may be indicated. This includes newspaper, radio and television advertisements, as well as advertisements within a firm — notice boards or newsletters, for example. Advertisements cannot define or describe a position on the basis of sex, and if the job was previously carried out by one sex, it must be made clear that the job is now open to both.

The 1998 Act encompasses the wider grounds of discrimination. Thus, an advertisement is discriminatory not only if it discriminates on the grounds of the sex of the individual, but also with regard to an individual having a particularly relevant characteristic in relation to any of the other grounds of discrimination, or if the advertisement is descriptive of a post or occupation previously held or carried out by a member of one sex or by individuals having the characteristic. Unless such an advertisement indicates a contrary intention, the advertisement shall be taken to be an indication to discriminate.

If the employer is advertising the position internally, the same equality rules apply and a statement that the position is open to both male and female candidates, married and single is required. It is an offence under the 1998 Act to make a statement knowing it to be false in such a publication or display; such an offence carries a considerable fine (see Chapter 24).

Examples of discriminatory advertising include "female supervisor" in a health and fitness clinic (*Cork Examiner Publications Ltd., Fitzsimons Flynn & Co. and An Employer* v *The Employment Equality Agency* EE 13/1990). In this case, the equality officer recommended that a notice be published on the appointments pages of the *Cork Examiner* once every week for a period of four weeks, drawing the attention of employers to the 1977 Act and stating that certain sections of the Act in relation to occupational qualifications had been repealed (i.e. there was provision that certain establishments were excluded because persons of one sex required special care on the grounds of decency and privacy).

In another case, a company was looking for full-time and part-time store detectives in ladies' fashion stores. The advertisement stated that "this position may be of particular interest to married women" (*Independent Newspapers Ltd., Group 4 Securitas Ireland Ltd.* v *The Employment Equality Agency* EE 19/1991 DDE 1/1993). This advertisement was considered discriminatory and the Labour Court determined that Independent Newspapers publish four times a banner on the top of their recruitment page, stating: "All positions advertised on this page are required to be open to male and female candidates"; and another advertisement stating: "In accordance with the Employment Equality Act, 1977, *The Irish Independent* is committed to ensuring that recruitment advertisements do not give the impression of a preference for candidates of one sex or marital status rather than the other". The company placing the advertisement had to contribute £500 towards the cost of the latter advertisement.

The 1998 Act provides for a fine on summary conviction of up to £1,500 and/or one year's imprisonment, or on conviction on indictment to a fine not exceeding £25,000 or to imprisonment for a term not exceeding two years or both.

Employers also cannot discriminate in terms of education requirements for a job. In one particular case, a certain certificate was required, which a female candidate did not have, though she did have a higher one. Women had been excluded from that particular training course which the employer required. This was considered to be discriminatory (*Landy* v *CERT Ltd.* EE 20/1983 DEE 2/1984).

Arising from the new legislation, employers would be well advised to advertise through the medium that will attract the widest possible audience — for example, national newspapers — although it would be generally reasonable to advertise in a provincial newspaper. Whilst this may well be more costly, employers cannot then be accused of being deliberately selective in their advertising; for example, an employer could well be exposed to allegations of religious discrimination if the job was advertised in a catholic parish magazine. If pictures/ photographs are used, they should reflect diversity and if the employer is registered with Rehab, it should show the logo "Positive to Disability".

Again, the equality legislation not only applies to the prospective employer placing the advertisement, but also to the publisher (e.g. newspaper) and advertising agency. If the employer is advertising the position internally, the same equality rules apply and a statement that the position is open to all qualified persons is required.

Under the 1998 Act, the Circuit or High Court may, on the application of the Equality Authority, order that a person is not to be appointed to a position where there are grounds for believing that the advertisement may be in contravention of the Act, pending the decision of the Director of Equality Investigations or as the court otherwise (s. 10(5)) orders (see Chapter 24, "Employment Equality Claims").

EMPLOYMENT AGENCIES

Employment agencies and other employment-related services shall not discriminate on the terms on which they offer their services. This provision does not apply if the employer can lawfully refuse to offer employment (see below) and the agency or service relies on such a statement from the prospective employer. The 1998 Act provides for a fine on summary conviction of up to £1,500 and/or one year's imprisonment, or on conviction on indictment to a fine not exceeding £25,000 or to imprisonment for a term not exceeding two years or both.

The 1998 Act provides that it is lawful for an employment agency to provide services exclusively for persons with disabilities or any such group (e.g. Rehab).

EXCLUSIONS

The 1998 Act provides an exclusion for people working outside Ireland where there are laws and customs that only allow a person of one sex to do the duties concerned. Such an exception might arise in respect of women working in certain Middle Eastern countries.

There are also certain circumstances where a person's sex may be taken as a genuine occupational qualification, such as modelling, acting, the provision of personal services (e.g. nursing, though both men and women can train as midwives), the prison service and the Garda Síochána (where the duties of the post include "guarding, escorting or controlling violent persons, or quelling riots or violent disturbances" and so forth). This would also include the direct supervision of prisoners dressing and undressing, the carrying out of personal searches and the interviewing of persons in relation to sexual offences.

In addition, there may be differences in height requirements. There is also provision for recruitment being open to men or women when there are insufficient numbers of one sex in the Garda Síochána or prison service. Exclusions also apply where because of the nature of the employment it is necessary to provide sleeping and sanitary accommodation for employees on a communal basis and it would be unreasonable to expect the provision of separate accommodation.

There are also exclusions in respect of the other grounds of discrimination:

- No employer is required to recruit an individual to a position if the individual will not undertake the duties attached to that position or will not accept the conditions under which those duties are required to be performed or is not fully competent and available to undertake the duties attached to that position having regard to the conditions under which the duties are required to be performed.

- Persons with disabilities shall be regarded as fully competent to undertake any duties with the provision of special treatment or facilities. An employer shall do all that is reasonable to provide the treatment or facilities (see Chapter 10 and also Chapter 2 in respect of pre-employment medicals).

- No employer shall be obliged to recruit an individual if the employer is aware of a criminal conviction arising from any form of sexual behaviour which is unlawful, or possesses other reliable information that the individual engages in or has a propensity to engage in any such behaviour — in other words, the recruitment and ongoing employment of paedophiles or such persons.

- A religious, educational or medical institution that is under the direction or control of a body established for religious purposes or whose objectives include the provision of services in an environment which promotes certain religious values shall not be taken to discriminate against a person if it gives more favourable treatment on the religion ground to an employee or a prospective employee over another person where it is reasonable to do so to maintain the religious ethos of the institution, or it takes action which is reasonably necessary to prevent an employee or a prospective employee from undermining the religious ethos of the institution (e.g. a Roman Catholic school wishing to employ a Roman Catholic teacher).

The Supreme Court, in *Campaign to Separate Church and State in Ireland Ltd. and Others* v *The Minister for Education, the Attorney General, The Most Reverend Cathal Daly and Others* ([1998] 3 IR 321), considered whether the payment of salaries to chaplains in community schools out of public funds was in breach of Article 44.2.2° of the Constitution of Ireland which provides: "The State guarantees not to endow any religion." In summary, the Supreme Court held that this Article was not designed to render the payment of monies to a denominational school for educational purposes unlawful. Article 44.2.2° must be read within the context of Article 42.2, which contemplated children receiving religious education in schools recognised or established by the State but in accordance with the wishes of the parents. Parents have the right to have religious education provided in the school their child attends and are not obliged to settle merely for religious instruction. Further, the system of salaried chaplains must be available to all community schools of whatever denomination on an equal basis in accordance with their needs and it would be constitutionally impermissible for a chaplain to instruct a child in a religion other than its own without the knowledge and consent of its parents.

• The only ground of discrimination that is applicable to employment for the purposes of a private household is the sex ground, hence a private household will not be liable for alleged discrimination on any other ground.

• It shall not be discriminatory on the age ground to set in relation to any job a maximum age for recruitment which takes into account the cost and time of training and the time period prior to retirement age when the employee will be effective in the job.

• There may be provisions relating to residence, citizenship and proficiency in the Irish language in respect of the holding of an office in the Civil Service, the Garda Síochána, the Defence Forces, a local authority, a harbour authority, a health board or vocational education committee, or as a teacher in a primary or post-primary school. There is no prohibition on having various educational or vocational requirements and the various professional or vocational bodies may require a person to have the appropriate qualification. These provisions will not allow any discrimination on the grounds of sex.

A group of employees in Wales considered that they were refused employment as house assistants in a residential home because they did not speak Welsh. They brought their claim to an industrial tribunal under the Race Relations Act, 1976. The UK EAT held that the local authority were not in breach of the Act, but even if they had been, the requirement that the applicants speak Welsh was justifiable (*Gwynedd County Council* v *Jones and Another* [1986] ICR 833, and see Chapter 10). This case is interesting, because such issues could arise in Gaeltacht areas where applicants for jobs may not speak Irish but it may be a reasonable requirement for the job.

JOB TITLE

The 1977 and 1998 Acts also provide that if there is a job description or job title which implies that the applicant should be of a particular sex, or that in the past the job was mainly carried out by a person of one sex — for example, a foreman or "head waiter/manager", (*Inde-*

pendent Newspapers (Ireland) Ltd. and Irish Banqueting Services Ltd. v *Employment Equality Agency* EE 17/1991 DEE 3/1993) — then the advertisement should contain a statement that the position is open to both sexes.

The 1998 Act also provides that any such reference in relation to the description of the post would also refer to characteristics in relation to any other grounds of discrimination.

APPLICATION FORMS

If application forms are used by an employer, all prospective employees who ask for a form should receive one. It is important that an employer briefs all staff who are in contact with prospective candidates on equality requirements; for example, a prospective candidate who telephones should not be told "the company is looking for men for this job" or "the job is only for Irish people" or "it is only for locals" or "foreigners would not get on too well here". The form should not contain questions which are discriminatory or which could give rise to discrimination; for example, asking the prospective employee whether he or she is married or single or how many children he or she has (*Barrington* v *The Medical Council* EE 9/1988).

Technically, it may be lawful to ask these questions on an application form, but one must consider whether the questions are necessary in order to find the best person for the position. By asking these questions, employers may be unnecessarily exposing themselves to claims of discrimination. Details of marital status and numbers of children are only appropriate when a candidate has accepted the job offer and the information is needed for pension/life assurance purposes.

Application forms are not to be recommended, as there is a very real risk that in asking questions to elicit information, employers may be exposed to asking for unnecessary information. Many application forms require applicants to attach a photograph of themselves; however, such a procedure may well expose the employer to allegations that there is discrimination on grounds of race, religion, age or disability in the recruitment process.

Curriculum Vitae

Requiring applicants to send a curriculum vitae is by far the most preferred method of job application. Applicants often voluntarily provide employers with a large amount of information using this method, such as marital status, religion (by the school they went to), date of birth and perhaps an indication of their politics by their extra-curricular activities. However, in time, prospective employees will be including less and less personal detail in their curriculum vitae.

INTERVIEWS

There have been several cases relating to access to employment and selection arrangements. The first key case was that of *Chaney* v *University College Dublin* (EE 15/1983), where the claimant alleged that the prospective employer had refused her access to employment because she was married and had children. She maintained that she had been asked at the interview how many children she had and how she proposed to have them cared for. Apparently, these questions were not asked of the male candidates, and it was considered that the questions were reasonable only if asked of both male and female candidates. In some situations, it may be quite permissible for a prospective employer to find out if a candidate is married; for example, if the surname on the application is different from that on professional certificates (*Tuite* v *The Coombe Lying-in Hospital* EE 17/1985). However, certain questions — such as "How will you be able to cope with being a housewife and working?"; or "What does your husband think about you working and studying?" (in relation to postgraduate study); or "Are you thinking of getting married?"; or "Do you intend having children?" — would be considered to be discriminatory on the basis of sex and marital status, as the case may be.

The noting of the claimant's marital status was considered proof that discriminatory questions were asked at interview, as there were no similar notes of other candidates (*Phelan* v *Michael Stein Travel* [1999] ELR 58).

Under the UK Race Relations Act, 1976, the UK Court of Appeal said that to prove discrimination, the claimant had to show that an employer's decision was made on the grounds of colour, race, nationality, or ethnic or national origins, and not merely that the decision was made on the basis of personal characteristics which might be associated with a particular racial group. In *Perera* v *Civil Service Commission and Another (No. 2)* ([1988] ICR 428), the claimant was a 42-year-old qualified advocate from Sri Lanka who came to England in 1973. He became an Executive Officer in the Civil Service and was called to the English Bar. In 1977 he applied for the position of legal assistant in the Civil Service. He was interviewed and assessed as unsuitable by the interview board. He considered he was discriminated against under the Race Relations Act, 1976, by taking into account factors relating to experience in the UK, command of English, British nationality and age. It was held that he was not discriminated against.

Words or acts of discouragement could constitute less favourable treatment, but where the questions could be asked of any candidate, they may not be discriminatory. In *Simon* v *Brimham Associates* ([1987] ICR 586), the claimant attended for a job interview with the respondents, a firm of employment consultants. When he refused to discuss his religion, the interviewer conceded that he did not have to do so, but explained, without knowing whether or not the claimant was Jewish, that the job was with an Arab company and that if he was of the Jewish faith it could preclude his selection. The claimant, who was Jewish, terminated the interview and brought a claim under the UK Race Relations Act, 1976, on the basis of race discrimination. This Court of Appeal judgement may have been surprising, but if faced with such facts in Ireland, based on the various sex discrimination cases, such questions could well be discriminatory.

Of course, it is perfectly reasonable for an employer to assess whether a prospective employee will be able to carry out their job duties. At interview, therefore, the job and its requirements should be fully explained and all the candidates asked whether they believe they would have any difficulty in doing the job, obviously after a period of appropriate training. All candidates should also be asked if there is anything else that they wish to add to the interview or say to their prospective employer. If there are further selection tests, it should be ensured that they are also free of discriminatory bias.

If interviewing persons where there is a presumption that their Sabbath is on a Friday/Saturday, there should not be any automatic assumption that they will be unavailable to work on those days. To avoid a potential claim for indirect discrimination, the employer should have sensible business reasons for hours of work.

In the UK case of *O'Driscoll* v *The Post Office* (Case No. 25671/89, noted in Bourne and Whitmore, 1997, p. 140), the interviewer asked an Irish applicant "Do you have a problem with the drink over here?"

— meaning, he claimed, "Is the Guinness as good?" The applicant, who understood the question as arising from the common stereotype of the Irish as being prone to drink problems, was awarded £600 for injury to feelings, because the question gave the impression of racial stereotyping and could have resulted in a poorer subsequent interview performance.

Employers should ensure that they keep the notes of the interview for at least 12 months following a letter to an unsuccessful candidate, and the notes for a successful candidate should be placed in their personnel file. A person has six months within which to bring a claim under the Employment Equality Act. The time limit may be extended where a person has "reasonable cause" for the delay (see Chapter 24, "Employment Equality Claims" and note the extended provisions in the 1998 Act).

"MARRIAGE BAR"

Prior to the early 1970s, in many employments, especially in the public service, women had to resign on marriage. In *Aer Lingus Teo* v *The Labour Court* ([1990] ELR 125), the Supreme Court considered that the compulsory retirement of 24 air hostesses (the complainants) was a discriminatory act relating to marital status, but it was not illegal. This case concerned the subsequent re-employment of these air hostesses on first a temporary, then permanent basis, in the mid-1980s, though all their previous service would not be considered for seniority purposes. The 1977 Act does not have a retrospective effect.

More recently, the "marriage bar" issue surfaced again, as women who had to resign on marriage wished to return to their previous job in the public service. In one particular case, the claimant, who had been employed as a Higher Tax Officer in the Revenue Commissioners, resigned on marriage in 1969. In 1973, the "marriage bar" was abolished and certain provisions permitted married women to be re-admitted to their jobs on grounds of hardship or if they became widowed. The claimant applied for reinstatement in January, 1990. She was advised that she could only be reinstated on grounds of hardship (for which she would have to show evidence of her circumstances) or if she was widowed. She brought a claim under the 1977 Act, and the Employment Equality Agency also made a complaint to the Minister for Finance on her behalf, alleging that the Minister procured discrimination by having such discriminatory rules for reinstatement. The equality officer considered that there was discrimination towards the claimant arising from her marital status. However, the equality officer's ruling of reinstatement was overturned. The Labour Court did not award her compensation, as it is not a case where compensation should be awarded to one claimant (*Moran* v *The Revenue Commissioners* DEE 5/1993; and *Employment Equality Agency* v *The Minister for Finance* EE 21/1991 [1993] ELR 129).

Section 11 of the Civil Service Regulation Act, 1956, as amended by section 4 of the Civil Service (Employment of Married Women) Act, 1973, was repealed by the Civil Service Regulation (Amendment) Act, 1996. The Civil Service Regulation Act, 1996, was enacted following the Labour Court determination in the above case (*Moran* v *the Revenue Commissioners* (DEE 5/1993)) in which the Labour Court stated that the Minister for Finance should at the earliest opportunity introduce the appropriate legislation to repeal the statutory provisions governing reinstatement.

The 1996 Act repealed the provisions in 1973 Act and the Minister announced that the next two series of clerical and executive officer competitions would compose special sub-panels of former civil servants. These individuals would be chosen without regard to their marital status or sex.

MOBILITY

An employer must not discriminate on the presumption that a woman would be less able to travel as part of the terms and conditions of employment. This could also apply on the age ground or indeed disability. In one particular case, the claimant considered that she had been discriminated against for the position of customer service agent. The employer had a condition of employment that employees must be mobile and be available for work both in Ireland and Great Britain. Interestingly, the equality officer accepted that the reason for her non-selection was that she was not able to comply with the mobility requirement, which the equality officer accepted to be an essential requirement of the job. Nonetheless, the equality officer considered that there had been discrimination at the job interview, and the claimant was awarded a small sum of compensation (*A Prospective Female Employee* v *A Company* EE 12/1989).

AGE

It is discriminatory to have certain age limits for positions. This issue has arisen in particular where married women wish to return to the workforce having raised their family. The key case on age limits was *North Western Health Board* v *Martyn* ([1987] IR 565), where the upper age limit of 27 years was considered to be discriminatory because the age was too low for many married women to re-enter the workforce, having fulfilled family responsibilities. Even though this decision was based on the actual facts of that particular case, the age limit requirement for such positions has now been raised.

The 1998 Act provides that an employer may not discriminate on grounds of age, although there may be exclusions as stated above (e.g. entry requirements for the employment concerned).

PREGNANCY

An employer may not refuse a prospective employee a position solely on the basis that she is pregnant. The European Court of Justice in the *Dekker* case (*Dekker* v *Stichting Vormingscentrum Voor Jong Volwassenen (VJW–Centrum) Plus* [1991] IRLR 27) considered that an employer is in direct contravention of the principle of equal treatment if they refuse to enter into a contract of employment with a candidate solely because of possible adverse consequences of employing a pregnant woman. In Ireland, prior to *Dekker*, it was considered to be indirect discrimination, since this obviously affects more women than men. In *Geraghty-Williams* v *An Foras Forbartha* (EE 6/1981 DEE 4/1982), the claimant was offered employment subject to a satisfactory medical report. The medical report stated that she was pregnant but otherwise in good health. The offer of employment was withdrawn. The Labour Court determined that the withdrawal of an offer of employment because the employee was pregnant was indirect discrimination. Also, the postponement of employment pending the completion of pregnancy was considered to be indirect discrimination (*Cassidy* v *Pan American Airways Inc.* EE 3/1989).

In another case, the claimant contended that she had been offered employment but when she told her prospective employer that she was expecting a baby within the next month, she was allegedly advised that the company could not guarantee her employment when the baby was born. There was considerable conflict of evidence in this case, but nonetheless the Labour Court considered that there was indirect discrimination and awarded the claimant £5,500, recommended that she be appointed to the next suitable vacancy in the branch concerned and that on reappointment her service be backdated to January 1988. The Labour Court reduced her financial award as, during the course of the proceedings, she had refused part-time work (*Power Supermarkets Ltd. t/a Quinnsworth* v *Long* EE 15/1991 DEE 2/1993).

PHYSICAL REQUIREMENTS

If there is a stipulation that a person must be of a particular height, it must clearly be an essential requirement for the job. In one case, CIE required that bus conductors should be at least 5'5" tall; the claimant, who was smaller than 5'5", claimed she had worked for a number of years as a bus conductor in the UK and that it did not affect her ability to do the job. The Labour Court considered that the requirement to be 5'5" was not an essential one (*Smith* v *CIE* EE 4/1979 DEE 1/1979). However, in another case, physical strength was considered an essential requirement for the position of fire-fighter (*Gibney* v *Dublin Corporation* EE 5/1986). As stated above, there may be specific requirements for the Garda Síochána and the prison service in relation to height requirements for men and women.

TERMS AND CONDITIONS

Terms on which employment is offered also cannot be discriminatory. For example, there have been situations where married women were indirectly discriminated against in respect of their access to full-time employment by a requirement that there be a lay-off period between part-time and full-time employment. In *Employment Equality Agency* v *Packard Electrical (Ireland) Ltd., the IT&GWU, and the AT&GWU* (EE 14/1985), female employees alleged that part-time employees on the twilight shift (mainly married women) were barred from entry to full-time employment. This practice arose from a clause in the union/ management agreement which provided that employees who had been laid off or made redundant from the twilight shift were not permitted to apply for full-time work with the company until a period of 26 weeks had elapsed from the date of redundancy. Furthermore, if such employees made application for full-time work, they would automatically be removed from the twilight shift recall list. The equality officer considered that this clause was not an essential requirement and that it was indirectly discriminatory against married women. The practice was to be discontinued immediately and the next 30 appointments for full-time positions (subject to suitability) were to be made from the twilight shift within three months from the date of recommendation.

The 1998 Act provides that an employer may have different terms and conditions for employees if it is genuinely based on their relative seniority or special treatment in the case of an employee with a disability.

PROCEDURE AND REDRESS

The 1998 Act provides for considerable changes in the procedures for bringing a discrimination claim, including a new provision for mediation, if the parties so wish, the office of Director of Investigations, the Labour Court, and appeals to the courts. There are also special procedures for equality claims based on gender, and new time limits and redress depending on whether the claim is under the gender ground or any of the other grounds of discrimination.

The 1998 Act provides a general right to "material information", which may give reasons for applying certain practices or procedures (s.76). However, where a person considers that they may have been discriminated against by, or in the course of an interview conducted on behalf of the Civil Service or Local Appointments Commissioners (other than recruitment or selection in respect of their own staff), the Minister for Defence (for the Defence Forces) or the Commissioners of the Garda Síochána (for the Garda Síochána), then "material information" (i.e. reason for non-appointment, etc.) will not include communications with external advisors or if it goes beyond the "permitted information". "Permitted information" is information which identifies the successful and unsuccessful candidates by reference to their sex, or the other eight discriminatory grounds. Hence, the prospective employer may only have to answer specific questions on the discriminatory grounds and not matters of security, for example.

It should be noted that where a person considers they have a claim against any of these bodies or persons, the claim in the first instance should be referred to the Commissioners, the Minister for Defence or the Commissioner of the Garda Síochána, as appropriate. This is dealt with in detail in Chapter 24, "Employment Equality Claims".

EQUAL STATUS BILL, 1999

This Bill was originally published on 5 February 1997 and provided for equality in the provision of services. This Bill was not enacted further to a full reference to the Supreme Court in June 1997, arising from the fact that there were sections in the Bill that had the same drafting as in the original Employment Equality Bill, which itself fell (*In the Matter of Article 26 of the Constitution of Ireland and In the Matter of the Equal Status Bill, 1997* [1997] ELR 185). The grounds of discrimination are the same as in the Employment Equality Act, 1998. The Bill was re-published on 15 April 1999. However, it is worth noting that the Equal Status Bill affected "firms" of partnerships (i.e. individuals who share in the capital and profits of the business). This form of business arrangement frequently applies to various professional groups — solicitors, doctors, accountants, veterinary surgeons, engineers and so forth. The Bill provided that the firm shall not discriminate in relation to:

(a)   The admission of a person as a partner or a member of the firm or the terms or conditions applicable to a partner or member of the firm;

(b)   The status of a partner or member of the firm in relation to the work done by the firm or the sharing in the capital and profits of the firm, or

(c)   The expulsion of a partner or member from the firm or any other sanctions against the partner or member.

This section is mentioned here because for some groups, discrimination in respect of partnerships is a form of "employment" discrimination. In other words, firms will have to be more transparent in their admission arrangements. There cannot be direct or indirect discrimination in respect of admission to partnerships and the grounds for decision for admission will now effectively be open for inspection.

General References

Bourn, C. and J. Whitmore (1997), *Anti-Discrimination Law in Britain*, 3rd edition, London: Sweet and Maxwell.

Callender, R. and F. Meenan (1994), *Equality in Law between Men and Women in the European Community: Collection of Texts and Commentary on Irish Law*, Martinus Nijhoff Publishers and Office for Official Publications of the European Communities.

Curtin, D. (1989), *Irish Employment Equality Law*, Dublin: The Round Hall Press.

Gunnigle, P., N. Heraty and M. Morley (1997), *Personnel and Human Resource Management: Theory and Practice in Ireland*, Dublin: Gill and Macmillan.

Hemming, J. (ed.) (1997), *Discrimination in the Workplace: A Practical Guide*, John Wiley and Sons Ltd.

Meenan, F. (1997), *Employment and Social Provisions of the Treaty of Amsterdam*, Dublin: Institute of European Affairs.

Chapter Two

THE CONTRACT OF EMPLOYMENT AND DATA PROTECTION

All employees work under a contract of employment, which in legal terms is called a contract of service. Frequently employees state that they "have no contract". What they are really saying is that they "have no *written* contract". A contract may be in writing or verbally agreed between the parties. There are many different forms of contract:

1. A written/oral contract providing ongoing employment;

2. A fixed-term contract (e.g. for one year or other specified period);

3. A specified purpose contract (e.g. to work on a specific project);

4. An independent contractor's agreement, which is not an employer/employee relationship (and is therefore not a contract of service but a contract for services).

It is always advisable to have a written contract or agreement between the parties. The Unfair Dismissals Acts, 1977 to 1993, contain particular requirements concerning fixed-term and specified purpose contracts which must be complied with if an employer seeks exclusion under that Act for unfair dismissal claims at the end of those contracts. These provisions are considered in Chapter 3, "Temporary and Part-time Employment".

Once the employer has made the decision to hire the successful candidate, a written offer of employment may be sent out. A contract of employment does not have to be long, complicated or very legalistic. It should set out in comprehensible language the key terms and conditions. The contract and agreement for employment only come into being once the contract has been accepted and signed by the employee. Obviously, a prospective employee does not have to accept the offer of employment and in the case of failure to do so, there is no employment contract between the parties. In other words, there must be offer and acceptance.

However, an employer can send out an offer of employment and then change their mind. It is extremely difficult for the employer to withdraw the offer at this time, yet it may be done if the employee has not accepted it. An employee who has accepted the contract would be entitled to the requisite notice period provided for in the contract should the employer wish to terminate the contract.

Before an offer of employment goes out, an employer should ask for the prospective employee's consent to check all relevant references (see below). If this is not feasible, the employer should only send out the contract of employment subject to a satisfactory medical examination and satisfactory references. It is recommended that an employer request that an employee undergo a general medical examination to determine that the employee is in good health. The employer may nominate the doctor and generally carries the cost of the examination. The doctor should be fully aware of the nature and requirements of the work concerned. If, for example, the prospective employee has a bad back and the job involves lifting heavy objects, the employer should be very cautious about hiring that person because this disability may cause problems later on in employment. It would then be arguable that any absenteeism arising from the condition would not be reason for a fair dismissal, as the employer was in full knowledge of the condition and that this issue is implied into the contract of employment (see Chapter 17, "Unfair Dismissal"). Should the potential employee be pregnant, this is not a sufficient reason for the employer to withdraw the offer of employment (see Chapter 1, "Recruitment and Equality").

However, any prospective employer must ensure compliance with the Employment Equality Act, 1998, in particular with the provisions that a person cannot be discriminated against in respect of their disability, which has a wide definition. In *"X" v Commission of the European Communities* ([1995] IRLR 320), X applied for work with the Commission as a typist. He did not pass the written test, but was invited to undergo a medical examination with a view to being employed for six months as a member of the Commission's temporary staff. During the course of the medical examination, X declined the suggestion that he should be screened for HIV antibodies. Blood tests were ordered and the medical officer concluded X was suffering from "full-blown AIDS". He was rejected for employment on the grounds that he was physically unfit. The Commission held that the compulsory HIV screening was abandoned in 1988. X brought a case before the Court of First Instance on grounds that he had been subjected to an AIDS screening test without his consent contrary to Article 8 of the European Convention on Human Rights. The Court of First Instance dismissed his application for an annulment of the decision not to employ him and for damages. On appeal, the ECJ annulled the decision of the Commission not to employ him but did not award damages. The Court stated that the right to respect for private life, embodied in Article 8 of the European Convention, is one of the fundamental rights protected by the legal order of the EU. It includes in particular a person's right to keep his state of health secret. It was accepted that the pre-recruitment medical examination serves a legitimate interest of the Community Institutions and if the person concerned, after being properly informed, withholds his consent to a test which the medical officer considers necessary in order to evaluate his suitability for the post, the Institutions cannot be obliged to take the risk of recruiting him. Nevertheless, that interest does not justify the carrying out of a test against the will of the person concerned.

A medical practitioner retained by a company to carry out pre-employment medical assessments is not under a duty of care to a job applicant in assessing suitability for employment, even though it is reasonably foreseeable that the applicant might suffer economic loss of the opportunity of employment. In *Kapfunde* v *Abbey National plc and Daniel* ([1998] IRLR 583), the plaintiff applied to Abbey National for a permanent post as cashier where she was already employed on a temporary basis. She completed the company's standard confidential medical questionnaire and disclosed that she suffered from an illness which resulted in absenteeism. She was sent to Dr Daniel for a pre-employment medical. On his advice, Abbey National rejected her application. She subsequently brought negligence proceedings against Abbey National and Dr Daniel for economic loss she suffered as a result of not getting the job, maintaining that the doctor owed her a duty of care in that he failed to exercise the skill and care to be expected of an occupational health physician and that he was a servant of the company. The Court of Appeal held that the doctor did not owe a duty of care to the plaintiff when she carried out an assessment of her medical history and recommended that she was not suitable for permanent employment because she was likely to have a higher than average absence level.

In some cases there may be a union/management agreement in place which sets out all the terms and conditions of employment. In that case, the offer letter may only have to state the job title, date of commencement and salary of the prospective employee concerned. Of course, a copy of the agreement should be sent with the offer letter. Alternatively, if there is a staff manual setting out all the terms and conditions of employment, the same situation may apply.

REFERENCES

There is no legal obligation on an employer to provide an employee, a former employee, a prospective employer or an employer with a written or oral reference. However, if an employer does provide a reference, it must be accurate as was considered in *Spring* v *Guardian Assurance plc and Others* ([1994] IRLR 460). His former employer was asked to give a reference and gave one as follows:

> Mr Spring held the position of Sales Manager until he was asked to leave in August of this year. His former superior has stated in writing that he was seen by some of the sales staff as a person who consistently kept the best leads for himself with little regard for the sales team that he was supposedly to manage; and his former superior has further stated that he is a man of little or no integrity and could not be regarded as honest . . .

Obviously the prospective employer decided to have no dealings with Mr Spring and he subsequently failed to secure appointments with two other insurance companies who received references on the same terms. Mr Spring sought damages from Guardian Assurance for economic loss (i.e., earnings which he would have had but for the reference). He claimed the reference was a malicious falsehood and/or negligent misstatement and/or breach of terms to be implied in his contract (that any reference given would be compiled with all reasonable care). The House of Lords held:

1. An employer who provides a reference concerning an employee or former employee to a prospective employer owes a duty of care to

the employee regarding the preparation of the reference and may be liable to the employee/former employee in damages for any economic loss suffered as a result of negligent misstatement.

2. The duty of the employer is to take reasonable care in compiling or giving a reference and in verifying the information on which it is based. If a reference is inaccurate, it is clearly foreseeable that the employee may be caused financial loss as a result of failing to obtain the new employment.

3. Even though there are the torts of defamation and injurious falsehood, the tort of negligence should be extended to protect the employee or former employee where the giver of a reference has acted unreasonably and carelessly; without an action for negligence, an employee may be left with no practical prospect of redress even though the reference may have permanently prevented him from obtaining employment in his chosen vocation.

4. The employee or former employee is not already adequately protected by the law of defamation as the employee would have to show malice in order to defeat the employer's defence of qualified privilege. Malice is very hard to prove, hence there is a disproportionate burden on the employee.

5. The recognition of the existence of a duty of care on the employer in relation to an employment reference does not undermine the law of defamation.

6. The imposition of a duty of care in the preparation of employment references is not prevented by the principle of public policy relating to the need for free and frank communication on relevant matters which underlies the defence of qualified privilege in the law of defamation.

7. An employee will have a remedy in negligence only if he established that the inaccurate reference was due to the employer's lack of care. There can of course be no action for negligence if the statement is true.

8. There are circumstances in which it is necessary to imply a term into the contract of employment that the employer will provide the employee with a reference at the request of the prospective employer, the reference to be prepared on careful inquiries which

an employer must make. This implied term refers to a class of employee where it is normal practice to require a reference from a previous employer before employment is offered and where the employment cannot be expected to enter that type or class of employment except on the basis that the former and the prospective employer, within a reasonable time after termination of employment, have a full and frank discussion.

In *Coote* v *Granada Hospitality Ltd* ([1998] IRLR 656), the European Court of Justice held that EC Directive 76/207/EEC, on the implementation of the principle of equal treatment for men and women, requires that Member States introduce into their national legal systems measures to ensure judicial protection for workers whose employer, after the employment relationship has ended, refuses to provide references as a reaction to legal proceedings brought to enforce compliance with the principle of equal treatment. Ms Coote brought a claim of sex discrimination, alleging dismissal because of pregnancy, which was subsequently settled. She sought employment through two employment agencies but she attributed her failure in finding employment to the fact that her former employer did not give her a reference. Whilst this case does not state that references have to be given, it does state that former employers cannot obstruct a dismissed employee's attempt to find new employment (see also Chapter 9, "Equality between Men and Women").

WORK PERMIT

The current labour shortage has resulted in a number of changes in the granting of work permits. Until recently, any non-European Economic Area (EEA) national (those who are not nationals of EU Member States together with Iceland, Norway and Liechtenstein) was required to apply for a work permit to the Department of Enterprise, Trade and Employment. Once issued, the permit is valid for one year and the employee must re-apply if they wish to continue to work.

However, the Department of Enterprise, Trade and Employment (following discussions with the Department of Justice, Equality and Law Reform) now advises that there are changes to work permit requirements in Ireland. There are now a number of categories of non-EU nationals who previously required work permits in order to take up employment in the State but now do not require such permits (Information Note, Department of Justice, Equality and Law Reform, 1 April 1999). They are as follows:

- Work permits are no longer required for persons who are posted for a maximum of four years for intra-corporate transfers, where the international company has a presence or proposes to establish a presence in Ireland.

- Persons who have been given permission to remain in the State because they are married to Irish nationals, or are a parent of an Irish citizen or have been given temporary leave to remain in the State on humanitarian grounds, having been in the asylum-seeking process. However, it is important to note that they have the permission of the Minister for Justice, Equality and Law Reform to remain in the State within the meaning of the Aliens Act, 1935, and the Aliens Order, 1946 to 1999.

- Persons sent to Ireland for training for a maximum period of three years, whether or not it entails work at an Irish-based company. Letters from the person's overseas employer and host will be required.

In respect of intra-corporate transfers, it will now be sufficient for the employee to have a letter from the employer stating that the individual has been sent on secondment to Ireland for a specific purpose and period of time. The Irish company to whom the employee has been seconded should send a confirming letter. Such letters must be original and must contain contact references should the Aliens Office need to find details.

It should be noted that a work permit does not necessarily allow such a person to enter or reside within the State; this is under the control of the Immigration Authorities at the Department of Justice, Equality and Law Reform. Employees must register with the Aliens Office if they work in Dublin or with the local Garda Station if outside the Dublin area, where an immigration stamp, valid until a specified date, will be put on their passport.

If an employee does not fall within the scope of the above rules, the employer will have to apply for a work permit (i.e., where the employee is not an EEA national) with the Department of Enterprise,

Trade and Employment. Before a work permit is issued, the Minister will have to be satisfied that every effort was made to recruit a qualified EEA national to the position. The proposed employment of such a person is usually in highly specialised positions. Application should be made at least ten weeks prior to proposed commencement of employment. Such permits are granted for one year but may be renewed.

EMPLOYEES OR INDEPENDENT CONTRACTORS

The difference between an employee and an independent contractor is often difficult to interpret. A person who is an employee and works under a contract of service — provided they have sufficient service — falls within the scope of employment protective legislation namely, the Unfair Dismissals Acts, the Minimum Notice and Terms of Employment Acts, Redundancy Payments Acts and the legislation dealing with maternity, adoptive and parental leave. An independent contractor is not an employee and thus does not fall within the scope of protective legislation. Independent contractors are essentially self-employed and sell their services to clients, thus they work under a contract *for services*. Examples of independent contractors are generally professionals and tradespersons; for example, solicitors, doctors, various other consultants, plumbers, electricians and so forth.

Generally, courts and tribunals are more inclined towards considering a person an employee as distinct from an independent contractor. In *Henry Denny & Sons (Ireland) Limited t/a Kerry Foods* v *The Minister for Social Welfare* ([1998] IR 34), the Supreme Court considered the difference between a contract of service and a contract for services. The issue concerned whether shop merchandisers are employees or not. If they were employees, they were insurable persons for the purposes of social welfare. In this case, the merchandiser was employed on yearly contracts which specifically stated that she was not an employee but an independent contractor and was liable for her own tax affairs. In holding that the merchandiser was an employee, Keane J considered:

> . . . while each case must be determined in the light of its particular facts and circumstances, in general a person will be regarded as providing his or her services under a contract of service and not as an independent contractor where he or she is performing those

services for another person and not for himself or herself. The degree of control exercised over how the work is to be performed, although a factor to be taken into account, is not decisive. The inference that the person is engaged in business on his or her own account can be more easily drawn where he or she provides the necessary premises or equipment or some other form of investment, where he/she employs others to assist in the business and where the profit which he/she derives from the business is dependent on the efficiency with which it is conducted by him or her.

In *E.P. Ó Coindealbháin (Inspector of Taxes)* v *Mooney* ([1990] IR 422 at p. 424), the difference between a contract of service and a contract for services was considered by Blayney J:

Where the agreement creating the relationship between the parties is expressed in writing . . . the entire agreement between the parties is to be found in the writing, so it is the unique source of their relationship: it follows that it is from its terms alone that the nature of the relationship can be determined.

In the *Kerry Foods* case (above), Murphy J considered that the contract was not "the unique source" of the relationship between the parties. He further confirmed that the Social Welfare Appeals Officer was correct in his conclusion that he was required to consider "the facts or realities of the situation on the ground" to enable him to reach a decision as to whether the merchandiser was an employee or an independent contractor. Further, it is important to ascertain the true bargain between the parties rather than rely on the labels ascribed to them.

In the case of *Tierney* v *An Post* ([1999] ELR 65) the plaintiff was appointed a postmaster by the former Department of Posts and Telegraphs in 1983. His employment was stated to be an unestablished one in his contract. This was a phrase which was not generally used to describe an independent contractor, but rather a non-permanent civil servant. Reference was also made in the rules contained in the Postmaster's Manual, which formed part of the agreement between the parties. McCracken J was of the view that An Post exercised a very strict control over the way the Postmaster did his work and pointed out that in the section which dealt with discipline, the word "dismissal" was used on several occasions, a word which clearly relates to a contract of service. It was held that the Postmaster was an employee.

The Employment Appeals Tribunal also considers issues such as whether the "employee" receives holidays, sick pay and pensions. A person who is in receipt of such benefits, it may be assumed, is an employee working under a contract of service. In *Irish Press Limited v Kelly* ((1986) 5 JISLL 170), the claimant had been an association football correspondent for the *Sunday Press* since 1952. It was contended that he was not an employee, as he only worked part-time and did not have income tax or PRSI deducted from his earnings. The Circuit Court overturned the Tribunal determination (which had held that he was an employee) and considered that Mr Kelly was not an employee. Clarke J in summary raised the following questions:

1. Does the sports editor have to accept his articles?

2. Would Mr Kelly be in breach of contract if he did not provide the newspaper with an article?

3. Could the newspaper get an injunction if he gave the article to another journal?

The questions were answered in the negative as each party was a free agent. Each was free to accept or to refuse work. There was a fresh offer and acceptance on each occasion. Accordingly, there was a contract for services. Clarke J also considered *In the matter of The Sunday Tribune Limited (in liquidation)* ([1984] IR 505), and compared the *Sunday Press* contributor with a freelance contributor.

In the *Sunday Tribune* case, Carroll J considered that a former employee who had been employed on a shift basis as a sub-editor, being required to attend the newspaper premises at a specified time, and who had to work under the guidance and instructions of a chief sub-editor, was an employee, as was a journalist who was paid a fixed sum each week for writing a weekly column and had to attend editorial conferences. However, a person who furnished regular articles, where each has been commissioned separately, was not considered to be an employee and was considered to be a freelance contributor.

There are special regulations for self-employed commercial agents (see European Communities (Commercial Agents) Regulations, 1994 (SI No. 33 of 1994)) where there is a written agreement between the parties. An agency contract for a fixed period, which continues to be performed by both parties, shall be deemed to be converted into an agency contract for an indefinite period. On termination of the agreement, either party is then entitled to notice depending on the length of the contract. Of course, the agreement can be immediately terminated where either party is in breach of the agreement or where exceptional circumstances arise.

STATUTORY REQUIREMENTS

Written Statement of Terms and Conditions of Employment

The Terms of Employment (Information) Act, 1994, arises from an EC Directive (91/533/EEC) which provides that an employer is obliged to inform an employee of the terms and conditions of employment. (The 1994 Act repealed sections 9 and 10 of the Minimum Notice and Terms of Employment Act, 1973, which provided that an employer had to provide a more limited written statement if requested.) The Act applies to employees who are normally expected to work over eight hours per week and have been in continuous employment for one month. It also applies to agency workers.

Section 3 of the Act provides that an employer must give the following information in writing to an employee within two months of commencement of employment. This legislation only applies to employees recruited after the commencement of the Act (16 May 1994) unless a current employee requests such information, in which case the information would have to be provided within two months of the request. The information to be included is as follows:

1. The full names of the employer and employee;

2. The address of the employer in the State or, where appropriate, the address of the principal place of the relevant business of the employer in the State or the registered office (within the meaning of the Companies Act, 1963);

3. The place of work or, where there is no fixed or main place of work, a statement specifying that the employee is required or permitted to work at various places;

4. The title of the job or nature of the work for which the employee is employed;

5. The date of commencement of the employee's contract of employment;

6. In the case of a temporary contract of employment, the expected duration thereof or, if the contract of employment is for a fixed term, the date on which the contract expires;

7. The rate or method of calculation of the employee's remuneration;

8. The length of the intervals between the times at which remuneration is paid, whether a week, a month or any other interval;

9. Any terms or conditions relating to hours of work (including overtime);

10. Any terms or conditions relating to paid leave (other than paid sick leave);

11. Any terms or conditions relating to:

    a) incapacity for work due to sickness or injury and paid sick leave, and

    b) pensions and pension schemes;

12. The period of notice which the employee is required to give and entitled to receive (whether by or under statute or under the terms of the employee's contract of employment) to determine the employee's contract of employment, or where this cannot be indicated when the information is given, the method for determining such periods of notice.

13. A reference to any collective agreements which directly affect the terms and conditions of the employee's employment including, where the employer is not a party to such agreements, particulars of the bodies or institutions by whom they were made (e.g. Labour Court, joint labour committees — see Chapter 7, "Collective Bargaining").

This statement must be signed and dated by the employer. If there are changes in the terms and conditions, the employee must be so advised within one month. This provision does not apply to changes in legislation or collective agreements.

There are also detailed provisions for employees who will be working outside the State for over one month. Information such as the period of employment outside the State, the currency in which they will be paid, any benefits in cash or in kind and the terms and conditions, where appropriate, governing the employee's repatriation must be given prior to departure.

The information provided must be retained by the employer for one year following termination of the employee's employment. The Act provides for a complaints procedure (see Chapters 22 and 23).

Dismissal Procedure

Section 14 of the Unfair Dismissals Act, 1977, provides that an employer must give an employee in writing the procedure that the employer will observe before and for the purposes of dismissing the employee. This document must set out the agreed written procedure between the employer and a registered trade union (see Chapter 7, "Collective Bargaining") or what has been the custom and practice in the employment. If there is no written agreement, the employer may write one and, if the employee accepts it, it will be deemed written procedure for the purposes of the Act. This must be given to the employee within 28 days of commencement. If the employer varies or alters the procedure, a written copy of the alteration must be provided to the employee within 28 days. The Unfair Dismissals (Amendment) Act, 1993, provides that if an employer fails to comply with the dismissal procedure, the failure will be taken into account when awarding redress to the unfairly dismissed employee. The Code of Practice on Disciplinary Procedures contains general guidelines on the application of disciplinary procedures and the promotion of best practice in giving effect to such procedures. These principles and procedures should apply unless alternative agreed procedures exist in the workplace (Industrial Relations Act, 1990; Code of Practice on Disciplinary Procedures (Declaration) Order, 1996, SI No. 117 of 1996).

LEGAL CONTRACT

Before one considers the terms of the contract of employment, it must above all be a legal contract. It cannot be tainted with an illegality, such as an agreement between the employer and employee to avoid the payment of income tax/PRSI. If an agreement is tainted with such illegality, an employee will not be able to sue on the basis of the contract (see *Lewis* v *Squash (Ireland) Ltd.* [1983] ILRM 363). The Unfair Dismissals (Amendment) Act, 1993, provides that, even if the contract is illegal, an unfairly dismissed employee will be entitled to redress for unfair dismissal. However, the rights commissioners, the Employment Appeals Tribunal or the Circuit Court will have authority to refer the file to the Revenue Commissioners or the Department of Social, Community and Family Affairs (see Chapter 17, "Unfair Dismissal").

EXPRESS AND IMPLIED TERMS

Express terms are the key terms unless legislation provides otherwise (for example, through minimum statutory requirements for notice, holidays and maternity leave).

Implied terms are those that are taken as being in existence between the parties, to include that the employer will provide work for the employee; will pay wages to the employee; will indemnify the employee against all costs, expenses and any claims against the employee which arise from the employee's duties; and will provide a safe place of work and safe equipment. Equally, the employee will serve the employer (and not give the work to anybody else); will do the work in a competent manner; will be loyal to the employer and be confidential about the work; will not act in such a manner as causes a conflict of interest with the employer; will be honest and will work in a safe manner.

Legislation also imposes implied terms into the employment contract, namely, the equal pay and equal treatment legislation. When the Employment Equality Act, 1998, comes into operation, each employment contract will have equal remuneration and equality clauses covering all nine grounds of discrimination as provided for under the Act. The Unfair Dismissals Acts provide that procedural agreements must be complied with and such compliance will be taken into account in awarding compensation under the Acts. Thus the employer must act in a reasonable and fair manner towards the employee and, of course, there also exists a constitutional right to fairness.

While the above are the statutory requirements, it is prudent for an employer to spell out completely the terms and conditions of employment.

It is advisable for an employer to provide an employee with a full contract of employment. This does not have to be a detailed legal document — it may be a letter, for example. However, it is recommended that it be given to the employee in writing and explained to the employee as well.

KEY CLAUSES IN THE CONTRACT OF EMPLOYMENT

Employer

The correct name and title of the employer should be fully stated, e.g. "ABC Limited, having its registered office/business address at . . . " If the employer has a number of companies, the employee should be advised that it may be necessary to work for such associate or subsidiary companies as the employer so decides.

Job Specification

The employer should also advise the employee as to what the job position is and provide the employee with a job specification. A job specification should set out all the duties that are required of the employee and may be an appendix to the contract of employment. While the job specification should set out all the duties, it should be acknowledged by both parties that, over time, the specific requirements of the job may change (e.g. upgrading of technology) and that the employee will carry out all reasonable requests of the employer. Of course, a genuine redundancy situation may arise if the employer requires a person with higher qualifications (see Chapter 18, "Redundancy").

Date of Commencement and Job Title

An employer should always provide a date of commencement of employment, that is, the date when the employee starts working for the employer. This point appears deceptively simple, but difficulties can arise because, over the passage of time, people can forget the date of commencement. It could be important should there be a claim for redundancy or unfair dismissal because of service requirements under these Acts.

The job title is usually clear enough because that was the position that was advertised; nonetheless, it should be stated in the contract of employment. Also, the employee should be told to whom they will be reporting; that is, the title of the person who has responsibility over the department. It is advisable to state that this may change over time.

Probation

A contract usually includes a probationary period at commencement of employment, usually for a period of six months. The purpose of probation is to ensure that the employee is capable of doing the job and to assess whether the employee can work harmoniously with fellow workers in the employment concerned. An employer should have provision to extend the probationary period at their discretion. Of course, during the probationary period the employer should ensure that the employee receives all necessary training and assistance in learning the new job. The Unfair Dismissals Acts provide that the probationary period cannot be longer than twelve months, as an employee who is dismissed having one year's service can bring a claim under the Acts. Thus, an employer cannot avoid the provisions of the Acts by keeping an employee on continuing probation.

Hours of Work

An employer should specify the hours of work and the times that are allowed for breaks and lunch. The Terms of Employment (Additional Information) Regulations (SI No. 49 of 1998) provides that, effective from 1 March 1998, employers should provide a written statement containing particulars of the times and durations of the rest periods and breaks referred to in s. 11 (daily rest period), s. 12 (rest and intervals at work) and s. 13 (weekly rest periods). Employees who commenced employment prior to that date should receive such information within two months of their request. If an employee is required to work overtime, it should be clearly stated, as should the rate of pay for such overtime. It is important to note that all requests for overtime be reasonable, in other words, all employees must be given adequate notice. In executive positions, it is normally expected that the employee works in excess of the basic hours with no extra payment.

An employee may have to work on shift. The shift rota should be clearly stated as well as breaks and whether overtime is required from time to time. Employers should also comply with the Organisation of Working Time Act, 1997 and various registered agreements (see Chapter 13, "Organisation of Working Time").

Of course, there are groups of employees who are not covered by the Act. These include persons who decide their own working time (e.g. senior executives).

Remuneration

An employer has an obligation to pay an employee for their services. The contract should state the salary or the rate of pay per week/hour; for example, £12,000 gross per annum subject to PAYE and PRSI. The timing of the payment should be stated, e.g., on the last date of every month, on every Friday, etc. An employer may state when the salary will be reviewed — every April, for example, or as agreed between management and the trade unions. The method of payment should also be agreed; for example, by credit transfer or by cheque as the case may be (see Chapter 6, "Payment of Wages"). If there are bonus payments or commission paid, the method of calculation and when paid should be clearly spelt out. An employer may pay for VHI (up to a certain level of benefit or in full), provide for profit sharing, share options and so forth.

Any deductions from wages or salary (other than income tax or PRSI) must be clearly stated in the contract, giving authorisation to the employer to deduct such monies.

Expenses

In some positions, an employee may need to travel in connection with their employment, in the case of a salesperson, for example. If the employee is to use a company car, it should be noted whether they have a full driving licence with no endorsement(s). If the employee is to use their own car on company business, the company should be indemnified against any claim. The indemnity should be noted on the employee's insurance certificate, which must be shown to management before the employee's car is used on company business. The rate of payment per mile should also be advised to the employee. There should be a statement to the effect that the company will only meet receipted expenses, and the procedures in place for claiming such outlay should be outlined.

If there is travel involved, the employer should specify whether it is to be economy or executive class (in the case of air and train travel) and whether there has to be prior written permission in the case of air travel.

Sick Pay

There is no statutory obligation on an employer to pay an employee sick pay in the event of absence from work due to illness. However, if there is a sick-pay scheme in place, an employer must give the employee the written details. Sick-pay schemes can be quite simple; for example, an employee may be entitled to up to six weeks full pay per year, but must reimburse the employer with the sum received for disability benefit. An employee who is ill for longer will have to rely on disability benefit only. Disability benefit is now subject to income tax. Some employers may provide that such an arrangement lasts for the first 26 weeks of illness and that the employee then moves on to the income continuance scheme, where such a scheme exists. An income continuance scheme is invariably linked into the pension scheme and is underwritten by an insurance company.

An employer should have certain rules in the event of an employee being sick and not available for work, such as having to contact a specified person by a certain time. Also, there is usually a requirement for employees to provide a medical certificate (stating the illness and the likely date of return to work) if they are out sick for more than three consecutive dates. If an employee is out for a long period, an employer may require weekly certificates. If an employee has consistent intermittent absenteeism, or if through illness is no longer capable of performing their job, employment may be terminated (see Chapter 17, "Unfair Dismissal"). It is a commonly held view that an employee's employment may not be terminated if they are out sick and have sent in medical certificates. This is not necessarily so, provided the employer has used fair procedures leading up to termination.

Holidays

Employees who have worked are entitled to statutory paid annual leave and public holidays under the Organisation of Working Time Act, 1997. Most employments have holiday provisions over and above that contained in the holidays legislation. Holidays are considered in more detail in Chapter 4.

Right to Search

An employer may incorporate into the contract the right to search an employee's person or property while on the company's premises or upon leaving the premises. An employer must obtain the employees' agreement to search, either in the employment contract or through the company rules, as otherwise the employer would commit a trespass to the person. This type of clause is more typically used in manufacturing or retail employments where there is a marketable commodity.

Lay-Off/Short-Time

An employer cannot lay off or put staff on short-time if there is no such provision in the contract of employment (or in the union–management agreement). Lay-off or short-time usually arises where there is insufficient work as a result of an economic downturn, or where there has been a fire in the factory or a shortage of raw material or some other unexpected problem. Lay-off means that the employee is advised that there will be no work for a period of time, and short-time may mean that the employee may only have work for half days or three days per week. Under the Redundancy Acts, short-time is defined as a situation where an employee works for less than half their normal working hours. There is no statutory provision requiring that notice be given to the employee. However, it is good practice to provide as much notice as is reasonable. The employer should also advise employees why such lay-off/short-time is necessary, that it is a genuine intention that it will not continue for too long and that it will be reviewed within a specified period of time.

An employer should take care in the selection of employees for lay-off or short-time. For example, it would be discriminatory just to choose part-time women employees or a particular grade of employee. Of course, it can be justified to choose certain groups for specific reasons, as long as it is not discriminatory.

An employee who has been on lay-off/short-time for a period of time may claim a statutory redundancy payment (see Chapter 18, "Redundancy").

Also, if an employer realises that there will be no work in the future for employees still on lay-off/short-time, then such employees must receive monies in lieu of notice and statutory redundancy. Lay-off/short-time may not be used as a means of avoiding notice entitlements (see Chapter 16, "Notice").

Health and Safety

The contract should have a positive statement that the company is committed to fulfilling its obligations under the Health, Safety and Welfare at Work Act, 1989, and that it has prepared a safety statement. The safety statement sets out the rights and responsibilities of both the company and its employees in achieving and maintaining a healthy and safe workplace. The statement identifies the material hazards within the workplace and the steps the company has taken to protect employees from them. The employee should receive and sign the safety statement on commencement of employment (see Chapter 15, "Health and Safety in the Workplace").

Trade Union Membership

It may be a condition of employment that an employee remain at all times during the course of employment a benefit member of a particular trade union and that the employer recognises a particular union for negotiation purposes (see Chapter 7, "Collective Bargaining"). If there is to be a deduction of wages for union dues, the employee may acknowledge and agree to that in the contract of employment.

Retirement Age

Employment contracts should state the normal retirement age, particularly for permanent employees. Generally, the normal retirement age in Ireland is the 65th birthday. Retirement age is not necessarily the same as pension age, as the pension scheme could technically provide for an earlier pension age than retirement age. For practical purposes, however, pension and retirement ages are the same. Upon reaching the retirement age, the employee's contract of employment comes to an end by operation of law, so there can be no viable claim for unfair dismissal or redundancy.

Pension

There is no statutory obligation on an employer to provide a pension for employees. However, if there is a pension scheme, either contributory or non-contributory, the employer must give the employee a copy of a summary of the key provisions (see Chapter 14, "Pensions").

Grievance Procedure

During the course of employment, an employee may have genuine grievances which they wish to raise with management. It is important that such matters be dealt with speedily in order to avoid an escalation of the issue. A grievance procedure should be simple and clear, and should provide that, in larger employments, the employee first approaches their supervisor and if the matter is not resolved at that level, then it may be referred to higher management. In small employments, such formality may not be necessary, because there may only be two levels of employee; namely, management and staff. It is important that the employee has a right of representation at all times (e.g., a colleague or shop steward). If matters cannot be resolved locally, there should be provision to refer the matter to a rights commission, the Labour Relations Commission, an equality officer or the Employment Appeals Tribunal, as appropriate (see Chapter 8, "Trade Disputes"). It is recommended that there be a procedure for dealing with allegations of sexual harassment or harassment/bullying generally. The grievance procedure may be amended to deal with such matters (see Chapter 1, "Equal Treatment", and Chapter 17, "Unfair Dismissal").

Notice

The contract may state that the Minimum Notice and Terms of Employment Acts will apply to this employment. This in effect means that the statutory notice provisions will apply. An employer may provide for a longer period of notice over and above the statutory minimum; for example, three months' notice. There should also be provision that the employer may pay monies in lieu of notice. It should also be stated for the purposes of clarification that an employee who is dismissed for reasons of gross misconduct is not entitled to notice or monies in lieu of notice. There may also be a provision that both parties may agree to waive the notice period or monies in lieu of notice (see Chapter 16, "Notice").

Even an employee who is dismissed during the probationary period is entitled to statutory minimum notice, provided that the dismissal is not the result of misconduct. If an employer provides for a longer period of contractual notice, it may only apply once the probationary period is over and the employee is confirmed in employment.

Dismissal/Disciplinary Procedure

As discussed above, the Unfair Dismissals Acts require the employer to provide the employee with the dismissal procedure. The Code of Practice on Disciplinary Procedures contains guidelines on the application of such procedures which may be used in the contract of employment and applied in any disciplinary situation (see Industrial Relations Act, 1990; Code of Practice on Disciplinary Procedures (Declarations) Order, 1996, SI No. 117 of 1996). Normally the dismissal procedure also includes information concerning disciplinary actions. It should be noted that the purpose of the procedures is not to terminate employment but to give the employee a warning that improvement is needed. It is recommended that the disciplinary/dismissal procedure be kept as simple as possible; if the procedure is unduly complicated, it may result in ambiguity and unnecessary problems.

The employer should clearly state the grounds for dismissal; for example, misconduct (e.g. theft, violence, falsifying clock-cards, being under the influence of alcohol while on the company premises); absenteeism, both prolonged and intermittent; poor work performance; bad time-keeping; redundancy; and any other substantial reason.

The essence of a disciplinary/dismissal procedure is balance and fairness to the employee concerned. It is a commonly held view by employees that one verbal and two written warnings can result in them being "fairly" dismissed. This is not necessarily the case, and if a claim under the Unfair Dismissals Acts were brought, there might well be a finding of "unfair dismissal". It depends entirely on the facts and the circumstances. In cases of gross misconduct — theft of company property, for example — there is no necessity at all for warnings. A thorough and fair investigation of the issue, with the opportunity for the employee to state their case (with representation) is called for. If the employer is satisfied that on the balance of probabilities the employee was involved in theft, the employment may then be terminated.

If matters cannot be resolved locally, there should be provision to refer the matter to a rights commissioner, the Labour Relations Commission, an equality officer or the Employment Appeals Tribunal, as appropriate (see Chapter 8, "Trade Disputes").

The key components of a disciplinary procedure are counselling, verbal warning, written warnings, a final written warning, suspension with or without pay (see Chapter 6, "Payment of Wages") and provision for representation. Procedural fairness is considered in more detail in Chapter 17, "Unfair Dismissal".

The Unfair Dismissals (Amendment) Act, 1993, provides that, when awarding compensation, the adjudicating bodies will take into account the compliance or the failure to comply by the employer with written dismissal procedures.

Secrecy and Confidentiality

While confidentiality about an employer's business is an implied term of the contract of employment, it is nonetheless prudent to include a clause stating that the employee shall not disclose any aspect of the employer's business to any third party except with the employer's prior written permission.

In some employments, the employer may have a separate agreement containing clauses relating to secrecy, confidentiality, restraint of trade or competition (i.e. a secrecy agreement).

The Whistle Blowers Protection Bill, 1999, is a Private Member's Bill published on 24 March 1999. The purpose of the Bill is to provide protection from civil liability to employees who make certain disclosures, to their employer or to somebody other than their employer, "reasonably and in good faith" in relation to the conduct of the business and affairs of their employers. The Bill lists the chief regulatory authorities of the State to whom or which disclosures may be made under the Bill (when enacted), including the Central Bank, Health and Safety Authority, the Garda Síochána, etc. The type of information covered by the Bill includes, for example, such information as amounts or relates to or supports an allegation that a criminal offence has been, is being or is likely to be committed; that there has been a failure to comply with legal obligations; or that the health and safety of an individual is being endangered. Protection against unfair dismissal is provided for.

Competition

The Competition Acts, 1991–1996, have raised problems concerning restraint-of-trade or non-competition clauses in contracts of employment. Restrictive covenants concern the right of a former employee to compete with their former employer after they have left their employment.

Section 4(1) of the 1991 Act provides that:

> all agreements between undertakings, decisions by associations of undertakings and concerted practices which have as their object or effect the prevention, restriction or distortion of competition in trade of any goods or services in the State or any part of the State are prohibited and void.

The Competition Authority, which "polices" the Acts, has issued guidelines in respect of such clauses in contracts of employment. These guidelines have no legal standing but are extremely useful. A non-competitive clause in a contract of employment is considered permissible because an individual who is an employee is not an "undertaking" — that person is working solely for the employer concerned. Thus there is no requirement for such contracts to be notified to the Authority.

However, an employee who leaves their employment to set up their own business would then be considered to be an "undertaking". If the former employer then tried to enforce the non-competitive clause, it would restrict competition. The clause would also be notifiable under the Act. While it is arguable that such an agreement between a former employer and employee would not have a major effect on competition, nonetheless there could be considerable impact, depending on the industry/service and the nature of the employee's work. A large number of restraint-of-trade clauses generally, or in one industry or service would restrict competition. In summary, an employer cannot have a clause that would distort competition in the market. Of course, the Authority can grant an exemption in respect of some clauses.

Leaving aside the Competition Act, one must also consider the general common law provisions on restraint-of-trade clauses. In summary, the employer must have a legitimate interest to protect; the restraint must be reasonable in terms of the conduct sought to be restricted; the duration and the geographical extent of the restriction must be reasonable. In *Premier Dairies* v *Doyle and Others* ([1996] 1 ILRM 363), the Supreme Court held that:

> while it is arguable that all covenants in restraint of trade are *prima facie* unlawful, here the restraint was for such a short duration and to such a limited area that in the absence of any other factors, the matter would be governed by the principle that where parties agree for valuable consideration that something shall not be done, it is appropriate for the Court to give effect to this negative bargain by means of an interlocutory injunction.

The defendants were independent contractors who distributed milk in the Dublin area and agreed that they would not, within a period of twelve months following termination, engage in or be associated with the distribution of any products in the area which compete or are likely to compete with Premier's contracts without prior written consent. Premier could terminate the contract if there was a breach, to include the non-payment of monies. The contractors subsequently purchased milk from another dairy and attempted to entice their old customers away from Premier. Generally speaking, the courts do not like enforcing such clauses and the clauses must be reasonable. Accordingly, it is generally provided that, if the courts delete such a clause, the balance of the contract remains enforceable.

Copyright/Patents

If the employee has to write or prepare materials in the course of their employment, the contract should clearly state that the copyright vests in the employer.

If it is envisaged that the employee will be writing articles for journals or will give lectures, there may be a statement that the employee may only do so with the prior written permission of the managing director. Further, if a text is published it should clearly state that "any views expressed are the author's own".

If an employee is involved in designing or adapting products, it should be clearly stated that all inventions shall be assigned to the employer. There should be a statement that all documents (including copies) of all memoranda and other pertinent materials be handed over on termination of employment.

Company Directors

The Companies Act, 1990, provides that shareholders are entitled to inspect (without charge) a copy or a memorandum of the terms of a director's contract of employment. Such documents must be kept at the registered office, the principal place of business or the place where the register of shareholders is kept. A holding company must also keep such memoranda of directors of subsidiary companies. However, disclosure in such case is not required where the contract has less than three years to run or can be terminated within 12 months with no compensation.

Relocation

An employer may provide that the employee, if requested, work elsewhere in Ireland (or abroad) with a specified period of notice and that all reasonable relocation expenses will be paid.

Arbitration

Generally, contracts of employment do not provide for arbitration clauses, because the Arbitration Acts, 1954–1980, do not apply to such contracts. There are special arrangements in the public and civil services. If a registered agreement forms part of the conditions of employment, the Labour Court may interpret the agreement (see Chapter 7, "Collective Bargaining").

Applicable Law

Should an employee have to work abroad for part of the contract, it is advisable to state the applicable law, i.e., that of the Republic of Ireland.

Attestation Clause

It is important for the employer to provide an attestation in the contract. Again, this can be extremely simple, with a statement that the employee accepts and agrees to be bound by the terms and conditions of employment. The employee should sign the letter/agreement and it should also be signed by the employer. One must stress that the employee should be fully aware of and understand all the terms and conditions of employment before signing the contract.

Summary

The above are the key points in relation to a contract of employment. An employer may also wish to provide a copy of the company rules within the contract of employment, in relation to such matters as shift-working, clocking procedure, details of notification if there is sickness, details of misconduct and gross misconduct, company cars, expenses, confidentiality, restraint of trade clauses and the safety statement.

Two copies of the contract should be sent to the prospective employee — one copy to be signed and returned to the employer by a particular date and the other to be held by the employee. If the terms and conditions are contained in a union–management agreement or a staff manual, a written statement stating that the employee understands and accepts the terms and conditions as contained in the agreement or staff manual should be sent back to the employer.

The employer may also request the employee to send with the acceptance letter their birth certificate, P45 form from the previous employment, and written evidence of trade union membership (if appropriate).

Once everything is in order and the employee commences employment, it is advisable for an employer to have a period of induction/training, so that the employee may be made aware of the custom and practice of the firm.

VARIATION OF CONTRACT

The terms of a contract of employment may not be varied without the agreement of the parties. A breach of a term of a contract may result in an employee resigning and claiming constructive dismissal (see Chapter 17, "Unfair Dismissal").

STATUTORY GUARANTEES ON TERMS AND
CONDITIONS OF EMPLOYMENT

Re-organisation of public enterprises and statutory guarantees were considered in two Irish cases, most recently in *Rafferty, Ward and The National Bus and Rail Union* v *Bus Éireann / Irish Bus* ([1997] 2 IR 424). Section 14 of the Transport (Reorganisation of Coras Iompair Éireann) Act, 1986, provides in summary that every person who was an employee of Coras Iompair Éireann (CIE) immediately before vesting day would become an employee of Irish Bus. Section 14(5) then provides that every person who immediately before vesting day is an officer or servant of CIE shall not when they move to Irish Bus receive a lesser scale of pay or be brought to less beneficial conditions of service unless there is a new collective agreement negotiated with any recognised trade union. Section 14(6) provides that scales of pay and conditions of service shall continue to apply until a new collective agreement is negotiated. Irish Bus produced a viability plan, which recommended significant alterations to the way Irish Bus was operated. This plan resulted in bus drivers spending a minimum of 85 per cent of their time driving and engaging in other duties for the remainder of their shifts. There followed various meetings between the NBRU and Irish Bus. Irish Bus indicated that parts of the plan would be implemented without agreement. The first two named plaintiffs were drivers and with the NRBU applied for judicial review, as they believed there was an attempt to introduce less beneficial conditions of service. Kelly J dismissed the application and considered:

> That the provisions of s. 14(5) will remain in force until the last officer or servant of CIE leaves the payroll. Interestingly, whilst the terms and conditions may not be reduced or lessened there is the possibility that they may be lessened if brought about by a collective agreement (which could be against the wishes of an individual employee). S. 14(6) was obviously transitional in nature until such time as pay and conditions are varied.

Conditions of Service/Work Practices

Kelly J noted that there did not appear to be a decision to date as to whether there was a difference in law between conditions of service and work practices. He referred to Blayney J in *Ó Cearbhaill* v *Bord Telecom Éireann* ([1994] ELR 54), where it was noted at p. 61:

It seems to me that conditions of service are conditions which one would expect to find in a contract of employment between employer and employee. Any terms which it would be normal to include in such a contract would be entitled to be so described and in considering what these terms might be, what has to be borne in mind is the nature of the contract of employment — it is a contract between an employer and a single employee. Each employee has an individual contract, so the conditions of service would have to be appropriate to such a contract.

Would a term dealing with an employee's prospects of promotion come into this category? In my opinion it would not. It does not concern the immediate relationship between the employer and employee as would, for example, the rate of pay, hours of work, length of holidays, sick leave, pension rights, etc. It relates rather to the general manner in which the employer's business is structured and managed. If an employer were to make it the subject of the contract of employment of individual employees he would be unable to change it without the consent of each of them. No employer would be prepared to restrict his freedom that way. For this reason it seems to me that it would be wholly inappropriate to include a prospect of promotion in a contract of employment and so it could not be considered as being a condition of service. It is simply an incident of a person's employment depending entirely on how the employer's business is structured and subject to change since the employer is under no obligation not to alter the structure of the business.

Kelly J therefore considered that there is a difference in law between conditions of services and work practices. He believed that, in addition to conditions stated above, a basic job description applicable to a post is a condition of service and at common law an employee is not required to do a fundamentally different job from that contracted for. He also referred to the English decision of *Cresswell* v *Board of Inland Revenue* ([1984] 2 All ER 713), where the plaintiffs objected to the introduction of computerisation on the grounds that it would be in breach of their terms of service to introduce it without their consent. Their claim was dismissed on the basis that employees did not have a vested right to preserve working obligations completely unchanged as from the moment they commenced work. Hence, in the *Rafferty* decision, Kelly J asked the question:

> Is the effect of the changes promulgated by the respondent such as
> to result in the bus driver doing a different job or is it merely to
> bring about a situation where they will be doing recognisably the
> same job in a different way?

If it is a different job, it is unlawful within the meaning of s. 5 of the
1986 Act without the consent of trade unions. If they are doing the
same job in a different way it does not attract such statutory protection and is lawful. The alterations to the job did not affect the rate of
pay, length of holidays, sick leave or pension rights. They were still
bus drivers. Also the altered duties only were required to be done
when the drivers were idle and yet paid, therefore there was no
change in the conditions of employment which thus were not protected by s. 14(5).

The Finance Act, 1997, provided for certain tax exemptions where
there is an agreement with employees for restructuring. The relief
applies where a company which is faced with an actual or imminent
substantial adverse change in its competitive environment, restruc-
tures its operations to ensure its survival, by agreement with the
workforce, and receives a certificate from the Minister for Enterprise,
Trade and Employment, certifying that it may be treated as a qualifying company for the purposes of the relief. According to the Department of Finance, the relief covers sums to a maximum of £20,000
effective from 21 July 1999. This is based on a 20 per cent pay cut
and the use of the exemptions for redundancy payments of £8,000
plus £600 per year of service but in this instance only applies to a
maximum of 20 years' service (IRN 29, 29 July 1999).

PERSONNEL RECORDS AND DATA PROTECTION

Personal data on employees kept on computer or word processor disk
are covered by the Data Protection Act, 1988. Data kept on manual
files are not covered under the Act. Personal data means "data relating to a living individual who can be identified either from the data or
from the date in conjunction with other information in possession of
the data controller". Such personal information may include details of
an employee's health, family and social circumstances, political opinions, racial origin, religious or other beliefs, sexual life or criminal
convictions. Certain data are exempt from the terms of the Act, such

as data for the purpose of safeguarding the State, data required by law to be made available to the public and so forth.

Employers who keep ordinary personnel data relating to employees including such matters as absence/injury records, disciplinary records, etc. are not covered under the Act, as such data would not be deemed "sensitive".

The 1988 Act has a number of definitions, including the *data controller* (who can be an individual, firm or other body) who controls the contents and use of personal data. A *data processor* is a person who processes the personal data on behalf of the data controller. It does not include an employee of a data controller who processes such data in the course of their employment, as when data are sent out to third parties for processing.

The Act gives a right to every individual who establishes the existence of personal data to have access to such data and to have inaccurate data rectified or erased. It also imposes obligations on data controllers and data processors to ensure that such data are kept accurate and up-to-date and for lawful purposes. There must also be sufficient security measures taken so that data are not disclosed.

Data Protection Commissioner

The Data Protection Commissioner has been appointed under the Act to supervise the operation of the legislation and to investigate complaints. Certain categories of data controllers and data processors are required to register with the Data Protection Commissioner. If an employer keeps normal personnel records (which do not comprise sensitive data), then there is no requirement to register.

Data controllers and data processors required to register include:

1. All public authorities.

2. All financial institutions, life assurance and insurance companies or businesses that are wholly or mainly involved in direct marketing, credit referencing or collecting debts.

3. Data controllers who keep personal data relating to racial origin, political opinions, religious or other beliefs, physical or mental health, sexual life, or criminal convictions. This can be collectively called sensitive data.

4. Data processors whose business consists wholly or partly of processing personal data on behalf of data controllers; for example, computer bureaux.

5. Data controllers or data processors who may be prescribed under the Act by the Data Protection Commissioner with the consent of the Minister for Justice.

An employer who does not fall within the above categories is not obliged to register with the Data Protection Commissioner.

Duties of Data Controller

Data controllers and processors have a duty of care towards the individuals in regard to sensitive data, and must abide by the Data Protection Principles:

1. "Fairly obtaining and processing" principle — an employee should be told why the information is needed and what use it may be put to, and assured that the information will not be used for any other purpose.

2. The data will not be used or disclosed in any manner incompatible with those purposes; for example, data collected on employees for personnel administration should not be used for direct mailing.

3. The data must be accurate, up-to-date, adequate, relevant and not excessive in relation to that purpose.

4. The data must be in proportion to the use to which they are put or to be put; for example, some personal details may be irrelevant.

5. The data must not be kept for longer than is necessary, as they may become out of date or irrelevant.

Data controllers and processors are required by the Act to maintain appropriate security against unauthorised access to, alteration, disclosure or destruction of data. Examples of such security requirements would be the use of code words, passwords or restriction of physical access.

Access to Data

An employee may ask to find out data on their personnel file. In the normal course, this should not cause any problems because it may merely contain medical certificates or warnings. However, if there are "personal data" on the file, an employee may request access of such data under the provisions of the Act. If the request is not answered, the employee may refer the matter to the Data Protection Commissioner and the employer may be guilty of an offence.

FREEDOM OF INFORMATION ACT, 1997

The Freedom of Information Act was enacted on 21 April 1997 and most public bodies became subject to the provisions of the Act on 21 April 1998. Local authorities and health boards became subject to its provisions by Ministerial Order on 21 October 1998 (Freedom of Information Act, 1997 (Sections 6(4), 6(5) and 6(6)) Regulations, 1998 (SI No. 516 of 1998). Public bodies covered under the Act are classified under various headings in the Act. They include:

- All Government Departments;

- Various state agencies (e.g. the Blood Transfusion Service Board, Central Statistics Office, the Civil Service Commissioners, the Competition Authority, the Employment Equality Agency, the Local Appointments Commissioners, the Pensions Board);

- Local authorities; and

- Health boards.

The purpose of the Act is to enable members of the public to obtain access (to the greatest extent possible consistent with the public interest and the right to privacy) to information in the possession of public bodies and to enable persons to have inaccurate personal information relating to them in the possession of such bodies corrected.

The key aspects of the Act are that there is a legal right:

1. For each person to access information held by such public bodies, subject to various exceptions.

2.   To have personal information in relation to themselves which is held by a public body amended where it is incomplete, incorrect or misleading.

3.   To obtain reasons for decisions of public bodies which particularly affect an individual. In an attempt to help people to focus their request for information, public bodies are required to publish a booklet containing information on their structures, functions and the categories of information they hold.

Appeal System

An independent appeal system has been set up to oversee decisions by public bodies under the Act. The new Office of Information Commissioner has been established with a mandate to report on the operation of the Act generally.

Definition of "Records"

"Records" held by a public body include all non-personal "records" created after the commencement of the Act; non-personal records created prior to the Act, where these are necessary to understand later records; and personal records regardless of when they were created. Personal records can generally only be accessed by persons to whom they relate.

"Record" is defined as follows:

> Any memorandum, book, plan, map, drawing, diagram, pictorial or graphic work or other documents, any photograph, film, or recording (whether of sound or images or both), any form in which data (within the meaning of the Data Protection Act, 1988), are held, any other form (including machine-readable form) or thing in which information is held or stored manually, mechanically or electronically and anything that is part or a copy in any form, of any of the foregoing or is a combination of two or more of the foregoing.

The Right of Access

A request must be received in writing specifying the record sought under the provisions of the Act. It must contain sufficient particulars to enable the record to be identified. If a person requesting wishes to be given access to the information in a particular form, he or she must specify that form in a letter.

The head of the public body (or the person to whom the function has been delegated) must acknowledge receipt of the request in writing within two weeks. This acknowledgement must include a summary of the rights of review under the Act and the failure by a public body to respond may be regarded as a refusal of the request.

The public body must decide whether to agree or to refuse the request within four weeks of the receipt of the request. In circumstances where sufficient particulars are not included in the request, the public body is obliged to help the person requesting to draft a revised request with better particulars of the information sought. The four-week period can be extended under certain circumstances for a further four weeks. Notification of the decision is required and, in cases of a refusal or deferral of access, the letter must set out reasons for the refusal or deferral in a summary of the rights to review.

Where the request for disclosure is granted, the letter informing the person requesting must specify whether a fee has been charged in respect of the granting of the request; the date on which, and the form and manner in which the access to the record concerned will be offered; and the fact that the records will be kept available for four weeks for the purpose of such access.

Where the request for disclosure is granted, the public body may give access to the record by providing the person with a copy of the record or an opportunity to inspect it.

There is an independent appeal system available to the head of the public body / Information Commissioner and to the High Court in cases of a refusal or deferral of access, a grant of partial access, or a grant of access in form other than that which was sought by the person requesting.

There is provision for fees chargeable in respect of access.

Personal Records

A public body shall refuse a request for personal information unless it is the individual themselves who is requesting the information (or that person has consented to such a request), or where the information relates to a group and is available generally to the public or where it is necessary to avoid a serious or imminent danger to the life or health of the individual.

The definition of "personal information" in the Act includes information about an identifiable individual that would, in the ordinary course of events, be known only to the individual or members of the family, or friends of the individual, or information that is held by a public body on the understanding that it would be treated by it as confidential. Such information includes:

- The educational, medical, psychiatric or psychological history, financial affairs, religion, sexual orientation, age or marital status, and the employment or employment history of the individual.

- Personnel records of the individual, which are defined as follows (s. 6(6)(a)):

> a record relating wholly or mainly to one or more of the following, that is to say the competence or ability of the individual in his or her capacity as the member of the staff of a public body or his or her employment or employment history or an evaluation of the performance of his or her function generally or a particular such function as such a member,

which was created more than three years before the commencement of the Act, provided that the records are not used or proposed to be used in a manner that would affect the individual. It was noted by the Minister, at the time of the Seanad debates, that civil servants will have access to their files only going back three years but, if there is anything there that has obstructed their promotion, they can see the full file.

Information concerning a record of a medical or psychiatric nature (including social work) relating to the person requesting may not be released if the head of the public body considers it might be prejudicial to the individual's physical or mental health, wellbeing or emotional condition.

There are certain exempt records under the Act, which include records held by courts of tribunal relating to proceedings in the court of tribunal.

The Act provides that individuals have the legal right to have personal information relating to themselves amended where it is incorrect, incomplete or misleading. Such amendment can be effective by altering the records so as to make the information complete and correct, by adding to the record a statement of the reasons why the record is incomplete, incorrect or misleading or by deleting the incorrect information from the record.

Where a record is amended, the public body concerned is required to take reasonable steps to notify any individual to whom access to the record was granted and any public body to whom a copy of the record was given of the amendment made. Public bodies are under an obligation to revert to the individual with a decision as to whether the information will be amended within four weeks of receiving the request and an independent appeals process is available against any refusal to amend the record.

General References

Clark, R. (1990), *Data Protection Law in Ireland*, Dublin: The Round Hall Press.

Data Protection Commissioner (1988), *Guide to the Data Protection Act, 1988,* Dublin, December.

Crump, D. and D. Pugley (1997), *Contracts of Employment,* 7th edition, London: Butterworths.

Forde, M. (1982), *Employment Law*, Dublin: The Round Hall Press.

Lavery, P. (1996), *Commercial Secrets: The Action for Breach of Confidence in Ireland*, Dublin: Round Hall Sweet & Maxwell.

McDonagh, M. (1998), *Freedom of Information Act, 1997, Law Statutes Annotated*, Dublin: Sweet and Maxwell.

McDonagh, M. (1998), *Freedom of Information Law in Ireland*, Dublin: Round Hall Sweet and Maxwell.

O'Mara, C. (1994), "New Regulations Establish Protection for Commercial Agents", *Commercial Law Practitioner*, June.

Chapter Three

TEMPORARY AND PART-TIME EMPLOYMENT

The terms "part-time" employment, "temporary" employment "casual" employment, "short-term" employment and "seasonal work" are not legal descriptions. There is, however, provision for the description of "zero hours" contracts in relation to working practices in the Organisation of Working Time Act, 1997 (see Chapter 13). Such employees have increasing protection under employment legislation. Indeed, most temporary employment arrangements should have a written statement of terms and conditions of employment.

The Worker Protection (Regular Part-time Employees) Act, 1991, came into force on 6 April 1991 (excluding redundancy and maternity, which came into force in June 1991). This Act provided that employees not previously protected under the (then) Unfair Dismissals Act, 1977, the Redundancy Payments Acts, 1967–1984, and the Minimum Notice and Terms of Employment Acts, 1973–1984, are covered provided they are normally expected to work at least eight hours per week and they have the appropriate service for the particular Act. In this book, rather than providing a separate chapter on the 1991 Act, the amendments that have been made to the various pieces of protective legislation are included in the appropriate sections. However, there are still questions raised in relation to certain types of employment, which shall be considered here.

"CASUALS"

There is no definition for "casual" employment. In practice, such workers are on standby to do work as required with no fixed hours or attendance arrangements. Nonetheless, it has been accepted that such workers are "employees" within the meaning of protective legislation. For example, the status of "permanent casuals" was considered in *Byrne* v *Gartan Ltd.* (1048/1983) where it was held that the claimant, a "casual" waitress, was considered to be an employee since over the years the expectation arose of her availability for work. There is no provision which would prevent a casual employee working for a number of different employers, provided of course there is compliance with the Organisation of Working Time Act, 1997 (see Chapter 13).

The Organisation of Working Time Act, 1997 (section 18), applies to an employee whose contract of employment requires them to make themselves available to work for:

1. A certain number of hours ("the contract hours"); or

2. As and when the employer requires the employee; or

3. A combination of "contract hours" and as and when the employer requires the employee.

This situation does not apply where the employer has previously retained the employee to do work of a casual nature on occasions whether or not the employee would have a reasonable expectation of work.

Where the employee has not been required to work at all in the week, the employee is entitled to the lesser of 25 per cent of the contract hours (or 25 per cent of the hours during which such work was done) *or* 15 hours' pay. Hence, if an employee is required to be available for 48 hours in a week, the employee would be entitled to 12 hours' pay, even if not called in.

Alternatively, where the employee has been required to work for less than 25 per cent of the "contract hours" or where such work has been done in the employment, they will be paid for 25 per cent of the hours of that work. The maximum percentage hours is again 15 hours. Hence the employee will be entitled to either 15 hours' pay or 25 per cent of the "contract hours" or the time worked, whichever is the lesser.

These provisions obviously do not apply where the employee was on lay-off or short-time during the week in question or there has been an emergency or accident in circumstances outside the employer's control. If an employee is not available due to illness or for some other reason, they are entitled to no such payment. Also this section does not apply to employees who are required to be "on call" for emergencies, for example. In such cases, the employees usually receive an "on call" allowance in addition to normal pay.

This will not affect a contract of employment that entitles the employee to be paid wages by the employer by reason alone of the employee making themselves available for work at the time and place concerned.

Zero Hours Contracts

The case of *Ocean Manpower Limited* v *MPGWU* ([1998] ELR 299) considered the issue of zero hours contracts, where the union sought on behalf of the worker concerned entitlement to benefit from the zero hours provision in section 18 of the Act and accordingly that the worker be paid the minimum of 15 hours' pay for each week since 30 September 1997. The company rejected the claim on the grounds that the worker's casual status precluded any entitlement under the Act. The agreement between the Union and the company clearly required employees to remain available for work during defined periods. They are also required to report to the company's premises at a specified time for the purpose of being allocated work. Furthermore, failure on an employee's part to report as required might be the subject of disciplinary proceedings under the agreement. While these obligations might not be rigidly enforced by the company, they remained part of the agreement and were a requirement in the employees' contract of employment. The Labour Court was satisfied that section 18 of the Act applied.

> It seems clear to the Court that the floor payment provided for by section 18(2) should be calculated by reference to the number of hours which the employee may be required to work in a week and not to the number of hours over which they are required to be available to undertake that work. It is noted that the agreement provides that normal working hours are to be from 8 a.m. to 5 p.m. for a five-day week. On this basis the rights commissioner's calculation of a floor payment of 10 hours or 9¾ hours in the case of a 39-hour week is correct. The rights commissioner is also correct in stipulating that where an employee does not present himself for work on any day (or days) of the week, the entitlement should reduce by 20 per cent (or multiples of 20 per cent as the case may

be). Also where an employee works in any day or days of the week, no entitlement arises once the basic entitlement has been exceeded.

AGENCY WORKERS

Agency workers are persons who register with employment agencies that make temporary workers available to a third party (the hirer), the classic example being "agency temps", often secretaries. The legal status of such work is both complicated and unfortunate, and the law in Ireland (*The Minister for Labour* v *PMPA Insurance Co. under administration* (1986) 5 JISLL 215) is that the agency temp is not an employee of the hiring company and thus does not have any protection under the legislation. If they were to be considered employees of anyone, it would be of the employment agency.

The Unfair Dismissals (Amendment) Act, 1993, provides that agency temps placed by an employment agency under the Employment Agency Act, 1971, shall be entitled to bring unfair dismissal claims for redress against the hiring company, i.e. the employer with whom they are placed. Of course, the agency temp must have the necessary service under the unfair dismissals legislation. The Terms of Employment (Information) Act, 1994, makes provision for a written statement of terms and conditions of employment provided that the employee has worked for four weeks. The responsibility to provide the statement is with the "employer" and the person liable to pay the wages of the individual who does the work. Therefore, if an individual is placed by an agency and is an "agency temp", then the agent should be responsible for the provision of the statement.

TEMPORARY EMPLOYMENT

In order to fall within the scope of protective legislation, a temporary worker must be an employee working under a contract of employment (of service) and must normally be expected to work at least eight hours per week. However, it should be noted that that worker must have the requisite period of service under the relevant legislation, namely: Unfair Dismissals Acts (one year); Redundancy Payments Acts (two years); and Minimum Notice and Terms of Employment Acts (13 weeks). There must be continuity of service and, in relation to seasonal employment, it is not sufficient for an employer to state that the contract comes to an end at the end of every season (for example in certain manufacturing industries and the hotel industry). The Employment Appeals Tribunal has considered that if the person works year-in year-out, or there is a pattern of such working, when that person is not working it is deemed to be a period of lay-off and continuity is preserved (*Roscrea Meat Products* v *Mullins and Others* UD 347/1983, and *Cowman* v *Bon Voyage Travel Ltd.* 1054/1983). Furthermore, the 1993 Unfair Dismissals Act provides that if an employee is re-employed within 26 weeks of dismissal, their continuity of service is not broken (see Chapter 16, "Notice"). Employers cannot dismiss and re-employ employees in order to avoid liability under the Acts.

FIXED-TERM CONTRACTS

One Fixed-Term Contract

The Unfair Dismissals Act, 1977, does not apply to the non-renewal of a fixed-term or a specified purpose contract, provided the contract is in writing, signed by both parties and states that the Act will not apply to the termination of the contract.

Section 2(2)(b) of the 1977 Act provides that the Act shall not apply in relation to:

> . . . dismissal where the employment was under a contract of employment for a fixed term or a specified purpose (being a purpose of such a kind that the duration of the contract was limited but was, at the time of its making, incapable of precise ascertainment) and the dismissal consisted only of the expiry of the term without its being renewed under the said contract or the cesser of the purpose and the contract is in writing, was signed for or on behalf of the employer and by the employee and provides that this Act shall not apply to a dismissal consisting only of the expiry or cesser aforesaid. . . .

In *O'Mahony* v *College of the Most Holy Trinity* ([1998] ELR 159), Trinity College Dublin argued that the Act did not apply to the claimant because he was employed for a three-year fixed-term contract and thus excluded by virtue of Section 2(2)(b) of the Act. In 1991, the College decided to appoint a full-time lecturer in psychol-

ogy. This position was advertised as being "tenable for an initial period of three years".

The claimant, a distinguished psychologist, replied to the advertisement, and was sent certain documentation, including a document
setting out conditions of employment, covering such matters as pension, which had all the appearances of relating to a permanent post.
The College said that he should have received another document, setting out the terms and conditions for a three-year contract, and it
seems that there was a clerical error in dispatching the papers to
him.

The claimant maintained that he arrived at the interview under
the impression that he had applied for a permanent position, although subject to a probationary period. It was pointed out to him
that all that was on offer was a three-year fixed-term contract. There
was the possibility of renewal at the end of that period, and also the
possibility that the post might be made permanent (subject to advertisement).

The claimant accepted the letter dated 18 October 1991, offering
him the appointment. This letter formed the contract of employment,
subject to the conditions of appointment attached thereto. An extract
was noted:

> As this appointment is for the fixed period . . . the provisions of
> the Unfair Dismissals Act (1977) will not apply to a dismissal con-
> sisting only of the expiry of the fixed term. . . . The lecturer's ap-
> pointment will be terminable by three months' notice from either
> side. Such notice to take effect on March 31st, or June 30th, or De-
> cember 31st.

The claimant was advised that he would not be re-employed at the
expiry of the three-year term. Because the post itself was not going to
be renewed, he was given a redundancy payment. The claimant argued (*inter alia*) that the contract he was employed under was not a
genuine fixed-term contract, as it contained both a notice provision
and also a probationary clause, and that there was not a genuine redundancy as the lectures were continuing. The Tribunal was of the
view that the redundancy defence would not succeed, as the fact that
a person is not replaced does not necessarily mean that it is a genuine redundancy. However, the Tribunal determined that by virtue of
Section 2(2)(b) of the 1977 Act, the Act does not apply to the termina-

tion of the contract. The Tribunal also held that even though there was both a probationary and a notice clause, that this did not destroy the fixed-term nature of the contract.

Non-renewal of Second or Subsequent Fixed-Term Contract

The Unfair Dismissals (Amendment) Act, 1993, extends s 2(2)(b) as follows:

> Provided that where, following dismissal consisting only of the expiry of the term of the contract of employment . . . (the "prior contract") without the term being renewed under the contract or the cesser of the purpose of the contract:
>
> (i)   the employee concerned is re-employed by the employer concerned within 3 months of the dismissal under a contract of employment such as aforesaid made between the employer and the employee (the "subsequent contract") and the nature of the employment is the same as or similar to that of the employment under the prior contract;
>
> (ii) the employee is dismissed from the employment;
>
> (iii) the dismissal only consisted of the expiry of the term of the subsequent contract without the term being renewed under the contract or the cesser of the purpose of the contract; and
>
> (iv) in the opinion of the rights commissioner, the Employment Appeals Tribunal, the Circuit Court or as the case may be, the entry by the employer into the subsequent contract was wholly or partly for or was connected with the purpose of liability under the Act —
>
> then:
>
> a)   this Act shall, subject to the other provisions thereof, apply to the dismissal, and
>
> b)   the term of the prior contract and any of the antecedent contracts shall be added to the subsequent contracts for the purpose of ascertainment under the Act of the period of service of the employee with the employer and the period so ascertained shall be deemed for these purposes to be one of continuous service.

The main area of concern is the non-renewal of a second or subsequent fixed-term contract. From an employer's viewpoint, the issue is problematic, as the Employment Appeals Tribunal may view the periods of employment as continuous unless there is good reason for the termination (or non-renewal) of the contract, and it could be held to be an unfair dismissal.

The Employment Appeals Tribunal has stated that employers may not use the device of a fixed-term contract to avoid the unfair dismissals legislation. In *FitzGerald* v *St Patrick's College* (UD 244/1978) where the claimant was a lecturer who had been employed on a series of fixed-term contracts that were eventually not renewed, the Chairman of the Tribunal stated:

> . . . if the mere expiry of a fixed term contract of employment were to be regarded as a substantial ground for the non-renewal of employment, the Unfair Dismissals Act, 1977, could be rendered abortive in many cases. An employer could side-step its provisions by employing his employees on fixed-term contracts only. Then, to get rid of an employee, on whatever grounds, be they trivial or substantial, fanciful or solid, fair or unfair, he need only wait until that employee's fixed-term contract expired, and then refuse to renew it.

Accordingly, employees working on repeated fixed-term contracts are covered under the unfair dismissals legislation, though they need to have at least one year's continuous service before they could bring a claim under the Unfair Dismissals Act.

The principles laid down by the Employment Appeals Tribunal have now been incorporated in the Unfair Dismissals (Amendment) Act, 1993. The Act provides that employers cannot avoid liability under the unfair dismissals legislation by employing their staff on such contracts. Thus, if there are two or more fixed-term contracts (i.e. re-employment within three months of the expiry of the first contract of any subsequent contract), then the adjudicating body may examine any second or subsequent contract to see if the employer was trying to avoid the legislation. Obviously, this only applies where the dismissal arises because the term of the contract has come to an end and there has been no renewal. These new rules are complicated and to date there is no determination from the Employment Appeals Tribunal interpreting them.

The Maternity Protection Act, 1994, applies to female employees working under a fixed-term contract. However, if the fixed term comes to an end during maternity leave, then the contract expires at that time.

Even though a contract is for a fixed term, it is strongly recommended that a notice clause be included in it. If, for example, the contract were for three years and the employer terminated it after six months — the employee would be entitled to sue for the balance of the contract, that is, for two-and-a-half-years' pay, in the absence of such a provision.

SPECIFIED PURPOSE CONTRACTS

These are entered into in order to complete a special project. They must be used carefully, however, because if an employee were employed to do a specific job and spent time doing other work, it may render the contract void. The employee may then fall within the scope of the Unfair Dismissals Act if there is a claim on termination, presuming the employee has the requisite one year's service.

Of course, an employer could well use the defence of redundancy if a claim is brought for unfair dismissal following the non-renewal of a second or subsequent contract. Further, an employer could be liable for a redundancy payment if the employee has 104 weeks' continuous service and there is a genuine redundancy situation on the expiry of a specified purpose contract (see Chapter 18, "Redundancy"). The provisions under the Unfair Dismissals (Amendment) Act, 1993, equally apply to specified purpose contracts.

TEMPORARY OFFICERS

Officers of health boards, local authorities and vocational education committees were excluded from the scope of the Unfair Dismissals Act, 1977. Problems have arisen in the case of temporary doctors and nurses and other temporary professional staff in the health boards, as they are deemed officers; for example, in *Western Health Board* v *Quigley* ([1982] ILRM 390) where the claimant, a nurse, had been employed as a temporary officer for many years and did not fall within the scope of the Act.

The Unfair Dismissals (Amendment) Act, 1993, makes provision that temporary officers of health boards fall within the scope of the unfair dismissals legislation.

In *Buckley* v *Southern Health Board* (MN293 UD110/96) (Circuit Court, Clifford J, unreported, 16 December 1998) (on appeal) the claimant was employed as a temporary full-time consultant psychiatrist from 20 March 1989 to 31 August 1995. The Tribunal were satisfied that at all times the reality of the position was that the post held by Dr Buckley was held temporarily, pending it being filled on a permanent basis.

In summary, the facts of the case were that Dr Buckley was employed on the basis of a series of fixed-term contracts. The Health Board hoped to create a permanent post at some stage, but claimed that this was delayed as a result of an overall review of its services and by efforts to get sanction for the filling of the position on a permanent basis.

The Tribunal was satisfied that Dr Buckley could not reasonably have got the impression that the temporary status had changed or had been converted into a permanent status of one other than temporary and was satisfied that at no stage did the Health Board act or conduct itself towards Dr Buckley in any manner such as would have entitled her to consider that a temporary status had changed. Therefore, when the Health Board had a successful candidate, they were entitled to terminate Dr Buckley's contract.

It would have been *ultra vires* for the Health Board to unilaterally confirm "permanent" status on a person in Dr Buckley's position. The Health Board would only fill the position in a permanent way by going through the Local Appointments Commission procedure and the Tribunal relied on the authority of *Western Health Board* v *Quigley* ([1982] ILRM 390), where Barrington J stated:

> A Health Board has no power to employ staff to carry out the duties of officers without going through the procedures laid down under the Local Authorities (Officers and Employees) Acts for the appointment of such staff.

The Tribunal further relied on the reasoning of Gleeson J in the case of *Ponnampalam* v *Mid-Western Health Board* (UD 300/79 Circuit Court, Gleeson J, 26 March 1980), which was an appeal to the Circuit

Court under the Unfair Dismissals Act, 1977. In that judgement, the former chairman of the Employment Appeals Tribunal stated as follows:

> I am satisfied that even if the Unfair Dismissals Act applied, section 6(4)(d) applies and makes the claimant's dismissal not unfair because I find that it resulted wholly from the claimant's inability to continue to work, without the employers contravention of the restriction imposed on them as a Health Board by Section 14 of the Health Act namely the sanction of Bord na nOspidéal.

The Unfair Dismissals (Amendment) Act, 1993, extended the protection of the unfair dismissals legislation to temporary officers of Health Boards. It was covered by the legislation and the Tribunal found that the recent aforesaid Section 6(4)(d) of the Unfair Dismissals Act, 1977, covered the position and meant that the dismissal was not unfair. Clifford J, on appeal to the Circuit Court, held that the Health Board had a duty to make a permanent appointment to the post and that it came within s 6(4) of the 1977 Act.

In *Orren* v *Western Health Board* (UD 268/96 and MN 676/96), the claimant had been employed by the respondent Health Board as Consultant Immunologist in an acting capacity from 1 April 1994. Her employment continued in an acting capacity by way of a number of contracts, which operated consecutively, until her employment was terminated on 31 December 1995. In the course of this period of employment, the position had been advertised by the Health Board on two separate occasions through the Local Appointments Commission in compliance with their legal obligations under Section 6 of the Local Authority Officers and Employees Act, 1926, and under Sections 15 and 18 of the Health Act, 1970. In the first competition, the claimant was unable to apply, because the upper age limit was too low. After representations by the claimant, the age limit was raised for the second competition and the claimant applied and was interviewed for the position. Unfortunately, she was not successful. The permanent post was offered to another doctor, with effect from January 1996, and the claimant was advised by letter of 11 October 1995. However, due to difficulties with his existing contract of employment, that doctor could not take up his position with the respondent Health Board until June 1996. The claimant became aware of this and offered to remain on until the new doctor was in a position to commence his duties. The respondent, however, discontinued the claimant's employment at the end of 1995 with the expiry of her final contract. The claimant was advised of this position in advance, per the respondent's letter to her of 31 October 1995.

The Tribunal was satisfied, from a substantive point of view, that the Health Board would have had substantial grounds to terminate the employment of the claimant under the circumstances in which the Local Appointments Commission had recommended the appointment of a person to fill the post of Consultant Immunologist. The decision to terminate the claimant's employment would be reasonable in these circumstances. However, the evidence before the Tribunal was such that the issue was not so clear-cut. The failure of the respondent to address the issue of keeping the claimant in employment until such time as the person recommended by the Local Appointments Commission could take up his post, led the Tribunal to the conclusion that the claimant was not dealt with fairly, as from 1 January 1996 to 1 June 1996, the services provided by the claimant were needed by the respondent. There was no good reason as to why the claimant could not have been kept in employment until 1 June 1996. Accordingly, the Tribunal was satisfied that in the light of this knowledge, the decision to terminate the claimant's employment on 31 December 1995 was procedurally unfair. Under the circumstances, there was no effective way of implementing either re-engagement or re-instatement, having regard to the legal strictures placed on the respondent. The Tribunal determined that the sum of £25,692 be paid to the claimant, being the sum equivalent to what she would have received for the five months.

Officers of vocational education committees established under the Vocational Education Acts, 1930-1944 are excluded from the jurisdiction of the Unfair Dismissals Acts, 1977-1993. The definition of "officer" is seen within the context of "eligible part-time teachers" who are teachers who receive pro-rata rights to permanent full time teachers who are officers of the vocational education committees. In *Hanley* v. *Co. Mayo VEC* ([1999] ELR 10), the claimant, an eligible part-time teacher who taught secretarial skills, was made redundant because there was a drop in numbers taking such classes. Section 23 of the Vocational Education Act, 1930 provides that each vocational educational committee shall appoint inter alia officers and servants as appropriate. In this case, the claimant was a part-time teacher from

1972-1989 and was not an officer during that time. In 1989 she became an eligible part-time teacher. The Employment Appeals Tribunal considered that she was not an officer, because all the provisions in the 1930 Act regarding appointment, removal from office and so forth did not apply. For example, permanent whole-time teachers were not made redundant in the event of their work diminishing; they would be re-deployed or re-trained. The Tribunal considered that there was no difference between her pre- and post-1989 position. Hence she was not an "officer".

APPRENTICES

The Unfair Dismissals Acts do not apply to the dismissal of a person who is or was employed under a statutory apprenticeship (i.e. an apprenticeship under the Industrial Training Act, 1967, as amended) if the dismissal takes place within six months after the commencement of the apprenticeship or within one month after the commencement of the apprenticeship or within one month after the completion thereof. The 1993 Act provides that an apprentice can bring a claim if dismissed for trade union membership or activity even though the apprentice does not have one year's service.

The Redundancy Payments Act, 1967, provides that an apprentice can be dismissed within one month of the completion of the apprenticeship and not be entitled to a redundancy payment. Employers must ensure that when they look at the date of such dismissal, they include the notice period — in other words, it must expire prior to the end of that one month.

It should also be noted that, should an employee go on maternity leave during the apprenticeship period, the apprenticeship can be lengthened to cover the period of time which she has lost while out on maternity leave.

Some apprenticeships are called statutory apprenticeships under the Industrial Training Act, 1967. With its attendant regulations, the Act provides for certain rules covering designated apprenticeships, which include engineering, construction, electrical, printing, motor, furniture and dental craftspersons. These rules govern the length of the apprenticeship, age of entry and qualifications. An apprentice may be dismissed without notice for grave misconduct or wilful disobedience in the course of employment, either during or after the ex-

piry of the period of probation. An apprentice may be dismissed for
any other reason with one week's notice. In all other cases, an employer will have to give one month's notice to FÁS. This is considered
in more detail in Chapters 17 and 18 on Unfair Dismissal and Redundancy.

EQUALITY

There are no service requirements for employees in respect of the
current equal pay or equal treatment legislation. The equal pay legislation provides that an employer can pay different rates of pay on
grounds other than sex; however, an employee working part-time
should not be paid on a lower pro-rata rate, presuming that they are
doing "like work" with a full-time male employee (e.g. *St Patrick's
College* v *Nineteen Female Employees* EP 4/1984 DEP 10/1984).
Equally, there cannot be any differentiation in treatment between
part-time and full-time employees; for example, selecting part-time
female employees for redundancy instead of male full-time employees
(*Two Employees* v *Michael O'Neill and Sons Ltd.* DEE 1/1988). Of
course, the Employment Equality Act, 1998, will extend the further
grounds of discrimination to temporary and part-time employees, as
there are no service requirements.

JOB-SHARING

Job-sharing as a form of work arrangement has been receiving considerable attention in recent years. It may be defined as one full-time
permanent post with benefits being shared by (usually) two employees. There are many permutations and combinations of job-sharing.
It provides for considerable flexibility for employees who wish to work
only part-time, though they are working within the confines of a full-
time post.

  The European Court of Justice held in the case of *Hill and Stapleton* v *The Revenue Commissioners* ([1998] IRLR 466) that Article 119
of the Treaty and the rules regarding equal pay must be interpreted
as meaning that where a greater percentage of women than men are
employed on a job-sharing basis, the pay increments awarded by reference to time actually worked to those exercising the right to move
from job-sharing to full-time work may not be organised in such a
way that the individuals concerned are placed at a lower grade in the

pay scale than other workers on full-time work who have the same length of service measured in years.

Access to job-sharing was considered in the *Minister for Justice, Equality and Law Reform and Others* v *Hand* (DEE 5/1998) where Ms Hand considered she was indirectly discriminated against because the Department did not give her a job-sharing position. The claimant maintained that discrimination occurred because she was required to work full-time. The equality officer held in her favour, but the Labour Court overturned the decision on appeal. The Labour Court considered that Ms Hand sought to impose a condition on her return to work that she be offered work at the level of Assistant Principal in a job-sharing capacity. The Department did try to facilitate the claimant but was unable to do so. The job-sharing arrangement in the Civil Service was created to benefit employees who wished to work part-time for domestic or personal reasons. It did not create an automatic entitlement to such posts but was subject to availability and suitability. In this instance, the claimant wanted to return following maternity leave and a career break and was advised her position was suitable for job-sharing. As the claimant had a senior job, the number of job-sharing posts was limited. There were a number of trawls through available posts but these yielded no results. The Labour Court found that the position of Assistant Principal was essentially a full-time one at this time. It was determined that there was no discrimination under the Employment Equality Act, 1977. (However, arising from an earlier mishandling, which was not discriminatory, the claimant should not be disadvantaged in respect of any financial loss, for a specific time period.)

Other examples of cases involving job-sharing are *An Post* v *O'Connor* (DDE 1/1998), which concerned an employee who wished to have full pay for maternity leave even though she was a job sharer. She maintained that the case of *Gurster* v *Freistaat Bayern* (C1/85) applied in that she should have been credited for service as if she had worked full hours. However, the Labour Court did not consider that the employer had breached the principles of the *Gurster* decision.

The *Gurster* decision was also raised in the case of the *Office of the Revenue Commissioners, Department of Finance* v *Flood* (DEE 3/1998) where the Labour Court considered the issue of discrimination and job-sharing. The claimant alleged that she had suffered discrimination, as her service during her period at work in a job-sharing capacity was only credited for promotional purposes as service at the rate of part-time working. The claimant's case was that the "requirement" that she be working in full-time service in order to obtain promotion was discriminatory, as a disproportionate number of women working for the Revenue Commissioners were unable to comply, since almost all of the part-time workers were women. She further claimed that the "requirement" impacted more on married women than on single women.

The equality officer rejected her claim on the basis that the statistics that had been produced did not show that a substantially greater number of women than men were affected by the requirement to work full-time and that, in the absence of statistical information in relation to marital status of those affected by the requirement, it would be unsafe to find in favour of the claimant. The decision of the European Court in the *Gurster* case was handed down on 2 October 1997, two years after the recommendation of the equality officer. As a result of that decision and following a directive from the Minister for Finance, the practice of which the claimant complained had ceased. From 1 December 1997, service in a job-sharing capacity in the public service was credited as full-time service for the purposes of promotional competition in the civil service.

The Court was satisfied therefore that the claimant suffered no loss as a result of the former alleged discriminatory practice of the Revenue Commissioners.

EMPLOYEE PARTICIPATION

The Worker Participation (State Enterprises) Acts, 1977 to 1991, provide for the election of temporary employees of designated state enterprises to the board of directors. In order to vote in such elections, an employee must be aged between 18 and 65 years and have one year's service, and in order to stand for such election, the employee must have three years' service. Participating employees are normally expected to work at least eight hours per week (see Chapter 12, "Employee Participation").

EU DIRECTIVE ON PART-TIME WORKERS

Directive 97/81/EC implements the Framework Agreement agreed between the European social partners on part-time work, which was agreed on the 6 June 1997 and should be implemented into Irish law by 20 January 2000. There is provision that member states may have a maximum of a further year to take into account special difficulties (inter alia).

The Framework Agreement on part-time work is contained in the Annex to this short Directive. The Preamble provides that this Agreement is a contribution to the overall European strategy on employment and part-time employment, which has had an important impact on employment in recent years. The Agreement sets out the general principles and minimum requirements relating to part-time work and to provide for the elimination of discrimination against part-time workers and to assist the development of opportunities for part-time working on a basis acceptable to employers and workers.

The purpose of the Framework Agreement is to:

1. Provide for the removal of discrimination against part-time workers and to improve the quality of part-time work;

2. Facilitate the development of part-time work on a voluntary basis and to contribute to the flexible organisation of working time in a manner that takes into account the needs of employers and workers.

The Agreement applies to

1. Part-time workers who have an employment contract or employment relationship as defined by the law, collective agreement or practice in force in each member state;

2. Member States after consultation with the social partners may, for "objective reasons", exclude wholly or partly part-time workers who work on a casual basis. Such objective reasons must be reviewed periodically to ensure they remain valid.

"Part-time worker" is defined as an employee whose normal hours of work are less than the normal hours of work of a "comparable full-time worker". Hours of work are calculated on a weekly basis or on an average over a period of employment up to one year. The term "comparable full-time worker" means a full-time worker in the same establishment having the same type of employment contract or relationship, who is engaged in the same or a similar work/occupation, due regard being given to other considerations, which may include seniority and qualifications/skills. If there are no comparable full-time workers in the same establishment, the comparison shall be made by reference to national law or politics.

The principles of non-discrimination are:

1. "Part-time workers" shall not be treated in a less favourable manner in respect of employment conditions than comparable full-time workers, solely because they were part-time, unless different treatment is justified on objective grounds.

2. Where appropriate, the principle of pro-rata time (*prorata temporis*) based conditions shall apply. This means that pay conditions shall be pro-rated on time worked as compared to full-time workers. The arrangements for the application of this clause shall be in accordance with national law. There is provision that access to particular conditions of employment may be subject to a period of service, time worked or earnings qualification. Such qualifications shall be reviewed periodically for the purposes of non-discrimination.

Member States and the social partners shall identify and review obstacles of a legal or administrative nature that may limit the opportunities for part-time work and, where appropriate, eliminate them.

A worker's refusal to transfer to full-time work from part-time work or vice versa shall not constitute grounds for a valid dismissal. This would be subject to the operational requirements of the establishment. However, employers should give consideration to employees who wish to transfer from full-time to part-time work that becomes available; requests from workers who wish to transfer from part-time to full-time work or to increase their working time; the provision of timely information or the availability of part-time and full-time work and transfer from full-time to part-time work or vice versa at all levels in the establishment; and opportunities for part-time workers for vocational training to enhance career opportunities and occupational mobility. All such information should also go to trade unions.

There shall be procedures for the settlement of disputes and grievances. The Agreement shall be reviewed five years after the Council decision.

EU DIRECTIVE CONCERNING THE POSTING OF WORKERS IN THE FRAMEWORK OF THE PROVISION OF SERVICES

Directive 96/71/EC was adopted in order to cover the temporary posting of a worker, employed by an employer in one Member State of the EU under a contract regulated by that Member State, to a second Member State where the work is actually carried out. The purpose of this Directive is to remove obstacles to the free movement of persons and services and it must be in force by 16 December 1999.

A "posted worker" means a worker who for a limited period carries out his work in the territory of a Member State other than the state in which he normally works. Further, the definition of a worker is that which applies in the law of the Member State to whose territory the worker is posted.

The Directive is both obligatory and permissive, in that the second Member State has to apply certain minimum standards of its labour law and collective agreements to the posted worker but is allowed apply other standards or indeed exclude the posted worker from those other standards as it may choose.

This Directive applies to all undertakings established in a Member State where there is

• The posting of workers to the territory of another Member State to work for them and under their direction under a contract between the employer who has made the posting and the party for whom the services are intended;

• The posting of workers to an establishment or undertaking owned by the group in the territory of a Member State provided there is an employment relationship between the undertaking making the posting and the worker during the period of the posting; or

• A temporary employment undertaking or placement agency, and a worker is hired out to a user undertaking, established or operating in the territory of a Member State, provided there is an employment relationship between the temporary employment undertaking or placement agency and the worker during the period of the posting.

Undertakings established in a non-Member State must not be given more favourable treatment than undertakings established in a Member State.

Terms and Conditions of Employment

Member States shall ensure that, whatever the law applicable to the employment relationship, the undertakings must guarantee workers posted to their territory the terms and conditions covering the following matters which are laid down in the Member State where the work is carried out (either by law or by collective agreement):

- Maximum work period and minimum rest periods

- Minimum paid annual holidays

- Minimum rates of pay, including overtime rates (this does not apply to supplementary occupational retirement pension schemes)

- The conditions of hiring out of workers, in particular the supply of workers by temporary employment undertakings

- Health, safety and hygiene at work

- Protective measures with regard to the terms and conditions of employment of pregnant women or women who have recently given birth, of children and of young people

- Equality of treatment between men and women and other provisions of non-discrimination.

With the exception of the building industry, Member States can also exclude from the provision of the application of this Directive the initial assembly and first installation of goods where this is an integral part of a contract for the supply of goods and necessary for bringing the goods supplied into use and carried out by skilled or specialist workers of the supplying undertaking, provided the posting does not exceed eight days.

DRAFT EU AGREEMENT ON FIXED-TERM CONTRACTS

There is currently a proposal for a Council Directive concerning the framework agreement on fixed-term work, concluded by UNICE,

CEEP and the ETUC (Brussels 28 April 1999) COM (99 203 Final). This draft framework agreement is to improve the quality of fixed-term work, by ensuring the application of the principle of non-discrimination, and to establish a framework to prevent abuse arising from the use of successive fixed-term employment contracts or relationships. It is envisaged that this agreement will apply to all fixed-term workers, with the exception of vocational training relationships and apprenticeship schemes and employment contracts concluded within the framework of a specific public or publicly supported training, integration and vocational retraining programmes. "Fixed-term worker" means a person having an employment contract or relationship entered into directly between an employer and a worker, where the end of the employment contract or relationship is determined by objective conditions such as reaching a specific date, completing a specific test, or the occurrence of a specific event. For the purposes of comparison, a "comparable permanent worker" means a worker with a work contract or relationship of an indefinite duration, in the same establishment, engaged in the same or similar work/occupation, due regard being given to qualifications and skills. The draft agreement provides for the principle of non-discrimination where fixed-term workers shall not be treated in a less favourable manner than comparable permanent workers on the basis that they are employed on a fixed-term contract. Member States shall introduce measures to prevent abuse arising from the use of successive fixed-term employment contracts or relationships obviously where there are no legal measures in place. Such measures can include objective reasons justifying the renewal of such contracts or relationships, the maximum duration of successive fixed-term employment contracts or relationships and the number of renewals of such contracts or relationships. There is also provision that employers shall inform fixed-term workers about vacancies that become available in the firm so that they have the same opportunity to secure permanent positions as other workers. Fixed-term workers shall also be taken into consideration in calculating numbers in a company for the purposes of worker representative bodies.

General References

Hepple B. and P. O'Higgins, (1981), *Employment Law*, 4th edition, Dublin: Sweet and Maxwell.

Leighton, P. (1986), "Job-sharing", *Industrial Law Journal*, No. 3.

Meenan, F. (1985), "Temporary and Part-time Employees", *Gazette of the Incorporated Law Society of Ireland*, July/August.

Redmond, M. (1983), "Beyond the Net: Protecting the Individual Worker", JISLL 1.

SECTION TWO

TERMS AND CONDITIONS OF EMPLOYMENT

Chapter Four

ANNUAL LEAVE, PUBLIC HOLIDAYS AND JURY SERVICE

The need for an employee to reconcile work and family responsibilities and the need for rest and recreation are essential for everybody in employment and are so recognised by the legislation. Over the years, this annual leave entitlement has been extended through various national and local agreements, legislation and an EC Directive. In some employments, the amount of annual leave is based on length of service or seniority within the employment. The EU Directive concerning certain aspects of the organisation of working time (93/104/EC) came into operation in Ireland (in respect of holiday provisions) under the Organisation of Working Time Act, 1997, on 30 September 1997. This Act provides for a statutory minimum of annual leave of four weeks to be applied over a transitional period of three years (Organisation of Working Time Act, 1997 (Commencement) Order, 1997, SI No. 392 of 1997). In *Ocean Manpower Ltd.* v *MPGWU* ([1998] ELR 299), the Act provides for a minimum entitlement, which can be improved upon by agreement. However, enhanced terms are not recoverable by the enforcement procedures established by the Act.

That Act repeals the Holidays (Employees) Act, 1973, and Section 4 of the Worker Protection (Regular Part-Time Employees) Act, 1991 (which provided for annual leave and public holiday benefits for regular part-time employees).

The Organisation of Working Time Act (holiday provisions — sections 19–23) applies to all employees (of any age) working under a contract of employment, to include all State employees — civil servants, employees of local authorities, health boards, harbour authorities, vocational education committees — and includes agency workers (the person who pays the wages, i.e., the employment agency or the hiring company). These provisions do not apply to members of the Garda Síochána and the Defence Forces.

ANNUAL LEAVE

The statutory minimum for annual leave is four working weeks in a leave year, subject to the transitional provisions in respect of leave years 1997/1998, 1998/1999 and 1999/2000 (see below). The full entitlement of "four working weeks" came into effect on 1 April 1999.

An employee has the following entitlements equal to:

1. Four working weeks in a leave year in which the employee works at least 1,365 hours (unless it is a leave year in which the employee changes employment);

2. One-third of a working week for each month in the leave year in which the employee works, at least 117 hours, or

3. Eight per cent of the hours the employee works in a leave year (but subject to a maximum of four working weeks).

If more than one of the above provisions applies to an employee, and where the period of annual leave is not identical, then the employee is entitled to the greater period of leave.

The reference to "working week" refers to the number of days the employee usually works in a week.

Leave Year

In practice, the leave year may vary from employment to employment. Some employments use the statutory definition of the leave year, which is 1 April to 31 March. Others may use the calendar year, 1 January to 31 December, and many manufacturing companies use 1 August to 31 July in the following year.

Entitlement

All "hours" that are worked, including overtime, are included for the purposes of calculating annual leave entitlement. Of course, time spent on annual leave is time worked. An employee who works for eight or more months in a leave year, subject to any provisions of an employment regulation order, registered employment agreement, collective agreement or any agreement between the employee and the employer, is entitled to two unbroken weeks' leave. Payment for annual leave must be made before annual leave actually begins.

If a female employee (or in the case of the death of the mother, the father of the child) has 14 weeks' maternity leave, it is included for the purpose of building up holiday entitlement. Thus, she is entitled to annual leave as well as maternity leave. Similar provisions apply to female employees (or sole male adopters) for the ten weeks' adoptive leave. However, time spent on additional maternity/adoptive leave — that is, up to an extra four weeks' (unpaid) leave — is not included for computation of leave. Time spent on parental leave and *force majeure* leave also builds up entitlement to holidays.

Method of Calculating Pay for Annual Leave

Pay for annual leave must be paid in advance of going on leave and be at the normal weekly rate or, as the case may be, at a rate which is proportionate to the normal weekly rate.

The Organisation of Working Time (Determination of Pay for Holidays) Regulations, 1997 (SI No. 475 of 1997), provides the methods for calculating the "normal weekly rate of pay" as follows:

1. If the employee's pay is calculated wholly by reference to a time rate or a fixed rate or salary that does not vary in relation to the work done, the normal weekly rate of pay shall be the sum (including any regular bonus or allowance which does not vary in respect of work done by the employee but excluding pay for overtime) that is paid in respect of normal weekly working hours last worked by the employee before the annual leave (or portion of annual leave) commences or the cesser of employment occurs;

2. If the employee's pay is not calculated as above, then the normal weekly rate of pay shall be the average weekly pay (excluding any pay for overtime) calculated over the period of:

   • Thirteen weeks ending immediately before the annual leave (or the portion of leave) commences or cesser of employment; or

   • If no time was worked during that period, then the period of 13 weeks ending on the day time was last worked by the employee before the annual leave (or portion of leave) commences or cesser of employment.

This second method of calculation would apply where an employee may be paid by basic salary and a variable commission and thus an average of the commission payable would be paid.

This method of calculation would also apply where an employee did some extra work and/or took extra responsibility. If this takes place during the 13 weeks prior to annual leave, the employee would get an average amount of that "extra pay". There is no statutory provision for including earnings arising from overtime. However, it would be the general practice, which the Labour Court has upheld, that "regular and rostered" overtime should be included in pay for annual leave.

Sickness

If an employee has been absent through illness during the leave year and, for example, has not worked 117 hours in each calendar month or where no hours are worked at all, then the employee may not be entitled to annual leave for that period. The employee may be entitled to eight per cent of the hours worked. However, if the employee has worked 1,365 hours in the total leave year, then that employee would still be entitled to the full leave. An employee who does not work for the 1,365 hours is only entitled to pro-rata leave for the time actually worked.

If an employee claims to have been ill during annual leave and is so certified by a medical practitioner, then that day or those days shall not be included in the employee's annual leave. Accordingly, the employee would then have extra days' entitlement.

Timing of Leave

The Act provides that the employer decides when the employee can take annual leave. The employer must take into account:

1. The need for the employee to reconcile work and any family responsibilities;

2. The opportunities for rest and recreation available to the employee.

The employer must consult with the employee or the employee's trade union at least one month before leave is to be given. Leave must be given in the annual leave year or, with the consent of the employee, within the six months following the leave year.

If an employer fails to give an employee annual leave within the appropriate time, the employer must pay the employee an amount equivalent to the holiday pay which would have been received if the employee had been allowed to take holidays in the normal way. The employee may also refer a complaint to the rights commissioner or the Employment Appeals Tribunal (as appropriate).

There is no provision in the Act where an employee can get "double payment" — that is, doing paid work for the employer during what should be holiday time and receiving holiday pay as well. Thus, assuming that the employer provides the employee with time off for annual leave (during the leave year or within six months of the end of the leave year, with the consent of the employee) and the employee does not take it, the employee could forfeit the leave. Of course, employers must ensure that the employee has the opportunity to take leave; otherwise the employee may bring a complaint to a rights commissioner or the Employment Appeals Tribunal, as appropriate.

In practice, a number of employments (particularly manufacturing companies) close for specified periods during the year; for example, the first two weeks in August and perhaps a week at Christmas. Generally, there can be flexibility about the timing of annual leave.

A registered agreement, employment regulation order or collective agreement may vary these legal rules about the granting of the period of unbroken annual leave for various categories of employees.

When granting annual leave, account must be taken of the pattern that a part-time employee works. For example, if the employee works three days per week, the annual leave would be over those three days. In other words, the annual leave must be given over the same days/hours that the employee works. Public holidays (see below) or sick days are not included for annual leave.

Cessation of Employment

The 1997 Act also provides that, when an employee ceases employment, any outstanding annual leave entitlement arising in the current leave year and the previous leave year must be paid by the employer. The employee should receive compensation for the loss of the annual leave proportionate to the normal weekly rate of pay had they been granted the leave.

PUBLIC HOLIDAYS

There are presently nine public holidays as listed in the Second
Schedule to the Organisation of Working Time Act, 1997.

- New Year's Day — 1 January

- St Patrick's Day — 17 March

- Easter Monday

- First Monday in May

- First Monday in June

- First Monday in August

- Last Monday in October

- Christmas Day — 25 December

- St Stephen's Day — 26 December.

The Minister may by regulation nominate any other day to be a public holiday or may substitute any of the above days with another day.
For example, New Year's Eve (31 December) 1999 was declared a
one-off, special public holiday in celebration of the Millennium (Organisation of Working Time (Public Holiday) Regulations, 1999 (SI
No. 10 of 1999)).

If a public holiday falls on a Sunday, it is automatically transferred to the next weekday — that is, a Monday. Good Friday and
Christmas Eve are not public holidays and an employee who does not
work those days must treat them as days of annual leave. Some contracts of employment state that the employment will be closed on
those days and they are deemed days of annual leave.

All whole-time employees are entitled to public holidays. Part-
time employees must have worked at least 40 hours during the five
weeks ending on the day before that public holiday. There is no public
holiday entitlement for an employee who is absent from work immediately before the public holiday where such an absence:

1. Is in excess of 52 consecutive weeks by reason of an injury sustained by the employee in an occupational accident (within the
   meaning of Chapter 10, Part II of the Social Welfare (Consolidation) Act, 1993);

2. Is in excess of 26 weeks by reason of an injury sustained by the employee in any accident (excluding a) above) or by reason of any disease from which the employee suffers or suffered;

3. Is in excess of 13 weeks for any absence authorised by the employer including a lay-off, but excluding absences under a) and b) above; or

4. Is due to a strike in the business or industry in which the employee is employed.

The employer can decide the manner in which the public holiday shall be given. The employer's options are:

1. A paid day off on the holiday, or

2. A paid day off within a month, or

3. An extra day's annual leave, or

4. An extra day's pay.

An employee may, at least 21 days prior to the public holiday, request the employer to make a determination as to the manner in which the public holiday will be granted. The employee must be notified of the decision at least 14 days before the holiday. If the employee fails to comply with the request, then the entitlement of the employee shall be to a paid day off on the public holiday or, if the employee is already entitled to a paid day off on that day, then the employee will get an additional day's pay.

If the public holiday falls on a day on which the employee would not normally work a full day, the 1997 Act provides that the employee is still entitled to a "full day's pay".

Rate of Pay

The Organisation of Working Time (Determination of Pay for Holidays) Regulations, 1997 (SI No. 475 of 1997) regulates pay for public holidays. Employees who work or who are normally required to work on a public holiday would be entitled to a day's pay for the public holiday.

1. The employee will be entitled to the sum (including any regular bonus or allowance the amount of which does not vary in relation

to the work done by the employee but excluding any pay for over-time) paid to the employee in respect of the normal daily hours last worked by the employee before that public holiday.

This matter was considered by the Labour Court in *Cadbury Ireland Ltd* v *SIPTU and ATGWU* (DWT 993), where the dispute concerned payment for the August public holiday weekend in 1997, when the night shift workers transferred to day shift. Cadbury's maintained that the employees should be paid for an eight-hour day for the public holiday as was the custom and practice. All employees who work during the shut-down period of two weeks commencing on the August public holiday sign a separate contract of employment for the two-week period and work day-shift only — eight hours per day. The unions maintained that workers coming off shift should receive ten hours' pay for the public holiday, based on the normal daily hours worked by an employee prior to the public holiday. The Labour Court determined that if the employees normally worked on a Monday, then they would be entitled to the amount received in respect of the normal daily hours worked by them on the last working day of the previous week — which was ten hours' pay. If they did not normally work on a Monday, then they should be paid one-fifth of a week's pay — i.e. for eight hours. (It should be noted that this matter was the subject of a rights commissioner hearing, under the Industrial Relations Acts, 1946–1990, in August 1997, prior to the commencement of the 1997 Act.)

2. In any other case, the employee will be entitled to the average daily pay (excluding any pay for overtime) calculated

    •   Over the period of 13 weeks ending immediately before that public holiday; or

    •   If no time was worked by the employee during that period, over the period of 13 weeks ending on the day on which time was last worked by the employee before that public holiday.

Employees who are not normally required to work on a public holiday will be entitled to one-fifth of the normal weekly rate of remuneration for the public holiday.

If an employee does not work on a public holiday, then:

1. The employee will be entitled to one-fifth of the sum (including any regular bonus or allowance the amount which does not vary in relation to work done by the employee but excluding any pay for overtime) paid in respect of the normal weekly hours last worked by the employee before that public holiday,

2. In any other case, the relevant rate in respect of that public holiday equal to one-fifth of the average weekly pay (excluding any pay for overtime) of the employee calculated

    *   Over the period of 13 weeks ending immediately before the public holiday, or

    *   If no time was worked by the employee during that period, over the period of 13 weeks ending on the day on which time was last worked by the employee before that public holiday. However, such an amount shall not exceed any sum which the employee would be entitled to if the calculation for employees normally required to work on a public holiday were to apply.

Calculation for Job Sharers

If an employee

1. Does not work or is not normally required to work on a public holiday; and

2. The employee is required to work half the time required to be worked by a whole-time employee (doing identical or similar work); and

3. The pay is calculated in accordance with a fixed rate or salary,

then the relevant rate of pay in respect of the public holiday shall be one-tenth of the sum (including any regular bonus or allowance, the amount of which does not vary in relation to work done but excluding pay for overtime) that is paid in respect of the last two weeks of normal working hours worked by the employee before that public holiday, provided that the relevant rate to which the employee would be entitled is not more than half the relevant rate they would have received for working on that day.

Church Holidays

An employer may substitute a church holiday for a public holiday as long as the employee is given 14 days' advance notice (this is not applicable to Christmas Day or St Patrick's Day). Such church holidays include 6 January, Ascension Thursday, the Feast of Corpus Christi, 15 August, 1 November and 8 December. These days cannot be substituted when they fall on a Sunday (the feasts of Ascension and Corpus Christi always fall on a Thursday). These days are feast days of the Roman Catholic Church but there is provision for the Minister to vary such days by regulation.

Bank Holidays / "EC" Days

It is common usage for employees to talk about "bank holidays" or "EC" days. Such descriptions have no legal meaning.

Cessation of Employment

If a full-time employee leaving employment ceases to be employed during the week ending on the day before a public holiday, and if the employee has worked for the employer during the four weeks preceding that week, then the employee shall be entitled to compensation for their loss of entitlement on the basis of an additional day's pay at the appropriate daily rate.

Insolvency

If the employer has become insolvent, an employee can claim for holiday pay due under the Protection of Employees (Employers' Insolvency) Acts, 1984–1991. Up to a maximum of eight weeks' holiday pay due is allowed and the limit for any week's holidays due is £300 per week (see Chapter 21, "Employer Insolvency").

Maintenance of Entitlement

Employees who are on maternity or adoptive leave maintain their public holiday entitlement.

RECORDS

All annual leave and public holiday records should be maintained by the employer at the place where the employee works and retained for a period of at least three years for inspection by the Department of

Enterprise, Trade and Employment. If the employee works at two or more premises or places, then the premises or place where the activities of the employee is principally directed or controlled is the place where the records should be kept. If the employer fails to keep adequate records, the employer shall be guilty of an offence. Where there is a failure to keep records, then in any proceedings before a rights commissioner or the Labour Court, the onus of proof that the provisions of the Act were complied with lies with the employer.

OFFENCES

Under the Organisation of Working Time Act, 1997, failure to keep records of leave is an offence. Proceedings must be initiated within 12 months of the offence by the Minister for Enterprise, Trade and Employment. A person who is guilty of an offence is liable to a fine of IR£1,500.

Under the Holidays (Employees) Acts, 1973–1991 (which was only repealed on 30 September 1997), the failure to allow leave within a specified period, to pay for annual leave or public holidays, or to keep records of leave, are offences. Proceedings must be instituted within 12 months of the offence. The person prosecuting is technically the Minister for Enterprise, Trade and Employment. A person who is guilty of an offence is liable to a fine of £25 or, in the case of a second or subsequent offence (under the same heading), the sum of £50.

PROCEDURES

An employee can refer a complaint under the Organisation of Working Time Act, 1997, in respect of entitlement to annual leave, times and pay for annual leave, entitlement in respect of public holidays and compensation for holidays on cesser of employment.

Notices of complaint must be put in writing and referred to a rights commissioner within six months of the alleged contravention. The six-month time limit may be extended to twelve months if there is reasonable cause. The rights commissioner shall hear the complaint and decide as to whether the claim was well founded; require the employer to comply with the relevant provisions; and award compensation of up to two years remuneration, as it is just and equitable. The rights commissioner's recommendations may be appealed to the Labour Court within six weeks of the date of the recommendations.

The Labour Court may hear the appeal and issue its determination. This determination is final when appealed to the High Court, on a point of law only.

Enforcement

If a rights commissioner's recommendation has not been carried out in accordance with its terms (and the time period in the appeal has expired), then the Labour Court may hear evidence of its non-implementation and issue a determination. If the determination is not implemented within six weeks of the date of communication, then application may be made to the Circuit Court for an Order enforcing the determination.

Employment Appeals Tribunal

If an employee is bringing proceedings to the Employment Appeals Tribunal under the Unfair Dismissals Acts, 1977–1993, the Adoptive Leave Act, 1995, the Maternity Protection Act, 1994, the Payment of Wages Act, 1991, the Redundancy Payments Acts, 1967–1991 (*inter alia*), then the employee may at the same time make application for their "holiday claim" to be heard and to seek appropriate relief. The time limits under the above enactments will not apply to the holiday claim.

Chapter 22 ("The Labour Relations Commission and the Labour Court") and Chapter 23 ("Employment Appeals Tribunal") consider procedures in further detail.

Complaints prior to 30 September 1997

If an employee has a complaint relating to a date prior to the date of commencement of the 1997 Act, they may refer the complaint to the Conditions of Employment Section of the Department of Enterprise, Trade and Employment. If there is a case to answer, the Department may send an inspector to the employer's premises. The Minister may issue proceedings under the Holidays (Employees) Acts, 1973–1991, or the 1997 Act, as appropriate.

There may also be provision for proceedings where there is a breach of registered employment agreement or an Employment Regulation Order.

Rights commissioners are not permitted to hear disputes concerning holiday matters in relation to a group of employees, but there does not appear to be anything prohibiting a rights commissioner from hearing an individual grievance. The rights commissioner may issue a recommendation, which may be appealed to the Labour Court. The Labour Court may issue a "binding" recommendation, which is not enforceable in the courts. There is nothing to stop a claim under the industrial relations "path" and also a legal claim through the courts.

Holiday pay is deemed to be "wages" under the Payment of Wages Act, 1991, and an employee may pursue a claim for non-payment of holiday pay under that Act within six months of the contravention of the 1991 Act. Such a claim would be useful where there is a contractual right (as opposed to the statutory right under the 1997 Act) to holiday pay outstanding (see Chapter 6, "Payment of Wages").

JURY SERVICE

Most individuals are called for jury service at some stage in their working lives unless they are ineligible for some reason. Jurors attend court in criminal and civil (e.g. defamation) proceedings in order to decide the facts of the case. Members of the Defence Forces, those concerned with the administration of justice and persons who are mentally or physically incapable are ineligible for jury service. There are other professional categories that are excused as of right; namely doctors, nurses and principals of schools and colleges. A person who has been in prison may be disqualified from jury service. A person who has served (or attended to serve) on a jury in the previous three years may be excused by the county registrar. A judge at the end of a trial may also excuse a juror from service for a period of time.

Thus, an individual who does not fall into one of the above categories may be called for jury service if they are aged between 18 and 70 years and are on the Dáil Electoral Register. The Juries Act, 1976, provides the legislation relating to the qualification for service and selection of jurors. The country registrar selects persons to be called for jury service.

Any person, summonsed as a juror, who fails without reasonable excuse to attend court, shall be liable to a fine not exceeding £50.

It is an employer's duty to allow employees to attend for jury service. However, if it is not practicable because of the nature of an employee's work, or if it is an extremely busy time at work, a letter from the employer should be sent to the county registrar explaining the reason for the request to excuse the employee. A person who has not been excused by the county registrar may appeal to the court to which they have been summonsed to attend. The court's decision is final.

An employee or an apprentice shall be treated as employed or apprenticed during any period when absent from employment in order to comply with a jury summons. Thus, an employee or an apprentice is entitled to pay while on jury service. The Act does not provide a method of calculating such payment. Obviously, there is an entitlement to basic pay. It is more difficult to work out pay where an employee is at the loss of overtime pay, commission, shift premiums or other bonuses. In such circumstances, it would be reasonable for the employer to average such pay. Another difficulty that can arise is if the employee is working on night shift and is called to jury service during the day. Clearly, both may not be possible, so an employee should not be expected to work all night after attending in court during the day.

Frequently, an employee may be excused from jury service by the court at 11 a.m. in any morning of required service. Obviously, the employee should report to work as soon as reasonable that same day. The county registrar's office can provide a statement with details of an employee's attendance on jury duty if so required.

General References

Kerr, T. (1998), *Organisation of Working Time Act, 1997*, Dublin: Sweet and Maxwell.

Chapter Five

MATERNITY, ADOPTIVE AND PARENTAL LEAVE

MATERNITY LEAVE

The Maternity Protection Act, 1994, implements EC Council Directive 92/85/EEC (19 October 1992) (The Pregnant Workers' Directive). The Act came into effect on 30 January 1995 (SI No. 16 of 1995). The Directive provided for measures to encourage improvements in the safety and health at work of pregnant workers and workers who have recently given birth or are breastfeeding. The Irish Maternity Protection of Employees Acts, 1981 and 1991, are repealed.

Application of the Act

This Act covers all female employees (and male employees on the death of the mother following the birth of the child for the balance of the maternity leave or additional maternity leave) from the first day of employment working:

1. Under a contract of service to include all civil servants, members of the Garda Síochána and the Defence Forces;

2. As officers or servants of a local authority, vocational educational committee, local authorities, harbour authorities and health boards;

3. As apprentices;

4. As "agency temps", and the person who is liable to pay the employee's wages is the person deemed to be the employer;

5. On fixed term contracts. However, where the fixed term expires before the last day of maternity leave, then the maternity leave shall expire on the same day on which the contract expires.

Time Off

An employee is entitled to *paid* time off from her work during "normal working time" for ante-natal and post-natal medical checks. "Normal working time" does not include overtime where, in the month prior to taking time off, the employee has worked less than 20 hours overtime. The employer pays for this time off. The right to time off for "medical or related appointment" is subject to an employee giving written notification of the date and the time of the appointment to her employer at least two weeks beforehand. If the appointment is urgent, the employee must advise her employer within one week after the appointment, and give an indication of the circumstances for the non-compliance.

In addition, the employer may require the employee to produce an appointment card or similar document indicating the time and date of the appointment, confirming the pregnancy or specifying the expected week of confinement. This provision does not apply to the first medical appointment in relation to the pregnancy.

Paid time off for post-natal care relates to the period of 14 weeks following the birth of the baby. Again, the employee should give her employer two weeks' notice of the appointment.

There is provision for such circumstances as may occur if, through no fault of her own, she could not comply with the notification; she should then give her employer evidence of her appointment within one week of the appointment.

The Regulations governing such time off are the Maternity Protection (Time Off for Ante-Natal and Post-Natal Care) Regulations, 1995 (SI No. 18 of 1995), which came into effect on 30 January 1995.

Length of Maternity Leave

Maternity leave is for 14 consecutive weeks and there is no obligation on the employer to pay an employee when she is on maternity leave. The leave commences when the employee decides but the normal pattern is four weeks' leave before the baby is born and ten weeks' afterwards. The Pregnant Workers' Directive provides that a woman must take at least two weeks' leave prior to the baby being born and two weeks' after the baby is born. If the baby arrives late and she is left with less than four weeks to the end of the maternity leave then the leave can be extended up to a maximum of four weeks. If there are medical reasons, maternity leave can commence at an earlier date, and where the medical certificate is issued and shown to the employer, she is deemed to have complied with the notification procedure even though she may not have informed her employer of her pregnancy.

Fixed-term contract employees are afforded protection until the fixed term expires.

Notification to Employer

Maternity leave is subject to the pregnant employee

1. Notifying her employer of her intention to take leave at least four weeks before the commencement of maternity leave

2. Giving to her employer or producing for her employer's inspection a medical certificate confirming the pregnancy or the expected week of confinement. "Confinement" and "date of confinement" are defined in section 41 of the Social Welfare (Consolidation) Act, 1993. Confinement is defined as "labour resulting in the issue of a living child, or labour after 24 weeks of pregnancy resulting in the issue of the child whether alive or dead". "Date of Confinement" is defined as "where labour began on one day resulting in the issue of a child on another day, to the date of the issue of the child or, if a woman is confined of twins or a greater number of children, to the date of the issue of the last of them".

The employee may revoke her maternity leave notification.

If the baby is born at least four weeks before the expected date of confinement, the employee shall be deemed to have complied with the notification requirement provided that she notifies her employer within 14 days of the baby being born. Her maternity leave will be deemed to have commenced on the earlier of either the date when she commenced maternity leave or the date of confinement.

Additional Maternity Leave

Additional maternity leave is frequently known as "unpaid maternity leave" because there is no social welfare payment during this period. An additional period of four weeks may be taken immediately following the maternity leave period. It should not be confused with extended maternity leave as described above. The employee is entitled to take additional maternity leave, regardless of whether her maternity leave has been extended or not.

Entitlement of Father

Where the mother has been delivered of a living child before the fourteenth week following confinement and where the mother dies, then the father (provided he works under a contract of employment) is entitled to leave during (a) any weeks between the week of confinement and the end of the tenth week following confinement; or (b) where the mother dies after the tenth week, then the balance of weeks up to the fourteenth week (i.e. during additional maternity leave).

The father must notify his employer in writing of the death of the mother as soon as he intends to take leave and the length of leave to which he believes he is so entitled. He should provide a copy of the death certificate of the mother and the birth certificate of the child as soon as possible. The leave shall commence within seven days of the mother's death.

The father may be entitled to a further four weeks' leave where he commences leave before the tenth week following confinement. Of course, the father must notify his employer that he is taking such additional leave at least four weeks before his expected date of return to work. The father may revoke his notification to take leave.

It should be noted that any time off under this Act should not be used in computing the 48-hour week reference period under the Organisation of Working Time Act, 1997.

Entitlement to Social Welfare Maternity Allowance

In order to be entitled to the social welfare maternity allowance, the individual must be employed and have paid *either* at least 39 PRSI contributions in the 12-month period before leave commences *or* at least 39 weeks' contributions since starting work *and* have at least 39 weeks paid or credited in the relevant tax year before maternity leave commences. The social welfare scheme provides that women get 70 per cent of their earnings (i.e. by dividing gross earnings in the relevant tax year by the number of weeks worked in that year) subject to a minimum payment of £86.70 and a maximum payment of £162.80 per week (based on earnings up to £12,094.00 per annum) (Social

Welfare Consolidated Payments Provisions) (Amendment) (No. 4) (Maternity and Adoption Benefit) Regulations, 1997, SI No. 249 of 1997). The appropriate form must be completed and sent to the Maternity Benefits Section of the Department of Social, Community and Family Affairs at least 10 weeks before the confinement.

In the case of an early miscarriage, there is no maternity benefit payable. Maternity benefit becomes payable in respect of stillbirths after 24 weeks of pregnancy.

The Social Welfare Act, 1997, extended maternity benefit of 14 weeks to self-employed persons who meet the eligibility criteria. In summary, the self-employed contributor must have 52 paid contributions in either of the two complete contribution years preceding the beginning of the benefit year in which the confinement begins. This came into effect on 9 June 1997.

Half-rate maternity benefit is payable if the recipient is receiving One Parent Family Allowance, Survivors' Contributory Pension, Widows' Non-Contributory Pension, Deserted Wife's Benefit or Prisoner's Wives Allowance.

A person that cannot meet the PRSI contribution conditions is still entitled to maternity leave and may be entitled to a supplementary payment from a health board, but this payment is means tested.

A number of employers actually "pay" their female employees while on maternity leave. In other words, they "top-up" the social welfare monies, usually by paying the employee's salary in the normal way and having the employee reimburse the employer with the social welfare monies. It should be noted that there is absolutely no obligation on the employer to pay monies to an employee while on maternity leave.

Leave to Protect Health and Safety

Section 18 of the Maternity Act provides for health and safety leave, where there is a risk to a pregnant employee or one who has recently given birth. Such leave applies to:

1. A pregnant employee who has notified her employer of her condition;

2. An employee who has recently given birth (i.e. during the previous 14 weeks) and whose employer has been informed of her condition; and

3.   An employee who is breastfeeding, i.e. has given birth at least 26
     weeks earlier and who has informed her employer of her condi-
     tion.

General Duties of Employer

It shall be the duty of every employer to carry out a risk assessment
to the health and safety of employees who are pregnant or breastfeeding resulting from any activity at the employees' place of work
which is likely to involve a risk of exposure to an agent, process or
hazardous working conditions. Preventative and protective measures
must be taken to ensure the health and safety of pregnant and
breastfeeding employees. These are listed in the First Schedule to the
Safety, Health and Welfare at Work (Pregnant Employees, etc.)
Regulations, 1994 (SI No. 446 of 1994). (which regulations were technically made under the Safety, Health and Welfare at Work Act,
1989). These regulations are in addition to Regulation 10 of the
Safety, Health and Welfare at Work (General Application) Regulations 1993 (SI No. 44 of 1993), which provides that every employer
must have a written risk assessment of the risks to safety and health
and must provide for protective measures in the preparation of the
Safety Statement.

These agents, processes and working conditions apply to all pregnant and breast-feeding employees. The *agents* are listed as:

1.   *Physical agents* including those causing foetal lesions or likely to
     disrupt placental attachment (or both), and in particular shocks,
     vibration, movement, handling of loads, noise, extremes of cold or
     heat;

2.   *Biological agents* (a "micro-organism . . . which may be able to
     provoke an infection, allergy or toxicity") including bacteria, vi-
     ruses and fungi, of risk groups 2, 3 and 4 within the meaning of
     Regulations 2(1) of the Safety, Health and Welfare at Work (Bio-
     logical Agents) Regulations, 1994 (SI No. 146 of 1994); and

3.   *Chemical agents* to include certain listed dangerous substances,
     chemical agents listed in First Schedule to the Safety, Health and
     Welfare at Work (Carcinogen) Regulations, 1993 (SI No. 80 of
     1993), mercury and mercury derivatives, carbon monoxide, etc.

Industrial processes are listed in the First Schedule of the Safety, Health and Welfare at Work (Carcinogen) Regulation, 1993 (SI No. 80 of 1983); for example, work involving exposure to aromatic poly-cyclic hydrocarbons present in coal, soot, tar, pitch, fumes and dust; work involving exposure to dusts, fumes and sprays produced during the roasting and electro-refining of cupro-nickel mattes and so forth.

Working Conditions specifically refers to underground mining work.

In addition to the above, the employer must specifically assess any risk to the health and safety of a pregnant employee from an agent or working condition specified in Part A of the Second Schedule result-ing from any activity in the place of work. The employer must also ensure that such an employee is not required to perform duties for which the assessment reveals such risk. The list of *agents* in Part A of the Second Schedule is as follows:

1. *Physical agents*: work in a hyperbaric atmosphere, such as in pressurised enclosures or underwater diving;

2. *Biological agents*: toxoplasma or rubella virus, unless the preg-nant employee is proved to be adequately protected against such agents by immunisation; and

3. *Chemical agents*: lead and lead derivatives insofar as these agents are capable of being absorbed by the human organism.

Working conditions again specifically refers to underground mining work.

There must be a specific assessment in relation to employees who are breastfeeding in relation to *chemical agents* (lead and lead de-rivatives insofar as these agents are capable of being absorbed by the human organism) and in respect of *working conditions* (underground mining work).

Where the risk assessment reveals a risk to the employee's safety or health and it is not practical to ensure the safety or health of such an employee through protective or preventative measures, then the working conditions or hours should be adjusted so that the exposure to such risk is avoided or, where this is not possible, the employee should be provided with other work. The safety representative shall be advised of the results of this risk assessment.

Night Work

If a doctor certifies that a woman should not perform night work during pregnancy or within 14 weeks of the birth, then the employer shall not oblige her to do night work during that period and shall transfer her to day work. If this is not possible, she shall be granted leave or extended maternity leave. "Night work" means work during the hours between 11 p.m. and 6 a.m. on the next day where the employee works at least three hours during those times as a normal course, or where at least 25 per cent of the employee's monthly working time is performed during these hours.

Pregnant women and nursing mothers shall be able to lie down to rest in appropriate conditions (Safety, Health and Welfare at Work (General Application) Regulations 1993 Schedule 4 (SI No. 44 of 1993)).

Entitlement to Health and Safety Leave

An employee is entitled to health and safety leave (see section 18 of the Maternity Act) where the employer is required to move an employee from her normal work, whether as a result of a risk assessment or because the employee cannot be required to perform night work, but

1. It is not technically or objectively feasible for the employer to move the employee as required by the Regulations; or

2. Such a move cannot reasonably be required on duly substantiated grounds; or

3. The other work to which the employer proposes to move the employee is not suitable for her (i.e. the work must be suitable for the employee concerned and appropriate for the employee to do in all the circumstances).

This health and safety leave covers the whole period beginning with the employee's pregnancy, continuing beyond any confinement until she ceases to be an employee who has recently given birth or an employee who is breastfeeding.

The Maternity Protection (Heath and Safety Leave Certification) Regulations, 1995 (SI No. 19 of 1995) provides the certificate which the employer must give the employee if she is going on this leave (see form, pages 135–7).

The employer shall pay the employee for the first 21 days of this leave and the employee shall be entitled to a social welfare payment in respect of the balance. Obviously, she must advise her employer as soon as practicable should she cease to be pregnant/breastfeeding or, if the employee considers that she is no longer vulnerable to the risk, she shall notify her employer as soon as reasonably practicable. The employer shall then notify her in writing that she can resume work in her job. The employer must have no reason to believe that the employee will be vulnerable. The leave shall end within seven days of the employer notifying her of her return to work (or earlier). The Regulations covering such payments are the Maternity Protection (Health and Safety Leave Remuneration) Regulations, 1995 (SI No. 20 of 1995).

The employee shall be entitled to three times her normal weekly pay for the first 21 days of such leave — i.e., three weeks' pay. When the 21 days of health and safety leave are not consecutive, then if there is a period of 14 consecutive days, the employee will be entitled to twice her normal weekly pay and then the appropriate daily rate; if during the 21 days there is a period of seven consecutive days, then the employee is entitled to her normal weekly pay and her daily rate thereafter; if there is a period of six consecutive days, then the employee will be entitled to the daily rate of pay.

The "appropriate daily rate" equals to her normal weekly pay divided by the number of days which she works in a normal working week; if she does not work a set number of days, divide by five. If an employee does not work (e.g. on a Sunday) there is a nil payment.

The normal weekly pay of an employee, where it is at a fixed rate and for a fixed number of hours, is her normal pay less overtime; pay excludes monies for night work, shiftwork, working unsociable hours or for being on call.

If an employee either was not working during "the basis week" or else worked fewer than her normal hours, the normal weekly pay is the average over the previous 26 weeks worked, excluding overtime pay.

If the employee has worked for less than 26 weeks, the average shall be decided by the use of the number of weeks she has worked. In this situation, "pay" means monies she is entitled to under her contract of employment but excludes nightwork, shiftwork, working unsociable hours and standby or on-call pay.

In *James Coffey and Dame Street Hair Studios* v *Byrne* ([1997] ELR 230), the employee hair stylist contended that she was entitled to health and safety leave. In May 1995 she became pregnant and informed her employer; she had a viral infection and was out sick for part of June 1995; she returned, suffered a relapse and was then out in July 1995. She received the "all clear" from her doctor in August 1995 in respect of the viral infection; however, he did advise her that, given her working conditions, it would be detrimental for her to return to work. She maintained that she had to work long hours standing and that the staff room was small and unventilated and there was no hot water for the staff. The ventilation was poor overall in the salon and she had suffered from asthma and chest infections. The employee obtained forms in respect of an application for health and safety leave. She was informed that her employer would not sign the forms and that she could not expect her job to be kept open. She was also informed that she was at no risk in the hair salon.

The employee could not get health and safety benefit until her employer completed the forms. Previous employees who were pregnant made no complaint about the working conditions. The employer then said that he only received the medical certificate at the rights commissioner hearing. The employer was unaware that he had to carry out a risk assessment.

The Employment Appeals Tribunal said the employer was aware of the pregnancy in August 1995 and had been requested to carry out a risk assessment, which was not carried out. It therefore followed that the employee was not provided with the results of any such risk assessment or any measures to be taken by the employer pursuant to the 1994 Regulations. The offer of reduced hours was not sufficient to discharge the duties imposed on the employer to carry out a risk assessment. The consequent failure to provide the employee with details of the measures to be taken established the right of the employee to protective leave under section 18 of the Act. The employee was awarded compensation of £2,703.

Employment Protection during Leave

Protective leave comprises maternity leave, additional maternity leave, father's leave (where the mother dies before the end of the tenth week) and health and safety leave.

The employee remains in the employment during any leave or time off under the Act, so statutory and contractual rights are protected during that time. Notices of termination of employment (from employer or employee) given during leave and to take effect during leave or after the end of leave are void, and thus the employee would remain in employment. An employee cannot resign during a period of leave or time off, and an employer cannot terminate an employee's employment during leave or time off. Any period of probation, training or apprenticeship stands suspended during absence on leave and the employee then gets the balance due to her on her return from leave.

The 1994 Act also provides that if an employer imposes a suspension on an employee or gives notice to terminate their employment and if the notice is due to expire during the employee's absence from work, then the notice is extended for any balance period after the leave.

During the period of additional maternity leave, father's leave (over the 14 weeks) and his extra four weeks' leave, the protection is more limited. The employee's continuity of employment for statutory rights (unfair dismissal, minimum notice redundancy) is protected. However, this leave would not be reckonable service for redundancy payment purposes. There would be no entitlement to annual leave in respect of this additional four weeks, but the public holiday entitlement remains, by virtue of the person still being in employment.

No period of leave under this Act can be deemed to be sick leave or annual leave.

Remuneration

An employee is only entitled to remuneration from her employer when she is on natal care absence or for the first three weeks of health and safety leave.

An employee is not entitled to any remuneration from her employer when she is on leave other than as stated above. There is no definition of "remuneration" in the 1994 Act. Previously under the 1981 Act, "remuneration" was broadly interpreted by the Employment Appeals Tribunal to include company car and attendance bonuses. In one particular case, the Tribunal considered that a company car was remuneration and thus it could be withheld from the employee during maternity leave (*McGivern* v *Irish National Insurance Co. Limited* P 5/1982). An attendance bonus is not considered payable during maternity leave even though an employee is deemed to be in employment during such leave (*Memorex Media Products* v *Byrne and Others* P 9/1986).

Employees on maternity leave are also entitled to any pay increases that arise before or during maternity leave (*Gillespie* v *Northern Health and Social Services Board* [1996] IRLR 214).

Right to Return to Work

There is a general right to return to the same job for employees who have been on maternity leave. This also applies if there has been a transfer of business while the employee was on leave. If, for example, in order to give an employee suitable work during pregnancy she had been in a job different from her usual one, she is still entitled to return to her old job. If that is not possible, the employer must provide suitable alternative work. Alternative work must be work that is suitable to the particular employee and appropriate for her in the circumstances. The Act does not define "suitable alternative work", but it specifies that the terms and conditions of the new contract as regards the place of employment, the capacity in which she is to be employed and the monetary and other terms of employment, must not be substantially less favourable than those of her previous job.

A number of cases have gone to the Tribunal under this particular heading. In one case, the employee had worked as a switchboard operator and upon returning from maternity leave was offered alternative work in the company's accounts department, in the same grade with no loss of pay. The company had originally advertised her original position internally as a temporary position but found nobody suitable. They then approached the National Manpower Service but their applicants only wanted permanent employment. The employer then offered someone the position on a permanent basis. The claimant was unhappy with this decision and sought reinstatement to her original position. The Tribunal considered that the inconvenience arising out of the new arrangement was greater to the employee than to the employer, and thus awarded her with reinstatement in her original job (*O'Brien* v *Harrington and Goodlass Wall Ltd.* P 2/1981).

In another case, an employee had originally worked as an accounts clerk and was offered the position of receptionist on her return from leave. She did not want to work as a receptionist and resigned her employment. In this particular case, the claimant was awarded £8,000 by the Tribunal (*Butler* v *Smurfit Ireland Ltd. t/a Paclene Co. Ltd.* P 3/1988).

Notification Requirements

The employee has to notify her employer in writing four weeks before the date on which she expects to return to work. If there is a problem with this notification — either there is a failure to give the notification or it is late — the rights commissioner or the Employment Appeals Tribunal may extend the four-week time limit for giving notification. However, if there are not reasonable grounds for the failure to give notification or the breach of the time limit, these matters will be taken into account if there is a termination of the employee's employment and if there is a claim for unfair dismissal.

Dismissal and Maternity Matters

It is an unfair dismissal to dismiss an employee arising from her pregnancy, giving birth or breastfeeding, or the exercise or purposed exercise of her rights (or his, in exceptional circumstances) under the Maternity Protection Act, 1994. The 1994 Act amends the Unfair Dismissal Acts, 1977–1993.

Under the 1994 Act, if an employee is not permitted to return to work, she is deemed to have been dismissed on the expected date of return and the dismissal shall be deemed to be an unfair dismissal unless, having regard to all the circumstances, there were substantial grounds justifying the dismissal.

If an employer is hiring an employee to cover for maternity leave, the employer shall have to provide the "new employee" with a written contract stating that the employment will terminate when the other employee returns from protective leave and further that the dismissal is only to facilitate the "old" employee's return to work.

Complaints and Disputes

A dispute may be referred to a rights commissioner within six months of the employer being informed of the initial circumstances of the dispute. This time limit may be extended to 12 months under exceptional circumstances. The rights commissioner may award up to 20 weeks' remuneration. Such recommendation may be appealed to the Employment Appeals Tribunal (within four weeks) and from there to the High Court on a point of law only. The Maternity Protection (Disputes and Appeals) Regulations, 1995 (SI No. 17 of 1995) apply; see Chapter 23.

Of course, any termination of employment shall fall within the scope of the unfair dismissals legislation.

ADOPTIVE LEAVE

The Adoptive Leave Act, 1995, grants adoptive leave to women employees on a similar basis to maternity leave. It also applies to male employees in certain circumstances (see Chapter 1, "Recruitment and Equality"). The Act came into operation on 20 March 1995 (Adoptive Leave Act, 1995 (Commencement) Order (SI No. 64 of 1995). The minimum period of leave provided in the Act is ten weeks, during which the employee will receive a social welfare payment. There is also an optional four weeks' additional unpaid leave. The principles of the Act and the notification requirements are similar to those of the Maternity Act.

Application of the Act

This Act covers exactly the same categories of female employees (and sole male adopters) from the first day of employment as under the Maternity Protection Act, 1994.

"An employed adopting mother" means a female employee in whose care a child (of whom she is not the natural mother) has been placed or is being placed with a view to the making of an adoption order, or to the effecting of a foreign adoption or following any such adoption. "Adopting father" means a male employee in whose care a child has been placed or is to be placed with a view to the making of an adoption order, or to the effecting of a foreign adoption or following any such adoption where the adopting mother has died. "A sole male adopter" means an adopting father outside the meaning of this Act and in whose care a child has been placed or is to be placed with a view to the making of an adoption order or to the effecting of a foreign adoption or following any such adoption. More usually, such a person is the child's father or male relative of the child or a widower. Orders may be granted under the Adoption Act, 1991, regardless of a person's marital status. A *"foreign adoption"* is defined under section 1 of the Adoption Act, 1991, and in summary applies where a child is adopted outside the State and where *inter alia* the adoptive parent(s) take on all parental rights and duties.

Notification Requirements

The adopting mother may be granted 10 weeks' leave, commencing on the day the child is placed for adoption. An employee who wishes to avail of leave in respect of an adoption (other than a foreign adoption) must

1. Notify her employer, as soon as reasonably practicable but not later than four weeks before the expected date of placement, of her intention to take leave;

2. Then as soon as reasonably practicable notify her employer of the expected date of placement;

3. Provide her employer with the certificate of placement as soon as is reasonably practicable but not later than four weeks after the date of placement.

In relation to a foreign adoption, the employee must

1. Notify her employer, as soon as reasonably practicable but not later than four weeks before the expected date of placement, of her intention to take leave;

2. Then as soon as reasonably practicable notify her employer of the expected date of placement; and

   (i) Provide the employer with a copy of the declaration made pursuant to the Adoption Act, 1991 (section 5 (1)(iii)(II)) before the date of placement, and

   (ii) Provide the employer with written details of the placement as soon as reasonably possible after the day of placement.

If the day of placement is postponed the commencement of the period of adoptive leave shall be postponed subject to the employee notifying the employer of the expected new day of placement as soon as possible. Any notification can be revoked.

Additional Adoptive Leave

An employed adopting mother or sole male adopter who has taken adoptive leave may be entitled to an additional four weeks' leave known as additional adoptive leave. This follows directly on adoptive leave. Notification of intention to take such leave must be given in writing to the employer at the same time as notification of taking adoptive leave or not later than four weeks before the expected date of return to work following on adoptive leave. This notification may be revoked by notification in writing not later than four weeks before the expected date of return to work following on adoptive leave.

In the case of a foreign adoption, where the adopting mother or sole male adopter requires additional adoptive leave before the date of placement to allow familiarisation with the child to be adopted, some or all of the additional adoptive leave may b taken before the date of placement. This period of additional adoptive leave shall expire immediately before the date of placement. This entitlement shall be subject to the adopting mother or sole male adopter notifying their employer in writing at least four weeks before the date on which he or she intends to take additional adoptive leave. The employer must be in receipt of a copy of the declaration under section 5(1)(iii)(II) of the Adoption Act, 1991. This notification may be revoked.

Entitlement of Father

Where an adopting mother dies, the adopting father shall be entitled to adoptive leave from his employment as follows

1. Ten weeks, or

2. The balance of the ten-week period, or

3. Such other period as the Minister for Enterprise, Trade and Employment may determine in consultation with the Ministers for Social, Community and Family Affairs and the Minister for Finance.

The adoptive leave shall commence within seven days of the death of the adopting mother or on the date of placement, whichever is the later.

The adopting father must give written notification to his employer as soon as he reasonably can before the commencement of the leave. Where the adopting mother dies after the date of placement, he must give written notification of his intention to take leave no later than the date of commencement of leave. The employer must also be notified of the date of placement. The employer must be in receipt of the certificate of placement as soon as is reasonably practicable, but not later than four weeks after the date of placement or the commencement of the leave, whichever is the latter.

In the case of a foreign adoption, the employer must be in receipt of a copy of the declaration under section 5(I)(iii)(II) of the Adoption Act, 1991, as soon as is reasonably practicable but not later than four weeks after the commencement of the leave. The employer must also be provided with details of the placement as soon as is reasonably practicable. The employee must, if requested, provide the employer with a copy of the death certificate of the adoptive mother as soon as is reasonably practicable.

The adopting father may revoke the notification.

Where the date of placement is postponed, commencement of adoptive leave shall also be postponed, provided that the adopting father notifies his employer of the expected new day of placement as soon as is reasonably practicable.

Additional Adoptive Leave for Father

An adopting father is entitled to additional adoptive leave where the adopting mother has died. It may comprise

1. Four weeks, or

2. Any balance period of four weeks following the ten weeks' adoptive leave, or

3. Such other period as the Minister for Enterprise, Trade and Employment may determine in consultation with the Ministers for Social, Community and Family Affairs and the Minister for Finance.

The adopting father must give notification to his employer as soon as is reasonably practicable before the commencement of the additional leave. Where the adopting mother dies after the date of placement, the adopting father must notify the employer of his intention to take leave no later then the date he commences leave.

The adopting father must also notify the employer of the expected date of placement.

The employee must give his employer the certificate of placement within four weeks of the date of placement or within four weeks after the commencement of the additional leave, whichever is the later.

In the case of a foreign adoption, the employee must give his employer a copy of the declaration under section 5(I)(iii)(II) of the Adoption Act, 1991, as soon as is reasonably practicable but not less than four weeks after the commencement of the leave, and must also give his employer details of the placement as soon as is reasonably possible.

Additional adoptive leave shall commence within seven days of the death of the adoptive mother or, where the adoptive father was on adoptive leave, immediately following adoptive leave.

A notification for additional adoptive leave may be revoked in writing.

An adoptive father is entitled to additional adoptive leave before the day of placement in the case of a foreign adoption where the adopting mother has died. This is for the purposes of familiarisation with the child who is to be adopted. This leave is subject to:

1. Having notified his employer before the date of placement as soon as is reasonably possible of his intention to take such leave; and

2. Causing his employer to be supplied with a copy of the declaration made pursuant to section 5(I)(iii)(II) of the Adoption Act, 1991, as soon as reasonably practicable but not later than four weeks after commencement of the leave; and

3. Where the employer requests the death certificate of the mother.

The period of additional adoptive leave shall commence immediately on the death of the mother. Notification of such leave may be revoked in writing.

Where the expected day of placement is postponed, commencement of the period of additional adoptive leave shall also be postponed, provided that the adopting father notifies his employer of the new day of placement as soon as is reasonably possible.

Placements of less than Fourteen Weeks' Duration

Where the placement is of less than 14 weeks' duration, the adopting parent shall notify his/her employer in writing of the date of termination of the placement as soon as is reasonably practicable but not later than seven days after the termination of the placement. This does not apply in the event of the death of the child.

Following on receipt of the notification, the employee shall return to work as soon as is convenient for the employer but not later than the date on which the notified period of adoptive or additional adoptive leave has expired. An employee shall give one week's notice of the day she is required to return to work.

In the case of a foreign adoption where an adopting parent takes additional adoptive leave before the day of placement and no placement takes place, she shall return to work on the day the notified period of leave expires and shall notify her employer of the intended date of return as soon as is reasonably practicable.

A rights commissioner or the Employment Appeals Tribunal may extend time for the service of notice by an adopting parent where the employee has failed to give notice within the time limits specified. Further, in the absence of reasonable grounds, failure to give notice within the time limits are matters which may be taken into account by a rights commissioner or the Employment Appeals Tribunal where they are awarding reinstatement, re-engagement or compensation.

Time off under the Adoptive Leave Act is not included for the purposes of calculating the reference period of 48 hours under s. 15 of the Organisation of Working Time Act, 1997.

Certificate of Placement

The health board or the registered adopting society shall, if the adopting parent so requests, give them a certificate of placement no later than seven days following the receipt of the request.

The certificate of placement shall state the following:

1. The date on which it is issued

2.   The day of placement

3.   The sex and date of birth of the child

4.   The name and address of the adopting parent or parents.

The employee has a right to return to work, subject to four weeks' written notification before her expected date of return. This notification shall be confirmed at least two weeks before the expected date of return. There is provision for the rights commissioner or the Employment Appeals Tribunal to extend these time limits.

Where the placement of a child was not arranged by the health board or by a registered adoption society and where an application for an adopting order was received by An Bord Uchtála (The Adoption Board) from an adopting parent(s), the Bord shall issue a certificate of placement to the adopting parent(s), on request.

Employment Protection during Leave

The employee remains in the employment during any leave under the Act, so statutory and contractual rights are protected during that time (section 15). Notices of termination of employment (from employer or employee) given during leave and to take effect during leave or after the end of leave are void, and thus the employee would remain in employment. An employee cannot resign during a period of leave and an employer cannot terminate an employee's employment during leave. Any period of probation, training or apprenticeship stands suspended during absence on leave and the balance due continues on the return from leave.

The Act also provides that if an employer imposes a suspension on an employee or gives notice to terminate their employment and if the notice is due to expire during the employee's absence from work, then the notice is extended for any balance period after the leave.

During the period of additional adoptive leave, the protection is more limited. The employee's continuity of employment for statutory rights — unfair dismissal, minimum notice redundancy is protected. However, this leave is not reckonable service for redundancy payment purposes. There would be no entitlement to annual leave in respect of this additional four weeks, but the public holiday entitlement remains, by virtue of the person still being in employment.

No period of leave under this Act can be deemed to be sick leave or annual leave.

Remuneration

Employees are not entitled to any remuneration from their employer when on adoptive leave. There is no definition of "remuneration" in the Act, so the same comments in relation to remuneration under the Maternity Protection Act, 1994 (see above) apply.

Right to Return to Work

There is a general right to return to the same job for employees who have been on adoptive leave. This also applies if there has been a transfer of business while the employee was on leave. The same provisions apply to return to work after adoptive leave as apply after maternity leave (see above).

Disputes Procedure

Disputes may be referred to a rights commissioner or the Employment Appeals Tribunal within six months (with provision for extension of time in exceptional circumstances) from the date the employer receives notification from the adopting parent. The rights commissioner's recommendation may be appealed to the Tribunal within four weeks of the date of communication of the recommendation. The Tribunal determination may be appealed to the High Court on a point of law only, or the Tribunal may request the Minister to refer the matter to the High Court on a question of law. Compensation may be up to a maximum of 20 weeks' remuneration (see Chapters 22 and 23).

PARENTAL LEAVE

The Parental Leave Act, 1998, came into operation on 3 December 1998, further to the Parental Leave Directive (Council Directive 96/34/EC). This Directive puts into effect the framework Agreement on parental leave concluded by the social partners at European level; the parties being UNICE (the Union of Industrial and Employers' Confederation of Europe), the CEEP (the European Centre of Public Enterprise) and the ETUC (the European Trade Union Confederation). However, the Irish Government sought the benefit of Article 2(2), which provides that Member States may have additional time to put the Directive into effect if this is necessary to implement the legislation. The purpose of this framework agreement is to reconcile work and family life and to encourage the introduction of new flexible ways of organising work and time that are better suited to the changing needs of society.

Presently in Ireland there is provision for career breaks (more usually for public service employees), compassionate leave (two/three days on the death of a close relative) or other forms of contractual arrangements with employers. There may be the maintenance of continuity/computation of service for the purposes of the Minimum Notice and Terms of Employment Acts, 1973–1991 (see First Schedule, paragraph 10), the Unfair Dismissals Acts, 1977–1993, and the Redundancy Payments Acts, 1967–1991 (see Schedule 3 paragraph 8(c), which provides for protection of up to 13 weeks for agreed leave of absence). However, there is no statutory entitlement to such career breaks.

Entitlement to Parental Leave

An employee who is the natural or adoptive parent is entitled to 14 weeks' unpaid leave from his or her employment to enable him or her to take care of the child. The employee must have at least one year's continuous service and any period of leave is not transferable between parents. The entitlement to parental leave shall only apply in respect of a child born on or after 3 June 1996 or a child in whose case an adoptive order has been made on or after that date.

A period of parental leave shall end on either the date the child is five years of age or where a child is the subject of an adoption order and who has reached three years but has not reached eight years on or before the date of the making of the adoption order, not later than the expiration of the period of two years beginning on that date. An employee shall only be entitled to leave as a natural or adoptive parent, but not as both. Where there is a multiple birth, it shall be deemed to be one child.

If an employee does not have one year of continuous service with his or her employer on the latest day for commencing parental leave but has completed three months of such employment, the person shall be entitled to parental leave of 1 week for each month of continuous employment that he or she has completed with the employer.

Nature of Parental Leave

Parental leave may consist of

1. A continuous period of 14 weeks or

2. With the agreement of the employer (individually or collectively), a number of periods of leave each of which comprises

   a) Days off;

   b) Hours off; or

   c) A combination of either.

Thus an employee may work shorter weeks or part-time, using up the hours to the maximum of 14 weeks' leave at average weekly working hours in the period of 14 weeks continuously prior to the commencement of leave. If the employer and employee cannot agree the hours, then it is 14 times the average number of hours per week during which the employee worked in each of the periods of 14 weeks ending before commencement. In determining the period of 14 weeks or the period of one-year holidays (including public holidays), sick leave, maternity leave, adoptive leave, or *force majeure* leave shall be excluded and a corresponding number of days shall be included instead. Time spent on parental leave is deemed to be time spent at work.

If an employee is entitled to parental leave in respect of more than one child, the period of parental leave in any period of 12 months shall not exceed 14 weeks or periods comprising the 14 weeks.

If any holidays (including public holidays) fall during a period of parental leave, and if the employee would have been working but for the leave and the holiday, the holidays shall be added to the period of parental leave. There shall be no break in continuity of employment.

Notice of Parental Leave

If an employee proposes to take parental leave, he or she shall give written notification of the proposal to the employer as soon as reasonably practicable but not later than six weeks before the commencement of such leave. The notice must be signed by the employee and state that date of commencement of leave, its duration and the manner in which it is proposed to be taken. An employee may revoke this notice. If an employee does not comply with the notification and takes leave, the employer may treat it as parental leave. The employer should give a copy of this notice to the employee. If the employer requires, where there is an adoption order, the employee must provide the date of birth and the date of the order, and in any other case the date of birth.

The Confirmation of Parental Leave

The employer shall give the employee a confirmation document (signed by the employer) which shall state the date of commencement of the leave, its duration and the manner in which it is to be taken.

Postponement, Curtailment or Variation of Leave

When the signed confirmation document is issued, the employee will not be entitled to work during the period of parental leave. Following on the date of confirmation, the leave or part of it may be curtailed as may be agreed between the parties. The form of leave may also be varied as agreed. The confirmation document may be amended accordingly.

Where parental leave is curtailed, the balance of parental leave that has not been taken may be taken at a future date to be agreed between the parties.

Postponement by Employer

If an employee gives notification of a proposal to take leave and if the employer believes that the taking of parental leave would have a substantial adverse effect on the operation of the business, profession or occupation by reason of seasonal variations in the volume of work concerned, the unavailability of a person to carry out duties of the employee, the nature of the duties, the number of employees, or if there are other employees on parental leave at the same time, the employer may at least four weeks before the commencement of leave postpone the commencement of leave for no longer than six months. This postponement will not apply where a confirmation document has been signed by employer and employee. However, before giving the employee such notice, the employer must consult with the employee. If the child has reached the maximum age, this is ignored in such circumstances.

Abuse

Parental leave is granted so that a parent can look after their child. Where an employer has reasonable grounds for believing that the leave is not being used for care of the child, the employer may by notice in writing terminate the leave. Then the employee shall not be entitled to return to work or receive pay until the end of the leave period which shall not be deemed parental leave.

If an employee gives his or her employer notice to take leave and if the employer believes that the employee is not entitled to such leave, the employer may refuse such leave. The employer must give a written statement with a summary of the grounds for refusing leave.

Employment Rights

The employee is deemed to be in employment during parental leave and all employment rights are protected. However, there is no right to remuneration or pension benefits, to include obligation to pay any contributions in respect of the employment. Any time spent on parental leave is separate from any other leave, including sick leave, annual leave, adoptive leave, maternity leave and *force majeure* leave.

If an employee who is on probation, in training or apprenticeship takes parental leave and if the employer considers that the employee's absence would not be consistent with the probation, training or apprenticeship, then the probation, training or apprenticeship shall be suspended. The 14 weeks (or whatever period) shall then be added to the end of the probation, training or apprenticeship.

Leave on Grounds of *Force Majeure*

An employee shall be entitled to leave with pay from their employment for *force majeure* leave where, owing to an injury or illness of a relation, the presence of the employee is required.

Relations are defined as

1. A person of whom the employee is the parent or the adoptive parent

2. The spouse of the employee or a person with whom the employee is living as husband or wife

3. A person to whom the employee is *in loco parentis*

4. A brother or sister of the employee

5. A parent or grandparent of the employee and

6. Other persons as may be prescribed by reputation under the Act.

Where an employee proposes to take *force majeure* leave, as soon as reasonably practicable either before or after taking the leave, they should give notice in writing to the employer of their proposal to take this leave. The notice shall specify the dates of the proposed leave and provide a summary of the reasons for the proposed leave. Persons on *force majeure* leave shall be deemed to be in employment during such leave.

This leave shall not exceed three working days in any period of 12 consecutive months or five days in any period of 36 consecutive months. If an employee was out for part of such a day, it will be deemed to be one full day. In the event of a dispute, the employee would be required to furnish the employer with a medical certificate containing particulars of the injury or illness and the length of time the person has suffered and is likely to suffer incapacity as a result. (Form of Notice is in Parental Leave (Notice of Force Majeure Leave) Regulations, 1998 (SI No. 454 of 1998).)

Return to Work

Employees are entitled to return to work following on the expiry of the leave. They are entitled to return to their own job on the same terms and conditions with their employer (or its successor following the transfer of a business). If the employee was not working in their usual job prior to leave, they are still entitled to return to their usual job or the job held just before leave as soon as reasonably practicable. If there is an interruption or cessation of work and it is reasonable to expect the employee to return to work, then the employee shall return to work as soon as possible after resumption of such work in the employment.

If the employer cannot permit the employee to return to his usual work, then the employer is entitled to offer suitable alternative employment on substantially not less favourable terms.

Records and Review

Employers shall keep all records of parental and *force majeure* leave to include periods of employment and the dates and times where employees were on such leave. Such records shall be kept for eight weeks. Notices shall be kept for one year. An employer who contravenes these provisions shall be guilty of an offence and liable on summary conviction to a fine not exceeding £1,500. Inspectors within the meaning of the Organisation of Working Time Act, 1997, may exercise their powers under this Act. The Minister for Justice, Equality and Law Reform may bring proceedings and prosecute under the Parental Leave Act.

The Minister shall review the Parental Leave Act between two to three years after commencement and consult with representatives of both employers and employees. The Minister shall prepare a written report and lay it before each House of the Oireachtas.

Disputes and Redress

All disputes under the Parental Leave Act may be referred by either party within six months of the occurrence of the dispute to a rights commissioner, except for disputes relating to dismissal including a dispute within the meaning of the Unfair Dismissals Acts, 1977–1993; a question under section 39(15) of the Redundancy Payments Act, 1967; or a dispute to which section 11 of the Minimum Notice and Terms of Employment Acts, 1973–1991. This does not refer to a member of the Defence Forces.

A decision of a rights commissioner may be appealed to the Employment Appeals Tribunal within four weeks of the date of the recommendation. A determination of the Employment Appeals Tribunal may be appealed to the High Court on a point of law.

The rights commissioner or Tribunal may order either or both of the following:

1. The granting of parental leave of such length to be taken at a specified time and in a specified manner;

2. An award of compensation in favour of the employee concerned not exceeding 20 weeks' remuneration.

General References

Health and Safety Authority (1996), *Pregnant at Work: A Guide to the Safety, Health and Welfare at Work (Pregnant Employees, etc.) Regulations, 1994*, Dublin: HSA.

Kerr, A. (1996), *Adoptive Leave Act, 1995, Law Statutes Annotated*, Dublin: Sweet and Maxwell.

Kerr, A. (1996), *Maternity Protection Act, 1994, Law Statutes Annotated*, Dublin: Sweet and Maxwell.

Kerr, A. (1998), *Parental Leave Act, 1998, Law Statutes Annotated*, Dublin: Sweet and Maxwell.

SCHEDULE

CERTIFICATE OF RISK, NON-FEASIBILITY OF PROVIDING OTHER WORK AND GRANT OF LEAVE ON HEALTH AND SAFETY GROUNDS

Maternity Protection Act, 1994

I Employee Details

Figures   Letters

Name: _____ RSI Number: | | | | | | | | | | |

Employee's Occupation: _____

The employee named above has notified me that:

she is pregnant   ❏}
she has recently given birth❏} **tick as appropriate**
she is breastfeeding   ❏}

Is employee employed under a fixed-term contract?   Yes ❏   No ❏

Day   Month   Year

If "Yes", state date contract ends | | | |

II Certification of Risk

Please complete either (a) — *workplace risk* or (b) — *nightwork risk*

(a)   The following *risk(s)* to the employee named above has/have been identified arising from a risk assessment undertaken in accordance with Regulations under the Safety, Health and Welfare at Work Act, 1989.

List risk(s) _____

_____

_____

Specify the reasons why it is not possible to eliminate the risk(s):

_____

_____

(b) The employee named above is required to perform *nightwork* (i.e. work between the hours of 11 pm and 6 am where the employee normally works at least three hours in the said period or at least 25% of her monthly working time in that period) and the medical registered practitioner named below has certified that the performance of night work poses a risk to the employee's health/safety and furthermore it is not feasible to transfer the employee to work.

Name of medical registered practitioner: _____

III Certification of Non-feasibility of Other Work and the Granting Of Leave

As a result of the risk(s) identified above and, arising from Regulations on Safety, Health and Welfare at Work (Pregnant Employees, etc.) (S.I. No. 446 of 1994) and the Maternity Protection Act, 1994 for the reason(s) indicated as applying below the employee has been granted leave on health and safety grounds because: **(tick as appropriate)**

(i) it is not technically or objectively feasible to move
    the employee   ❏

(ii) such a move cannot be required on duly substantiated
    grounds   ❏

(iii) the other work proposed for the employee is not
    suitable for her   ❏

IV Supplementary Information

Date of commencement of leave on health and safety grounds

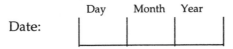

Date: Day   Month   Year

Expected duration of leave (in weeks): _____

                                                    Day   Month   Year
Expected date or *date*
of confinement as appropriate

	Day	Month	Year

Date of last day of 21 days health and safety leave during which payment by employer applies

V Declaration

I/We declare that the details I/We have given above are true and complete.

I/We undertake to inform the Department of Social Welfare immediately in the event of notifying the employee to return to work where:

- the risk to the employee no longer exists
- other work becomes available for the employee

Signed by or on behalf of Employer: Company's Name:

_____   _____

_____   Address: _____

Position: _____

	Day	Month	Year

Date:

Employer's Registered Number: _____

Date ....

Telephone Number: _____   Employer's Official Stamp

Chapter Six

PAYMENT OF WAGES

Happily, the manner of the payment of wages and procedures for resolution of disputes have now reached more modern standards. Prior to the enactment of the Payment of Wages Act, 1991, the previous legislation governing deductions from wages rested in laws passed in the Georgian and Victorian eras. Known as the Truck Acts, which have since been repealed, they provided that the payment of wages to manual workers was to be in "coin of the realm". They also limited the circumstances in which deductions could be made from manual workers' wages so that certain abuses could be limited.

PAYMENT OF WAGES ACTS

The Irish Payment of Wages Act, 1979 (see below) provided a more modern manner of payment of wages for manual workers than previously, as long as there was an agreement between employers and employees. Nonetheless, this legislation did not provide very practicable procedures for the modern cashless environment. Cheques and credit transfers were now acceptable as long as there was an agreement. It also established that all employees were entitled to a written statement of deductions from their pay; for example, PAYE, PRSI and other deductions such as VHI and trade union dues.

The 1979 Act has now been repealed (with all the previous legislation), but it must be noted that all agreements for manual workers that came into force under the 1979 Act are still applicable, unless agreed otherwise.

The Payment of Wages Act, 1991, came into force on 1 January 1992. The 1991 Act provides for transitional arrangements for employees who were paid their wages in cash before the coming into operation of the Act. Such employees are entitled to continue to receive cash wages until they reach an agreement with the employer for the payment of wages by one of the accepted methods of payment in the new Act. An employee who enters into an agreement to be paid wages by cheque under the 1979 Act and now wishes to revert to cash payment may do so. The right to change payment to cash would be included at the end of the agreement. If there is no termination date to the agreement, there must be four weeks' notice to end the agreement. It is an offence for an employer to be in breach of these provisions and such a breach may result in a fine of up to £1,000.

Thus, from 1 January 1992, the method of payment for all manual employees has been what is agreed between employer and employee as stated in the employment contract (or the union/ management agreement where this is incorporated into the contract of employment).

The 1991 Act established for the first time a range of rights for all employees relating to the payment of wages. Neither an employer nor an employee can "contract out" of the provisions of this Act. The key rights established under the Act are:

1. A right to a readily negotiable mode of wage payment (e.g., cheque, credit transfer, payable order or such other methods that may be added to the list from time to time),

2. A right to a written statement of wages, conditions and deductions, and

3. Protection against unlawful deductions from wages.

The Act covers all employees who are:

1. Working under a contract of employment or apprenticeship,

2. Employed through an employment agency or through a subcontractor, and

3. In the service of the State, including members of the Garda Síochána, the Defence Forces, civil servants, employees of any local authority, health board, harbour authority or vocational education committee.

MEANING OF WAGES

Wages are defined as:

1. Normal basic pay as well as any overtime;

2. Shift allowances or other similar payments;

3. Any fee, bonus or commission;

4. Any holiday, sick pay or maternity pay;

5. Any other form of payment (e.g. degree allowance in respect of pay as a secondary school teacher; *O'Sullivan* v *Department of Education* (PW 2/97));

6. Any sum payable to an employee in lieu of notice on termination of employment.

However, the following payments are not regarded as wages:

1. Expense payments incurred by employees in carrying out their employment;

2. Any payment by way of pension, allowance or gratuity in connection with the death, retirement, or resignation of the employee or compensation for loss of office. (In *Dunne* v *Department of Defence* (PW 7/95), a statutory deduction in respect of the Widows' and Children's Pension Scheme was held to be outside the jurisdiction of the Act, as it was not "wages" within the meaning of the Act);

3. Any payment relating to the employee's redundancy;

4. Any payment to the employee otherwise than in the employee's capacity as an employee;

5. Any payment-in-kind or benefit-in-kind;

6. Repayment of loans to employees as individuals — other than as a benefit under a loan scheme.

MODES OR METHODS OF WAGE PAYMENTS

The legally acceptable modes of wage payment include:

1. Cheque and bank draft drawn on any of the commercial banks or a Trustee Savings Bank;

2. Payable order warrant issued by a Minister of the Government or a public authority;

3. Postal order, money order, paying order warrant issued by or drawn on An Post;

4. Credit transfer to an account specified by the employee;

5. Cash.

Employers are required to make alternative arrangements for wage payment where a strike or other industrial action affects banks or other financial institutions so that cash is not readily available to employees who are paid by a non-cash method. In these circumstances, wages must be paid with the employee's consent by one of the other legally acceptable modes of wage payment. If the employee does not agree to same, the employer must pay the wages in cash.

If an employer pays wages to an employee otherwise than by one of the above-stated methods, or contravenes these special arrangements in the event of a bank dispute, it shall be an offence and the employer is liable to a fine of up to £1,000.

RIGHT TO A WRITTEN STATEMENT

All employees are entitled to a written statement showing (a) the gross amount of wages payable and (b) the nature and amount of any deduction from that gross amount. This statement must be given at the time of payment when the employee is paid by cheque, cash, postal or money order. If the employee is being paid by way of credit transfer, this statement must be given to the employee as soon as possible after payment.

There is an obligation on the employer to treat the information contained in the pay statement as confidential. A statement of wages which includes an error or omission is a valid statement of wages provided that it can be shown that the error or omission was due to a clerical mistake or was made accidentally and in good faith. Obviously, the mistake should be rectified as soon as possible.

An employer who contravenes this provision can be liable to a fine of up to £1,000.

DEDUCTION FROM WAGES

An employer may only make deductions from wages (or receive any payment from an employee) if:

1. The deduction or payment is required or authorised to be made by or under statute (e.g., PAYE or PRSI); or

2. The deduction or payment is required or authorised to be made under the term of the contract of employment (this term must have been in force at the time the deduction was made or the payment received, e.g. employee pension contributions, deductions for till shortages); or

3. There is an advance written agreement from the employee, (e.g. VHI premiums, trade union dues).

In *Murphy* v *Ryanair plc* (PW 2/92) the employee was suspended without pay for one week. There was no provision for the deduction in the contract of employment or in a written statement prior to the suspension. The EAT held that the employee was entitled to be paid for that week.

In the case of *Curust Hardware Limited* v *Dalton* (PW 1/92) on the termination of the claimant's employment, the employer deducted a sum of £820 (one month's pay plus a bonus of £20) because she had failed to give the period of notice under her contract of employment. On 9 March 1992, the claimant gave two weeks' notice, which was to expire on 20 March 1992. She gave notice to the Company Secretary, who said he would inform the Director. She had been offered a new job starting two weeks hence. Her Director was away during the week commencing 9 March 1992 and he returned on 16 March; he said nothing about her notice. The following day, 17 March, was a public holiday and she was sick for 17, 18, 19 and 20 March. When she went to collect her P45 and her wages, she discovered that one month's pay plus bonus had been deducted.

Her contract provided for one month's notice; there was no express provision in the contract that a deduction in wages could be made for failure to give notice. Therefore, this provision was not expressed and could not be implied. The Tribunal ruled that the claimant was to receive the monies for the period during which she worked, the bonus and for holiday pay due.

Payments under a sick pay scheme are deemed to be wages under section 1(1)(a)(20) — see *Department of Defence* v *O'Riordan* (PW 3/92). It should be noted that overpayments — i.e. the employer paid too much — are not covered within the jurisdiction of the Act.

In the case of *Walsh* v *Komac Construction and Civil Engineering Limited* (PW 2/95) the claimant's wages and holiday cheque "bounced". The Tribunal treated this as an unlawful deduction.

Special restrictions are placed on employers in relation to deductions (or the receipt of payments) from wages which:

1. Arise from any act of the employee (e.g. till shortages, bad workmanship, breakages), or

2. Are in respect of the supply to the employee by the employer of goods or services which are necessary to the employment (e.g. the provision or cleaning of uniforms).

Any deduction (or payment) from wages of the kind described above must satisfy the following conditions:

1. The deduction (or payment to the employer) must be provided for in the contract of employment, either in writing or orally

2. The amount of the deduction (or payment to the employer) from wages must be fair and reasonable having regard to all the circumstances, including the amount of the wages of the employee

3. The employee must be given, at some time prior to the act or omission (e.g. till shortage) or the provision of the goods or services (e.g. uniform cleaning), written details of the terms of the contract of employment governing the deduction (or payment to the employer) from wages.

Where a written contract exists, a copy of the terms of the contract that provide for the deduction (or payment) must be given to the employee. In any other case, the employee must be given written notice of existence and effect of the terms. Written notice must be given in the case of each deduction. The deduction cannot take place more than six months after the employee's act or omission has become known to the employer. Where there is a series of deductions arising from the same incident, the first deduction must take place within six months of the incident. The deduction in respect of service provided by the employer must also take place within six months.

An employer making a deduction arising from a till shortage (for example), must give the employee a written statement at least one week before the deduction takes place, including the reason for, and the amount of, the deduction. Of course, the deduction cannot exceed the amount of the employer's loss.

Similarly, a deduction arising from a service provided to the employee — for example, uniform cleaning — cannot be for more than the cost of the service. The employer must give a receipt for the amount of the deduction.

DEDUCTIONS AND PAYMENTS OUTSIDE THE APPLICATION OF THE ACT

The provisions on deductions do not apply to:

1. Statutory deductions (e.g. PAYE, PRSI, reimbursement of social welfare payments to the Minister for Social Welfare). The employer must have authorisation for such deductions (e.g. Certificate of Tax Free Allowances).

2. Deductions paid over to a third party (e.g. trade union subscriptions, VHI premiums, contributions to a group savings scheme, etc.). This kind of deduction remains outside the application of the Act, provided that the employer pays the correct amount over to the third party by the appropriate date. The employer should also be in receipt of a notice from the third party (e.g. the VHI) that such monies are due and owing by the employee.

3. Deductions for the overpayment of wages or expenses, as long as the amount deducted does not exceed the amount due to the employer.

4. Deductions or payments arising from a strike or industrial action in which the employee has been involved. The deduction or payment must arise because of the employee's involvement in such action. In *Beaumont Hospital* v *McNally and Others* (PW 29–33/96), the Employment Appeals Tribunal considered that the non-payment for the period of the employees' work-stoppage from 8.30 a.m. to 12.30 p.m. on 26 March 1996 fell outside the scope of

the Act as it concerned terms or conditions of the effective employment which come within the definition of "strike" and "industrial action".

5. Statutory disciplinary proceedings. A deduction from the wages of an employee in consequence of any disciplinary procedure, if those proceedings were held by virtue of a statutory provision; for example, the Garda Síochána (Discipline) Regulations, 1989.

6. Deductions or payments arising from a court order in the unusual cases where a court has awarded damages to an employer against an employee (e.g. statutory redundancy monies paid back to the employer after an employee has been reinstated following a redundancy dismissal). There must, of course, be prior written consent from the employee.

7. Deductions or payments arising from certain specific court orders (for example, an Attachment of Earnings Order to pay maintenance to the spouse of an employee).

WAGE DEFICIENCY

Non-payment of wages, or any deficiency in the amount of wages due to an employee on any occasion, is regarded as unlawful unless the deficiency or non-payment is attributable to an error of computation.

In the event that an employer decides unilaterally to reduce an employee's wages or remuneration (i.e. without the employee's agreement) then the employee may decide to take a claim under the Payment of Wages Act, 1991 (not applicable where the reduction is a benefit-in-kind; for example, a company car); or sue for breach of contract in a court of appropriate juridisdiction; or, if the breach is fundamental, resign and claim that they have been constructively dismissed under the Unfair Dismissals Acts, 1977–1993. It must be emphasised that such a resignation must be a last resort and the employee may not necessarily succeed in such an action (e.g., the employer may argue that they had little option, arising from a downturn in business, with the only other option being redundancy).

INSPECTION PROCEDURE

Authorised officers appointed by the Minister for Enterprise, Trade and Employment have inspection powers under the 1991 Act. They have power of entry to the employer's premises at all reasonable times, and the power of inspection to see if the Act has been complied with. The time limit for subsequent criminal proceedings is 12 months from the date of the offence.

REDRESS AND COMPLAINTS PROCEDURE

An employee may complain to a rights commissioner where there has been an alleged unlawful deduction or the employer required an unlawful payment from the wages of the employee. Such complaint must be made within six months of the alleged breach of the Act. The claimant may be awarded:

a) The net amount of the wages (after the making of any lawful deductions) in the week preceding the deduction; or else

b) If the amount is greater than (a), then twice the amount of the deduction or payment.

The rights commissioner's recommendation may be appealed to the Employment Appeals Tribunal (see Chapter 22, "The Labour Relations Commission and the Labour Court", and Chapter 23, "The Employment Appeals Tribunal").

It must of course be noted that if a person brings a claim under the Payment of Wages Act and if the rights commissioner has issued a recommendation, then in such circumstances the employee cannot recover such an amount in court against the employer for breach of contract. Alternatively, if the employee has proceeded to the courts for breach of contract, once the court hearing has commenced, the rights commissioner may not issue a recommendation.

OVERPAYMENT OF WAGES

As stated above, an overpayment of wages does not fall within the scope of the Act, so if an employee is overpaid wages in error, then it depends on whether it is a mistake of law or of fact. If the overpayment is a mistake of law, then the sum is not recoverable but if it is of

fact, then the sum may be recoverable. In *Avon County Council* v
Howlett [1983] IRLR 171, a teacher on sick leave following an accident was regularly overpaid by mistake. The Council became aware
of this mistake when over £1,000 had been overpaid, and sought to
have the money repaid. The overpayment was as a result of a mistake of fact on the part of the Council, in that it failed to realise that
Mr Howlett had been off sick for more than six months. He had spent
the money, believing it to be his. Mr Howlett refused to return the
money and the County Council issued proceedings which finally resulted in a judgment of the Court of Appeal, holding that the County
Council were estopped from reclaiming the monies which the teacher
received based on the employer's representations. It was also held
that if an employer overpays an employee, the employer will be estopped from succeeding in the claim if the following conditions are
satisfied:

1. The employer has led the employee to believe that they are enti-
    tled to treat the money as their own;

2. The employee receiving the money has in good faith altered their
    position as a result;

3. The overpayment was not caused primarily by the fault of the
    employee.

The Court intimated that that, if the employee still had the money in
his possession, the decision might have been different.

General References

Crump, D. and D. Pugley (1997), *Contracts of Employment*, 7th edition, London: Butterworths.

Hepple, B.A. (1981), *Hepple and O'Higgins Employment Law,* 4th edition, London: Sweet and Maxwell.

Kerr, T. (1991), *Irish Law Statutes Annotated, The Payment of Wages
Act*, London: Sweet and Maxwell.

Langford, K. (1996), "Keeping Pay Deductions Within The Law", *Irish
Law Times*, June.

Lockton, D. (1994), *Employment Law*, London: Macmillan Professional Masters.

Chapter Seven

COLLECTIVE BARGAINING

Collective bargaining and its voluntary nature is the keystone of Irish industrial relations. The term "collective agreement" is defined in the Anti-Discrimination (Pay) Act, 1974, as "an agreement relating to terms and conditions of employment made between parties who are or represent employers and parties who are or represent employees". There is also a definition of collective agreement in the Organisation of Working Time Act, 1997, which provides for an agreement by or on behalf of an employer on the one hand, and by or on behalf of a body or bodies representative of the employees to whom the agreement relates on the other hand. There is also a different definition in the Protection of Young Persons (Employment) Act, 1996, which defines a collective agreement as "by or on behalf of an employer on the one hand and by or on behalf of a trade union or trade union representative of the employees to whom the agreement relates on the other hand". This last definition clearly refers to trade unions but the other definition would include staff associations or "excepted bodies" under the Trade Union Act. Under the Employment Equality Act, 1998, "collective agreement" is technically undefined but includes employment regulation orders and registered employment agreements (see below).

VOLUNTARISM

In essence, industrial relations in Ireland have been characterised by legal abstention, whereby both employers and employees are free to enter into negotiations and to regulate their own respective rights and behaviour. An employee has the constitutional right to join a trade union (Article 40.4.1). However, there is no duty placed on an employer to negotiate with a trade union (*Abbott and Whelan* v *ITGWU and Others* [1982] 1 JISLL 56). An employer is entitled to refuse representation by a solicitor where procedures provide for trade union representation only (*Devoy* v *The Rt-Hon The Lord Mayor, Alderman and Burgesses of Dublin and Others* (1994–95) 10 JISLL 304 at p. 309, HC, per Carroll J); of course, natural and constitutional justice must be adhered to.

In *The Association of General Practitioners Ltd. and Others* v *Minister for Health* ((1994–95) 10 JISLL), the High Court considered whether the Minister had a legal obligation to consult with The Association of General Practitioners when conditions of service for doctors in general medical practice for the supply of general medical services was being considered. Section 26 of the Health Act, 1970 provided that the health boards may make arrangements with doctors to carry out GMS services, but the terms and conditions for the doctors are determined beforehand by the Minister. The Act imposes no express obligation on the Minister to consult the medical profession, their representatives or anyone else before deciding on the appropriate terms and conditions. The Minister did consult with the Irish Medical Organisation, which represents the majority of doctors participating in the scheme (approximately 75 per cent). The doctor plaintiffs argued that they were being penalised as a result of their insistence that they were not represented by the IMO. O'Hanlon J, in refusing the application of the Association of General Practitioners, relied on *Inspector of Taxes* v *Minister for Public Service* (unreported, 24 March 1983, HC, Murphy J). Murphy J referred to *Abbott* v *ITGWU*, where McWilliam J said, "There is no duty placed on any employer to negotiate with any particular citizen or body of citizens" and Murphy J held that the decision by the Minister for Public Service, on the ground of established administrative practice, to allow recognition to one association only in respect of each grade, represented a proper discharge of any contractual obligation which he owed to a staff association seeking recognition.

O'Hanlon J also stated (in *The Association of General Practitioners Ltd and Others* v *Minister for Health* at p. 274):

> . . . I do not consider that there is any obligation imposed by ordinary law or by the Constitution on an employer to consult with or negotiate with any organisation representing his employees or some of them, when the conditions of employment are to be settled or reviewed. The employer is left with freedom of choice as to

whether he will negotiate with any organisation or consult with them on such matters, and is also free to give a right of audience to one representative body and refuse it to another, if he chooses to do so.

The claim by the Association of General Practitioners was not sustainable. Of course, it was noted that if there was a mass exodus of members from the IMO and a corresponding influx of members to the plaintiff Association, then the Minister might consider it appropriate to replace the IMO with the Plaintiff Association when the Agreement has run its course or has been determined by notice.

"Voluntarism" is becoming more and more of a misnomer, because individual employment rights are increasingly protected by statute with a basic "floor of rights". Such basic rights as holidays, hours of work and redundancy must be within the statutory framework.

Negotiations on the amount of salary and wages are "voluntary", yet in recent years centralised bargaining has resulted in the Programme for National Recovery (PNR), the Programme for Competitiveness and Work (PCW), the Programme for Economic and Social Progress (PESP) and now Partnership 2000. This Agreement provides for some local bargaining and includes not only pay matters but also provision to amend various pieces of employment legislation. Generally, employment legislation provides for more and more reference of issues to third parties at the instigation of the parties involved.

INDUSTRIAL RELATIONS ACTS

The Industrial Relations Acts, 1946 to 1990, provide the framework for the collective bargaining process. The 1990 Act defines "worker" as (s. 23(1)):

> . . . any person aged 15 years or more who has entered into or works under a contract with an employer, whether the contract be for manual labour, clerical work or otherwise, whether it be expressed or implied, oral or in writing, and whether it be a contract of service or of apprenticeship or a contract personally to execute any work or labour including, in particular, a psychiatric nurse employed by a health board and any person designated for the time being . . . [employed under the Defence Act, 1954 or employed

under the State (other than established civil servants)] but does not include:

a) a person who is employed by or under the State

b) a teacher in a secondary school

c) a teacher in a national school

d) an officer of a vocational education committee, or

e) an officer of a school attendance committee.

Local authority (including health board) officers are now covered within the meaning of "worker" and thus are now covered under the Labour Court/Labour Relations Commissioners (including rights commissioners) industrial relations machinery. They were previously covered by a conciliation and arbitration scheme (Industrial Relations Act, 1990 (Definition of "Worker" Order, 1998 (SI No. 264 of 1998))).

In order to give an overview of the Irish system of collective bargaining, we must refer back to the enactment of the Industrial Relations Act, 1946, which essentially legislated for industrial relations dispute resolution machinery within the framework of "voluntarism". That Act is extremely significant in our history and, despite some amendments, is still the key Industrial Relations Act for dispute resolution, leaving aside issues of trade disputes within the context of strikes. The Act, which was novel for its time, set up the Labour Court to deal with a rush of wage claims expected following the price/wages freeze and the lifting of the statutory orders after the Second World War.

The Labour Court's key function is in the settlement of trade disputes. The Court is arranged into three divisions consisting of a chairperson and two deputy chairpersons with six ordinary members, three employer representatives and three employee representatives. Such persons are appointed by the Minister for Enterprise, Trade and Employment, though the Irish Business and Employers' Confederation and the Irish Congress of Trade Unions provide the Minister with their nominees. While it may be called the "Labour Court", it is not a court of law and its recommendations are not legally binding (although it does have adjudication in relation to equality and working time matters — see Chapters 9, 10 and 13). Nonetheless, the

Court has power to summon witnesses, hear evidence on oath and, in certain circumstances, issue binding recommendations.

The key provision of the Industrial Relations Act, 1969, was the establishment of the office of rights commissioner, which hears matters relating to individual grievances.

The Industrial Relations Act, 1990, set up the new industrial relations framework under the Labour Relations Commission and amended various parts of the earlier Acts. The 1990 Act provides new trade dispute legislation, having repealed the Trade Disputes Act, 1906 (as amended in 1982) (considered in the next chapter). The Labour Relations Commission comprises a chairperson, representatives of both sides of industry and two independent members who are appointed by the Minister for Enterprise, Trade and Employment. The Commission also appoints a chief executive. The Commission has under its umbrella the conciliation, rights commissioner and equality services (see Section 4, "Industrial Relations and Adjudicating Bodies" where all aspects are considered in more detail). The Commission also has power to publish Codes of Practice (see Chapter 8, "Trade Disputes"). A dispute which affects the public interest may be referred by the Minister to the Commission or to the Labour Court. However, it should be noted that the Labour Court is essentially a "court of appeal" within the industrial relations framework.

The Labour Relations Commission investigates and conciliates disputes. The Labour Court may not investigate a dispute until it has received a report from the Commission stating that it cannot resolve the matter and that both parties request the Court to investigate it. In certain circumstances, there may be direct reference to the Labour Court either by the workers concerned or by both parties (in respect of a certain issue in a dispute). There has to be agreement to accept the Court's recommendation.

TRADE UNIONS

The Trade Union Act, 1941, sets out the provisions for registration of trade unions and the granting of a licence which authorises negotiation on terms and conditions of employment. There are certain "excepted bodies" who may lawfully negotiate wages or other conditions of employment without holding a negotiation licence; for example, the civil service, teachers' groups and so forth. An "excepted body" also includes an association, all the members of which are employed by the same employer.

It should be noted that if a union failed to have a balloting procedure in place by 18 July 1992, in accordance with the 1990 Act, it lost its negotiation licence.

In order to obtain a licence, a trade union must have rules on the entry and cessation of membership. The list of members must be available for inspection. At least 18 months before a new union applies for a licence, it must notify the Minister for Enterprise, Trade and Employment, the ICTU and any trade union to which its members also belong, as well as place the appropriate notice in the press. There must also be an appropriate balloting procedure. The new union must have at least 1,000 members resident in the State for the previous 18 months and at the date of application, and deposit between £20,000 and £60,000 (depending on the size of the membership) with the Registrar of Friendly Societies.

A Code of Practice on the Duties and Responsibilities of Employee Representatives and the Protection and Facilities to be afforded them by their Employer came into effect on 25 June 1993 (SI No. 169 of 1993). The main purpose of this Code is to set out for the guidance of employers, employees and trade unions the duties and responsibilities of employee representatives (shop stewards) and the protection and facilities that should be afforded them to enable them to carry out their duties in an effective and constructive manner. The Code underlines the importance of such representatives in our system of industrial relations and in the resolution of disputes/grievances, and the manner in which their duties are discharged significantly affects the quality of management/labour relations in their establishments for its efficient operation and future development.

The principal duties and responsibilities of employee representatives include:

1. Representing members fairly and effectively in relation to matters arising within the undertaking or establishment in which they work and which concern employment and conditions of employment;

2. Participating in negotiation and grievance procedures as provided for in employer/trade union agreements or in accordance with

recognised custom and practice in the undertaking or establishment in which they work;

3. Co-operating with the management of the undertaking or establishment in ensuring the proper implementation and observance of employer/trade union agreements, the use of agreed dispute and grievance procedures and the avoidance of any action, especially unofficial action, which would be contrary to such agreements or procedures and which would affect the continuity of operations or services;

4. Acting in accordance with existing laws and regulations, the rules of the union and good industrial relations practice; liaising with and seeking advice and assistance from the appropriate full-time trade union official;

5. Having regard at all times to the safe and efficient operation of the undertaking or establishment;

6. Subject to any other arrangements made between an employer and a trade union, employee representatives should conform to the same job performance standards, company rules, disciplinary conditions and other conditions of employment that are comparable to employees in the undertaking or establishment in which they work.

If an employer considers that an employee representative is acting beyond the normal authority of a union representative or in a manner which is damaging to the establishment, then the employer should in the first instance take the matter up with the employee representative concerned and failing satisfactory resolution take the matter up with the appropriate trade union.

The election or designation of employee representatives must be in accordance with the trade union rules or the union/management agreement. The representatives must be actually representative of the employees concerned (taking into account the size of the employment, the number of trade union members employed and the structure of trade union organisation in the employment) and should normally have a minimum of one year's service in the particular employment. The appointment should be confirmed in writing by the trade union and they shall be given appropriate advice and training by the union. The employer must provide the representative with relevant information concerning the procedures for communicating with management representatives and may provide additional training.

The Code provides protection for employee representatives in that they may not be dismissed or suffer any unfavourable change in their conditions of employment or unfair treatment including selection for redundancy because of their status or activities as employee representatives or suffer any action prejudicial to their employment because of their status or activities as employee representatives without prior consultation taking place between management and the trade union. If an employee is dismissed arising from such activities, the representative should normally be reinstated. These provisions are without prejudice to the provisions of the Unfair Dismissals Acts, 1977–1993.

There should be agreements between management and the employee representatives ensuring the provision of reasonable facilities for the employee representatives. Such facilities should enable them to carry out their duties promptly and efficiently and regard must be had for the size of the employment concerned — facilities include necessary time off to a reasonable extent as long as there is prior permission (this time off would include trade union meetings and training courses); the question of payment of wages for the time off should be the subject of discussion in advance. Employee representatives should be granted reasonable access to all workplaces and to management in order to carry out their functions. In the absence of check-off arrangements, employee representatives may by prior agreement be permitted to collect union dues regularly. Employer and trade unions should agree arrangements for the posting of trade union notices relating to the normal activities of the union in a place where employees have access. Employee representatives acting on behalf of their trade union should be permitted to distribute non-political news-sheets, pamphlets, publications and other documents relating to normal trade union activities amongst the members of the union in the workplace, obviously taking into account the orderly operation and tidiness of the workplace.

TRADE UNION RECOGNITION

Trade Union Recognition Report

The High Level Group on Trade Union Recognition was set up under Paragraph 9.22 of Partnership 2000. The paragraph provided that, in order to assist employers, employees and unions, the industrial relations system and institutions would be modernised during the period of Partnership 2000. The Group involved the Departments of the Taoiseach, Finance, Enterprise, Trade and Employment, ICTU, IBEC and IDA Ireland, to consider the detailed proposals submitted by ICTU on the Recognition of Unions and the Right to Bargain. As of August 1999, this Report has not yet been implemented.

An initial report was issued in early 1998, but it coincided with the Ryanair strike in Dublin Airport, which closed the Airport for two days in early March of that year.

The Group produced its Second Report in March 1999. The Report provided that, where negotiated agreements are in place, the most effective means of resolving differences between employers and trade unions representing employees is by voluntary collective bargaining. Where there is not a negotiated agreement in place and where there is no collective bargaining, the matter can be referred to the Labour Relations Commission, which will appoint an officer from its Advisory Service to assess the issues in dispute and work with the parties in an attempt to resolve the issues. If there is no early resolution, a "cooling-off period" will come into effect. During this time, the Advisory Service will continue to work with the parties, and IBEC and ICTU may become involved. If matters resolve, the Labour Relations Commission will disengage and may make proposals for the peaceful resolution of future grievances/disputes. If matters remain unresolved, the Labour Relations Commission will make a written report to the Labour Court which, having considered the matter, will issue a recommendation. It was recommended that these general principles should be incorporated into a Code of Practice under the Industrial Relations Act, 1990 (s. 42).

Voluntary Process Not Complied With

If the voluntary process has not been complied with, and where a trade union so requests, the Labour Court will be empowered to summons parties to attend before it where:

- An employer has failed to follow the steps outlined in the above voluntary process;

- Appropriate internal procedures and mechanisms have failed to resolve the issue; and

- There is no recourse to industrial action during the process.

In such cases, the Labour Court will conduct an investigation into the matters in dispute, taking into account all labour practices in the employment, and will issue a recommendation. In the event that the parties fail to resolve the issues within the framework of the Labour Court recommendation, the Labour Court following a review of the matter will issue a determination, which shall be binding for one year only. If matters are not resolved during that year, following a further review the Court may issue a binding determination. This would require amendment to the Industrial Relations Act, 1946.

Individual Representation: General Principles and Fair Procedure

The Code of Practice on Disciplinary Procedures (SI No. 117 of 1996) provides for the essential elements of fair procedures. The Group noted that procedures should be updated periodically so that they are consistent with changed circumstances in the workplace, developments in employment legislation and case law and good practice generally. It was recommended that IBEC and ICTU, together with the industrial relations machinery of the State, should take steps to promote awareness of the rights of individuals to natural justice and the adoption of fair procedures.

Disputes of "Special Importance"

The Group noted that there are disputes of "special importance" that impact on essential services or cause widespread disruption to business and the general public, which can arise due to the absence of agreed mechanisms or a willingness to bargain or a failure to avail of the services of the Labour Relations Commission or the Labour Court. It was recommended that parties involved in providing essential services agree amendments to their disputes procedures to adopt the key provisions of the voluntary Code of Practice (SI No. 1 of 1992).

Trade Union Recognition Bill, 1998

The Trade Union Recognition Bill, 1998, was published on 3 February 1998 but has not been passed into law. This was a Private Member's Bill that provided a mechanism to resolve disputes concerning failure by employers to recognise a trade union.

The definition of trade union includes "staff associations" or other excepted bodies within the meaning of s. 6 of the Trade Union Act, 1941. The union must be representative of a substantial number of employees or category of employees. It was noted in the Explanatory Memorandum that this was in line with the decision in *Federation of Irish Rail and Road Workers* v *Great Southern Railway* ([1942] Ir Jur Rep 33), where a union that represented about one-third of employees was sufficiently representative for the purposes of a statutory provision. Further, such a dispute may not be referred, if there is an existing union recognised in respect of such employees.

It was proposed that such disputes should be referred initially to the Labour Relations Commission and if the dispute is not resolved, to the Labour Court, which would investigate and issue a recommendation. The Labour Court could order the taking of a ballot of the employees. If the Labour Court recommendation was not complied with or if it did not resolve the dispute, the Labour Court after a further hearing could make an employment regulation order, which might include provision for statutory consultations and disciplinary representations as well as pay and conditions. Such employment regulation orders are enforceable under the Industrial Relations Acts, 1946–1990.

Once a union is recognised by an employer, the Bill proposed that the employer must negotiate with it in good faith in respect of the pay and conditions of its members, consult with the trade union where legislation requires such consultation and provide the opportunity to be represented in respect of any disciplinary proceedings.

There was also provision that, if an employee was dismissed in respect of reasons related to the seeking of union recognition, it would be an unfair dismissal for the purposes of the Unfair Dismissals Act, 1977. Also, there was provision for the extension of the definition of "trade dispute" in the Industrial Relations Act, 1990, to include trade recognition disputes.

If this Bill had been enacted, it would have undermined the voluntarism of Irish industrial relations as enshrined in the Industrial Relations Act, 1946.

JOINT LABOUR COMMITTEES

The Industrial Relations Act, 1946, empowered the Labour Court to set up a Joint Labour Committee (JLC) on the application of an organisation representing workers, a trade union or the Minister for Enterprise and Employment. The purpose of a JLC is to regulate conditions of employment and minimum rates of pay for workers engaged in certain forms of activity. There are JLCs covering some of the following forms of activity: Contract Cleaning (City and County of Dublin), Retail Grocery and Allied Trades, Law Clerks, Hairdressing (Dublin and Cork), Provender Milling and so forth.

The Labour Court will not establish a JLC unless it considers that the application is well founded and is made by an organisation or a group representing such workers or employers, and that either:

1. There is substantial agreement between such workers and their employers to the establishment of a joint labour committee, or

2. The existing machinery for effective regulation of remuneration and other conditions of employment of such workers is inadequate or is likely to cease or to cease to be adequate, or

3. Having regard to the existing rates of remuneration or conditions of employment of such workers or any others, that it is expedient that a joint labour committee be established.

The Labour Court will consider the issue and, after consultation with the parties, prepare a draft establishment order. Then the Court will publish a notice stating that it intends to hold an inquiry into the application for a JLC; the day, time and place where the inquiry will be held (not earlier than 30 days or later than 60 days from the date of publication); and where draft copies of the establishment order can be obtained.

All objections to the draft must be in writing, listing the grounds of objection to the establishment of the JLC. The objections will be considered by the Court on the day of the inquiry. If the Court is satisfied about matters, the order will be published and become effective not later than 42 days afterwards.

The constitution and proceedings of JLCs are governed by the Fifth Schedule to the Industrial Relations Act, 1990. A JLC comprises an independent chairperson appointed by the Minister for Enterprise and Employment and an equal number of employer and worker representatives who are appointed by the Labour Court.

JLCs issue Employment Regulation Orders (EROs) which set out minimum rates of pay for all workers covered by the JLC. The proposals of an ERO must be published, stating where copies of the proposals may be obtained and that representations may be made within 21 days of the publication. The proposed ERO is then submitted to the Labour Court, which may refer the proposals back to the JLC or give effect to them from whatever date the Court considers appropriate. The JLC does not have to republish its amended proposals, though they do have to go back to the Court for the making of an order.

If there is already a registered employment agreement (see below) in place and there is agreement with both sides, the provision of an ERO may be waived as long as the terms and conditions of employment are not less favourable than those of the ERO.

An inspector may institute proceedings against an employer for breach of an ERO and a worker may also institute civil proceedings against their employer. Breach of an ERO is an offence and the employer may be liable to a fine of £750.

The Labour Relations Commission may carry out periodic reviews to see whether new JLCs should be established and to review existing committees. Also, the Labour Court may ask a JLC for a report on the industry for which it was established. The independent chairperson may also ask the members for such a report.

JOINT INDUSTRIAL COUNCILS

Joint Industrial Councils (JICs) are permanent, voluntary joint negotiating bodies whose main purpose is the promotion of harmonious relations between employers and employees. The procedures of the Council must provide that during the course of a trade dispute, a lockout or a strike cannot take place until the matter has been considered by the Council. The Labour Court does not register such

groups unless it is satisfied that they are substantially representative
of a particular class, type or group of worker and their respective employers.

REGISTRATION OF COLLECTIVE AGREEMENTS

The Industrial Relations Act, 1946 (as amended by the 1990 Act),
provides that a collective agreement may be registered with the Labour Court, making it legally binding upon the parties. These are
known as registered agreements and they provide for certain basic
terms and conditions of employment. Such agreement is defined in
the 1946 Act as

> . . . an agreement relating to the remuneration or the conditions of
> employment of workers of any class, type of group made between a
> trade union of workers and an employer or trade union of employ-
> ers, or made at a meeting of a joint industrial council between
> members of the council representative of workers and members of
> the council representative of employers.

The Acts provide for certain requirements to be complied with before
these agreements can be registered. The agreements apply to all
workers of the particular category who need not necessarily be represented at the negotiation process before the Labour Court.

Before an agreement can be registered, the Labour Court must be
satisfied that the parties to the agreement are substantially representative of such workers and employers. All practical details of applicants must be given (e.g. names and addresses) the extent to which
there is agreement and the grounds for establishing that the applicants are substantially representative of such employees.

A 1992 High Court judgment declared the registered agreement in
the security industry as null and void due to "rubber stamping" by
the Labour Court. It was also considered that neither fair procedures
nor appropriate registration formalities were complied with. The parties were represented by the Federated Union of Employers (FUE)
(now IBEC), who represented five firms where 1,000 of the 2,700
static guards were employed, and the Irish Transport and General
Workers' Union (now Scientific Industrial and Professional Trade
Union). An organisation called the National Union of Security Employers (NUSE) challenged the validity of the agreement, which was

registered in 1984, on the basis that the objections of certain employers in the security industry were not considered by the Court and that FUE did not substantially represent the majority of employers in the security industry (*National Union of Security Employers* v *The Labour Court, Ireland and the Attorney General*, High Court (1994–1995) JISLL 97). (As a sequel, the Security Industry Joint Labour Committee Establishment Order (SI No. 377 of 1998) came into effect on 16 October 1998.)

There has been ongoing concern over the years that such agreements are not constitutional, but this issue was not addressed in this judgment.

Two parties may consent to such registration or, where there are more than two parties involved, there must be substantial agreement between them. The agreement must apply to all workers of a particular type, group or class and their respective employers. The Court must be satisfied that it would be a desirable practice or that it would be expedient to have a separate agreement for that group, class or type of worker. The agreement cannot have the intention of restricting employment or causing unduly costly work practices. The agreement must provide that if there is a trade dispute, a strike or lockout shall not occur until the dispute resolution provisions in the agreement have taken place. The contents of the agreement become the contractual provisions of the employment contract.

Before the agreement is registered, the Labour Court must ask the parties to publish particulars of the agreement so that it will be brought to the attention of all the parties who will be covered by it. This is extremely important because all employers and employees who may not be party to the original application will be covered by the agreement when it is registered. The Court will not register the agreement until 14 days have elapsed from the date of the publication. If there is an objection to the registration of the agreement, the Court will have to hear all such objections and then make its decision. Once the Court is satisfied that all aspects of the Act have been complied with, the agreement shall be placed on the Register of Employment Agreements.

The Labour Court is considered the body for the interpretation of registered agreements. If the interpretation of a registered agreement arises before a court of law, it may be referred to the Labour Court if the Court so wishes.

There is provision for the variation or amendment to registered agreements. If variation is requested, the Court shall hear all the parties and then decide. This is a frequent occurrence in matters such as pay. A variation order is then registered along with the original agreement and becomes part of the registered agreement.

If there is a breach of the agreement and a complaint to the Court, both parties will be heard (should they so wish) and the Court shall make the appropriate order so that the agreement is complied with if the complaint is well founded.

The 1990 Act provides that an employer must keep all the necessary records to show that a registered agreement is being complied with. Such records must be kept for three years and an employer who fails to do so may be liable to a fine of £500. If records are falsified, there is liability to a fine of £1,000.

If a sum is due to a worker by an employer arising from a registered employment agreement, or if there is a breach of such an agreement, an inspector can institute proceedings for the recovery of the sum of the enforcement of the condition on behalf of the worker. A worker can also institute proceedings on their own behalf.

There are also provisions stating that there cannot be the maintenance of a strike (out of the union funds) where an employer is being made to agree to pay levels or work conditions other than those contained in the agreement. In such situations, the Court may order the union not to assist the maintenance of such a strike or may cancel the agreement. If there is a breach of this order, the party may be guilty of a criminal offence (£1,000 and £200 fines per day for a continuing offence). If a strike continues after such an order, and the issue does not relate to pay or conditions of employment, then the payment of strike benefits is not considered to be "assistance or maintenance" within the meaning of the Act.

A registered agreement may be cancelled by a joint voluntary application of the parties concerned. Also, the Court may cancel an agreement if there is a substantial change in the trade or industry covered. Equally, an agreement registered for a specific period and still in force at the end of the period will continue to remain in force until it is formally cancelled. It can be cancelled after three months' notification to the Court where there is agreement between the parties.

MINIMUM WAGE

The Minister for Enterprise, Trade and Employment appointed the Minimum Wage Commission in July 1997 under the Chair of the then Chairperson of the Labour Court, Ms Evelyn Owens. Its terms of reference was to advise on the way to implement the commitment to a national minimum hourly wage; to examine the range of possible mechanisms for determining and implementing minimum wage-fixing machinery; to study any measures that may have an adverse impact on employment and competitiveness; and to consult with the social partners before finalisation of their report.

The rate decided by the Commission was £4.40 per hour. Subsequently, an inter-departmental group of civil servants was set up to consider implementation. Such implementation would require legislation and consideration would have to be given to the definition of "employee", to include agency workers, but possibly excluding statutory apprentices and close relations working for each other. The definition of working time would be as defined in the Organisation of Working Time Act, 1997.

The calculation of pay would have to be considered. The Group felt that all "gross payments which can be regarded as making up the rate for the job" should be taken into account, such as the basic rate, bonus, allowances for special duties and commission, piece and incentive rates, shift premium, etc. (but excluding overtime premiums). The value of board and lodging may be included but employer pension contributions may be excluded.

The inspectorate in the Department would monitor the application of such future legislation with a complainant having the option of going to an inspector or a rights commissioner, with a right of appeal to the Employment Appeals Tribunal.

The Minister for Enterprise, Trade and Employment has announced that the minimum wage would indeed be set at £4.40 per hour, effective from 1 April 2000 (see various issues of *Industrial Relations News*: No. 29 of 1997; No. 1 of 1998 — *Britain's Minimum Wage Bill to set parameters for Ireland?;* Nos. 24 and 25 of 1999).

General References

Kerr, A. (1991), *The Trade Union and Industrial Relations Acts of Ireland*, Dublin: Sweet and Maxwell.

McCarthy, C. (1977), *Trade Unions in Ireland, 1894–1960*, Dublin: Institute of Public Administration.

Murphy, Thomas V. and William K. Roche (eds.) (1997), *Irish Industrial Relations in Practice*, 2nd Edition, Dublin: Oak Tree Press in association with the Graduate School of Business, UCD.

Report of the Commission of Inquiry on Industrial Relations (1981), Dublin: Stationery Office.

Chapter Eight

TRADE DISPUTES

INDUSTRIAL RELATIONS ACT, 1990

The Industrial Relations Act, 1990, came into operation on 18 July 1990. This complex legislation is the outcome of various different proposals and much discussion, including recommendations by the commission of Inquiry on Industrial Relations, which reported in July 1981. The Trade Disputes Act, 1906, as amended (the Trade Disputes (Amendment) Act, 1982, extended the scope of the 1906 Act) has been repealed in full.

There have been a number of key cases giving consideration to the Act, in particular the Supreme Court judgment in *Halligan & Others v Nolan Transport (Oaklands) Limited* ([1998] ELR 177) which considered the definition of "trade dispute" and the application of the provisions on balloting. Many of the rulings of the High Court during the 1970s and 1980s have now become statutory provisions in the 1990 Act; for example, the provisions relating to places where picketing is permitted and the numbers that may be involved.

The purpose of the Act is to make better provision for promoting harmonious relations between workers and employers and to amend the industrial relations and trade union legislation generally. In this chapter, trade or industrial disputes are considered. Legislation affecting trade unions themselves and general industrial relations (collective) bargaining have already been considered.

DEFINITIONS

As with all pieces of legislation, the definitions in the Act (s. 8) are important and considered first.

Employer

"A person for whom one or more workers work or have worked or
normally work or seek to work having previously worked for that
person."

Worker

"Any person who is or was employed whether or not in the employment with whom a trade dispute arises, but does not include a
member of the Defence Forces or of the Garda Síochána."

This appears to be a very loose definition and one fears it will be open
to wide interpretation. There is no specific reference to a contract of
service (contract of employment). Accordingly, the courts may consider that independent contractors fall within the definition of
"worker". If that is the case, there is no major change from the 1906
Act. However, individuals who are seeking employment would appear
to be excluded.

As stated in the definition, members of the Garda Síochána are
excluded from the provisions of the 1990 Act. This resulted in their
use of "Blue Flu" days in respect of their pay dispute in 1998. These
"Blue Flu" days involved gardaí telephoning in sick as an uncertified
sick leave day. (*Industrial Relations News* No. 1 of 7 January 1999
notes that the total number of days could amount to 7,000 days for
each of the two days of action).

In *Westman Holdings Ltd.* v *McCormack and Others* ([1991] ILRM
833), six of the defendants were employed by a company called Alma
Taverns Ltd. as bar and restaurant staff in an establishment in Dublin known as Judge Roy Beans, occupied by that company under a
lease. The lease expired on 1 March 1991 and the business was taken
over by the immediate landlords, Westhall Property Co. Ltd., who
also took over the employment of the worker defendants.

On 15 March 1991, Westhall entered into a contract with Westman Holdings to sell the premises. Westhall terminated the employment of all its employees and business ceased on 5 April 1991. Prior
to that, each of the employees had received a sum of money and
signed a form acknowledging that this was in full discharge of all
claims that they may have against Alma and Westhall. An official of
the workers' trade union, INUVGATA, made a claim that its member
employees of Westhall were entitled to continue in the employment of

Westman under the provisions of the European Communities (Safeguarding of Employees on the Transfer of Undertakings) Regulations, 1980. Westman rejected the claim and the worker defendants commenced an official union picket of the premises.

Westman made a successful *ex parte* application to have the picketing removed on 11 April. On the hearing of the matter, an interlocutory injunction was granted, restraining the defendants from picketing the premises. That decision was appealed to the Supreme Court, which considered that, on the balance of convenience, the injunction against picketing should continue until the full hearing of the case. The Court acknowledged that there were fair reasons for such a hearing, however, including consideration as to whether Westman would be deemed to be their employer and whether there was a transfer of business within the meaning of the 1980 Regulations.

Trade Dispute

> "Any dispute between employers and workers which is connected with the employment or non-employment, or the terms or conditions of, or affecting the employment of any person."

This definition excludes "worker v worker" disputes. It obviously does not *only* apply to "employer v worker" disputes, however, as it can include disputes involving former workers (thus including dismissal in the widest sense, e.g. employees having a dispute over future redundancy payments) or indeed workers employed by some other employer. The terms or conditions of employment include all matters either expressed or implied in the contract of employment.

The Supreme Court in *Halligan and Others* v. *Nolan Transport (Oaklands) Limited* ([1998] ELR 177) considered two issues:

1. Whether or not a dispute existed;

2. Whether or not the Union was entitled to authorise strike action having regard to the manner in which the secret ballot was conducted and the manner in which those voting actually voted.

The background of the case was as follows.

Nolan Transport, a family firm, employed 55 drivers and in December 1992 some of these drivers wished to join a trade union, as they apparently had a grievance concerning pay and conditions. Following a meeting attended by James Halligan, Henry Nolan and five other drivers, a SIPTU official wrote to the company on 18 January claiming that his union had accepted into membership "a large number of your company employees" and seeking a meeting "to set in train the necessary steps to establish what we hope will be a good working relationship". There was also telephone communication between a union official and the Chief Executive. The next day, 19 January 1993, some of the drivers met Mr James Nolan (the father of the Chief Executive and other family members of management) in the company yard. He was not involved in the management of the company but worked as a labourer for the company. Mr Halligan and a number of his colleagues maintained that they were dismissed by the father or alternatively that the conduct of the father and the other members of the Nolan family on 19 and 20 January 1993 led them to believe that they had been so dismissed. There was subsequent picketing.

On 24 January 1993, a further meeting of the members of the Union was held in Waterford and a decision was made to hold a ballot for industrial action (although there were only five members and two Union officials at that meeting). Twenty-three members voted in the ballot. By way of circular letter, the company informed its employees that they did not have to be a member of a union to work for the company and requested each employee to sign and return the letter to the company if they were satisfied with their conditions of employment. All of the office staff signed the form and all but four or five of the drivers likewise signed. There was then a meeting of the Waterford branch of the Union on 31 January 1993 at which seven driver members were present with a Union official and the Branch Secretary. The votes were counted and the result, as declared and circulated, was that 20 had voted in favour of strike action and three against. A further meeting of the members was called for 7 February. On 2 February, strike notice was served for 11 February. Between 2 and 10 February, there was considerable activity. The Union initiated a trenchant campaign in support of the planned industrial action, whilst the overwhelming majority of drivers expressed dissatisfaction with it. A petition dissociating themselves from industrial action and expressly refusing to withdraw their labour on 11 February 1993 was signed by 48 of the company drivers. There was a further Union meeting on 7 February at which 16 drivers were present. There was considerable controversy as to what took place at the meeting; during the course of the Court proceedings, 11 drivers gave evidence to the effect that they did not understand the result of the ballot because they were aware they had themselves voted against industrial action.

On the expiration of the strike notice, a picket was placed on the company premises on 11 February 1993. Three of the defendants picketed the premises. Notwithstanding the picket, the business of the company continued and indeed its turnover increased. It was noted that the industrial action appears to have been particularly abrasive. Picketing continued and finally an application for an interlocutory order to restrain such picketing was made in March 1994. Keane J, on 22 March 1994, held that he was prepared to make an Order restraining any picketing other than peaceful picketing at the plaintiff's premises (reported in (1994–1995) 10 JISLL 105).

Nolan Transport then brought proceedings against named officials, employee members of SIPTU (who had been employed as advisers) and SIPTU itself for a declaration that their actions in endorsing industrial action against the company were unlawful in that they constituted a wrongful inducing of breaches of the company's commercial contracts and interference with business relations; further, that the industrial action was in breach of SIPTU's rules. Nolan Transport also applied for an injunction restraining SIPTU from committing acts of intimidation against their employees, servants or agents and from imposing or seeking to impose an embargo on Nolan Transport's business, whether by communication with their customers, business associates, consignors, consignees or otherwise; and seeking damages for unlawful interference with its trade or business, for interfering with its business relations and economic interests, and for defamation and/or malicious falsehoods.

Following a 28-day hearing, during which nearly 100 witnesses were called, Barron J delivered his judgment in the High Court on 20 December 1994, expressly rejecting the claim that the drivers had been dismissed by the father. He held that the father did not have authority to dismiss employees and that the drivers recognised that this was so ((1994–1995) 10 JISLL at page 114). He therefore held that there was no *bona fide* trade dispute, as he considered that the Union never regarded the issue of dismissals as more than an event to use to its advantage and that that part of the dispute was not pursued *bona fide* to get the two men back to work (one other man was not prevented from working) but as part of a policy to take all the drivers into membership. A claim to negotiate on behalf of all the workers in a particular employment is an attempt to deprive those who are not members of their right of free association (at page 163).

Barron J also gave consideration to the matter of secret ballots (see below). He found that it necessarily followed from the evidence that the result of the ballot that had been declared on 31 January was dishonest and an inescapable conclusion reached that the ballot had been "rigged". If a twelfth driver had voted against industrial action (and there was evidence that he did), then the vote would have been against industrial action.

Barron J awarded the company a sum of £601,000 damages against the defendants — of that sum, £25,000 was expressly attributed to the defamation and malicious falsehoods; £400,000 to loss of profits and £176,000 to additional fuel costs. In addition, an injunction was granted restraining the picketing of the plaintiff's premises or otherwise engaging in industrial action against the company. The Union and its members appealed that judgment to the Supreme Court.

The Supreme Court gave consideration to the matter of whether there a trade dispute existed. Murphy J asked the question as to whether Mr James Halligan or Mr Henry Nolan or their Union believed that the three employees or some of them had been dismissed from their employment with the company in January 1993. It was clear that the father did not himself have the power to dismiss employees and the question remained as to what the employees reasonably understood as a result of the clear but crude message given to them by the father. It is further noted that they did not consult with their Union officials that evening nor when they were advised to turn up for work the following day and "verify whether or not they had been dismissed". The inference to be drawn from the events of 19 January was that the father purported to dismiss the three employees although he had no authority to do so. It was further noted that whilst the father was infuriated by the trade union activities of the particular employees, there was no suggestion that any of them did anything on the evening in question to provoke the father or to engage in any argument with him. Murphy J stated:

> If he had the authority which he purported to exercise, the words spoken would have constituted a dismissal. The contention made by the Company that the dismissals were contrived by the employees does not seem to be supported by any version of the facts.

Murphy J continued by considering the meaning of a *"bona fide* trade dispute". He said:

> If employers and workers both acknowledge themselves to be engaged in any trade dispute, there is no difficulty in describing it as a *bona fide* trade dispute. But a *bona fide* trade dispute may also exist where one party denies that there is any dispute and the other believes that he has been wronged and is in dispute as a result. On the other hand, an outside party or "meddler" who had no legitimate interest of his own to protect but who . . . stirred up trouble in a business for reasons of malice or spite could not claim to be engaged in any *bona fide* trade dispute. . . . If, however, a *bona fide* trade dispute does exist between an employer and workers, some of whom happen to be members of a trade union, the trade union is entitled, within the Constitution and the law, to support its members who are in dispute. That, in doing this, it may be partly motivated by the aim of impressing its members and other workers and enhancing its own reputation and membership appears to me to be quite irrelevant as long as it acts within the law and does not intend to infringe the constitutional right of each worker to join or not to join a trade union as he himself thinks best.

He said therefore it follows that the members, official and the union were entitled to the statutory immunities conferred on those engaged in activities in furtherance of a trade dispute save insofar as those privileges were removed or restricted by the Industrial Relations Act, 1990.

Industrial Action

> "Any action which affects or is likely to affect, the terms or conditions, whether express or implied, of a contract and which is taken by any number or body of workers acting in combination or under a common understanding as a means of compelling their employer, or to aid other workers in compelling their employer, to accept or not to accept terms or conditions of or affecting employment".

This definition is extremely broad, even broader than a similar definition contained in the Unfair Dismissals Acts, 1977 to 1993. It also refers to collective industrial action as opposed to action by an individual employee. The definition encompasses action such as "work-to-rule" and a "go slow". If employees wish to engage in such industrial action, they will have to comply with requirements of the legislation, such as holding secret ballots, which are discussed below.

The bank strike of 1992 resulted in claims in respect of industrial action and breach of contract. In *Browne and Jones* v *Governor and Company of the Bank of Ireland; Loftus and Bredin* v *Ulster Bank Limited* ((1994–1995) 10 JISLL 47), the issue of alleged breach of the contract of employment and industrial action was considered. In early 1992, the Irish Bank Officials Association (IBOA) embarked upon limited industrial action whereby its members were involved in a total ban on overtime; hours of work were strictly limited and there would be no sale of assurance or insurance products. By March 1992, the IBOA had instructed its members not to maintain records of data relating to fees, charges or commission in respect of certain products and services. The Bank of Ireland sent a form to be signed by virtually all its employees as follows:

> During the course of the current dispute I undertake to carry out my normal duties in accordance with normal requirements and not to engage in industrial action.

Ulster Bank sent out a similar form as follows:

> I confirm that I will work normally and honour the full terms of my contract of employment.

Employees were advised that if they did not send back the form by a certain date it would be presumed that such employees were acting in

support of or engaging in industrial action and would have their salaries reduced by 20 per cent. The plaintiffs, all members of the IBOA,
refused to sign the form. None of the plaintiffs was engaged in the
relevant duties of the position of bank official, as one would normally
understand it to mean at the time; for example, one was working in
fraud prevention, another in the stationery department. During the
relevant period prior to full strike action, the plaintiffs carried out
their normal duties. Nonetheless, there was a 20 per cent reduction
in their salary over a period of about three weeks. The Court considered that there were three questions to be answered:

1. Did the refusal of the plaintiffs or any of them to sign the pledge
   of loyalty constitute a breach of their contracts of employment?

2. Had the defendant Banks the right to deduct a proportion of each
   of the plaintiff's salary because of their refusal to sign?

3. If the signing of the pledge was merely for the purpose of getting
   the Banks out of a logistic difficulty, were the plaintiffs or any of
   them obliged to assist the banks out of such difficulty?

Ballagh J of Dublin District Court did not consider the refusal to sign
to be a breach of contract and he saw no reason for the officials to re-
confirm their contract of employment. Prior to the commencement of
the all-out strike, none of the plaintiffs was in breach of their contract
of employment. The banks were not entitled to deduct such monies
and awarded the plaintiffs decrees for the amounts deducted (see also
Maher v *Allied Irish Banks plc* [1998] ELR 204; and *O'Donovan* v *Allied Irish Banks plc* [1998] ELR 209).

Strike

> "A cessation of work by any number or body of workers acting in
> combination or a concerted refusal or a refusal under common un-
> derstanding of any number of workers to continue to work for
> their employer done as a means of compelling their employer, or to
> aid other workers in compelling their employer, to accept or not to
> accept terms or conditions of or affecting employment".

The key issue in this definition is that the purpose of the strike must
be to compel an employer to accept or not to accept certain terms and
conditions of or affecting employment. By implication it excludes

strikes which are purely political, such as a general strike or demonstration concerning income tax matters.

IMMUNITIES

The legislation does not give a positive right to strike, but trade union members, officials of trade unions and trade unions themselves who take industrial action in furtherance or contemplation of a trade dispute have immunity or protection under the legislation (section 13). In other words, they cannot be sued for taking part in such action. Of course, such persons are required to comply with the balloting and notice requirements as provided for in the legislation.

This immunity or protection applies only to "authorised" trade unions (including its officials and members), that is, trade unions which hold negotiation licences. There is no change on this point from the previous legislation.

However, like all general rules, there are exceptions. Accordingly, such persons in dispute may be sued for damages or there may be proceedings by way of injunction if, for example:

1. It is not a genuine trade dispute, e.g. a political action as discussed above (see definition of strike/industrial action);

2. The balloting and notice procedures have not been complied with;

3. Non-peaceful picketing takes place;

4. The industrial action amounts to an inducement to breach a commercial contract or there is an unlawful interference with a trade or business.

These issues were considered in the case of *G&T Crampton Limited* v *Building and Allied Trades Union & Others* ([1998] ELR 4) where Cramptons, a building company, had contracted to construct a building by a particular date subject to substantial penalty clauses for delay in performance of the contract. The defendant bricklayers working on the site claimed that they were employees of Cramptons and not employed by a subcontractor. When that subcontractor completed its phase of the building, the subcontractor terminated the employment of all its bricklayers on the site. The next phase of the building commenced with a new subcontractor who did not employ any of the bricklayers, who then placed a picket on the site. No work was carried out on the site from that time and Cramptons were unable to obtain deliveries of materials. Cramptons applied for an interlocutory injunction restraining the bricklayers and their union from engaging in industrial action on their site and interfering with their business. Laffoy J granted Cramptons their interlocutory injunction restraining the trade union and its members from watching or besetting or picketing the site and from interfering with access to or egress from the site. Thus, judgment was upheld by the Supreme Court. In so holding, section 19(2) of the Act was considered, which provides:

> Where a secret ballot has been held in accordance with the rules of a trade union . . . the outcome of which . . . favours a strike or other industrial action [and] gives notice of not less than one week to the employer concerned of its intention to do so, a court shall not grant an injunction restraining the strike or other industrial action where the respondent establishes a fair case that he was acting in contemplation or furtherance of a trade dispute.

Consideration would have to be given to whether the three preconditions were applied (i.e. a secret ballot favouring industrial action, giving the requisite notice). If these conditions have been fulfilled, the Court must then decide whether the union has established a fair case that it was acting in contemplation or furtherance of a trade dispute. If all these conditions were fulfilled, then Cramptons' application would be turned down. Laffoy J considered that:

> There was no evidence whatsoever before the Court as to the outcome of the secret ballot conducted by the union and, in particular, there is no evidence that the outcome favoured picketing the site.

Arising from this, it was held that the union was not entitled to rely on section 19(2) and Cramptons' case falls to be decided on the ordinary principles applicable to applications for interlocutory injunctions (*American Cynamid Co.* v *Ethicon Limited* [1975] AC 396, as adopted by the Supreme Court in *Campus Oil Ltd.* v *Minister for Industry and Energy (No. 2)* [1983] IR 88). The issues to be decided were whether there is a fair issue to be tried between the parties and whether damages would be an adequate remedy for Cramptons. It was affirmed by the Supreme Court that there was a fair issue to be tried, damages were not an adequate remedy and that the balance of convenience was in favour of the granting of the injunction pending the full hearing of the case for a permanent injunction.

Trade unions themselves cannot be sued for damages in respect of a tort (a civil wrong) pursued in contemplation or furtherance of a trade dispute, provided, of course, that they have an honest and reasonable belief that the action is in contemplation or furtherance of such trade dispute. Of course, if it is an action for defamation or for breach of contract, the trade union can be sued.

INDIVIDUAL WORKERS

One of the major changes in the 1990 legislation concerns disputes relating to an individual worker. The legislation is quite clear in that it refers to "one individual worker" and not to group disputes. Section 9(2) states:

> Where in relation to the employment or non-employment or the terms or conditions of or affecting the employment of one individual worker, there are agreed procedures availed of by custom or in practice in the employment concerned, are provided for in a collective agreement, for the resolution of individual grievances, including dismissals . . .

Thus, if such procedures are not applied, the employee will not have the benefit of the immunity. This means that the employer may seek an injunction to stop the picketing and may sue for damages caused by it.

If at any stage an employer fails or refuses to comply with such procedures, the employee will have the benefit of the immunity even though the full procedures will not have been exhausted. The procedures referred to in the Act are not specified, but would include reference to such persons or bodies as a rights commissioner, Labour Relations Commission, the Labour Court, an equality officer or the Employment Appeals Tribunal.

Thus, it is important and indeed practicable for both employer and employee to include a specific reference to the mandatory referral of disputes to third parties in the contract of employment and/or collective agreement. Indeed, having such mandatory referral can assist the speedy defusing and resolution of disputes. Interestingly, even though the Unfair Dismissals Acts, 1977 to 1993, provide for an appeal from the Employment Appeals Tribunal to the Circuit Court, such appeal to the courts is excluded under the provisions of the 1990 Act. Thus, following on the hearing of an unfair dismissals case by the Employment Appeals Tribunal, the former worker can picket the premises of their former employer and have immunity under the Act.

SECRET BALLOTS

A major change in Irish trade dispute legislation concerns the provisions of secret ballots. Trade unions must now have a pre-strike secret ballot rule in their rulebooks. If a trade union fails to provide for such rules, the union shall cease to be entitled to hold a negotiation licence.

The Act (Section 14) provides that the rules of every trade union must contain certain provisions, which are in summary:

1. No strike or other industrial action will take place without a secret ballot;

2. All members whom it is reasonable for the union to believe will be called upon to engage in the strike or other industrial action must be given a fair opportunity of voting;

3. Notwithstanding a majority vote favouring industrial action, the committee of management of a trade union will have full discretion in relation to the organisation of industrial action; and

4. A trade union must make known to the members entitled to vote in the ballot the results as soon as practicable after the vote.

Obviously, balloting must take place before primary or secondary picketing (see below) takes place. There may be a number of ballots — for example, one in the employment where the original trade dispute exists and a second ballot in another workplace if there is to be secondary picketing.

Following a ballot for industrial/strike action, the trade union must give an employer one week's (seven days') notice of such action.

The *Nolan Transport* case (see above) also considered the matter of the secret ballot. Murphy J stated:

> It has been said that section 14 . . . requires that industrial action
> should be authorised by a secret ballot but such a statement is
> misleading. The statute requires that the rules of the trade union
> should contain provisions in relation to such ballots and imposes
> sanctions for the failure either to have such rules or to observe
> them. On the face of it, the participation by a trade union in or its
> support for a strike or other industrial action without the author-
> ity of a secret ballot of its members would be a matter of internal
> management of the affairs of the union and constitute a breach of
> contract between the executive of the union and the membership
> rather than a breach of statutory duty.

However, the requirement to hold a secret ballot also confers rights
and duties on "outsiders". Individuals may lose their statutory protection where they engage in industrial action "in disregard of or contrary to the outcome of a secret ballot". Technically, unions
themselves are not penalised. If a union were to engage in industrial
action in disregard of the wishes of its members in a secret ballot, it
would not forfeit the immunities conferred upon it. Instead, it would
risk the loss of its negotiating licence. In the *Nolan Transport* case,
either no secret ballot was held or else a secret ballot "in its outcome"
authorised the industrial action, so that there was no question of the
individual appellant acting in disregard of the resolution of their colleagues. This would be the case even if the evidence justified the conclusion that the majority of the employee members of the union voted
against industrial action. From the point of view of the union, the
holding or not holding of the secret ballot or the manner in which it
was held does not impinge in any way on the rights of the union towards the company employers. It was further held that the party re-
sisting the application for an interlocutory injunction (more usually
the union) is the party that must show that the statutory balloting
provisions have been complied with.

The Supreme Court noted that such events should never occur
again and unions should comply with their own regulations. Finally,
Murphy J stated: "Furthermore, they owe it not only to themselves
but also to their members and the public to be in a position where
they can comfortably demonstrate such compliance."

AGGREGATE BALLOTING

The issue of aggregate balloting can arise where there are a number of trade unions in a workplace. The Act does not require that aggregate balloting take place, however. If only one union votes, members of other unions would be expected to work in the normal way — that is, pass the picket and not take part in industrial action.

The Act contains complex provisions on the aggregation of votes in a multi-union ballot. The effect of these provisions is to give a trade union the right to allow its members to take industrial action where a majority of all the workers in the plant have voted in favour of such action, but where the members of the union concerned have voted against it.

A union that is affiliated to the Irish Congress of Trade Unions cannot vote in favour of supporting a strike organised by another trade union unless such action has been sanctioned by ICTU.

BALLOTING SANCTIONS

If a trade union fails to hold a secret ballot, or if one week's strike notice is not given, or if the ballot is flawed (e.g. the proper electorate was not balloted, members were not notified or if the members balloted on a different issue), the strike/industrial action may not attract the immunities under the legislation. The employer may seek an *ex parte* injunction (i.e. without notifying the trade union/members in dispute) restraining such action.

The Registrar of Friendly Societies may revoke the licence of a trade union if it fails to hold a secret ballot in accordance with legislation after being instructed to do so.

PICKETING

Section 11(1) of the Act provides:

> It shall be lawful for one or more persons, acting on their own behalf or on behalf of a trade union in contemplation or furtherance of a trade dispute, to attend at, or where that is not practicable, at the approaches to, a place where their employer works or carries on business, if they so attend merely for the purpose of peacefully obtaining or communicating information or of peacefully persuading any person to work or abstain from working.

Workers are thus confined to picketing at their place of work (unless
they fall within the secondary picketing exemption, which is considered below). The picketers must be attending "in contemplation or
furtherance of a trade dispute" and they must also be "acting on their
own behalf or on behalf of a trade union". This applies to both official
and unofficial picketing. They can only picket their employer, not associated companies of their employer. Again, this provision reflects
the stated position of the High Court over the last number of years.
An employee can picket at branches of their employer's business, but
not at premises of associated companies.

This provision raises a question about the position of workers who
are employed by one company but who work at the premises of another. It is likely to provide major scope for interpretation. For example, it would affect an employer with a small head office and workers
in various locations, such as in the catering and cleaning industries.
Accordingly, can such workers only picket the head office of their employer or can they picket the various sites where they work? If, for
example, all the service workers were employed in Dublin it would be
[reasonably] practicable for them to picket the head office in Dublin.
However, if the employer had employees scattered all over the country, it would not be practicable for them to travel to Dublin to picket
the head office. It would make more sense for them to picket the place
where their employer "carries on business". The next wording we
have to consider is the meaning of "carries on business". Is it merely
the business functions of a head office or is it where the business contracts are actually performed?

The courts will likely take a wide interpretation of where "it is
practicable" to picket. In other words, if there are numerous country
locations or city centre locations, picketing would be allowed in the
place where the employee works and carries out the business of the
employer.

The definition of "employer" also raises the issue of what happens
to a prospective employee who has unsuccessfully sought employment. The position would appear to be that the prospective employee
cannot picket the employer as the prospective employer was never
actually in employment.

Industrial Estates and Shopping Centres

The Act provides that an employee must picket at the premises where the employer carries on business or, if that is not practicable, "at the approaches to" the premises.

In the past few years, the picketing of shopping centres or industrial estates has been problematic. Such complexes are usually owned by financial institutions, investment companies or other bodies, and the employers who have shops or factories in the complex are their tenants. Thus, for example, staff picketing outside a shop within the shopping centre were seen as trespassing, and picketing outside the shopping centre itself obviously affected all other traders. Usually, the matter was resolved by the owners of the centres giving permission to picket on the premises, thus resolving the issue of trespass and the effect it might have had on general business in the centre.

In effect, the 1990 Act states the existing legal position and provides a right to picket the approaches to a complex. Of course, picketers at various entrances would clearly have to name the employer with whom they were in dispute. Further, it would be reasonable to have only two picketers at each entrance.

Secondary Picketing

Secondary picketing occurs where workers in dispute with company X picket company Y with a view to bringing about a withdrawal of labour or a disruption of business, thus adding to the pressure on company X to reach a settlement. Company Y will normally have a connection with company X, whether as a customer, a supplier or a competitor.

Generally, under the 1990 Act, all secondary picketing is unlawful (s. 11(2)). However, secondary picketing may be lawful if the picketers:

> believe at the commencement of their attendance and throughout the continuance of their attendance that that employer has directly assisted their employer who is a party to the trade dispute for the purpose of frustrating the strike or other industrial action.

For example, if company Y was merely trying to gain more business at the expense of a competitor, then the secondary picketing would not be lawful. It would only be lawful where the "second" employer frustrated the strike by actively providing services on behalf of the employer.

Persons who wish to engage in secondary picketing have to prove that the "second" employer is trying to frustrate the strike. In other words, the onus of proof will be on the picketers and must be sustained throughout the period of secondary picketing.

Balloting provisions are of particular importance to secondary picketing. Not only will the issue be balloted on by the employees in the primary dispute, but the union members in the secondary employment will have to ballot.

There is one exception to the general provisions on secondary picketing. Action taken by an employer in the health services in order to maintain life-preserving services shall not constitute action which "assists" an employer who is party to a dispute.

Both the wording of the Act on secondary picketing and also balloting provisions in relation thereto will undoubtedly provide ample scope for litigation and judicial interpretation.

CODES OF PRACTICE

In February 1991, the Minister for Labour requested the Labour Relations Commission to prepare codes of practice on disputes procedures and levels of cover which should be provided in the event of disputes arising in essential services. In preparing this Code, the Commission had consulted with and taken into account the views of ICTU, FIE (now IBEC), the Department of Finance, the Department of Labour, the Local Government Staff Negotiations Board, the Labour Court and representatives of the International Labour Organisation. The draft code was accepted by the Minister for Labour who made an order under Section 42 of the Industrial Relations Act, 1990, namely Industrial Relations Act, 1990, Code of Practice on Dispute Procedures (Declaration) Order, 1992 (SI No. 1 of 1992).

The Code "recognises that the primary responsibility for dealing with industrial relations issues and the resolution of disputes rests with employers, employer organisations and trade unions". The Code covers disputes procedures, including procedures in essential services. The Act provides that such Code(s) shall be admissible in evidence before a court, the Labour Court, the Labour Relations

Commission, a rights commissioner or an equality officer and shall be used in deciding on the issue concerned.

The key issues were to make provision for written procedures that would resolve the matters in dispute in a peaceful manner and to avoid the need for any of the parties to resort to actions that would lead to a disruption of supplies and services, or a loss of income to employees and of revenue to employers. In order to achieve this aim, the procedures provide for discussion at the earliest possible stage with a view to the parties reaching agreement and thus avoiding industrial action. These principles cover all employments, irrespective of their sector or size, and written procedures should be given and explained to all employees. There should also be an appropriate timescale within which the procedures should be effected. The procedures should also take into account the use of the State industrial relations machinery — namely, the Labour Relations Commission, the Labour Court, the rights commissioner service, the equality service and the Employment Appeals Tribunal. Of course, the procedures should be reviewed from time to time to ensure that they remain effective.

Dispute procedures should provide:

1. That the parties will refrain from any action which might impede the effective functioning of these procedures;

2. For co-operation between trade union and employers on appropriate arrangements and facilities for trade union representatives to take part in agreed dispute procedures;

3. For appropriate arrangements to facilitate employees to consider any proposals emanating from the operation of the procedures.

The Code also provides general guidance to employers and trade unions on the arrangements necessary to ensure minimum cover of service for disputes that could have serious or adverse consequences for the community or the business/service concerned and its employees. There is also a joint obligation on employers and trade unions to have contingency plans to deal with any emergency that may happen in an industrial dispute.

In employments providing an essential service in particular, management and unions should make arrangements covering:

1. The maintenance of plant and equipment;

2. All matters concerning health, safety and security;

3. Special operational problems that exist in continuous process in-
    dustries;

4. The provision of urgent medical services and supplies; and

5. The provision of emergency services required on humanitarian
    grounds.

If there are no dispute procedures in place, the Code provides that
they should be put in place and should cover both individual and collective procedures. If procedures are in place, both employers and
trade unions should take whatever steps are required to ensure that
the principles in the Code are incorporated within them. The agreements should include appropriate levels of management and trade
union representation at various stages in the procedure.

ESSENTIAL SERVICES

The Code of Practice described above provides additional procedures
and safeguards for the peaceful resolution of disputes involving essential services. These would include services whose cessation or interruption could endanger life, or cause major damage to the national
economy or widespread hardship to the community, such as the
health services, energy supplies (including gas and electricity), water
and sewage services, fire, ambulance and rescue services and certain
elements of public transport.

Over the last two years, there have been a number of disputes in
the public sector covering essential services, including the nurses' pay
dispute (note that there was a Commission on Nursing to investigate
and recommend on the profession generally but the Report recommended that pay be considered by the Labour Court), the Garda
Síochána (with their "Blue Flu" days), more recently the fire-fighters'
dispute and of course the closure of Dublin Airport for a weekend
arising from a dispute in the airline, Ryanair.

In their report into the latter dispute, the Inquiry Team concluded
that there should be an "urgent review of the adequacy of existing
contingency plans to deal with a major industrial dispute at the air-

port", to include the issue that the Inquiry believed that it was an act of gross misconduct for employees to violate their airside security clearance and demonstrate on the airside and that such action warranted instant dismissal. Therefore the Inquiry believed that airport-based companies should amend their disciplinary procedures accordingly. There should also be registration with the Labour Court of employer/union agreements of airport-based employers to ensure that there are proper dispute resolution procedures in place and that these are complied with. If such an agreement is not registered with the Labour Court or the companies are non-union, there should be a mechanism whereby there should be adherence to the Code of Practice on Dispute Procedures, either through the contractual arrangement or through a change in the Airport bye-laws (see *Industrial Relations News*, No. 45 of 26 November 1998).

Additional procedures should be introduced in these employments, recognising the joint responsibility of employers in trying to resolve disputes without recourse to strikes or other forms of industrial action. Employees should be fully aware of the nature of the service that they are providing and its relationship with the community. Also, any major changes affecting employees' interests should involve consultation with the trade unions within the agreed procedures. Unless there are other procedures in place, agreements negotiated on a voluntary basis should include one of the following provisions to eliminate or reduce the risk to essential supplies or services arising from industrial disputes:

1. Acceptance by the parties of awards, decisions and recommendations which result from the final stage of the dispute settlement procedure where these include investigation by an independent expert body such as the Labour Court, an agreed arbitration board or tribunal or an independent person appointed by the parties (some semi-state bodies — the ESB, for example — have internal industrial relations machinery); or

2. A specific undertaking in agreements that, should one of the parties decide that an award, decision or recommendation emerging from the final stage of the dispute settlement procedure is unsatisfactory, it will agree on the means of resolving the issue without recourse to strike or other forms of industrial action; such agreements to include a provision for a review of the case by an agreed

recognised body after 12 months, which would represent a final determination of the issue; or

3. Provision that the parties to an agreement would accept awards, decisions or recommendations resulting from the operation of the final stage of the dispute procedure on the basis that an independent review would take place at five-year intervals to examine whether the employees covered by the agreement had been placed at a disadvantage and, if so, to advise on the changes necessary to redress the position, taking into account economic and financial considerations.

If the parties have not concluded an agreement taking into account one of the above options and there is a serious threat to the continuity of essential supplies and services, and if the Labour Relations Commission is satisfied that all available disputes procedures have been used to try to effect a settlement, the Commission shall then consult with the Irish Business and Employers' Confederation (IBEC, formerly FIE) and the ICTU. The objective would be to secure their assistance and co-operation for whatever measures may be necessary to resolve the dispute. This may include a continuation of normal working for a period of not less than six months in order for the parties or the State industrial relations machinery to effect a full and final settlement of the issues concerned.

General References

Forde, M. (1991), *Industrial Relations Law*, Dublin: The Round Hall Press.

Kerr, A. (1991), *The Trade Union and Industrial Relations Acts of Ireland with Commentary*, Dublin: Sweet and Maxwell.

Kerr, A. and G. Whyte (1985), *Trade Union Law in Ireland*, Dublin: Professional Books.

McCarthy, C. and F. von Prondzynski (1988), *Employment Law in Ireland*, 2nd edition, Dublin: The Round Hall Press.

Report of the Commission of Inquiry on Industrial Relations, Stationery Office, Dublin, July 1981.

Chapter Nine

EQUALITY BETWEEN WOMEN AND MEN

EQUAL REMUNERATION

Article 119 of the Treaty of Rome provides that men and women should receive equal pay for equal work. In Ireland, equal pay legislation came into effect on 31 December 1975 as a result of the application of EC Directive 75/117/EEC. The Anti-Discrimination (Pay) Act, 1974, brought the Directive into effect and provided that an equal pay clause is implied into each and every contract of employment. Thus there cannot be unfavourable treatment in relation to pay between men and women. Over the last 25 years, a large number of women have successfully claimed for equal pay against their employer, and such claims (with arrears of "equal pay") have cost employers substantial sums.

At the time of writing, the 1974 Act was still in force, but it was due to be repealed by the Employment Equality Act, 1998, which was expected to commence in October 1999. Whilst the 1998 Act alters existing equality legislation, the changes in respect of sex discrimination reflect the provisions of the Treaty of Rome and the original Directives on equal pay and equal treatment, with the interpretation of the various judgements of the European Court. Arising from these changes, this chapter will include equal pay and sex discrimination; reference will be made to the current Anti-Discrimination (Pay) Act and the Employment Equality Act, 1977, but the major references in the text will be to the equal pay and equal treatment provisions of the Employment Equality Act, 1998. Of course, all the cases cited will still be applicable under the new legislation. Relevant case law under the 1974 and 1977 Acts will therefore be referred to. The additional grounds of discrimination provided for in the Employment Equality Act, 1998, will be considered in Chapter 10.

STRUCTURE OF THE EMPLOYMENT EQUALITY ACT, 1998

The Employment Equality Act, 1998, is divided into seven Parts. Part I comprises definitions for the purposes of the complete Act. Part II contains general provisions in respect of discrimination, to include the grounds where discrimination is taken to occur; the definition of "like work"; discrimination and employment agreements; advertising; employment agencies; vocational training; membership of various bodies; liability and obligations of employers; and compliance with legislation.

Part III contains specific provisions regarding equality between men and women, to include the application of the equality principles to both men and women; entitlement to equal remuneration; implied term in the contract of employment to equal remuneration; equality clause relating to gender issues; indirect discrimination on the gender ground; sexual harassment; positive action on equal opportunities; the exclusion of discrimination in certain employment; provision for special treatment for pregnancy, etc.; and finally special provisions in relation to the Garda Síochána and the prison service.

Part IV provides specific provisions regarding equality between the other categories of persons, in relation to discrimination on the following grounds: marital status, family status, sexual orientation, religious belief, age, disability, race and membership of the Traveller community. There is provision for entitlement to equal remuneration; an equality clause relating to non-gender issues, indirect discrimination, harassment in the workplace, positive action and various exceptions in dealing with family, age or disability; special provisions for persons with disabilities; and various other exclusions.

Part V establishes the Equality Authority, setting out its membership, functions and powers. Part VI provides for equality reviews, action plans and review of the legislation. Part VII provides for remedies and enforcement, noting that there are alternative adjudicating procedures in respect of sex discrimination cases.

DEFINITION OF DISCRIMINATION

For the purposes of the 1998 Act, discrimination shall be taken to occur where, on any of the discriminatory grounds, one person is treated less favourably than another is, has been or would be treated. In relation to the "gender ground", it is where one person is a woman and the other person is a man. The other discriminatory grounds are considered in Chapter 10. The Act refers to persons for this section as "A" and "B", i.e. where A is a woman and B is a man or vice versa. Hence the use of such references in the sections of the Act.

It is important to note that the matters dealing with discrimination based on sex are contained in Part III of the Act (sections 18–27) and that the 1974 and 1977 Acts are fully repealed. Throughout this chapter, references are made to cases that were heard by equality officers, the Labour Court, and the various courts under the 1974 and 1977 Acts, where they are still applicable.

ENTITLEMENT TO EQUAL REMUNERATION

Article 1 of EEC Directive 117/1975 provides:

> The principles of equal pay for men and women outlined in Article 119 of the Treaty . . . mean for the same work or for work to which equal value is attributed, the elimination of all discrimination on grounds of sex with regard to all aspects and conditions of remuneration.

Section 19(1) of the 1998 Act provides that:

> It shall be a term of the contract under which A is employed that, subject to this Act, A shall at any time be entitled to the same rate of remuneration for the work which A is employed to do as B who, at that or any other relevant time, is employed to do like work by the same or an associated employer.

The 1998 Act provides the right of men and women to receive the same rate of remuneration if employed on "like work" by the same (or an associated) employer. A man and a woman perform "like work" where both perform the same duties under the same or similar conditions; where the work performed is of a similar nature with any differences being infrequent or of small importance in relation to the work as a whole; or where the work is equal in value, judged by the demands it makes in terms of skill, responsibility, working conditions and physical or mental effort. There is no longer a requirement that the claimant and the comparator have to work in the same "place" (i.e. city, town or locality).

The 1998 Act provides for elimination of both direct and indirect discrimination, thus eliminating the earlier confusion as to whether indirect discrimination was technically provided for in the 1974 Act.

CLASS ACTIONS

Class actions are not allowed under the 1998 Act; hence each claimant must make their own individual claim, stating their name, the basis of the claim and the name of the comparator(s) (*Verbatim Limited* v *Ray Duffy, The Labour Relations Commission and SIPTU and Margie Ryan and Others* (1994–95 10 JISLL 172).

PART-TIME EMPLOYEES

There are no service requirements in the Employment Equality Act, 1998. Part-time women workers cannot be discriminated against on pay matters just because they are part-time; it must be justified on other grounds (*Bilka-Kaufhaus GmbH* v *Weber von Hartz* [1986] ECR 1607). In *St Patrick's College, Maynooth* v *19 Female Employees* (EP 4/1984, DEP 10/1984), the equality officer considered that the employees' lower rate of pay was on the basis of indirect discrimination because they were part-time employees. They were successful in their claim, which was upheld by the Labour Court. In the case of *Kowalska* v *Freie und Hansestadt Hamburg* ([1990] IRLR 440), the Advocate General of the European Court of Justice, in summary, considered that Article 119 must be interpreted as prohibiting provisions in a collective agreement which would indirectly discriminate against a group of workers in matters of pay. Thus, part-time workers must be treated the same way as full-time workers on a proportional basis. Of course, pay can be different as long as it is on "grounds other than sex".

This legislation applies to both men and women. The basis of the dispute must first be raised with the employer and if equal pay is denied, then the dispute can be referred to an equality officer. Marital status of the claimant or the comparator does not matter. Claims are initially referred to an equality officer; if either party is dissatisfied with the equality officer's recommendation, they may appeal it to the Labour Court. A claimant who is awarded equal pay is entitled to three years' difference (between themselves and the comparator) in the rate of pay prior to the referral of the claim to the equality officer and all pay differences from the date of referral (provided, of course, there is the necessary service). Section 4 explains procedures in equal pay claims before the Director of Equality Investigations, mediation equality officers, the Labour Court and the Circuit Court.

APPLICATION

The Acts have wide application and cover all employed persons in both the public and private sectors. "Employed" means employed under a contract of service (i.e. a contract of employment, either oral or written) or apprenticeship or a contract personally to execute any work or labour (section 19(2) of the 1998 Act).

The definition of "employed" would appear to apply to certain self-employed persons and independent contractors, as long as such persons "personally execute" the work concerned; in other words, it would not cover the staff of an independent contractor. A solicitor who was a partner in a firm was not covered under the Act (*P.C. Moore & Co.* v *Flanagan*, EP 13/1978, DEP 12/1978), but a senator of the Oireachtas was (*Department of Public Service* v *Robinson* EP 36/1978 DEP 7/1979). "Agency temps" are not currently included under the legislation, because in law they are deemed to be neither employees of the hiring company (i.e. the place where they work) nor of the employment agency. This issue has yet to be tested under the equality legislation. The husband of a deceased employee bringing a claim would be entitled to the same pensions benefits as those enjoyed by the survivors of the married male employees (*EEA* v *University College, Galway* EP 18/1984 DEP 2/1985).

A former employee can also bring a claim (*Revenue Commissioners* v *O'Sullivan* EE and EP 10/1983 DEP 7/1983). In addition, the equality officer in *Byrne* v *Champion Fire Defence Ltd.* (EP 8/1985) considered that a woman is entitled to the same rate of pay as a man who previously performed the same job, and furthermore that both persons do not have to be employed at the same time.

The definition of employer is broad and includes associated employers (e.g. a company with a subsidiary or a holding company with a number of subsidiaries). Thus, for example, a woman may work in one company and the male comparator in another company. In the case of *Clonskeagh Hospital* v *Two Telephonists* (EP 40/1979), the equality officer considered that the women who worked in one hospital could compare themselves with the male comparator who worked in another of the same health board.

REMUNERATION

The definition contained in section 2 of the 1998 Act is:

> In relation to an employee, [remuneration] does not include pension rights but, subject to that, includes any consideration, whether in cash or in kind, which the employee receives, directly or indirectly, from the employer in respect of the employment.

Thus, remuneration not only includes basic pay but also accommodation, bonus earnings, commission payments, marriage gratuities, overtime payments, permanent health insurance, redundancy payments and sickness payments.

Pension rights are to be excluded under the new legislation (they were included under the 1974 Act and there were a number of cases; these are now considered in chapter 14). Matters in relation to pensions will have to be dealt with under the Pensions Acts, 1990–1996. Pension rights are defined as:

> A pension or any other benefits flowing from an occupational pension scheme.

The Labour Court has interpreted "remuneration" to mean that the employee's total package is not the issue but instead each and every aspect of remuneration must be equal where there is "like work", unless there are "grounds other than sex".

Accommodation

In a number of cases, it has been established that accommodation that is "part and parcel" of a job should be seen as part of remuneration (*CIE* v *IT&GWU*, DEP 1/1978). In *Metropole Hotel* v *Seven Female Waitresses* (EP 19/1986 DEP 4/1987) the waitresses in question were in receipt of a lower basic rate of pay than the waiter comparator, but they received accommodation and thus the hotel argued that they were in fact receiving equal remuneration. The Labour Court determined that this view was incorrect as the Act provided for "the same rate" of remuneration. The claimants were awarded the same basic rate of pay.

Bonus Payments

Bonus payments should be the same for men and women who are doing "like work". In one particular case, female workers maintained that they were discriminated against because their production bonus commenced at 80 per cent performance while the male comparators were at 70 per cent, and women could only earn their maximum bonus at 117 per cent performance while the men did so at 120 per cent. The Labour Court considered that the women were entitled to be paid their production bonus at the same minimum level of performance (*Lissadell Towels Ltd.* v *IT&GWU* EP 10/1986 DEP 3/1989).

Commission

Commission is clearly part of remuneration, so it must be applied in the same way.

Marriage Gratuities

Before the removal of the "marriage" bar, which formerly required women employees to resign upon marrying, many public and private sector employments paid to those women marriage gratuities based on pay and service. Following the removal of the "marriage bar" during the 1970s, many employers continued to pay the gratuities in certain circumstances (for example, to women who had been in employment prior to the changes and who still wished to avail of the gratuity on marriage).

In a number of cases, men maintained that they were entitled to the marriage gratuity and were thus being discriminated against. In the *Bank of Ireland* case, the claimant was employed from 1969 until his retirement in 1984; he married in 1980 and, before he left the Bank, wrote requesting payment of his marriage gratuity. At that time, the marriage gratuity was only payable to certain female employees. He then brought a claim under the 1974 Act and both the equality officer and the Labour Court held in his favour. The Bank appealed the case to the High Court. Costello J held that this higher payment to such female officials was not because they were women but because they fulfilled certain conditions, namely (a) they were married and (b) had entered the service of the Bank before 1974. Thus the difference in pay was "on grounds other than sex" (*Bank of Ireland* v *Kavanagh* (1987) 6 JISLL 192 EP 11/1985 DEP 10/1985) and since followed, for example, in *Deeney* v *National Irish Bank* (EP 4/1991).

Overtime Payments

These have been accepted as part of remuneration, but like bonus and commission payments must be applied equally where employees are doing "like work".

Permanent Health Insurance

Membership of a permanent health insurance scheme or income continuance plan has also been clearly established as part of remuneration. The practice of excluding female employees in respect of disabilities arising from pregnancy or childbirth was considered discriminatory (*Shield Insurance Co. Ltd.* v *Two Female Employees*, EP 8/1984 and *McCarren & Co. Ltd.* v *Jackson* EP 5/1987).

Redundancy Payments

Lump sum redundancy payments in excess of statutory redundancy are part of remuneration and thus cannot be discriminatory on the basis of gender.

However, situations can arise where different payments are made to men and women and such payments may not be discriminatory. In the case of *Grant, Barnett and Co.* v *Leonard* (EE 7/1983 DEE 7/1983), ten of the staff were declared redundant. Union and management negotiated a severance package of two and a half weeks' pay per year of service, which was accepted by a number of employees. However, three others, including two men, rejected the offer and negotiated a higher package for themselves. The claimant then contended that she had been discriminated against compared to her male colleagues, as they got a higher package. The claim was brought under the 1977 Act and the equality officer considered that the claim did not fall within the scope of that Act. On appeal, the Labour Court agreed that the payment did not come within the scope of the 1977 Act, but the criteria used to calculate the payment did. Nevertheless, the Court did not consider that the payment was discriminatory, as it had nothing to do with the claimant's sex.

The payment of *ex gratia* payment to female part-time workers was at issue in another case where the claimants maintained that the

computation of their voluntary redundancy package was unfair because they only received credit for one year's service for two years'
part-time work. The male comparators were full-time employees and
at the date of redundancy the women were also in full-time employment. The equality officer considered that the claim fell within the
scope of the 1974 Act, but the claim was not upheld, as the company
was actually calculating the *ex gratia* payment on the basis of the full
weekly rate of pay. The equality officer calculated that if the claimants' package were calculated on the same basis as the men, they
would in fact be in receipt of a higher payment and no account would
be taken of the fact that part of their service was part-time (*Packard
Electric (Ireland) Ltd.* v *38 Female Employees* EP 3/1992).

Uniforms

The definition of remuneration includes "any consideration . . . which
an employee receives . . . in respect of his employment from his employer". In a number of cases, the meaning of "consideration" was discussed and in one case was defined as "some advantage moving from
one party to a contract to the other party to the contract in return for
something given or promised by the other party under the contract"
(*Educational Building Society* v *Male Employees* EP 9/1987).

In that case, the female employees received a jacket, two skirts
and five blouses or £45 in lieu of the blouses on an annual basis. The
male employees considered that they were entitled to a uniform or
monies as well. The equality officer considered that the employer was
not giving the women uniforms in return for something given or
promised under the contract because they were employed in the first
instance subject to the condition that, where provided, uniforms must
be worn. Thus the provision of free uniforms does not constitute remuneration where it is a condition of employment.

In another case, there was a dispute concerning a claim by female
catering employees who had to wash their own "easy-care" overalls
while the male catering assistants' cotton coats were laundered free
of charge. As a result of this arrangement, the women considered
they received less pay than the men, even though they were doing
"like work". The equality officer stated:

> I consider that irrespective of whether or not the employer, in
> laundering the uniforms of the males, is giving the males an ad-

vantage or benefit, the employer is not providing the laundering of
the uniforms in return for something given or promised by the
employee under the contract. In fact, both the male and female
employees are employed in the first instance subject to the condition that they wear the uniforms provided by the employer in the
course of their duty and that they must appear clean at all times
in order to comply with the hygienic standards set by the employer. Consequently, I find that as the male comparators were
employed subject to the condition that they wore a uniform which
had to be clean, the provision of laundered uniforms to the male
employees concerned did not constitute any part of the consideration which they received in respect of their employment.

Accordingly, the female claimants did not have an entitlement under
the Act to have their uniforms laundered by the company or to be
reimbursed for the expenses incurred in laundering the uniforms
(*British Home Stores (Dublin) Ltd.* v *127 Female Catering Assistants*,
EP 1/1988). However, a weekly uniform cleaning allowance was considered to be remuneration as it was a monetary payment (*Group 4
Securitas (I) Ltd.* v *26 Female Store Detectives* EP 3/1991 — part of
this recommendation was appealed (DEP 6/1991) but the Labour
Court determination did not affect the uniform payment).

Private Health Insurance

Many employers provide VHI, or other private health insurance cover
for employees as part of their remuneration package. In the case of
Gypsum Industries plc v *Ormiston* (EE 16/1992) the employer agreed
to pay the VHI subscription for employees whose earnings exceeded
the limit for free medical care. If an employee's earnings fell below
the limit for one year, the company would fund VHI cover for that
year only. In this case, the employee had been earning more than the
health service limit in 1988 but, because of maternity leave, fell below the limit in 1990, and the special concession was then applied for
1991. In 1991, the health service income limit was abolished and the
company provided one year's transitional arrangement after which
this arrangement was to cease. The claimant was not entitled to this
transitional year, as her cover at the time arose from the special concession. She claimed that her loss of that transitional year was discriminatory, as the reason for her reduced earnings was her
maternity leave. The equality officer accepted her argument and she

succeeded in her claim of discrimination (although this was a case under the Employment Equality Act, 1977, she nonetheless received the same value of the VHI cover).

COLLECTIVE AGREEMENTS

Most collective agreements which form part of an employee's contract of employment simply describe the rates of pay, hours of work, leave arrangements, fringe benefits, work practices, disciplinary procedures and related matters. It is implied into each contract of employment that there is an entitlement to equal remuneration and equal treatment. If there is a discriminatory clause in the agreement, it shall be deemed null and void. The 1998 Act provides for a mechanism to make application to the various adjudicating bodies (see Chapter 24, "Employment Equality Claims").

COMPARATOR

The 1998 Act provides that discrimination on the ground of gender shall be taken to occur where a woman is treated less favourably than a man or vice versa. They must be employed by the same or an associated employer. Two employers are taken to be associated if one is a body corporate over which the other either directly or indirectly has control, or if both are bodies corporate of which a third person has direct or indirect control. However, two employees will not be taken to do "like work" unless they both have the same or reasonably comparable terms and conditions of employment. A comparator must be a real individual rather than a hypothetical member of the opposite sex. The comparator need not have been employed at the same time, however. In the *Polymark* case, it was considered that claimants cannot change their comparator once the claim has commenced, as to do so would constitute a new claim (*State (Polymark (Ireland) Ltd.) v The Labour Court and IT&GWU* [1987] ILRM 357).

In *Brides and Others* v *the Minister for Agriculture* ([1998] ELR 125), it was considered that the claimants and the comparators were not employed by the same or an associated employer and thus not entitled to equal pay. The claimants were employed as poultry officers in the Department of Agriculture and the male comparator was employed by Teagasc (the agricultural advisory body which was not controlled by the Department of Agriculture) as an agricultural development officer.

Under the 1998 Act, the claimant and the comparator are no longer required to be employed in the same "place", as under the 1974 Act. Hence, there can now be claims within a group of companies with varying locations within the State.

RELEVANT TIME

The 1998 Act provides that there is an entitlement to equal remuneration where the claimant and comparator are employed by the same or an associated employer to do like work at that or at any other relevant time. "Relevant time" means three years before and three years after the employment to do "like work". Hence, the claimant and comparator do not have to be employed at the same time but may have been employed to do "like work" at any time before that or any time after. The provision in the Act contains no specific requirement that a comparator must be employed at the same time as a claimant. In one case in which this issue arose, the equality officer concluded that "nothing in the Act" suggested "that a woman cannot be entitled to the same rate of pay as a man who had previously performed the same job as her" (see *Champion Fire Defence*, above). Though it was held that the man and woman need not be employed at the same time, the job cannot have significantly changed and must still be of equal value.

"LIKE WORK"

There are three definitions of "like work" in section 7 of 1998 Act:

> Two persons shall be regarded as employed on like work where:
>
> a) Both perform the same work under the same or similar conditions, or each is interchangeable with the other in relation to the work;
>
> b) The work performed by one is of a similar nature to that performed by the other and any differences between the work performed or the conditions under which it is performed by each either are of small importance in relation to the work as a whole or occur with such irregularity as not to be significant to the work as a whole; or

c) The work performed by one is equal in value to that performed by the other, having regard to such matters as skill, physical or mental requirements, responsibility and working conditions.

Where an agency worker is required to do like work, it may only be compared with another agency worker.

The three definitions of "like work" are considered separately.

Exactly the Same Work

The work actually performed and the conditions under which it is performed by the claimant and the comparator must be virtually identical. In the early years of the Act, there were a large number of claims under this heading, though now claims are far more likely to be brought on grounds of similar work or work of equal value. Generally speaking, claimants would be wiser to claim all three forms of "like work" if they are unsure. In one case where the employer argued that a claimant's work was not the same as that of her comparator because the comparator had a liability for additional attendance and duties, it was found that in practice the work performed was substantially the same. Equal pay was therefore awarded on the basis of the actual work situation rather than additional work, which rarely occurred (*Department of Posts and Telegraphs* v *Kennefick* EP 9/1979 DEP 2/1980).

Similar Work

This definition in the Act applies where work is broadly similar; where differences occur only infrequently and are of small importance in relation to the work as a whole. This means that there can be differences as long as they remain "of small importance". However, even an occasional difference can make the work dissimilar if it is sufficiently important in relation to the job as a whole.

There have been several key cases in this area, such as *Toyota Motor Distributors Ireland Ltd.* v *Kavanagh* (EP 17/1985 DEP 1/1986) and *Dowdall O'Mahony & Co. Ltd.* v *9 Female Employees* (EP 2/1987 DEP 6/1987). In the *Dowdall O'Mahony* case, women on a lower grade maintained that they were doing like work under section 3(b) with men in a higher grade. The Labour Court considered the following points:

1. Was the work performed by each claimant similar in nature to that performed by each comparator?

2. Were there any differences between the work performed by each claimant and each comparator?

3. Did the differences occur infrequently?

4. Were the differences of small importance in relation to the work as a whole?

The Labour Court found as follows:

1. The work performed was of a similar nature. The claimants and comparators each performed general operative factory work and the Court took the view that the intention of section 3(b) is to cover claims from persons employed in such situations, as opposed to persons employed on the same work, which is covered by section 3(a) — two bus conductors, for example — or work that is not the same or similar which is covered by section 3(c) — a clerical worker and a general operative worker, for example.

2. The Court found that there were differences between the work performed by each claimant and each comparator.

3. These differences occurred on an ongoing basis and therefore occurred frequently.

The Court further stated that the Act did not state a basis for assessing what is or is not of small importance. Therefore, this must be a matter for judgement. If the company had a job classification system which was free of sex bias, then that would be used. In the *Dowdall O'Mahony* case, the Court had difficulty in assessing what criteria were used in assessing the work classified as grade 1 (the claimants) and that of grade 2 (the male comparators). Thus, in the absence of such criteria, the Court decided that it had to examine the work and make a judgement based on its own experience of grading structures, salary scales and rates of pay. The Court then sought (a) to identify the differences and (b) to decide whether or not these differences were of such importance that they would normally be used as the basis for establishing a different grade, salary scale or rate of pay, irrespective of the sex of the workers concerned.

In this case, the major difference that the Labour Court saw related to the physical demands of the jobs performed by the claimants and comparators. The Court considered that this difference was not significant and did not justify a difference in pay. Thus the claimants and the comparators were doing "like work" and equal pay was awarded.

Carroll J in *An Comhairle Oiliúna Talmhaíochta* v *Doyle and Others* (High Court, unreported, 13 April 1989) considered that, in order to make a finding under section 3(b), the Labour Court must find:

1. That the work is of a similar nature; and

2. That (a) either there are no differences in the work performed or the conditions under which it is performed by each or (b) any differences are either infrequent or of small importance in relation to the work as a whole.

The Supreme Court considered the issue of whether work was of a "similar nature" in *O'Leary* v *The Minister for Energy, Transport and Communications* [1998] ELR 113. The claimants, working at Dublin Airport, claimed equal pay under the Anti-Discrimination Pay Act, 1974, contending that they carried out work of a "similar nature" as two male radio operators and that any differences in the work occurred only infrequently and were of small importance. The equality officer concluded that the work was of a similar nature, but that the comparators' work frequently differed from the applicants' and the differences that occurred were of more than small importance in that they required the comparators' additional qualifications and skills. The equality officer therefore recommended that the claimants and the comparators did not do "like work". On appeal, the Labour Court upheld this finding. On further appeal, the High Court held that there was no discrimination and this was then appealed to the Supreme Court on the grounds that the Labour Court had given inadequate grounds for its decision. The Supreme Court dismissed the appeal, reasoning that, for the claims to succeed, it would have to be established that the applicant and the comparators were engaged in "like work". The Supreme Court stated that to liken patently different categories of work one with another by reference to the demands which they make on skill, effort and responsibility of the workers involved may be a difficult task. Where, however, as in the present case, there is at the very least a significant degree of similarity between the work performed by the claimants and comparators, it should be an easier task to compare the demands which each makes on those engaged in its performance. The possibility of establishing equality of demands or identifying the basis for any inequality must be enhanced in proportion to the degree of similarity between the allegedly different works. According to the Supreme Court, there was no doubt that the Labour Court fully intended to endorse the findings and conclusions of the equality officer and that there was ample evidence to support the decisions reached. (This case is also considered in Chapter 23 on procedural issues.)

Equal Value

This definition allows for comparisons to be made between jobs that are radically different in content. For example, the claimant and the comparator may be in different grades and, indeed, may have different value to the employer, but their jobs require the same skill, responsibility, physical or mental effort and equality of working conditions.

Section 7(3) of the 1998 Act provides that if a worker is earning less remuneration than their comparator and the work that they are doing is *higher* in value than that carried out by the comparator, then for the purposes of the Act the work performed by the claimant is regarded as work of equal value. This confirms the decision of the European Court of Justice in the case of *Murphy and Others* v *An Bord Telecom Éireann* (EP 28/1983 DEP 6/1984 [1986] ILRM 483 [1988] 1 CMLR 1 879, High Court, unreported, April 1988 and DEP 7/1988). This equal pay case was referred by the High Court to the European Court of Justice for its opinion, after both the equality officer and the Labour Court held that "work of higher value" does not come within the scope of the Act. In this case, the claimant and 28 other women were employed as factory workers engaged in such tasks as dismantling, cleaning, oiling and reassembling telephones and other equipment. They were claiming the right to be paid at the same rate as a male worker employed in the same factory as a stores labourer who was engaged in cleaning, collecting and delivering equipment. The key point here was whether "work of higher value" came within the meaning of the principle in the EC Treaty of equal pay for equal work. Keane J stated that "the words [equal in value] should not be used so as to require a mathematical exactitude of equality having regard to the statutory context in which they are used" (at p. 486).

The High Court asked the ECJ for its interpretation of Article 119 as follows:

> Does the community law principle of equal pay for equal work extend to a claim for equal pay on the basis of work of equal value in circumstances where the work of the claimant has been assessed to be of higher value than that of the person with whom the claimant sought comparison?

The ECJ considered that:

> Article 119 of the EEC Treaty must be interpreted as covering the case where a worker who relies on that provision to obtain equal pay within the meaning thereof is engaged in work of higher value than that of the person with whom a comparison is to be made.

Thus, such employees did fall within the scope of Article 119 and therefore of the 1974 Act. The High Court then referred the case back to the Labour Court for determination on the basis that the claimants and the comparators were doing "like work".

The principle of equal pay for work of equal value was upheld in the case of *Sweeney* v *The Labour Relations Commission and the Department of Enterprise and Employment* (EP 10/1997 and DEP 5/1998) where the Head of the State's Equality Service was awarded equal pay with her three male comparators who were directors of other services within the Labour Relations Commission. The claimant was employed at the grade of assistant principal and received an allowance for higher duties. The three named male comparators were all graded principal officers. Subsequently, Ms Sweeney applied to the Labour Court for the implementation of this decision and she also appealed it on the basis that for the equality officer's recommendation to be properly implemented, she should not only obtain equal pay but be graded as a principal officer as well. The Court was satisfied that the claim before the equality officer was a claim for "remuneration" and the issue of grading was not raised at the time. It then considered whether a finding in relation to a "rate of remuneration" would also encompass a finding in relation to grading. On the basis of the *Defrenne* v *Sabena* (ECJ 149/77) judgment, in which the ECJ held that ". . . Article 119 of the Treaty cannot be interpreted as prescribing, in addition to equal pay, equality in respect of the other working conditions applicable to men and women", the Labour Court concluded that the recommendation cannot be interpreted as having extended to the question of grade.

JOB EVALUATION

The 1998 Act does not specifically provide for job evaluation. (The 1974 Act did not either require or prohibit the use of job evaluation.) Such schemes have been considered in a number of cases, but they have not generally formed the basis of any recommendation or determination from equality officers or the Labour Court. Invariably, both the employer and the claimant(s) provide their own job evaluation reports and use such reports as the basis of their arguments.

The Court made its attitude to job evaluations clear at a relatively early stage, when it said that, in effect, in assessing a case, evaluations would be one of a number of considerations to be borne in mind, but not the determining one. The results may, or may not, contain an element of bias based on sex, but they should not be ignored.

The Act does not provide any assistance as to how jobs should be assessed and compared in terms of the provisions of section 3(c) (namely, skill, responsibility, mental and physical effort and working conditions). In every case, the equality officer and the Labour Court (as the case may be) compare and contrast the claimant and the comparator under each heading and then weigh up all the factors to see if the work is equal in value. It is not a mathematical process, so objective judgment must be used. In the case of *Pauwels Trafo (Ireland) Ltd.* v *15 Women Catering Machine Operators* (EP 48/1981), the equality officer stated:

> There is no method by which the equality officer nor any assessor can determine with mathematical precision that the woman's work and the man's work come out exactly the same. The equality officer must therefore take a practical approach to the work under examination and determine whether the total package of every individual's work under examination can be reckoned as being of equal value in terms of section 3(c).

OBJECTIVE JUSTIFICATION

In the *Royal Copenhagen* case, which concerned equal pay and piece-work schemes, the European Court of Justice stated:

> Since Article 119 of the Treaty is mandatory in nature, the prohibition on discrimination between men and women . . . extends to all agreements which are intended to regulate paid labour collectively, as well as contract between individuals . . . the fact that rates of pay have been determined by collective bargaining or by negotiation at local level may be taken into account by the national court as a fact in its assessment whether differences between the average pay of two groups of workers are due to objective factors unrelated to any discrimination on grounds of sex. *(Specialarbbejderforbundet I Danmark v Dansk Industri acting for Royal Copenhagen* [1995] IRLR 649)

The case of *Flynn and Others v Primark t/a Penneys Ltd.* ([1996] ELR 78 [1997] ELR 218 [1998] ELR 94 [1999] ELR 89), concerned female applicants, who were sales and clerical assistants, who claimed equal pay with their male comparators, male storemen. Initially, it was found by the equality officer and the Labour Court that, although they were performing like work, there were reasons other than sex for the pay difference. The pay difference was as a result of five productivity agreements concluded between 1974 and 1979, when the male storemen had considerable industrial relations strength. Also, the rates of pay of the two groups of employees were negotiated by different trade unions and through different industrial relations channels. The Labour Court determination was appealed to the High Court and Barron J held that the Labour Court had failed to apply the correct principle of law. He considered that once there was a finding of like work, the Labour Court was obliged to determine whether the difference in pay was gender-based. If the Labour Court found that the practice was not in reality a way of reducing levels of pay of one group of employees, it should then see whether the differences in pay were objectively justifiable. In this case, the only justification could be on economic grounds and it should exist at the date of the determination. It should be noted that Barron J considered the fact that the rates of pay did not in themselves objectively justify the practice. Various judgments of the European Court of Justice were considered, including *Enderby v Frenchay Health Authority and Sec-*

retary of State for Health ([1993] IRLR 591). The European Court of Justice considered the fact that the respective rates of pay of two jobs of equal value — one carried out almost exclusively by women and the other predominantly by men — were arrived at by collective bargaining processes which, although carried out by the same parties, were distinct and conducted separately and without any discriminatory effect within each group, was not sufficient objective justification for the difference in pay between the two jobs.

Barron J stated ([1997] ELR 218 at p. 223):

> Once there was a finding of like work, it was for the National Court — in our jurisdiction the Labour Court — to determine whether the difference was in fact gender-based and not in reality merely an indirect way of reducing the level of pay of a group of workers exclusively or predominately of one sex. It is only when they find that not to be the reality that a decision must be made that there is an objectively justifiable reason for the difference in pay. The appellants say that this reason must exist at the date of the determination. It seems to me that this should be so, since otherwise the employer would be relying upon a factor which no longer exists.

The case was sent back to the Labour Court. The Labour Court considered that the differences in pay between the clerical assistants and the storemen were objectively justified on economic grounds, as the productivity agreements generated continuing economic benefits for Penneys. Also, if the higher rate of pay was taken back from the comparators, it would lead to serious difficulties. This determination was appealed to the High Court on a number of grounds, to include that the Labour Court determination was based on an unsustainable finding of fact, as not all the comparators were party to the productivity agreement, and there was no consideration as to whether the differences in pay were objectively justified on economic grounds. Instead, it considered whether the changes in work practices provided the employer with benefits; the Labour Court should not have considered the implications of taking away the higher rate of pay from the male comparators and finally held that the difference in negotiation procedure could not constitute an objective justification.

Laffoy J dismissed the appeal on the basis that:

> The difference in pay was objectively justifiable between the two groups on economic grounds at the time the agreements were achieved and it continues to be objectively justifiable. It was further noted that the comparison was between groups of workers and not between individual members of one group and the other group and it was therefore immaterial that some of the comparators did not participate in the productivity agreements.

The Labour Court correctly found that the differential between the two groups was historically objectively justifiable on economic grounds.

The employers did not subjectively put a higher value on the work of the male storemen than on the work of the female claimants. However, the storemen had more to bargain with, hence they had to be paid higher wages to achieve flexibility and productivity. This differential had to be ongoing to maintain productivity and flexibility.

The Labour Court was correct in considering what would happen if the difference in pay was removed from the male comparators, in that the reversion to the original practices would be economically imprudent for the employer.

The legal points show that if there is a finding of "like work", there must be an objective justification for any pay differences, and the fact that there may be different industrial relations negotiations does not absolve the employer or indeed the unions in this matter. Hence, it is arguable that the defence of collective bargaining may not be viable.

All rates of pay should be objectively justifiable. The European Court of Justice made it clear in the *Danfoss* case that where an employer had a system of remuneration which was not "transparent" (i.e. there were no clear grounds for assessing the pay structure) it must prove that its salary practice was not discriminatory if a woman showed that for a relatively large number of employees, the average wages of women were less than those of men. In this case, the employer paid the same basic salary to employees in the same salary class, but there was a collective agreement between the employers' association and the trade union which provided for salary supplements to employees based on their mobility, training and length of service. The result was that the average wage of men was 6.85 per cent higher than that of the women (*Handelsandog Kontor-*

funkionaerenes Forbund i Danmark v *Dansk Arbedsgiverforening (for Danfoss)* [1989] IRLR 532.

GROUNDS OTHER THAN GENDER AND DEFENCES TO AN EQUAL PAY CLAIM

In summary, the 1998 Act allows differences in pay where there are "grounds other than sex". Section 19(5) provides that:

> . . . nothing in this Part shall prevent an employer from paying, on grounds other than the gender ground, different rates of remuneration to different employees.

Where a term of a contract or a criterion applies to all employees (or a group of employees) to include A and B (i.e. the claimant and comparator) and where the remuneration for employees who fulfil the term or criterion is different from those who do not and is such that the proportion of employees who are disadvantaged by the term or criterion is substantially higher in the case of those of the same sex as A than in those of the same sex as B, which cannot be justified by objective factors unrelated to A's sex, then each shall be treated as fulfilling the term or criterion which results in the higher remuneration (s. 19(4)).

There have been numerous examples where equality officers or the Labour Court have considered that such grounds would be as follows:

1. *Service*: This may be applied where rates of pay are tied into annual increments (e.g. *Inter-Beauty (Ireland) Ltd.* v *Bobbett*, EP 41/1981).

2. *Age*: An age-related structure would not constitute discrimination as long as it was based on age and not sex (*Irish Plastic Packaging* v *IT&GWU*, EP 25/1978). However, when the 1998 Act is in operation, this could be discrimination based on age. There is also provision for age-related scales to be abolished within three years of the operation of the Act.

3. *Attendance duties*: A liability to work extra hours may justify a higher rate of pay. In *Department of Posts and Telegraphs* v *POMSA* (EP 7/1977), the male telephonists were paid a higher rate of pay because they had a more onerous attendance liability.

This was rejected by the equality officer, as (*inter alia*) the male night telephonists retained a higher basic rate of pay while on day duty and the female day telephonists also had a liability to work unsociable hours.

4. *Capacity for extra duties*: In *Dunnes Stores (Parkway) Limerick Ltd.* v *28 Female Employees* (EP 6/1987), the male comparators performed extra duties over and above their main work and thus the claimants were not entitled to equal pay. It should be noted that the extra duties must actually be performed; it is not sufficient to have a liability to do extra duties.

5. *"Red-circling"*: Frequently, employees have a personal rate of pay because of particular circumstances that are not based on sex. For example, in *Schiesser (International) Ireland Ltd.* v *217 Female Employees* (EP 11–15/1988 DEP 1/1989) one of the male comparators was not working the full range of duties because of illness, yet he retained his original rate of pay. Hence an employee whose work is overvalued is said to be "red-circled".

In *Micromotors Groschopp (Ireland) Ltd.* v *IT&GWU* (EP 18/1986 DEP 5/1987), there was a new job evaluation scheme following the introduction of equal pay. At that time, it was found that 16 men and one woman were overrated. They were allowed to retain their "old" rates of pay on a personal basis. The claim concerned four women who compared themselves with a number of the "red-circled" males. In the case of three of the claimants, they had been appointed to their existing grades subsequent to the job evaluation exercise. This was accepted by the equality officer as being based on grounds other than sex, hence their claims failed. However, the fourth claimant had been employed at the time of the job evaluation and her work had not changed since. It was accepted that she was doing "like work" with the male comparators and that if she had been male, her rate of pay prior to the job evaluation would have been the same as the men's. She was therefore awarded equal pay with the men and the Labour Court upheld this decision.

In *Eastern Health Board/St Brendan's Hospital* v *Coffey and Others* (EP 8/1990 DEP 5/1991), the male comparators stated that they were not aware of any red-circling agreement. Thus, the defence of grounds other than sex failed.

The Labour Court awarded £100,000 to each claimant in *Department of Tourism, Transport and Communications* v *Four Workers* [1998] ELR 1. The claimants were employed as communications assistants and the male comparators as radio officers with an approximate salary difference of £10,000 per annum. The female claimants had been reassigned on health grounds to less demanding work in the accounts department in a particular station that provides communications and weather services for transatlantic aircraft. Their salaries were red-circled to ensure that they suffered no loss. In rejecting this argument, the Labour Court found that the two positions as a matter of course were retained for male radio officers who were not available for shift work. The Court was satisfied that the work for radio officers in the accounts department was not dependant on any special arrangement to protect their pay while they were unfit to do their normal work. Instead, it was a rate for men working in accounts who had previously been working as radio officers.

6. *Part-time employees*: Such employees are entitled to a pro rata payment for the same work done by full-time employees (for example, *St Patrick's College, Maynooth*, case above).

7. *Actuarial factors*: There cannot be sex-based differential factors in the calculation of benefits under an income continuance scheme. Furthermore, as a result of the EC Directive on Equal Treatment in Occupational Social Security Schemes, there can be different premium payments for men and women but they cannot result in different payments.

8. *Grading structure*: The employer must be able to show that the work in all grades has been evaluated in a non-discriminatory manner and that pay differences would be the same if men were in the lower grades and women in the higher ones. In such situations, there would be no discrimination. However, there have been a number of successful "equal value" claims brought by women in lower grades against men in higher ones.

9. *Qualifications*: It has been considered that superior qualifications can be grounds for higher pay (*Department of Agriculture* v *Instructors in Farm Home Management and in Poultry Keeping*, EP 32/1978, DEP 10/1979, and see also *An Comhairle Oiliúna Talmhaíochta* v *Doyle and Others*, High Court, unreported, Carroll J, 13 April 1989). However, if there is an all-female wage scale, such differences cannot be relied on.

10. *Collective bargaining*: This has already been discussed above under "Objective Justification".

EQUAL TREATMENT

The purpose of the Employment Equality Act, 1977, is to ensure equal treatment in relation to certain employment matters. This Act came into force on 1 July 1977 and was enacted on foot of EC Directive (76/207/EEC) on the implementation of the principle of equal treatment for men and women as regards access to employment, vocational training and promotion and working conditions. That Directive recites the purpose of the social action programme of achieving equality between men and women and identifies the principle of equal treatment (Article 2(1)) as meaning "that there should be no discrimination whatsoever on grounds of sex either directly or indirectly by reference in particular to marital or family status".

The European Court of Justice judgment in the case of *Marleasing SA* v *La Commercial Internationale de Aliamentacion SA* ([1990] ECR 4135) confirmed that national courts are bound to interpret their national laws in the light of the wording and purpose of the relevant EC directive (this was accepted by Murphy J in *Nathan* v *Bailey Gibson Ltd., The Irish Print Union and the Minister for Labour* [1993] ELR 106, [1996] ELR 114).

It should be noted that the 1977 Act does not refer to family status. Since any reference to childminding arrangements is discriminatory, it would logically follow that reference to matters of status or children is also discriminatory. However, the 1998 Act does refer to family status (see Chapter 10).

The Act does not cover pay matters, as they are specifically covered under the Anti-Discrimination (Pay) Act, 1974. As previously discussed in Chapter 1, it is unlawful to discriminate on grounds of sex or marital status, either directly or indirectly. Unlike the 1974

Act, there is no requirement for a specific male comparator and neither Act makes provision for a "hypothetical male", though under the 1977 Act there must be some evidence that the claimant was treated in a materially different manner from somebody of the other sex or of the same sex but of a different marital status. In Chapter 1, "Recruitment and Equality", the key principles of the Act were considered on the basis of how they relate to recruitment and access to employment generally.

All employees fall within the scope of the Act as they will under the 1998 Act. There are no restrictions in respect of length of service, hours of work, or place of employment. Although not tested, it would appear that independent contractors providing services to an employer fall within the scope of the 1997 Act, as do their employees in respect of services to another employer.

INDIRECT DISCRIMINATION AND STATISTICS

The definition of indirect discrimination, which has already been considered, introduces proportionality into indirect discrimination cases. Statistics have become part of the evidence in such cases. Statistics typically relate to company figures, though in some cases national statistics have been used. Barron J in *North Western Health Board* v *Martyn* ([1985] ILRM 226 (HC)) stated that statistics must be used in evidence. He stated:

> There must be evidence and generally this evidence will be statistical. For example, if a condition is imposed which makes it difficult for women to comply, then two sets of statistics must be considered:
>
> 1. The statistics of the particular application for employment;
>
> 2. The actual statistics of an application for similar employment on the same conditions but without the impugned condition.
>
> If it is found that the proportion of men to women applicants in the first set of statistics is 80/20 and the second set of statistics 60/40, then as a matter of fact the particular requirement is one which discriminates against women. Obviously, it may be extremely difficult in practice to obtain the latter set of statistics, but that does not absolve the Tribunal hearing the matter from

seeking to obtain evidence which is as near as possible to such statistics.

This case concerned the issue of age limits and recruitment to employment for women who had been affected by the "marriage bar". The ruling was overturned by the Supreme Court, but that Court did not overturn the requirement to have proper statistical evidence. The case of *Employment Equality Agency* v *Packard Electric (Ireland) Ltd.* (EE 14/1985) concerned an allegation that there was indirect discrimination because of a "condition" that persons who worked on the twilight shift had to be laid off for 26 weeks before they could apply for full-time employment. The twilight shift mainly comprised married women and thus they felt that they were being discriminated against. The equality officer's recommendation showed the detailed statistical evidence required — namely, the numbers of single men and women and married men and women employed, and the number of persons who normally would apply for full-time employment, broken down according to the person's sex and marital status and those that could apply for full-time employment if the offending condition were dispensed with.

The case of the *Revenue Commissioners* v *Irish Tax Officials' Union* (EE 6/1986, DEE 2/1987) used a more sophisticated statistical technique, the chi-square test. This case concerned an allegation that there was discrimination in relation to promotion where there was a panel of suitable persons drawn up for promotion and more men than women were placed on the panel. The Labour Court considered that the outcome of the interviews did not make statistical sense, as there had been more female than male applicants. This particular test was used in order to find out whether the observed frequencies (i.e. of successful applications) differed substantially from the expected frequencies (or results). The test showed that a higher number of women should have been successful; thus there was an indication that discrimination was likely to have been present at interview. The Labour Court subsequently determined that two women, in order of merit, be placed on the panel for promotion.

In the case of the *Central Statistics Office (CSO)* v *O'Shea* (EE 7/1987), national unemployment statistics were considered, as the claimant maintained that she was discriminated against in obtaining employment with the CSO, as she was required to have been in re-

ceipt of unemployment benefits. This requirement was found to have
been indirectly discriminatory against women because of social welfare regulations which made it difficult for married women to be registered as unemployed (see Callender and Meenan (1994)).

The High Court has accepted the use of statistics in assessing
proportionality in looking at the requirement to hold a union card in
order to be available for promotion. The figures considered include
the number of existing employees in the company who were members
of the Irish Print Union (all male) and the membership of the IPU
broken down into male and female which showed that there was a
much higher number of males. This showed that the requirement to
hold an IPU card had a disproportionately greater impact on women
than it did on men (though this case was decided against the employee appellant on different grounds) *(Nathan v Bailey Gibson Ltd.
and the Minister for Labour* above).

EFFECTS OF PAST DISCRIMINATION

We are still contending with the effects of past discrimination and
undoubtedly it will take a working generation before it is resolved. In
particular, reference must be made to the "marriage bar", where
women who married in the late 1960s and early 1970s now want to
return to the workforce after having reared their children. The issue
of age limits and the effect of losing seniority on return to work has
already been considered.

EQUAL OPPORTUNITIES AND POSITIVE ACTION

There is no definition of positive action in the equality legislation.
The 1998 Act provides that the provisions of the Act are without
prejudice to measures to promote equal opportunity for men and
women, in particular by removing existing inequalities which affect
women's opportunities in the areas of access to employment, vocational training and promotion and working conditions. There is provision for the Equality Authority to carry out equality reviews (in
respect of all grounds of discrimination) which includes an audit of
the level of equal opportunity and an examination of the practices
and procedures in the employment concerned and the subsequent
application of an equality plan. The Equality Authority may carry out
such an equality review and action plan where the business employs

over 50 persons (this is considered in more detail in Chapter 25, "The Employment Equality Agency and the Equality Authority").

In the introduction to its "Model Equal Opportunities Policy" (1991), the Employment Equality Agency (EEA) states: "Our legislation is a useful standard-setter, but it does not by itself tackle the systematic discriminatory character of a traditional sex-segregated labour market".

The Second Commission on the Status of Women recommended that the EEA (or the Commission's proposed Equality Commission) have statutory powers under the legislation to draw up a Code of Practice on equality matters. Such a Code would be admissible in any equality proceedings.

The EEA defined the positive approach as one that:

> in the first instance means management and unions working to create a climate where all staff are aware that the sex and marital status of a person is not a factor in any management decision regarding, for example, who to recruit, who to train, who to promote.

> The second feature of a genuinely positive approach involves management and unions taking positive action to remove any existing discrimination or imbalance based on sex and to promote equal opportunities in the organisation.

In its Model Policy, the EEA includes draft statements in relation to the following: selection, advertising, application forms, shortlisting for interview, testing, interviewing, promotion, training, placement, mobility, work experience, work and family responsibility, pay and benefits in kind and so forth. There is also a guide to assist in the monitoring of an Equal Opportunities Policy.

Many large employers not only have positive action programmes but also have various "family friendly" initiatives that provide for various forms of work-sharing, part-time work, career breaks and so forth. *Equality News*, the quarterly publication of the Employment Equality Agency, has numerous excellent articles on such initiatives. Trade unions have been continually highlighting the importance of equality in the workplace and employ women's officers and hold women's conferences. Furthermore, all the unions have been particularly active in bringing equal pay and equal treatment cases. The employers' body, IBEC provides various guidelines and assistance to employers in respect of equal opportunities.

SEXUAL HARASSMENT

For the first time in Irish law, sexual harassment has been defined in the Employment Equality Act, 1998 (s. 23(3)).

Sexual harassment is defined as follows:

a) Any act of physical intimacy by B towards A;

b) Any request by B for sexual favours from A; or

c) Any other act or conduct of B (including without prejudice to the generality, spoken words, gestures or the production, display or circulation of written words, pictures or other material);

shall constitute sexual harassment of A by B if the act, request or conduct is unwelcome to A and could reasonably be regarded as sexually, or otherwise on the gender ground, offensive, humiliating or intimidating to A.

Sexual harassment constitutes discrimination (on the gender ground) by A's employer where A is employed or in the course of A's employment, B sexually harasses A and either (s. 23(1)):

1. A and B are both employed at that place or by the same employer; or

2. B is A's employer; or

3. B is a client, customer or other business contact of A's employer and the circumstances of the harassment are such that A's employer ought reasonably to have taken steps to prevent it.

This extends to any person with whom the employee is likely to come in contact in the course of business. This includes the seeking or using of any service provided by an employment agency and participation in vocational training.

Sexual harassment may also arise where (s. 23(2)):

1. B sexually harasses A, whether or not in the workplace or in the course of A's employment; and

2. A is treated differently in the workplace or otherwise in the course of A's employment by reason of A's rejection or acceptance of the sexual harassment or it could reasonably be anticipated that A would be so treated.

It shall be a defence for the employer to show that all reasonable steps were taken:

1. To prevent A being treated differently in the workplace in the course of employment and if and so far as any such treatment has occurred, to reverse the effects of it; and

2. To prevent B from sexually harassing A (or any class of such persons).

Accordingly, it is recommended that employers have a procedure to deal with allegations of sexual harassment, which must of course be applied (see below).

Although sexual harassment was not specifically defined or mentioned in the 1977 Act, there have been numerous cases concerning alleged sexual harassment brought before the equality officers and the Labour Court. The Labour Court has stated that:

> . . . freedom from sexual harassment is a condition of work which an employee of either sex is entitled to expect, and that denial of such freedom contravenes the 1977 Act (*Garage Proprietor* v *A Worker* EEO 2/1985).

In the European Commission Code of Practice, sexual harassment is defined as "unwanted conduct of a sexual nature or other conduct based on sex affecting the dignity of women and men at work".

The EEA has defined sexual harassment as behaviour which includes:

> . . . unreciprocated and unwelcome comments, looks, jokes, suggestions or physical contact which might threaten a person's job security or create a stressful or intimidating working environment ("A Model Sexual Harassment Policy — Sample Policy Outline", in EEA, 1991).

Equality officers and the Labour Court have considered sexual harassment to be direct discrimination. Most cases to date have concerned sexual harassment between men and women — the matter of harassment between members of the same sex is unclear. Such harassment was claimed between women (as a second allegation against the company) in one case, but the Labour Court made its decision on the basis of harassment by a male visitor who was not an employee of the company (*A Company* v *A Worker*, EEO 3/1991 — see below). In another case, the alleged harassment had been by the managing director's husband, who was an independent contractor who frequently visited the premises (*A Company* v *A Worker* DEE 2/1988).

The types of behaviour that have been held to constitute sexual harassment vary widely. It can range from direct, persistent, unwanted physical contact and sexual advances, to unsolicited comments, suggestions, jokes and looks of a sexual nature. It need not be physical or verbal. It can even by symbolic in form to have the effect of intention and psychological effects (see *A Limited Company* v *One Female Employee*, 1989 — Confidential Recommendation). However, the key point is that the activity must be unwanted, unwelcome and unsolicited. Agreement between employees obviously would not constitute harassment. In summary, it must undermine the person's job security and provide an intimidating working environment.

The first Irish case involving sexual harassment concerned a 15-year-old girl working as a shop assistant/petrol pump attendant. She worked there for about seven months and maintained that she had been sexually harassed by her employer. She resigned and claimed constructive dismissal. The Labour Court awarded her £1,000 (above, EEO 2/1985).

Another case concerned the alleged harassment of the secretary to a general manager where she alleged that she had been continually harassed by both the company secretary and the general manager. She maintained that the harassment had been so bad that it adversely affected her health and that she was left with no option but to resign and claim constructive dismissal. The alleged harassment in this case involved instances of physical touching and assault, the use of crude language with sexual connotation, the display of an offensive calendar and a Christmas card with a double meaning. The employee had complained to a previous general manager, but matters got worse on the appointment of a new one (the employee was awarded £4,000 as she had incurred little loss having obtained alternative employment (*A Company* v. *A Worker* EEO 3/1991).

The Labour Court has taken a wide view of sexual harassment, and it is not necessarily caused directly by the employer or an employee within the company. In fact, it can happen where a person enters the premises at the invitation of the employer and harasses an employee (*A Company* v *A Worker* DEE 3/1991).

An employee who considers that she is being harassed at work should invoke the grievance procedure and report the matter to her manager, if at all possible. In smaller employments, this may not be possible, particularly if the person who is harassing her is her manager. Nonetheless, the matter should be reported so as to try to avoid resigning. In one case, the Labour Court determined that the claimant had produced no evidence that she had complained to her employer that she was being harassed (DEE 2/1988 above).

The Employment Equality Agency has published a Model Policy in order for employers to recognise that sexual harassment will not be tolerated in the workplace. The Model provides a positive statement that sexual harassment will not be tolerated, definitions of sexual harassment, an outline of the responsibility of management and staff and procedures should an employee consider that they have a grievance in this regard.

The EC Recommendation and Code of Practice on Protecting the Dignity of Women and Men at Work (OJ No. 19/1, 24/2/92) may also be applied through the Code of Practice agreed between employers and employees issued by the then Minister for Equality and Law Reform in September 1994. The European Commission Code described its objectives as "to encourage the development and implementation of policies and practices which establish working environments free of sexual harassment and in which women and men respect one another's human integrity". It is noted in the Code of Practice that sexual harassment results primarily from abuse of power, in that this type of behaviour is frequently experienced by employees who are junior to the alleged perpetrator in the employment power structure.

The 1998 Act identifies that sexual harassment may occur not only in the workplace but also outside of the workplace (e.g. in a hotel) and the degree of control available to the employer in the particular circumstances would be relevant. The person allegedly harassing the employee may be a non-employee (e.g. a client, customer or supplier). Section 15 of the Act provides that an employer may be vicariously liable for the acts of its employees, whether or not it was done with the employer's knowledge or approval (this, in effect, will overturn the point of law in *The Health Board* v *B.C.* [1994] ELR below).

Employers should issue a policy statement expressing the employer's commitment to providing a working environment free of sexual harassment. There should be a statement that sexual harassment will be considered to be a disciplinary offence and subject to normal disciplinary sanctions, to include such disciplinary action that shall be taken against the perpetrator if sexual harassment is taken to have occurred; there shall be no victimisation of the complainant or of an employee who gives evidence; employees should be reassured that complaints of sexual harassment will be treated with sensitivity and confidentiality and that all necessary support and services (e.g. counselling) will be available. Complaints procedures should also be put in place, with informal and formal procedures. It is important that all procedures should be based on fair procedures and natural justice and that everybody be entitled to representation. If the complaint is not upheld, it should be noted that it may have been a genuine complaint as opposed to being malicious. Of course, the reason for a malicious complaint should equally be investigated and treated accordingly. It should be noted that existing grievance procedures can be used, with appropriate amendments.

The issue of vicarious liability was considered above and it was particularly noted in *The Health Board* v *B.C. and the Labour Court*, where it was held that an employer may not be vicariously liable for the employee's wrongful acts. Vicarious liability in this context is where an employer may be liable for the wrongs committed by their staff if the wrongs are committed during the scope of employment.

The next point to consider is in what context employers can be held liable for the torts or wrongs of independent contractors.

Costello J, in *The Health Board* v *B.C. and the Labour Court*, stated:

> In the absence of express statutory provision, the law in this country in relation to the liability of an employee for the tortious acts (including statutory torts) of his employee is perfectly clear — an employer is vicariously liable where the act is committed within the scope of his employment. . . . An employer may, of course, be vicariously liable when his employee is acting negligently, or even

> criminally. . . . But I cannot envisage any employment in which
> they are engaged in respect of which a sexual assault could be re-
> garded as so connected with it as to amount to an act within its
> scope.

The matter of same-sex harassment must be considered. For example, in *Brookfield Leisure Ltd.* v *A Worker* (EEO 12/1993), the Labour
Court determined that dismissal arising from an employee's sexual
orientation did not fall within the scope of the Employment Equality
Act, 1977. In *Smith* v *Gardner Merchant Ltd.* ([1998] IRLR 510), the
UK Court of Appeal held that harassment of a homosexual because of
their sexual orientation is not sex discrimination. However, discrimination against a transsexual fell within the scope of the Equal
Treatment Directive (*P* v *S and Cornwall County Council* [1996]
IRLR 347). Matters of discrimination on grounds of sexual orientation are considered in Chapter 10, "Other Grounds of Discrimination".

Instead of proceeding under the legislation, a claimant may bring
a claim at common law for breach of contract arising from sexual
harassment (*Butler* v *Four Star Pizza Limited*, March 1995).

One notable case, which was not brought under the legislation,
was that of *Reilly* v *Bonny* (High Court, November 1997, reported in
The Irish Times, 20 November 1997) which was probably the first
civil action by judge and jury concerning sexual assault in the workplace. The plaintiff had worked in Mr Bonny's pub "Bonny and Clyde"
and claimed that he had sexually assaulted her while she worked in
the pub between September 1992 and May 1993; she denied any
wrongdoing, said she wanted to kill herself and had spent time in
psychiatric care. The case heard by judge and jury found that Mr
Bonny had assaulted Ms Reilly, the assault was sexual in nature and
that it had violated the plaintiff's constitutional rights to sexual integrity. She was awarded £135,000 in compensatory damages and
£5,000 in aggravated damages plus costs.

Of course, if a person may not bring their claim under the Employment Equality legislation, they can instead bring a claim under
the Unfair Dismissals Acts, 1977–1993, where relevant. However,
there would have to be a constructive dismissal resulting in the
claimant leaving the employment, which is not always the most satis-

factory approach but it does leave the claimant with the option of raising wider issues than gender under the legislation.

VOCATIONAL TRAINING

The Employment Equality Act, 1998, provides that no vocational education body can discriminate in respect of courses offered, including access to the courses and the terms and manner in which they are offered to persons over the statutory school leaving age of 16 years. The key case in this area concerns access to physiotherapy training at University College, Dublin, which used to be available only to female students. In *UCD* v *Corrigan* (EE 13/1979 DDE 6/1980), the male claimant was denied access to the physiotherapy school. The Labour Court considered that this was discriminatory and determined that the claimant be accepted for the course in the next academic year. In *Trinity College, Dublin* v *McGhee* (EE 1/1989), the claimant successfully maintained that she was discriminated against at interview for a place in the college's Diploma in Theatre Studies course because she was asked questions concerning her marital status.

There are certain exclusions in the 1998 Act (section 12) in respect of hospitals or schools established for religious purposes or which provide services in an environment which promotes certain religious value in respect of discrimination on the religious ground only (considered further in Chapter 10). However, this exclusion may not be used on the gender grounds; it applies to religion only.

PERSONAL SERVICES AND OCCUPATIONAL QUALIFICATIONS

The Employment Equality Act, 1998, does not apply to discrimination on the gender ground in employment which consists of the performance of services of a personal nature such as the care of elderly or incapacitated persons in their own home, where the sex of the employee constitutes a determining factor.

The Act provides that there are certain circumstances where "personal services" are performed, making it "necessary to have persons of both sexes engaged in such duties" (Section 25(4)). Both men and women can work as nurses, for example, but there may be certain circumstances where only male nurses are appropriate; for example, in some areas of psychiatric nursing. This provision may also apply where because of the nature of employment it is necessary to provide living accommodation for employees on a communal basis and it would be unreasonable to expect provision of separate accommodation of that nature or impracticable for the employer to so provide.

As stated in Chapter 1, there are certain circumstances where a person of a particular sex is required for a job — modelling or acting, for example — and also in respect of certain duties in the Garda Síochána and the Defence Forces.

DRESS

The issue of discrimination can arise in respect of "dress". For example, in one case it was considered discriminatory that women were not allowed to wear trousers or jeans at work (*Norwich Union Insurance* v *131 Female Clerical Staff* EE 19/1981). In another case, where women were provided with free uniforms but men were not (or given compensation in lieu of uniforms), it was not considered discriminatory. The equality officer decided that since it was a condition of the women's employment to wear uniforms or "appropriate dress" it was not discrimination within the meaning of the Anti-Discrimination (Pay) Act, 1974 (*Educational Building Society* v *Male Employees* EP 9/1987; see earlier).

PREGNANCY AND ADOPTIVE LEAVE

The Unfair Dismissals Acts, 1977 to 1993, provide that if a dismissal results from pregnancy or matters connected therewith, it is an unfair dismissal.

In *Browne* v *Rentokil Ltd.* ([1998] IRLR 445), the employer operated a rule where, if an employee was out sick continuously for more than 26 weeks, they were dismissed. Ms Browne was absent from work for a number of pregnancy-related causes and was subsequently dismissed. The European Court of Justice held that the Equal Treatment Directive (76/207/EEC) precludes the dismissal of a female employee at any time during pregnancy for absences due to incapacity for work caused by illness resulting from that pregnancy. Also, the fact that a female worker is dismissed during her pregnancy on the basis of a contractual term (in this case the 26-week rule in the employing company), which provides that the employer can dismiss an employee of either sex is immaterial. Hence, dismissal of a pregnant woman at any time due to incapacity for work caused by an illness resulting from that pregnancy is contrary to the Directive.

In *Boyle* v *Equal Opportunities Commission* ([1998] IRLR 55), the Equal Opportunities Commission provided for a maternity scheme of three months and one week's maternity leave on full pay. However, if the women were not to return to work and work for at least one month following on maternity leave, they would have to repay the monies. Also, staff who were not entitled to paid leave of absence whilst retaining their contractual rights had no entitlement to remuneration during the first 14 weeks of leave. These provisions were at variance with the contractual entitlement of those who were ill, who were entitled to a full salary for six months in any 12-month period and then half-pay for a maximum period of 12 months in any four-year period. The European Court of Justice held that, under the Pregnant Workers Directive, there is nothing prohibiting an employer, where they have paid more than the statutory entitlement, from obtaining a refund of monies if the employee does not work the required period following on maternity leave. There is nothing prohibiting an employer from bringing forward the maternity leave period where the employee states that the maternity leave is to commence in the six-week period preceding childbirth. If the employee has been on sick leave with a pregnancy-related illness and if she gives birth during that six weeks, there is nothing precluding the employer from bringing forward the date on which her maternity leave commences to the beginning of the sixth week prior to the birth or the beginning of the sick leave period, whichever is the later. Further annual leave may accrue during the 14-week maternity leave but it does not accrue during any additional maternity leave. A provision that prohibits a woman from taking sick leave during the 14 weeks' maternity leave is in breach of the Directive. However, in the *Hoj Pedersen* case (*Handel-Og Kontorfunktionaernes Forbund I Danmark, acting on behalf of Hoj Pedersen* v *Faellesforeningen For Danmarks Brugsforeninger* [1999] IRLR 55), it was held that it is contrary to Article 119 of the Treaty and to the Equal Pay Directive (75/117/EEC) to provide that a pregnant woman who, before the beginning of her maternity leave, is unfit for work due to a pregnancy-related illness, is not entitled to receive full pay from her employer where if she just suffered from an "ordinary" illness, she would receive full pay from her employer.

Further, it is in breach of the Equal Treatment Directive and the Pregnant Workers Directive (92/85/EEC) for an employer to send a woman home from work who is pregnant and fit for work without paying her full salary. This would arise in such a situation where an employer considers that they cannot provide the employee with work. However, this decision could be open to question if, for example, there is a genuine lay-off situation.

Hence it may be concluded that there is a difference between the rights of pregnant workers (i.e. those who have not yet gone on maternity leave) and the rights of women on maternity leave. Therefore, any adverse treatment based on pregnancy is sex discrimination under Article 119 of the Equal Treatment Directive and the Pregnant Workers Directive. Women on maternity leave are not "workers" but have special protection under the Pregnant Workers Directive as a result of their biological condition, which provides them with a right to maternity leave and protection against dismissal. Women on maternity leave cannot claim that they have been treated differently to men who are off work due to illness.

In *Webb* v *EMO Air Cargo (UK) Ltd.* (No. 2) ([1995] ICR 1021), the claimant was employed to replace an employee of the company who was on maternity leave; she then became pregnant herself. She was dismissed, which was in breach of the Equal Treatment Directive.

The Adoptive Leave Act, 1995, provides that an employee is entitled to 10 weeks' adoptive leave. Many large employments provide for adoptive leave on the same basis as maternity leave (see Chapter 5, "Maternity, Adoptive and Parental Leave").

The provision of adoptive leave for fathers has been the subject of much case law in recent years, where there was provision in the contract of employment or collective agreement for adoptive leave only for mothers. This in fact was historical, where employers tried to provide the same rights to adoptive mothers as natural mothers. There was also an anomaly in the 1977 Act, which specifically did not provide for special terms for adoptive mothers. The Employment Equality Act, 1998, has dispensed with this anomaly and provides

> Nothing in this Act shall make it unlawful for an employer to arrange for or provide treatment which confers benefits on women in connection with pregnancy and maternity (including breastfeeding) or adoption.

Hence the numbers of cases where the courts accepted that fathers should be paid for adoptive leave where there was such a clause in the contract of employment. In *Aer Rianta* v *37 Male Employees* (EE 11/1987 [1990] ILRM 193 DEE 3/1990) male employees considered that the failure to provide for paternity leave was discriminatory. The Labour Court did not agree, however.

It is discriminatory for an employer to provide adoptive leave for women employees only. The High Court considered in the case of *O'Grady* v *Telecom Eireann* that the essential issue of law was section 16 of the Employment Equality Act, 1977. Bord Telecom gave adoptive leave of 10 weeks (with a further four weeks' unpaid leave) to women employees only. Mr O'Grady, a night telephonist, and his wife went to Romania and adopted a child in May 1991. He was refused adoptive leave. The claimant contended that pregnancy and childbirth applied to the biological relationship between a mother and a child and were not wide enough to capture the non-biological relationship between a mother and child whom she had adopted — Murphy J said that he could find no justification for interpreting the word "childbirth" as if it were the word "maternity" or otherwise interpreted to include adoption. Accordingly, the discrimination was not permitted by the statutory exemption (*O'Grady* v *An Bord Telecom Eireann*, High Court, Murphy J, April 1996, unreported). The Supreme Court confirmed that if adoptive leave is part of the conditions of employment, then it should be equally applicable to male and female employees ([1998] ELR 61). This judgment was followed in the cases of *Dublin Institute of Technology, CDVEC* v *Doolan* (DEE 8/1998) where a college lecturer was awarded £6,500; and *Eastern Health Board* v *Merriman*, where a senior health board official was awarded 10 weeks' adoptive leave (EE 10/1998).

Pregnancy and access to employment has already been discussed in Chapter 1. In summary, an employer may not have a requirement that an employee "not be pregnant", as this could constitute indirect discrimination, since it only affects women.

In *University College, Dublin* v *Zeuli* (EE 4/1987), it was considered that rostering arrangements should be made that facilitated a nursing mother.

MOBILITY AND TRANSFER

The issue of mobility has arisen from a particular case involving a claim of alleged discriminatory questions at interview. However, the equality officer considered that there was a requirement for mobility in the job, and that the reason for the applicant's non-selection was that she was unable to comply with the mobility requirement. This was seen as an "essential requirement" for the job (*A Company* v *A Prospective Female Employee*, EE 12/1989; see Chapter 1, "Recruitment and Equality").

Internal transfer within a company or organisation would fall within the scope of this legislation. In one particular case, a claimant was refused a transfer because the employer did not consider it appropriate that a secretary should work in the same sensitive area as her husband. The equality officer considered that such a policy was intended to apply to all relatives and was not confined to married women. Thus there was no direct or indirect discrimination (*NIHE* v *Bolton*, EE 7/1984).

A policy of transferring employees from one location to another in Ireland or abroad must apply to both male and female employees. All employees must get equal chances of promotion and experience. One exception would be sending female employees to a country outside the State where there are laws and customs allowing a person of only one sex to do the duties concerned, as is the practice in certain Middle Eastern countries.

SENIORITY

Loss of seniority has caused difficulties for women, in particular where they had been obliged to resign on marriage and subsequently return to work. For example, if they were re-employed, previous service was excluded for seniority purposes (see, for example, *Aer Lingus Teo.* v *Labour Court and Others* ([1990] ELR 113); as the claimants had "less" service, they were not working on the "better" routes as their service prior to marriage was excluded for seniority purposes).

OVERTIME

Both male and female employees should have equal access to overtime. There cannot be rostering arrangements that would discriminate against women and deny them equal access to overtime (*Cork Corporation* v *Cahill and Others* EE 17/1984 DEE 1/1985 (1987) 6 JISLL 172). The same situation applies to shift rosters.

SHORT-TIME/LAY-OFF

If an employer finds that, because of economic circumstances, staff have been put on short-time or lay-off, the employer must ensure that the same rules for selection are applied to both male and female employees. For example, it would be discriminatory for an employer to put a female employee on lay-off or short-time because the employer takes the view that her husband may be working.

SAFETY

An employer must comply with the Organisation of Working Time Act, 1997, and the Safety in Industry Acts, 1955 and 1980 (and also the Safety, Health and Welfare at Work Act, 1989). Night work for women is permitted. The safety legislation states that women may only lift 16 kilos. However, an employer must take reasonable steps to provide for the employment of women without being in breach of the Acts, for example, by providing lifting equipment so that there will not be a breach of the 16-kilo weight limit (see *Tayto Ltd.* v *O'Keefe and Others*, EE13/1985; and Factories Act, 1955 (Manual Labour); Maximum Weights and Transport Regulations, 1972 (SI No. 283 of 1972)). The Second Commission of the Status of Women recommended that the weightlifting exemption (16 kilos) be valid where an employer can show that all necessary steps have been taken to reduce the incidence of manual handling and the carrying of loads. This would include the organisation of teamwork and the provision of mechanical aids and devices.

There are other discriminatory provisions in force, for example, the prohibition of women working underground in a mine (Employment Equality Act, 1977 (Employment of Females in Mines Order, 1985, SI No. 176 of 1985)).

REDUNDANCY

There must be fair selection for redundancy. In one key case, the selection for redundancy of part-time women employees instead of full-time male employees was considered to be indirect discrimination, as more married women worked on a part-time basis than men (*Michael O'Neill and Sons Ltd.* v *Two Female Employees* DEE 1/1988).

Discrimination in respect of age limits, minimum height and strength have already been considered in Chapter 1.

DISCIPLINARY MEASURES

A disciplinary or dismissal procedure should be exactly the same for male and female employees. Furthermore, disciplinary measures which are stricter than those applied to male employees cannot be imposed on a female employee.

VICTIMISATION

A person cannot be victimised for having brought an equal pay or equal treatment claim. The case of *SIPTU* v *Dunne* ([1993] ELR 65) concerned the victimisation which resulted from the denial of promotion after the referral of an equal pay claim. The equality officer considered that the onus was on the employer to give a reasonably credible explanation for the interview board's selection, which it failed to do. The claimant succeeded in her claim and the equality officer recommended the creation of a new post with the difference in pay from the date of the non-promotion. She was also awarded £3,000 for distress and loss of status. In *Commissioner, An Garda Síochána, Minister for Justice, Equality and Law Reform* v *Garda Mary Flynn* (DEE 9/1998), Garda Flynn considered that she was victimised and left without appropriate work to do for a considerable period of time after she brought an equal treatment claim. She further maintained that her immediate superiors had adopted a negative attitude towards her from that time, which coloured their input to the promotions interview panel and thereby ultimately negatively affected her chances of promotion. The Labour Court had access to Promotional Assessment forms for 1995, 1996 and 1997. No records were available for 1994 and the interview took place in 1994. It was considered that there was a negative view in 1996 but not in 1997 as a result of the

glowing reports of a subsequent superior who credited her with quali-
ties which she was not been credited with before. The evidence also
included an assessment given directly to the Court by a former Assistant Commissioner who had worked closely with the claimant. It was
clear that there was a period of time when the claimant's superiors
had a very negative view about her, which was at variance with a
number of other superior officers. The key question was: was the
claimant victimised? The Court found that on the balance of probabilities and without any other clear explanation for the totally con-
flicting views, the claimant was victimised following the issue of
proceedings in 1993.

Victimisation and Dismissal

Under the 1998 Act (or, indeed, under the previous legislation), an
employee cannot be dismissed for bringing a sex discrimination
claim, giving evidence in such proceedings, or giving notice that they
are going to bring a claim or give such evidence. If dismissed, an employee can either be reinstated (i.e. get their job back with no loss),
re-engaged (i.e. get a similar position with or without loss of pay) or
be awarded compensation so that they have been at no loss. Such a
dismissal is also a criminal offence.

DISMISSAL

There have been relatively few cases of employees claiming retaliatory or discriminatory dismissal, constructive or otherwise. These
cases mainly concerned employees who were dismissed within the
one-year period from the commencement of their employment. More
usually, persons who are claiming that they were unfairly dismissed
will bring their claim under the Unfair Dismissals Acts, 1977 to 1993,
as the ostensible reason for their dismissal may be something else —
lack of performance, for example. An employee is not entitled to receive redress for dismissal under both the equality and the unfair
dismissals legislation.

In one case, an employee dismissed from temporary employment
contended that the company had a preference for a male employee;
the dismissal was considered discriminatory and she was awarded
£4,000 (*Irish TV Rentals* v *Brady* EEO 1/1984 EE 5/1985 DDE
8/1985). In another case, an allegation of retaliatory dismissal arose

from a part-time employee who had applied for full-time employment. She brought proceedings to the effect that she was discriminated against at interview and succeeded in that claim. She was subsequently dismissed from her temporary employment and brought successful dismissal proceedings (*University College, Dublin* v *A Female Worker*, EEO 5/1983; and *University College, Dublin* v *Chaney* EE 15/1983; see Chapter 1, "Recruitment and Equality").

Constructive dismissal claims have primarily arisen in the context of allegations of sexual harassment. There were a number of cases brought against the State airline company Aer Lingus concerning access to part-time work for cabin crew staff (800 staff) (*Aer Lingus* v *Coman, Delsgaauw, O'Dwyer and Stewart*, EEO 4, 5, 6 and 7/1998). In 1992, an agreement was reached between Aer Lingus and the cabin crew on part-time work options for cabin crew employees providing that a minimum of five per cent of cabin crew may be facilitated to avail of the option of part-time work. Part-time work options are granted for a period of 12 months and allocation is based on seniority. In the spring/summer of 1996, four female members of cabin staff resigned from their employment maintaining that the refusal of part-time work/long-term special leave for family responsibilities constituted constructive dismissal on the grounds of sex and marital status under the Employment Equality Act, 1977. Aer Lingus argued that it was required to have sufficient numbers of fully trained, competent and experienced staff for its schedule and to comply with strict safety requirements. Therefore it was not feasible for the airline to grant unlimited access to part-time work, but it was willing to seek agreement on flexible working. The Labour Court did not consider that the scheme was directly discriminatory. Indirect discrimination was then considered. The Court noted that the scheme was only guaranteed to five per cent of the permanent cabin staff and the key question was whether the five per cent restriction was essential or not. If it was essential, there was no question of discrimination. If it was not essential, the question of whether it affected more women than men or more married than unmarried persons would arise. The Court was satisfied that the five per cent arrangement was essential given the relief arrangements available at the time and for its operational and economic viability. Accordingly, the Court found that the restriction of the scheme to five per cent was not discriminatory and the claims were dismissed. It was noted in the determination that the parties had negotiated increased part-time work options.

If an employee is dismissed in circumstances amounting to victimisation, then the employer shall be guilty of an offence and if a prosecution is proved that the employee was dismissed and the employee sought redress under the Act, or opposed anything unlawful under the Act, or gave evidence in any criminal or other proceedings under this Act or gave notice to any of such matters, then the main reason for the dismissal is victimisation. On conviction for an offence, the Court, if it considers that the Labour Court would have power to make an order for reinstatement or re-engagement of the employee, may give such an order. The Court may also, in addition to imposing a fine for an offence, order that compensation be paid to the employee. Compensation will be the amount that the adjudicating authorities can award under the Act or, if the order is made by the District Court, £5,000 (i.e. to the limit of the District Court jurisdiction). The employer may appeal against the conviction. Equally, an employee may appeal in respect of the amount of compensation awarded. A person found guilty of an offence shall be liable on summary conviction to a fine not exceeding £1,500 or to imprisonment for a term not exceeding one year or both or on conviction on indictment to a fine not exceeding £25,000 or to imprisonment for a term not exceeding two years.

PROCUREMENT OF DISCRIMINATION

The 1998 Act provides that a person cannot procure or attempt to procure another person to do anything that constitutes discrimination which is unlawful under the Act or constitutes discrimination for the purposes of enforcement under the Act. Anyone who does so shall be guilty of an offence.

Union/management agreements can unintentionally give rise to discrimination where certain practices are agreed between an employer and the trade union. For example, in the case of *Employment Equality Agency* v *Packard Electric Ireland Ltd., the IT&GWU, and the AT&GWU* (EE 14/1985) part-time women were denied immediate access to full-time employment on foot of the union/management agreement. In another case, both employer and union required the employees to hold a certain union card for specific jobs (see the *Bailey*

Gibson case, above). More recently, the Minister for Finance, in his supervisory role over the public service, was considered to procure discrimination in relation to the re-employment of married women who had resigned because of the "marriage bar" (*Department of Finance, the Revenue Commissioners* v *A Worker* EE 20 and 21/1991 and DEE 5/1993).

The Second Commission on the Status of Women recommended that there be a mechanism that would allow the Labour Court to declare null and void any collective agreement that was contrary to the provisions of the 1974 or 1977 Acts.

PROCEDURES

Under the 1998 Act, the claimant has "a right to information" (see Chapter 24, "Employment Equality Claims"). There are two different sets of procedures under the 1998 Act. A claim may be referred to the Director of Equality Investigations or, if the parties agree, the claim may be referred to mediation, where it may or may not be resolved. In the event of no reference to mediation or where mediation has not produced an agreement, the Director of Equality Investigations may investigate the claim and issue a decision. Such decision may be appealed to the Labour Court, whose determination may be appealed to the Circuit Court. Dismissal claims are referred direct to the Labour Court. Equal treatment claims must be referred in writing within six months of the last act of alleged discrimination unless there are exceptional circumstances. Gender discrimination claims may be referred to the Circuit Court, which may request the Director of Equality Investigations to investigate the claim. Procedures are considered in detail in Chapter 24.

General References

Callender, R and F. Meenan (1994), *Equality in Law between Men and Women in the European Community: Collection of Texts and Commentary on Irish Law*, Luxembourg: Martinus Nijhoff Publishers and Office for Official Publications of the European Communities.

Curtin, D. (1989), *Irish Employment Equality Law*, Dublin: The Round Hall Press.

Employment Equality Agency (1991), *Equality at Work: A Model Equal Opportunities Policy* (including a grievance procedure for sexual harassment), Dublin: EEA.

Finucane, K. and B. Buggy (1996), *Irish Pensions Law and Practice*, Dublin: Oak Tree Press.

Harvey, N. and A. Twomey (1995), *Sexual Harassment in the Workplace: A Practical Guide for Employers and Employees*, Dublin: Oak Tree Press.

Meenan, F. (1997), "Employment Equality and Collective Bargaining: The Irish Experience" in F. Meenan (ed.), *Legal Perspectives: The Jurisdiction of the Employment Relationship*, Vol. 5, Proceedings of Fifth IIRA European Regional Industrial Congress, Dublin: Oak Tree Press.

Chapter Ten

OTHER GROUNDS OF DISCRIMINATION

AMSTERDAM TREATY

Article 13 of the EC Treaty as amended by the Treaty of Amsterdam, which came into effect in May 1999, provides:

> Without prejudice to the other provisions of this Treaty and within the limits of the powers conferred by it upon the Community, the Council, acting unanimously on a proposal from the Commission and after consulting the European Parliament, may take appropriate action to combat discrimination based on sex, racial or ethnic origin, religion or belief, disability, age or sexual orientation.

This reflects the human rights dimension of the European Union as in Article 6 (formerly Article F) of the Common Provisions of the Treaty:

> The Union is founded on the principles of liberty, democracy, respect for human rights and fundamental freedoms, and the rule of law, principles which are common to the Member States.

The Treaty stresses the respect of the fundamental rights guaranteed by the European Convention of Human Rights, 1950.

Article 136 of the EC Treaty outlines the fundamental social rights as determined by the European Social Charter and Community Charter — that is, to promote employment; improve living and working conditions in order to make possible their harmonisation while the improvement is being maintained; ensure proper social protection; secure a dialogue between management and labour; and develop human resources with a view to lasting high employment and the elimination of social exclusion.

In the employment context, relevant rights are the rights to freedom of peaceful assembly, association and the right to equality of opportunity without any distinction such as race, colour, ethnic, national or social origin, culture or language, religion, conscience, belief, political opinion, sex, marital status, family responsibilities, sexual orientation, age or disability, and the right to information, consultation and participation in respect of decisions affecting the interests of workers.

EMPLOYMENT EQUALITY ACT, 1998

The Employment Equality Act, 1998, provides that an employer cannot discriminate on the following grounds: sex (see Chapter 9), marital status, family status, sexual orientation, religion, age, disability, race or for being a member of the travelling community. Each contract of employment shall be deemed to contain a non-discriminatory equality clause and an equal remuneration term. At the time of writing, the Act is due to come into operation in October 1999. This chapter will give consideration to these new grounds of discrimination in employment.

Equality Clause Relating to Non-gender Issues

Each contract of employment shall be deemed to include a non-discriminatory equality clause (s. 30(1)). It should be noted that, for explanatory purposes in the Act, there is reference in this Part to two persons, one denoted as being "C" and the other as being "D"; for example, where C and D have different marital statuses or C and D have different religious beliefs or C has a religious belief and D does not and so on, making reference to all the grounds of discrimination (section 28(1)). Such a clause (which is separate from remuneration and pension rights) has the following effect, that if (s. 30(2)):

a) C is employed in circumstances where the work done by C is not materially different from that done by D in the same employment, and

b) At any time C's contract of employment would (but for the non-discriminatory equality clause):

(i) contain a term which is or becomes less favourable to C than a term of a similar kind in D's contract of employment; or

(ii) not include a term corresponding to a term in D's contract which benefits D,

then the terms of C's contract of employment shall be treated as modified so that the term in question is not less favourable to C or, as the case may be, so that they include a similar term benefiting C.

A non-discriminatory clause will not operate in relation to a difference between C's and D's contracts of employment if the employer proves that the difference is genuinely based on grounds other than a different marital status, a different family status, different sexual orientations, different religious beliefs, different ages, persons with different disabilities, different race, colour, nationality or ethnic or national origins or if one person is a member of the traveller community and the other is not, or any combination of those factors.

Entitlement to Equal Remuneration

It shall be a term of the contract of employment under which C is employed that C shall be entitled to the same rate of remuneration for the work that C is employed to do as D, who at that time or at any relevant time is employed to do like work by the same or an associated employer (s. 29(1)). Further, if the employees are working for associated employers, C and D shall not be regarded as doing like work unless they both have the same or reasonably comparable terms and conditions of employment. The "relevant time" is the three years which precede (on or after the commencement of this section of the Act) or the three years which follow the particular time.

The entitlement to equal remuneration is as follows (s. 29(4)):

Where a term of a contract of employment or a criterion applied to employees (including C and D):

a) applies to all employees of a particular employer or to a particular class of employees (including C and D);

b) is such that the remuneration of those who fulfil the term or criterion is different from those that do not;

c) is such that the proportion of employees who can fulfil the term
    or criterion is substantially smaller in the case of the employ-
    ees having the same relevant characteristic as C when com-
    pared with the employees having the same relevant
    characteristic as D; and

d) cannot be justified as being reasonable in all the circumstances
    of the case;

then for the purposes of [the equal remuneration term], C and D
shall each be treated as fulfilling or, as the case may be, as not fulfilling the term or criterion, whichever results in the higher remuneration.

Of course, an employer may pay different rates of remuneration to
different employees on grounds other than the discriminatory
grounds.

General Exceptions

An employer may provide a benefit to an employee in respect of
events related to members of the employee's family or any description of members (e.g. special leave in the case of illness) and a benefit
to or in respect of a person as a member of an employee's family (e.g.
private health insurance). "Member of the family" in relation to any
person means that person's spouse, or a brother, sister, uncle, aunt,
nephew, niece, lineal ancestor or lineal descendant of that person or
that person's spouse.

Harassment in the Workplace

Harassment is forbidden in respect of any of the other grounds of discrimination — in other words, there cannot be discrimination in relation to any of the discriminatory grounds. This concept must be
considered in relation to alleged "bullying" in the workplace, which
may result in stress, which is considered in Chapter 15, "Health and
Safety in the Workplace".

Sexual harassment is defined as any act or conduct of E (the employer, another employee or a client, customer or other business contact), including spoken words, gestures, or the production, display or
circulation of written words, pictures or other material, if the action
is unwelcome to the recipient and could be regarded in relation to the

relevant characteristic of the recipient as offensive, humiliating or intimidating to C.

An employer may defend a claim for alleged harassment by ensuring that there are proper policies in place to ensure that persons are not treated differently in the workplace and to prevent harassment.

Marital Status

Marital status is defined as "single, married, separated, divorced or widowed". An employer may not discriminate where two persons have a different marital status. However, a benefit to an employee on or by reference to an event occasioning a change in the marital status of the employee (e.g. a wedding present) is excluded from the scope of the Act.

Family Status

Family status means responsibility:

a) As a parent or as a person *in loco parentis* in relation to a person who has not attained the age of 18 years; or

b) As a parent or the resident primary carer in relation to a person of or over that age with a disability which is of such a nature as to give rise to the need for care or support on a continuing, regular or frequent basis.

A "resident primary carer" is a primary carer in relation to a person with a disability if the primary carer resides with the person with the disability.

There is an exception to this ground where an employee who has family status is given a benefit intended directly to provide or assist in the provision, during working hours, of care for a person for whom the employee has responsibility (e.g. childcare facilities).

Sexual Orientation

Sexual orientation means heterosexual, homosexual or bisexual orientation.

The 1998 Act provides that a person cannot be discriminated against based on their sexual orientation. Such a ground does not fall within the scope of the Equality Directives as discussed below; hence, sexual orientation as defined in the Act is one of the new grounds of discrimination. Indeed, the Labour Court held that a dismissal arising from sexual orientation did not come within the scope of the Employment Equality Act, 1977 (*Brookfield Leisure Ltd.* v *A Worker*, EEO 12/1993). In this instance, the claimant did not have one year's service; however, if a claimant does have over one year's service, they may claim for unfair dismissal under the Unfair Dismissals Acts, 1977–1993. The ECJ has ruled that Community law does not specifically prohibit discrimination against transsexuals. The Court ruled in favour of the claimant in *P* v *S and Cornwall County Council* ([1996] IRLR 347) and stated the scope of the Directive cannot be confined simply to discrimination based on the fact that a person is of one or the other sex: "In view of its purpose and the nature of the rights which it seeks to safeguard, the scope of the Directive is also such as to apply to discrimination arising, as in this case, from the gender reassignment of the person concerned." The Court also stated that discrimination against the transsexual claimant constituted a form of direct discrimination because she had been treated differently according to whether she was perceived as a man or a woman. In essence, the claimant was allowed act as her own comparator. Previously, transsexuals had lost claims of direct sex discrimination due to an "equal misery" argument, by which male to female transsexuals and female to male transsexuals would be dismissed from employment and that the discrimination was not due to sex but to something else (i.e. the sex change). Hence, discrimination in respect of transsexuals falls within the scope of the Equal Pay and Equal Treatment Directives, as opposed to non-gender discrimination. However, the ECJ did not follow this judgment in *Grant* v *Southwest Trains* (see below).

The ECJ has stated that same-sex relationships do not fall within the scope of the Equal Pay Directive. In *Grant* v *Southwest Trains* ([1998] IRLR 206), Ms Grant's employment contract with Southwest Trains provided reduced rate travel concessions to the employee's spouse or "common law opposite-sex spouse". Ms Grant, a clerical worker, lived in a stable relationship with a female partner. She sought the travel concessions for her partner, which was refused by Southwest Trains. Ms Grant maintained that this was in breach of Article 119 and the EC Treaty, which stated that there should be equal pay without regard to sex and of the Equal Pay Directive. She argued that the denial of the travel concession constituted direct sex discrimination, because "but for" her sex as a female the benefits would be granted. It should be noted that the male employee who had previously held Ms Grant's position had an unmarried female partner who had received the concession. She further argued that this was sex discrimination based on sexual orientation discrimination. The Human Rights Committee of the International Convention on Civil and Political Rights has found that its prohibition on sex discrimination includes sexual orientation. The Advocate General recommended in favour of Ms Grant. Advocate General Elmer cited *P v S and Cornwall*; he argued that direct discrimination was present in this case and that Article 119 should be interpreted broadly to prohibit discrimination based on sexual orientation. The Court subsequently rejected this recommendation and ruled against both of Ms Grant's arguments. It ruled that this discrimination was not direct sex discrimination and that this was due to the traditional "equal misery" argument. In this case, the EC Commission agreed that Article 119 (now Article 141) prohibited discrimination based on sexual orientation. However, it did argue that Ms Grant's discrimination was not discrimination based on sexual discrimination, but it was based on the fact that Ms Grant was not involved in a traditional heterosexual relationship and this type of discrimination was different to discrimination based on sexual orientation. If such a case were brought in Ireland, following the implementation of the 1998 Act, such a claim may well succeed.

Religion

The *religion ground* means where one person has a different religious belief from the other or where one has a religious belief and the other has none. "Religious belief" includes a person's religious background or outlook.

A religious, educational or medical institution which is under the direction or control of a body established for religious purposes or whose objectives include the provision of services in an environment which promotes certain religious values shall not be taken to discriminate against a person if:

1. It gives more favourable treatment, on the religion ground, to an employee or a prospective employee over that person where it is

    reasonable to do so in order to maintain the religious ethos of the
    institution; or

2.   It takes action, which is reasonably necessary to prevent an em-
    ployee or a prospective employee from undermining the religious
    ethos of the institution.

The issue of access to employment and religious issues was considered generally in Chapter 1, "Recruitment and Equality". A collective
agreement between the Minister for Education, the Association of
Secondary School Teachers of Ireland and the Council of the Management of Catholic Secondary Schools made provision for teachers
who had already commenced employment within Catholic secondary
schools, thereby placing the teachers on a panel so that when a permanent post came up in a Catholic school it would be offered to
members of the panel on a seniority basis. The teachers had to fulfil
various service requirements to be placed on the panel. In *Greally* v
*Minister for Education, Ireland, the Attorney General and the Asso-
ciation of Secondary Teachers of Ireland* ([1999] ELR 106), the plaintiff, a secondary school teacher and a practising Catholic, claimed he
was denied the pursuing of his career because of this scheme.
Geoghegan J refused the application on the basis that this arrangement was reached on the normal basis of industrial relations discussions. Membership of the panel was not based on religious profession,
belief or status; it was based on degrees of experience in Roman
Catholic Schools. This scheme secured jobs for those who had a legitimate expectation of permanent posts in the Catholic school system, while protecting the Catholic ethos of the school. In respect of
the plaintiff's argument that he was denied the right to earn a livelihood, Geoghegan J considered:

> The plaintiff's right to earn a livelihood is not infringed in my
> view. The panel systems apply to all teachers though the supple-
> mentary panel arrangements do not apply to all kinds of schools.
> Because a person has a right to a particular livelihood, it does not
> mean that he has a right to receive employment from any par-
> ticular employer. As I have already explained, the Minister has no
> interest in preventing the Catholic employers from employing
> anybody they like. The conditions in the supplementary panel sys-
> tem are conditions laid down by those employers in consideration

of their agreement to honour the system and in assertion of the right to maintain denominational schools. No Minister prevented the plaintiff achieving panel rights. He failed to get panel rights because of his own desire to get employment on a temporary basis in Catholic schools. As it turns out, the plaintiff's livelihood is in no way affected because he has achieved an excellent job with excellent prospects in the community school sector.

In *O'Neill* v *Governors of St Thomas More Roman Catholic Voluntary Aided Upper School and Another* ([1997] ICR 33), initially an industrial tribunal in the UK dismissed a claim of sex discrimination on the grounds that the plaintiff had not been dismissed because she was pregnant but because the pregnancy was by a Roman Catholic priest and had become public knowledge, making her position as a teacher of religious education untenable. However, on appeal it was considered that the reason for her dismissal was based on sex discrimination. This case may be considered along with the Irish case of *Flynn* v *Sister Mary Anna Power and the Sisters of the Holy Faith* ([1985] ILRM 336), where there was a dismissal of a pregnant teacher who had an affair with a married man in the same country town in which she taught. This was held to be a fair dismissal by Costello J in the High Court as, *inter alia*, the claimant knew that there were certain obligations on teachers in religious schools. That particular claim was brought under the Unfair Dismissals Act, 1977. Whilst of course it is an unfair dismissal to dismiss an employee arising from pregnancy or matters connected therewith, consideration may be given to bring a claim instead under employment equality legislation with unlimited compensation. It should be borne in mind that religious institutions may not discriminate on grounds of sex, even though they have the exclusion clause of being allowed protect their own religious ethos.

Age

The *age ground* is applicable between the ages of 18 and 65 years. This minimum age is not applicable in respect of access to vocational training.

It is not discriminatory on the age ground for an employer to pay different rates of remuneration or have different terms and condi-

tions of employment if the difference is based on their relative seniority or length of service in a particular post or employment.

In respect of access to employment, it will not be discriminatory to
set a maximum age in respect of any job which takes into account:

1.   Any cost or period of time involved in training a recruit to a stan-
     dard at which the recruit will be effective in that job; and

2.   The need for there to be a reasonable period of time prior to re-
     tirement age during which the recruit will be effective in that job.

It shall not constitute discrimination on the age ground to fix different ages for the retirement (whether voluntary or compulsorily) of
employees or any class or description of employees.

Age-related differences in remuneration must be brought to an
end within three years of the commencement of the Act. Discrimination may be permitted where there is clear actuarial or other evidence that significantly increased costs would result if the
discrimination were not permitted in those circumstances. This exemption applies to the disability ground where it is more likely that
costs would be involved. It is much more difficult to envisage what
costs may be involved in legislation where there is an exemption on
pension schemes. However, if community rating were to be applied to
medical health insurance and if it were paid by the employer, then
this should fall within this caveat. Of course, age and disability may
be linked, especially where we have such a wide definition of disability, as it is more likely that an employee may become ill with increased years.

It is expected that there will be an Age Discrimination Directive
in the latter half of 1999. This Directive would be under Article 13 of
the Treaty of Amsterdam, which gives the EU power to issue regulations on measures to prevent age discrimination.

It should be noted that under the Unfair Dismissals Acts, 1977–
1993, it is an unfair dismissal to dismiss an employee on the basis of
their age. Hence if an employee believes that they were dismissed on
the age ground, they will have to decide whether to bring an action
for unfair dismissal or for discrimination under the Employment
Equality Act, 1998. The redress will be the same. Provided that there
is not a resignation, the onus of proof will be on the employer in both
situations.

Disability

"Disability" (s. 2) is defined as:

a) The total or partial absence of a person's bodily or mental functions, including the absence of a part of a person's body;

b) The presence in the body of organisms causing, or likely to cause, chronic disease or illness;

c) The malfunction, malformation or disfigurement of a part of a person's body;

d) A condition or malfunction which results in a person learning differently from a person without the condition or malfunction; or

e) A condition, illness or disease which affects a person's thought processes, perception of reality, emotions or judgment or which results in disturbed behaviour;

and shall be taken to include a disability which exists at present, or which previously existed but no longer exists, or which may exist in the future or which is imputed to a person.

Section 16(3) of the Act states that:

a) A person who has a disability shall not be regarded as other than fully competent to undertake, and fully capable of undertaking, any duties if, with the provision of special treatment or facilities, such a person would be fully competent to undertake, and be fully capable of undertaking, those duties.

b) An employer shall do all that is reasonable to accommodate the needs of a person who has a disability by providing special treatment or facilities to which paragraph (a) relates.

c) A refusal or failure to provide for special treatment or facilities to which paragraph (a) relates shall not be deemed reasonable unless such provision would give rise to a cost, other than a nominal cost, to the employer.

An employer therefore should treat a person with a disability as being fully competent even if there has to be special treatment or facilities. An employer only has to provide special treatment or facilities if there is only a nominal cost involved.

In the Supreme Court case concerning the constitutionality of the original Employment Equality Bill, 1996 (*In the Matter of Article 26 of the Constitution of Ireland and In the Matter of the Employment Equality Bill, 1996*, [1997] ELR 132), a number of issues arose under this ground of discrimination.

It was raised that the definition of disability was too wide, as it referred to disabilities that may happen in the future, to the extent that virtually the entire population would be covered under the Act.

It was also raised that there was undue hardship on employers in the original drafting of the Bill, as they were required to bear what could be significant costs involved in providing appropriate facilities for disabled people without payment or compensation from the State and that this constituted an unjust attack on property. In particular, this would cause undue hardship to small firms. The Court stated that it was satisfied that:

> . . . the provisions constitute a delimitation of the exercise by employers of a right protected by that Article, i.e. the right to carry on a business and earn a livelihood. It is also satisfied that these limitations have been imposed by the Oireachtas with a view to reconciling the exercise of the rights in question with a specific aspect of the common good, i.e. the promotion of equality in the workplace between the disabled and their more fortunate fellow citizens. The issue which the Court has to resolve is as to whether the abridgement of those rights affected by these provisions constitutes an "unjust attack" on those rights in the case of individual employers, having regard to the manner in which it has been effected. . . . The Bill has the totally laudable aim of making provision for such of our fellow citizens as are disabled. Clearly it is in accordance with the principles of social justice that society should do this. But, *prima facie*, it would also appear to be just that society should bear the cost of doing it. . . . it attempts to transfer the cost of solving one of society's problems onto a particular group. The difficulty the court finds with the section is, not that it requires an employer to employ disabled people, but that it requires him to bear the cost of all special treatment or facilities which the disabled person may require to carry out the work unless the cost of the provision of such treatment or facilities would give rise to "undue hardship" to the employer.

It is noted that the wide definition of disability in the Bill meant that it would be impossible to know what the future costs would be. It was held that this section was repugnant to the Constitution. Hence the amendment to "nominal cost". It may be assumed in time that larger employments will have a higher obligation to provide for special treatment or facilities and "nominal cost" may have a different meaning in smaller and larger establishments. Under the UK Disability Discrimination Act, 1995, the Compliance Cost Assessment for the Act was £200 sterling per employee in the ten per cent of cases where changes were required (see Thomas, 1997, p. 50).

The case of *Kenny* v *Hampshire Constabulary* ([1999] ICR 27) was heard under the UK Disability Discrimination Act, 1995. The claimant suffered from cerebral palsy and needed assistance when going to the toilet, applied for a job with the information technology department and was accepted subject to appropriate arrangements being made for his needs. Attempts to find volunteers were unsuccessful, and an application for outside care support was made, but there were difficulties because of the cost. The offer of employment was withdrawn. The Employment Appeals Tribunal considered that the UK Act was intended to confine arrangements to job-related matters and to oblige employers to make adjustments to the way the job was structured and organised so as to accommodate those who could not fit into existing arrangements. Employers were not under a statutory duty to provide carers to attend to an employee's personal needs and therefore in this case the requirements to make adjustments did not apply. However, the issue as to whether the employer was justified in withdrawing the job offer and not considering interim arrangements had to be justified and was thus remitted to the industrial tribunal again for consideration.

Special Provisions

"Special treatment" under the Act may include hours of work that suit the person's disability (e.g. avoidance of rush hours in the city so that they may travel more easily or times to fit in with carers). Other examples may be that such an employee may be able to do more work in their own home and communicate via computer, etc. In some cases, the provision of hours suitable for treatment or rehabilitation may be allowed.

An employer may pay a different rate of pay to an employee with a disability if, because of the disability, the employee is restricted in their capacity to do the same amount of work or hours as a person who is employed to do work of that description but who does not have that disability.

An employer (or any other person) may provide special treatment or facilities for persons with disabilities as follows which:

1. Enables or assists that person to undertake vocational training, to take part in a selection process or to work; or

2. Provides that person with the training or working environment suited to the disability; or

3. Otherwise assists that person in relation to vocational training or work.

However, an employer does not have to recruit, employ, train or promote a person who will not or is unavailable to carry out the duties of a position or who will not accept the duties under which it is performed or who is not fully competent to carry out their duties.

A person who is without a disability (or who has a different disability) will not be entitled to the same remuneration, treatment or facilities.

What are the effects of the health and safety legislation of employing persons with disabilities? Employers may provide for various facilities to include special reserved car parking, access ramps, rails, wider doorways, special toilet facilities, various telephone, computer and other visual aids. Grants may be made available in respect of such changes if an employer is about to employ a person with a disability, an employee becomes disabled or a person with a disability is self-employed.

It should be noted that this is not always possible; if, for example, the employer rents the premises and there is no permission for changes in the premises from the landlord. There is provision in the UK Disability Discrimination Act, 1995, whereby the provisions of that Act override any lease.

In respect of disability, it should of course be noted that the Act does not cover pension schemes; hence the issue of disability in relation to actuarial matters will not arise specifically under the Act.

However, an employer may provide for pensions in such a case. Pension rights are defined as "a pension or any other benefits flowing from an occupational pension scheme". However, does this mean that income protection or disability plans/life assurance are excluded? If we look at the definitions in the Pensions Acts, 1990–1996, it includes income continuance schemes or life assurance, etc. It should be noted that it is envisaged that there will be a new Pensions Act to cover all these additional grounds of discrimination.

It should also be noted that the Defence Forces, the Garda Síochána and the Prison Service are exempt from these provisions.

Race

The Act prohibits discrimination on the "race" ground where two persons are of different race, colour, nationality or ethnic or national origins. These are not technically defined in the Act. It may therefore be useful to view the British Race Relations Act, 1976, as amended. The origins of the British legislation lay in earlier Acts to combat the racial discrimination that followed the various waves of post-Second World War immigration to deal with labour shortages. In this country, this aspect of the new legislation may indeed become more important with increased immigration and refugees and the current Irish labour shortage.

Such issues may now be considered in the light of the UK Race Relations Acts of 1968 and 1976 and in consideration of various terms.

"Ethnic" and "National Origin"

The judgment in *Mandla* v *Lee* ([1983] 2 AC 548) construed the word "ethnic" widely in a broad cultural and historic sense.

> A group is identifiable in terms of its ethnic origins if it is a segment of the population distinguished from others by a sufficient combination of shared customs, beliefs, traditions and characteristics derived from a common or presumed common past, even if not drawn from what in biological terms is a common racial stock. It is that combination which gives them a historically determined social identity in their own eyes and in the eyes of those outside the group. The have a distinct social identity based not simply on

group cohesion and solidarity but also on their belief as to their historical antecedents.

It has been noted that it is arguable that national origins are less important than religious groupings. Sikhs were held to be an ethnic group; however, Muslims were held to be a religious grouping. *Mandla* v *Lee* is the key UK case on the criteria to be applied in establishing as to whether an ethnic group exists.

In summary, it was considered that essential conditions included:

1. A long shared history, of which the group is conscious as distinguishing it from other groups, and the memory of which keeps it alive;

2. A cultural tradition of its own, including family and social customs and manners, often but not necessarily associated with religious observance;

3. Either a common geographical origin, or descent from a number of common ancestors;

4. A common language, not necessarily peculiar to the group;

5. A common literature peculiar to the group;

6. A common religion different from that of neighbouring groups or from the general community surrounding it;

7. Being a minority or being an oppressed or dominant group within a larger community.

A person may fall into this group, for example, by marriage or religious conversion, and it makes no difference.

Case law will have to develop in respect of this ground of discrimination, and it is possible that persons may belong under various headings. The 1998 Act provides specific and distinct protection for members of the travelling community, as discrimination against such persons is a specific ground of discrimination in the Act.

Positive Action

An employer may put in place measures in order to reduce or eliminate the effects of discrimination and to integrate into employment, generally into the workplace, or in particular areas of the workplace (s. 33):

1. Persons who have reached the age of 50 years;

2. Persons with a disability or any class or description of such persons; or

3. Members of the traveller community.

The State may provide for training or work experience for a disadvantaged group of persons.

Special Provisions

It is reasonable for there to be special provisions (s. 36) for the following:

1. Persons holding office under, or in the service of, the State (including the Garda Síochána and the Defence Forces) or otherwise as a civil servant, within the meaning of the Civil Service Regulation Act, 1956, or

2. Officers or servants of a local authority, for the purposes of the Local Government Act, 1941, a harbour authority, a health board or vocational education committee.

The provisions referred to above are those relating to all or any of the following:

1. Residence

2. Citizenship

3. Proficiency in the Irish language.

It shall not be unlawful to have any provision (whether in the nature of the requirement, practice or otherwise) in relation to proficiency in the Irish language with respect to teachers in primary and post-primary schools.

It shall not be unlawful to require in relation to a particular post

1. The holding of a specified educational, technical or professional qualification which is a generally accepted qualification in the State for posts of that description; or

2. The production and evaluation of information about any qualifi-
    cation other than such a specified qualification.

It shall not be unlawful for a body controlling the entry to, or carrying on of, a profession, vocation or occupation to require a person carrying on or wishing to enter that profession, vocation or occupation,
to hold a specified educational, technical or other qualification which
is appropriate in the circumstances.

  However, nothing in this section shall render lawful discrimination on the gender ground.

Occupational Qualification for the Post

Without prejudice generally in relation to discrimination on the age
ground, the disability ground or the ground of race, the relevant
characteristic shall be taken to be an occupational qualification for a
post on grounds of physiology or of authenticity for the purpose of
entertainment, if the nature of the post (s. 37(3)):

1. Requires the person having the same relevant characteristic (e.g.
    being of a particular colour, age, etc.) and

2. Would be materially different if such a person did not have the
    relevant characteristic.

In relation to discrimination on the religion ground or on the ground
of race, the relevant characteristic shall be taken to be an occupational qualification for a post where it is necessary that the post shall
be held because it is likely to involve the performance of duties outside the State in a place where the laws or customs are such that
those duties could not reasonably be performed by a person who does
not have that relevant characteristic or, as the case may require, by a
person who has a relevant characteristic (e.g. certain Middle Eastern
countries).

  Examples of occupational qualifications are similar to the sex occupational qualification for the post: acting, modelling or the provision of authenticity (e.g. a requirement for certain skills in oriental
cooking).

  None of these discriminatory grounds apply to employment of any
person for the purposes of a private household. The age grounds or

the disability grounds of discrimination do not apply for employment in the Defence Forces, the Garda Síochána or the prison service.

PROCEDURES

Under the 1998 Act the claimant has a right to information. There arc two different sets of procedures under the 1998 Act. If the parties agree, the claim may be referred to mediation, where it may or may not be resolved. In the event of no reference to mediation or where mediation has not produced an agreement, the Director of Equality Investigations may investigate the claim and issue a decision. Such decision may be appealed to the Labour Court, whose determination may be appealed to the Circuit Court.

General References

Bourn, C. and J. Whitmore (1996), *Anti-Discrimination Law in Britain*, 3rd edition, London: Sweet and Maxwell

Carolan, B. (1999), "Hope Fades for EU Recognition of Same-Sex Partnerships", *Law Society Gazette*, May.

European Commission (1999), *Affirming Fundamental Rights in the European Union,* Report of the Expert Group on Fundamental Rights, European Communities.

European Foundation for the Improvement of Living and Working Conditions (1997), *Combating Age Barriers in Employment, Research Summary*, Office for Official Publications of the European Communities.

Heffernan, L. (ed.) 1994, *Human Rights: A European Perspective*, Dublin: The Round Hall Press in association with the Irish Centre for European Law.

Meenan, Helen (1999), "Age Discrimination in the United Kingdom", *International Journal of Discrimination and the Law*, Vol. 3, Issue 4, pp. 227–48.

Thomas, G. (1997), *The New Law on Disability Discrimination*, London: Sweet and Maxwell.

Chapter Eleven

TRANSFER OF A BUSINESS

Decades ago, an employee had no rights on the transfer of a business. When a business was sold (and there was a new employer), the employee's contract of employment was terminated. Subsequently, redundancy, minimum notice and unfair dismissals legislation provided limited protection in ensuring continuity of service for an employee in the case of a transfer of a business. The European Communities (Safeguarding of Employees' Rights on Transfer of Undertakings) Regulations, 1980 (SI No. 306 of 1980) now attempts to protect employees' statutory and contractual rights in the event that the business is transferred as a going concern. These regulations (which arose from the EU Transfer of Undertakings Directive — 77/187/EEC) have succeeded to a limited extent, but they do suffer somewhat in their drafting from EU law into Irish law. However, there is a new Directive (98/50/EC), which should amend a number of the difficulties of the current legislation. This new Directive must be transposed into national law by 17 July 2001 (see page 272). Indeed, the Preamble to the new Directive notes that the Social Charter adopted on 9 December 1989 (points 7, 17 and 18) states that

> The completion of the internal market must lead to an improvement in the living and working conditions of workers in the European Community. The improvement must cover, where necessary, the development of certain aspects of employment regulations such as procedures for collective redundancies and those regarding bankruptcies. Information, consultation and participation for workers must be developed along appropriate lines, taking account of the practices in force in the Member States. Such information, consultation and participation must be implemented in due time, particularly in connection with restructuring operations

in undertakings or in cases of mergers having an impact on the employment of workers.

The purpose of these regulations is to protect employees' rights in the event of a transfer. They are almost identical to the original EC Council Directive, which is somewhat clearer and provides that the regulations apply to the transfer of an undertaking, business, or part of a business to another employer as a result of a legal transfer or merger. The Council Directive also states that it is necessary to provide for the protection of employees' rights in the event of a change of employer. In other words, they will retain their jobs and also seniority and continuity of service. These regulations also place an obligation on employers to inform and consult their employees' representatives in the event of a proposed transfer.

A TRANSFER

The term "transfers" is not defined in the regulations. However, the key point in relation to the transfer of a business is that there must be a change in the identity of the employer, and that the business be transferred as a going concern, as was considered by Barron J in *Nova Colour Graphic Supplies Ltd.* v *EAT and Another* ((1987) 6 JISLL 142).

It is generally considered that transfers of control in companies by means of share ownership or the mere transfer of assets does not constitute a transfer; for example, the lease of property or the sale of machinery. The case of *Guidon* v *Farrington* ([1993] ELR 98), highlighted that the reversion of a lease from a lessee back to the lessor of a property constituted a transfer of a business where the business was carried on. The facts of the case are that the claimant worked as a "night owl" in the Westmoreland Street premises of Local Stores (Trading) Ltd., t/a Seven Eleven, from 18 June 1990 until 23 March 1991. A receiver was appointed to the group of shops and the claimant was transferred to the Seven Eleven in the BP Petrol Station at Usher's Island where she worked as normal until 14 June 1991. She went into work on 17 June, when she was told by another employee that she no longer worked there. On 14 June, the lease of the petrol station reverted back to the landlords, Richard and Hugh Farrington, who were now running the business. The claimant maintained that the Transfer of Undertakings Regulations applied and also that she was entitled to one week's notice, which would bring her within the scope of the unfair dismissals legislation (see Chapter 17). The Tribunal considered that both the EC Directive and the regulations applied in this case and relied on two European Court of Justice cases, *Landsorganisationen I Danmark* v *Ny Molle Kro* ([1987] ECR 5465), and *Berg* v *Besselsen* ([1988] ECR 2559). The Tribunal considered that it was an unfair dismissal and she was awarded compensation. It is still important to ask the question: "Is there a change in the identity of the employer and is there a transfer of a business as a 'going concern'?" For example, is there a transfer of customer lists, debtors lists and so forth?

Another Irish decision concerned the application of the regulations to the "contracting out" of services by an employer. In this case, the employer, a shopping centre, had employed security staff but decided to contract out the work to a security firm instead. The security firm offered a position to the claimant, who had been employed by the shopping centre, but he refused because he was told he would be working in another location on a lower salary. He brought to the Employment Appeals Tribunal a claim for unfair dismissal, which was rejected. He referred the matter to the High Court for review. The key point in this case was whether "contracting out of the services" was a "legal transfer" within the meaning of the regulations. Relying on European Court of Justice judgments, Blayney J considered that there was a transfer of a business and that the Directive is applicable if the business retains its identity or if there is a change in the legal or natural person who is responsible for carrying on the business, regardless of whether ownership is transferred or not. It was considered that the business was the same as before, as exactly the same security services were being provided by five security guards. There had also been a change in the legal or natural person who was responsible for carrying out the business (*Bannon* v *Employment Appeals Tribunal and Drogheda Town Centre* [1993] IR 500).

This case was a watershed, because employees who are not offered employment in such circumstances may now successfully claim unfair dismissal based on these regulations. Heretofore, such persons were invariably in receipt of redundancy and there were usually no further claims.

The sale of a company by a receiver may also come within the scope of the regulations. In *Mythen* v *the Employment Appeals Tribunal (EAT), Butterkrust Ltd. and Joseph Downes & Sons Limited (in receivership)* ([1990] ELR 1), the claimant had been employed by Joseph Downes & Sons Ltd., which went into receivership. He received a statutory redundancy payment and was successful in obtaining minimum notice monies from the EAT. However, 40 of the Downes employees received offers of employment from Butterkrust, but Mr Mythen did not. He considered that he was unfairly selected for redundancy and brought an unfair dismissals claim against both companies. The Tribunal considered that he could not bring a claim under the regulations and the Unfair Dismissals Act, as the regulations had not amended that Act (or indeed any of the other protective legislation). He applied to the High Court for a review of the determination, and the High Court quashed the Tribunal decision. Accordingly, an employee who has lost his job as a result of a transfer could bring a claim under the relevant employment protection legislation, as well as relying on the transfer of a business regulations against either (or both) the transferor or transferee of the business (see Chapter 21, "Employer Insolvency").

In summary, the regulations provide that all the rights and obligations of the selling company arising from contracts of employment or employment relationships (this includes collective agreements/union management agreements) existing on the date of transfer shall be transferred to the purchaser. If the employee is employed on the date of transfer, there shall be no break in service or in continuity of service and all entitlements under the employee's contract of employment are automatically transferred. This would include not only wages/ salary, but also statutory obligations, such as service under the redundancy, minimum notice and unfair dismissals legislation, as well as matters like seniority.

One possible grey area regarding the transfer of business is in relation to pension schemes. This matter is unclear and pensions may be frozen as of the date of transfer. The Pensions Act, 1990, may be of some assistance, as the employees at least may now have transferable pension rights to be brought into a new scheme.

In the case of *Merckx and Neuhuys* v *The Ford Motor Company Belgium SA* ([1996] IRLR 467), the European Court of Justice ruled that Article 1(1) of Council Directive 77/187/EEC must be interpreted as applying where an undertaking holding a motor vehicle dealership for a particular territory discontinues its activities and the dealership is then transferred to another undertaking which takes on part of the staff and is recommended to customers without any transfer of assets. Two salesmen refused transfers to a new company, claiming redundancies instead, on the basis that their conditions of employment were to be substantially changed. Article 4(2) of the Directive requires the Member State to provide that where the contract of employment is terminated because the transfer involved had changed the level of remuneration awarded to the employee, the employers should be regarded as having been responsible for the termination. A change in the level of remuneration is a substantial change in working conditions within the meaning of Article 4(2).

RETENTION OF IDENTITY

The European Court of Justice in *Spijkers* v *Gebroeders Benedik Abattoir CV* ([1986] 2 CMLR 296 at 300), stated

> In order to establish whether or not such a transfer has taken place . . . it is necessary to consider whether, having regard to all the facts characterising the transaction, the business was disposed of as a going concern, as would be indicated *inter alia* by the fact that its operation was actually continued or resumed by the new employer, with the same or similar activities.

In *Ryan* v *Kelleher, Limerick Blood Transfusion Service (LBTS) and the National Blood Transfusion Service (NBTS)* (496/1991), the claimant was employed by Dr Sheila Kelleher and the LBTS as a laboratory technician who maintained his employment was terminated by reason of redundancy. Redundancy as a fact was disputed by the respondents, as it was argued that the claimant was not dismissed but was transferred to other suitable employment in the Mid-Western Health Board. The respondents argued that different parts of the business of LBTS were transferred to both the Mid-Western Health Board and also to the NBTS within the meaning of the Transfer of Undertakings Regulations and thus, as the claimant continued to be employed by the Mid-Western Health Board, no claim for redundancy could arise. The NBTS paid monies to Dr Kelleher and the LBTS for the acquisition of the business. The Mid-Western Health

Board disputed that there was a transfer of an undertaking, business
or part of a business. The business of Dr Kelleher and LBTS involved
the collection of blood, the provision of blood, blood products, blood-
grouping and cross-matching services to the Mid-Western Health
Board. Dr Kelleher and the LBTS ceased all operations on 31 January 1991 and as of 1 February 1991 the NBTS commenced the business of collecting blood in the area, with the same employees as
originally employed by the LBTS, and then provided the blood to the
Mid-Western Health Board. As of 1 February, the blood-grouping and
cross-matching services were now being carried on by the Mid-
Western Health Board with four of the five laboratory technicians
(who had no break in service) previously employed by Dr Kelleher
and the LBTS. The Tribunal referred to the *Spijkers* case [1986] ECR
1119 with regard to whether the business retained its identity.
Where the European Court of Justice stated that a major indicator is
if the "operation was actually continued or resumed by the new employer with the same or similar activities", the Tribunal considered
that there was a transfer of an undertaking within the meaning of
the transfer regulations and dismissed the claimant's redundancy
and minimum notice claims and confirmed that all the rights and
obligations of the transferor arising from the contract of employment
of the claimant existing on the date of transfer were transferred to
the Mid-Western Health Board.

Sub-contracting

In *Schmidt* v *Spar und Leihkasse der Frühren Amter Bordesholm,
Kiel and Cronshagen* ([1994] IRLR 302), the European Court of Justice held that the Transfer of Undertakings Directive can apply to
contracting-out of services such as cleaning operations, even where
the work was performed by a single employee before being contracted
out to an outside firm. Once again, the key point is whether the business retains its "identity". This is indicated, inter alia, by the actual
continuance or resumption by the new employer of the same or similar activities. Ms Schmidt was employed at the Savings and Lending
Bank as the only cleaner at a particular branch. In February 1992,
when the branch was refurbished and extended, she was dismissed
because the Bank decided to contract out the cleaning to the firm already responsible for cleaning most of its other premises. That firm

offered to employ Ms Schmidt at a higher monthly wage but she turned the offer down on the grounds that she would be receiving a lower hourly wage, since there was now a larger area to clean. She brought an action under German law on protection against dismissal, challenging her dismissal on the grounds that it was not socially justified. She initially lost her case and the matter was referred to the European Court of Justice with the following questions:

1. May an undertaking's cleaning operations, if they are transferred by contract to a different firm, be treated as part of their business within the meaning of Directive 77/187/EEC?

2. If the answer to question 1 is in principle in the affirmative, does that also apply if, prior to the transfer, the cleaning operations were undertaken by a single employee?

The Savings Bank maintained that the provision of cleaning services was neither its principal nor an ancillary operation. The transfer of a very small part of all the services, therefore, could not constitute a transfer of a part of a business within the meaning of Directive 77/187. The European Court of Justice ruled as follows:

> Article 1(1) of Council Directive 77/187/EEC of 14 February 1977, and the approximation of the laws of the Member States relating to the safeguarding of employees' rights in the event of transfers of undertakings, businesses or parts of businesses, is to be interpreted as covering a situation . . . in which an undertaking entrusts by contract to another undertaking the responsibility for carrying out cleaning operations which it previously performed itself, even though, prior to the transfer, such work was carried out by a single employee.

The factual reverse of *Schmidt* happened in *Francisco Hernandez Vidal SA* v *Gomez Perez* ([1999] IRLR 132) (joined cases C-127/96, C-229/96 and C-74/97), where the employers had contracted out their cleaning operations but then wanted to terminate the contract and look after their own cleaning. The ECJ ruled that "the decisive criterion for establishing if a transfer of undertaking" has taken place is "whether the entity in question retains its identity". An economic entity is "an organised grouping of persons and assets enabling an economic activity which pursues a specific objective to be exercised".

Therefore, for the Directive to be applicable, it must refer to more than one specific works contract. Finally, "the mere fact that the maintenance work carried out by the first cleaning firm and then by the undertaking owning the premises is similar does not justify the conclusion that the transfer of such an entity has occurred". However, in such cases there was deemed to be a transfer of a business.

In *Power* v *St Paul's Nursing Home and D&M Cleaning Ltd.* (UD 611/97), the nursing home subcontracted the cleaning of its premises to D&M Cleaning, having previously employed its own cleaners. D&M Cleaning interviewed all the cleaners and said that it was not prepared to acknowledge continuity of employment and that there would be a change to the terms and conditions of employment. The employees brought unfair dismissal claims. In respect of considering whether there was a transfer or not, the contractor said that St Paul's had transferred all its cleaning equipment to the contractor and that this was taken into account in the pricing of the contract. It was held that this was a transfer of a business, as the cleaning operations at St Paul's were capable of forming a separate economic entity, the fact that the contractor was willing to take on the employees (even though in breach of employment protection legislation) and the transfer of equipment.

In *Cunningham and O'Connor* v *Oasis Stores Limited* ([1996] ELR 183), following on various changes of ownership and a reorganisation of the management structure, the two claimants, a chief executive and area manager, were no longer required and hence there was a redundancy as the requirement for their kind of work had ceased or diminished. Dismissal for such reasons is allowed by the Directive.

Change of Contractor

The judgment in the case of *Süzen* v *Zehnacker Gebäudereinigung GmbH Krankenhaus Service* ([1997] IRLR 255), gave rise to considerable controversy and may have a huge impact on the protection of employees in the service industry, where contracts to provide services (e.g. cleaning) are lost and a new contract granted to another contractor. Putting it simply, the employees of the first contractor may not be entitled to remain in the same place of work with the new contractor. The ECJ stated:

> The mere loss of a service contract to a competitor cannot there-
> fore by itself indicate the existence of a transfer within the mean-
> ing of the Directive. In those circumstances, the service
> undertaking previously entrusted with the contract does not, on
> losing a customer, thereby cease fully to exist, and a business or
> part of a business belonging to it cannot be considered to have
> been transferred to the new awardee of the contract.

Zehnacker had a contract to clean a private church-run secondary school in Bonn Bad Godesberg. The school terminated the cleaning contract with Zehnacker with effect from 30 June 1994 and contracted out its cleaning to another contractor called Lefarth GmbH instead. Mrs Süzen was employed by Zehnacker and, together with seven other cleaners at the school, was dismissed when their employers lost the contract. She claimed that this dismissal was invalid, relying upon the Transfer of Undertakings Directive. The ECJ considered that the

> . . . Directive does not apply to a situation in which a person who
> had entrusted the cleaning of his premises to a first undertaking
> terminates his contract with the latter and, for the performance of
> similar work, enters into a new contract with a second undertak-
> ing, if there is no concomitant transfer from one undertaking to
> the other of significant tangible or intangible assets or taking over
> by the new employer of a major part of the workforce, in terms of
> their numbers and skills, assigned by his predecessor to the per-
> formance of the contract.

In *Cannon* v *Noonan Cleaning Ltd. and CPS Cleaning Services Ltd.* (RP 324/97 UD200/1997 and MN 591/97), CPS succeeded in obtaining the cleaning contract for Balbriggan Garda Station, which was formerly operated by Noonan Cleaning. Mrs Cannon had been employed by Noonan and she turned up for work with the new contractor who did not employ her. No tangible assets transferred between the two contractors. It would therefore appear that the Employment Appeals Tribunal had no alternative but to apply the *Süzen* case and the fact that the transfer of the intangible profit margin was not significant enough to be a major issue in the "transfer". However the Tribunal did voice concern over the willingness or otherwise of the new contractor to take over the workforce and stated:

There is no doubt that in a service undertaking the workforce and
its expertise constitute a major aspect of the undertaking but it is
difficult to understand how, where an employer refuses to take on
the workers of a previous contractor, he can escape the rigours of
the Directive, while a contractor who takes on a major part of the
workforce, perhaps out of magnanimity, will be caught by it. It
would seem that the Directive, in this former instance, has not
addressed the mischief in the law that it was intended to do.

The *Süzen* case was also applied in *Shiels and Others* v *Noonan
Cleaning and ISS Contract Cleaners Ltd.* (RP 180/97 UD 461/97 and
MN 754/97) where no assets were transferred and no employees were
taken on by the incoming contractor.

However, confusion still reigns, as in *Sanchez Hidalgo* v *Aso-
ciacion de Servicios* ([1999] IRLR 136) (joined cases C-173/96 and C-
247/96) and *Ziemann* (Case C-247/96), the ECJ held the replacement
of a sub-contractor with a new sub-contractor constituted a transfer
of a business as there was a transfer of an economic entity. The *Hidalgo* case concerned contracts to run home-help services for a local
authority in Spain, and *Ziemann*, the provision of a security service
at a medical supplies depot in the German army. An economic entity
was described as an organised grouping of people and/or assets enabling an economic activity with a specific objective to be carried out.

TERMINATION OF EMPLOYMENT ARISING FROM A TRANSFER

The primary purpose of these Regulations is to prohibit a purchaser
from dismissing employees because of the transfer of a business.
However, if dismissals arise for economic, technical or organisational
reasons, they may be permitted. If redundancies take place following
the transfer of a business, there should be no difficulty as long as
there is not unfair selection. This is extremely important, as the staff
in the two businesses would have to be looked at together to consider
the issue of selection. If employees consider that they have been dismissed because of a transfer, they may well have a cause of action
against both their original employer and the purchaser under the
Unfair Dismissals Acts, 1977 to 1993.

However, redundancies prior to the proposed transfer of a business may not be genuine within the meaning of the Redundancy
Payments Acts. This is a technical point but it is worth considering.

Of course, the reality of many redundancies that take place prior to the transfer of the business is that the employee receives not only his statutory entitlement, such as minimum notice, holidays and statutory redundancy, but also an ex-gratia lump sum. One of the provisions of receiving that lump sum would be that the employee would sign a discharge form provided that they had received the sums in full and final settlement of all claims. Section 15 of the Unfair Dismissals (Amendment) Act, 1993, amending the rules for continuity of service, provides that the transfer of a business does not break continuity of service for the purpose of unfair dismissal and minimum notice *unless* the employee received and retained a redundancy payment from the transferor (the employer) at the time of the transfer and by reason of the transfer.

This provision appeared to be at variance with the intention of the Directive in so far as it purported to allow a break in continuity of service and it was noted as such by the Employment Appeals Tribunal in *Brett & Others* v *Niall Collins Limited (in Receivership) and Oyster Investments Ltd.* (UD 929–934/1994). The film processing company Niall Collins Ltd. employed 50 staff and subsequently went into receivership. The receiver negotiated a contract to sell the company to Oyster Investments Ltd. This contract was concluded on 28 March 1994 but not formally signed until 29 March 1994. The receiver dismissed all the employees on 28 March and then some of the employees received a call to come back to work on 29 March 1994. Although slimmed down, the company was up and running again on 29 March. The Tribunal considered the fact that trading had ceased for some time at the date of the transfer did not imply that there was no transfer, and the fact that the goodwill or existing contracts are not transferred are not conclusive evidence against there being a transfer. The Tribunal stated:

> It is clear that the Directive preserves the continuity of the contract of employment where the business transferred maintains its identity. This does not mean that when the assets of the business are disposed of there is a transfer but if the assets are disposed of as a going concern and the operation "is resumed by the new employer with the same or similar activities", then that will constitute a transfer for the purposes of the Directive.

The Tribunal noted that:

> . . . where a company is put into liquidation or an employer is de-
> clared a bankrupt, the selling on of the assets of the insolvent per-
> son, natural or legal, is not a transfer of an undertaking for the
> purpose of the Directive. A receivership is, however, because the
> appointment of a receiver does not indicate in law that the com-
> pany is insolvent although it operates to that effect for the pur-
> poses of the Protection of Employees (Employers' Insolvency) Act,
> 1984.

The tribunal noted in this case that the business was sold as a going
concern and the only element missing was the fact that the employees did not transfer with the business. The receiver purported to
dismiss the staff by paying them redundancy and the only reason for
doing so was that the business would not have all the statutory liabilities that the staff attracted. Further, the receiver dismissed
them all on 28 March so that there was no real evidence that they
were dismissed for economic, technical or organisational reasons, as a
number of them were re-employed the next day. The Regulations
specifically prohibit dismissals by reason of a transfer. The Tribunal
considered the dismissal by reason of the transfer was null and void
and of no effect and, as redundancy requires a dismissal, the payment made was not a redundancy payment. Therefore section 15 of
the Unfair Dismissals (Amendment) Act, 1993, had no application in
this case.

Arising from this case, it is important to note that even if an employee is made redundant or dismissed and if they can show that it is
by reason of a transfer, then they may have continuity of service and
hence have protection under the various employment statutes without having to build up the necessary service (e.g. one year for statutory unfair dismissal).

The ECJ has also concluded that an employee cannot waive their
rights in relation to the Directive on the Transfer of a Business so
that they would be less well off with the new employer (*Foreningen of
Arbejdsledere i Danmark* v *Daddy's Dance Hall A/S* [1988] IRLR
315). Section 13 of the Unfair Dismissals Act, however, provides that
an employer may bring a claim if they feel that they have been denied representation or had to sign the agreement under duress (see
Chapter 17, "Unfair Dismissal").

CHANGE OF WORKING CONDITIONS

If, following on the transfer of employment, there is a change in working conditions (reduction in salary, change in seniority and so forth) it would be possible for the employee to resign and claim constructive dismissal (see *Power* v *St. Paul's Nursing Home and D&M Cleaning Ltd* above). However, such an approach without advice would be most imprudent. Such employees would be well advised to have recourse to the grievance procedure (if any), or failing that to refer the dispute to a Rights Commissioner/Labour Relations Commission to try and resolve the matter through negotiation.

DUTY TO INFORM AND CONSULT EMPLOYEES

The vendor and the purchaser are required to inform the employees or their representative in good time of the:

1. Reasons for the transfer;

2. Legal, economic and social implications of the transfer for the employees, and

3. Measures envisaged in relation to the employees.

These provisions are very general and there is no provision that employees have to receive the full details of the proposed transfer and all the legal and financial arrangements or that they have to be involved in them. Thus, generally, both vendor and purchaser only give the most general of information.

The employers do not have to state whether or not there will be redundancies, only what measures are envisaged in the organisation; for example, changing duties, changing seniority and other terms and conditions of employment.

As noted above, there is provision that the vendor/purchaser shall "consult" with the employee representative "in good time" if there are measures envisaged in relation to the employees. Unfortunately, "in good time" is not defined and employees are usually advised at the last moment about the proposed transfer. This is not necessarily the employers' fault because during delicate negotiations it may be imprudent for persons other than those negotiating the deal to be aware of it.

If the employees have no representatives, the vendor or the purchaser must give the employees a written statement outlining the above particulars, and notices containing these particulars must be displayed in the work place where the employees can read them. A sample letter from the vendor to the employee representative is given at the end of this chapter.

Employees who feel that their employer has not complied with the regulations can refer the matter to the Department of Enterprise, Trade and Employment for investigation. If an officer from the Department is of the opinion that a transaction constituted a transfer, that officer may request the parties to provide all relevant information, books or documents. An authorised officer shall be furnished by the Minister with a certificate authorising the exercise of the officer's powers; for example, for entry on to an employer's premises. If a person fails to respond and provide such information, that person shall be guilty of an offence and shall be liable on summary conviction for a fine not exceeding £300. However, this is not very satisfactory and it is always open to the employees to apply to the High Court for an order that the vendor and the purchaser comply with the regulations.

In addition to the obligation on the transferor and the transferee to inform and consult employees in undertakings where the Transnational Information and Consultation of Employees Act, 1996, applies, there is also the additional obligation to inform employees through the procedures provided for in that Act (see Chapter 12, "Employee Participation and Partnership").

EMPLOYMENT RIGHTS PROTECTION BILL, 1997

Arising from these various deficiencies, the Employment Rights Protection Bill, 1997, was published in December 1997 as a Private Member's Bill. The stated purpose of the Bill in the Explanatory Memorandum was to redress a serious defect in the Protection of Employment Act, 1977, and the European Communities (Safeguarding of Employees' Rights on Transfer of Undertakings) Regulations, 1980, namely that the existing law fails to provide adequate remedies for non-compliance. There is no right of an employee to compensation or to any other remedy for breach of the collective redundancy and transfer of undertakings laws.

The existing enforcement mechanism is that of criminal prosecution, which is unusual in the industrial relations context and is rarely used. In any event, a prosecution in itself confers no benefit on a wronged employee. The Bill proposed to provide proper compensatory and remedying mechanisms for contravention of the collective redundancy legislation and the regulations on transfer of undertakings.

The Bill provides that a dispute regarding compliance with the collective redundancies legislation, the transfer of undertakings regulations, or the relevant EU directives can be referred to a rights commissioner. Either side can appeal the findings of the rights commissioner to the Employment Appeals Tribunal. An appeal or reference on a point of law lies to the High Court.

Redress can include reinstatement, re-engagement or up to two years' remuneration. There were also provisions for enforcement and offences.

GENERAL OFFENCES UNDER THE REGULATIONS

If a person contravenes a provision of these regulations (other than non-provision of information as stated above), that person shall be guilty of an offence and shall be liable to a fine not exceeding £500 on summary conviction. The Minister may bring proceedings under the regulations but they must be instituted within 12 months of the date of the alleged offence.

PROCEDURES

If an employee considers that their job had been lost arising from a transfer of a business, that employee may bring a claim under the unfair dismissals legislation and any other relevant legislation.

AMENDING DIRECTIVE

Directive 98/50/EC of 29 June 1998, which amends the original Directive, must be in force in national law by 17 July 2001. The purpose of the new Directive is to amend the current Directive in the light of the impact of the internal market, the legislation of the Member States with regard to the rescue of undertakings in economic difficulties, the case law of the ECJ and the laws in the Member States. The following points are particularly noted:

- The legal concept of "transfer" must be clarified within the context of the current applicable Directive and the case law of the ECJ;

- The legislation must apply to private and public undertakings, whether or not they operate for gain;

- The word "employee" must be clarified within the light of case law of the ECJ;

- The exclusion of certain provisions of the Directive to ensure the survival of insolvent undertakings;

- The circumstances in which the function and status of employee representatives are to be preserved should be clarified;

- The necessity to ensure that the information and consultation requirements are complied with irrespective of whether the decision leading to the transfer is taken by the employer or by an undertaking controlling the transfer; and

- The circumstances in which employees must be informed where there are no employee representatives must be clarified.

In summary, this Directive applies "to any transfer of an undertaking, business, or part of an undertaking or business to another employer as a result of a legal transfer or merger". "Transfer" is then defined as follows: "where there is a transfer of an economic entity which retains its identity, meaning an organised grouping of resources which has the objective of pursuing an economic activity, whether or not that activity is central or ancillary". It should be noted that an administrative reorganisation of public administrative authorities or the transfer of functions between such authorities is not a transfer. The transfer must take place within the territorial scope of the Treaty (but does not apply to sea-going vessels). The Directive applies to all employees regardless of the hours they work or the nature of their employment contract (e.g. fixed term, etc.). Interestingly, following on the transfer, the new employer must observe the terms of any collective agreement until its expiry or the commencement of a new one. The Member States may limit the period for observing such collective agreements to one year. Unless Member States wish to provide for such application, it is specifically provided that the Directive does not apply to company pensions schemes (which are outside the statutory social security schemes in Member States). However, if Member States do not provide for the application of the Directive to pension schemes, they should make suitable alternative legislative provision for the protection of employees' pensions in the transferor's employment.

The general provisions in respect of employment protection are repeated. However, these provisions do not apply in respect of insolvency proceedings which have been instituted with a view to the liquidation of the assets of the transferor and is under the supervision of a competent public authority (which may be an insolvent practitioner authorised by a competent public authority — in the Irish case a liquidator or receiver appointed by the High Court). Of course, all employee entitlements shall be paid as provided in the Protection of Employees (Employers' Insolvency) Act, 1984, or else new terms and conditions may be negotiated to ensure the survival of the business or undertaking.

There may be agreed alterations to an employees' terms and conditions of employment where the transferor is in a situation of serious economic crisis, provided that the situation is declared by a competent public authority and open to judicial supervision on condition that such provisions already exist in national law by 17 July 1998.

General References

Byrne, G. (1999), *Transfer of Undertakings: Employment Aspects of Business Transfers in Irish & European Law*, Dublin: Blackhall Publishing.

Kerr, A. (1988), "Implementation of Directive 77/187 into Irish Law and Case Law of the Court of Justice", Irish Centre for European Law, *Acquired Rights for Employees*, Conference Papers, November.

McMullen, J. (1998), *Business Transfers and Employees' Rights*, Third edition, Dublin: Butterworths

McMullen, J. (1999), "The Application of the Acquired Rights Directive in Britain and Ireland", *Industrial Relations News*, IRN 12, 25 March.

Quinn, O. (1999), "Existing Duties of Employers to Consult with Trade Unions", *The Bar Review*, April.

LETTER TO EMPLOYEE REPRESENTATIVE FROM THE TRANSFEROR (VENDOR) WHICH SHOULD BE IN "GOOD TIME"

                                                        XYZ Limited
                                                        123 New St.
                                                        Dublin 4

                                                        [date]

Ms Joan Smith
A Union
Old Street
Dublin 1

Dear Ms Smith,

On behalf of the company, I am writing to you as my employees' union official to inform you that the company is being transferred to ABC Limited on [date]. I am obliged to write to you further to the Transfer of Undertakings Regulations.

The reason for the transfer of our business to ABC Limited is because both I and the other Directors are going to retire. ABC Limited will be carrying on the business of XYZ Limited as a going concern.
It is envisaged that there should be no legal, economic or social implications resulting from the transfer affecting your members at the date of transfer. The continuity of employment of your members shall not be affected. Furthermore, ABC Limited shall recognise the rights connected with the contract of employment and collective agreements on such transfer.

There are no further measures contemplated at this time in relation to your members other than a change in identity of their employer.

Yours sincerely

For and on behalf of XYZ Limited

Chapter Twelve

EMPLOYEE PARTICIPATION AND PARTNERSHIP

EMPLOYEE PARTICIPATION

The 1970s saw a major interest in employee participation at both board and sub-board level. The Worker Participation (State Enterprises) Act, 1977, provided for employee participation at board level in certain semi-state companies. In 1985, the Minister for Labour set up an Advisory Committee on Worker Participation, which included members from both sides of industry. The following were the terms of reference (see Morrissey, 1989):

1. To advise the Minister for Labour on the scope for the development of employee participation at sub-board level in different types of work organisation;

2. To promote interest in practical experimentation in workplace participation;

3. To identify research needs and make recommendations.

The Advisory Committee reported in 1986. There was apparent agreement as regards increased participation, and the majority considered that legislation should be introduced with reference to organisations in the private sector employing more than 100 people. Employer members of the committee considered that there should be a purely voluntary approach. The Committee also considered that participation at sub-board level should be reinforced and developed.

Subsequently, the Worker Participation (State Enterprises) Amendment Act, 1988, provided for sub-board level participation in certain semi-state companies and organisations. The Worker Protection (Regular Part-Time Employees) Act, 1991, extended the benefit of worker participation in the 1977 and 1988 Acts to include regular part-time employees, that is, employees who have 13 weeks' continuous service and who are normally expected to work at least eight hours per week. The Worker Participation Acts were subsequently amended by the Air Companies (Amendment) Act, 1993.

Board and Sub-board Participation in Semi-state Companies

The following semi-state companies include board participation:

> Bord na Móna, Córas Iompair Éireann, Electricity Supply Board, Aer Lingus Group plc, Aer Rianta, An Post, Bord Telecom Éireann (see below) and NET (Nitrigín Éireann Teo — employees of Irish Fertilizer Industries Limited may elect persons to the board of NET at one-third worker participation) and the National Rehabilitation Board (the Minister may vary the number of worker directors below the one-third arrangement but the number of worker directors cannot be less than two).

The Telecommunications (Miscellaneous Provisions) Act, 1996, provided for the transfer of certain duties of the Minister for Transport, Energy and Communications to the Director of Telecommunications Regulations. The 1996 Act also provides for additional provisions in respect of the appointment of worker directors to An Bord Telecom Éireann. The number of worker directors in any order under the Worker Participation (State Enterprises) Act shall not exceed one-third of the number that the Minister is entitled to appoint under the Articles of Association of the company. The first election was to have been in 1997 and then every four years. Where employee shareholding schemes have been established, the members of the scheme(s) may nominate to the Minister for appointment to be a shareholder of An Bord Telecom a shareholder of such scheme, or a person who is a former employee of the company (being a person who was entitled to vote in such election). Alternative directors may be appointed on the same basis. The Worker Participation (State Enterprises) Order, 1996 (SI No. 405 of 1996) fixed the number of directors as 12 and the number of worker directors as two.

The above list of companies may be extended by the appropriate Minister (depending on what government department controls the company) by regulation. Sub-board participation applies to all the above companies as well as the following list:

> ACOT, An Foras Talúntais, FÁS, Blood Transfusion Services Board, Board for the Employment of the Blind, Bord Fáilte Éireann, Bord Gáis Éireann, Bord Iascaigh Mhara, Bus Éireann, Bus Átha Cliath, Central Fisheries Board, CERT Limited, An Bord Tráchtála (now part of Enterprise Ireland), Dublin District Milk Board, General Medical Services (Payments) Board, Great Southern Hotels Limited, Hospitals Joint Services Board, Iarnród Éireann, Industrial Development Authority/Forbairt (the latter and parts of the former are now part of Enterprise Ireland), Forfás, Irish National Stud Company Limited, Irish Steel Limited, Kilkenny Design Workshops, Racing Board, RTÉ, Shannon Free Airport Development Company Limited, Údarás na Gaeltachta, VHI.

Two other companies with provision for board and sub-board participation have been subsequently privatised (B&I and Siúcre Éireann).

Board-Level Participation — Worker-Director

Initially, the appropriate Minister determines an election year for each particular semi-state body and also decides on the size of the board with the appropriate number of worker directors. For voting purposes, an employee must be over 18 years of age and be employed for at least one year. All full-time and regular part-time employees are eligible to vote.

There are extremely detailed regulations under the Acts providing for voting procedures to ascertain whether a majority of employees wish to proceed and vote for worker-directors. There are also detailed regulations for the conduct of a ballot and provision for postal voting.

A candidate for worker-director must be an employee who is aged between 18 and 65 years. Each candidate must be employed in a full-time capacity or as a regular part-time employee within the company for at least three years' continuous service. The candidate must be nominated by a "qualified body", which may be a trade union or any other body recognised for collective bargaining within the particular company.

Following the election, the Minister shall be informed of the successful candidates, who must then be appointed to the particular board. A worker-director is entitled to the same fees and expenses as other directors and this should not affect their normal remuneration.

A worker-director may resign their membership of the board by letter addressed to the appropriate Minister. Equally, a Minister may remove a worker-director from office.

Each particular company must take the appropriate steps to amend the memorandum and articles of association to conform with the legislation. Furthermore, each employer may be required by the Minister to bring the Act to the attention of their employees.

The Irish Aviation Authority Act, 1993, provides that the Worker Participation (State Enterprises) Act shall not apply to the Irish Aviation Authority.

Sub-Board Participation

The Worker Participation (State Enterprises) Act, 1988, provided for the introduction of sub-board participation arrangements in the state enterprises listed above. There is provision for the appointment of an "appropriate officer" who will have responsibility for the procedures in relation to sub-board participation. In summary, the appropriate officer is the company secretary (or whoever performs those functions) or the officer in the company who is acceptable to the trade union(s) or other groups recognised for collective bargaining purposes.

The consultative arrangements may be requested as follows:

1. A trade union(s) or any other recognised body within the company which represents a majority of employees (or an application signed by the majority of employees) may apply in writing to the appropriate officer of the company requesting sub-board participation; and

2. The appropriate officer must be satisfied that at least 15 per cent of employees sign the application. That officer must then take a poll of all employees to see if the majority is in favour of the establishment of main or sub-board participation. There are certain time limits within which the poll must be taken. If more than 50 per cent of employees are in favour, arrangements will be made to introduce sub-board participation. If 50 per cent or less are in favour, no further poll may be taken for four years from the date of the result.

The decision of the appropriate officer will be final and cannot be appealed in the event of a dispute concerning eligibility to sign applications for the original request, eligibility to vote at a poll and the clarity of meaning of the question on the ballot paper.

When sub-board participation is requested, the nature of the consultative arrangements by the employee representatives would include the following:

1. A regular exchange of views and clear and reliable information between management and employees on matters that are specified in the agreement;

2. Relevant information from management about certain decisions that are liable to have an effect on employees' interests;

3. Dissemination of information and views arising from the participation;

4. Provision for review and termination of the consultative arrangement;

5. Other factors which management and employees may decide between them.

Annual Reports

Since 1 January 1989, state enterprises to which the legislation applies must describe in the annual reports any action taken during the year to introduce sub-board participation as well as any new participation agreement or alternations made to an existing agreement.

State enterprises must carry the costs of all consultative arrangements.

Duties and Protection of Employee Representatives

In June 1993, the Minister for Enterprise and Employment introduced a Code of Practice under the Industrial Relations Act, 1990, on the duties and responsibilities, as well as the protection and facilities, to be afforded to employee representatives by their employers (SI No. 169 of 1993). This Code of Practice is admissible in any court or tribunal and may be extremely important should an employee be dismissed for trade union activities, provided that that employer is a properly elected employee/union representative.

Employee representatives are formally designated by a trade union and normally participate in negotiations about terms and conditions of employment, including any discussions about disputes or grievances. Representatives should normally have one year's service and be elected in accordance with the union rules or the union/management agreement. Their appointment should be confirmed in writing to the employer by the union, and the employer should advise the representative of the procedures for communicating with management. The number of representatives in any employment should have regard to the size of the employment and the number of trade unions/members.

The duties and responsibilities of employee representatives include:

1. Representing their members fairly and effectively;

2. Participating in negotiation and grievance procedures in accordance with the union/management agreement or the custom and practice of the employment;

3. Co-operating with management in ensuring that there is proper implementation and observance of trade union/management agreements;

4. Using agreed dispute and grievance procedures and the avoidance of action — in particular, unofficial action — which would be contrary to the agreements in place and which would affect the continuity of business;

5. Acting in accordance with the law and the rules of the union and liaising with the full-time union official.

In addition, the representatives should continue to do their own work in the normal way.

Employee representatives who carry out their duties in line with this Code of Practice should not be dismissed or suffer disadvantage as a result. If an employer considers that a representative is acting beyond that representative's usual authority, or in a manner which is damaging to the employer, the employer should raise the matter first with the representative and, if still dissatisfied, the matter should then be referred to the trade union. There is nothing prohibiting the employer from dismissing the representative, for example, if there were a genuine redundancy, as long as there is fair selection for redundancy.

The employer must afford the representative reasonable facilities so that the representative can carry out their duties; for example, reasonable time off (with appropriate employer permission) for trade union meetings and training courses. The representative should be given reasonable access to union members and, if there is a problem, reasonable access to management as well. The representative should also be allowed to collect union dues and distribute union information. The payment of wages/salary during time off for training courses and representation should be discussed in advance with management.

TRANSNATIONAL INFORMATION AND CONSULTATION OF EMPLOYEES ACT, 1996

This Act implemented Council Directive 94/45/EC, which provided for the establishment of transnational arrangements for the information and consultation of employees in Community-scale undertakings and Community-scale groups of undertakings. It also provided for the establishment of European Works Councils. These arrangements are for the purposes of providing information to and consultation with employees. These arrangements are not for the purposes of bargaining in respect of terms and conditions of employment, nor is there provision for trade union recognition. The Act came into operation on 22 September 1996 (Commencement Order (SI No. 276 of 1996)).

Employments could be exempted from the provisions of the Directive if they had an agreement covering the workforce which provided for the transnational information and consultation of employees prior to the commencement of the Act.

Under the Act, *Community-scale undertakings* are any undertaking with at least 1,000 employees within the Member States and where there are at least 150 employees in two Member States; while *Community-scale group of undertakings* are where there are at least 1,000 employees in the Member States and where there are at least 150 employees in a group undertaking in two Member States. "Community" refers to all the Member States of the European Union as well as Norway, Iceland and Liechtenstein, but excludes the United

Kingdom. There is an obligation (s. 8) either to establish a European Works Council or to make arrangements for the provision of information to and consultation of employees. The central management shall be responsible for the setting up of the various arrangements. If central management is not located within a Member State, then the central management's representative agent in a Member State shall be responsible, or failing that, the management in the Member State where there is the greatest number of employees. Then the management on its own initiative or at the written request of at least 100 employees spread over two undertakings in two Member States shall initiate negotiations for the establishment of an information and consultation arrangement (s. 10). These negotiations are to take place with a Special Negotiating Body whose function is to negotiate an agreement and structure for the negotiation and consultation arrangements (s. 11). Employee representatives shall be elected in accordance with the rules in the Act (First Schedule). The negotiation can lead to an arrangement of a European Employees' Forum, but the parties may also agree to establish one or more information and consultation procedures instead of such a Forum. If an agreement requires a Forum, the agreement shall make provision for the composition, the number of members, the allocation of seats and the term of office; the functions and procedure for information and consultation; the venue, frequency and duration of meetings; and the financial and other resources to be allocated to the Forum. If, alternatively, there is an agreement for procedures on consultation, provision must be made for procedures and the issues for information and consultation. The journal *Industrial Relations News* has published a number of these agreements (e.g. *The Dalgety European Forum Agreement* (see IRN 11, 13 March 1997)).

In the event that the Special Negotiating Body and the central management agree, or where central management refuses to commence negotiations within six months of the employees' request, or where after three years from the date of the request the parties were unable to conclude an agreement, then a European Works Council shall be established (s. 13 and Second Schedule). These are known as subsidiary requirements.

The European Works Council shall have at least three and not more than 30 employee members, who shall be elected in the same manner as those elected to the Special Negotiating Body. If there is no election, the members shall be appointed. There are additional provisions for extra members where there are large employments. Committees may be drawn up as appropriate. The European Works Council shall meet with central management at least once per year to be informed and consulted on the basis of a report drawn up by central management on the progress of the business and its prospects. Paragraph 5(2) of the Schedule provides:

> The meeting shall relate in particular to the structure, economic and financial situation and probable trends in employment, investments and substantial changes concerning the organisation, introduction of new working methods or production processes, transfer of production, mergers, cutbacks or closures of undertakings, establishments or important parts thereof, and collective redundancies.

Where there are exceptional circumstances affecting employees, in particular relating to relocation, closure of establishment or collective redundancies, the Works Council has a right to be informed and a right to meet central management. Central management shall meet all operating expenses and also the funding equivalent of one expert per meeting.

Any member of a Special Negotiating Body, a European Employees' Forum, a European Works Council or an employee's representative to an information and consultation procedure must not disclose any information given to him in confidence. Central management may withhold commercially sensitive information. Matters of information may be referred to an arbitrator appointed by the Minister. Employees' representatives are protected from dismissal, any change in their terms and conditions of employment or any other action prejudicial to their employment.

There is also provision for reference to an arbitrator of disputes concerning the interpretation or operation of agreements. If the parties cannot agree an arbitrator, then either party can make application to the Labour Court for the appointment of an arbitrator. Having heard the case, the arbitrator shall make their determination, which may only be appealed to a court on a point of law. There is also provision for offences, prosecution and penalties for various breaches under the Act (e.g. disclosure of financial information).

The Labour Court has issued a decision in one European Works Council case (noted in *SIPTU Report*, October 1998 at p. 15) concerning *Baxter Healthcare*. The case concerned the Baxter European Forum. The employees of the Irish operation are entitled to two representatives on the Forum. Management wanted one SIPTU representative and one non-union representative. The Labour Court recommended that the representatives be selected by a single election conducted by proportional representation, with all employees employed on the day of the election being entitled to vote. An "independent outsider" should be appointed to supervise the ballot and the names of the candidates and their location were to be the only information given on the ballot paper. In the event of both seats being filled by representatives of the one group, then the substitute delegate's seat should be filled from the other group.

Proposed Directive

There is a proposed EU Directive on information and consultation at national level, which may provide for such information and consultation in all EU firms where there are over 50 employees. The areas of consultation include economic/strategic matters, decisions on work organisation, contractual relations and trends in employment.

PARTNERSHIP 2000

The national agreement initiated in December 1996, "Partnership 2000 for Inclusion, Employment and Competitiveness", represented a strategic approach to lead the Irish economy and society into the twenty-first century and to provide for partnership arrangements in all aspects of working life. The key aspects of the agreement in relation to employee participation are as follows (Partnership 2000, 9.1):

> An objective of this Partnership is to extend partnership arrangements at enterprise level. Such arrangements are already taking place in different ways in a variety of employments. These arrangements have not been documented systematically and consequently are probably underestimated. International and domestic experience suggest that further development of the partnership approach at enterprise level will enhance the competitiveness of firms, the quality of

the work environment and the access of employees to lifelong learning.

The National Economic and Social Council (NESC) suggested that the challenge is to encourage firms, employees and unions to advance from experiment to comprehensive innovation; encourage the development of new models; and recognise the different starting points of different enterprises and employees. The NESC concluded that competitiveness can be greatly assisted by partnerships at enterprise level which provide a "potentially powerful means of accelerating innovation". The parties to Partnership 2000 subscribed to these conclusions and recommendations. The Government and Social Partners agreed that a National Framework be established to develop partnership at enterprise level and to provide encouragement, training, information and support to employers and employees/representatives. Partnership was defined as:

> . . . an active relationship based on recognition of a common interest to secure the competitiveness, viability and prosperity of the enterprise. It involves a continuing commitment by employees to improvements in quality and efficiency; and the acceptance of employers of employees as stakeholders with rights and interests to be considered in the context of major decisions effecting their employment.

> Partnership involves common ownership of the resolution of challenges, involving the direct participation of employees/representatives and an investment in their training, development and working environment.

The objectives of enterprise partnerships are:

- To enhance the prosperity and success of the enterprise;

- To create the basis and arrangements for discussion of major decisions affecting the organisation's future;

- To engage all stakeholders' ideas, abilities and commitment; and

- To enhance the quality of the work environment.

This National Framework for Partnership for Competitive Enterprises does not attempt to impose any single structure or model of

partnership. Topics appropriate for discussion at enterprise level include employee involvement for competitiveness; training; personal
development and support; equality of opportunities, representational
arrangements, forms of financial involvement (see below), occupational health and safety and the work environment, composition of
the workforce, co-operation with change including new forms of work
organisation, problem-solving and conflict avoidance and adaptabil-
ity, flexibility and innovation. The Social Partners (including IBEC
and ICTU) supported the establishment of the National Centre for
Partnership.

In order to provide for this Partnership in respect of tax-efficient
financial participation, recent Finance Acts have provided for tax efficient methods of saving and purchasing of shares in employing
companies. This is considered in Chapter 2, "The Contract of Employment".

FINANCIAL PARTICIPATION

There are many different forms of financial participation, including
profit-sharing, share ownership and share options. Financial participation may be defined as a share of the profit or wealth of an enterprise, distributed by employers in addition to wages and direct
incentives. Even before Partnership 2000, during the 1980s there
was considerable interest in the concept of profit-sharing. "Building
on Reality", the 1984–87 National Plan, stated:

> . . . if, through profit-sharing or employee shareholding, em-
> ployees share in profits, or own part of their own company,
> they have a strong incentive to take a more enlightened atti-
> tude to industrial change. By having a stake in the business in
> which they work, employees have a greater incentive to pro-
> mote increased efficiency and profitability in their companies.

Various forms of financial participation shall now be considered.

Share Options

Many employments provide for share options where an employee
may purchase shares in the future at the current price. This obviously provides for a gain where the shares increase in value over
time. Such purchases are usually "staggered" over a period of time.

There may be provision for the putting aside of monies to purchase shares in the future if the plan is approved by the Revenue Commissioners. The shares can be purchased at a time when the shares are high in value, thus increasing the gain.

There were special provisions for approved share option schemes under the Finance Act, 1986, but these provisions were repealed; hence the preferential rules contained in that Act apply to share options granted after 29 January 1992.

Save-as-You-Earn Schemes

The Finance Act, 1999, provided for a savings scheme with certain tax advantages so that employees may buy shares in the future. This is carried out by way of share option and the key tax advantage is that employees are granted an option to buy shares at a fixed price with their money saved under the scheme. The share price may be discounted as approved by the Revenue Commissioners. The actual share option is granted tax-free. There are two aspects to these Schemes:

1. An approved savings-related share option scheme;

2. A certified contractual savings scheme

Only money from such a savings scheme can be used to fund the purchase of shares allocated to employees under the share option scheme. The price at which shares may be purchased on exercise of the option must be separate on the date the option is first granted and it cannot be at a discount of more than 25 per cent from the market value of the shares at that time. No benefit-in-kind income tax is charged to the employee for receiving a share option in the first place and no income tax can be levied in respect of the discount received at the time the share option is exercised. However, if the shares are later sold at a profit, then this is subject to capital gains tax (currently at the rate of 20 per cent). An income tax payment may arise if the option is exercised within three years of it being granted.

The costs of establishing a savings-related share option scheme will be allowed as a deduction for corporation tax purposes. Contractual savings schemes set up in conjunction with these share option schemes also benefit from tax exemptions. Bonus or interest payments under these schemes are to be exempt from income tax if it is

used in conjunction with an approved share option scheme. Under
the scheme, employees may save for a period of three, five or seven
years. At the end of the savings period, the money may be taken out
the scheme as a cash lump sum without buying shares (allowing an
"out" clause if the share price happens to collapse in the meantime).
These schemes have to be approved by the Revenue Commissioners.
All employees and full-time directors must have access to the scheme
on similar terms. A qualifying period may be set but this may be no
longer than three years. (The qualifying period for the existing approved profit-sharing schemes is currently five years but this is also
to be reduced to three years.)

Employees and directors cannot take part in a scheme if they have
or have had in the previous 12 months more than 15 per cent of the
ordinary share capital in a "close company". A "close company" is defined as either the company in which the shares are bought, a company which controls the company in which the shares are bought or a
member of a consortium which owns that company.

The shares must be of a class quoted on a recognised stock exchange and must be in a company which is not under the control of
another company (unless of course the controlling company shares
are quoted on a stock exchange). This appears to effectively exclude
the small to medium-sized enterprise sector in the scheme.

Under normal circumstances, the share options must not be capable of being exercised more than six months after the bonus date (i.e.,
completion date of the contractual savings scheme). There may be
exceptions to this, which include death or cessation of employment
through injury, disability, redundancy or reaching pension age.

The maximum monthly savings allowed under the contractual
savings schemes is £250 and the minimum saving is £100, which may
be varied by the Minister for Finance.

Approved Profit Sharing

The Finance Act, 1982 (as amended by the 1997 Finance Act), provided for profit-sharing schemes. Such schemes allow employees to
receive profits of a company in shares. Such arrangements are tax
efficient if the shares are held for three years, as no income tax is
paid. If the shares are sold within two years, all tax benefits are lost.
The only liability is that, when the shares are sold, there is a capital
gains tax liability if there is an increase in value. Equally, the com-

pany receives tax relief on monies it puts into the scheme. These shares are the normal shares and must be issued on the same basis to all employees. Again, such an arrangement requires the establishment of a trust and the appointment of trustees. The maximum amount that may be transferred in any one year is £10,000.

Employee Share Ownership Plans

The Finance Act, 1997, as amended by the Finance Act, 1999, provides for employee share ownership plans. Under such a scheme the total workforce in an enterprise may purchase shares under a trust. Agreement is reached between the employee representatives and the employer so that employees may purchase equity in the company by way of trust and the Employee Share Ownership Trust is established with trustees. Trustees comprise employer and employee representatives and independent trustees approved of by the Revenue Commissioners. The Trust then purchases shares using funds arising from savings resulting from organisational change, agreed profit-share and bank loans. The trust may also secure the nomination of a board member of the company. If the shares remain in the trust and are not distributed, their value is free from income tax and capital gains tax. If the shares leave the trust through an approved profit-sharing scheme then they retain the income tax exemption but are only liable to capital gains tax for the last three years while they are in an approved profit-sharing scheme. These trusts are set up for 20-year periods, so that employees can cash their shares on retirement or on leaving the company. Such trusts were set up in Telecom Éireann and Aer Lingus.

It may be useful to note that the Taxes Consolidation Act, 1997, contains all the legislation then in operation in respect of such matters subject, of course, to amendment by subsequent Finance Acts.

Publication of Accounts

Employee representatives may find the publication of company accounts useful in negotiation. These accounts would be available in the Companies Office, Parnell Square, Dublin 1. The Companies (Amendment) Act, 1986, as amended by the European Communities Accounts Regulations, 1993 (SI No. 396 of 1993), translates the provisions of the Fourth EC Company Law Directive, which dealt with the content and publication of the annual accounts of public and private limited companies, into Irish law (excluding companies not trading for profit or companies not having a share capital for charitable/religious purposes). The relevant accounts are the balance sheets, profit and loss accounts and notes to these accounts. The format of such accounts is specified and there are certain rules concerning times to be declared in the accounts, valuation rules of assets and liabilities and the information to be provided by way of notes to the accounts. The Directive also provides regulations regarding the company's annual report and the auditors' report on the company's accounts. In essence, a true and fair view of the company's operations must be given and the Directive provides that there may be a departure from the Directive's provisions in order to give such a true and fair view.

General References

Brennan, N., F.J. O'Brien and A. Pierce (1991), *Financial Accounting and Reporting in Ireland*, Dublin: Oak Tree Press.

Brennan, N., F.J. O'Brien and A. Pierce (1992), *A Survey of Irish Published Accounts*, Second edition, Dublin: Oak Tree Press.

Courtney, T.B. (1994), *The Law of Private Companies*, Dublin: Butterworths.

"European Works Council: What the Delegates Say", *Industrial Relations News*, IRN 9, 26 February 1998.

Kelly, A. (1989), "The Worker Director in Irish Industrial Relations", in *Industrial Relations in Ireland, Contemporary Issues and Developments*, Department of Industrial Relations, UCD.

Kerr, A. (1990), *Worker Participation (State Enterprises) Act, 1988, Irish Law Statutes Annotated*, Dublin: Sweet and Maxwell.

Kerr, A. (1997), *Transnational Information and Consultation of Employees Act, 1996, Irish Law Statutes Annotated*, June, Dublin: Sweet and Maxwell.

Kerr, A. and G. Whyte (1985), *Irish Trade Union Law*, Dublin: Professional Books.

Meenan, F. (1986), "Profit Sharing", *Gazette of the Incorporated Law Society of Ireland*, July/August.

Morrissey, T. (1989), "Employee Participation Sub-Board Level", in *Industrial Relations in Ireland, Contemporary Issues and Developments*, Department of Industrial Relations, UCD.

Partnership 2000 for Inclusion, Employment and Competitiveness, December 1996, Stationery Office, Dublin.

"Partnership: Myth or Reality?" *Industrial Relations News*, IRN 11, 13 March 1997.

Text of ICTU Guidelines on Gainsharing, Profit Sharing and ESOPs, *Industrial Relations News*, IRN 15, 22 April 1999.

"The Dalgety European Forum Agreement", Supplement, *Industrial Relations News*, IRN 11, 13 March 1997.

Chapter Thirteen

ORGANISATION OF WORKING TIME

ORGANISATION OF WORKING TIME ACT, 1997

The Organisation of Working Time Act, 1997 (and Regulations made under the Safety, Health and Welfare at Work Act, 1989) transposes into Irish law Council Directive 93/104/EC concerning certain aspects of the Organisation of Working Time. In essence, it provides for the 48-hour week and there are transitional provisions for this from 1998 to 2001. The 1997 Act repeals the Conditions of Employment Acts, 1936 and 1944, the Night Work (Bakeries) Acts, 1936–1981, and the Shops (Conditions of Employment) Act, 1938 and 1942, which regulated the hours of work in industry and shops respectively. There are also Codes of Practice under the legislation (e.g. the Code of Practice on Compensatory Rest, SI No. 44 of 1998 below). The various provisions of the Act came into operation on 30 September 1997, 30 November 1998 and 1 March 1998 (The Organisation of Working Time Act, 1997 (Commencement) Order 1997 (SI No. 392 of 1997)).

The 1997 Act also repeals the Holidays (Employees) Acts, 1973–1991 and section 4 of the Worker Protection (Regular Part-Time Employees) Act, 1991, in respect of holidays (see Chapter 4).

As stated, this Directive was adopted as a health and safety measure on the basis of Article 118a of the EC Treaty, which provides (*inter alia*):

> . . . Member States shall pay particular attention to encouraging improvements especially in the working environment, as regards the health and safety of workers, and shall set as their objective the harmonisation of conditions in this area, while maintaining the improvements made . . .

In the *United Kingdom of Great Britain and Northern Ireland* v *Council of the European Union* ([1997] IRLR 30), the UK applied to the ECJ requesting it to annul the "Working Time Directive" or to annul various provisions to include breaks, weekly rest periods, that Sunday be included in weekly rest periods, the 48-hour working week and the four weeks' paid annual leave, on the basis that the Directive had not been adopted correctly. The application was essentially on the basis that there was no genuine and objective link between health and safety and working time. The Court turned down the application (except for the issue of Sunday working; see below) on the basis that the Directive had been adopted correctly and that:

> There is nothing in the wording of Article 118a to indicate that the concepts of "working environment", "safety" and "health" as used in that provision should . . . be interpreted restrictively, and not as embracing all factors, physical or otherwise, capable of affecting the health and safety of the worker in his working environment.

In summary, the Organisation of Working Time Act, 1997, provides statutory rights for employees in respect of rest, maximum working time and holidays and the key provisions are as follows:

- Maximum average net weekly working time of 48 hours;

- A daily break of 11 consecutive hours;

- Rest breaks while at work;

- A weekly break of 24 consecutive hours;

- Maximum average night working of eight hours;

- Maximum hours of work for night workers engaged in work involving special hazards or a heavy physical or mental strain — an absolute limit of eight hours in a 24-hour period.

Transitional Provisions

The 48-hour working week came into effect generally on 1 March 1998; however, there are transitional provisions which provide that employees may work up to 60 hours per week from 1 March 1998 to 28 February 1999; and up to 55 hours per week from 1 March 1999 to 29 February 2000. The 48-hour week comes into effect in respect of all employees who fall within the scope of the Act on 1 March 2000.

However, to work the maximum permitted hours during 1998 and 1999, an agreement must be reached by the parties and approved by the Labour Court. The Fifth Schedule to the Act details the procedures to be observed in implementing the transitional provisions.

Variation of Working Time

The specific provisions of the Act relating to rest times may be varied by Regulations; through legally binding collective agreements made under the Act and approved by the Labour Court; through registered employment agreements or employment regulation orders; or where there are unforeseeable circumstances (e.g. emergencies).

The rest times and averaging periods for weekly working hours may be varied as follows:

Section 6(1) provides for circumstances:

- Where Regulations exempt certain activities from rest breaks, daily and weekly rest periods (see General Exemption Regulations (SI No. 21 of 1998) below);

- Where collective agreements providing for a similar exemption have been concluded by the parties and approved by the Labour Court (registered employment agreements and employment regulation orders may also provide for the variation orders, but not of the working time provisions).

Section 6(2) provides for circumstances:

- Where shift workers who can change shift and cannot themselves avail of the rest period are exempted (in respect of the daily and weekly rest periods);

- Where persons employed in activities consisting of periods of work spread out over the day are exempted (in respect of the daily and weekly rest periods);

- Where employers are exempted from the obligation to provide daily and weekly rest periods and rest breaks due to exceptional circumstances or an emergency, including an accident or an imminent risk of an accident, or otherwise to the occurrence of unusual and unforeseeable circumstances beyond the employer's control.

Where statutory rest times are varied in any of the circumstances mentioned above, the employer must ensure that the employee has available to themselves:

1. Equivalent compensatory rest; or

2. Where this is not possible for objective reasons, appropriate protection.

General Principles of and Arrangements for Equivalent Compensatory Rest and Appropriate Protection

The Code of Practice on Compensatory Rest (Organisation of Working Time (Code of Practice on Compensatory Rest and Related Matters) (Declaration) Order, 1998 (SI No. 44 of 1998)) was prepared by the Labour Relations Commission. This Code of Practice was developed in agreement with IBEC, ICTU, the Labour Court, the Department of Enterprise, Trade and Employment and the Irish Co-operative Organisation Society. The National Authority of Occupational Safety and Health was also consulted. The failure on the part of an employer to comply with the Code will not render the employer liable to criminal or civil proceedings; however, the Code shall be admissible before a court, a Rights Commissioner or the Labour Court in proceedings under the 1997 Act.

The Code states that appropriate rest breaks are vital for the health and safety of the worker and are important in the efficient and effective operation of the workplace. Exempted employees who lose out on their statutory rest entitlements should receive compensatory rest as soon as possible afterwards. However, there is no specific time period within which compensatory rest must be given under the Act or the Directive.

The Code of Practice usefully sets out examples of compensatory rest for a number of different work situations, and they are as follows:

Example 1

> *An exempted employee works Monday to Friday, 9.00a.m. to 5.30p.m. He/she works in an industry which cannot be interrupted on technical grounds (an exempted activity). For two weeks per month, that employee is "on call" for maintenance work. On Wednesday night, he/she is called out to perform emergency work. The callout commences at 8.30p.m. and finishes at 11.30p.m. The employee's entitlement to 11 hours' consecutive rest is interrupted. Prior to the callout, the employee had received three hours rest and after the callout he/she received 9.5 hours rest. In total, the employee received 12.5 hours rest; therefore no further entitlement to rest arises as an exemption applies (see sections 2(7)(i) and 2(7)(ii) of this Code).*
>
> *If no exemption applied, then the employee is entitled to the full 11 consecutive hours' rest from the end of the callout.*

Example 2

> *Under an exemption provided for in a collective agreement approved of by the Labour Court, an employee is permitted to work 14 consecutive 8-hour days. In those circumstances, the employee, in respect of that period, has a minimum entitlement of two periods of 24 hours' compensatory rest plus two periods of 11 consecutive hours' daily rest. The employee is given three consecutive periods of 24 hours off immediately after the 14 consecutive working days. This goes beyond the requirement to give two periods of 24 hours' compensatory rest preceded by the relevant daily rest requirement and is, therefore, acceptable.*

Example 3

> *An employee is entitled to a break of at least 15 minutes after working for 4½ hours. If an exemption applies, the taking of the break may be delayed but compensatory rest should be provided. In this circumstance, the employee is given a later break of 15 minutes or breaks totalling 15 minutes by way of compensatory rest before the end of the day. No further compensatory rest is required.*

Example 4

> *An exempted employee works a three-cycle rotating shift pattern:*
>
> | | |
> |---|---|
> | Week 1 | *8 a.m. – 4 p.m.* |
> | Week 2 | *4 p.m. – 12 a.m.* |
> | Week 3 | *12 a.m. – 8 a.m.* |
>
> *In a 5-over-7-day roster, no changeover provides for less than 48 hours' rest. Therefore, no entitlement to compensatory rest arises. In a 6-over-7-day roster, however, the changeover between week 2 and week 3 provides only for 24 hours' rest.*
>
> *In this circumstance, the exempted employee is entitled to compensatory rest of 11 consecutive hours.*

The Code of Practice states that the 11 consecutive hours' interval between shifts is required for reasons of health and safety to ensure that employees have a minimum period of sleep. From a health and safety point of view, it is dangerous for employees to miss out on a minimum number of hours' sleep and then report to work. When there is any variation of the 11 hours of statutory rest permitted under the Act, the employer should ensure that the health and safety requirements for adequate compensatory rest are sufficient in the circumstances pertaining in that employment. This is equally applicable to the weekly rest provision. Consideration should be given to the distance between home and employment in order to ensure that adequate rest is obtained.

Typically in industry, callout arrangements provide for eight hours' consecutive rest before returning to work. Such arrangements will, where the exemption is applicable, continue to be acceptable provided that the compensatory rest requirements are fulfilled.

Where variation of the weekly statutory rest periods is permitted under the 1997 Act, the employer concerned should have regard to the circumstances pertaining in that employment and to the health and safety requirements for adequate rest for their employees.

If it is not possible for an employer to provide the equivalent rest period, the employer may make arrangements for compensation, which shall not be monetary compensation or some other material benefit. However, it may be something that will improve the physical conditions or amenities at work. A common sense approach should be taken by employers and employees in this situation, taking into account the circumstances in the employment and health and safety. Such compensation may include:

1. Enhanced environmental conditions to accommodate regular long periods of attendance at work;

2. Refreshment facilities, recreational and reading material;

3. Appropriate facilities/amenities such as television, radio and music;

4. Alleviating monotonous work or isolation;

5. Transport to and from work where appropriate.

The Department of Enterprise, Trade and Employment has set up a Monitoring Committee to discuss and resolve operational problems in relation to the legislation.

Application of the Act

The Act applies to all work with the exception of the Garda Síochána and the Defence Forces (subject to an order amending same).

Part II of the Act (minimum rest periods and other aspects of working time) shall not apply to:

- Persons engaged in sea fishing, other work at sea, or the activities of a doctor in training; or

- A person who is employed by a relative (spouse, father, mother, grandfather, grandmother, stepfather, stepmother, son, daughter, grandson, granddaughter, stepson, stepdaughter, brother, sister, half-brother or half-sister) and is a member of that relative's household, and whose place of employment is a private dwelling house or a farm in or on which the person and the relative reside; or

- A person the duration of whose working time (except any minimum period of time that is stipulated by the employer) is decided by themselves whether or not provision for the making of such decision is made in their contract of employment.

The Minister for Labour, Trade and Consumer Affairs (Enterprise, Trade and Employment (Delegation of Ministerial Functions) (No. 2) Order, 1997 (SI No. 330 of 1997)), after consultation with any other Government Minister, may by regulation exempt persons from the application of the Act from the following activities:

- Involving or connected with the transport (by whatever means) of goods or persons; or

- In the civil protection services where, if the provisions of Act were to apply, the efficient operation of the service concerned would be adversely affected.

Of course, the provisions in relation to holidays shall apply (see Chapter 4).

Some of these exemptions have been set out as follows:

1. The Organisation of Working Time (Exemption of Transport Activities) Regulations, 1998 (SI No. 20 of 1998), provides that persons employed in a transport activity as defined shall be exempt from the application of the Act in respect of the daily rest period, rests and intervals at work, weekly rest periods, weekly working hours and nightly working hours. These exemptions only apply if the person is fully engaged in that particular industry. The defined activities include any continuing activity (including safety) consisting of or connected with any vehicle, train, vessel (including the navigation of inland waterways) or any other means of transport of goods or persons. However, employees who carry out an administrative function that is not directly related to the operation of such transport do not fall within this exemption.

    In *Coastal Line Container Terminal Limited* v *SIPTU* (DWT 994) the substance of the complaint was that the employee crane drivers were not provided with compensatory rest under paragraph 4 of the Working Time (General Exemptions) Regulations, 1998 (SI No. 21 of 1998). The employer maintained that such employees were excluded as they fell within the scope of the Organisation of Working Time (Exemption of Transport Activities) Regulations, 1998 (SI No. 20 of 1998). The employer operates a terminal at Dublin Port where the transport of container goods to and from the UK are loaded and discharged by the employee crane drivers.

In summary, the Court determined that the employees are dock workers and involved in the provision of services at harbour as contained in paragraph 3(d)(ii) of the General Exemption Regulations (SI No. 21 of 1998). Therefore they are not covered by the exemptions. Accordingly, the employer should ensure that each of the crane drivers has available a rest period and break so as to comply with the provisions of the Working Time (General Exemptions) Regulations, 1998 (SI No. 21 of 1998).

2. The Organisation of Working Time (Exemption of Civil Protection Services) Regulations, 1998 (SI No. 52 of 1998), provide that the same exemptions apply to the following specified activities:

(i) The activity of a person employed in a prison (including St Patrick's Institution) or places of detention (provided under Section 2 of the Prisons Act, 1970), that involves the maintenance of security in that prison or place of detention or the control or care of prisoners and which cannot be carried on within the normal rostering schedules applicable to that prison or place of detention;

(ii) The activity of a person employed by a fire authority (within the meaning of the Fire Services Act, 1981) in the position commonly known as retained fire-fighter;

(iii) The activity of a person, other than a member of the Garda Síochána, employed as an authorised officer (within the meaning of the Air Navigation and Transport Acts, 1950 to 1988 and any enactment amending or extending those Acts);

(iv) The activity of a person employed by Dublin Port Company as a member of its Harbour Police;

(v) The activity of a person employed in the Irish Marine Emergency Service not being an activity of a clerical nature.

3. The Organisation of Working Time (General Exemptions) Regulations, 1998 (SI No. 21 of 1998) which came into effect on 1 March 1998, provide that the following group of persons will be exempt from the applications of Section 11 (daily rest period), Section 12 (rest and intervals at work), Section 13 (weekly rest periods) and Section 16 (nightly working hours). The employee must be "wholly or mainly employed" in the activity concerned. The ex-

emptions also do not apply if an employee falls within a class of
employee covered under a joint labour committee or is a special
category worker (e.g. an employee whose work involves special
hazards or heavy physical or mental strain). The group of activities are:

(i)   An activity in which the employee is regularly required by the
      employer to travel distances of significant length, either from
      their home to the workplace or from one workplace to another
      workplace (e.g. salespersons);

(ii) An activity of a security or surveillance nature, the purpose of
      which is to protect persons or property which requires the
      continuous presence of the employee at a particular place or
      places, and, in particular, the activities of a security guard,
      caretaker or security firm.

(iii) Activities in the economy or public service where the rate of
      production or the nature of services will vary from time to
      time and where there should be continuity of production or
      service, in particular in any of the following: persons working
      in a hospital or residential institution, services at a harbour
      or airport, production in the media and telecommunications
      industries, provision of ambulance, fire and civil protection
      services, production, transmission or distribution of gas, wa-
      ter or electricity, collection of household refuse, operation of
      an incineration plant, any industrial activity which for tech-
      nical reasons cannot be interrupted, research and develop-
      ment, agriculture and tourism.

Regulation 5 of the Regulations provides that:

1. An employer shall not require an employee to whom this exemption applies to work during a shift or other period of work that is
   of more than six hours' duration without allowing them a break of
   such duration as the employer determines;

2. In determining the duration of such a break, the employer shall
   have due regard to the need to protect the health, safety and com-
   fort of the employee and the general principle concerning the prevention and avoidance of risk in the workplace.

Regulation 4 of these Regulations provides that if an employee is not entitled, by reason of this exemption, to the rest period and break, the employer shall ensure that the employee has available to themselves a rest period and a break that in all the circumstances can reasonably be regarded as equivalent to the first mentioned rest period or break.

Regulation 6 of the Regulations provides that nothing in the Regulations shall override a provision or provisions of a more beneficial kind to the employee concerned which is or are contained in:

1. A collective agreement referred to in section 4(5) of the Act;

2. A registered employment agreement; or

3. An employment regulation order.

Daily Rest Period

An employee shall be entitled to a rest period of not less than 11 consecutive hours in each period of 24 hours during which he or she works for his or her employer.

Employees covered under the Organisation of Working Time (Exemption of Transport Activities) Regulations, 1998 (SI No. 20 of 1998), the Organisation of Working Time (General Exemption) Regulations (SI No 21 of 1998), and the Organisation of Working Time (Exemption of Civil Protection Services) Regulations, 1998 (SI No. 52 of 1998) are exempted from this provision.

Rest and Intervals at Work

An employer shall not require an employee to work for a period of more than four-and-a-half hours without allowing them a break of least 15 minutes.

An employer shall not require an employee to work for a period of more than six hours without allowing them a break of at least 30 minutes. Such a break may include the 15-minute break. A break allowed to an employee at the end of the working day shall not be regarded as satisfying either of these requirements. The Minister may make regulations in respect of a specified class of employee that the minimum period of a break shall be more than 30 minutes but under one hour.

The Organisation of Working Time (Breaks at Work for Shop Employees) Regulations, 1998 (SI No. 57 of 1998), provides that shop employees whose hours of work include the period from 1.30 p.m. to 2.30 p.m. shall, after six hours work, be allowed a break of one hour which must commence between those hours. However, the break may not occur at the end of the working day. A *shop* includes:

1. Any premises in which any retail trade or business (this is defined as a barber or hairdresser, the business of hiring goods otherwise than for use in a trade or business, a pawnbroker or the business of retail sales by auction) is carried on;

2. Any premises in which goods are received direct from customers for cleaning, repairing, altering or laundering;

3. Any wholesale shop (means any premises occupied by a wholesale dealer or merchant where goods are kept for sale wholesale to customers resorting to the premises);

4. Any warehouse occupied:

    (i) for the purpose of a retail trade or business, by the person carrying on such retail trade or business; or

    (ii) by a wholesale dealer or merchant for the purposes of the business carried on by him or her in a wholesale shop;

but does not include

1. Premises which are not used as part of a shop or wholesale shop

2. Any premises or part of the premises which is used for a hotel, the preparation of food or catering, or any business carried on pursuant to an intoxicating liquor licence.

Weekly Rest Periods

A *daily rest period* is a period of 11 hours in any 24-hour period in which the employee works for their employer. In each period of seven days, an employee shall in addition be entitled to a rest period of at least 24 consecutive hours. An employer may, however, provide the employee a second 24-hour rest period in the following period of seven days, rather than this 24-hour break in every seven days. In other words, 48 hours in a fortnight, provided that the daily rest period of 11 hours immediately precedes the 48 hours off. Unless an employee is obliged by their contract of employment to work on a Sunday, one of the rest periods must include a Sunday.

In *The United Kingdom of Great Britain and Northern Ireland* v *Council of the European Union* (see above), the European Court of Justice held that there was no explanation as to why Sunday as a weekly resting day is more closely connected with the health and safety of workers than any other day.

Employees covered under the Organisation of Working Time (Exemption of Transport Activities) Regulations, 1998 (SI No. 20 of 1998), the Organisation of Working Time (General Exemption) Regulations (SI No 21 of 1998), the Organisation of Working Time (Exemption of Civil Protection Services) Regulations, 1998 (SI No. 52 of 1998) are exempted from this provision.

Sunday Working

Section 14 of the 1997 Act sets out the statutory rights for employees in respect of Sunday working. In essence, there is a premium for Sunday working. Any employee who is required to work on a Sunday and where the fact that they have to work on a Sunday has not been taken into account in the determination of their pay, shall be compensated by:

1. The payment to the employee of a reasonable allowance having regard to all the circumstances, or

2. Increasing the employee's rate of pay by a reasonable amount having regard to all the circumstances, or

3. Granting the employee reasonable paid time-off from work having regard to all the circumstances, or

4. A combination of two or more of the above means.

Where there are proceedings before a rights commissioner or the Labour Court that this section of the Act has not been complied with, then the adjudicating bodies shall compare the complainant's value or rate of pay to a comparable employee in the same sector of industry.

In *Group 4 Securitas* v *SIPTU* (DWT 996), an individual employee applied for an increase in the £5.00 Sunday premium which is paid to all employees in unionised employment in the security industry. The rate was originally agreed in 1984. Both parties agreed that this was a test case, which would have implications for the security industry in general. The rights commissioner issued her decision on 15 December 1998. The rights commissioner held that it was not a valid claim. The Court determined that section 14(1) of the Organisation of Working Time Act, 1997, clearly states that where an employee's pay has not taken account of the requirement to work on Sunday, they shall be compensated. However, in this case the employee was paid an allowance for working on Sundays and therefore did not have a case under the Act. Further, the Court did not consider that section 14, under which the claim had been brought, allows for a claim for enhancement of the rate.

Sunday Working in the Retail Trade

A Code of Practice on Sunday working in the retail trade was made on 19 November 1998 (SI No. 444 of 1998) in relation to the Sunday work supplemental provisions. In the preparation of the Code of Practice, submissions were sought from IBEC, ICTU, MANDATE and SIPTU. Such views were taken into account in the preparation of the Code of Practice. The retail trade comprises many varied groups of businesses such as drapery, grocery, hardware or fast food, operating in diverse business environments.

The Code is designed to assist employers, employees and their representatives in observing the 1997 Act in relation to Sunday working in the retail trade and to ensure that best practices are operated by all employers for those employees who service that sector of industry through Sunday working. Sunday hours of work and rostering arrangements have a significant impact on the quality of life of workers as well as being important to the efficient operation of the enterprise. Therefore, there should be discussion and consultation between the employer and employee and their representatives, as appropriate. Failure to observe the Code shall not render a person liable to civil or criminal proceedings. However, the Code shall be admissible in evidence before a court, the Labour Court or a rights commissioner in proceedings under the Act.

General Principles of Compensatory Arrangements for Sunday Working in the Retail Trade

The following are guidelines on compensatory arrangements for Sunday working:

> Where a collective agreement exists between an employer and a trade union representing employees or employees who are not unionised, there should be no alteration except through standard negotiation mechanisms. Where there is no collective agreement, best practice should be set by compensation arrangements provided for in a collective agreement applying to comparable employees in the retail sector.

Agreements should take the following into account

1. A premium payment will apply to Sunday working; the nature and value of this premium rate should be negotiated between employers and employees or their representatives;

2. Existing employees should have the option to volunteer to opt into working patterns, which include Sundays on a rota basis and form part of a regular working week (i.e., being required to work no more than five days out of seven);

3. Newly recruited employees may be contracted to work Sundays as part of regular rostered working pattern;

4. Employees who have a minimum of two years' service on a Sunday working contract should have the opportunity to seek to opt out of Sunday working for urgent family or personal reasons, giving adequate notice to the employer;

5. Meal breaks on Sundays should be standardised in line with the other working days of the week;

6. All employees should have the opportunity of volunteering to work on the peak Sunday trading days prior to Christmas, in addition to their normal working week. In these circumstances length of service will not be the overriding criterion for selection for Sunday working.

The Labour Relations Commission will provide assistance to employees and trade unions and employees who are not unionised in the negotiation of collective agreements on compensatory arrangements for Sunday working. The Protection of Workers (Shops) (No. 2) Bill, 1997 was published in December 1997 providing that an employee shall not be obliged to work on a Sunday without their consent.

Weekly Working Hours

An employer shall not allow an employee to work in each period of seven working days more than an average of 48 hours calculated over the following *reference period* (s.15):

1. Four months, or

2. Six months — for those employed a distance from their place of work (e.g. salesperson), security industry, activities where there is a need for continuity of production or service (e.g. hospitals, care institutions, docks, airports, the media, essential services, research and development, agriculture), where there is a foreseeable surge of activity (particularly in agriculture, tourism or the postal services) or where there are exceptional circumstances or emergency.

    Employees working in a prison or place of detention, firefighters, authorised officers under the Air Navigation and Transport Acts, 1950–1988, harbour police in Dublin Port and persons (other than clerical staff) employed in the Irish Marine and Emergency Service who fall within the Organisation of Working Time (Exemption of Civil Protection Services) Regulations, 1998 (SI No. 52 of 1998), and also persons working in the transport sector where there is a continuity of regularity of service (Organisation of Working Time (Exemption of Transport Activities) Regulations, 1998 (SI No. 20 of 1998) do not fall within the scope of this provision of the Act.

3. Nightworkers' work is averaged over two months (s. 16).

A *reference period* may not include any period of annual leave, absence from work under the maternity, adoptive leave or parental leave legislation or sick leave.

Nightly Working Hours

Night work means work carried out during *night-time*, which is defined as the period between midnight and 7 a.m. on the following day (s.16). A *night worker* means an employee:

1. Who normally works at least three hours of their daily working time during night-time; and

2. The number of hours worked by the employee during night-time, in each year, equals or exceeds 50 per cent of the total number of hours worked by them during that year.

An employer shall not permit a night worker, in each period of 24 hours, to work:

1. In a case where the work done by the worker in that period includes night work and the worker is a special category night worker, more than eight hours; and

2. In any other case, more than an average of eight hours, that is to say an average of eight hours calculated over a period (the reference period) that does not exceed:

    (i) Two months; or

    (ii) Such greater length of time as is specified in a collective agreement that for the time being has effect in relation to that night worker and which stands approved of by the Labour Court under section 24 of the Act.

A *special category night worker* means a night worker with respect to whom an assessment carried out by their employer (pursuant to a requirement of regulations under section 28(1) of the Safety, Health and Welfare at Work Act, 1989, in relation to the risks attaching to the work that the night worker is employed to do) indicated that that work involves special hazards or a heavy physical or mental strain.

The days or months of a *reference period* are consecutive days and months. A *reference period* shall not include:

1. Any rest period granted to the employee under section 13(2) except so much of it as exceeds 24 hours;

2. Any rest periods granted to the employee under section 13(3) except so much of each of those periods as exceeds 24 hours;

3. Any period of annual leave granted to the employee in accordance with the Act except for annual leave in excess of that provided for under the Act to be given to the employee;

4. Any absences from work by the employee authorised under the Maternity Protection Act, 1994, the Adoptive Leave Act, 1995, and the Parental Leave Act, 1998;

5. Any sick leave taken by the employee.

Employers of persons employed in activities concerned by SI Nos. 20, 21, and 52 of 1998 are exempted from the provisions of section 16.

PROVISION OF INFORMATION IN RELATION TO WORKING TIME

An employer must notify an employee in advance of the hours which an employer will require the employee to work, subject to unforeseen circumstances. Thus, if the contract of employment, any regulation order, registered employment agreement or collective agreement does not specify the normal or regular starting or finishing times of work of an employee, the employer shall notify the employee of the starting and finishing times at least 24 hours before the first day or the day in each week that the employee is required to work.

If the employer requires the employee to work additional hours, the employer shall give the employee at least 24 hours' notice before the first day or the day in the week which the employee is required to work. Notification may be given by posting a notice in a conspicuous position in the place of the employee's employment.

ZERO HOURS WORKING PRACTICES

The Organisation of Working Time Act, 1997 (section 18), contains provisions whereby an employee may be paid when their contract requires them to be available for a specified or unspecified number of hours, even though they may not actually be called upon to work. These practices, known as "zero hours working", are considered in detail in Chapter 3, "Temporary and Part-time Employment".

COLLECTIVE AGREEMENTS

A "collective agreement" is defined in the Act as

> . . . an agreement by or on behalf of an employer on the one hand, and by or on behalf of a body or bodies representative of the employees to whom the agreement relates on the other hand.

The Labour Court may approve a collective agreement on an application of the parties (after consultation with the representatives). The Court will not approve an agreement unless the following conditions are fulfilled:

1. In respect of collective agreements, referring to compensatory rest periods, daily rest period, rest and intervals at work and weekly rest periods, weekly working hours and nightly working hours, the Labour Court must be satisfied that it is appropriate to approve of the agreement in relation to the provisions of the Council Directive (i.e. the Working Time Directive) permitting the entry into collective agreements for the purposes concerned;

2. The agreement has been concluded in a manner usually employed in determining the pay or other conditions of employment of employees in the employment concerned;

3. The employee representative is an authorised trade union or an "excepted body" (see Chapter 8) which is sufficiently representative of the employees;

4. The agreement is in such a form as appears to the Labour Court to be suitable for the purposes of the agreement being approved under the Act.

If an agreement is approved and it is then varied by the parties, any other parties may apply to the Labour Court to have the varied agreement approved. The Labour Court may withdraw its approval of a collective agreement if it considers that that there are sufficient grounds.

The Labour Court has an application form (Form 1) (see pages 317–21) for application for approval of a Collective Agreement under the Act where the employees are represented by a trade union or an "excepted body". Form 2 covers applications for the approval of variations to collective agreements. There are also provisions for transitional provisions where an employee has consented to a notice (i.e. a non-collective individual agreement). These notices may be approved by the Labour Court, but from 1 March 2000 only collective agreements covering employees who are members of trade unions or excepted bodies may be approved by the Labour Court (Form 3). A division of the Court considers at a private meeting whether the agreement complies with the Act. If the agreement complies with the Act, the Court issues an Approval and notes in the register of agreements. The Labour Court has published a guide to its Functions and Procedures under the 1997 Act, which includes a sample collective agreement concerning working time and rest arrangements under the exemption provisions as well as sample letters of explanation from the union/excepted body and sample letter of consent from the employee. (There are similar documents from employer to employee and vice versa where there is no trade union/excepted body.)

Records

Employers must keep records of details of the hours of work and details of holidays for its employees at the place where the employee works or the main place where they work for the previous three years to show compliance with the Act (or earlier legislation).

DISMISSAL

An employer shall not penalise an employee for having in good faith opposed by lawful means an act that is unlawful under the 1997 Act. If an employee is penalised by dismissal within the meaning of the Unfair Dismissals Acts, 1977–1993, then relief may not be granted under the Organisation of Working Time Act and under the Unfair Dismissals Acts, 1997–1993, in that an employee cannot obtain redress under both Acts.

COMPLAINTS PROCEDURE

The Act sets out a complaints procedure for dealing with the various complaints that may arise under the Organisation of Working Time Act, 1997. Complaints may be made to a rights commissioner within six months of the alleged contravention. There is provision for an extension of this time limit to twelve months after the six months where there is reasonable cause. Rights commissioner's recommendations may be appealed to the Labour Court within six weeks of the date of the recommendation. A Labour Court determination may be appealed to the High Court on a point of law by the Minister, at the request of the Labour Court, or by either party to the proceedings. There is provision for the implementation of rights commissioners' recommendations or Labour Court determinations (see Chapter 22, "The Labour Relations Commission and the Labour Court" and Chapter 23, "Employment Appeals Tribunal", for further detail).

PROTECTION OF YOUNG PERSONS (EMPLOYMENT) ACT, 1996

The purpose of the Act is to provide for the implementation of the EC Directive on the protection of young people at work (No. 94/33/EC of 22 June 1994). The Act also repeals and replaces the Protection of Young Persons (Employment) Act, 1977, and came into operation on 2 January 1997 (Protection of Young Persons (Employment) Act, 1996 (Commencement) Order, 1996 (SI No. 371 of 1996).

The Act generally prohibits the employment of children but specifies the circumstances in which an employer may employ a child. A "child" means a person who is under 16 years of age or the school leaving age, whichever is the higher. The Minister for State at the Department of Enterprise, Trade and Employment may authorise, by licence, in individual cases, the employment of children (and by regulation children over 13 years) in cultural, artistic, sports and advertising activities which are not harmful to safety, health or normal development and which are not likely to interfere with attendance at school, vocational guidance or training programmes.

Abstract of Protection of Young Persons (Employment) Act, 1996

The Protection of Young Persons (Employment) (Prescribed Abstract) Regulation, 1997 (SI No. 3 of 1997), provides that the Abstract must be displayed at all principal entrance(s) to work premises where persons under 18 are employed. The sections on age limits and maximum hours of work per week as are follows:

Abstract: Summary of Main Rules on Employing People under 18

Age Limits

For a regular job, the general minimum age is 16. Employers can take on 14- and 15-year-olds on light work:

* Part-time during the school term (over 15 years only);

- As part of an approved work experience or educational programme;

- During the school holidays, provided there is a minimum three-week break from work in the summer.

Any child under 16 may be employed in film, theatre, sports or advertising under licence.

Maximum Hours of Work per Week

Under-18s may not be employed for more than 40 hours a week or 8 hours a day, except in a genuine emergency. The maximum weekly working hours for 14- and 15-year-olds are:

	Age 14	Age 15
Term-time	Nil	8 hours
Holiday work	35 hours	35 hours
Work experience	40 hours	40 hours

Early Morning and Night Work

The hours permitted are:

	Age Under 16	Age 16 and 17
Early morning	after 8 a.m.	after 6 a.m.
Night work		
With school next morning	up to 8 p.m.	up to 10 p.m.
With no school next morning (e.g. holidays, weekends)	Up to 8 p.m.	Up to 11 p.m. (and not before 7 a.m. next morning)

Rest Breaks

	Age Under 16	Age 16 and 17
30 minutes break after working	4 hours	4½ hours
Every 24 hours	14 hours off	12 hours off
Every 7 days	2 days off	2 days off

Exclusions

The Protection of Young Persons (Employment of Close Relatives) Regulations 1997 (SI No. 2 of 1997) provides that the provision on the prohibition of employment of children (s. 3), the duties of an employer in respect of obtaining of details in respect of date of birth (s. 5), the minimum hours (s. 6 (1)(a)) and the inclusion of time spent on vocational training as working time (s. 11), do not apply in respect of the employment of close relatives. The Protection of Young Persons (Employment) (Exclusion of Workers in the Fishing and Shipping Sectors) Regulations, 1997 (SI No. 1 of 1997), provides that where a young person is employed in these sectors and is assigned to work between the hours of 10 p.m. in any one day and 6 a.m. on the following day, they will get compensatory rest.

A child over 14 years may be employed to do non-industrial light work outside of the school term, provided that the hours of work do not exceed seven hours in any day or 35 hours in any week. The work must not be harmful to the safety, health and development of the child. During the summer holiday period, the child is prohibited from doing any work for a period of at least 21 days. A child over 15 years may do light non-industrial work for up to eight hours per week during school term time. A child over 14 years and in full-time secondary education may be employed as part of a work experience or educational programme for up to eight hours in any day or 40 hours in any week. An employer may employ a child over 15 years to participate in a training or work experience programme arranged or approved by the Minister or FÁS for up to eight hours in any day or 40 hours in any week.

The hours of work and night work provisions shall not apply to members of the Defence Forces in certain circumstances and subject to certain conditions. Any time spent by a young person working under a combined work/training scheme or in-plant work experience scheme is deemed to be working time.

Duties of Employer

Before employing a young person or child, the employer must obtain a copy of the birth certificate or other satisfactory evidence of age and, when employing a child, must obtain the written permission of the parent or guardian. The employer is required to maintain a register containing details of time worked, rates of pay and total pay in relation to every young person or child so employed.

There is a prohibition on double employment. However, it is allowed as long as the total hours worked do not exceed the maximum allowed under the Act. It will be a defence to any proceedings taken against an employer for a breach of the Act to show that the breach resulted from an emergency situation. An employer must keep records, for at least three years, to show that there is compliance with the Act. If a person is guilty of an offence under the Act, they shall be liable on summary conviction to a fine not exceeding £1,500 and, should there be a continuation of the offence, £250 per day for every day the offence continues. There are provisions for the bringing of complaints under the Act, by the young person, their parent or guardian, to a rights commissioner, and appeals to the Employment Appeals Tribunal (see Chapters 22 and 23).

General References

Kerr, T. (1996), *Protection of young Persons (Employment) Act, 1996: Law Statutes Annotated*, Dublin: Sweet and Maxwell.

Kerr, T. (1998), *Organisation of Working Time Act, 1997: Law Statutes Annotated*, Dublin: Sweet and Maxwell.

Labour Court (1997), *Labour Court: Guide to its Functions and Procedures*, November, Dublin: Labour Court.

Form 1

THE LABOUR COURT

ORGANISATION OF WORKING TIME ACT, 1997

Application to the Labour Court for Approval of a Collective Agreement under *Section 24* and/or the *Fifth Schedule* to the Organisation of Working Time Act, 1997

This form applies only to collective agreements and should be used where the employees concerned are represented by a trade union or an "excepted body"*. If no union or excepted body is recognised by the employer in respect of the category of employees concerned, Form 3 should be used.

---

(1): Employer *(name and address, and name, address and telephone no. of person to contact):*

---

(2): Union(s) or Excepted Body/Bodies* *(name and address, and name, address and telephone no. of person(s) to contact):*

---

(3): Number of Employees affected by this Agreement:
(Please note that if the Agreement provides for an average working week of more than 48 hours in the year commencing 1st March, 1998 and/or the year commencing 1st March, 1999, under the transitional provisions of the Fifth Schedule to the Act, the names of the employees to whom it applies must be included in the Agreement - see (6) or (7) below and the confirmation at the end of this form.)

---

(4): Date of the Agreement:

---

(5): Details of the type of Employment covered by the Agreement *(a general description of the type of work covered by the agreement will normally be sufficient. If the work involves danger to the employees, the information should be sufficiently detailed to enable the Court to consider safety implications):*

(6): Day Workers - Working Hours and Rest Periods

(a) Average Working Week *(in hours - covering only time spent carrying on the work. Please insert figure for each of the years below):-*

> **Year commencing 1st March, 1998** *(Transitional provisions in the Fifth Schedule to the Act provide for a maximum average of 60 hours per week in the year)*:
>
> **Year commencing 1st March, 1999** *(Transitional provisions in the Fifth Schedule to the Act provide for a maximum average of 55 hours per week in the year)*:
>
> **Year commencing 1st March, 2000, onwards** *(Maximum average 48 hours per week)*:

(b) Averaging period for determining the Working Week *(maximum 12 months)*:

(Please give reasons if the averaging period exceeds 4 months, or 6 months for certain employments - see explanatory Guide.)

(c) Rest Arrangements *the statutory minimum rest requirements are: daily rest - 11 hours per 24-hour period; weekly rest - 24 hours per week, preceded by 11 hours' daily rest; rest breaks - 15 minutes where 4½ hours have been worked and 30 minutes (which may include the 15-minute break) where 6 hours have been worked.) Certain activities or employments are exempted from these requirements, either under the Act itself or by Regulations - see explanatory Guide - although compensatory rest must be provided.)*

Does the agreement provide for rest arrangements which do not meet the minimum statutory requirements? Please indicate YES [ ] or NO [ ]

If the answer to the question above is "YES", please complete the following:

> **Breaks during Working Day:**   ......hours/minutes every .....hours/minutes
>
> **Daily Rest Period:**   ......hours every 24 hours
>
> **Weekly Rest Period:**   ......hours every .....days
>
> **Compensatory Equivalent Rest Arrangements:**

(7): Night Workers - Working Hours and Rest Periods *(If this section does not apply, please leave it blank.)*

(a) Average Working Week *(in hours - covering only time spent carrying on the work. Please insert figure for each of the years below)*:-

Year commencing 1st March, 1998 *(Transitional provisions in the Fifth Schedule to the Act provide for a maximum average of 60 hours per week in the year)*:

Year commencing 1st March, 1999 *(Transitional provisions in the Fifth Schedule to the Act provide for a maximum average of 55 hours per week in the year)*:

Year commencing 1st March, 2000, onwards *(Maximum average 48 hours per week)*:

(b) Averaging period for Determining the Working Week *(maximum 12 months)*:

(Please give reasons if the averaging period exceeds 2 months - see explanatory Guide.)

(c) Rest Arrangements *(the statutory minimum rest requirements are: daily rest - 11 hours per 24-hour period; weekly rest - 24 hours per week, preceded by 11 hours' daily rest; rest breaks - 15 minutes where 4½ hours have been worked and 30 minutes (which may include the 15-minute break) where 6 hours have been worked.) Certain activities or employments are exempted from these requirements, either under the Act itself or by Regulations - see explanatory Guide - although compensatory rest must be provided.)*

Does the agreement provide for rest arrangements which do not meet the minimum statutory requirements? Please indicate YES [ ] or NO [ ]

If the answer to the question above is "YES", please complete the following:

Breaks during Working Day: ......hours/minutes every .....hours/minutes

Daily Rest Period: ......hours every 24 hours

Weekly Rest Period: ......hours every .....days

Compensatory Equivalent Rest Arrangements:

3

(8): <u>Does the Agreement contain an exemption from paragraph 2(b) and (c) of the First Schedule to the Act?</u> *(Under the First Schedule, there is an automatic yearly increase in the minimum legal holiday entitlement, from 15 days (the minimum in 1996) to 20 days in 1999. A collective agreement may provide for exemption from paragraph 2(b) and (c) of the Schedule, which provides for interim increases up to 1999. An exemption would mean that the employees' minimum legal holiday entitlement would remain unchanged until 1999, when it would increase directly to 20 days.)*

   <u>Please indicate</u> YES [ ] or NO [ ]

(9): <u>Please describe the procedures followed in reaching the Agreement</u> *(the Act requires the Labour Court to be satisfied that the Agreement has been reached in "a manner usually employed in determining the pay or other conditions of employment of employees in the employment concerned"):*

Chapter Fourteen

PENSIONS

A good pensionable job may be everybody's dream, especially in the public service or in "safe" private employment. Generally speaking, pension schemes in the public service were considered to be a major benefit and indeed nowadays more and more employers in the private sector are providing pension schemes for their employees. In the early 1990s, it was considered that that no job was "safe" or protected from the ravages of recession, as was reflected in the number of persons made redundant. Equally, in the late 1990s, there is more emphasis on fixed-term contracts, part-time work and so forth. Thus, in the last number of years there has been considerable focus on pension schemes. However, employees who are fortunate in belonging to a company pension scheme as part of their terms and conditions of employment frequently do not understand the intricacies of pensions.

There is no obligation on an employer to provide a pension scheme for employees. Indeed, up to the enactment of the Pensions Act, 1990, there was little regulation of pension schemes. This Act has gone some way in regulating pension schemes and also in implementing EC Directive 86/378 on equal treatment for men and women in occupational pension schemes. There have been subsequent amendments to the 1990 Act with the Pensions (Amendment) Act, 1996.

As previously considered, the Terms of Employment (Information) Act, 1994, provides that if there is a pension scheme, the employer must provide an employee with details describing it. This is usually done by way of a summary booklet given to employees (see Chapter 2, "The Contract of Employment"). These booklets set out the terms of the pension scheme in a comprehensible manner and usually also provide details of the income protection plan in the event of illness and the life assurance policy (if any) at the same time.

Pension schemes are set up by an employer for employees (the beneficiaries) by means of a trust. A trust may be summarised as an obligation whoro a porson (the trustoe) holds property (trust property) for the benefit of others (the beneficiaries). Employees are members of the pension scheme, though technically this is quite distinct from their contract of employment.

Pension schemes — voluntary schemes set up by an employer — are usually called occupational pension schemes because the scheme has been "approved" (or the employer is in the process of seeking "approval") under the Finance Act, 1972 (as amended).

"Approved" pension schemes receive special tax advantages, namely that an employer's contributions (at present up to 15 per cent of gross salary — see below) are tax deductible. A pension scheme may or may not be a contributory one where the employee also contributes. An employee may make additional voluntary contributions if the scheme allows for this. The pension scheme must provide for benefits to the employee or to the surviving spouse, children, dependants and personal representatives, as the case may be. It should be noted that the Finance Act, 1999, provides for new tax rules for pensions for the self-employed, directors of family companies and employees who are not members of an occupational pension scheme. A percentage (which increases in accordance with age) can be set aside each year as pensions contributions and this is fully tax deductible, up to an income limit of £200,000 per annum.

The maximum benefit a retiring employee can receive is two-thirds of their final salary (i.e. as denoted for pension purposes), though an employee who does not have the full 40 years' service could be entitled to less. There should also be provisions in relation to the age of retirement and what benefits are paid to an employee's widow/widower and dependants. A scheme may allow the employee to take a lump sum up to one-and-a-half-times their final salary upon retirement. Again, this is reduced if there are less than 40 years' service.

In the event of early retirement, voluntary redundancy schemes, or where for example there are negotiations in respect of a termination payment, the value of the pension is extremely important and the purchase of additional years of service may be a major part of negotiations. Hence, independent pension and taxation advice is crucial.

THE PENSIONS BOARD

The 1990 Act provided for the establishment of the Pensions Board. The Board comprises a chairperson and 12 members who represent the pensions industry, the Ministers for Finance and Social, Community and Family Affairs, employers, trade unions and the various relevant professions.

The Pensions Board has been entrusted to carry out the following functions:

1. To monitor and supervise the operation of the Act and pensions developments;

2. To advise the Minister for Social, Community and Family Affairs on pension matters and on standards for schemes;

3. To issue guidelines on the duties of pension scheme trustees and to encourage the provision of appropriate training facilities for trustees;

4. To publish reports;

5. To perform such other tasks at the Minister's request.

The trustees of a pension scheme are required to register the scheme with the Board.

PRESERVATION OF PENSION ENTITLEMENTS

Until the preservation of benefits provisions in the Act came into force, there was a major difficulty for employees who were members of occupational pension schemes. Upon their departure from the company, these employees frequently left behind their years of pensionable service.

The preservation provisions came into force on 1 January 1993 and apply to persons with five or more years' service in a particular pension scheme. However, in order to benefit from this provision, two out of the five years must be after 1 January 1991.

This in effect will mean that schemes will be required to preserve the pension entitlements of its members if they leave their employment after 1 January 1993 but before pensionable age. In other words, such persons will have a pension entitlement preserved for

them until they reach normal pensionable age in respect of that particular scheme.

The alternative forms of preservation are for employees to have
the choice of having a transfer payment, equivalent to the actuarial
value of their preserved benefit entitlement, transferred to the
scheme of their new employer, or else the trustee may purchase an
approved annuity bond underwritten by a life assurance office.

From 1 January 1996, there must also be an annual revaluation of
any preserved benefits in the pension scheme at the annual rate of
the consumer price index or by four per cent, whichever is the lesser.
All additional voluntary contributions which an employee has added
to the scheme shall be treated in the same manner.

The downside of this legislation is that employees leaving their
jobs, especially younger employees, who would have preferred to have
their pension contributions returned to them (if it was a contributory
scheme) no longer can, if they have more than five years' service.

Disputes on these issues may be referred to the Pensions Board.
There is a right of appeal from a decision of the Board to the High
Court on a point of law only.

FUNDING STANDARD

Pension schemes (as long as they are not defined as contribution
schemes — see explanation in Lynch and Kelly, 1990, pp. 25–32) are
now required to have a minimum funding standard and an actuary
must provide an actuarial funding certificate for all schemes currently in existence. The first certificate must be provided within a
period of three-and-a-half years after the date of the previous certificate. If it is a new scheme, there must be a funding certificate submitted within three-and-a-half years of the scheme's commencement.

There are detailed provisions in the Act setting out the funding,
which are governed by the Occupational Pensions Scheme (Funding
Standard) Regulations, 1993, and the Amendment Regulation of 1998
(SI No. 419 of 1993 and SI Nos. 320 and 568 of 1998). The key objective is to ensure that there are sufficient assets within the scheme to
secure the pensions for existing beneficiaries, and following a period
of ten years, the benefit expectations of active members relating to
their periods of scheme membership. In other words, there must be

complete cover for all liabilities of the scheme, and if there is not, the scheme must have full cover within a period of ten years.

The initial actuarial certificate must certify that sufficient assets exist to cover 100 per cent of the following benefits:

1. Pensions in the course of payment;

2. Additional benefits which were provided by way of additional voluntary contributions or in respect of transfer rights from another scheme (i.e. where a new employee comes into the scheme with transfer rights from another pension scheme);

3. Any remaining benefits accrued under the scheme in respect of service after 1 January 1991.

DISCLOSURE OF INFORMATION IN RELATION TO SCHEMES

The trustees of a pension scheme must now provide financial and other information about the scheme to members, prospective members, their spouses and authorised trade unions. The information should include the rules of the scheme, its administration and financial basis, and any individual rights and obligations arising under it. There is provision in the Family Law Act, 1995, in cases of judicial separation (and foreign divorces) for a pensions adjustment order, which is essentially a re-arrangement of pension benefits in favour of the other spouse and dependants. There are also similar provisions in respect of divorce in the Family Law (Divorce) Act, 1996.

There must also be annual reports in respect of each scheme year after 1 January 1991. The information required includes a trustee's report, an investment report, audited accounts in respect of the scheme year, a copy of the auditor's report and a copy of the latest actuarial funding certificate. There is an exclusion from this provision in respect of certain schemes.

TRUSTEES OF PENSION SCHEMES

The Act outlines the general statutory duties of trustees of occupational pension schemes. Such duties are:

1. To ensure that the contributions due to the scheme are paid into the fund and are properly invested;

2. To ensure that the benefits of the scheme are paid as they become due;

3. To ensure that proper membership and financial records are kept;

4. To register both the scheme and all the names of trustees to the scheme with the Pensions Board. All existing schemes had to register by 1 January 1991.

The duties of a trustee are onerous, with a considerable degree of responsibility. Briefly, the general duties of a trustee are to:

1. Inspect the trust deed;

2. Ensure that all the property is vested in the names of the trustees;

3. Carry out strictly the terms of the trust;

4. Exercise a duty of care;

5. Ensure that there is no delegation of the trustee's duties;

6. Be sure there is no conflict of interest;

7. Act in good faith;

8. Provide information on the pension scheme;

9. Invest trust monies properly;

10. Apply to the High Court where there is doubt as to the interpretation of a trust deed.

Since 1 January 1994, employee members of pension schemes may elect member trustees, provided that the election process is initiated by at least 15 per cent of the members or by trade unions representing at least 50 per cent of the members. This is applicable to schemes where there are at least 50 members, or in directly invested schemes of not less than 12 members (SI No. 376 of 1996).

EQUALITY

Women are no longer "birds of passage . . . who come for a short time and then fly off to get married and bring up their children" (Lord

Denning in *Worringham* v *Lloyds Bank Ltd.* ([1981] ECR 767 and Curtin, 1989). Article 119 (now Article 141 following the Treaty of Amsterdam) of the EC Treaty provides that there must be equal pay between men and women. In *Defrenne* v *Sabena* (Case 80/70 — "*Defrenne I*"), the ECJ held that retirement schemes in the public sector were not subject to the requirements of Article 119, as it did not constitute a direct or indirect payment to the worker. In *Defrenne II* (Case 43/75) ([1976] 2 CMLR 98), the ECJ ruled that article 119 had direct effect to ensure the protection of rights of individuals in respect of equal pay. (This issue arose as Belgium had not implemented equal pay legislation at the time.) Over the years, it has evolved from case law that pension benefits fall within the scope of equal pay. The European Court judgment in *Bilka-Kaufhaus GmBH* v *Weber von Hartz* ([1986] 2 CMLR 701) has confirmed that in EU law, occupational pension schemes and the rules governing them fall within the scope of Article 119 (now 141). The rules governing pension schemes were considered an integral part of the contract of employment and the benefits paid under the scheme constituted remuneration.

The relevant pieces of Irish legislation are:

1. The Anti-Discrimination (Pay) Act, 1974, deals with all matters relating to pay including occupational pension schemes. As previously noted, this Act applies to full-time and part-time employees. Hence, part-time employees are entitled to pensions provided they do "like work" with their comparator (see *Bilka Kaufhaus*, above). Equality officers and the Labour Court have given wide latitude to the definition of remuneration, including contributions to pension schemes, survivors' benefits and access to schemes.

2. The Employment Equality Act, 1977, deals with equal treatment in employment. However, this Act specifically excludes matters dealing with occupational pension schemes.

3. The Employment Equality Act, 1998 (yet to be implemented, this will repeal the above two Acts), specifically excludes matters in relation to pensions, hence there will have to be a new statute to deal with matters in relation to equality and to determine whether the other grounds of discrimination (e.g. age, disability etc.) shall also be discriminatory grounds in respect of pensions. The definition of "remuneration" in the 1998 Act states that it

does not include "pension rights", which are defined as "a pension or any other benefits flowing from an occupational pension scheme".

4. The Pensions Acts, 1990–1996, provide that there must be equal treatment between men and women (both full-time and part-time) in relation to "occupational benefit schemes". EC Directive 86/378 was brought into Irish law by Part VII of the Pensions Act, 1990, as amended by the 1996 Amendment Act (and Occupational Benefit Schemes (Equal Treatment) Regulations, 1992 (SI No. 365 of 1992)).

There have been several Irish cases, which may be summarised under the 1974 and 1977 Acts as follows:

1. *ASTMS* v *Linson* (EP 1/1977 DEP 2/1977), where there were both different entries and retirement ages to and from the scheme. The Labour Court determined that there should be equal pension benefits for men and women.

2. *Department of the Public Service* v *Robinson* (EP 36/1978 DEP 7/1979), considered equality of survivors' benefits, namely that then Senator Mary Robinson maintained that the non-provision of a widowers' pension was discriminatory. It was held that the provision of benefits to dependants was part of an employee's remuneration.

3. In *University College, Dublin* v *IFUT* (EP 7/1979 DEP 17/79), the Labour Court considered that the provision of a Contributory Widows' and Children's Plan for men only was discriminatory.

These Irish cases have targeted the root of the problems in equal treatment in pension schemes. However, they do not assist in finding solutions.

EC Directive 86/378 provides that occupational pension schemes must comply with the principle of equal treatment between men and women. The Directive provides that discriminatory provisions must have been removed from pension schemes by January 1993.

The Directive applies to group occupational pension schemes, not individual/one-member schemes. The principle of the Directive is to exclude discrimination based on sex or marital status connected with:

1. Scope and access to the scheme;

2. Obligation and calculation of contributions to the scheme;

3. Calculation and duration of benefits to the member and their spouse and dependants; and

4. Retirement from the scheme.

The intent of the Pensions Act is to provide that there cannot be discrimination, either direct or indirect, on the basis of sex in respect of any matter relating to an "occupational benefit scheme". "Occupational benefits" are defined as meaning "benefits, in the form of pensions or otherwise, payable in cash or in kind in respect of:

1. Termination of service;

2. Retirement, old age or death;

3. Interruptions of service by reason of sickness or invalidity;

4. Accidents, injuries or diseases arising out of or in the course of a person's employment;

5. Unemployment; or

6. Expenses incurred in connection with children or other dependants."

and includes any other benefit corresponding to a benefit under the social welfare or maternity legislation.

There are certain exceptions to this rule, however, such as defined contribution schemes with different treatment, which may be explained on actuarial grounds. For example, there is a presumption that women live longer than men; therefore they will receive benefits for longer. The problem then arises that if the pension payment is the same, then women must either make higher contributions or retire later from their job. This problem will have to be addressed in the near future in relation to equality and pension schemes. There must also be equal retirement ages, though this has not caused a major problem in Ireland, as relatively few schemes provided for a lower retirement age for women, and furthermore, Ireland's social welfare code does not discriminate on ages for retirement or receipt of old age pensions.

These issues were considered in the UK case of *Barber* v *Guardian Royal Exchange Assurance Group* ([1990] ECR 1889). When Mr Barber was made redundant, the company rules allowed that members of the pension scheme were entitled to an immediate pension at 55 years for men and 50 for women. All other staff received cash benefits and a deferred pension at age 62 for men and 57 for women. Mr Barber was aged 52 when he was made redundant and thus was not in receipt of a pension. The Court held that such pension benefits fall within the scope of Article 119; an age condition that varies in relation to a person's sex is contrary to Article 119. Article 119 cannot be relied upon prior to the date of this judgment (17 May 1990), however, unless legal proceedings had already been instituted. As this case rules that the principle of equal pay applies to each aspect of remuneration, there may well be a real question to be answered in respect of apparent discrimination where there are defined contribution schemes that have been excluded from the equality principles of the 1990 Act.

An employee who is absent from work because of pregnancy, maternity leave or for family reasons (e.g. on parental leave) does not lose occupational benefit entitlements (see the definition above) for that period provided that the scheme allows for same. This is very important, because the Maternity Protection Act, 1994, the Adoptive Leave Act, 1995, and the Parental Leave Act, 1998 provided that women who were on such leave were not entitled to any remuneration and their employer did not have to make any contribution to the occupational benefit scheme for that period.

Disputes on alleged discrimination in relation to access to occupational pension schemes may be referred to an equality officer, the Labour Court and the High Court, as laid down in the 1990 Act, which is the same as under the Anti-Discrimination (Pay) Act, 1974 (see Section 4). The Labour Court may:

1. Determine whether a rule in a scheme complies with the principle of equal treatment.

2. Determine whether any such rule is null and void.

3. Determine whether the terms of a collective agreement, employment regulation order or contract of employment comply with the principle of equal treatment. The Pensions (Amendment) Act,

1996, provides that where a term of the contract of employment (whether express or implied), a rule or an agreement does not comply with the principle of equal treatment, it shall be rendered null and void (insofar as it does not comply) with effect from 17 May 1990. The more favourable treatment that has been afforded to men (or vice versa to women) shall be afforded to women as the case may be. The employer shall take such measures as are necessary to give effect to this requirement. This applies to the period 17 May 1990 to 31 December 1998, or in the case of unequal retirement ages, 31 December 2017.

4. Determine whether an employer has provided equal access to a scheme.

5. Recommend a specific course of action to resolve any of the above breaches of the legislation.

Certain disputes in relation to "occupational pension schemes" may be referred to the Pensions Board by the trustees. Such references should include whether the scheme is a defined contribution scheme for this part of the Act, whether any rule of an occupational pension scheme complies with the principle of equal treatment and whether and to what extent any such rule is rendered null and void by compulsory levelling-up provisions.

The ECJ held in *Vroege* v *NCIV Instituut voor Volhuisvesting BV and Another* ([1994] IRLR 651) that an occupational pension scheme which excludes part-time workers will contravene Article 119 if the exclusion affects more women than men, unless of course there are objective reasons on grounds other than sex. Equal treatment in respect of the right to join such schemes may go back to 8 April 1976, the date of the *Defrenne* decision, which held that Article 119 has direct effect. Of course, if, for example, part-time employees were excluded from membership of a scheme in contravention of Article 119, then the employee must pay all appropriate monies to the scheme (*Fisscher* v *Voorhuis Hengelo BV and Another* [1994] IRLR 662).

Dismissal

If an employee is dismissed for having in good faith notified the Pension Board of an alleged breach of the pensions legislation; made to the Board a report concerning misappropriation of resources of a pension scheme or a voluntary report of any matter concerning the state and conduct of a scheme; made a reference under the Acts (e.g. an equality claim); gave evidence of any proceedings under the Act; or gave notice to the employer of their intention to do any of these matters — in such cases, the employer shall be guilty of an offence and the employee may be reinstated, re-engaged or awarded compensation up to a maximum of 104 weeks' remuneration by the Labour Court. The employer may also have to pay a fine (which amount the employee may appeal to the High Court or to the Circuit Court (as appropriate)). Even where there has been a dismissal and no prosecution has been brought, the Labour Court, having heard the claim, can order reinstatement, re-engagement or a fine (compensation up to 104 weeks' remuneration) and if the employer does not comply with such an order within two months the employer shall be guilty of an offence and subject to a fine and /or imprisonment. Such a claim must be made to the Labour Court within six months of the date of the right of appeal to the Circuit Court.

DEATH BENEFIT

Frequently, a pension scheme will include a death benefit plan, should the employee die in service before the normal pension age. Obviously, the provisions and monies payable depend on the scheme itself, but usually the deceased's dependants receive a defined amount of monies in respect of the employee's pensionable service.

INCOME CONTINUANCE PLAN

Frequently, as an addition to a pension arrangement, there is provision for an income continuance plan, whereby an employee who is continuously disabled for over 26 weeks would be entitled to an income continuance payment. This payment only lasts as long as the person is ill and can only continue up to pension age.

Finally, it is strongly recommended that a person should get professional advice from an expert on pensions should that person have any questions in relation to their pension scheme.

General References

Callender, R. and F. Meenan (1994), *Equality in Law between Men and Women in the European Community — Collection of Texts and Commentary on Irish Law,* Martinus Nijhoff Publishers and The Office for Official Publications of the Commission of European Communities.

Curtin, D. (1989), *Irish Employment Equality Law*, Dublin: The Round Hall Press.

Finucane, K. and B. Buggy (1996), *Irish Pensions Law and Practice*, Dublin: Oak Tree Press.

Forde, M. (1992), *Employment Law*, Dublin: The Round Hall Press.

Kenny, P. (1993), "The Pension Act, 1990: Preservation Regulations", *Industrial Relations News, IRN 6*.

Lynch, C., and R. Kelly (1990), *Pensions Act, 1990, Law Statutes Annotated*, Dublin: Sweet and Maxwell.

Pensions Board Annual Report and Accounts (1998).

Chapter Fifteen

HEALTH AND SAFETY IN THE WORKPLACE

The key pieces of legislation covering health, safety and welfare at work are the Safety, Health and Welfare at Work Act, 1989, and the Safety, Health and Welfare at Work (General Application) Regulations, 1993 (SI No. 44 of 1993), which came into effect on 18 February 1993. In recent years, there have also been many changes to the law, including the Occupier's Liability Act, 1995, which came into operation on 17 July 1995; and there have been various other new Regulations concerning health and safety in the workplace. The Maternity Protection Act, 1994, which was enacted on foot of an EC Health and Safety Directive (92/85/EEC) contains provisions to protect pregnant women (and women who have recently given birth) in the workplace. There have also been claims in respect of occupational stress, which as an illness is in its legal "infancy" and indeed may well become a major issue over the next few years. More recently, the whole area of "bullying at work" has also come to the fore and will be considered in this chapter.

There have been numerous other Acts over the years, including the Factories Act, 1955, and the Safety in Industry Act, 1980. There are also other Acts covering working in mines and quarries (Mines and Quarries Act, 1965), the handling of dangerous substances (Dangerous Substances Acts, 1972 and 1989), matters concerning fire safety (Fire Services Act, 1981) and numerous regulations covering various aspects of health and safety, such as the lifting of weights.

The original Acts covered safety in industry and thus all employments were not covered. The 1989 Act provided a major reform of key recommendations from the Barrington Report, which resulted from the Commission of Inquiry on Safety, Health and Welfare at Work. In summary, the Barrington Report recommended that framework legislation be put in place covering all workplaces (i.e. including agriculture, fishing, forestry, transport, laboratories and hospitals) and not merely to cover industry (some 20 per cent of the workforce). The Report stated:

> Our Report is characterised by a certain distrust of legalism. We doubt if safety and health can be advanced by an excessive reliance on detailed and increasingly complex regulations imposed on workplaces from outside. Rather, we see the problem in terms of reform within the workplace, based on clearer ideas about the responsibilities of employers, workers, the self-employed and others. The law has a role to play . . . [in] setting a framework within which managers and workers operate, but is no substitute for a sense of commitment based on responsibilities which are clearly defined and understood.

One major recommendation was that the system must be preventative and the Report stated:

> It is not merely that prevention is better than cure. Once an accident has happened there is often no cure. If the system is to be preventative, safety must be a feature in the planning of factories and systems of work. This idea governs all our recommendations.

Arising from these views, the 1989 Act was enacted as a framework Act and contains the key principles of health and safety in the workplace. The Act contains the statutory duties of employers and common law duties of care. There are additional obligations on manufacturers, suppliers, designers and builders, and all persons are required to consider the impact that their place of work or articles used at work have on the public or visitors to the premises, including independent contractors.

It should be noted that the 1989 Act did not repeal all of the earlier legislation, much of which is still in force with the various regulations made thereunder. Thus the legislative arrangements are somewhat complicated, though the Health and Welfare at Work Act, 1989 (Repeals and Revocations) Order, 1995 (SI No. 357 of 1995) was used to activate the repeal or revocation of certain provisions of existing Acts so as to avoid overlapping or duplication of the 1989 Act and the General Applications Regulations, and to repeal other existing enactments which are obsolete (e.g. the Office Premises Act, 1958, and numerous sections of the 1955 Act).

NATIONAL AUTHORITY FOR OCCUPATIONAL
SAFETY AND HEALTH

This independent Authority, known as the Health and Safety Authority, was set up under the Act and it took over the functions of the industrial inspectorate at the Department of Labour. The Authority comprises a chairperson and ten ordinary members appointed by the Minister for Enterprise, Trade and Employment.

The functions of the Authority are to:

1. Make adequate arrangements for the enforcement of the 1989 Act and all other statutory provisions;

2. Promote, encourage and foster the prevention of accidents and injury to health at work in accordance with the provisions in the 1989 Act;

3. Encourage and foster activities and measures which are directed towards the promotion of safety, health and welfare of persons at work;

4. Make arrangements as it considers necessary in order to provide information and advice on health and safety matters;

5. Make all the necessary arrangements to undertake, promote, sponsor, evaluate and publish the results of research, surveys and studies relating to hazards and risks to the safety and health of persons at work or arising from work activities;

6. Draw up codes of practice.

The Authority has considerable powers of enforcement and its inspectors may enter premises and inspect all documents and the actual workplace itself. The inspector may be accompanied by a member of the Garda Síochána if there is reasonable belief that there will be a serious obstruction to the inspector in the course of their duties. An inspector may issue an improvement notice if the inspector is "of the opinion" that there has been a breach of the "relevant statutory provisions" or if an improvement plan has not been submitted. A person who is aggrieved by an improvement notice may apply to the District Court within 14 days of the notice being served. The District judge may confirm the notice, cancel it or make any necessary modification. If matters are not resolved, the inspector may issue a prohibition notice. Failure to comply with a prohibition notice may lead to imprisonment or a fine of up to £1,000. Application may be made to the District Court within seven days of its service to have it cancelled or modified. Finally, if matters are still unresolved, application may be made to the High Court for an order restricting or prohibiting the use of a place of work. This can be done by way of an *ex parte* application; in other words, the other side does not have to be notified. The significance of a failure to remedy matters is increased at each stage in the process.

There were a number of High Court applications by the Authority in respect of construction sites and breach of safety regulations at the end of 1997.

GENERAL DUTIES OF EMPLOYERS

The Act sets out the statutory duties of care, but these provisions are only recognisable by the courts in respect of criminal proceedings (as outlined above) (s. 6). The breach of any of these provisions does not give a cause of action in civil proceedings. Thus, one has to fall back on the common law duties of care (that is, the rules that have been built up by the courts over the years). Nonetheless, such duties as described in the Act may be used as a good summary of the general duties of care. It is worthwhile stating the exact provisions of such duties:

1. It shall be the duty of every employer to ensure, so far as is reasonably practicable, the safety, health and welfare at work of all his employees.

2. Without prejudice to the generality of an employer's duty under subsection (1) the matters to which that duty extends include in particular:

a)   as regards any place of work under the employer's control, the design, the provision and the maintenance of it in a condition that is, so far as is reasonably practicable, safe and without risk to health;

b)   so far as is reasonably practicable, as regards any place of work under the employer's control, the design, the provision and the maintenance of same means of access to and egress from it;

c) the design, the provision and the maintenance of plant and machinery that are, so far as is reasonably practicable, safe and without risk to health;

d) the provision of systems of work that are planned, organised, performed and maintained so as to be, so far as is reasonably practicable, safe and without risk to health;

e) the provision of such information, instruction, training and supervision as is necessary to ensure, so far as is reasonably practicable, the safety and health at work of his employees;

f) in circumstances in which it is not reasonably practicable for an employer to control or eliminate hazards in a place of work under his control, or in such circumstances as may be prescribed, the provision and maintenance of such suitable protective clothing or equipment, as appropriate, that are necessary to ensure the safety and health at work of his employees;

g) the preparation and revision as necessary of adequate plans to be followed in emergencies;

h) to ensure, so far as is reasonably practicable, safety and the prevention of risk to health at work in connection with the use of any article or substance;

i) the provision and the maintenance of facilities and arrangements for the welfare of his employees at work; and

j) the obtaining, where necessary, of the services of a competent person (whether under a contract of employment or otherwise) for the purpose of ensuring, so far as is reasonably practicable, the safety and health at work of his employees.

Employers and self-employed persons also have a duty towards persons who are not employees — visitors or independent contractors, for example.

More recently, harassment or bullying in the workplace has become a major issue. It is appropriate in this context to use the first statutory definition of "harassment" as provided in the Employment Equality Act, 1998 (yet to be implemented). This is not the definition of sexual harassment in the workplace which is specifically provided for under the Employment Equality legislation but it is a useful definition of harassment generally which, under that Act, applies to the various other discriminatory grounds aside from gender, i.e., marital status, family status, sexual orientation, religion, age, disability, race and membership of the traveller community.

However, there may of course be more general matters of harassment and these may be summarised as follows. If, at a place where X is employed in the workplace or otherwise in the course of X's employment, another individual harasses X by reference to the relevant characteristics and both are employed at that place by the same employer or where the other individual is the complainant's employer or where the alleged harasser is a client, customer or other business contact of X's employer and the circumstances of the harassment are such that X's employer ought reasonably to have taken steps to prevent it, then for the purposes of this Act, the harassment constitutes discrimination by X's employer in relation to X's conditions of employment on whichever discriminatory ground is relevant to persons having the same relevant characteristic as X.

Of course, this applies whether X is in the workplace or not and where X is treated differently in the workplace because of their rejection or acceptance of the harassment. It is immaterial whether the parties are related or they have the same relevant characteristics. Harassment may be considered as any act or conduct (including spoken words, gestures, or the production, display or circulation of written words, pictures or other material if the action or other conduct is unwelcome and would reasonably be regarded in relation to the relevant characteristic as offensive, humiliating or intimidating to the recipient. It shall of course be a defence for an employer to show that they took all reasonable steps and therefore it would be recommended to employers that they have a procedure generally to deal with alleged harassment/bullying/intimidation in the workplace. Such procedure could be used generally in respect of sexual harassment, harassment under the various other grounds of discrimination under the Employment Equality Act, 1998, or indeed any general grounds of intimidation.

GENERAL DUTIES OF EMPLOYEES

The 1989 Act also sets out the statutory duties for employees and the same provision applies that these are enacted for the purpose of criminal proceedings. However, they are of more importance within the context of discipline and dismissal for the purposes of the Unfair Dismissals Acts, 1977 to 1993 — that is, if there is a breach of one of these provisions, it may prove reasonable grounds for dismissal.

Again the provisions of the Act (s. 9) are worth noting:

1. It shall be the duty of every employee, while at work:

a) to take reasonable care for his own safety, health and welfare and that of any other person who may be affected by his acts or omissions while at work;

b) to co-operate with his employer and any other person to such extent as will enable his employer or the other person to comply with any of the relevant statutory provisions;

c) to use in such manner so as to provide the protection intended any suitable appliance, protective clothing, convenience, equipment or other means or thing provided (whether for his use alone or for use by him in common with others) for securing his safety, health or welfare while at work; and

d) to report to his employer or his immediate supervisor, without unreasonable delay, any defects in plant, equipment, place of work or systems of work, which might endanger safety, health or welfare of which he become aware.

(2) No person shall intentionally or recklessly interfere with or misuse any appliance, protective clothing, convenience, equipment or other means or thing provided in pursuance of any of the relevant statutory provisions or otherwise, for securing the safety, health or welfare of persons arising out of work activities.

SAFETY STATEMENT

A safety statement is management's written programme for safeguarding health and safety in the workplace. All employers have a general obligation to provide a safety statement, which must specify the manner in which safety, health and welfare at work is to be adhered to. The safety statement may be used in evidence in any criminal or civil proceedings (e.g. for personal injury arising from an accident). The safety statement must identify hazards and provide an assessment of the risks to safety and health. However, the General Application Regulations, 1993, provides that:

> it shall be the duty of every employer in preparing a safety state-
> ment (a) to be in possession of an assessment in writing of the risk
> to safety and health at the place of work . . . such risks to include
> any which puts groups of employees at unusual risk, and
> (b) to decide on any protective measures to be taken and if neces-
> sary, the protective equipment to be used.

Thus, employers must show in writing how they carried out the assessment. A hazard is anything that can potentially cause harm —
these are classified as physical and chemical hazards and biological
agents. Human factors must also be taken into account when identifying hazards. Workers should be mentally and physically capable of
doing their jobs in safety. Vulnerable groups include pregnant
women, young workers, older workers and people with disabilities.

If there is a hazard present, the next step is to consider the likelihood of it causing an accident. In other words, carry out a "risk assessment". Depending on the nature of the workplace and the
inherent hazards, it is this writer's opinion that a professional engi-
neer, chemist or relevant expert be retained to advise in this regard.

The statement must specify:

1. The arrangements and resources provided for safeguarding the
    safety, health and welfare of persons employed at a place of work
    to which the safety statement relates;

2. The co-operation required from employees as regards safety,
    health and welfare; and

3. The names and job titles where applicable of the persons respon-
    sible for the performance of tasks assigned to them by the said
    statement.

If an inspector considers that a safety statement is inadequate, they
may direct that it be revised and the employer must so comply within
30 days. The company director's report must provide an evaluation on
safety in the company for the period covered by the report.

SAFETY REPRESENTATIVE

Every employer must consult with their employees to ensure their
health, safety and welfare at work and to take into account any representation that they may have. Employees may select their own

safety representative. A safety representative shall have a right to information in so far as it is reasonably practical to ensure employees' safety and health in the workplace. All employers must inform the safety representative when an inspector enters the workplace for an inspection.

A safety representative has the following powers:

1. To make representations to an employer on any aspects of safety, health and welfare at the place of work.

2. To investigate accidents and dangerous occurrences, provided that the representative shall not interfere with or obstruct the performance of any statutory obligation required to be performed by any person under any of the relevant statutory provisions; for example, a safety representative cannot prevent a safety inspector from investigating an accident.

3. To make oral or written representations to inspectors on matters of safety, health and welfare at work.

4. To receive advice and information from inspectors on matters of safety, health and welfare at work.

5. To carry out inspections subject to prior notice to the employer and to agreement between the safety representative and the employer as to frequency. The parties shall consider the nature and the extent of the hazards in the place of work in determining the frequency of inspections.

6. To investigate potential hazards and complaints made by any employee whom the representative represents relating to that employee's health, safety and welfare at the place of work, subject to prior notice to the employer, and in circumstances in which it is reasonable to assume that risk of personal injury exists.

7. To accompany an inspector on any tour of inspection other than one made for the purpose of investigating an accident.

GENERAL DUTIES OF DESIGNERS, MANUFACTURERS AND OTHERS

Again, these duties contained in the Act are only referable in the context of criminal proceedings. Thus, there are duties on the manufacturers, designers, importers and suppliers of goods, such as adequate testing, updating of information, the necessary research to eliminate hazards and so forth.

THE "GENERAL APPLICATION" REGULATIONS

The Safety, Health and Welfare at Work (General Application) Regulations, 1993 (SI No. 44 of 1993) came into effect on 18 February 1993. The regulations are extremely lengthy and detailed but everybody, employers and employees, would be well advised to read them. These Regulations extend the requirements of the 1989 Act, which as previously stated is a framework Act, and also implement EC Directive 89/391/EEC on the introduction of measures to encourage improvements in the health and safety of workers in the workplace. The regulations also implement various other related EC Directives.

In summary, the regulations impose general and specific obligations on employers with regard to the evaluation and reduction of exposure of employees to occupational risks and hazards in the workplace. Equally, employees have to co-operate with their employers on their health and safety in the workplace. Existing legal obligations relating to the safe use of electricity, the provision of first-aid facilities and notification of accidents and dangerous occurrences to the Authority are revised and updated. The cost of any measures relating to health and safety shall be borne by the employer alone, including the cost of all safety clothing, etc. The Regulations have detailed provision concerning:

1. Requirements for all workplaces — for example, with regard to temperature, lighting, rest rooms, washrooms and so forth, with specific regulations for older and new premises with a cutoff date of 31 December 1992;

2. Work equipment requirements for equipment used for the first time before and after 31 December 1992;

3. Listing of work activities which require personal protective equipment;

4. Listing of safety equipment for various parts of the body, such as head or feet, with requirements for various different types of work;

5. Matters that have to be considered for the manual handling of loads;

6. Minimum requirements for all display screen equipment and work stations; and

7. Listing of dangerous occurrences, such as flammable substances.

ACCIDENT NOTIFICATION

Where an accident happens:

*   At a person's place of work and the individual dies or is prevented from carrying out his work for more than three days following the accident; or

*   Where a person who has an accident at a place related to their work or work activity dies or suffers an injury or condition and requires treatment from a doctor as an in- or outpatient; or

*   If there is a dangerous occurrence (e.g. collapse of scaffolding);

Then the responsible person (e.g. the employer) shall notify the Authority. In the case of death, the Authority must be advised by the quickest possible method of the name of the deceased, brief particulars and the location of the accident. As soon as practicable, a full report should go to the Authority of the death, injury or condition. In the event of a death, the scene of the accident must not be tampered with until an inspector has inspected the site.

A delayed death (where the injured person dies within a year of the accident) must also be advised to the Authority. Records of accidents must be kept for ten years. There are statutory forms from the 1993 Regulations, which must be used to notify the Authority.

MATERNITY PROTECTION ACT, 1994

This Act was passed to implement EC Council Directive 92/85/EEC. It came into effect on 30 January 1995 (SI No. 16 of 1995). In the area of health and safety, the most important aspect is that this Act provided for the first time for what is known as "health and safety leave". An employer is obliged to carry out a risk assessment in respect of effects on pregnant employees or mothers who have recently given birth or are breastfeeding. An employee is entitled to such leave when the employer is required to move her from normal work as a result of a risk assessment or because she cannot be required to perform or provide night work *and* where it is not technically or objectively feasible for the employer to move the employee or such a move cannot reasonably be required on duly substantiated grounds or the other work to which the employer proposes to move the employee is not suitable (see Chapter 5 on the Maternity Protection Act, 1994).

PROTECTION OF YOUNG PERSONS (EMPLOYMENT) ACT, 1996

The Protection of Young Persons (Employment) Act, 1996, provides that an employer must carry out a risk assessment in respect of the employment of children or young persons (Safety, Health and Welfare at Work (Children and Young Persons) Regulations, 1998 (SI No. 504 of 1998). The risk assessment is in relation to the young person's lack of experience or maturity, exposure to physical, biological and chemical agents or work processes and work. The Regulations contain a detailed list of the various agents and work processes. The risk assessment looks at all aspects of the work; if there is a situation where it is considered that the work is beyond the physical or mental capacity of the child, involves the risk of accident or exposure to radiation, etc., then the child or young person should not be employed. The employer also has an obligation to inform a child or young person of any risk identified and where a child is being employed, the parent or guardian must be informed as well. Also, where there is a risk, there must be health surveillance. If the child or young person is to do night work, there must be a free assessment of their health beforehand. The result of such tests should be given to the young person and to the parent or guardian of a young person.

WELFARE AT WORK

The Safety, Health and Welfare at Work (Miscellaneous Welfare Provisions) Regulations, 1995 (SI No. 358 of 1995) repeal relevant sections of the Factories Act, 1955, the Office Premises Act, 1958 and the Safety in Industry Act, 1980. The Regulations provide for a number of employer duties.

Cleanliness

Every employer must ensure that:

1. Every place of work shall be kept in a clean state and accumulations of dirt, refuse, trade refuse and waste shall be removed at least once every day by a suitable method, and

2. The floor of every workroom shall be cleaned at least once every week by a suitable method.

Facilities for Sitting

Every employer should provide reasonable opportunities for sitting as long as it does not affect their work. If a substantial proportion of the work can be done sitting, then there should be suitable facilities for sitting.

Supply of Drinking Water

Every employer must ensure that there is an adequate supply of wholesome drinking water maintained at suitable points conveniently accessible to all employed persons.

Facilities for Taking Meals, etc.

Every employer must ensure that

1. Suitable and adequate facilities for boiling water and taking meals are provided and maintained for the use of employed persons, or

2. Employed persons have reasonable access to other suitable and adequate facilities for the taking of meals.

There must also be a safe location to eat meals.

The 1993 Regulations also provide that there should be comfortable and safe workstations with safe and suitable chairs. There should be at least 4.65 square metres of floorspace for each office worker; a comfortable temperature of at least 17.5°C; adequate lighting; washing facilities. In respect of VDUs, the 1993 Regulations require employers to carry out a risk assessment of VDU work-stations to include keyboard, VDU screen, printer, workchair, workdesk and the actual environment. Eye tests must be provided at regular intervals for each employee before commencing display screen work or if the employee experiences visual difficulties which may be due to VDU work.

ANTI-SMOKING PROVISIONS

The Tobacco (Health Promotion and Protection) Regulations, 1995 (SI No. 359 of 1995), came into force on 1 January 1996 (with the exception of provisions for restaurants, which came into effect on 1 May 1996). These Regulations revoke the 1990 Regulations. The relevant Act is the Tobacco (Health Promotion and Protection) Act, 1988. In summary, a person cannot smoke in any common/public areas or rooms in any building occupied by the state or any statutory body; crèches/kindergartens; schools (except staffrooms); teaching areas of third level institutions; any food preparation area of restaurants, cafés, etc.; waiting rooms of railway and bus stations; spectator areas of sports halls; cinemas, theatres and other places of entertainment; hospitals, nursing homes and other places of care; public areas of banks; hairdressers. Of course, facilities may be provided for staff or patients who smoke. Smoking is prohibited in any public transport vehicle. The non-smoking area in restaurants, canteens etc., must be at least on half of the seating; there are, however, provisions for inspection by the health board, which may provide for a larger "smoking area".

COMMON LAW

General Duty of Care

The common law duty of care runs alongside the health and safety legislation. As stated above, the various statutory duties of employers and employees are not admissible in a civil action for damages (though the safety statement is) and thus it is important to consider the common law duties.

It is settled law that "the duty of an employer towards a servant is to take reasonable care for the servant's safety in all the circumstances of the case". This principle was further clarified by Henchy J in *Bradley* v *CIE* [1976] IR 217 at page 223, where he stated:

> The law does not require an employer to ensure in all circumstances the safety of his workmen. He will have discharged his

> duty of care if he does what a reasonable and prudent employer
> would have done in the circumstances.

In that case, the claimant was a signalman whose duties included servicing lamps on certain signals at the top of vertical signposts. He reached each lamp by climbing the half-inch round steel rungs of an almost vertical steel ladder attached to each signal post. While descending the ladder, his right foot slipped on a rung; he fell to the ground and was injured. He claimed damages and the High Court jury found that CIE had been negligent in failing to provide a safe place of work. Evidence was given that Mr Bradley's fall would have been prevented if an elliptical steel cage had been attached to the ladder so that he could go up and down in the cage. He was awarded damages.

On appeal to the Supreme Court, it was held that the suggested steel cage had not been shown either to have been one which was commonly used by other railway operators or one a reasonably prudent employer would think was necessary for the protection of his employees. The High Court award was overruled.

In *Brady* v *Beckman Instruments (Galway) Inc.* [1986] ILRM 361, the plaintiff contracted a form of dermatitis as a result of inhaling certain fumes. It was considered that the plaintiff had very little exposure, and his injury was "unique and improbable as not to be one which could be said to have been reasonably foreseeable by his employers" (page 363). Therefore, it is not sufficient for the injured employee merely to seek damages on a bare allegation of negligence. An employee must make sure to state how and why the employer was in breach of their duty of care. Equally, the duty varies according to the employee's circumstances. Accordingly, an employee's lack of work experience, expertise, youth or physical disability may be taken into account in assessing the duty of care owed by the employer.

The duty of care is further considered under the following headings:

Competent Staff

An employer owes a duty to use due care to select proper and competent staff. However, before an employer is liable, the employer must be aware of their incompetence. In the case of *Hough* v *Irish Base Metals Ltd.* (8 December 1967 and reported on page 323, McMahon and Binchy, 1990) the Supreme Court held that certain "larking" for a bit of fun did not constitute a breach of duty of care. In this case, an employee was injured when jumping away from a gas fire which had been placed near him for "a bit of devilment" by another employee. As no evidence was given of lack of supervision, there was no liability.

This duty is to be distinguished for vicarious liability, where the employer will be responsible for the torts (wrongs) of fellow employees of the injured employee in the course of their employment.

Safe Place of Work

The employer must ensure that a reasonable safe place of work is provided and maintained for employees. It is not sufficient to show that the employee was aware of the danger of the premises. The test that is applied is that of reasonable foresight on the part of the employer. However, an employer is not entitled to expect employees to act in the interests of their own safety. Premises that are not under the employer's control may cause problems; for example, delivering goods to customers' premises. There is no definite answer to this problem but the general principle is that where there is no liability on the customer's part, freedom from liability will also extend to the employer.

Proper Equipment

An employer has the duty to take "reasonable care to provide proper appliances and to maintain them in a proper condition and so to carry on his/her operations as not to subject those employed by him/her to unnecessary risk". Equally, an employer may be liable for the failure to provide equipment essential to the safety of the employee or the failure to maintain equipment in a safe condition.

Safe System of Work

Once again, "safe" means what is reasonable under the circumstances. "System" may be loosely defined as a method of doing work. Therefore, "If an accident causes injury to a workman and the accident results from a risk of an unsafe system of work, against which the employer should have, but did not, take reasonable precautions to guard, then the employer is liable for damages" (*Kinsella* v

Hammond Lane Industries Ltd. 96 ILTR 1 at page 4). Examples of failure to provide a safe system would include unstable scaffolding.

CONTRIBUTORY NEGLIGENCE

In any civil proceedings for damages, the employer must have some evidence that the employee contributed to the accident, otherwise this contention will not be accepted by the court. However, the courts are aware that the employer sets standards of care and that the employee, in the employee's own economic interests, may be obliged to accept a less than adequate level of safety. In *Steward* v *Killeen Paper Mills Ltd.* ([1959] IR 436 at page 450), an employer customarily failed to keep in its correct place a protective guard on a dangerous machine in a paper mill and thus caused the employee operating the machine to take a chance in grabbing at paper and injuring himself. Kingsmill-Moore J stated: "Where it can be shown that a regular practice exists unchecked, it is difficult to convict of contributory negligence a workman who follows such practice."

Other matters, such as an employee's failure to wear protective clothing or to comply with safety requirements, would constitute contributory action on the employee's part.

BULLYING

The Health and Safety Authority has defined "bullying" in the workplace as:

> repeated aggression, verbal, psychological or physical, conducted by an individual or group against another person or persons.

Isolated incidences of aggressive behaviour, while not to be tolerated, should not be described as bullying. Only inappropriate aggressive behaviour, which is systematic and ongoing, is regarded as bullying. The Authority has published a booklet which has been drawn up by the Employment Equality Agency, the Departments of Justice, Equality and Law Reform, and Enterprise, Trade and Employment, the Labour Relations Commission, IBEC and ICTU.

Examples of bullying behaviour include verbal abuse, threats, jokes, isolation or exclusion from social activities, pestering people,

imposition of impossible deadlines, giving one individual all the un-
pleasant work and so forth.

The nature of "bullying" can take many different forms and this is
in no way a complete list. It must of course be noted that these are
grey areas which are not necessarily easy to identify. However, "bullying" should not be confused with authoritarian management of an
operation. In essence, "bullying" is more in the nature of intimidation
and victimisation in the workplace.

There are groups of employees who may be more vulnerable to
this form of behaviour; for example, employees lower down the hier-
archy; employees who have unreasonable targets/deadlines to meet;
employees who challenge management's authority when, for example,
they are not provided with the necessary resources to carry out their
job in a professional manner; or employees who lack a certain level of
education. Many trade disputes concerning trade membership and
recognition may lead to intimidation and aggression in the workplace. There are other groups of employees who may be specifically
vulnerable, such as employees with a physical or learning disability,
persons of different religious or political beliefs or sexual orientation
and so forth. These latter groups should have a remedy in respect of
the provisions combating harassment in the Employment Equality
Act, 1998.

"Bullying" can manifest in various illnesses, which may be considered to be personal injuries. Of course, if the employee believes that
they have been injured, then there will have to be the necessary
medical certification to confirm such illness and the cause of it. There
is also the issue of ongoing anxiety of the employee. This is obviously
not going to assist any firm or organisation, because the employee
who is living in a constant state of anxiety is not capable of giving of
their best.

Many employments now have procedures in place not only to deal
with allegations of sexual harassment but also harassment generally.
Indeed, it is a good defence for an employer to state that there is such
a procedure in place when there are allegations of such harassment.
Of course, the procedure must actually be implemented and this will
become more standard practice when the Employment Equality Act,
1998, is implemented. When dealing with such allegations, all appropriate procedures should be put in place, such as advice, counselling
and so forth. It is in everyone's interests that the matter be resolved

as soon as possible. In matters that are not easily resolved, a proper investigation should take place with members of management (not involved in any allegations) hearing the allegations and giving all parties rights of representation and the right of cross-examination for the other party. It is important that all fair procedures should be applied.

An employer also has an obligation to look after the health, safety and welfare at work of all employees under the general health and safety provisions in the General Application Regulations, where there is an obligation to develop an adequate prevention policy in relation to health, safety and welfare at work, to include working conditions and so forth.

In one of the first reported cases, *Saehan Media Ireland Ltd.* v *A Worker* ([1999] ELR 41), the Labour Court stated that:

> . . . work-related stress is recognised as a health and safety issue and employers have an obligation to deal with instances of its occurrence which may be brought to their attention.

In this case, the claimant was employed as head of security and reported directly to the HR Manager. In referring his case to the Labour Court, he alleged that intimidatory remarks were levelled at him by the HR Manager. This was denied by the company, which claimed that there was no intimidation, bullying or harassment. Further, the worker claimed that the company's grievance procedure made no provision for cases where a problem concerned an employee's immediate superior, that he had raised the issue on a number of occasions with senior management but received no reply and that the intimidation to which he was subjected had affected his health. The Labour Court held that the incidents in themselves did not amount to bullying, as that term was generally understood. However, work-related stress was a health and safety issue which management had an obligation to deal with. The employer's failure to respond within the terms of the grievance procedure represented a serious omission, which may have exacerbated the worker's condition. Compensation was awarded in the sum of £500.

STRESS IN THE WORKPLACE

Employers have both a statutory and a common law duty of care to
their employees. This duty is not only related to stress, but may also
cover "work-related stress", which is a more recent phenomenon and
may provide fertile grounds for claims.

The Health and Safety Authority in their booklet, "Workplace
Stress", acknowledged that workplace stress is becoming an increasing concern for both employers and employees. Indeed, it has to be
stated that more and more employees are considering that they may
well have claims for compensation in respect of stress in the workplace. The Health and Safety Authority has recently defined workplace stress as arising "when the demands on a person exceed their
capacity to meet them". They say that causes of stress in the workplace include shift work, faulty work organisation, changes in work
practices, poor working relationships, poor communications, lack of
control, ill-defined work roles, dull repetitive work, highly demanding
tasks, direct interface with the public, etc.

They further state that stress can contribute to any of the following conditions: increased heart disease, increased digestive problems,
skin problems, anxiety, depression, irritability, fatigue, loss of job
satisfaction, increased accidents, substance abuse (including alcohol
and cigarettes).

Within the organisation, stress can lead to increased absenteeism,
low motivation, reduced productivity, reduced efficiency, faulty deci-
sion-making and poor industrial relations.

The Health and Safety Authority states that safeguards and controls must be implemented primarily at organisational level which is
ususally the (apparent) source of the problem. This may involve
changes in working conditions, organisations and structures. These
changes may need to be supported by a programme of individual
coping strategies.

Whilst there have been relatively few actions in this area, this
writer considers that it will be of major importance in the future. The
matter of stress surfaces in particular in cases of individual grievances with the workplace and potentially where there are constructive dismissal claims. It would be fair to say that if employers do not
handle general grievances or work situations which may lead to constructive dismissal (breach of contract), they will be open to claims to

the effect that stress at the workplace has caused the employee injury and illness.

Within recent UK case law, the first case of importance was *Johnstone* v *Bloomsbury Health Authority* ([1991] 2 All ER 293; [1991] 2 WLR 1362). In this case, the plaintiff doctor, a senior house officer, alleged that as a result of working in excess of 88 hours per week, his employers were in breach of their implied duty under his contract of employment with them to take reasonable care for his safety. The Health Authority maintained that these were the hours that he was contracted to work. His contract provided that the standard working week was 40 hours and that he was to be on call for a further 48 hours. He claimed that as he had inadequate sleep he became ill. Technically, this set of proceedings was complicated but the key points were that it was held that the Health Authority were not entitled to require the doctor to work for so many hours in excess of his standard working week as would foreseeably injure his health.

The issue of causation was considered in *Petch* v *Customs and Excise Commissioners* ([1993] ICR 789). Mr Petch, who was a civil servant, claimed damages for negligence against the defendants for causing him to have a mental breakdown by the volume and stressful character of his work. In 1974 whilst working he had a mental breakdown which resulted in his taking sick leave, returning to work in 1975. He was transferred to another department and in 1983, he became ill again and finally retired on medical grounds in 1986. He maintained that the two breakdowns were due to pressure of work. Dillon LJ approached the issue of breach of duty as follows:

> . . . I take the view, in the light of the general circumstances of this case and the other findings of the judge which I have set out, that unless senior management in the defendant's department were aware, or ought to have been aware that the plaintiff was showing signs of impending breakdown or were aware or ought to have been aware that his workload had carried a risk that he would have a breakdown, then the defendants were not negligent in failing to avert the breakdown of October 1974.

The facts suggested that there were no signs of a breakdown and that his workload did not carry a real risk. However, in relation to the second breakdown, the duty of care:

> . . . extended to taking reasonable care to ensure that the duties
> allocated to him did not bring about a repetition of his mental
> breakdown of October 1974.

However, he did not succeed in his case, as the defendants did as
much as they could reasonably be expected to do to dissuade the
plaintiff from coming back to work.

In the "landmark" decision of *Walker* v *Northumberland County
Council* ([1995] 1 All ER 737), Coleman J saw no reason why "the risk
of psychiatric damage should be excluded from the scope of an employer's duty of care". The plaintiff was employed by the defendant
local authority as an area social services officer from 1970 until December 1987. He was responsible for managing four teams of social
services fieldworkers in an area that had a high proportion of childcare problems. In 1986, the plaintiff suffered a nervous breakdown
because of the stress and pressures of work and was off work for
three months. Before he returned to work, he discussed his position
with his superior who agreed that some assistance should be provided to lessen the burden of the plaintiff's work. In the event, when
the plaintiff returned to work, only very limited assistance was provided and he found that he had to clear the backlog of paperwork that
had built up during his absence while the pending childcare cases in
his area were increasing at a considerable rate. Six months later, he
suffered a second mental breakdown and was forced to stop work
permanently. In February 1988, he was dismissed by the local
authority on the grounds of permanent ill health. He brought an action against the local authority claiming damages for breach of its
duty of care, as his employer, to take reasonable steps to avoid exposing him to a health-endangering workload.

Coleman J held that where it was reasonably foreseeable to an
employer that an employee might suffer a nervous breakdown because of the stress and pressures of their workload, the employer was
under a duty of care, as part of the duty to provide a safe system of
work, not to cause the employee psychiatric damage by reason of the
volume or character of the work which the employee was required to
perform. On the facts, prior to the first illness, it was not reasonably
foreseeable to the local authority that the plaintiff's workload would
give rise to a material risk of mental illness. However, as to the second illness, the local authority ought to have foreseen that if the

plaintiff was again exposed to the same workload, there was a risk that he would suffer another nervous breakdown, which would probably end his career as an area manager. The local authority ought therefore to have provided additional assistance to reduce the plaintiff's workload, even at the expense of some disruption of other social work and, in choosing to continue to employ him without providing effective help, it had acted unreasonably and in breach of its duty of care. It followed that the local authority was liable in negligence for the plaintiff's second nervous breakdown and that accordingly he was entitled to damages.

In summary, a number of factors must be considered when approaching this type of situation:

1. If an employee advises their employer that they have an unreasonable volume of work to do, then the employer should investigate the matter.

2. If an employee who has never shown signs of "stress" before and has a good mental history takes sick leave as a result of stress or if they have a breakdown, the employer may have a case to answer. Of course, medical evidence would be absolutely vital.

3. If there has already been a breakdown and there is a history of re-employment, then the employer must be extremely careful and changes must be made so that a further breakdown does not occur.

4. The net effect of the *Walker* case is that if an employee does have a breakdown, if the employer takes them back to work, the employee may become ill again and may have to go on income continuance.

5. Finally, in summary, employers will have to be even more careful in dealing with claims of alleged sexual harassment or constructive dismissal, as the issue of stress-related illness is more likely to arise.

CONTRACT OF INSURANCE

When an employer takes out employer liability insurance, that employer is entering into a contract with the insurance company. From the employer liability point of view, certain aspects of the standard contract are worth noting:

1. The employer subjugates the right to conduct or control on their own behalf any claim made under the policy. In effect, this means handing over the running of the insurance claim to the insurers' solicitors, and that the insurance company will be the decision-maker as regards the substance or otherwise of the claim.

2. It will ensure that employees other than those working under a contract of service (for example, independent contractors) are covered. If they are not so covered, there could well be a claim against the company's public liability policy.

CLAIMS FOR PERSONAL INJURY AND TIME LIMITS

The Statutes of Limitation, 1957 and 1991, provide that a claim for personal injury as a result of negligence, nuisance or breach of duty must be brought within three years from the date of cause of action accrued or the date of knowledge, if later, of the person injured. Personal injuries include any disease and any impairment of a person's physical or mental condition.

The "date of knowledge" (section 2 of the Statute of Limitations (Amendment) Act, 1991, which was passed into law on 10 July 1991) refers to the date on which the individual first had knowledge of the following facts:

1. That the individual actually had been injured;

2. That the injury in question was significant;

3. That the injury was attributable in whole or in part to the act or omission which is alleged to constitute negligence, nuisance or breach of duty;

4. The identity of the defendant; and

5. If it is alleged that the act or omission was by another person, then the identity of that person and the facts supporting the bringing of an action against that person.

The "knowledge" includes what the injured person should know from facts that are observable or ascertainable to that person with medical or other expert advice. A person has to take all reasonable steps to obtain that knowledge.

In cases where the claim is statute-barred, there is nothing prohibiting the person bringing their claim because the argument of time limits is a defence to a claim. There is the possibility that the defence may not be allowed.

Normally in personal injury cases, little time elapses between a prospective plaintiff suffering an injury and appreciating that they have a cause of action in respect of it. Occasionally, however, a person may contract a disease that is slow to manifest itself, or a comparatively trivial incident may lead after many years to epilepsy or some cancerous condition. For example, in case of pneumoconiosis and asbestosis, substantial injury to the lungs may be in existence for years before it is actually discovered. The time limit would run from the date of discovery of the alleged injury. In these situations, a person would have to take all reasonable steps to obtain medical advice. In the case of failure to do so, then the time limit would run from the date the person suspects the condition.

If a person dies within the three-year limitation period, such proceedings for alleged injury must be brought within three years from date of death, or from the date that the personal representative became aware of the facts of the case, whichever is the later.

COURT PRACTICE AND PROCEDURE

Frequently, a notice of claim will commence with the employer receiving a letter from the employee's solicitor referring to the incident, asking for an admission of liability and agreement to pay substantial damages within seven days, otherwise proceedings will be issued and served on the employer. At this point, an employer should notify the insurers and send them a copy of the letter. Furthermore, records (if any) should be searched to check the date of the accident.

Assuming that the employer has not admitted liability and the employee wishes to proceed with a claim, the employee must decide in what court to commence proceedings, which is determined by the financial jurisdiction of each court;

1. District Court (up to £5,000);

2. Circuit Court (between £5,000 and £30,000);

3.   High Court (any amount over £30,000).

At this stage, there are certain court documents that must be served on each party before the case is ready to go into court. The real purpose of these documents is for both parties to find out about the circumstances of the alleged accident and loss.

Briefly, the necessary documents for each court are:

1.   *District Court*: (a) Civil Process; (b) Notice of Intention to Defend; (c) Counterclaim. These pleadings are usually not complicated and can be dealt with expeditiously.

2.   *Circuit Court*: (a) Civil Bill; (b) Notice of Appearance; (c) Notice for Particulars; (d) Defence; (e) Notice for Trial. These pleadings take approximately six months if done expeditiously. The timing of the hearing will depend on the circuit, that is, the length of the lists of cases awaiting hearing.

3.   *High Court*: (a) Plenary Summons; (b) Notice of Appearance; (c) Statement of Claim; (d) Notice for Particulars; (e) Reply to Particulars; (f) Defence; (g) Reply; (h) Notice of set-down for trial. These pleadings take about six to eight months if done expeditiously. The case then goes into the list and it takes nine to twelve months before the matter comes up for hearing; however, there can be very long delays.

It might be noted that all the above are routine court documents. In many cases, there may also be third party proceedings (that is, a second defendant). This would necessitate further documentation.

Employer Position

The insurance company's solicitor and counsel will act on the employer's behalf and handle all court documentation. However, it is important that an employer request that all court pleadings be conducted as speedily as possible, the reason being that if damages are awarded or if the case is settled, such monies will be computed on the basis of loss. Thus, the shorter the time, the less loss will be incurred. Loss will comprise not only lost earnings but account will also be taken of the physical condition of the employee, the state of the labour market, and non-pecuniary loss, such as payment for suffering, loss of amenities, loss of life expectation. Employers should ensure that they are fully informed of all documents that are exchanged between the parties. Many cases do not go to full hearing as they may either be settled at the initial stages of the pleadings or else at the door of the court.

Costs

Costs are also a major item in any of these cases, as there are legal costs and witness costs. Both sides may retain (depending on the circumstances) solicitors, one senior counsel and one junior counsel, and expert witnesses including medical consultants, engineers and actuaries.

DISMISSAL DURING PROCEEDINGS AGAINST EMPLOYER

It is a common occurrence that an employee alleges involvement in an accident at work and then goes out sick for a considerable time. During their absence, they may bring proceedings against their employer for negligence, claiming damages. Faced with such circumstances, employers frequently leave employees "on the books" and do not apply normal procedures for long-term absenteeism. The result is that when the employee's injury claim is completed (either goes to court or is settled) they will look for their job back. From an employer viewpoint, such a position is unenviable because the employer is not in a good position to dismiss, since fair procedures have not been applied. In such a situation, the employee usually claims they are fit to return to work. I would go a step further and state that if there was a dismissal and the employee brought a claim under the Unfair Dismissals Acts, 1977–1993, then they may well succeed in their case and may indeed be awarded re-employment or more usually re-engagement. On balance, the most practical thing for the employer to do is to have the employee medically examined, taking them back only if they are certified as fit to return. An assessment about future employment can be made at that stage. In any event, the insurance company may increase the company premium or indeed refuse to cover the particular employee. If the employee is certified unfit to return, the employer may have no option but to terminate the employment. There is no obligation on the employer to find alternative work or "light work". However, if there is custom and practice in the em-

ployment to provide alternative work, the employer should do everything reasonable to find other suitable work for the employee.

Thus, when an employee goes out sick following an alleged accident, an employer is advised to follow and apply normal absenteeism
procedures. The employer may then be in a position to dismiss the
employee and successfully defend an unfair dismissal claim. It can be
argued that the act of dismissal can lead to further problems insofar
as the employee may receive more in damages because of the loss of
their job. Of course, the company premium could also be affected.
From an employment law viewpoint, however, it is more prudent to
follow normal absenteeism/dismissal procedures should a dismissal
arise. Employers should make clear the reason for dismissal; that is,
incapability to perform the job, as opposed to dismissal due to the
employee taking legal proceedings against the employer.

I should state that in my recent experience, there have been quite
a number of cases where employees have been out sick for some considerable time and, in accordance with company rules, they have
been paid for the first 26 weeks (or one year) of their absence. After
this stage, consideration has to be given to the income continuance
scheme. If the insurance company accepts that the employee is ill and
incapable of returning to work in the foreseeable future, then they
can receive income continuance. However, there have been a large
number of cases where the medical referees of insurance companies
have certified that the employee is fit to go to work. There may then
be a dilemma, as the employer and the insurers express two quite
opposite views. This is quite common and there have been cases
where employees are subsequently dismissed and only receive State
disability benefit. They bring unfair dismissals claims and obviously
if they maintain that they are not fit to work, they cannot really be
awarded any compensation because they are not available to do the
job for which they were employed. In these situations, the Employment Appeals Tribunal privately requests the employer to make all
the necessary appeals to the insurance company to see if they will get
further medical opinion to show that the employee is unfit for work.
If this arrangement is not put in place, in this writer's opinion, there
would be an award for re-engagement and the employer would be left
with a choice either to re-employ the employee at some time in the
future or else to expend further legal costs in appealing the matter to
the Circuit Court, where the same award may be made.

OCCUPIERS' LIABILITY ACT, 1995

This Act, which became law on 17 July 1995, provides that an occupier of premises also owes a statutory duty towards three classes of entrant: visitors, recreational users and trespassers. A "visitor" means an entrant who is lawfully on the premises of the occupier, e.g. persons entering the premises lawfully in the normal course of business. The duty owed to visitors is to take reasonable care that they and their property do not suffer injury or damage by reason of any danger existing on the premises of the occupier. This is very like the standard duty of care in ordinary negligence and of course this may be affected by a plaintiff's contributory negligence. A "lower" duty of care is afforded to recreational users and trespassers.

The Act provides that there must be written notices that are simple, clear, reasonable, placed in a prominent position and carefully drafted to enable occupiers to restrict, modify or exclude their duties under the Act. For example, notices must be prominently displayed at entrances. However, obviously an owner cannot then intentionally injure or act in a reckless manner towards a visitor.

An occupier will not be liable for damage or injury done to an entrant on the premises by an independent contractor, provided of course that all reasonable care was used when engaging the independent contractor. Of course, this is not applicable if the occupier knows (or indeed ought to have known) that the work was not properly done.

Finally, it is vital to have the appropriate employer and public liability insurance in place.

General References

Brady, C. and A. Kerr (1994), *The Limitation of Actions*, 2nd edition, Dublin: The Incorporated Law Society of Ireland.

Hall, G., "The Occupiers' Liability Act, 1995: Modification of Occupier's Duty to Entrants", *GILSI*, Vol. 89, No. 5, pp. 189–90.

Health and Safety Authority (1995), *Guide to the Safety, Health and Welfare at Work Act, 1989 and the Safety, Health and Welfare at Work (General Application) Regulations, 1993*, Dublin: HSA.

Health and Safety Authority (1999), *Bullying at Work*, Dublin: HSA.

Health and Safety Authority (no date), *Workplace Stress*, Dublin: HSA.

McMahon, Bryan (1995), "Occupiers' Liability Act, 1995", *GILSI*, Vol. 89, No. 9, pp. 353–5.

McMahon, B. and W. Binchy (1990), *Irish Law of Torts*, 2nd Edition, Dublin: Butterworth (Ireland) Ltd.

Mesham, John (1995), "A flood of claims?", *Solicitors' Journal*, 20 July, p.732.

Murphy, Dan (1995), "Irish Law on Health, Safety and Welfare at Work", *Medico-Legal Journal*, Vol. 1, No. 1, p. 24.

Shannon, G. (1998), "Employers' Liability and Safety Statement: Part I and II", *Commercial Law Practitioner*, Vol. 5, Nos. 9 and 10.

White, J.P.M. (1989), *Irish Law of Damages for Personal Injury and Death*, Dublin: Butterworths.

White, J.P.M. (1994), *Civil Liability for Industrial Accidents*, Dublin: Oak Tree Press.

SECTION THREE

TERMINATION OF EMPLOYMENT

Chapter Sixteen

NOTICE

An employer or employee who wishes to terminate the contract of employment must give the requisite notice unless agreed otherwise. Prior to the enactment of the Minimum Notice and Terms of Employment Act, 1973, it was the common law that decided what was the acceptable period of notice to terminate the contract of employment. That period was decided on the basis of the position that the employee held and the frequency of payments; for example, monthly, weekly, or hourly. Thus, if an employee were paid weekly, the notice period would be one week, though an employee who was an executive may be entitled to a few months' notice. In the case of *Tierney* v *Irish Meat Packers* (High Court, unreported, Lardner J, 1989, and noted at ((1989) 8 JISLL 59) an employee with nine years' service as group Credit Controller was given the statutory minimum notice of six weeks. The High Court considered that this was not reasonable, so he was awarded six months' notice.

The common law entitlement to notice was considered further in *Lyons* v *M.F. Kent (International) Ltd.* ([1996] ELR 103) where it was considered that the notice period had to be decided on what was reasonable in all the circumstances. Each case had to be decided on its own merits and by reference to modern standards. In this case, Costello P considered the fact that the plaintiff who claimed wrongful dismissal (common law entitlement to notice) was a professionally qualified person who carried on his profession in Ireland before being sent abroad for the company. His work status and level of responsibility was also relevant. Combining all these factors, a twelve-month notice period (i.e. loss only) was applied.

The Minimum Notice and Terms of Employment Act, 1973, provides basic notice periods, based on length of service, which an employer must give unless, of course, the employee is dismissed for misconduct.

The Act also provides the period of notice that an employee who is resigning must give an employer. Furthermore, it provides that an employee is entitled to a written statement of the terms and conditions of
employment (see Chapter 2, "The Contract of Employment").

STATUTORY MINIMUM NOTICE

The Act covers all employers and all employees who are normally expected to work over eight hours per week (the 1973 Act was amended
in 1984 to bring the weekly threshold down from 21 to 18 hours, and
then in 1991 to include regular part-time employees, thus reducing
the threshold to eight hours). There are certain exclusions, to include
the employer's immediate family if living with the employer and employed in the same house or farm; civil servants; members of the
permanent Defence Forces and the Garda Síochána; and seamen
signing on under the Merchant Shipping Act, 1894.

NOTICE TO EMPLOYEES

To dismiss an employee who has been in continuous service for 13
weeks or more, the employer must give a minimum period of notice
based on the employee's length of service, as follows:

• 13 weeks' to 2 years' service — 1 week

• 2 to 5 years' service — 2 weeks

• 5 to 10 years' service — 4 weeks

• 10 to 15 years' service — 6 weeks

• 15 or more years' service — 8 weeks.

Service is continuous unless an employee is dismissed or leaves voluntarily. It is not usually affected by strikes, lockouts, lay-offs or
dismissal followed by immediate re-employment. These rules have
been further amended by the Unfair Dismissals (Amendment) Act,
1993; namely, that if an employee receives and accepts a statutory
redundancy payment from the transferor of a business at the time of
the transfer and by reason of the transfer, then service is broken.
However, note the reasoning of the Employment Appeals Tribunal in
Brett v *Niall Collins Ltd.* (UD 929/94), where it was of the opinion

that this provision ran contrary to the Acquired Rights Directive, as transfer of ownership of a firm or part of a firm does not break continuity of service (see Chapter 11, "Transfer of a Business"). A series of fixed-term (or specified-purpose) contracts with renewals may constitute continuous service (see Chapter 3, "Temporary Employment" and Chapter 16, "Unfair Dismissal" for the new provisions in the Unfair Dismissals (Amendment) Act, 1993, in respect of renewal of fixed-term and specified-purpose contracts). The rules of continuity of service are contained in a schedule to the Act (which has been amended by the Unfair Dismissals Acts, 1977–1993). It might also be noted that the 1993 Act provides that continuity of service is not broken if an employee has been re-employed within 26 weeks after dismissal, if it was for the purpose of avoiding liability under the unfair dismissals legislation.

There are also rules for computable service contained in the Act. These are the actual periods of service used to assess an employee's entitlement to the various periods of notice. This should not be confused with continuous service, as if an employee's service is broken, the period of computable service has to start over again. Periods of service that are not computable include: (a) any week in which an employee is not normally expected to work eight hours; (b) any period of lay-off; sickness or injury; (c) any agreed absence over 26 weeks; or (d) any absence due to a strike in the employment.

CONTRACTUAL NOTICE

The law provides that an employee is entitled to the longer of contractual notice or statutory minimum notice. The 1973 Act provides the statutory minimum notice to which an employee is entitled. However, if the contract of employment provides for a longer period of notice, then that is the notice period to which the employee is entitled. Similarly, if the contract of employment provides for one month's notice and an employee has over 10 years' service, the Act will apply, thereby giving the employee an entitlement to six weeks' notice.

NOTICE AND FIXED-TERM CONTRACTS

A perennial question arises with regard to fixed-term contracts: does such a contract require the inclusion of a notice period as, if there is a notice period, can it genuinely be considered a fixed-term contract? It was confirmed in *O'Mahony* v *College of the Most Holy Trinity*, [1998] ELR 159, that there is no firm decision in the Irish courts, but the determination considered a number of English judgments, including *Dixon* v *the BBC* [1979] QB 546, where Lord Denning MR considered that:

> The words "fixed term" means a specified term, even though it is determinable by notice within that term.

The Irish Employment Appeals Tribunal accepted this ruling, as most contracts for a specified or "fixed" term contain provision for termination by either party. Such provisions for termination within the term do not change the nature of the term. It is well established that the common law is reluctant to force someone to work against their will and if an employee was locked into a fixed-term contract, with no right to resign, this fundamental freedom would be negated. Equally, therefore, if an employee can terminate the contract, then the employer must also be able to bring the contract to an end. The Employment Appeals Tribunal in this case determined that a notice period in a fixed-term contract does not exclude the fact that it is a genuine fixed-term contract.

NOTICE TO EMPLOYER

An employer is entitled to one week's notice from an employee who has been in continuous employment for 13 or more weeks and wishes to end a contract of employment, unless of course the contract of employment provides for a longer period of notice.

LAY-OFF OF EMPLOYEE

An employee who has been put on lay-off and is subsequently made redundant by the employer is still entitled to notice monies. In other words, lay-off cannot be used as a mechanism to avoid paying statutory notice (*Industrial Yarns* v *Greene* [1984] ILRM 15). However, an employee on lay-off who then claims redundancy may not be entitled to monies in lieu of notice unless the lay-off was seen as a method of avoiding the payment of notice monies.

MISCONDUCT

If an employee is dismissed for "misconduct", the employer does not have to give any notice or monies in lieu of notice. The term "misconduct" has led to confusion, because it is not defined in the Act and we must look to the common law for a suitable definition. The High Court in *Brewster* v *Burke and the Minister for Labour* ((1985) 4 JISLL 98) accepted a UK definition of "misconduct":

> It has long been part of our law that a person repudiates the contract of service if he wilfully disobeys the lawful and reasonable orders of his master. Such a refusal fully justifies an employer in dismissing an employee summarily.

In this case, the employee maintained that he was entitled to compensation for notice based on his length of service, but the employer stated that he was not so entitled as he had failed to comply with a reasonable order. The Employment Appeals Tribunal decided that the employee was entitled to compensation for notice and the High Court, in considering the UK precedent, agreed with the EAT determination.

The Tribunal has generally taken a narrow view of the meaning of the term "misconduct". It would include violence and theft, but may not include refusal by an employee to accept reasonable instructions, being late, dismissal arising from conflict of interest, and so forth.

WAIVER OF NOTICE OR PAYMENT IN LIEU OF NOTICE

On termination of employment, an employer or an employee may waive their right to notice or an employee may accept payment in lieu of notice. However, both parties must be in agreement to such an arrangement. Failing that, an employee is entitled to stay on and work during the notice period, though the practicalities are that there may be no work for the employee, and indeed it is usually beneficial for the employee to receive payment in lieu of notice as notice monies (up to £8,000, plus £600 for each complete year of service) may be paid without any reduction of income tax or PRSI (see Chapter 20, "Taxation of Termination Payments").

RIGHTS OF EMPLOYEE DURING NOTICE

During the notice period, the employee is entitled to normal pay and any other rights, such as sick leave, pension contributions, or company car, on the basis that the employee is available and willing to work even though work may not be provided. An employee is entitled to the benefit of monies in lieu of notice, even if that employee is on lay-off during the notice period (*Irish Leathers Ltd.* v *Minister for Labour* (1986) 5 JISLL 211). In *Irish Shipping Ltd.* v *Byrne, the Minister for Labour and Others* ((1987) 6 JISLL 177), Lardner J considered that the employees were not entitled to compensation for loss of minimum notice. Following a winding-up order and the appointment of a liquidator, the employees were re-employed on a day-to-day basis and worked for a longer period than their statutory entitlement and received their usual pay. They were not considered to have had any loss and thus no compensation was awarded.

HOLIDAYS

Holidays may run concurrently with the notice period, provided that the employee is still in employment — the reason being that under the Organisation of Working Time Act, 1997, the employer may decide when holidays may be taken.

MATERNITY, ADOPTIVE AND PARENTAL LEAVE

Where an employee is entitled to return to work following maternity adoptive or parental leave, but is not permitted to do so, the date of termination of the contract is the "due date of return". Hence there is no entitlement to notice (s. 40(3) of the Maternity Protection Act, 1994, and s.30 of the Adoptive Leave Act, 1995, and s. 25(3)(c) of the Parental Leave Act, 1998).

NOTICE AND REDUNDANCY

All periods of notice under the Minimum Notice and Terms of Employment Acts, 1973–1991, the Redundancy Payments Acts, 1967–1991, the Protection of Employment Act, 1977, and contractual notice run concurrently. For example, a company letting go a large number of staff must give the Minister for Enterprise, Trade and Employment at least 30 days' notice under the Protection of Employment

Act, 1977 (Collective Redundancies). An employee with between five and ten years' service would be entitled to two weeks' notice under the Redundancy Acts and would also be entitled to four weeks' notice under the Minimum Notice and Terms of Employment Act. In this situation, however, the employee would be entitled to four weeks' notice, as all the periods of notice run together, plus an additional two days' notice under the Protection of Employment Act.

Another example would be an employee who had three months' notice in the contract of employment and over 15 years' service. The employee may have eight weeks' statutory minimum notice plus two weeks' redundancy notice, but in this situation should be given three months' notice and need only receive the RP1 (Notice of Redundancy) two weeks before the actual termination. If a person is entitled to contractual notice, it is considered that the statutory part of their notice is that period prior to the termination of employment. Thus, an employee who receives the contractual period of notice and is let go prior to its completion (presuming that it is longer than the statutory period of notice) is entitled to the balance under the Minimum Notice and Terms of Employment Act (*Jameson* v *MCW Ltd*. M 878/1983).

NOTICE MUST BE CERTAIN

While notice does not have to be in writing, it must be specific and certain. It is not sufficient for an employer to tell an employee that the employee is going to be dismissed, without giving the actual date.

The High Court has clarified this point by confirming that notice must be certain. In *Bolands Ltd. (in receivership)* v *Josephine Ward and Others* ([1988] ILRM 382), the receiver informed employees that their employment was terminating on a specific date, with a notice period complying with statutory minimum notice. However, the receiver decided to continue trading in the hope that he would be able to obtain a purchaser and the original notice was extended week-by-week for some time. When the employees were terminated, they maintained that they had not received their statutory minimum notice. They appealed to the EAT and were successful (and were awarded full monies in lieu of notice less one week), and the High Court accepted the EAT decision. However, the receiver appealed to the Supreme Court, which considered that they had been in receipt of their minimum notice as the receiver had acted in good faith in granting the extensions; it was clear that the employees knew that they were under notice and that they were benefiting from the notice extensions.

CONSTRUCTIVE DISMISSAL

An employee who resigns and claims constructive dismissal under the Unfair Dismissals Acts, 1977 to 1993, even if successful, is not entitled to statutory minimum notice (*Halal Meat Packers (Bally-haunis) Ltd.* v *Employment Appeals Tribunal* [1990] ELR 49).

NOTICE CANNOT BE WITHDRAWN

Notice of termination of employment cannot be withdrawn except by agreement between the parties.

REMEDIES

If either party is disputing their right to notice, the length of notice or the calculation of continuous service, the issue may be referred to the Employment Appeals Tribunal for determination. Any person who is dissatisfied with the Tribunal's decision — or the Minister for Enterprise, Trade and Employment at the request of the Tribunal — may refer an issue to the High Court on a point of law (see Chapter 23, "Employment Appeals Tribunal").

The vast majority of cases that are brought to the Employment Appeals Tribunal under this Act are in relation to a person's entitlement to notice; for example, an employee given four weeks when they should have been entitled to six, or not getting the necessary amount of pay during the notice period, and so forth. Invariably, these cases under the Minimum Notice Act go hand-in-hand with a claim under the Unfair Dismissals Acts and the Redundancy Payments Acts.

The Employment Appeals Tribunal only has authority to grant statutory minimum notice, and thus an employee who has an entitlement to more than statutory notice will have to bring their claim to the appropriate court — namely, the District Court for sums up to £5,000, the Circuit Court for sums up to £30,000 and the High Court for larger amounts.

COMPENSATION

The Tribunal may dismiss a claim by an employee, or it may award compensation for any loss arising from the employer not giving notice. Social welfare receipts — unemployment benefit or assistance — are not deducted from such an award (*Irish Leathers Ltd.* v *Minister for Labour* (1986) 5 JISLL 211). However, an employee who is ill and not available for work during the notice period is not entitled to any compensation, as that employee is deemed unavailable for work. For the same reason, an employee on strike during the notice period has no entitlement to compensation.

An employee who is working during the notice period, and in receipt of at least the same earnings as they would have received from their previous employer, has no entitlement. However, if the employee receives less money, they would be entitled to the difference, as compensation in this Act is based on "loss".

SETTLEMENTS

If there is a settlement on termination of employment which includes notice monies, it is extremely important to state that fact fully in the settlement agreement, and the amount of monies the employee received. Furthermore, such an arrangement must be fully explained to an employee so that they understand that they cannot subsequently claim that they are entitled to statutory notice monies. If such an agreement was not explained to the employee and there was no specific provision for notice monies, the employee could successfully bring a minimum notice claim to the Employment Appeals Tribunal.

General Reference

Kerr, T. (various years), "The Year in Review" in *Journal of the Irish Society of Labour Law*, Vols. 1–8.

Chapter Seventeen

UNFAIR DISMISSAL

The Unfair Dismissals Act came into force on 15 April 1977 and was a major watershed in Irish employment law. For the first time, an employee claiming unfair dismissal was entitled to a statutory remedy; namely, reinstatement, re-engagement or a maximum of 104 weeks' remuneration. Since then, there have been several amending Acts: the Protection of Employees (Employers' Insolvency) Act, 1984, which reduced the hourly threshold; the Worker Protection (Regular Part-Time Employees) Act, 1991, which extended the scope of the unfair dismissals legislation to cover regular part-time employees; and finally the Unfair Dismissals (Amendment) Act, 1993, which made a number of key amendments. The 1993 Act applied to all dismissals on or after 1 October 1993.

Prior to the enactment of this legislation, an employee who considered that they were unfairly dismissed could only pursue an action through the courts for wrongful dismissal — a more lengthy and expensive process. Furthermore, the employee would technically only be entitled to damages in respect of their lost notice as provided under their contract of employment if they did not get the requisite notice. They may also be entitled to other damages; for example, relocation expenses. However, a person bringing such a claim must mitigate their loss (e.g. by seeking suitable alternative employment). In such cases, each case must be considered on its facts and merits. Application could also be made for so-called "stigma" damages, as in the UK case of *Malik and Another* v *Bank of Credit and Commerce International SA* (in compulsory liquidation) ([1997] IRLR 462), which arose due to the collapse of the bank and the knowledge in the public arena that the bank had been operating in a dishonest manner. The former employees felt that their chances of future employment were jeopardised as a result. The House of Lords held an employee can recover such damages.

However, this remedy was quite impractical for the ordinary working person, as the costs of the case may well be greater than the amount that they succeeded in being awarded. Actions for wrongful dismissal or breach of contract may be taken by executives with long notice periods. This action may also be used by employees who have less than the required service under the Act, but such cases are relatively infrequent. There are other forms of employment that are not covered under the Unfair Dismissals Acts, 1977–1993, including full-time officers of health boards, officers of vocational education committees and civil servants who are employed under statute (e.g. the Vocational Education Acts, 1930–1944, Local Government Act, 1941) where their employment may only be terminated by the responsible Minister. If there is redress in respect of such dismissal, it is usually to the High Court, where fair procedures or indeed the decision to dismiss may be challenged. However, more recently applications have been made to the High Court to restrain the decision to dismiss in cases where an employee considers that fair procedures and natural justice have not been applied (these cases are considered below).

The 1993 Act provides that if a rights commissioner has issued a recommendation under the Act, or if a Tribunal hearing has commenced, the employee cannot obtain damages at common law for wrongful dismissal. Alternatively, if a court hearing has commenced for wrongful dismissal, the employee will not be entitled to redress under the unfair dismissals legislation.

Furthermore, the 1993 Act provides that if a Rights Commissioner has issued a recommendation or has commenced a hearing in respect of a dismissal, the dispute cannot also be referred to a Rights Commissioner or the Labour Court under the Industrial Relations Acts, 1946 to 1990. Alternatively, if a Rights Commissioner has made a recommendation or if a hearing has commenced before the Labour Court under the Industrial Relations Acts, then the employee is not entitled to redress under the unfair dismissal legislation.

APPLICATION OF THE ACT

Obviously, there must be a dismissal before a claimant can obtain redress under the Act. Dismissal (s. 1 of 1977 Act) occurs where:

1. The contract of employment was terminated by the employer, whether notice was given or not;

2. The employee had no option but to resign because of the conduct of the employer (constructive dismissal — see below); or

3. A fixed-term or specified-purpose contract was not renewed (see Chapter 3, "Temporary Employment").

If a former employee does not come within the scope of the Unfair Dismissals Acts, a claim for redress cannot be pursued. Accordingly, the substantive facts or the reason for dismissal cannot be determined by the adjudicating body which may be the Rights Commissioner, the EAT, the Circuit Court or High Court.

CONTRACT OF EMPLOYMENT

A claimant must have been an employee under a contract of service, whether written or oral. This has already been discussed in Chapters 2, "The Contract of Employment", and 3, "Temporary Employment". If the employee died subsequent to the dismissal, the claim may be brought by the personal representative of the deceased employee.

Usually, there is no difficulty in deciding who the employer was (see also Chapter 23, "Employment Appeals Tribunal"), as one merely has to look at the contract of employment or some other document, such as an "offer of employment" letter or payslip. However, in a few cases, the identity of the employer was not clear, as transpired in *Allison* v *Incorporated Law Society of Ireland and Laurence Cullen, President* (UD 492/1986). In summary, the claimant acted as secretary to the president for his term of office, which lasted for one year. She had worked for two previous successive presidents and was paid directly by the president's professional offices, yet worked on the Law Society premises. The presidents were reimbursed to the value of 85 per cent of her salary by the Law Society and she received a P45 from the president at the end of each term of office. The president for 1986, Laurence Cullen, entered in negotiation with her but decided not to employ her. The Tribunal considered that she was not an employee of Mr Cullen and stated that "it appears to us that the true employer was and remained until termination, the Society, and . . . that succeeding Presidents acted as agents of the Society". The case shows that the Tribunal is likely to take the "fairest" view as to who the employer was.

The 1993 Act (s. 13) has extended the scope for who may be considered an employee, namely that for the purposes of the unfair dismissals legislation, "agency temps" will now be considered employees of the hiring employee if they are placed by an employment agency. Of course, such employees will have to have worked the necessary service and hours (e.g. *Bourton* v *Narcea Ltd. and AIBP* UD 186/1994, it was considered that Narcea was an agency who hired out boners to Anglo-Irish Beef Processors meat plants. The claimant was employed by Narcea, but on foot of the provision in the 1993 Act, Bourton was deemed an employee of AIBP for the purposes of the Act.

CONTINUITY OF SERVICE

An employee who does not have the requisite one year's continuous service cannot fall within the scope of the Act. The unfair dismissals legislation provides that the rules for assessing and computing periods of service are contained in the First Schedule of the Minimum Notice and Terms of Employment Acts, 1973 to 1991. These rules have already been discussed in Chapter 16, "Notice". The 1993 Act provides that the dismissal of an employee followed by their re-employment by the same employer within 26 weeks will not break their continuity of service if the dismissal was connected with the avoidance of liability under the Act.

However, an employee who maintains that he or she was unfairly dismissed by reason of trade union membership or activities (s. 14 of the 1993 Act), pregnancy or was denied her entitlement under the maternity legislation (s. 6(2)(a) of the 1977 Act as amended by s. 38(5) of the Maternity Protection Act, 1994) or entitlement to parental leave or *force majeure* leave (s. 6(2)(b) of the 1977 Act as amended by s. 25(2) of the Parental Leave Act, 1998) does not have to have one year's service.

The Worker Protection (Regular Part-time Employees) Act, 1991, has added further complexity to issues of continuity. First, a regular part-time employee must have one year's service under the Act to bring an unfair dismissals claim. However, if the employee maintains that they were dismissed by reason of trade union membership or activities, they must have 13 weeks' service.

AGE

The Act does not apply to persons who were under 16 years of age on the date of their dismissal. An employee who has reached 66 years, or normal retirement age, on the date of their dismissal also may not bring a claim under the Act. The normal retirement age is usually the 65th birthday. However, if the employer specified retirement age as 60 years and an employee was dismissed on their 60th birthday, they would not fall within the scope of the Act. Arising from this provision, it is important that the contract of employment states clearly the retirement age. If, for example, the retirement age was specified as 67 years, then equally the employee could not bring a claim under the Act because the employee had exceeded the 66-year limit. (In one unusual case the Tribunal accepted that the age of 20 years was the normal retirement age for the category of employment that the employee was in (*Humphries* v *Iarnród Éireann*, UD 1099/1988).)

Retirement age was considered in the High Court case of *Donegal County Council* v *Porter and Others* ([1993] ELR 101) where a number of fire-fighters with long service were dismissed on the ground that they had reached 55 years. There were no written contracts and there was no reference to a specific date of retirement. Their expectation was that they would work until they reached 60 years, presuming they were capable of performing their duties. The Department of the Environment issued a circular letter recommending a retirement age of 55 years and the Council decided to implement its terms. Flood J stated that the attempt to force them into retirement at 55 years was an attempt to alter unilaterally the contractual situation and would be a breach of contract unless it could be lawfully sustained. As there were no substantial grounds justifying the dismissal, reinstatement was ordered.

HOURS

In summary, a person is normally expected to work at least 18 hours per week, or eight hours per week in the case of a regular part-time employee. This is a result of the Worker Protection (Regular Part-time Employees) Act, 1991, which brought regular part-time employ-

ees within the application of the Unfair Dismissals Acts, provided
they have the necessary service.

The law does not specifically provide for averaging the hours over
a period of time (*McFadden* v *Ryan t/a Zodiac Apparel*, M 294/1981).
The only practical way of determining the hours is to look at the
hours actually worked and the custom and practice associated with
the duties (for example, regular compulsory overtime). As a rule of
thumb, an employee who more often than not worked over eight
hours per week would fall within the scope of the Act, even though
there was the odd week where fewer hours were worked.

In *Edwards* v *Aerials and Electronics (Irl) Ltd.* (UD 302/1985), it
was held that as neither employer nor employee could provide evidence as to hours worked, the hours were deemed indeterminable
and the claim failed. However, this was an extremely unusual situation.

Where an employee actually works a limited number of hours but
is "on-call" for a number of hours, the "on-call" hours are deemed to
be working hours. Accordingly, such employees as nurses, fire-
fighters, etc. may fall within the scope of the legislation (*Bartlett* v
Kerry County Council, UD 178/1978 and *Donegal County Council* v
Porter and Others, above).

ILLEGALITY

There are certain types of contract that are forbidden at common law
and are therefore illegal; for example, contract to defraud the Revenue. The first such case was *Lewis* v *Squash (Irl) Ltd.* (UD 146/1982
and [1983] ILRM 363), where the claimant received in addition to his
salary of £14,000 the sum of £2,000 for "expenses". The Tribunal
found that the £2,000 was in fact a salary increase, though it was not
returned to the Revenue by the company or the employee as part of
his salary. The Tribunal found that the contract of employment was
tainted by an illegality and therefore unenforceable.

A valid and enforceable contract of employment must therefore
exist upon which the claim under the Act is founded. In *Morris* v
Peter Keogh (Upholsterers) Ltd. (UD 947/1984) there was a perfectly
valid and enforceable contract. In that case, the employee while in
employment claimed unemployment benefits. The Tribunal consid-

ered that the employee's wrongful declarations made his contract of employment unenforceable and the claim failed.

In *Wosser* v *Dublin Corporation* (UD 42/1989) the Tribunal considered that social welfare fraud, even where admitted, was a matter for the Department of Social Welfare. The 1993 Act (s. 7) provides that if an employee has been unfairly dismissed and if there was a term or a condition of the contract of employment which breached the Income Tax Acts or the Social Welfare Acts, then the employee will be entitled to redress for dismissal. The adjudicating bodies shall send the file to the Revenue and/or the Department of Social, Community and Family Affairs. Previously, if there was such a breach, the employee was not entitled to any redress.

TIME LIMITS

In summary, the claim for the unfair dismissal must be brought to a Rights Commissioner or the Employment Appeals Tribunal within six months of the date of dismissal. The 1993 Act provides that the time limit may be extended up to 12 months from the date of dismissal as long as a Rights Commissioner or the Tribunal is satisfied that there were "exceptional circumstances" preventing the service of the claim within the first six months of the date of dismissal. The meaning of "exceptional circumstances" was considered by the Tribunal in *Byrne* v *P.J. Quigley Ltd.* ([1995] ELR 205) as follows at p. 207:

1. The words "exceptional circumstances" are strong words and should be contrasted with the milder words "reasonably practicable in the case" . . . "Exceptional" means something out of the ordinary. At least the circumstances must be unusual, probably quite unusual, but not necessarily highly unusual.

2. (a) In order to extend the time, the Tribunal must be satisfied that the exceptional circumstances "prevented" lodging the claim within the general time limit. It is not sufficient if the exceptional circumstances caused or triggered the lodging of the claim.

    (b) It seems to follow that the exceptional circumstances involved must arise within the first six months, "the period aforesaid". If they arose later, they could not be said to "prevent" the claim being initiated within that period.

This is considered in detail in Chapter 23, "Employment Appeals Tribunal".

SETTLEMENT

Section 13 of the Unfair Dismissals Act states that:

> a provision in an agreement (whether a contract of employment or not and whether made before or after the commencement of this Act) shall be void in so far as it purports to exclude or limit the application of, or is inconsistent with, any provision of this Act.

In effect, this means that there cannot be an agreement between an employer and employee to contract out of this legislation. Such agreement would be rendered void and unenforceable under the Act.

Such attempted "contracting out" could be contained in a contract of employment or in an agreement on termination of employment. The exceptions as provided by the Act are fixed-term or specified-purpose contracts, though there may not be a series of such contracts.

This appears to be a straightforward provision (a similar one is contained in the Redundancy Payments Acts), yet such agreements have raised key legal issues. The first is the equitable principle of promissory estoppel. To put this simply, if a termination agreement is entered into prior to any statutory proceedings, and the employee then brings a claim under the Act, the employee is estopped from denying the agreement and its validity. Thus, the claimant should not be able to pursue a claim under the Act. (If there is an agreement on the basis of redundancy with an ex gratia payment, note the provisions of the Employment Protection Order, 1996 — see Chapter 19, "Collective Redundancies".)

The Tribunal has taken different approaches to such agreements. In *Kehoe* v *Memorex Media Products Ltd*. (UD 222/1987), the estoppel argument was accepted by the Tribunal. In this case, the claimant had received statutory redundancy and an *ex gratia* sum "in full and final settlement of all matters on termination of employment". The claimant argued that she entered into the agreement under duress. There was no evidence of duress and the claim fell on the issue of estoppel. However, in *Dempsey* v *Memorex Media Products Ltd*. (UD 306/1987) which had similar facts to the Kehoe case, the Tribunal side-stepped the legal theory of estoppel and appeared to be more pragmatic as to how they approached the claim. The Tribunal heard all the evidence and held that there was a genuine redundancy, thus a "fair" dismissal.

One interpretation of this section has meant that if a settlement is arrived at, the Tribunal may rely on this section and hear the substantive part of the case and rule thereon.

In practical terms, this issue can arise where an employee's contract is about to be terminated for any reason, although it more usually happens in a redundancy situation where monies are offered to the employee on the basis of a "full and final settlement". This situation is commonplace. It can be generally stated that such an agreement would stand up as long as the employee is fully advised of their rights by a solicitor or their union official. An employee can still bring a claim under the Act, but the chances of success are slim if the employee was fully advised prior to the signing of the agreement.

The early case of *Eate* v *Semperit (Ireland) Ltd.* (UD 46/1977) was most interesting. Prior to his dismissal, the claimant accepted a sum of money, which was to be in full and final settlement of any outstanding claims he may have had against the company. The Tribunal did not accept this agreement as valid and, relying on Section 13, held that the claimant was unfairly dismissed, though he was not entitled to additional compensation.

However, if such an agreement is entered into following the initiation of proceedings or after a Rights Commissioner's hearing, the Tribunal would more than likely hold that the agreement did not exclude or limit the application of the Act (*Doyle* v *Pierce (Wexford) Ltd.*, UD 50/1979).

Another option, usually unpopular because of the preference of the parties to have such agreements shrouded in secrecy (e.g. the employer may not wish to create a precedent), is, after the initiation of proceedings, to "register" the agreement with the Tribunal. The Tribunal would not register such an agreement and issue a determination thereon unless it was satisfied that the employee, in particular, was fully represented and was satisfied as to its terms. Such an arrangement would not be considered to limit the operation of the Act.

In the early years of the operation of the Act, where there was a settlement of a claim prior to a hearing, the Tribunal invariably issued a determination stating that there was a settlement to the satisfaction of the parties, sometime including the details. From the early

1980s onwards, the practice of issuing such determinations stopped, probably as a result of the requested secrecy of the parties (usually the employer)

The key term of the settlement agreement is that the claimant withdraws proceedings under all the Acts under which they have claimed and that the agreement be kept confidential to the parties. It is normal to have a settlement agreement that would provide, for example, that the former employee signs an agreement with the following wording:

> I .... accept the sum of £xxx in full and final settlement of all statutory, contractual and any other claims arising from my employment with .... Ltd.

However, the Tribunal has taken the opposite view in a number of cases, even where it has been satisfied that the employee agreed to the settlement. Further, the employee must have had full knowledge that such sum was final settlement of, in particular, all statutory claims arising from the employment and that the employee could not then bring a claim under the 1977 Act. The employee should have been in receipt of legal or trade union advice so that there would be no element of duress. Employers should make provision for an employee who is receiving a settlement or termination of employment and subsequently comprising his statutory entitlements should have a full opportunity to receive all appropriate legal/trade union advice.

EXCLUSIONS

Certain categories of employees (Section 2) are excluded under the Acts, including:

- Members of the Defence Forces and the Garda Síochána.

- Civil servants; in *Central Bank of Ireland* v *Gildea* ([1997] ELR 238), where the claimant was employed as a Central Bank security guard and the issue arose as to whether he was employed "by or under the State". He was dismissed for alleged gross misconduct and brought an action under the Unfair Dismissals Acts. The Central Bank claimed that the Bank was an integral part of the Government of the State and that the civil service Regulations applied to its employees and hence he was employed "by or under the State". Keane J, however, stated that Central Bank employees were "in no different position from those employed in a vast range of what have come to be called 'semi-state bodies', the employees of which, by specific legislative provision, be deemed to be civil servants but who, in the absence of any such provision, are not to be so regarded". It was held that he could claim under the Unfair Dismissals Acts, as he was not a civil servant employed by or under the state. However, it should be noted that unestablished civil servants may fall within the scope of the legislation (e.g. industrial workers in the Office of Public Works).

- Officers of local authorities;

- Officers of vocational education committees (but "eligible part-time teachers" may fall within the scope of the Acts — see *Hanly* v *County Mayo Vocational Educational Committee* ([1999] ELR 10) — and "part-time" teachers may be excluded from the scope of the unfair dismissals legislation — see Chapter 3, "Temporary and Part-time Employment");

- Officers of health boards (except for temporary officers);

- FÁS trainees and apprentices (if employed by FÁS); and

- Close relatives of an employer who reside in the same house or farm with the employer.

DISMISSAL DURING PROBATION OR TRAINING

The Act does not apply to the dismissal of an employee during a period of probation or training if the contract is in writing and the duration of the probation or training is one year or less and is so stated in the contract.

The Act does not apply in relation to the dismissal of an employee during the period of employment when the employee is undergoing training for the purpose of becoming qualified or registered as a nurse, pharmacist, health inspector, medical laboratory technician, occupational therapist, physiotherapist, speech therapist, radiographer or social worker.

DISMISSAL DURING APPRENTICESHIP

If an employee is employed as a statutory apprentice (under the Industrial Training Act, 1967) the Act will not apply to their dismissal if the dismissal takes place during the first six months of the apprenticeship or within one month after the completion of the apprenticeship.

In *MacNamara* v *Castlelock Construction & Development Ltd.* (UD 808/1984), it was contended that the claimant, employed as a third-year apprentice, fell outside the scope of the Act because he had between six months' and one year's service. It was held that he had a viable claim.

PERSONS WHO WORK OUTSIDE THE STATE

The Act does not apply to the dismissal of an employee who:

1. Ordinarily worked outside the State unless the employee was ordinarily resident within the State during the term of the contract; or

2. Was domiciled in the State during the term of the contract and the employer (if an individual) was ordinarily resident in the State during the term of the contract, or if it is a company, it had its principal place of business in the State during the term of the contract.

In *Dignam* v *Sisk Nigeria Ltd. and John Sisk and Son Ltd.* (UD 125/1983), the claimant originally worked for John Sisk and Sons Ltd. and then applied for the position of contracts manager with Sisk Nigeria Ltd., a company incorporated in Nigeria with its sole area of business there. The claimant was not dismissed by John Sisk and Sons Ltd., but by Sisk Nigeria Ltd. Accordingly, the Tribunal had no jurisdiction and the claimant did not fall within the scope of the Act. In *Kelly* v *Aer Rianta International CPT* ([1998] ELR 170), the claimant was employed in Moscow and was dismissed. However, he fell within the scope of the Act, as he retained domicile in Ireland and intended to return.

DIPLOMATIC IMMUNITY

This issue was considered by the Supreme Court in the case of the *Government of Canada* v *Employment Appeals Tribunal and Brian*

Burke ([1992] ELR 29). In this case, the employee was employed as a driver with the Canadian Embassy in Dublin between June 1986 and May 1988, when he was dismissed. He brought proceedings under the Minimum Notice and Terms of Employment Act, 1973, and also the Unfair Dismissals Act, 1977, before the Employment Appeals Tribunal. The Canadian Government submitted that the Tribunal had no jurisdiction to hear the claims, which were rejected, and the Tribunal went on to award the claimant compensation in the sum of £10,200. This determination was referred to the High Court by the Canadian Government for judicial review. In the High Court ([1991] ELR 57), McKenzie J considered that the Tribunal was justified in proceeding to hear the claims, since the doctrine of absolute sovereign immunity had no application in the modern world. However, the Supreme Court thought otherwise and considered that the employment of an embassy chauffeur is within the sphere of governmental or sovereign activity and that the doctrine of restrictive immunity applied. Accordingly, because of this doctrine, such an employee has no cause of action against his employer.

The principle of sovereign immunity operated to deprive the Tribunal of jurisdiction in *Geraghty* v *Embassy of Mexico and Another* ([1998] ELR 310). It was further determined that while a waiver of sovereign immunity could be inferred from the claimant's contract of employment, any waiver of the principle must be express. In *Zimmerman* v *Der Deutsche Schuliverein Ltd.* ([1999] ELR 211), the claimant, a civil servant of the Federal Republic of Germany, was employed as a principal in a secondary school. Some of the teaching staff including the principal were employed by the German State and some by the Irish State. The Tribunal held that it had jurisdiction to hear the claim as he had a separate legal relationship with the company limited by guarantee which owned the school.

CONSTRUCTIVE DISMISSAL

Constructive dismissal arises where an employee is left with no option but to resign because of the employer's breach of contract. It is defined in the Act as:

> . . . the termination by the employee of his contract of employment with his employer whether prior notice of the termination was or was not given to the employer, in circumstances in which, because

of the conduct of the employer, the employee was or would have
been entitled, or it was or would have been reasonable for the employee, to terminate the contract of employment without giving
prior notice of the termination to the employer.

In strict legal terms, the concept of "constructive dismissal" is difficult. However, the tests applied to "constructive dismissal" may be
summarised as the contract test and the reasonableness test (see
Redmond, 1999).

The contract test was summarised by Lord Denning MR in *Western Excavating (ECC) Ltd.* v *Sharp* ([1978] ICR 121):

If the employer is guilty of conduct which is a significant breach
going to the root of the contract of employment, or which shows
that the employer no longer intends to be bound by one or more of
the essential terms of the contract, then the employee is entitled
to treat himself as discharged from any further performance.

Alternatively, the reasonableness test asks whether the employer
"conducts himself or his affairs so unreasonably that the employee
cannot fairly be expected to put up with [it] any longer, [if so] the
employee is justified in leaving".

The Tribunal has not detailed which test it has applied in constructive dismissal cases. However, examples would be where employers have changed the employee's terms and conditions (for
example, demotion), or where "life at work" has become so intolerable
that the employee feels that there is no other option but to resign
their employment.

In these cases, the onus is first on the employee to prove that they
were dismissed, and then on the employer to show that it was a fair
dismissal.

The first key case, which is still the classic example of constructive
dismissal, was *Byrne* v *RHM Foods (Irl.) Ltd.* (UD 69/1979). The
claimant was employed as a secretary working for a marketing manager. The marketing manager was suspended, but the managing director assured the claimant that her own job was safe. Subsequently,
however, the keys of the marketing manager's filing cabinet were
taken away and the claimant was given no work and had no contact
with her colleagues. When her telephone was disconnected, she felt
that she had no other option but to resign. The Tribunal, in uphold-

ing her claim, held that this was not a genuine resignation and commented that:

> [the claimant's] continuous isolation without knowledge of what
> was going on or contact by any person [made it] reasonable and
> understandable her confidence and trust in her employer should
> be undermined to the extent that she could tolerate it no longer.

Another case is *Gallery* v *Blarney Woollen Mills Ltd.* ([1990] ELR 143). In this case, the claimant was employed as a manager at the Kilkenny Shop at the time of the takeover by Blarney Woollen Mills Ltd. Prior to the transfer, she maintained that she was totally responsible for the operation of the Dublin shop. Following on the takeover, she considered that her position and duties had become unclear and her authority was being undermined by decisions taken by the new head of retail in the Blarney Group. She was advised after a number of weeks that the new management was not happy with her performance. She wrote to the head of retail asking for a written confirmation of the terms and conditions in her contract and also asked for an indication that the company placed full trust and confidence in her. The reply was unsatisfactory and the claimant wrote again saying that if she did not receive a written reply dealing with various points raised she would be forced to take steps to protect her position. She then received a reply requesting a meeting to discuss the matter with her. She responded by stating that the company's conduct amounted to constructive dismissal and she resigned.

The company referred the Tribunal to the cases *of Conway* v *Ulster Bank* (UD 474/1981) and *Beatty* v *Bayside Supermarket* (UD 142/1987). Both these cases clearly established that, where there is a union/management agreement containing a grievance procedure, such procedure should be substantially followed by employees when they consider that there is a breach of contract by their employer.

The Tribunal, however, considered that this was a constructive dismissal and stated that "the respondent company acted unreasonably in its dealings with the claimant and she became frustrated, leaving her with no option but to resign".

There are a considerable number of cases where an employee resigns and then claims constructive dismissal. In such situations, the Tribunal can hold there was a clear resignation and therefore there was no dismissal. However, in certain cases — for example, if an employee just "walks off" the job — the Tribunal could hold that there was no dismissal and no resignation. Accordingly, it could be argued that the employee is still employed.

It should be noted that there is no provision for "self-dismissal". In other words, an employer cannot state to an employee that if that employee does not do something or does not come in to work that it is deemed to be a "self-dismissal". There is no such thing; either the employer or the employee must actually terminate the contract of employment.

Finally, an employee who is aware that there is a breach of contract should not live with such a breach for too long, because it could then be considered to be acquiescence to the breach of contract.

Constructive Dismissal and Harassment

The issue of "harassment" or "bullying" in the workplace can be considered within the context of "constructive dismissal". Bullying itself is dealt with in Chapter 15. In respect of "constructive dismissal" arising from bullying in the workplace, the issue can be looked at in terms of breach of contract of employment. The employer has a duty of care to look after the health and safety of employees in the workplace, and this includes prevention of bullying. This duty is implied into the contract of employment by statute (see Chapter 15). This issue therefore goes to the root of the contract and, essentially, such cases can be treated as constructive dismissal. Obviously, in such instances it would be vital for the employee to avail of the grievance procedure and only after the exhaustion of such procedure, without a satisfactory outcome, can an employee resign and claim constructive dismissal. It must be noted that the onus of proof will be on the employee to prove that it was a dismissal.

In *Leeson* v *Glaxo Wellcome Ltd.* ([1999] ELR 170), the claimant was private secretary to the managing director, who retired in 1996. A new Managing Director was then appointed, who then had a number of concerns about her work, including her timekeeping. The claimant subsequently went sick and there then followed correspondence where she alleged she had been bullied and victimised. The claimant resigned and claimed unfair dismissal. The Tribunal allowed her claim and awarded her £22,500. It considered that there was an obligation on the employer to have procedures to resolve such problems. On appeal, the circuit court considered that it was entirely appropriate that the managing director offer criticism of her work with a view to bringing changes. It was considered that it was not reasonable for her to terminate her employment.

DISMISSAL ARISING FROM LOCKOUT OR STRIKE

The 1993 Act has amended the 1977 Act by providing that the lockout of an employee shall be deemed to be a dismissal. If, at the end of the lockout, the employee is not reinstated or re-engaged (the meaning of which was extended by the 1993 Act and considered below under Redress) and one or more others were reinstated or re-engaged, it would be considered an unfair dismissal.

The 1993 Act provides that the dismissal of an employee for taking part in a strike or industrial action is an unfair dismissal if at least one other employee was not dismissed for the same action, or if another employee was reinstated or re-engaged. The date of reinstatement or re-engagement is the date as agreed between the employer and employees, or if there is no agreement, the date on which reinstatement or re-engagement was offered to the majority of the workforce.

If a particular employee is dismissed for taking part in a strike and other employees are not so dismissed, it would be an automatically unfair dismissal. However, if during the course of a strike or other industrial action, there was abusive behaviour from an employee, it could be a fair dismissal.

If one looks closely at this section of the Act, it is arguable that if an employer dismissed all employees who were on strike or taking part in an industrial action, it could be considered a fair dismissal. However, this is obviously problematic and not advisable.

UNFAIR DISMISSAL

The substantive part of the 1977 Act (s. 6) provides that all dismissals are deemed "unfair" unless there were substantial grounds justifying the dismissal. There are certain grounds which constitute "fair" dismissal, namely dismissal arising from the employee's capability, competence, qualifications, conduct, redundancy and where the employee's ongoing employment was in contravention of statutory provisions. The Act contains a number of grounds where a dismissal is deemed unfair, as discussed below. It should also be noted that a person may maintain that they were dismissed in respect of any of the grounds of discrimination under the Employment Equality Act, 1998, but a person may not proceed under the Unfair Dismissals Acts *and* the Employment Equality Act, 1998, where the employee has instituted proceedings at common law for wrongful dismissal and the hearing of the case has begun; a Rights Commissioner has issued a recommendation under the Unfair Dismissals Acts; or the Tribunal has commenced hearing into the matter of the dismissal.

Membership of a Trade Union or Involvement in Trade Union Activities

An employee cannot be dismissed because of trade union membership or because of a proposal that they or another employee became a member of a trade union. However, this only applies if the activity is engaged in outside normal hours of work or during the hours at work when it is allowed. The employee does not have to have one year's continuous service to bring a claim for this reason, and the age limits also do not apply for this form of claim.

The burden of proof would be on the claimant to show that the employer was aware that they were a member of a trade union or engaged in such activities.

In the case of *Wixted* v *Sang Mann* ([1991] ELR 208), the claimant joined a trade union because of poor working conditions. Subsequently, the union wrote to management requesting a meeting to discuss the wages and conditions of employment of their members. The claimant was dismissed and at the Tribunal the employer maintained that he was dismissed for poor work performance. The Tribunal did not accept this and considered that he was dismissed wholly or mainly because of his trade union activities.

In a similar case, *White* v *Simon Betson* ([1992] ELR 120), the claimant was only employed for one month when his employment was terminated. The claimant maintained that his weekly wage was agreed when he started work, but that he was then paid irregular amounts at regular intervals. He was out sick for a few days (having provided a medical certificate) and he was given his wages and told not to come into work any more. The claimant advised the Tribunal that some three days prior to his termination, he had become a member of SIPTU. SIPTU had written to the employer requesting a discussion on the claimant's conditions of employment. The employer again maintained that there was poor work performance and that he had made up his mind to terminate the employment on the first day that the employee was out sick. Furthermore, he maintained that he had received no letter from SIPTU until after the termination of the employment. The Tribunal considered that the correspondence had been received prior to the termination of the employment and that the decision to dismiss was as a result of his trade union membership and was therefore unfair.

One has to say generally that the Tribunal is very conscious of the constitutional right to be a member of a trade union.

Religious or Political Views

It would be an automatically unfair dismissal if an employee were dismissed because of their religion or politics. The dismissal of an employee because of their religion is problematical, however. In the case of *Merriman* v *St James's Hospital* (Circuit Court, Clarke J, 24 November 1986), the claimant, a hospital attendant, was dismissed because she refused to bring a crucifix and candle to a dying patient. When subsequently asked why by the nurse in charge, the claimant replied that she was a Christian and that it was not the Word of God to do so, and that she did not adore false gods. There were subsequent meetings and correspondence between the parties and finally she was asked to resume duty as long as she was prepared to bring a crucifix and candle to a patient's bedside if so instructed. After additional discussion, however, she was dismissed.

The judgment notes that it is the practice to bring a crucifix and candles to the bedside of a Catholic patient who is dying and to assist in various other religious rites and services which are made available for patients in the hospital. The attendant does not have to participate personally but only to assist. Clarke J ordered her re-engagement, that she did not have to participate in a religious rite or ceremony and that in her case the carrying of the crucifix and candle be dispensed with. She advised the Court that she was unwilling to attend patients at their religious services. In effect, this meant that her terms and conditions would be different from the other hospital attendants. She was awarded £800 compensation.

Civil or Criminal Proceedings

It would be deemed an unfair dismissal if an employee were dismissed because they might threaten or institute civil proceedings against the employer, or if the employee were likely to be a witness in such proceedings. Equally, in relation to criminal proceedings against the employer, if the employee were dismissed after making statements to the prosecuting authority, it would be an unfair dismissal.

An example would be if an employee has been out ill for some considerable time because of a work-related accident and subsequently institutes proceedings against the employer. The employer may have decided that the employee is no longer capable of performing the job and dismiss the employee. If so, the employer can only dismiss by reason of absenteeism and not because the employee has proceeded to take action for damages.

Race, Colour or Sexual Orientation

An employee cannot be dismissed by reason of their race or colour. It should be noted that there may be some future developments on this point as was envisaged under the Equal Status Bill, 1991, namely that there can be no discrimination against persons on any grounds. The 1993 Act also provides that an employee cannot be dismissed because of their sexual orientation.

Age

The 1993 Act provides that an employee cannot be dismissed because of age. This in no way affects the provision that an employee must be aged between 16 years and normal retiring age (or 66 years) before they fall within the scope of the Act. This amendment may have far-reaching effect, particularly in cases where employees maintain that the reason that they were selected for redundancy was because of their age. In a number of redundancy cases, the Tribunal has been of the view that the real reason for dismissal was "age". In *Kerrigan* v *Peter Owens Advertising and Marketing Limited* (UD 31/1997) the claimant, an Advertising Account Director, was advised that due to loss of clients the company would have to make him redundant. Initially, the company said the redundancy had to do with cost cutting. Subsequently, he was advised the reasons for his dismissal were costs, re-organisation, age, etc. In evidence, the claimant said that in addition to concern about losing clients, his age was a factor, as their clients wanted to deal with a 30-year-old Account Director. The Tribunal determined that he was unfairly dismissed and no redundancy situation existed, as the requirements of the business had not ceased or diminished at the time. This dismissal arose wholly or mainly from his age. The Tribunal also considered that "age" was a factor in the selection for redundancy of a boat mechanic aged 51 years (*O'Donnell v Royal National Lifeboats Institute*, UD 533/1995, see below).

Membership of the Travelling Community

The 1993 Act provides that an employee cannot be dismissed because they are a member of the travelling community.

Of course, if an employee is dismissed by reason of their religion, age, race, sexual orientation or membership of the travelling community, they may choose between a claim under the Unfair Dismissals Acts or the Employment Equality Act, 1998 (when in operation). If the person has less than one year's service, they can only claim under the 1998 Act.

Pregnancy, Maternity, Adoptive Leave and Parental Leave

An employee cannot be dismissed by reason of her pregnancy or related matters. Also, an employee cannot be dismissed for pursuing her entitlement to maternity leave under the Maternity Protection Act, 1994.

The various Acts providing for such leave are considered in Chapter 5. Further, the matter of pregnancy dismissals are considered within the meaning of the Equal Treatment Directive and also the "Pregnancy Directive". Of course, the Maternity Protection Act, 1994, amended the Unfair Dismissals Acts, 1977–1993. In the event of a dismissal arising from pregnancy, consideration will have to be given as to which piece of legislation the claim will be under. In the future, such claims will be under the Employment Equality Act, 1998, with the potential of unlimited compensation.

Again, the burden of proof is on the employee to prove that she was dismissed by reason of her pregnancy. However, if she is incapable of performing her job, the burden of proof is on the employer.

As stated above, an employee cannot be denied maternity rights. In the case of *Maxwell* v *English Language Institute* ([1990] ELR 226), the claimant had been employed as a secretary for a short time, though there was a conflict of evidence as to whether she was employed on a probationary or a permanent basis. Nonetheless, she submitted a maternity allowance claim form to her employer, who failed to complete it. She subsequently advised her employer that she intended taking maternity leave and was dismissed. The employer maintained that her work was unsatisfactory but he had never disciplined her. It was considered that she was dismissed by reason of her pregnancy.

In the case of *Flynn* v *Sister Mary Anna Power and the Sisters of the Holy Faith* ([1985] ILRM 336), the claimant considered that she was dismissed by reason of her pregnancy. She was a secondary school teacher in a New Ross convent school living with a married man in the town and was pregnant by him. The school manager wrote to her (following a meeting some months earlier) requesting her resignation because of complaints by certain children's parents about her "lifestyle" and her "open rejection of the norms of behaviour and the ideals which our school exists to promote". Costello J considered (in summary) that it was a fair dismissal and that her pregnancy was not the cause (since her work had deteriorated and there were also complaints about her living with a married man). Also, the claimant knew that there were certain obligations on teachers in religious schools, even though there were no written statements to that effect in her contract of employment. Furthermore, an employee's conduct in sexual matters outside the place of employment may justify dismissal if it is capable of damaging the employer's business, and in this case her lifestyle might damage the school's efforts to foster certain norms of behaviour and religious tenets that the school was established to promote.

This case may now be considered within the context of the new Employment Equality Act, 1998 (see Chapter 10).

BURDEN OF PROOF

There is a presumption under the Act that all dismissals are deemed unfair, except (a) where dismissal is not in dispute (for example, where the claimant has resigned and is claiming constructive dismissal); and (b) where there are jurisdictional points at issue (for example, the employee's continuity of service or time limits). In cases where the employee proves that neither of the above applies, however, the burden of proof shifts on to the employer to prove that the dismissal was fair.

FAIR PROCEDURES

An employer must be reasonable in regard to all the circumstances, and thus the constitutional right to fair procedures must be applied. In other words, the employee is entitled to be aware of all the evidence against them and to respond to any allegations. Recently, there have been a number of cases where application has been made to the courts to prevent a dismissal where there has been an alleged breach of fair procedures. There is usually an interlocutory application made to the High Court requesting reinstatement of the employee plaintiff with payment to the employee of their remuneration pending a full hearing of the case before the Court. It should be noted that such applications must be considered with extreme caution; they are still rare and may not be successful. Such cases are usually settled between the parties. Indeed, this is an area of law which has seen major developments in the last five years of the century.

The common law does not order specific performance of the contract of employment or a contract for personal service; for example, that the court should order reinstatement. However, in certain circumstances, the court can state that there is a breach of fair procedures and order that the employee continues to be paid pending the full hearing of the action. It is both undesirable and generally impossible to compel an unwilling party to maintain continuous personal relations with another.

The first Irish case, *Fennelly* v *Assicurazioni Generali SPA* ((1985) 3 ILT 73), was a most unusual case where the plaintiff had a fixed term contract for 12 years when the employer terminated the contract. Costello J considered that there was a fair question to be tried that the contract had been invalidly terminated. It was held that he would be paid until the full hearing of his case as he would be left without a salary and nothing to live on, which would be disastrous.

There followed almost a decade until the recent group of cases. In *Shortt* v *Data Packaging Ltd.* ([1994] ELR 251) the plaintiff entered

into a three-year fixed-term contract in 1988 as managing director of
Data Packaging. The contract provided that it would continue after
the period of three years if the parties so elected and any continuation was to be deemed to be employment of indefinite duration termi-
nable by six months' notice. He continued on until 11 January 1994,
when he was advised by telephone by the company chairman that he
was to be made redundant owing to company restructuring. This was
confirmed by letter; the termination was to be of immediate effect
and the plaintiff was directed by make arrangements for the collection of his personal belongings and to vacate his office. He vacated
the premises immediately and did not return. By Notice of Motion
dated 7 February 1994, he sought the following orders and reliefs:

1. An injunction restraining the defendants from appointing any
   person other than the plaintiff to the plaintiff's position as managing director of the defendant company pending the trial of the
   action;

2. An order that the defendant continue to pay the plaintiff all salary accruing from 11 January 1994 to trial of the action;

3. An order that the defendant fund until the trial of the action all
   of the plaintiff's VHI premiums, his pension, life assurance and
   death-in-service benefit by paying all instalments and premiums.

4. An order that the defendant be restrained pending the trial of the
   action or until further order in the meantime from dissipating or
   reducing the plaintiff's pension benefits in any mode whatsoever.

Keane J held:

1. That the plaintiff had made out a fair issue to be tried as to the
   legality of the purported termination of his employment contract;

2. That removal from office must comply with the principles of
   natural justice;

3. That damages would not be an adequate remedy in circumstances
   where the plaintiff would be totally without remuneration until
   the trial of the action;

4. That the balance of convenience was in favour of the granting of an injunction pending the hearing in order to preserve the status quo.

In *Doyle* v *Grangeford Precast Concrete Limited* ([1998] ELR 260) the plaintiff was employed as safety officer on terms agreed in July 1997. In September 1997, he received a letter of appointment setting out his terms and conditions of employment; these differed from his original agreement. He refused to sign these terms and his employment was terminated. The plaintiff brought proceedings to restrain the employer from dismissing him. In the Circuit Court, Buttimer J granted an injunction requiring the employer to pay his salary pending the hearing of the action (as to whether he was properly dismissed or not). The plaintiff had to undertake to carry out his duties as required. The injunction was granted because there was a significant issue to be tried between the parties at the hearing of the action. It would have been unjust to leave the plaintiff without income with only the prospect of an award of damages at the trial, having regard to the fact that trust and confidence between the parties may not have broken down; that the situation could be salvaged by some mediation; that injunctive relief would be granted; and he would have to carry out duties as required. On appeal to the High Court, the Order was varied such that the defendants were not required to supply the plaintiff with any benefits of his employment other than his salary unless he performed services for them pursuant to his undertaking to that effect:

1. Trust had irretrievably broken down between the plaintiff and the defendant, who would never again enjoy the relationship of employer and employee. The plaintiff's likely remedy, if successful in the action, would be in damages rather than in reinstatement.

2. There was a fair issue to be tried as to the notice to terminate the plaintiff's employment and as to the legality of the said termination, including his entitlement to natural justice.

In *O'Malley* v Aravon School Ltd. (High Court, Unreported, Costello P, 13 August 1997), an interlocutory injunction was refused to restrain the dismissal of a school principal, as there was a loss of confidence in her.

In *Maher* v *Irish Permanent plc (No. 1)* ([1998] ELR 77) Laffoy J granted the Plaintiff, a branch manager with the building society, an Order restraining the Irish Permanent from taking steps to dismiss him, save in accordance with the disciplinary code and the principles of natural justice. When the Defendant subsequently instituted disciplinary proceedings, he commenced another High Court action and sought an interlocutory injunction restraining the disciplinary proceedings. His application was refused by Costello P in the High Court on 7 October 1997 (No. 2 [1998] ELR 89. This judgement is interesting as it indicates a reluctance to anticipate a breach of rules or of natural justice by a domestic-disciplinary tribunal. In this regard, Costello P refused to rule that hearsay evidence should be excluded from the hearing:

> I cannot hold that hearsay evidence should not be accepted under any circumstances at tomorrow's hearing in Killarney. I cannot assume that the person holding the hearing will act unfairly. His duty is to hold a fair hearing and to produce a fair result. It may well be that it would be wrong to accept hearsay evidence in certain circumstances . . . I cannot assume that the defendant is going to act in a grossly unfair manner.

Costello P relied on the judgement of Henchy J in *Kiely* v *Minister for Social Welfare* ([1977] IR 267) as follows:

> Tribunals exercising quasi-judicial functions are frequently allowed to act informally — to receive unsworn evidence, to act on hearsay, to depart from the rule of evidence, to ignore courtroom procedures, and the like — but they may not act in such a way as to imperil a fair hearing or a fair result.

In *Mooney* v *An Post* ([1998] ELR 238) the plaintiff was employed as a postman and was in receipt of complaints concerning alleged tampering and non-delivery of postal packets. This resulted in an investigation by An Post and by the Garda Síochána. Criminal charges were preferred against the plaintiff and he was acquitted in December 1985. Over the years, there was considerable correspondence between the plaintiff and An Post, including the provision of the Book of Evidence, witness statements with names blacked out and other detailed information. The plaintiff denied the various allegations and requested that an inquiry be convened, presided over by an independent chairman with the facility to cross-examine witnesses. An Post refused this request but did offer to meet with him; he was dismissed in March 1987 and he brought proceedings before the High Court which were subsequently appealed by the plaintiff to the Supreme Court. The Supreme Court held that the plaintiff had been adequately informed of the allegations; that he had been afforded ample opportunity to rebut and make representations and that such representations were to be taken into account by An Post.

There were two main legal issues: whether the plaintiff was entitled to rely upon his acquittal in the criminal case to defeat the civil complaint against him; and whether he was entitled to have the complaint investigated at an oral hearing before an independent chairman. The mere fact that a person is acquitted on a criminal charge is not a bar to the bringing of a civil complaint against him. Failure to prove a matter beyond reasonable doubt does not preclude its proof on the balance of probabilities. The difference between employee and office holder was not the determining issue as to whether the issues of constitutional and natural justice apply. An employee may be entitled to natural and constitutional justice with regard to his dismissal but the requirements will depend on the circumstances of the case. For example, where an employment is terminated pursuant to statutory procedures, it will ordinarily be sufficient for the employer to show compliance with the procedure. The two maxims *nemo iudex in sua causa* ("no man can be a judge in his own case") and *audi alteram partem* ("hear the other side") seldom apply to employment situations. An employee is entitled to fair procedures, but what fair procedures will depend upon the circumstances surrounding the proposed dismissal. At a minimum, the employee is entitled to be informed of the charges against him and to be given an opportunity to answer them and to make submissions. The plaintiff was entitled to know the charges of misconduct against him and to be given an opportunity to answer them and to make submissions. The plaintiff was entitled to know the charges of misconduct against him but was not entitled to a hearing before the Board of An Post, nor to see the investigating officer's report. The plaintiff had been given the benefit of fair procedures. The circumstances of dismissal were relevant to the plaintiff's claim for an oral hearing before an independent arbitrator. The right to silence, on which the plaintiff had properly relied in the criminal case, does not apply to dismissal proceedings, which are essentially civil in nature. It was not sufficient for the plaintiff simply to deny and demand that the defendant prove the allegations. Furthermore, the defendant was not in a position to set up a tribunal with power to subpoena witnesses. Having received complaints, which called into question the integrity of the postal service and which it could not responsibly ignore, An Post was entitled to a proper explanation from the plaintiff, which it did not receive.

This judgment is particularly useful, as it clearly sets out the rights and obligations of both employer and employee in respect of investigations and fair procedures. It also sets out the difference between a person's right to silence in criminal matters and to the employer's entitlement to an explanation.

The 1993 Act attaches even greater statutory importance to fair procedures, as it provides that the adjudicating body may consider the "reasonableness . . . of the conduct of the employer (whether by act or omission) . . . in relation to the dismissal . . .". Account will also be taken of any union/management agreement or custom and practice in the employment concerned, or to a Code of Practice relating to dismissals approved by the Minister for Enterprise and Employment (see Industrial Relations Act, 1990; Code of Practice on Disciplinary Procedures (Declaration) Order, 1996, SI No. 117 of 1996 — see below). The net effect of these provisions is that the Tribunal (and other bodies) will be even more strict and there will be greater compensation or a higher likelihood of re-employment being awarded to an unfairly dismissed employee.

CODE OF PRACTICE ON DISCIPLINARY PROCEDURES

The main purpose of this Code of Practice is to set out for the guidance of employers, employees and their representatives the general principles that should apply in the operation of disciplinary procedures and the promotion of best practice in giving effect to these procedures. Of course, these procedures only apply if there are no alternative agreed procedures in the employment concerned that conform to these general provisions. Procedures are necessary to ensure both that discipline is maintained in the workplace and that disciplinary measures can be applied in a fair and consistent manner. The

Code states that the procedures applied must comply with the general principle of natural justice and fair procedures, which include that:

1. The details of the allegations or complaints be put to the employee concerned;

2. The employee concerned be given the opportunity to respond fully to any such allegations or complaints;

3. The employee concerned is given the opportunity to avail of representation;

4. The employee concerned has the right to a fair and impartial determination of the issues being investigated, taking into account the allegations or complaints themselves, the response of the employee concerned to them, any representations made by or on behalf of the employee concerned and any other relevant or appropriate evidence, factors or circumstances.

It is recommended that the allegations or complaints be set out in writing, that the source of the allegation or complaint be given or that the employee concerned be allowed confront or question witnesses.

The Code of Practice provides that disciplinary action may include:

1. An oral warning;

2. A written warning;

3. A final written warning;

4. Suspension without pay (but note that this may be in breach of the Payment of Wages Act, 1991, and an employer may be in breach of contract so such a course of action is not advisable);

5. Transfer to another task, or section of the enterprise;

6. Demotion (again extreme caution is recommended here, as it may result in a justifiable resignation and claim for constructive dismissal; hence such a provision must be in the employee's contract of employment);

7. Some other disciplinary action short of dismissal;

8. Dismissal.

It is noted in the Code of Practice that the steps will be progressive; however, there may be instances where more serious action, including dismissal, is warranted at an earlier stage. An employee may be suspended on full pay pending the outcome of an investigation into an alleged breach of discipline.

The purpose of a disciplinary procedure is not to terminate an employee's employment but rather to assist the employee in their performance. Where there is a serious issue such as alleged theft, the employer should suspend the employee with pay, pending a full and thorough investigation. The employee should have the opportunity to be represented. An employer does not have to decide the guilt or innocence of an employee but can make the decision to dismiss on the balance of probabilities that the person "committed an offence". In cases of poor performance, an employee should be brought through the whole disciplinary process, making sure that the employee is given every opportunity to improve with adequate training.

It is also absolutely vital that an employee brought through the disciplinary process be clearly advised of the next stage in the process if there is no improvement. If a final written warning is given, an employee should be clearly told that if they do not improve within a certain period of time, they will be dismissed.

FAIR DISMISSAL

The Act provides a number of grounds that may constitute a fair dismissal. This section of the Act is important, so the relevant subsections are quoted in full.

> 6(1) Subject to the provisions of this section, the dismissal of an employee shall be deemed, for the purposes of this Act, to be an unfair dismissal unless, having regard to all the circumstances, there were substantial grounds justifying the dismissal. . . .

> 6(4) Without prejudice to the generality of subsection (1) of this section, the dismissal of an employee shall be deemed, for the purposes of this Act, not to be an unfair dismissal, if it results wholly or mainly from one or more of the following:

a) the capability, competence or qualifications of the employee for performing work of the kind which he was employed by the employer to do,

b) the conduct of the employee,

c) the redundancy of the employee, and

d) the employee being unable to work or continue to work in the position which he held without contravention (by him or by his employer) of a duty or restriction imposed by or under any statute or instrument made under statute. . . .

Incapability

Incapability was defined by the Employment Appeals Tribunal in the case of *Reardon* v *St Vincent's Hospital* (UD74/1979): "Incapability may be generally defined as long-term illness." Generally speaking, there is nothing prohibiting an employer dismissing an employee for long-term absenteeism when it can be established that there is no reasonable return date to work.

In the case of *Bolger* v *Showerings (Ireland) Ltd.* ([1990] ELR 184), Lardner J set out the key requirements (in summary) that an employer will have to comply with in order to have a fair dismissal, namely:

1. It was the ill-health which was the reason for his dismissal;

2. That this was substantial reason;

3. That the employee received fair notices that the question of his dismissal for incapacity was being considered; and

4. That the employee was afforded the opportunity of being heard.

This case also established that where there is no dispute between the parties as to the incapacity of the employee, it is not necessary to await medical tests before the decision to dismiss. A note of caution must be added to this last statement, as one obviously has to look at each case on its own merits. However, if the employee has been out from work for an unreasonable length of time and cannot give a return date, dismissal may be reasonable.

One myth that still prevails is that an employee who is out sick and has handed in medical certificates cannot be dismissed. This is a total fallacy. Equally, employers may well ask, after what period of absenteeism may the employee be dismissed? There is no answer to this either, but an employer must be reasonable and have carried out all necessary enquiries to see when the employee can return to work. If there is no reasonable return date and if the employee has been out for a lengthy period, then dismissal may be permissible. Extreme caution should be exercised at all times, however.

It is well established that for an employee who is no longer capable of performing their duties, there is no obligation on the employer to provide "light work" or alternative duties (*Gurr* v *The Office of Public Works* [1990] ELR 42).

There are many other forms of absenteeism besides long-term, such as intermittent absenteeism with a variety of illnesses or a pattern of being absent on Fridays and Mondays or on a Tuesday after a long weekend. Employers do not have to tolerate this either, but again, all fair procedures and warnings must be exhausted. For example, a pattern as discussed above may be as a result of alcoholism, and if so the employer should ensure that the employee is referred to necessary treatment centres to try and combat this illness. Still, if attendance does not improve, an employer may terminate the employment following appropriate warning procedures.

Employers have lost many cases by not complying with reasonable procedures; for example, not asking the employee for a reasonable return date or not sending the employee to a company doctor in order to establish the true medical position and a prognosis for a return date to work.

If an employer has a sick pay scheme, an employee may not abuse it, for example, by working while on sick leave. Again, it is well established that this may be fair ground for dismissal.

Competence

A person's lack of competence as a ground for dismissal may be extremely hard to prove, especially where one is dealing with employees whose duties are in "grey" areas, such as executive staff. Often, decisions on competence may be subjective rather than objective.

The case of *O'Donoghue* v *Emerson Electric (Ireland) Ltd. t/a Thermodisc Ireland* (UD 177/1986) highlights the issue of competence. The claimant had been a managing director of the US subsidiary since 1984. His summary dismissal arose from the company's performance compared with projected targets supplied to the IDA. The claimant was not aware of these targets, though he was deemed responsible for not achieving them. His production goals were based on his own targets supplied to the US parent, which were exceeded. There was alleged poor performance in the 1986 financial year. However, the Tribunal considered that no reasonable decision to dismiss could be based on the information available before the expiry of the first quarter of the company's financial year. It was also considered that the employee had no clear warning of dissatisfaction or an opportunity to improve the performance of the company. The claimant was held to have been unfairly dismissed and was awarded compensation in the sum of £52,542. This award included a deduction as the Tribunal considered that the claimant contributed 30 per cent to his dismissal because he had failed to resolve friction between two managers in the Irish operation. This shows that the Tribunal accepts that a manager must apply certain managerial skills.

This decision highlighted the requirement for fair procedures and warnings where one is dealing with alleged poor company performance, and in particular that an employee with responsibility for reaching certain targets must have full knowledge of such targets. This decision counteracts the view that one cannot use the same procedures when dealing with management.

The Tribunal observed that:

> . . . we are satisfied that the respondent, far from giving the claimant any clear warning or proper opportunity to improve the performance at the Irish plant to the satisfaction of the American management, did not express its dissatisfaction to him in clear terms. Isolated passing comments on some details cannot be constructed as warnings, or indeed expressions of dissatisfaction, especially against a background of sometime fulsome praise.

In the case of *Richardson* v *H. Williams & Co Ltd.* (UD 17/1979), the claimant was dismissed because the company had been dissatisfied with his work performance over a period, in particular in relation to his authorising payment of accounts by cheque while not following the company procedure. He was also lacking in carrying out freshness checks (i.e. on perishable items). The Tribunal noted that the claimant was not given an opportunity to defend himself and the Tribunal applied the following principles:

a) Where an employee has been given a justified warning that,
    unless his work improved in a specific area, his job would be
    in jeopardy, then it follows that such employee must be given:

    (i) A reasonable time within which to effect such improve-
         ment;

    (ii) A reasonable work situation within which to concentrate
         on such defects;

b) If an employee improves in the complained-of area to the rea-
    sonable satisfaction of the employer, and such defect is not
    repeated, then such a warning cannot be solely relied on in
    relation to a dismissal for other reasons.

In the case of *O'Neill* v *Bus Éireann* ([1990] ELR 135), O'Malley J in
the Circuit Court stated that he was referred to the case of *Alidair
Ltd* v *Taylor* ([1978] ICR 445), where Lord Denning MR made a
statement which is appropriate:

> whenever a man is dismissed for incapacity or incompetence, it is
> sufficient that the employer honestly believes on reasonable
> grounds that the man is incapable or incompetent. It is not neces-
> sary for the employer to prove that he is in fact, incapable or in-
> competent.

Judge O'Malley considered that:

> this is a very wide statement and I do not entirely agree with it;
> but it does lay down the grounds for a proper approach for a Court
> which is considering the results of the deliberation of an Indus-
> trial Tribunal. It also indicates that it is irrelevant whether or not
> fair procedures were adopted in arriving at the decision that the
> party in question was incompetent.

The Employment Appeals Tribunal did look into whether there was a
fair enquiry or not, and O'Malley J considered that it was more for
the High Court to assess whether their decision was correct. Once a
court is satisfied that there were grounds for the belief that an employee was incompetent, the procedures adopted in arriving at that
belief are only relevant to justify that belief.

Qualifications

An employee may be fairly dismissed if he does not have the requisite qualifications for performing the work for which he was employed. This issue arises rarely, because it would more than likely involve a redundancy situation in which an employer wanted to obtain a person with the necessary higher skills.

In *Ryder and Byrne* v *Commissioners of Irish Lights* (High Court, Costello J, 16 April 1980, unreported), the employer had a requirement for two of its staff to obtain higher technical qualifications within a reasonable time. They failed to comply with the requirement and it was considered a fair dismissal.

In *Coyle* v *Dun Laoghaire Vocational Education Committee* (UD 993/1996), the claimant was not given sufficient time to obtain the qualification that the VEC required him to have. Further, he was not advised that he would be dismissed. It was held to be an unfair dismissal.

Conduct

An employee may be dismissed by reason of their conduct or "misconduct", though the term "misconduct" is not contained in the Act. Misconduct is a very broad term and may include the following:

- Abuse of sick pay schemes

- Clocking offences

- Conflict of interest

- Theft/irregularities

- Refusal to obey reasonable instructions

- Violence.

This is obviously not a comprehensive list, but provides a good indication of what may be construed as misconduct.

In the case of *Dunne* v *Harrington* (UD 166/1979), the Tribunal clearly set out its reasoning in cases of dishonesty, and this approach should be carried out by employers in all situations which may lead to a conduct dismissal:

1.   We do not consider our function to be the establishment of guilt or innocence;

2.   We do not seek to impose on an employer or employee a standard of behaviour so high as of itself to be unfair;

3.   Faced with a problem requiring investigation, an employer may investigate it:

   a)   personally in a fair and reasonable manner, i.e. as fully as is reasonably possible, confronting the "suspected" employee with "evidence", checking on and giving fair value to the employee's explanations or comments and allowing the employee to be represented at all such meetings/ confrontations if the employee requests it or a union/ management agreement requires it and to produce "counter-evidence" . . .

   or

   b)   to rely on the reports of others. If he does so without confronting the accused employee with the contents of same, without hearing, investigating and giving value to his replies, giving him reasonable opportunity to produce rebutting "evidence" and to be represented if the employee feels this to be desirable, then such employer breaches a fundamental rule of natural justice, viz. that the other party (i.e. the employee in these circumstances) should be heard.

   In short, an employer acting on the reports of third parties and not acquainting the employee of same does so at his peril if it results in the dismissal of that employee. We wish to make it clear that we are basing our comments on an internal inquiry of an industrial or business nature . . .

4.   Faced with the information amassed by a fair and reasonable investigation, an employer should apply himself to it in a fair and reasonable way (as a prudent and concerned employer would) and reach his conclusion as to the appropriate disciplinary measure which should of course relate reasonably to the "offence" . . .

Some areas of misconduct will now be considered:

Abuse of Sick Pay Schemes

As stated above, it is established that an employee cannot abuse the sick pay scheme. A typical example would be an employee who maintains that they are sick and then works for somebody else. In the case of *Hardy* v *Cadbury Ireland Ltd.* (UD 727/1983), the claimant was out sick yet was allegedly collecting clothes for friends and bringing them to the dry cleaners for a charge. The employee was dismissed for being in breach of the sick pay scheme and the Tribunal upheld the dismissal.

Clocking Offences

An example of this would be clocking another employee's card to give the impression that the latter had worked overtime. This is clear misconduct and may be dismissible, as it is a breach of the trust the employer had in the employee. Equally, the completion of overtime sheets when the overtime was not actually worked would be in breach of trust (*Grimes* v *Otis Elevator Group Ireland* UD 292/1988).

Conflict of Interest

An employee may not act in conflict of their employer's interests. An employee has a duty not to compete with their employer and not to divulge confidential information or trade secrets. In *Shortt* v *Smurfit Corrugated Ireland Ltd.* (UD 540/1986), the claimant was employed as a specialist designer of rubber stereos which are used in the printing on cardboard boxes. It was established that he was providing a similar service to the company's competitors and the Tribunal upheld his dismissal. The Tribunal also took a dim view of a claimant who worked as a butcher in a co-op store and then established his own butcher's shop only yards away from his employer (*Whitty* v *Waterford Co-Operative Ltd.*, UD 192/1986 and UD 764/1986 — there were procedural difficulties in this case, hence two claims).

Theft / Irregularities

Generally speaking, in a dismissal arising from an alleged theft, the value of the goods taken is immaterial, because if the employer has reasonable belief that goods were taken at all, there is a clear breach of trust.

If there are criminal proceedings pending, an employer should nonetheless carry out a full investigation, and not await the outcome of those proceedings. An employer can terminate employment on the reasonable belief that an employee committed the offence and does not decide the guilt of the employee. Of course, if an employee is acquitted by the courts, the employer may be in a difficult situation.

These problems were highlighted in *Sheehan* v *H.M. Keating & Son Ltd.* ([1993] ELR 12), where the claimant was dismissed for allegedly stealing tyres which were the property of the company. It was submitted on behalf of the claimant that the dismissal had been delayed and the company stated that this was at the request of the Garda Síochána so that they could facilitate their investigation. In fact, the Garda investigation was not completed until November 1991, yet the employee was dismissed in July of that year and the company had completed its investigation the month before. The Tribunal considered that in June there were grounds to justify dismissal by reason of gross misconduct, but as fair procedures where not applied, it was an unfair dismissal. However, since the claimant contributed 100 per cent to his dismissal, he received a nil award.

In *Hestor* v *Dunnes Stores Ltd.* ([1990] ELR 12), on the other hand, the employer applied fair procedures and it was shown that if an employee cannot offer a reasonable explanation, there may be a justifiable dismissal. Employees in this company were entitled to purchase goods subject to certain procedures and supervision from management. The claimant took a packet of ham, as well as packets of chips and burger buns from stock. The chips and buns were paid for but the packet of ham was allegedly concealed under the claimant's arm. She was confronted by a security officer and presented the items that had been paid for, then the ham fell to the floor. The claimant was questioned and she gave no reasonable explanation other than that she forgot about the ham. The Tribunal considered that it was a fair dismissal and this was upheld by Clarke J in the Circuit Court where he considered the issue was not whether or not she stole the ham, but whether it was reasonable or not to dismiss her having regard to her conduct.

PERSONS REPORTING CHILD ABUSE

The Protections for Persons Reporting Child Abuse Act, 1998, which came into force on 23 January 1999, provides protection from civil liability to persons who report child abuse "reasonably and in good faith" to designated officers of health boards or any member of the Garda Síochána. "Designated officers" include social workers, child care workers, public health nurses, hospital consultants, non-consultant hospital doctors, all other health boards, medical and dental personnel, community welfare officers, speech and language therapists, all health board nursing personnel, physiotherapists, psychologists, psychiatrists, occupational therapists, ambulance personnel, health education officers, play therapists, substance abuse counsellors, care assistants and home helps. The chief executive officer of each health board in the State must appoint specific health board personnel as "designated officers" (as designated by the Minister for Health) to receive reports under the Act.

The main provisions are as follows:

1. The provision of protection to persons who report child abuse from penalisation by their employers;

2. The creation of a new offence of false reporting of child abuse.

The Act provides protection from civil liability for persons who acting "reasonably and in good faith" report to a designated officer of the health board or any member of the Garda Síochána their opinion that

1. A child has been or is being assaulted, ill-treated, neglected or sexually abused; or

2. A child's health, development or welfare has been or is being avoidably impaired or neglected.

It provides protections from discrimination or dismissal from their employment for employees who acting "reasonably and in good faith" report child abuse to a designated officer of a health board or to the Garda Síochána. An avenue of redress for such employees who have been discriminated or dismissed is by way of complaint to a Rights Commissioner. There is also provision for an appeal from the decision of the rights commissioner by either party to the Employment Appeals Tribunal. The section provides that the Rights Commissioner shall investigate the complaint and direct that specific action be taken by an employer who has contravened the Act (e.g., reinstatement, re-engagement or pay compensation to an employee who was penalised by way of dismissal).

This provision also provides that in respect of an unfair dismissal within the meaning of the Unfair Dismissals Acts, 1977 to 1993, relief may not be granted to an employee in respect of that dismissal both under this Act and also under the Unfair Dismissals Acts.

There is provision for appeals and enforcement, as under the Terms of Employment (Information) Act, 1994, shall apply as they apply for the purposes of that Act with the modifications as detailed.

There is a new offence of false reporting of child abuse where a person makes a report to the appropriate authority "knowing the statement to be false". The penalty for conviction of such offence is a fine or imprisonment. There is a time limit within which proceedings for an offence under this section must be taken.

There is a saving provision, which specifies that the statutory immunity provided under the Act for persons reporting child abuse is additional to any defences already available under any other enactment or rule of law in force immediately before the passing of the Act.

REDUNDANCY

The redundancy of an employee may be a good defence to an unfair dismissals claim. In order for an employee to bring a claim under the Unfair Dismissals Acts, they must have one year's service. However, an employee who has been made redundant does not necessarily have to fall within the application of the Redundancy Payments Acts, 1969 to 1991. In other words, even though an employee has not been in receipt of statutory redundancy payment, that employee can still bring a claim for unfair dismissal on the basis that it was not a genuine redundancy; in other words, that the dismissal was for some other reason. The Unfair Dismissals Act does not state that it has to be a redundancy within the meaning of the Redundancy Payments Acts, though the definition of redundancy in those Acts would be applied (see definition on page XX, Chapter 18, "Redundancy").

In a number of cases, the employee has successfully maintained that statutory redundancy as a reason for dismissal was a "sham" or a "cloak". One particular case, *Edwards* v *Aerials and Electronics (Ireland) Ltd.* (UD 236/1985), highlights this issue. This case shows the problem of making an employee redundant within the context of a reorganisation. The claimant was managing director of the Irish subsidiary of a company based in Belfast. It was decided to cut the overheads of the Dublin company, which was losing money, by removing a tier of management and running the company from Belfast. The claimant contended that he was not dismissed by reason of redundancy but for some other reason, maintaining that there had been a change in attitude towards him. He gave evidence that there had been disagreements at board level and that more recently he was not allowed to visit suppliers and that decisions were being made about the company with which he as managing director did not agree.

The Tribunal was of the view that:

> the claimant had raised major doubts as to whether the redundancy was genuine. We recognise that the function of a full-time managing director no longer exists but we must direct our minds to the cause-and-effect relationship between redundancy and dismissal. The issue was whether he was dismissed because the employer had decided to reorganise the structure of the company, or whether a decision was taken to dismiss him for some other reason. In other words, was the reorganisation a cause or a consequence? On balance, we are inclined to the latter view.

This decision demonstrates that if an employee is made redundant it must be based on genuine grounds for redundancy and not as a "cloak" for some other reason. In other words, if a company wishes to have a reorganisation, it must show the requirements for same and not use it as a vehicle for dismissal for any other reason, such as incompetence.

In *St Ledger* v *Frontline Distribution Ltd*. (UD 56/1994) the Tribunal stated that redundancy is "impersonal and it involves change. . . . Impersonality runs through the five definitions in the Act . . . change also runs through the five definitions."

UNFAIR SELECTION FOR REDUNDANCY

A person bringing a claim maintaining that it was not a genuine redundancy may also claim that they were unfairly selected for redundancy. The 1977 Act states as follows:

[where] if an employee was dismissed due to redundancy but the circumstances constituting the redundancy applied equally to one or more other employees in similar employment with the same employer who had not been dismissed, and either:

a) the selection of that employee for dismissal resulted wholly or mainly from one or more of the matters specified in sub-section 2 [clarified below] of this section or another matter that would not be a ground justifying dismissal; or

b) he was selected for dismissal in contravention of a procedure (being a procedure that has been agreed upon by or on behalf of the employee and by the employee or a trade union, or an excepted body under the Trade Union Acts, 1941 to [1990], representing him or has been established by the custom and practice of the employment concerned) relating to redundancy and there were no special reasons justifying a departure from that procedure;

then the dismissal shall be deemed, for the purposes of this Act, to be an unfair dismissal.

This means that if an employee is selected for redundancy because of trade union membership or activities, religious or political opinions, involvement in civil or criminal proceedings against an employer, race or colour, pregnancy, or the denial of maternity rights, sexual orientation, age or membership of the travelling community, it will be an unfair selection. Such grounds for selection are rare and in most cases an employee may not have the necessary proof to substantiate the claim.

We will now look at the issue of the actual selection for redundancy. An employer must comply with the custom and practice or the procedure agreed in a union/management agreement unless there were special reasons to depart from it.

Again, the best way of considering this issue is to paraphrase the wording in the Act:

1. The employee must have been dismissed because of redundancy;

2. The circumstances constituting the redundancy must have applied equally to one or more other employees;

3. Those other employees must have been employed in employment similar to that of the claimant and with the same employer;

4. The selection of the dismissed employee must have resulted wholly or mainly from one or more of the grounds for unfair dismissal (see above);

5. Alternatively, the employee must have been selected for dismissal in contravention of a procedure agreed upon by or on behalf of the employer and the employee or a trade union, or established by custom or practice in the employment concerned relating to redundancy and where there were no special reasons to depart from the said procedure.

An employer will have to show that a redundancy situation existed at the date of dismissal. Therefore, if an employee is made redundant as a result of a downturn in business, management accounts will be needed for the period concerned to prove that fact (for example, balance sheets, sales reports and so forth).

The employer should also have full details of all other relevant employees and their job duties. Also, there should be copies of the employees' RP1, RP2 and other relevant documentation. There should also be evidence of the actual selection process (for example, copies of procedural agreements) and if there are none there should be details of the normal custom and practice in the particular employment. In other words, the employer should have looked at previous redundancies within the particular employment.

As in all dismissal cases, each case stands on its own merits but it is worthwhile illustrating a few examples. A good example of the "last in, first out" approach to redundancy selection is seen in the case of *O'Connor* v *SSIH (Ireland) Ltd.* (UD 50/1983). Here the Employment Appeals Tribunal held that in the absence of any union/management agreement, the custom and practice of "last in, first out" should be adhered to. In this particular case, the company contended that the claimant, who had six years' service was made redundant. The claimant stated that she had been employed as a clerk typist and had been promoted to receptionist and then promoted to stock control. There were three other women employed. Another employee with two years' service was employed as a receptionist, did stock control, typing, bookkeeping and answered the telephone. The bookkeeper had 12 years' service. The company stated that there was a redundancy situation and that there was not custom and practice of "last in, first out". The decision to keep the employee with two years' service was because she was particularly good. However, the company agreed that the claimant could have done her work and therefore was unfairly selected for redundancy and was awarded compensation.

On the other hand, it may be permissible to "keep the best". In *Cassidy* v *Smith and Nephew Southalls (Ireland) Ltd.* (UD 35/1983), the Tribunal considered that the company was entitled to select the claimant for redundancy rather than a particularly good employee.

The union and management agreement may contain various criteria for choosing somebody for redundancy, but the key issue is that there must be objective criteria; for example, the employee's level of attendance, competence, skills and flexibility.

However, in the case of *Kirwan* v *Iona National Airways Ltd.* (UD 156/1987), a pilot who was selected for redundancy on the basis of his productivity was considered to have been unfairly selected, as he was never informed that his low productivity was imperilling his position with the company.

In *Boucher and Others* v *Irish Productivity Centre* ([1995] ELR 205), there was an agreed plan to save the respondent, to include staff redundancies of 16 people, but there was no selection method. The chief executive had to select the employees for redundancy, which he achieved by a process of elimination. He selected those most suitable to stay with a balance of skills, flexibility and the ability to generate new business. The five claimants were selected. It was held to be an unfair dismissal, as the claimants were not advised of the assessment and should have been allowed give their views.

REDRESS

An employee who is unfairly dismissed is entitled to redress consisting of whatever the Rights Commissioner, the Employment Appeals Tribunal or the Circuit Court considers appropriate "having regard to all the circumstances". Although not stated in the Act, in practice this extends to the High Court, which hears appeals from the Circuit Court. Such appeals are full hearings of the case (not just appeals on a point of law). However, it should be noted that in *State (Irish Pharmaceutical Union)* v *Employment Appeals Tribunal* ([1987] ILRM 36), it was considered that the views of both sides should be considered before redress is awarded. Such redress may be reinstatement, re-engagement or compensation. The 1993 Act provides that where redress is being awarded, the Rights Commissioner, the Tribunal or the Circuit Court has to give reasons in the written order as to why either of the other two forms of redress was not awarded to the employee; for example, if compensation is being awarded, why reinstatement or re-engagement has not been awarded.

Re-employment

Over the last few years, and in particular from 1984, it has become apparent that in a high number of cases the remedy of re-employment has been awarded, the reasoning being that more than likely the employee will not yet have found alternative employment. Between 1989 and 1991, re-employment was awarded in approximately 30 per cent of cases where an employee was considered to have been unfairly dismissed. Undoubtedly, this was due to then current economic circumstances for the most part. Further, there has been consistent criticism over the last number of years that the Tribunal is awarding low amounts of compensation. Taking these two points into account, the Tribunal has become more likely to award re-employment. However, this remedy is more often applied to unskilled, semi-skilled or skilled workers in large employments rather than members of management or those in small employments.

Reinstatement

Section 7(1)(a) of the Act defines reinstatement as follows:

> Reinstatement by the employer of the employee in the position which he held immediately before his dismissal on the terms and conditions on which he was employed immediately before his dismissal together with a term that the reinstatement shall be deemed to have commenced on the day of the dismissal.

In effect, reinstatement means that an employee who has been unfairly dismissed is awarded their old position back immediately as if they were never dismissed. It is usually awarded where there is no blame attributable to the employee. This means that loss of earnings (net pay, i.e. gross weekly pay less income tax, PRSI and social welfare) must also be paid to the former employee. This would also include loss of pension contributions, if appropriate. Thus the employee should be at no loss whatsoever and their continuity of employment is retained. The application of reinstatement has been further extended by the 1993 Act and provides that if an employee is reinstated and if the terms and conditions are more favourable, then the new terms and conditions apply. The purpose of this extension would be so that the reinstated employee may receive the benefits of any favourable changes in terms and conditions of employment which applied to other employees.

In *McCrum* v *Initial Services Ireland Ltd.* (UD 693/1984), the company contended that the claimant's record of absence and late attendance were appalling. The claimant was given several warnings, culminating in a week's suspension. In the week prior to dismissal, she was absent for a number of days and was also late on two occasions. Finally, she was absent on a particular day and the company was informed by telephone that she was suffering from a toothache and would be consulting her dentist. The following day the claimant handed in her certificate from her dentist covering her absence for 10 days, that is, from the date she telephoned in. When she met the plant manager, she was informed that the company had already decided to dismiss her in view of her attendance records. The claimant was awarded reinstatement based on the fact that the company did not consider her excuse reasonable and had, in fact, already decided to dismiss her prior to such explanation. Furthermore, as the facts were not in dispute, the Tribunal decided that the claimant need not give evidence, as the employer had not discharged the burden of proof.

In *Reilly* v *Smurfit Cartons Ltd.* (UD 722/1983), the claimant was dismissed for being absent from work without permission and for falsification of clock cards. Two employees were involved in this incident; one was suspended for eight weeks, without pay, while the claimant was dismissed. It was contended that the claimant had a previous warning, but this was not available in evidence before the Tribunal.

The Tribunal considered that the claimant's conduct was of a serious nature, but the fact that he was dismissed while the other employee, who was guilty of the same conduct, was only suspended, was not satisfactory to the mind of the Tribunal. Accordingly, the claimant was also awarded reinstatement but was given the same period of suspension without pay as the other employee, that is, eight weeks. Thus, he was not to receive the full financial loss.

In considering these cases, both employees were unskilled workers who did not have alternative employment prior to the Tribunal hearing. Further, the Tribunal considered there was not a fair application of reasonableness by the employer and, accordingly, the employees were awarded reinstatement.

In *Rapple* v *Irish Press Newspapers* (UD 841/ 1995) the claimant was awarded reinstatement so that he could benefit from enhanced pension rights which arose out of the employer's liquidation.

Re-engagement

Section 7(1)(b) defines re-engagement as follows:

> Re-engagement by the employer of the employee either in the position which he held immediately before his dismissal or in different position which would be reasonably suitable for him on such terms and conditions as are reasonable having regard to all the circumstances.

In effect, this means that an employee either gets their old position back or else a different position which would be reasonably suitable for them on such terms and conditions as are reasonable.

The remedy of re-engagement is less clear than reinstatement and therefore the Tribunal in most cases explains what it means by it. The normal situation is that re-engagement of an employee does not break their continuity of service. However, in *Scott* v *Yeates & Sons Limited, Opticians* ([1992] ELR 83) the Tribunal clearly stated that there was a break in continuity. An employee who is re-engaged is not entitled to any loss of monies between the date of dismissal and the date of re-engagement. This remedy, which is applied more frequently than reinstatement, is usually awarded where the employee has contributed somewhat to their own dismissal. From the employee's point of view, it is obviously less satisfactory and, of course, it is less costly to the employer than having to reinstate the employee.

The Tribunal may order re-engagement on a final written warning arising from particular conduct; e.g., going underground in breach of procedures where there was a history of alcohol abuse but where the employer was in breach of application of the procedural agreement (*Mellett* v *Tara Mines Limited*. UD 375/1995).

This re-employment remedy has been consistently applied by the Tribunal in relation to dismissals where an employer has been in breach of procedure or natural justice in a "conduct" dismissal. It can also be applied in absenteeism dismissals where there is a breach of fairness, for example, not getting the up-to-date medical position of the employee before making a decision to dismiss. Again, the remedy is more usually applied in large employments.

Examples of where re-engagement was awarded, and the circumstances of such an award, will now be considered.

Procedures

In *Bolger* v *Dublin Sport Hotel Ltd.* (UD 45/1985), the claimant was dismissed from his position of assistant head waiter because he failed to report to work and was, in fact, working for another employer on that particular day. The Tribunal stated that in this case the company should have considered alternative options, namely, a period of suspension without pay and/or a final written warning. Though the Tribunal did note that the claimant's conduct was serious, it determined that the claimant be re-engaged.

This remedy may also be used where it is clear that the employee has committed serious misconduct yet the employer failed to use proper procedures to investigate the issue. The employer should consider the range of responses to such conduct, for example, suspension without pay/final written warning. The purpose of applying this remedy in such situations is to hold the status quo; in other words, the employee is re-employed and, depending upon the circumstances, fair procedures are applied to a further investigation and the employee could then be dismissed for a second time *(Whitty* v *Waterford Co-operative Society Ltd.*, UD 192/1986 and UD 764/1986).

Absenteeism

This remedy has been applied in a number of absenteeism cases. Indeed, the use of the re-engagement remedy is quite a normal approach to find an equitable solution. More than likely, the reason the Tribunal awards re-engagement to an employee who has been dismissed because of long-term absence is that the employee would not be entitled to compensation, since they may have been unavailable for work following on the dismissal and for the foreseeable future. Furthermore, if there was not sufficient up-to-date medical information at the date of dismissal, the employer may now have an opportunity of obtaining such information and, equally, the employee has a further chance of becoming medically fit in the intervening period.

In *McLoughlin* v *Celmac (Irl) Ltd.* (UD 799/1984), the claimant was dismissed because of illness-related absenteeism. The Tribunal noted that the company made the decision to dismiss without having up-to-date medical opinion with regard to his future availability for work. The Tribunal considered that the claimant should have been medically examined and there is an onus on an employer to get up-to-date medical evidence prior to making the decision to dismiss. In this case, the claimant was awarded re-engagement but he was to receive no monies from the date of dismissal to the date of re-engagement.

In *Walsh* v *A. Guinness Son & Co (Dublin) Ltd.* (UD 871/1985), the claimant, a storeman, had a very unsatisfactory attendance record and could give no firm indication as to when he would be fit for work. A decision was made to dismiss the claimant and subsequently a meeting was held with the union at which the claimant said he had been informed by his doctor that he would be fully fit to resume work. The company decided that the dismissal should stand. However, the Tribunal took the view that, in or about the time of the dismissal, there was a clear indication that the claimant would be fully fit within a short period. The Tribunal further considered that it was unreasonable to terminate his employment at that time in the light of the information then available. On reading the determination, it would appear that no up-to-date medical evidence was sought by the company on the claimant's medical condition. Accordingly, the Tribunal considered that re-engagement was the most appropriate remedy.

In some cases where absenteeism is the reason for dismissal, the Tribunal has taken a different approach to re-engagement. In *McGrane* v *Mater Private Nursing Home* (UD 369/1985), for example, the claimant was dismissed by reason of absenteeism. Noting that there was no definite pressure placed on the nursing home to replace the claimant, the Tribunal considered that she was unfairly dismissed. The Tribunal ordered re-engagement from such date as the claimant was certified fit to resume work, provided that she be so certified not later than 31 December 1985 (the determination was dated

9 October 1985). However, in the event of the claimant not being so certified within that period, the determination would fail. This means that re-engagement was awarded but the claimant had to be fit to resume work by a particular date to have any entitlement to return.

In *Heneghan* v *El Company Ltd.* (UD 253/1985), the Tribunal took the view that the claimant should be re-engaged. Part of the reasoning in this case was that the claimant — a machine operator — was not a key employee and that, in a company that employed about 400 people, it was not necessary or reasonable to terminate her employment. The claimant submitted to an examination by the company doctor (the company/union agreement provided for steps to be taken in these circumstances — presumably an independent medical examination). Shortly after her employment was terminated, she claimed she was fit to resume work.

COMPENSATION

From a review of the Annual Reports of the Employment Appeals Tribunal (see above), it appears that compensation amounts awarded under the Act are relatively low. For example, in 1996 the average compensation figure was £5,354, in 1991 the average compensation figure was £2,660, and in 1985 the average figure was £2,460. Over the last few years, the average has been creeping up slowly. It should be borne in mind that each case rests on its own merits and that compensation is based on the employee's salary and the employee's "loss". So, if an employee has been unfairly dismissed and obtains a job on the same rate of pay soon after their dismissal, their "loss" may be relatively low. Under the 1977 Act, the Tribunal (and the other adjudicating bodies) had to deduct social welfare receipts, earnings and tax rebates from the employee's net wage loss. The 1993 Act has remedied this situation and provides that social welfare receipts and tax rebates shall no longer be deducted from an employee's loss. Accordingly, in the future the compensation awards may be higher. However, in the current labour market, a claimant's loss may be curtailed due to the availability of employment and the obligation to mitigate loss.

Section 7(1)(c) of the Act defines compensation as:

> . . . payment by the employer to the employee of such compensation (not exceeding in amount 104 weeks' remuneration in respect

of the employment from which he was dismissed calculated in accordance with regulations . . .) in respect of any financial loss incurred by him and attributable to the dismissal as is just and equitable having regard to all the circumstances.

The maximum an unfairly dismissed employee may be awarded is 104 weeks' gross remuneration. Remuneration includes "allowances in the nature of pay and benefits in lieu of or in addition to pay". There are specific regulations to work out weekly wage and overtime, commissions etc. There are also specific provisions in the Act for the calculation of loss.

When an award of compensation is being made, account must be taken of the extent to which the financial loss was attributable to an act, omission or conduct on the part of the employer. The 1993 Act has extended this to include the extent to which the employer applied fair procedures in the union/management agreement or custom and practice in the employment concerned, and of course the Code of Practice on Disciplinary Procedures, and if there was a failure by the employer to set out the grounds for dismissal if requested by the employee. The effect of these provisions is that if an employer breaches fair procedure, there will more than likely be a higher award for the unfairly dismissed employee.

Loss

"Financial loss", in relation to the dismissal of an employee, includes

> any actual loss and any estimated prospective loss of income attributable to the dismissal and the value of any loss or diminution, attributable to the dismissal, of the rights of the employee under the Redundancy Payments Acts, 1967 to [1991], or in relation to superannuation.

Financial loss may be considered under the following headings:

1. *Actual loss*: This is the employee's loss from the date of dismissal to the date of the Tribunal hearing, that is, gross weekly pay less income tax, PRSI, income tax rebate received, unemployment benefit/assistance.

2. *Future loss*: This is loss attributable to future loss of earnings. In considering such loss, the Tribunal has to take into account fac-

tors such as the employee's future employment prospects, skill and age.

3. *Loss of rights under protective legislation and superannuation*: The employee, particularly one with long service, is awarded monies for the loss of protection under the Redundancy Payments Acts, 1967 to 1991, Unfair Dismissals Acts, 1977 to 1993, and the Minimum Notice and Terms of Employment Acts, 1973 to 1991. Such monies are frequently low but the dismissed employee will have to build up service in any new employment in order to fall within the scope of these Acts once again. For example, should a redundancy situation arise, the loss may be considerable as the employee may be the "last-in" in a new employment; therefore, the "last in, first out" principle would more than likely militate against that employee.

Although not specifically mentioned in the Act, the Tribunal has awarded nominal compensation for loss of statutory rights under the unfair dismissals and the minimum notice legislation. Pension loss may be the main contributor towards high awards, as the loss of pension rights is an extremely important factor in the assessment of compensation for unfair dismissal. The assessment of the loss is very difficult. The return of the employee's own contributions (less tax plus interest) is not sufficient to compensate for the loss of future pension rights. This has now changed, as an employee is entitled to a transfer value of the pension benefits or deferred pension built up from 1 January 1991. Thus, they may not lose out on past benefits but would still lose out on future benefits. One must also consider that it may take the employee approximately two years to belong to the pension scheme operated by their employer, or indeed the new employer may not operate a pension scheme (there is no requirement on an employer to provide one). A further basis for compensation would be if the previous employer operated a non-contributory pension scheme and the new employment operates a contributory scheme. Therefore, the additional cost of the new scheme would have to be considered.

It might be noted that there are very few cases where pension loss was awarded.

Maximum Award

An unfairly dismissed employee may be awarded a maximum of 104 weeks' gross remuneration. However, loss is actually computed on a net basis. A clear example of how the maximum may be awarded is as follows using the main headings in *Bunyan* v *United Dominions Trust (Ireland) Ltd.* (UD 66/1980) (note that since the 1993 Amendment Act, social welfare receipts and income tax rebates are not deducted; such figures are marked * below):

Calculation of annual remuneration:

1. Salary	£15,826
2. Annual bonus	£500
3. Company contribution to pension scheme	£3,000
4. Private use of company car	£2,000
5. Value of lunches and subscriptions	£200
6. Employer's PRSI	£701
Total Remuneration	*£22,227*

In this case, a pension was part of the employee's remuneration. Calculation of the employee's loss and pension was as follows:

Pension loss	£44,800
Actual loss, i.e. net remuneration less social welfare*	£19,558
Future loss (arising from dismissal measured over 5 years x £8,000)*	£40,000
Diminution of rights under protective legislation*	£160
Total Actual Loss	*£104,518*

Claimant's Contribution to the dismissal:

Less 45%	£47,033
Net Loss	£57,485
Statutory Maximum (2x £22,227)	£44,454
Total Compensatory Award	*£44,454*

The key point is that the deduction for contribution to the dismissal is taken from the total loss rather than from the maximum award. This concept was also applied in *Cavanagh* v *Dunnes Stores Ltd.* ([1995] ELR 164), where it was held that even though the claimant contributed to his dismissal by reason of his conduct, it was not sufficient to merit a deduction of the maximum award. In his case, it was £124,000.

A similar calculation was also used in *Moriarty* v *F.W. Woolworth plc* (UD 672/1984), where the claimant, dismissed for alleged irregularities, was awarded the maximum. The reason he was awarded the maximum (£34,840) was that the Tribunal considered he would not find suitable alternative work between then and retirement age.

The maximum was also awarded in the case of *Maugham* v *Janssen Pharmaceuticals BV* (UD 1127/1984), where the Tribunal considered in detail its reasoning for such award. The claimant, an administration manager with the company, was dismissed for alleged non-performance following the installation of a computer. In such cases, the Tribunal must consider the claimant's age, skills, length of service, and the general employment market and likely rates of pay should she find alternative employment. It considered that she would be unlikely to get as good a job again and that, as a career woman, she would likely seek and be available for employment until normal retirement age. She was awarded £38,722.

Deduction of Social Welfare

The Unfair Dismissals (Amendment) Act, 1993, provides that there shall be no deduction of social welfare monies or tax rebates from any compensation awarded under the Act in respect of a dismissal which took place on or after 1 October 1993. The 1977 Act had provided for social welfare monies to be deducted from compensation.

Employee Contribution to Dismissal

Section 7 of the Act refers to "compensation in respect of any financial loss incurred by him and attributable to the dismissal as is just and equitable having regard to all the circumstances". The Tribunal thus has discretion in its award of compensation; for example, it can deduct a percentage contribution if the employee has failed to mitigate their loss or if the employee has contributed to their dismissal.

Section 7(2) provides:

> Without prejudice to the generality of subsection (1) of this sec-
> tion, in determining the amount of compensation payable under
> the subsection referred shall be had to . . .

b)   The extent (if any) to which the said financial loss was attrib-
     utable to an action, omission or conduct by or on behalf of the
     employee;

c)   The measures (if any) adopted by the employee or, as the case
     may be, his failure to adopt measures, to mitigate the loss
     aforesaid . . .

and

f)   The extent (if any) to which the conduct of the employee
     (whether by act of omission) contributed to the dismissal. [(f)
     from 1993 Act].

In *Shiels* v *Williams Transport Group (Ireland) Ltd.* (UD 191/1984)
the claimant, an export manager, was dismissed for allegedly having
drugs on his employer's premises. The claimant admitted having
such illegal drugs and admitted using them at work. The company
procedures were faulty, however, as he was not interviewed by management. The Tribunal considered he was unfairly dismissed but he
contributed to his dismissal by 100 per cent. No redress was awarded.

This case shows that it is virtually impossible for an employer to
succeed in a case where there is a breach of fair procedure. The Tribunal repeated this approach in many other cases and in *Sheehan* v
H.M. Keating & Sons Ltd. ([1993] ELR 12), where the claimant had
been convicted of theft of company property after his dismissal. Prior
to the dismissal, the Tribunal considered that fair procedures were
not applied, but since he contributed 100 per cent to his dismissal, he
received a nil award. However, the Tribunal awarded minimum notice even though he was dismissed for alleged misconduct.

However, in *O'Loughlin* v *Climatic Building Systems Ltd.* (UD
600/1984), the general manager was dismissed for allegedly acting in
conflict with the interest of his employer. No proper investigatory
procedures — which would have taken two months — were applied
by the employer. The claimant was awarded only two months' net pay

because if the company had carried out a proper investigation, there may have been reasonable grounds for dismissal.

Mitigation of Loss

If an employee fails to mitigate their loss — for example, if an employee fails to look for another job — the Tribunal may take that into account and deduct a small percentage from the total award. Also, an employee who fails to register and collect unemployment benefit or assistance for a period of time after their dismissal cannot claim the full loss for that period. In other words, the Tribunal will only give that employee loss less the social welfare to which they would have been entitled (see non-deduction of social welfare above).

In *Cavanagh* v *Dunnes Stores Ltd.* ([1995] ELR 164) the claimant was awarded the sum of 104 weeks' gross remuneration. It was argued that he failed to mitigate his loss by setting up his own security company as opposed to looking for a job. This argument was not accepted by the Tribunal, as it was not accepted that he should obtain a job worth, say, £8,000 to £10,000 in the security industry.

Basic Award

The 1993 Act provides that if an employee has been unfairly dismissed but incurs no loss, then a basis award may be given. An example would be where an employee finds a similar job immediately after their dismissal and thereby incurs no loss. There would be provision for a basic award of up to four weeks' remuneration in such situations.

Reduction in Award — Redundancy

Frequently, a compensation award may be reduced because the employee would have been dismissed in any event by reason of redundancy. Such a factor was taken into account by the EAT in *Ryan* v *Noel & Francis O'Kelly t/a O'Kelly Bros.* (UD 1030/1983). The Tribunal found the claimant, a contracts manager/surveyor, to have been unfairly dismissed. He was awarded compensation from the date of dismissal to the date when he would have been made redundant in any event.

The *ex gratia* aspect of redundancy payment was considered in *O'Connor* v *Premier Dairies Ltd.* (UD 614/1984). Here, the claimant was dismissed by reason of redundancy, but the company broke an agreement with him to keep him on for temporary work. If he had been employed for one extra week, he would have been entitled to statutory redundancy pay and an *ex gratia* payment. The loss attributable to his unfair dismissal was one week's pay plus the *ex gratia* lump sum.

Taxation

The normal taxation rules on termination payments apply for Tribunal awards under the Unfair Dismissals Acts, 1977 to 1993, and the Minimum Notice and Terms of Employment Acts, 1973 to 1991 (see Chapter 20, "Taxation of Termination Payments").

Costs

In the EAT case of *Conway* v *Westair Aviation Ltd.* (UD 652/1983), the Tribunal awarded witness costs to the claimant as it considered that the company acted "frivolously or vexatiously". Such ruling was further to paragraph 19(2) of the Redundancy (Redundancy Appeals Tribunal) Regulations 1968 (SI No. 24 of 1968), incorporated into the Unfair Dismissal (Claims and Appeals) Regulations, 1977. Such costs may only be for travelling expenses or any other costs associated with the hearing. Legal costs are not included.

Procedures

The procedures applicable to bringing a case under the Unfair Dismissals Acts, 1977 to 1993 are considered in section 4.

General References

Department of Industrial Relations, UCD (1989), *Industrial Relations in Ireland: Contemporary Issues and Development* (see following chapter: T. Murphy, "The Impact of the Unfair Dismissals Act, 1977, on Workplace Industrial Relations"), Dublin: Department of Industrial Relations, UCD.

Employment Appeals Tribunal, *Annual Reports*, Dublin: Stationery Office.

Kerr, T. and D. Madden (1996), *Unfair Dismissal Cases and Commentary*, IBEC.

Mallon, T. and M. Bolger (1997), "Injuncting the Contract of Employment", *The Bar Review*, December.

Meenan, F. (1985), *A Survey of Unfair Dismissals Cases, 1977–1984*, Supplement to FUE Bulletin, June.

Murphy, T. (1984), "Restoring Management Prerogative: the Unfair Dismissals Act in Practice", *Journal of Irish Business and Administrative Research*, Vol. 6, No. 1, April; and reply: F. Meenan, "Restoring Management Prerogative", *Journal of Irish Business and Administrative Research*, Vol. 6, No. 2, October, 1984.

Redmond, M. (1999), *Dismissal Law in the Republic of Ireland,* second edition, Dublin: Butterworths.

Chapter Eighteen

REDUNDANCY

Statutory redundancy payments under the Redundancy Payments Acts, 1967 to 1991, are meant to compensate for the loss of security, seniority and other benefits which have built up in employment, for an employee whose position has become redundant. The statutory payment is relatively low, especially as it is calculated on an earnings ceiling of £300 per week (or £15,600 per year) (Redundancy Payments (Lump Sum) Regulations, 1994 (SI No. 64 of 1994). Therefore, many employees negotiate a severance payment that is higher than the statutory award, usually based on an employee's length of service.

The principal Redundancy Payments Act is the 1967 Act, which was amended by the 1971, 1973 and 1979 Acts. The Acts were also amended by the Protection of Employees (Employers' Insolvency) Act, 1984, and the Worker Protection (Regular Part-Time Employees) Act, 1991. The Redundancy Payments Acts are complicated and the purpose of this chapter is to look at their key provisions.

If an employer is making a number of employees redundant, the Protection of Employment Act, 1977 (as amended by the Protection of Employment Order, 1996, SI No. 370 of 1996) may apply. This Act provides for consultation between the parties beforehand and that certain notice must be given to the Minister for Enterprise and Employment (see Chapter 19, "Collective Redundancies").

DEFINITIONS OF STATUTORY REDUNDANCY

Redundancy is defined as meaning one of the grounds of statutory redundancy in Section 7(2) of the Redundancy Payments Act, 1967 (as amended by section 4 of the Redundancy Payments Acts, 1971).

. . . an employee who is dismissed shall be taken to be dismissed by reason of redundancy if the dismissal is attributable wholly or mainly to:

(a) The fact that his employer has ceased, or intends to cease, to carry on the business for the purposes of which the employee was employed by him, or has ceased or intends to cease, to carry on that business in the place where the employee was so employed; or

(b) The fact that the requirements of that business for employees to carry out work of a particular kind in the place where he was so employed have ceased or diminished or are expected to cease or diminish; or

(c) The fact that his employer has decided to carry on the business with fewer or no employees, whether by requiring the work for which the employee had been employed (or had been doing before his dismissal) to be done by other employees or otherwise; or

(d) The fact that his employer had decided that the work for which the employee has been employed (or had been doing before his dismissal) should henceforward be done in a different manner for which the employee is not sufficiently qualified or trained, or

(e) The fact that his employer has decided that the work for which the employee had been employed (or had been doing before his dismissal) should henceforward be done by a person who is also capable of doing other work for which the employee is not sufficiently qualified or trained.

A redundancy situation must arise at the date of dismissal. If it does not, a redundant employee may successfully bring a claim for unfair dismissal (e.g. *Glynn* v *Pepe (Ire) Ltd.* [1993] ELR 39).

The definition of "redundancy" was considered in *St Ledger* v *Frontline Distribution Ltd* (UD 56/94); the ruling in this case was published for future guidance, notwithstanding the case was settled between the parties. The facts were that the claimant, a warehouse supervisor, was dismissed and replaced by another employee, a Mr Kennedy who it was claimed was better trained to do the work. Mr Kennedy had passed an examination which might lead to a diploma.

The claimant provided full details of his career with job specification of the work he carried out whilst in employment. Mr. Kennedy reported to a different person and he could also do the job without the help of a part-time helper, but it should be noted that the company was not relying on the argument of a reduction in staff. The employer relied on the definition of redundancy at paragraph (e) and to a lesser extent at paragraph (d). The Tribunal considered the concept of redundancy as follows:

> Redundancy has two characteristics which are of importance in this case. It is impersonal and it involves change.
>
> Impersonality runs through the five definitions in the Act. Redundancy impacts on the job and only as a consequence of the redundancy does the person involved lose the job. It is worthy of note that the EC Directive on Collective Redundancies uses a shorter and simpler definition: "one or more reasons not related to the individual workers concerned".
>
> Change runs through all five definitions. This means change in the workplace. The most dramatic change of all is a complete closedown. Change may also mean a reduction in needs for employees, or a reduction in numbers. Definition (d) and (e) involve change in the way the work is done or some other form of change in the nature of the job. Under these two definitions, change in the job must mean quantitative change. Definition (e) must involve, partly, at least work of a different kind and that is the only meaning we can put on the words "other work". More work or less work of the same kind does not mean "other work" and is only quantitative change. In the event, the quantitative change in this case is in the wrong direction. A downward change in the volume of work might imply redundancy under another definition, (b), but an upward change would not.
>
> For redundancy to arise in the present case, the respondent would have to satisfy us that the nature of the job changed, and that in connection with the change, and only in connection with the change, Mr Kennedy had certain training that the claimant had not.

It was also noted by the Tribunal that redundancy did not arise in this case because there was no evidence that Mr Kennedy had any special training in the formal sense related to work experience. The company argued that Mr Kennedy had more ability. However, it was considered that "ability" is not the same as training. It is irrelevant whether Mr Kennedy is better able to do the work previously done by the claimant. To hold otherwise would be to deny the essential impersonality of redundancy.

This case was followed in *Coyle* v *Dublin Institute of Technology* (RP 67/98) where Mr Coyle was initially a part-time lecturer, then he became a yearly lecturer replacing a permanent staff member who was away. When the permanent staff member came back, Mr Coyle's employment was terminated. Hence, the key question was whether the job performed by Mr Coyle was the same as that position which he replaced. If the job was different, then once employment came to an end, the job was extinguished and therefore there was a redundancy. On the other hand, if the job was the same and he was merely temporary, then there was no redundancy. The Tribunal, relying on the *St Ledger* case (above), found that there was no significant different between the nature of the position held when Mr Coyle possessed it compared to his predecessor. It was also noted that there was no change in staff complement.

APPLICATION OF ACT

There are certain provisions which an employee must fulfil before being entitled to a statutory redundancy payment:

1. The employee must work or have worked under a contract of service or apprenticeship; however, the Acts do not apply to an apprentice who is being made redundant within one month of the completion of apprenticeship. The Acts also apply to a person who had worked under a fixed-term contract and the contract has expired, provided that there is a redundancy situation.

2. The employee was in employment which was insurable for all Social Welfare Benefits.

3. The employee must be aged between 16 and 66 years.

4. The employee must normally have been expected to work at least eight hours per week (this includes regular part-time employees).

5. The employee must have been continuously employed for 104 weeks between the ages of 16 and 66 years. This does not necessarily mean that an employee actually has to work the 104 weeks.

6. The employee must have been dismissed within the statutory definition of dismissal.

CONTINUITY OF SERVICE

The Acts have complicated rules which establish whether an employee has continuity of service and how to compute reckonable service in order to calculate redundancy payments. Nonetheless, there is a presumption in the Acts that all service is continuous unless proven otherwise; for example, if the employee had resigned or had previously received a redundancy payment from the same employer. This means that the burden of proof is on the employer to prove that service was broken. The Act states that "a person's employment during any period shall, unless the contrary is proved, be presumed to have been continuous".

The Employment Appeals Tribunal is very reluctant to determine that there is a break in continuity of service. The continuity rules are difficult but they may be summarised as follows, noting the overriding provision in paragraph 4 of the Second Schedule to the Act:

> For the purposes of this Schedule employment shall be taken to be continuous unless terminated by dismissal or by the employee's voluntarily leaving the employment.

Continuity is not broken by (a) sickness or injury of less than 78 weeks, or (b) lay-off, holidays, or authorised leave of less than 26 weeks. An employee who is absent because of illness and on an income continuance plan may be entitled to redundancy because, notwithstanding their illness, they are deemed to be an employee (*Gordon* v *Asahi Synthetic Fibres (Ireland) Ltd.* RP 29/98).

In *Irish Shipping* v *Adams and Others* ((1987) 6 JISLL 186), the High Court (on appeal from the EAT) considered continuity of employment in respect of seamen with periods of service at sea followed by periods when they were not actually working. The facts were that at the end of a tour of duty at sea, it was understood that the seamen would return to service again with Irish Shipping only, as soon as a

suitable vacancy arose. It was common to spend six months at sea
and four months on shore. The first few weeks on shore were paid
leave (holidays). Earlier, the Employment Appeals Tribunal relied on
the statutory presumption that there was continuity of employment
and various interruptions in service did not break continuity. It was
concluded that the periods spent on shore comprised holidays, the
balance being lay-off or agreed absence with the employer, presuming
the employee sought further service. Thus there was continuity of
service and an entitlement to statutory redundancy.

As stated above, the Tribunal is reluctant to consider that there
was a break in an employee's continuity of service. There have been
enormous difficulties in understanding the true meaning of these
rules, in particular. They may be best highlighted by the claims
brought under the Redundancy Payments Acts by former employees
of Gateaux who were terminated as a result of the closedown of the
company in autumn 1990. In this case, there were a large number of
employees with "casual" service who were on a recall list. They only
worked for varying parts of the year, depending on their seniority on
the list. Their employment usually came to an end before Christmas
and they were given notice of termination. They were given a new
contract for every period that they worked. The Tribunal relied on the
presumption that service was continuous. In their decision, the Tribunal did not refer to the stipulation that a break of over 26 weeks
lay-off meant that continuity would be broken. The Tribunal instead
appears to have relied on Rule 4 referred to previously — that "employment shall be taken to be continuous unless terminated by dismissal or by the employee's voluntarily leaving the employment".

Thus Rule 4 was overriding and there was never any termination
by either employer or employee and continuity was not broken (*Far-
rell* v *Gateaux Ltd.* 547/1990).

Continuity is also not broken by:

1.   Service in the Reserve Defence Force;

2.   Absence from work because of a lock-out by the employer or for
     taking part in a strike;

3.   Transfer of a business;

4. Protective leave (which includes maternity leave, additional maternity leave, and health and safety leave), natal care absence within the meaning of the Maternity Protection Act, 1994;

5. Adoptive leave or additional adoptive leave under the Adoptive Leave Act, 1995;

6. Parental leave or *force majeure* leave under the Parental Leave Act, 1998;

7. Reinstatement, and generally re-engagement, under the Unfair Dismissals Acts, 1977 to 1993;

8. Delayed receipt of the full statutory minimum notice;

9. Dismissal due to redundancy before reaching 104 weeks' continuous service and if there is a resumption of work within 26 weeks of the original termination.

RECKONABLE SERVICE

The rules for reckonable service are actually used to compute the period of service, which is then used to reach the statutory redundancy entitlement. The following periods of service are excluded:

1. Lay-off;

2. Absence from work due to a strike in the employer's business;

3. Absence from work due to strike or lockout in a business or industry other than that in which the employee is employed since 1 January 1968;

4. Authorised absence in excess of 13 weeks in a 52-week period;

5. Absence due to illness in excess of 26 weeks;

6. Absence in excess of 52 weeks due to occupational injury.

NO DISMISSAL

There are certain circumstances where there is not a dismissal and thus no entitlement to a redundancy payment within the meaning of the Acts:

if the employee's contract is renewed or if the employee is re-engaged under a new contract by the same employer and the new arrangement is to take effect immediately (i.e. the old contract is finished on a Friday and the next contract commences on the Monday); or

the renewal or re-engagement follows an offer in writing made by the employer before the ending of the current contract. The new contract must take effect immediately or not later than four weeks from the end of the previous contract.

Also, if there is a re-engagement by a different employer and the employment commences immediately upon the agreement of the parties confirming the terms and conditions of employment (with a written statement that service is continuous), then there is no entitlement to redundancy, as there is no dismissal.

An employee who unreasonably refuses an offer of re-employment may not be entitled to a redundancy payment. If the employee was offered re-employment on different terms and conditions within two weeks after the service of the Redundancy Notice (to take effect within four weeks), and if the employee unreasonably refuses the offer, then there is no entitlement to redundancy. An example of "different terms and conditions" would be a change in location. If the employee claims redundancy then, the employee's individual circumstances are taken into account as regards the physical practicalities of going to work in the new location; for example, if the employee had a car, it may be considered that it was an unreasonable refusal.

These issues were considered in a number of recent cases. The case of *Finn* v *Prescott Cleaners Ltd.* (RP 12/98) considered the issue of transferability between branches. The claimant commenced working for the company in 1985, stating that he would be prepared to work in any of the branches. His employment was confirmed in the Mullingar branch in 1985. The Mullingar premises was sold in 1997. The claimant elected to seek a finding that he was made redundant from his place of work. The new owner said that he was transferable and therefore not entitled to redundancy. It was held that he was entitled to redundancy as there was no written offer of re-employment.

In *Blade* v *Kerry Co-operative Dairies Ltd.* (RP 90/98), the claimant, a driver, was originally employed by Tuam Dairies, which was taken over by Kerry Co-operative Dairies. There was a flexibility clause in the union/management agreement whereby he could be required to move. There was a reduction in the number of drivers. He had to change his work schedule from Tuam to Galway as a relief driver. The Employment Appeals Tribunal determined that it would not be unreasonable to refuse the offer of alternative employment as a relief driver in Galway. The decision was on the basis that the issue of flexibility cannot be the defining issue where there has been a *de facto* reduction in the jobs of drivers. "Transfer of a Business" was considered further in Chapter 11.

REDUNDANCY DUE TO LAY-OFF OR SHORT-TIME

Lay-off is defined in the Acts as where an employee's employment ceases because the employer is not able to provide the employee with work and

> it is reasonable in the circumstances for the employer to believe that the cessation of employment will not be permanent and . . . the employer gives such notice to the employee prior to the cessation.

There is no specific period of notice laid down in the Act. The case of *Lawe* v *Irish Country Meats (Pig Meats) Limited* [1998] ELR 266 considered the matter of lay-off and the contractual right to payment during such lay-off. There was a background of industrial action in this case; the plaintiff had not been involved but he had been laid off for 10 days without pay. He sought payment for wages. It was alleged that a custom and practice had developed whereby workers could be laid off without pay where there was a shortage of raw material, a slackness of work or seasonal problems. Such lay-offs were normally done in consultation with the union, of short duration, and operated on a last-in, first-out basis. The District Court dismissed the claim but it was allowed on appeal to the Circuit Court. White J considered that it was an employer's fundamental obligation to pay the agreed remuneration for the times of work during which the employee is prepared to work. There is no general right at common law to lay-off without pay but it may be established by custom in limited circumstances (*Bond* v *CAV Ltd.* [1983] IRLR 360). If the lay-off at issue in this case was temporary, and a custom and practice which entitled the defendant to lay-off without pay applied; or if production problems arose as a direct result of the industrial dispute and notice was given that the lay-off was temporary, then the employer was entitled to lay-off without pay. However, in this case, the lay-off was as a result of the company decision to downgrade the plant, leading to job losses and possible closure. The employee's lay-off was not temporary but formed part of a winding down by the defendant of its workforce. It would have led to redundancy but for the acceptance by the workforce of a Labour Court recommendation which paved the way for a return to work. It was not a situation where, due to custom and practice, the company was entitled to lay-off without pay. Further, in circumstances where the redundancy did not occur, the employee's employment was continuous and he was entitled to pay for the period of lay-off (i.e. for 10 days subject to the normal deductions of PAYE and PRSI).

Short-time arises where there is a decrease in the employee's work so that the employee's pay is less than 50 per cent of their normal weekly remuneration. If an employee has been laid off or kept on short-time for four or more consecutive weeks, or for a series of six or more weeks (of which not more than three were consecutive) within a period of 13 weeks, then the employee may be entitled to a redundancy payment. The employee must give the employer notice of intention to claim redundancy payment (see the RP9 form on pages 459–60) after the expiry of either period, or not later than four weeks after the end of the lay-off or short-time.

Alternatively, the employee may give notice in writing to the employer (i.e. whatever notice is required under the contract, or else one week's notice, under the Minimum Notice and Terms of Employment Acts, 1973–1991) of their intention to terminate the contract. In this situation, the employee will not be entitled to notice or monies in lieu because the employee is terminating the contract of employment (provided that the lay-off or short-time is genuine and is not to avoid the payment of notice) (see *Industrial Yarns Ltd.* v *Greene* [1984] IRLM 15 and Chapter 16, "Notice").

The employer may issue a counter-notice stating that they will be able to provide at least 13 weeks' work commencing within a period of four weeks from the date of receipt of the claim. The employee must receive the counter-notice within seven days of the employee's intention to claim a redundancy payment. If the employer does not fulfil the counter-notice, the employee is entitled to redundancy.

REDUNDANCY PROCEDURE

Redundancy Notice

An employer who proposes to dismiss an employee must give their employee Notice of Redundancy — the RP1 form (see page 452). The employer must also send a copy of this form to the Minister for Enterprise, Trade and Employment.

This issue of notice is extremely important because the employee's entitlement to notice can be decided by the Minimum Notice and Terms of Employment Acts, 1973 to 1991, or the contract of employment. An employee is entitled to the benefit of the longest period of notice — that is, statutory notice or contractual notice — but, nevertheless, the RP1 form must be given at least two weeks before the date of redundancy dismissal (See Chapter 16, "Notice"). For example, if the employee is entitled to at least eight weeks' notice, the most practical thing for an employer to do is to give the employee the RP1 form at least eight weeks before the proposed date of redundancy.

If an employee will not accept the notice, the employer should send it by registered post to the employee and advise the Department of Enterprise, Trade and Employment that the employee would not accept it and that it was sent by registered post.

Time off

An employee who is being made redundant (i.e. who has 104 weeks' continuous service) is entitled to paid time off in order to look for a new job or to make arrangements for training for further employment. This time off is paid time off, but it must be reasonable.

Leaving Before Notice Expires

If an employee who has been given notice of dismissal wishes to leave before the notice has expired, they may terminate their employment in writing beforehand. This may be done by way of the RP6 form. However, this may only be done during the period of the notice to which the employee is entitled, called the "obligatory period" in the Act. If the employer has given notice over and above the employee's entitlement, the employee cannot give such a notice during that extra period; otherwise the employee would lose the redundancy payment. Of course, the employer may agree to bring forward the obligatory period of notice so that the employee can get the redundancy payment (see pages 457–8).

Redundancy Certificate

The employer must give the employee the Certificate of Redundancy (the RP2 form — see pages 453–4) on the date of dismissal.

It should be noted that Part 2 of this form (Employee's Receipt for Lump Payment) is only in respect of the statutory lump-sum payment. In other words, if an employee were receiving an *ex gratia* amount over and above the statutory lump sum, it should not be included on this form.

It is important that the employee actually receives the redundancy payment, because this form is deemed to be an acknowledgement thereof.

Part 3 of the form (Declaration by Employer) is the part where the employer declares that the employee was dismissed by reason of redundancy and that the employee is entitled to the lump sum which is set out on the form. Indeed, even if an employee is entitled to no lump sum at all, this should be so stated. The employer must sign this part of the form, stating their position held in the company and the date.

Statutory Redundancy Payment

An employee who has been dismissed (or who terminates their own employment as a result of lay-off or short-time) is entitled to a statutory redundancy payment as follows:

1. A half-week's normal weekly remuneration for each year of continuous and reckonable service between 16 years and their 41st birthday; plus

2. A week's normal weekly remuneration for each year of continuous and reckonable year of service between 41 and 66 years; plus

3. The equivalent of one week's normal weekly remuneration.

There are various complex rules for the calculation of the statutory redundancy payment, which is based on normal weekly remuneration, to take into account commission and other varied payments. The weekly wage which is to be used for the calculation of statutory redundancy is the wage applying on the date that the employee is declared redundant; that is, the date on which the employee is given the RP1 form (*Minister for Labour* v *Nokia Ltd.*, High Court, Costello, J., unreported, 30 March 1983 and noted (1984) 3 JISLL at page 49).

The statutory redundancy payment is subject to a ceiling of £15,600 per annum or £300 per week. Statutory redundancy payments are tax-free (see Chapter 20, "Taxation of Termination Payments").

Refusal of Employee to Accept Redundancy

As mentioned earlier, if an employee refuses to accept the redundancy notice, an employer may send such notice to the employee's home by registered post. The employer should simultaneously send a copy to the Minister. Equally, if an employee does not accept (and sign) the RP2 form and the redundancy monies, the employer should send same to the employee by registered post. The employer can still apply for the rebate (see below) by sending copies of all documentation and a copy of the cheque for redundancy monies to the Minister explaining that the employee would not accept redundancy and that all forms and payments were sent to the employee's home by registered post.

Employer's Rebate from the Social Insurance Fund

The employer applies to the Minister for Enterprise, Trade and Employment for the rebate from the Social Insurance Fund. This amounts to 60 per cent of the statutory redundancy payment paid to an employee (the rebate is only concerned with the statutory aspect of a redundancy payment). The employer completes the RP3 form (see pages 455–6).

If an employer fails to comply with the above provisions (i.e. the serving of the RP1 form), the Minister may reduce the amount of rebate payable to the employer to 40 per cent. The RP3 form must be sent to the Minister within six months of the date of payment of the redundancy lump sum, with a copy of the Redundancy Certificate.

Employers should note in claiming the rebate that the Department of Enterprise, Trade and Employment may check with the Revenue Commissioners and any other Government Department (e.g. Social, Community and Family Affairs) to see that everything is in order. For example, they may ensure that the employee got the appropriate period of notice, which shall be included in the P45 form.

SEVERANCE

Frequently an employer will pay an employee monies over and above statutory redundancy. In unionised employments, the employee's trade union may negotiate with the employer for a higher redundancy payment. There are many different formulae; for example, two weeks' pay per year of service plus statutory; or four weeks' pay per year of service plus statutory; or a lump sum based on a certain number of years' service, etc. Section 51 of the 1967 Act provides that "any provision in an agreement (whether a contract of employment or not) shall be void in so far as it purports to exclude or limit the operation of any provision of this Act".

Therefore, caution must be exercised in redundancy negotiations either to pay the statutory lump sum separately, or to specify that amount separately in any agreement so that the employee knows what the statutory payment is. In the *Minister for Labour* v *O'Connor and Irish Dunlop Company Ltd.* ((1985) 4 JILL 72), Kenny J, in his High Court judgment, stated:

> When an employer has failed to issue a redundancy certificate to an employee when dismissing him by reason of redundancy, compensation paid to the employee on dismissal for redundancy can be treated as payment by the employer of the statutory lump sum only when the employer proves to the satisfaction of the Tribunal (i) that the employee at the time of payment knew the amount of the statutory lump sum to which he was entitled at the date of the dismissal and (ii) that the employee agreed to accept the sum paid in discharge of his claim for the statutory lump sum.

In this case, the employee was made redundant and should have received £500, but he was not given an RP2 form. The employee did not know the exact amount of his statutory entitlement during the course of negotiations on his lump sum or when it was paid. It was held that he was entitled to the statutory lump sum in addition to the £500.

The ruling in *Talbot (Ireland) Limited* v *The Minister for Labour and Others* ((1985) 4 JISLL 87) by Barron J is also of importance. It concerned the closing down of the Talbot car assembly plant. Arising from a strike, there were negotiations between the company, the unions, the government and various State agencies, which resulted in letters of resignation from the employees and acknowledged payment of monies "in full and final settlement of any claim". The employees successfully brought claims for statutory redundancy to the EAT. The company appealed this decision to the High Court, and Barron J, in referring the matter back to the Tribunal for rehearing, stated that the Tribunal had to answer the following question:

> Was the claim to statutory redundancy payment discussed in the course of the negotiations leading up to the making of the agreement and the signing of the letters of negotiation?

The Tribunal reheard the whole case and determined that Talbot had discharged its liability under the Act and that the employees were in full knowledge of their legal position. There was no evidence that either the employees or their advisers were unaware of the manner in which statutory lump sums were calculated under the Acts. The document they signed was also important as it was acknowledgement of payment by Talbot of a stated sum

> as final settlement of any claim I have against the Company other than any payment outlined in 3 [training payment made during an extended notice period] of the above agreement or payments available to me as a member of the Talbot Works Pension Scheme.

Therefore there was no additional entitlement to statutory redundancy payments.

TAXATION

As stated above, statutory redundancy payments are tax-free. The Taxes (Consolidation) Act, 1997 (as amended), provide certain further allowances for employees on termination of employment. The first £8,000 of a termination payment, together with £600 for each complete year of service, may be paid tax-free. There is a further allowance of £4,000, making a total of £12,000 tax-free, provided that the employee has never claimed that extra relief before.

There is also Standard Capital Superannuation Benefit relief and Top Slicing relief (see Chapter 20, "Taxation of Termination Payments").

CLAIMS PROCEDURES

The Acts provide for Deciding Officers who are officials in the Department of Enterprise, Trade and Employment (Redundancy Section) who make decisions in relation to redundancy; for example,
whether the redundancy payment was correct, who the employer was
and any other matter under the Act. More usually, the deciding officers decide on the rebate to which an employee is entitled.

Usually, all claims under the Act are referred to the Employment
Appeals Tribunal for determination. Less frequently, appeals against
a deciding officer's decision, usually in respect of non-payment of the
rebate by the Social Insurance Fund, may be referred to the Tribunal.
Deciding officers may also refer matters to the Tribunal if they are in
doubt in a particular case.

An employee must refer a redundancy claim to the Tribunal
within 52 weeks of the date of dismissal or termination of employment after lay-off or short-time. The 52-week time-limit may be extended to 104 weeks if reasonable cause can be shown for the delay.

This is considered in more detail in Chapter 23, "Employment Appeals Tribunal".

NON-PAYMENT BY THE EMPLOYER

If an employee has not been paid statutory redundancy after taking
all reasonable steps (excluding legal proceedings), or if the employer
is insolvent or has died, an application may be made to the Social Insurance Fund for payment. The RP77 form and the RP14 form (see
pages 461–4) may be used. However, the more usual step is for the
employee to bring a claim to the Tribunal and to send the Determination to the Fund to request payment.

General References

Kerr, A. (1995), *Termination of Employment Statutes — Commentary*,
London: Sweet and Maxwell.

Department of
Enterprise, Trade
and Employment

FORM RP1

NOTICE OF PROPOSED
DISMISSAL FOR REDUNDANCY

REDUNDANCY PAYMENTS ACTS, 1967 TO 1991
An Roinn Fiontar, Trádála Agus Fostaíochta - Department of Enterprise, Trade and Employment

Note for employer: On the date that this notice is given by an employer to the employee a copy of it must be sent to the Minister for Enterprise, Trade and Employment at Davitt House, 65A Adelaide Road, Dublin 2. Failure to do this may lead to a reduction in rebate payable.

PLEASE COMPLETE THIS FORM IN BLOCK CAPITALS

Figures   Letter

EMPLOYER'S PAYE REGISTERED NUMBER

BUSINESS NAME OF EMPLOYER

BUSINESS ADDRESS

GIVE DETAILS OF TYPE OF BUSINESS IN WHICH REDUNDANCY ARISES

For Official Use

NACE

Figures   Letters

EMPLOYEE'S REVENUE AND SOCIAL INSURANCE (RSI) NO.

To   SURNAME

FIRST NAME

ADDRESS

SOCIAL WELFARE INSURANCE NUMBER
(If any)
Figures

SEX | Male | | Tick Appropriate Box
| Female | |

DATE OF BIRTH OF EMPLOYEE

Day | Month | Year

OCCUPATION _____

ADDRESS OF PLACE OF EMPLOYMENT

_____

_____

GIVE DETAILS OF THE REASON FOR REDUNDANCY

_____

_____

_____

For Office Use

MANCO

AREA

REASON

DATE OF COMMENCEMENT
OF EMPLOYEE'S EMPLOYMENT

Day | Month | Year

NUMBER OF HOURS NORMALLY
EXPECTED TO WORK PER WEEK

It is necessary to terminate your employment by reason of redundancy. In accordance with the provisions of the Redundancy Payments Acts, 1967 to 1991, I hereby give you notice that your employment will terminate on

Day | Month | Year

SIGNATURE OF EMPLOYER _____

POSITION HELD IN COMPANY _____

DATE OF NOTICE

Day | Month | Year

 Department of Enterprise, Trade and Employment

FORM RP2

REDUNDANCY CERTIFICATE

REDUNDANCY PAYMENTS ACTS, 1967 TO 1991
An Roinn Fiontar, Trádála Agus Fostaíochta - Department of Enterprise, Trade and Employment

Note: Before completing this form please refer to explanatory booklet.

PLEASE COMPLETE THIS FORM IN BLOCK CAPITALS

Figures   Letter

EMPLOYER'S PAYE REGISTERED NUMBER

BUSINESS NAME OF EMPLOYER _____

BUSINESS ADDRESS _____

_____

EMPLOYEE'S REVENUE AND SOCIAL INSURANCE (RSI)
NUMBER

Figures   Letters

To: SURNAME _____ FIRST NAME _____

SEX	Male		Tick Appropriate Box
	Female		

SOCIAL WELFARE INSURANCE NUMBER
(If Any)
Figures

DATE OF BIRTH
Day   Month   Year

OCCUPATION

For Official Use
MANCO

DATE OF COMMENCEMENT
Day   Month   Year

DATE OF TERMINATION
Day   Month   Year

NUMBER OF HOURS NORMALLY
EXPECTED TO WORK PER WEEK

PERIODS OF NON RECKONABLE SERVICE

	DAY	MONTH	YEAR		DAY	MONTH	YEAR	REASON
From				To				_____
From				To				_____
From				To				_____

1. CALCULATION OF STATUTORY LUMP SUM PAYMENT

Note: Regard should be had to ceiling on normal weekly remuneration.

Years

(i)   Total Reckonable Service _____

(excluding service before age of 16 and other non-reckonable service)

Weeks

(ii)   Number of weeks pay due _____

(iii)   Amount of Normal Week's Pay:

Gross Weekly Wage	Average Regular Overtime	Benefits In Kind	Total
£	£	£	£

(iv)   State ceiling on earnings applied for purposes of calculation if the statutory ceiling is lower than normal week's pay_____ £

(v)   Amount of Statutory lump sum payment to which employee is entitled_____ £

2. EMPLOYEE'S RECEIPT FOR LUMP PAYMENT

Note: In no circumstances should this receipt be used for any payment other than the statutory redundancy lump sum or part thereof. This receipt will not be accepted as valid unless the sum paid is inserted.

WARNING: DO NOT SIGN THIS RECEIPT UNTIL YOU ACTUALLY RECEIVE PAYMENT OF THE SUM BEING ACKNOWLEDGED.

I acknowledge receipt of a lump sum redundancy payment amounting to_____ £

DAY   MONTH   YEAR

Signature of Employee _____

3. DECLARATION BY EMPLOYER

I declare that the employee was dismissed by reason of redundancy, that the employee is entitled to a lump sum of the amount set out in Part 1(v) of this certificate, and that the employee was paid a lump sum of_____ £

(If no payment was made, please insert NIL.)

Signature of Employer_____

Date

Position held in Company _____

FORM RP3

| AN ROINN FIONTAR, TRÁDÁLA AGUS FOSTAÍOCHTA | DEPARTMENT OF ENTERPRISE, TRADE AND EMPLOYMENT |

EMPLOYER'S CLAIM FOR REBATE FROM THE SOCIAL INSURANCE FUND

REDUNDANCY PAYMENTS ACTS 1967 TO 1991

NOTES

Before completing this form please refer to explanatory booklet. A claim for rebate must be sent to the Minister for Enterprise, Trade and Employment addressed to his office in Dublin within six months of the date of payment of the redundancy lump sum. It must be accompanied by the copy of the Redundancy Certificate on which the employee has signed the receipt for the lump sum.

Please complete this form in BLOCK CAPITALS

Employer's PAYE Registered Number [| | | | | | | | |]
                           FIGURES   LETTER

Business Name of Employer

Business Address

To the Minister for Enterprise, Trade and Employment:-

I certify that the employees whose names are listed overleaf (and on continuation sheets numbered   to   ):—

   (i)   ceased employment on the dates on the attached Redundancy Certificates,

   (ii)   in accordance with the terms of the Redundancy Payments Acts, 1967 to 1991, were paid lump sums for which they have signed receipts on the attached copies of redundancy certificates and that these redundancy certificates are true copies of the certificates given to the employees concerned.

I understand that in order to establish my right to any rebate it may be necessary for you to refer to information given by me to the Revenue Commissioners and other Government Departments, and I hereby give my consent to the disclosure of such information for this purpose only. I also certify that none of the redundancy payments to which this claim refers is awaiting the decision of an Appeals Tribunal.

I claim rebate amounting to [£   ] and declare that no other claim for rebate has been made in respect of the service of these employees between the dates of commencement and termination on the attached redundancy certificates.

Signature of Employer   _____

Position held in Company _____ Date _____

RP3

CLAIM FOR REBATE FROM THE SOCIAL INSURANCE FUND

EMPLOYEE'S REVENUE AND SOCIAL INSURANCE (RSI) NUMBER	EMPLOYEE'S		AMOUNT OF REBATE CLAIMED £
	SURNAME	FIRST NAME	

FDU 5/93

FORM RP6
(Obligatory Period)

LEAVING BEFORE REDUNDANCY NOTICE EXPIRES

It may be that when you get form RP1 - Notice of proposed dismissal for Redundancy - you might wish to leave your employment sooner than the date of termination notified to you, e.g., to take up alternative employment. If you decide to leave, there is a risk that you may lose any entitlement to redundancy payments unless you notify your employer in writing and also comply with the general conditions on the back of this form. You may use this form for writing to your employer.

If after receipt of this notice your employer objects to your leaving your employment and you leave notwithstanding, you may have to prove to the satisfaction of the Employment Appeals Tribunal that your grounds for leaving were reasonable.

PART 1:
NOTICE TO AN EMPLOYER BY AN EMPLOYEE TO TERMINATE EMPLOYMENT
(SECTION 10 OF THE REDUNDANCY PAYMENTS ACT, 1967 AS AMENDED BY
SECTION 9 OF THE REDUNDANCY PAYMENTS ACT, 1979)

To: ....

....

(Name and Address of Employer)

With reference to your Notice of Redundancy (RP 1) dated...................proposing to terminate my employment on...................(date of termination notified), I hereby give you notice of my intention to anticipate dismissal by leaving on.....................(insert date on which you propose to leave). Note that *the date on which you give this notice and the date on which it expires must be within the obligatory period of notice*. Your employer's consent may be necessary to ensure this, see Part 3 of this form).

Revenue & Social Insurance No:........................   Signed: ....(Employee)

Social Welfare Insurance No:.............................   Date: ....

PART 2:
COUNTER-NOTICE BY EMPLOYER

To: ....

Name of Employee

I request you to withdraw your notice and to continue in my employment until the date on which my notice expires. If you do not withdraw your notice I will contest any liability to pay you a redundancy payment. My reason for objection is ....

....

Signed: ....(Employer)

Date: ....

PART 3:
CONSENT BY EMPLOYER TO ALTER DATE OF HIS DISMISSAL NOTICE SO AS TO
BRING EMPLOYEE'S ANTICIPATORY NOTICE WITHIN THE OBLIGATORY PERIOD.
(SECTION 9 OF THE REDUNDANCY PAYMENTS ACT 1979).

I agree that the date of termination notified on my notice of proposed dismissal (RP1) be altered to...............so that the giving of employee's notice to anticipate dismissal and the expiration date of his anticipating notice shall be within the obligatory period of notice.

Signed: ....(Employer)

Date: ....

EMPLOYEES PROPOSING TO ANTICIPATE THEIR REDUNDANCY NOTICE BY LEAVING SOONER THAN THE DATE OF TERMINATION NOTIFIED TO THEM ON FORM RP1 SHOULD READ THESE NOTES CAREFULLY BEFORE COMPLETING THE FORM OVERLEAF. *(This is not a statutory form and it is open to you to use an alternative means of communication with your employer, provided it is in writing).*

If you have been given Notice of proposed dismissal for Redundancy (Form RP1) and you wish to leave your job sooner than the date you are to become redundant *(as set out on the redundancy notice)* you should, if you want to preserve your entitlement to redundancy payment, fill in the form overleaf and send it or give it to your employer.

This must be done within (not before) your obligatory period of notice. Normally this period is the two weeks immediately before the date you are to become redundant but if you have been in the job for between 5 and 10 years, this period is extended to 4 weeks; if you have been in the job 10 to 15 years the period is 6 weeks and if you have been more than 15 years the period is 8 weeks. If your contract of employment lays down a longer period of notice, this longer period is the obligatory period of notice in your case.

You may leave your job before the date specified in your redundancy notice and still preserve your redundancy entitlement only if the dates on which you give notice and *on which you leave are within your obligatory period* of notice as set out in the previous paragraph. Furthermore if your employer give you a counter-notice in form similar to the "counter-notice by employer" overleaf you will not be entitled to redundancy payment if you unreasonably refuse to comply with his request. *(Any disputes on this matter may be referred to the Appeals Tribunal).*

If the date on which you wish to give notice is outside the obligatory period your employer may bring it within that period by agreement in writing to an alteration of the date of termination shown on his notice of dismissal (RP1). Part 3 of this form may be used for this purpose. You should obtain written agreement to alteration of termination date on employer's notice *prior to giving your anticipation notice,* and if your employer refuses to agree to such alteration you must wait until a date within the obligatory period before giving anticipatory notice.

NOTE FOR EMPLOYERS

If an employee under notice of redundancy leaves by his own decision before the date set out in his notice (RP1) without complying with all of the conditions set out above, he may not be entitled to a lump sum under the Redundancy Payments Acts. Should you pay an employee a lump sum to which he is not entitled because he has not complied with the procedures outlined on this form, you will not get a rebate from the Department of Enterprise, Trade and Employment unless the Employment Appeals Tribunal decides otherwise.

If you agree to an employee leaving before the date set out in his notice of redundancy (RP1), though within his obligatory period of notice, you must attach completed form RP6, or whatever written notice you have received from him, to your claim for rebate, as evidence of compliance with these procedures, otherwise you will not be paid rebate.

If the date on which an employee wishes to give you anticipatory notice is outside the obligatory period you may (though you are not obliged to) bring it within such period by alteration of the termination date on your dismissal notice. Your agreement to do so must be in writing. Part 3 of this form may be used for this purpose.

If you do *not* agree to your employee's leaving before the date set out in his notice of redundancy (RP1), though within his obligatory period of notice, you should, *before the expiration date of his anticipatory notice* give him counter-notice in writing. Part 2 of this form may be used for that purpose.

The redundancy lump sum will be based on the period: date on which service commenced to date of actual termination.

Issued by the Department of Enterprise, Trade and Employment
Davitt House, 65A Adelaide Road, Dublin 2

FORM RP9

AN ROINN FIONTAR, TRÁDÁLA AGUS FOSTAÍOCHT	DEPARTMENT OF ENTERPRISE, TRADE AND EMPLOYMENT

LAY OFF AND SHORT TIME PROCEDURES

NOTES

An employer may use Part A overleaf of this form to notify an employee of temporary lay off or temporary short time (lay off and short time are defined at the end of this page).

An employee may use Part B overleaf of this form to notify his / her employer of intention to claim a redundancy lump sum payment in a lay off or short time situation.

An employer may use Part C overleaf of this form to give counter notice to an employee who claims payment of a redundancy lump sum in a lay off / short time situation.

EMPLOYER'S PAYE REGISTERED NUMBER Figures Letter	ADDRESS OF EMPLOYEE
BUSINESS NAME AND ADDRESS OF EMPLOYER	
	SEX (TICK ✔ APPROPRIATE BOX) ☐ MALE ☐ FEMALE
	DATE OF BIRTH OF EMPLOYEE Day Month Year
DESCRIPTION OF BUSINESS IN WHICH REDUNDANCY ARISES	DATE OF COMMENCEMENT OF EMPLOYEE'S EMPLOYMENT Day Month Year
FOR OFFICIAL USE ONLY — NACE CODE	ADDRESS OF PLACE OF EMPLOYMENT
EMPLOYEE'S REVENUE AND SOCIAL INSURANCE (R.S.I.) NUMBER Figures Letters	
EMPLOYEE'S SURNAME	
EMPLOYEE'S FIRST NAME	FOR OFFICIAL USE ONLY — AREA CODE

DEFINITION OF LAY OFF AND SHORT TIME

A lay off situation exists when an employer suspends an employee's employment because there is no work available, when the employer expects the cessation of work to be temporary and when the employer notifies the employee to this effect.

A short time working situation exists when an employer, because he has less work available for an employee than is normal, reduces that employee's earnings to less than half the normal week's earnings or reduces the number of hours of work to less than half the normal weekly hours, when the employer expects this reduction to be temporary and when the employer notifies the employee to this effect.

PART A : Notification to employee of TEMPORARY LAY OFF or TEMPORARY SHORT TIME

Notification in respect of this part need not be in writing

It is necessary to place you on   ☐ **TEMPORARY LAY OFF**   ☐ **TEMPORARY SHORT TIME**
(Please tick ✔)

as and from   Day   Month   Year

by reason of _____

_____

I expect the LAY OFF / SHORT TIME to be temporary.

Signature of Employer _____ **Date** _____

PART B : Notice of Intention to claim Redundancy Lump Sum Payment in a LAY OFF / SHORT TIME situation

An employee who wishes to claim a redundancy lump sum because of lay off / short time must serve notice of intention to claim in writing within four weeks after the lay off / short time ceases. In order to become entitled to claim a redundancy lump sum on foot of a period of lay off, short time or a mixture of both, that period must be at least four consecutive weeks or a broken series of six weeks where all six fall within a thirteen-week period. An employee who wishes to terminate his contract of employment by reason of lay off or short time must give his employer the notice required by his contract or if none is required, at least one week's notice.

An employee who claims and receives redundancy payment in respect of lay off or short time is deemed to have voluntarily left his employment and therefore not entitled to notice under the Minimum Notice and Terms of Employment Act, 1973.

To *(Business Name of Employer)* : _____

I give you notice of my intention to claim a redundancy lump sum in respect of LAY OFF / SHORT TIME *(Delete whichever does not apply)*

                    Day   Month   Year   Day   Month   Year
        From   To

Signature of Employee _____ **Date** _____

PART C : Counter Notice to Employee's Notice of Intention to claim a Redundancy Lump Sum

Notification in respect of this part must be in writing and must be given to the employee within seven days of service of the employee's notice.

I contest any liability to pay you a Redundancy Lump Sum on the grounds that it is reasonable to expect that
                                                              Day   Month   Year
within four weeks of the date of service of your notice, namely   *(Date of Service),*

you will enter upon a period of employment of not less than thirteen weeks during which you will not be on lay off or short time any week.

Signature of Employer _____ **Date** _____

FDU91/120

**Department of
Enterprise, Trade
and Employment**

FORM RP14

Roinn Fiontar Trádála agus Fostaíochta

EMPLOYEE'S APPLICATION FOR LUMP SUM
FROM THE SOCIAL INSURANCE FUND

NOTES FOR EMPLOYEE

This form is to be used when applying to the Minister for Enterprise, Trade and Employment for payment of a redundancy lump sum from the Social Insurance Fund. You should only use this form if you have applied in writing to your employer for payment (Form RP77 may be used) and he has failed to pay the redundancy lump sum,

This Form must be accompanied by either a Redundancy Certificate or a favourable decision from the Employment Appeals Tribunal.

If you have applied in writing and your employer refuses to give you a Redundancy Certificate or ignores your application and you consider that you are entitled to a redundancy payment, you may appeal to the Employment Appeals Tribunal. If the Appeals Tribunal decides that you are entitled to a redundancy lump sum they will issue a decision which should be sent to the Minister for Enterprise, Trade and Employment with this form.

Please complete this form in BLOCK CAPITALS

Employer's PAYE Registered Number

FIGURES   LETTER

(Available on Notice of Dismissal (RP1), Redundancy Certificate (RP2) and P45)

Business Name of Employer

Business Address

If the employer is deceased, give the name and address of his representative. If the business is in liquidation or receivership, please supply the name and address of the liquidator or receiver. If the business has ceased trading but has not gone into liquidation or receivership, and the employer is no longer available at the business address, please supply the address at which he may be contacted.

Name

Address

Employee's Revenue and Social Insurance (R.S.I.) Number

| | | | | | | | | | | | | |
FIGURES   LETTERS

Surname

First Name

Address*

NON PAYMENT BY MY EMPLOYER DUE TO	TICK✓
LIQUIDATION	
RECEIVERSHIP	
BANKRUPTCY	
CLAIMS INSOLVENCY	
EMPLOYER DECEASED	
REFUSES TO PAY	
IGNORES MY APPLICATION	
OTHER REASON (GIVE DETAILS)	

PLEASE ATTACH: Notice of Dismissal (RP1) and Redundancy Certificate (RP2), or state Employment Appeals Tribunal Case

Number: _____ Decision Date: _____

I claim payment of a lump sum/part of a lump sum from the Social Insurance Fund by reason of default on the part of my employer.

I applied in writing to my employer for payment on _____ (Date).

SIGNATURE OF EMPLOYEE _____ **DATE** _____

A person who fraudulently applies to the Minister for a lump sum shall be guilty of an offence and shall be liable on summary conviction to a fine of up to £300.

*Please ensure that the employee's correct address is given on this form as the cheque in respect of the lump sum entitlement shall be posted to that address. Any changes of address must be notified immediately to the Redundancy Payments Section of the Department of Enterprise, Trade and Employment.

FORM RP77

EXPLANATORY NOTE FOR EMPLOYEE WHEN APPLYING
TO AN EMPLOYER FOR A LUMP SUM

This form may be used by an employee

A.   who considers that he is entitled to a redundancy payment and his employer has not acknowledged his entitlement by giving him

    (i)   Notice of proposed dismissal for Redundancy (Form RP1)
    (ii)   Redundancy Certificate (Form RP2)
    (iii)   Lump sum payment

If an employee has received (i) and (ii), or (ii) only but not (iii), he should apply in writing to his employer for payment.

B.   who considers that he has received an incorrect lump sum

C.   who has received a favourable decision from the Employment Appeals Tribunal on his redundancy appeal and who wishes to pursue the matter of payment of the lump sum, or an unpaid part of it, with his employer's representative.

Should a payment or a balance of payment be refused or this application be ignored by an employer, the following options are open to the employee:

If he has not received a Redundancy Certificate (Form RP2): he may apply to the Employment Appeals Tribunal for a declaration of redundancy or a declaration of the facts of redundancy. Form RP51A* should be consulted and used for this purpose.

If he holds a Redundancy Certificate or alternatively has received a favourable decision from the Employment Appeals Tribunal on his redundancy appeal: he may refer the matter to the Department of Enterprise, Trade and Employment, Davitt House, 65A Adelaide Road, Dublin 2, for further attention. Form RP14* should be consulted and used for this purpose.

IMPORTANT

1.   Record the date on which you apply for payment to your employer
2.   Allow a reasonable time, say 14 days, for the employer to deal with the matter before proceeding further.
3.   Do not use this Form for purposes other than applying to an employer for payment of a statutory Redundancy lump sum or balance of a lump sum.
4.   If dismissal arises in a lay-off or short-time situation consult Form RP9* in the first instance

NOTE FOR EMPLOYERS AND EMPLOYEES

The following informational booklets in particular on the Redundancy Payments Scheme may be of interest in connection with disputes.

Guide to the Redundancy Payments Scheme.
Explanatory Leaflet on the Employment Appeals Tribunal.

*Available from Employment Exchanges or from Department of Enterprise, Trade & Employment.

FORM RP77

REDUNDANCY PAYMENTS ACTS, 1967 TO 1990

A claim by an employee against an employer for a lump sum or part of a lump sum.

An employee who is in doubt about whether he has a valid claim or not can check against an informational leaflet on the qualifications - (see the footnote overleaf).

To: ....

....

....

Name and Address of Employer

I claim a lump sum payment/s balance of lump sum payment* from you in respect of my dismissal. My claim is based on the following grounds (tick whichever applies):

The grounds of my dismissal constitute redundancy but I have not received a redundancy notice/redundancy certificate* nor a lump sum payment. I request these. ☐

I have received a redundancy notice/redundancy certificate* but no lump sum payment. ☐

The lump sum which I received is incorrect. Particulars of the error are: ☐

....

....

I have received a favourable decision from the Appeals Tribunal in regard to my redundancy appeal and I now request to pay the lump sum due to me. ☐

Insurance No. ....   Signed...

Date:..   Address:...

....

....

....

*Strike out whichever is not applicable.

Form RP 51B

APPLICATION TO EMPLOYMENT APPEALS TRIBUNAL
UNDER REDUNDANCY PAYMENTS ACTS, 1967 TO 1991

NOTE: This form is to be used by an employee/employer when appealing against a decision of the Minister for Enterprise, Trade and Employment or a Deciding Officer in a matter of redundancy. (Form T1-A should be used by an employee when appealing against a decision of an employer).

Please tick (✓) whichever of the following boxes is appropriate to your appeal:

A. If you are an employee and you are disputing a decision of a Deciding Officer about:

    (i)   **who your employer is**   ☐

B. If you are an employer and you are disputing

    (ii)   **a decision by the Minister in relation to a rebate**   ☐

    (iii)   **a decision by a Deciding Officer in relation to (i)**   ☐

Name and Address of person making appeal

Phone No.

RSI No/Reg. (PAYE) No.

The grounds of my application are as follows:

_____

_____

_____

_____

_____

_____

_____

_____

_____

Name and address of any representative who has agreed at your request to deal with your appeal

Phone No.

Send this form to:

**Secretary,
Employment Appeals Tribunal
Davitt House
65A Adelaide Road
Dublin 2
Telephone: (01) 6614444
1890 220222 Lo-Call from outside (01) area**

Signed _____

Date _____

CAUTION: The Tribunal may award costs against a party who has acted vexatiously or frivolously in the matter of an appeal.

Chapter Nineteen

COLLECTIVE REDUNDANCIES

The Protection of Employment Act, 1977, as amended by the Protection of Employment Order, 1996 (SI No. 370 of 1996) provides for certain procedural requirements that an employer must follow in the event of collective redundancies. The 1977 Act implements EC Directive 75/129/EEC as amended by Directive 92/56/EEC, which came into Irish law on 9 December 1996 (see below). Both Directives have been consolidated into Council Directive 98/59/EC of 20 July 1998. The 1977 Act (as amended) does not apply to establishments employing less than 21 people.

"Collective redundancies" mean dismissals (see para. 5 of the 1996 Order) arising from redundancy during any period of 30 consecutive days where the employees (including temporary and "agency temps" (see para. 4 of the 1996 Order)) being made redundant are:

1. Five employees in an establishment employing 21–49 employees;

2. Ten employees in an establishment normally employing 50 to 99 employees;

3. Ten per cent of employees in an establishment normally employing 100 to 299 employees; or

4. Thirty employees in an establishment normally employing 300 or more employees.

Where there are at least ten dismissals in an establishment normally employing between 20 and 100 employees, then if there are at least five redundancies, any other dismissals shall be added for the purposes of the Act.

An "establishment" is defined as an employer or a company or a subsidiary company or a company within a group of companies, which can independently effect redundancies (para. 5 of the 1996 Order). In order to compute the number of employees normally employed, the average of the number employed shall be taken in each of the twelve months preceding the date on which the first dismissal takes effect.

It is important to note that this Act does not apply to the dismissal or termination of employees who were employed under a fixed-term or specified purpose contract, persons employed by the State, officers of local authorities and persons employed under the Merchant Shipping Act, 1894.

CONSULTATION

This Act provides that an employer proposing to create collective redundancies shall initiate consultations with "employees' representatives" with a view to reaching an agreement. "Employees' representative" means a trade union or staff association or a person or persons chosen by the employees likely to be affected by the redundancies to represent them.

The consultations should take place at the earliest opportunity and at least 30 days before the first dismissal takes effect. The subject matter of the consultation shall include the possibility of avoiding the proposed redundancies by reducing the number of employees to be dismissed or the redeployment or retraining of employees to be made redundant, and the basis on which particular employees will be made redundant (s. 9(2) as amended by para. 8 of the 1996 Order).

The employer is obliged to provide the employee representatives with all information in writing in relation to the proposed redundancies. Employers cannot raise the defence that it was a controlling body that made the decision and had all the information. Employer information must include:

1. The reasons for the proposed redundancies;

2. The number and descriptions or categories of employees whom it is proposed to make redundant;

3. The number of employees and descriptions or categories, normally employed;

4. The period in which it is proposed to effect the redundancies;

5. The criteria proposed for the selection of the workers to be made redundant, and

6. The method for calculating any redundancy payments other than those methods set out in the Redundancy Payments Acts, 1967–1991, or if an ex gratia payment is made, then the basis of the calculation must be given; for example, x weeks' pay per year of service.

An employer who does not comply with this consultation process shall be guilty of an offence and shall be liable to a fine of up to £500.

OBLIGATION ON EMPLOYER TO NOTIFY MINISTER

There is an obligation on the employer to notify the Minister for Enterprise, Trade and Employment of the proposed redundancies at the earliest opportunity, but at least 30 days before the first dismissal takes effect. This notification should be sent by registered post or delivered by hand. An employer who breaches this requirement may be guilty of an offence and liable for a fine of up to £500.

Statutory regulations (SI No. 140 of 1977) provide that certain particulars must be included in the notification to the Minister:

1. The name and address of the employer, indicating whether the employer is a sole trader, a partnership or a company;

2. Address of the establishment where the collective redundancies are proposed;

3. Total number of persons normally employed at that establishment;

4. Numbers and description or categories of employees whom it is proposed to make redundant;

5. Period within which the collective redundancies are proposed to be effected, stating the dates on which the first and final dismissals are expected to take effect;

6. Reasons for the proposed collective redundancies;

7. Names and addresses of the trade unions or staff associations representing employees affected by the proposed redundancies, and with which it has been the practice of the employer to conduct collective bargaining negotiations; and

8. The date on which consultations with each trade union or staff association commenced and the progress achieved in those consultations to the date of notification.

In the case of collective redundancies due to the closure of an employer's business following bankruptcy, winding up proceedings or a court order, the person looking after the affairs of the employer only has to provide the above information if requested.

The employee representatives may forward, in writing, to the Minister for Enterprise, Trade and Employment any observations relating to this Notification. It is important to note that collective redundancies shall not take effect before the expiry of the 30-day period beginning on the date of the Notification to the Minister. If the collective redundancies are effected by an employer before the expiry of the 30-day period, the employer shall be guilty of an offence and shall be liable to a fine not exceeding £3,000. However, where an employer is convicted of an offence in relation to a failure to supply employee representatives with certain information, or if collective redundancies take place before the 30-day notice expires, the employer may argue that there were substantial reasons relating to the business which made it impracticable to comply with these statutory requirements or there was a bankruptcy, insolvency or a court order. Records of collective redundancies should be retained by the employer for three years and if such records are not kept the employer shall be guilty of an offence and liable to a fine of up to £500.

FURTHER CONSULTATIONS WITH THE MINISTER

The Minister may request the employer to enter into consultations with the Minister or with an authorised officer in order to seek solutions to the problems caused by the proposed redundancies. Authorised officers are invariably civil servants of the Department of Enterprise, Trade and Employment, and they may enter the employer's premises and make enquiries to be satisfied that the Act is being complied with. Any person who obstructs the officers in the carrying out of their duties shall be guilty of an offence and liable to a fine of up to £500. Any proceedings for an offence under this Act will be prosecuted by the Minister and proceedings must commence within one year from the date of the offence.

Chapter Twenty

TAXATION OF TERMINATION PAYMENTS

Unlike monies received as damages in a personal injury action, monies received on termination of employment are taxable. These payments are frequently called ex-gratia payments or redundancy (excluding statutory redundancy) payments. However, there are certain exceptions or allowances. Such payments also include notice monies and awards under the Unfair Dismissals Acts, 1977 to 1993.

The tax provisions shall be considered first and then some practical examples are used to explain this taxation.

INCOME TAX

The provisions dealing with income tax are contained in s. 123 of the Taxes Consolidation Act, 1997, subject to the reliefs and exemptions in s. 201 (formerly sections 114, 115, Schedule III of the Income Tax Act, 1967, as amended by the Finance Act, 1993). The Taxes Consolidation Act, 1997 brought all previous legislation on income tax, etc., into one consolidating statute. Hence the "double" references. Section 123 brings within the tax charge any payments on retirement or removal from office or employment. The payment:

1. Must not be otherwise chargeable to income tax (e.g. salary, holiday pay);

2. Must be made directly or indirectly in consideration of the termination of employment or any change in its functions or emoluments, including payments in commutation of annual or periodic payments, whether chargeable to tax or not;

3. May or may not be in pursuance of a legal obligation;

4. May be for remuneration other than money (e.g. receipt of company car).

The individual receiving the monies or goods (e.g. company car) must be the holder or past holder of the employment.

In the following situations, the payment will be treated as being to the employee:

1. Payment given to the employee's executor or administrator (i.e. if the employee is deceased); or

2. To the employee's spouse or any relative or dependant; or

3. To any person to whom the payment is made on behalf of the holder or past holder of the employment.

Section 201 provides for certain further exemptions in respect of foreign employment, or payments made on termination of employment due to the employee's death, injury or disability. There is also relief in respect of certain approved pension schemes where the contribution by the employer was assessed as payments by the employee.

In *B.D. O'Shea (Inspector of Taxes)* v *Michael Mulqueen* (1994–95 10 JISLL 356), the issue was whether a lump sum payment of £325,000 to Mr Mulqueen on his retirement was exempt from income tax. The key question was whether the monies received were in respect of his illness or by way of redundancy package or offer just before his retirement in recognition of past service. Mr Mulqueen was head of Personnel for all employees in Ireland with Digital Equipment Corporation International BV. In early 1989, he had open-heart surgery and returned to work. However, in May 1991 his condition became serious enough for doctors to advise retirement and he resigned on 25 May 1991. The company responded by agreeing to his early retirement and stated that they would make an ex-gratia payment to him of £325,000 on his resignation on health grounds. He ceased work on 31 August 1991 and after his retirement his medical condition stabilised and became generally normal. At the end of 1990, there were difficulties in the world markets and Digital announced a voluntary severance plan; applications could be made between 14 and 18 January 1991. No person over 60 was entitled to apply; Mr Mulqueen attained 60 years on 28 December 1990.

The then section 115, the relieving section, provided:

> (1) Tax shall not be charged by virtue of section 114 in respect of the following payments, that is to say:

a) any payment made in connection with the termination of the holding of an office or employment by the death of the holder, or made on account of injury to or disability of the holder of an office or employment.

The Revenue Appeal Commissioner (and, on appeal, the Circuit Court) found that the payment was made because of early retirement due to ill health. The package was not given to him solely because of his retirement. Carroll J held that it fell within the meaning of section 115(1)(a) of the Income Tax Act, 1967. Accordingly, there was no charge to income tax.

RELIEF

Certain tax reliefs are available:

1. Statutory redundancy payments — that is, payments under the Redundancy Payments Acts, 1967 to 1991 — are tax free (s.203 of the 1997 Act).

2. The first £8,000 of a termination payment is tax-free. However, if an employee receives two or more payments from the same employer or an associated employer, the total exemption is still £8,000. This is effective from 1 December 1998 (s. 14, Finance Act, 1999).

3. There is also a tax-free allowance of £600 per year of service, effective from 1 December 1998 (s. 14, Finance Act, 1999). The total figure of £8,000 plus £600 per year of complete service is the basic exemption.

The basic exemption may be increased by £4,000 provided that:

1. The employee must not have claimed and received this increased amount before; and

2. The £4,000 increase is reduced in an equal amount by any tax-free lump sum such as commutation monies received from a pension fund either at the time of termination or receivable in the future under an approved pension scheme relating to the employment.

The practical application of all of this is that £6,000 (£8,000) (plus the additional benefit of £500 (£600) per year of service) can be paid directly to the employee. However, if the termination is for any sum above £6,000 (£8,000) plus the additional allowances in a termination situation (excluding statutory redundancy), approval must be granted by the Revenue Commissioners.

The letter sent by the employer to the Revenue would contain the following:

- Name and PRSI number of employee

- Name, address and RSI number of employer

- Date of termination

- Amount of termination payment excluding statutory redundancy

- Amount of notice monies paid if not included in the above

- Pension details to include:
  - ◊ Copy of the pension booklet
  - ◊ Monies to be paid arising from vested rights under the pension scheme.

Presuming no difficulties arise, the Revenue send an approval letter for payment within a few weeks.

If the necessary approval is not granted or if there is not sufficient time, the employer must deduct tax (on the basis of the employee's allowances) from the part of the lump sum over £6,000 (£8,000) (plus the additional £500 (£600) per year of service). If the employer does not deduct the tax, the employer will be liable for the amount not correctly withheld.

OTHER ALLOWANCES

Where a former employee has long service or is receiving a large severance sum, the simpler way of looking at taxation is to consider the tax exempt amount as being (a) £8,000 (plus £600 per year of service) or (b) Standard Capital Superannuation Benefit (SCSB). SCSB may be computed as:

$$\frac{A \times B}{15} - C$$

where
  A = average remuneration for the last three years of service
  B = number of complete years of service
  C = any tax-free sum received or receivable under an approved superannuation scheme

Example

An employee has worked for 20 years at an average salary for the last three years of £20,000 and has received £4,000 commutation from his pension scheme. He is to receive a termination payment of £21,000, excluding statutory redundancy but including monies in lieu of notice.

$$\frac{£20,000 \times 20}{50} - £4,000 = £22,666$$

Therefore the termination payment will be exempt from tax. (Under the normal relief, the employee would only have got £20,000, i.e. £8,000 plus £12,000 (£600 per year of service) plus £4,000 minus £4,000 (pension)).

However, if the employee had only 18 years service, the calculation would work out at:

$$\frac{£20,000 \times 18}{50} - £4,000 = £20,000$$

The employee would have to pay tax on the balance of £1,000 (i.e. £21,000–£20,000). In order to work out the tax on £1,000, the next relief shall be considered.

TOP SLICING RELIEF

When the taxable amount is arrived at, the employee will be taxed at their standard rate of tax, which may be even higher than the rate they normally pay because of the lump sum. However, the Top Slicing Relief ensures that the employee will be taxed at an average rate over the previous three years of assessment, rather than at their current rate of tax. This should have the benefit of reducing the amount of tax payable.

Top Slicing Relief may be computed as:

$$A - \frac{(P \times T)}{I}$$

where
> A = the additional tax which would be payable if the taxable lump sum were treated as income earned in the year of assessment (i.e. at the date of termination) over the amount which would be payable if the lump sum were not taxable.
> P = the taxable lump sum.
> T = the total amount of tax chargeable in respect of the total income of the employee for the five preceding years of assessment.
> I = the total taxable income for five preceding years of assessment.

The figure arrived at by applying this formula is deducted from the tax chargeable for the year of assessment to which the payment relates, i.e. at the beginning of the next tax year.

PRSI

A Class K contribution is payable by the employee on the amount of a lump-sum payment, subject to tax. This is presently 2.25 per cent.

SOCIAL WELFARE

A person who is unemployed and available for work is entitled to unemployment benefit or assistance. Persons under 55 years who receive redundancy payments in excess of £15,000 are disqualified from unemployment benefit for nine weeks from the date of termination. However, if the termination payment is marginally in excess of this figure, it would be advisable for an individual to seek advice from the Department of Social, Community and Family Affairs, as there is a possibility of flexibility in certain cases.

General References

Brennan, F. and S. Howley (1998), *Tax Acts: Commentary, 1998–1999*, Dublin: Butterworths.

Corrigan, K. (1983), "Taxation on Termination of Employment", 2 JISLL 37.

Kerr, T. (1984), "Taxation on Termination of Employment: The Commonwealth Perspective", 3 JISLL 23.

Ward, J. (1997), *Judge on Income Tax*, 1997–98 edition, Dublin: Butterworths.

Chapter Twenty-one

EMPLOYER INSOLVENCY

The financial position of employees who lose their jobs as a result of employer insolvency is substantially protected as a result of the Protection of the Employees (Employers' Insolvency) Act, 1984. The Act results from an EC Directive (80/087/EEC) relating to the protection of employees in the event of the insolvency of their employer. The Directive came into force in Ireland on 22 October 1983 and applies to insolvencies after that date.

State guarantees for employees if their employer becomes insolvent are provided for in the Act in relation to the non-payment of wages or salary, holiday pay, sick pay, monies in lieu of notice and any recommendation, determination or order in respect of unfair dismissal, wrongful dismissal, compensation for maternity, adoptive and parental leave claims. Pension matters are also covered, subject to a ceiling and time limits.

BANKRUPTCY

If an individual becomes bankrupt, all that individual's property vests in the Official Assignee in Bankruptcy. This is provided for in the Bankruptcy Act, 1988, which contains procedures for the administration of estates in bankruptcy cases.

LIQUIDATION

There are several different forms of liquidation, such as a creditors' voluntary winding-up or a members' voluntary winding-up (i.e. where there are not sufficient monies to pay debts), or a compulsory liquidation by the High Court. When such a liquidation arises, the business is no longer operating, so the contract of employment comes to an end. In some cases, the liquidator may carry on the business for some time and the employees may continue working for the liquidator under their contracts. In other cases, before a final order for liquidation, a provisional liquidator is appointed, and, presuming that person is running the business, the employees will work for them.

RECEIVERSHIP

If a creditor is not being paid, there is usually provision in the loan agreement for the appointment of a receiver. For example, a bank appoints a receiver whose duty it is to safeguard sufficient assets to protect the monies owing. The whole company may not be insolvent. A receiver goes in and runs the business as a going concern; this may have no effect on the employees, although usually a receivership is a forerunner to an insolvency. A body corporate under the Industrial and Provident Societies Acts, 1893 to 1978, is to be regarded as having become insolvent for the purposes of the 1984 Act on the day on which a winding-up order was made or a voluntary winding-up was passed (Protection of Employees (Employers' Insolvency) (Specification of Date) Regulations 1986 (SI No. 50 of 1986) and note SI No. 232 of 1985).

COURT EXAMINER

The Companies (Amendment) Act, 1990, made provision for the High Court to appoint an examiner when a company is in financial difficulties (e.g. as happened in 1990 with the Goodman companies) to see if the company can be saved and to enter into arrangements with creditors. Again, however, the examiner may consider that the company cannot be saved, and then there may eventually be a liquidation.

PREFERRED CREDITORS

An employee may be ranked as a preferred creditor on the insolvency of an individual or a company by virtue of the bankruptcy and companies legislation. Such legislation applies to certain named or preferred debts owed to employees.

Ranking before all other creditors, the liquidator's expenses must be paid, as must the Revenue Commissioners', if certain taxes are owed. For the other creditors, a preferred creditor ranks behind the holder of a fixed charge (e.g. on land) but in front of debenture holders secured by a floating charge (e.g. book debts) or unsecured creditors. Commercial agreements may have retention of title clauses by virtue of which the ownership of goods is held by the seller until the purchase price has been paid. Such a clause may confer a "super preferential" status on the seller, as they are not now part of the winding-up proceedings. Accordingly, if the purchaser becomes insolvent, there are fewer assets to realise for the benefit of employees.

The Bankruptcy Act, 1988 (individual employers), provides preferential status for the wages/salary of an employee for four months before the date the employer is adjudged to be bankrupt, subject to a maximum of £2,500. Holiday pay, sick pay and pension contributions are also covered and there are particular rules in the case of farm labourers.

The Companies Acts have similar provisions in respect of wages up to a maximum of £2,500. The Acts also cover arrears for holiday pay, sick pay and the provision of superannuation benefits, compensation and redundancy payments payable under the Unfair Dismissals Acts, 1977 to 1993, the Minimum Notice and Terms of Employment Acts, 1973 to 1991 and the Redundancy Payments Acts, 1967 to 1991, as preferred debts under the above legislation. However, it might be noted that an employee will receive their statutory redundancy lump sum from the Social Insurance Fund (see s. 39 of the Social Welfare Act, 1981).

Prior to the enactment of the 1984 Act, if there were insufficient funds to pay an award made by the Tribunal to an employee before the commencement of the winding-up, the employee would not be paid in full. If the award was made after the date of the winding-up, the employee would be an unsecured creditor and there would be no guarantee of sufficient funds to pay them. The payment of such sums is now guaranteed.

The above is a general explanation of a very technical area of law. However, the Act as regards employees' rights is a considerable improvement on the original position, as it guarantees employees' entitlements, subject to certain conditions.

DEFINITIONS

The 1984 Act has a number of definitions:

Employee

The definition of an employee is the same as in the Redundancy Payments Acts, 1967 to 1991, and now covers regular part-time employees. It also covers employees over the age of 66 years who are debarred from receiving payments from the Social Insurance Fund because they are not fully insurable because of their age (Protection of Employees (Employers' Insolvency) Act, 1984 (Amendment Order) Order, 1988 (SI No. 48 of 1988)).

Further, section 3 of the Act provides that the Act applies to all employees employed in employment which is insurable for all benefits under the Social Welfare Acts, 1981–1984.

"Insurable employment" is defined in s. 2 of the Social Welfare (Consolidation) Act, 1981, as a person over the age of 16 years and under pensionable age and is contingent upon employment in the State. This is modified by the Social Welfare (Contributions) (Amendment) Regulations, 1961 (SI No. 139 of 1961). Hence, persons who are ordinarily resident in the State are not thereby excluded from the status of employed contributor. However, where the period of absence exceeds 52 weeks, they are no longer entitled to the status of employed contributor. In *Kenny* v *Minister for Trade and Employment* ([1999] ELR 163), the applicant was employed by a limited liability company from 1978 to 1989. He carried out his work in Ireland from 1978 to 1984 and then moved to America for the company. His employment was terminated in America in 1989. He instituted proceedings for wrongful dismissal and was awarded £12,682 in 1996. Some days before the case was heard, the company went into voluntary liquidation and subsequently the liquidator maintained that the company did not have sufficient assets to pay him. Application was made to the Insolvency Fund and was refused. On application to the High Court, O'Sullivan J held he was not in insurable employment.

Insolvent

An employer is deemed to become insolvent if the employer is an individual (i.e. as opposed to a company) and has been adjudicated bankrupt, or has filed a petition for or has executed a deed of arrangement with their creditors, or if they have died and the estate is insolvent.

Date of Insolvency

The date of insolvency in the case of an individual is the date of adjudication, the date of filing the petition, the date of executing the deed of arrangement, or the date of death (as the case may be).

If it is a company (as defined by the Companies Act, 1963, as amended), the date of insolvency is the date a winding-up order is made, or a resolution for voluntary winding-up is made, or, if a receiver or manager has been appointed under a debenture secured by floating charge, or of the appointment of a provisional liquidator, then it is the date the receiver or manager is appointed. A cooperative is regarded as being insolvent on the day the manager or receiver is appointed.

The Minister for Enterprise, Trade and Employment may also specify by regulation the circumstances and date in which a specified class or description of employer is deemed to be insolvent. This is usually to cover a scenario where an employer has ceased trading and no formal bankruptcy or winding-up proceedings have been initiated.

EMPLOYEE'S RIGHTS

An employee (the applicant) may apply to the Minister on the prescribed form and the Minister shall pay the debts owed. However, the Minister must be satisfied that:

1. The applicant falls within the scope of the Act and the employer has become insolvent;

2. The date of insolvency is not earlier than 22 October 1983; and

3. On the "relevant date", the applicant was entitled to be paid the whole or part of any debt. In respect of an unfair dismissal, equality notice, maternity, adoptive or parental leave claim, this is the date of the Order awarding the compensation, or the date of the employer's insolvency, whichever is the later. In relation to the other debts, it is the date of termination of employment or the date of the employer's insolvency.

The payments are paid out of the Social Insurance Fund, which is funded by employer PRSI payments.

DEBTS

Where appropriate, the Social Insurance Fund pays debts under this Act. The amount payable to an employee in relation to a debt is based on £300 gross per week (if less than one week, it is on a proportional basis) (Protection of Employees (Employers' Insolvency) (Variation of Limit) Regulations, 1994 (SI No. 17 of 1990, as amended by SI No. 62 of 1994)). These Regulations are applicable where the date of termination of employment or of insolvency is on or after 1 May 1994. If the debt results from an award under the unfair dismissals or equality legislation, there cannot be a payment unless the time limit for bringing the appeal has expired or an appeal was made and withdrawn. Legal costs are not paid by the Fund; however, there is provision for the processing of entitlements (see form IP8). The debts covered in the Regulations are included under the following headings.

Normal Weekly Remuneration

This has the same meaning as in the Redundancy Payments Acts, 1967–1991. The applicant shall only be entitled to an amount in arrears for a period, or aggregate of periods of not more than eight weeks. In *Bollard and Others* v *Minister for Enterprise and Employment in the case of Irish Press Newspapers Ltd. (Liquidation/Receivership)* (I 13/96), "lieu days" and "lieu shifts" (where employees worked overtime or worked an additional shift to cover for illness) were considered "wages" for the purposes of the Act, as they were entitled to a day/shift off within 28 days, and if not a day's pay. "Bonus weeks", where employees worked on public holidays, were also considered to be "remuneration", as the payment was made in cash. The former employees also claimed for monies due under the National Agreement, as there was a "moral obligation" to pay them. The Employment Appeals Tribunal determined that the Act applied to debts, (i.e. monies legally due), hence no entitlement.

Sick Pay

This is arrears due for a period or periods not exceeding (in total) eight weeks under a sick pay scheme which forms part of an employee's contract of employment. These payments are only applicable for periods in which the employee was unable to fulfil the contract because of ill health and for sick pay to which the employee became entitled. Only the difference between disability or injury benefit and normal weekly remuneration is payable.

Court awards for arrears of wages and sick pay are also covered.

Holiday Pay

Holiday pay is defined as pay in respect of a holiday actually taken or any holiday pay which has accrued at the date of termination of the employee's employment. Such debt shall not exceed payment, in respect of a period of eight weeks, to which the employee became entitled during the relevant period. It also includes court awards for holiday pay.

The "relevant period" in all these cases means the 18 months before the date of insolvency or termination of employment.

Holiday pay is now covered under the Organisation of Working Time Act, 1997, and any compensatory awards from a rights commissioner, the Labour Court or the Employment Appeals Tribunal may be paid by the Social Insurance Fund.

Notice

An amount which an employer is required to pay under an award by the Employment Appeals Tribunal under the Minimum Notice and Terms of Employment Acts, 1973 to 1991.

Recommendation, Determination or Order under the Unfair Dismissal Acts, 1977 to 1993

Any amount which an employer is required to pay further to a recommendation of a rights commissioner, determination of the Tribunal or a Circuit Court order.

Wrongful Dismissal (Claim for Damages for Breach of Contract)

A court award for damages is also covered provided the employee was so entitled on the relevant date. However, the maximum amount payable will be limited to what the employee would have obtained as redress under the Unfair Dismissals Acts.

Compensatory Awards under the Maternity Protection Act, 1994, Adoptive Leave Act, 1995 and Parental Leave Act, 1998

Compensatory awards from a rights commissioner or the Employment Appeals Tribunal can be paid from the Social Insurance Fund.

Employment Regulation Order

Any amount that an employer is required to pay under an employment regulation order within the meaning of the Industrial Relations Acts, in relation to which proceedings have been instituted against the employer for an offence under section 45 (as amended) of the Act.

Equality Pay or Equality

Any amount specified in a recommendation, determination or order under the Anti-Discrimination (Pay) Act, 1974, or the Employment Equality Act, 1977, which an employer is required to pay further to an equality officer's recommendation or a determination by the Labour Court or a decision of the High Court. Also included are damages awarded under the 1977 Act, fines imposed under either the 1974 or 1977 Acts and compensation directed to be paid under the 1974 or 1977 Acts. Any amount, damages, fine or compensation under this heading is a debt only if the recommendation, decision, determination, award or order was made during or after the expiration of the relevant period.

When the Employment Equality Act, 1998, comes into effect, all orders, determinations and decisions shall fall within the scope of the 1984 Act (section 103 of the 1998 Act).

RIGHTS OF MINISTER

When the employee receives payment in respect of a debt, all rights and remedies in respect of that debt which the employee may have under the relevant company or bankruptcy legislation will be transferred to the Minister.

RELEVANT OFFICER

Payment will not normally be made from the Fund in respect of any debt until a statement of the amount of debt owed has been received from the relevant officer. The officer must furnish such statement when requested by the Minister.

A relevant officer may be an executor, an administrator, the official assignee or a trustee under an arrangement between an employer and its creditors under a trust deed executed by an employer, or a person designated by regulations under the Act for certain classes of employer. The Act provides that the Minister may appoint a person to be a relevant officer in circumstances where no formal bankruptcy or winding-up proceedings have been initiated. In *Minister for Labour* v *Thomas Grace, Liquidator, and Johnston, Mooney and O'Brien Ltd. (In Voluntary Liquidation)* [1993] ELR 50, O'Hanlon J confirmed that section 6(7) of the Act "gives exceptional power to the Minister to make a payment without awaiting the delivery of the said statement where a long delay has already taken place and he is satisfied that a payment under the section should be made".

PROCEDURE

The Protection of Employees (Employers' Insolvency) (Forms and Procedure) Regulations, 1984 (SI No. 356 of 1984 as amended by SI No. 349 of 1991) provide statutory forms which may be used to make a claim under the Act. Certain forms are to be completed by the employee and given to the employer's representative (e.g. receiver, liquidator, etc.). The representative then makes application on behalf of the employee for such payments.

Employee Forms

These forms are for the most part self-explanatory.

- *Form IP1*: Employee's application for a payment of arrears of wages, sick pay, and holiday pay owed by an insolvent employer (pages 491–3). There are no specific forms for claiming compensation under the maternity, adoptive and parental leave legislation but, as they are based on weeks of compensation, this form could be used.

- *Form IP2*: Employee's application for payment of a Tribunal award under the Minimum Notice and Terms of Employment Acts, 1973 to 1991 (pages 494–5).

- *Form IP4*: Employee's application for payment of arrears of statutory minimum wages, entitlements under the Anti-Discrimination (Pay) Act, 1974, Employment Equality Act, 1977, Unfair Dismissals Acts, 1977 to 1993, or court awards in respect of unfair/wrongful dismissal (pages 498–501). These forms will have to be amended to provide for entitlement under the Employment Equality Act, 1998.

The employee on signing these forms must:

1. Declare they have made no other applications;

2. State they are aware that their rights and remedies as a preferential creditor against the employer will be transferred to the Minister when paid (see below); and

3. State upon payment that there is no appeal pending and that they are not subject to appeal by anyone else.

Employer Forms

The relevant officer or employment representative completes the following forms:

- *Form IP3*: Application by an employer's representative for funds in respect of wages, sick pay, holiday pay and minimum notice awards (pages 496–7).

- *Form IP5*: Application by an employer's representative for funds to pay entitlements under an Employment Regulation Order, Unfair Dismissals Acts, 1977 to 1993, Anti-Discrimination (Pay) Act, 1974 and Employment Equality Act, 1977 (pages 502–3). These forms will have to be amended to provide for entitlement under the Employment Equality Act, 1998.

The employer's representative must:

1. Declare that to the best of their information the entitlements are correct;

2. Consent to disclose such information as may be necessary;

3. Undertake to distribute to employee(s) concerned the appropriate amounts which they receive as a result of this application;

4. Declare that they have not appealed or are not aware of any such appeal (on Form IP5);

5. Attach copies of IP1, IP2 and IP4 (as appropriate) signed by the employee;

6. State in whose favour the instrument of payment (e.g. cheque) should be drawn; and

7. Sign the Form IP3 or IP5.

The Minister, on receipt of the application, will pay such monies to the relevant officer (employer representative) unless there are particular reasons for making payment direct to the employee. Once the relevant officer has made payment to the employee, the Minister must be informed in writing, including details of any deductions made in relation to income tax, PRSI or pensions scheme contributions. The Act provides that the payment may be made by the Minister even though no statement has been supplied where:

1. A period of six months has elapsed since application but no payment has been made; and

2. The Minister is satisfied that the payment should be made; or

3. It appears to the Minister that there is going to be a further delay before a statement is received in relation to the debt.

The Minister may refuse an application completely or part thereof if there is collusion between the employee and the employer that such debt would be the subject of the application and the employer has the means to pay the debts or part thereof.

Information

The Minister may by notice in writing require the employer to provide relevant information including records kept pursuant to the Organisation of Working Time Act, 1997; that is, registers, wages sheets and so forth.

PENSIONS SCHEMES

There is provision for the payment of unpaid contributions to an occupational pension scheme which forms part of the contract of employment. Unpaid relevant contributions shall be paid out of the Fund. Relevant contributions are defined as contributions which were not paid by an employer in accordance with an occupational pension scheme either on the employer's own account or on behalf of an employee. An employee's contribution is only payable when that sum has been deducted from their pay. In *Re Cavan Rubber Ltd. (In Voluntary Liquidation)* [1992] ELR 79), the Tribunal determined the payment of both employer and employee pension contributions, even though the trust deed for the pension scheme was neither signed nor approved by the Revenue Commissioners, as the scheme fell within the definition of "occupational pension scheme" under the Act.

The sum payable in respect of unpaid employer contributions shall be the lesser of:

1. The balance of contributions remaining unpaid for the period of 12 months ending on the day prior to the date of insolvency; or

2. The amount certified by an actuary to be necessary for the purpose of meeting the liability of the scheme to pay the benefits provided by the scheme.

Unpaid contributions on behalf of an employee shall not exceed the amount prior to insolvency.

Procedure

The Protection of Employees (Employers' Insolvency) (Occupational Pension Scheme) (Forms and Procedure) Regulations, 1990 (SI No. 121 of 1990) provides statutory forms for making such claims:

*   *Form IP6*: This form is to be used in case of application for payment of (a) amounts deducted from pay of an employee in respect of contributions to the scheme which were not paid into the scheme; and (b) unpaid contributions of an employer on the employer's own account to an occupational pension scheme. Part 1 must be completed by a trustee, administrator or other person competent to act on behalf of the occupational pension scheme. Part 2 must be completed by the insolvent employer's representative (pages 504–7).

*   *Form IP7*: This is the Actuarial Certificate, which must be completed by the actuary. This Certificate must accompany the IP6

when a claim in respect of unpaid pension scheme contributions is being made. The actuary must sign the form giving details of their professional qualification and business name and address. The terms of the scheme must be attached to this Certificate (pages 508).

EMPLOYMENT APPEALS TRIBUNAL

Complaints may be made to the Employment Appeals Tribunal by (a) a person to whom the Minister has failed to make any payment; or (b) one who claims that any such payment is less than the amount that should have been paid.

Complaints under this Act shall only be heard in relation to the following debts:

- Remuneration

- Monies owing under sick pay schemes

- Holiday pay

- Unpaid pension contributions.

The complaint must be made within six weeks of the decision of the Minister further to an application for payment, or, if this time period is not practicable, within such period as the Tribunal considers reasonable. If the Employment Appeals Tribunal finds that the Minister is liable, a declaration shall be made to that effect.

Procedure

The statutory form for making such complaints to the Tribunal is form T1-C (available from the Employment Appeals Tribunal).

Appeal

Decisions of the Employment Appeals Tribunal may be appealed to the High Court on a point of law within 21 days of the decision.

Offences

Proceedings for an offence may only be instituted with the consent of the Minister. If a person making an application under the Act, whether for themselves or another person, knowingly makes a false statement, false representation or conceals a material fact, furnishes false documents or refuses or wilfully neglects to provide information, *inter alia*, such person shall be liable on summary conviction to a fine not exceeding £500. If an offence is committed by a body corporate, both the company and certain officers may also be liable.

General References

Barrett, G. (1996), *The Effects of Insolvency on the Contract of Employment*, (18) DULJ, Dublin: Round Hall Sweet and Maxwell.

Forde, M. (1991), Employment Law in Ireland, Dublin: Round Hall Press.

Keane, R. (1991), *Company Law in the Republic of Ireland*, Second edition, Dublin: Butterworths.

Kerr, A. (1995), *Termination of Employment Statutes: Commentary*, London: Sweet and Maxwell.

Form IP 1

AN ROINN FIONTAR AGUS FOSTAIOCHTA

DEPARTMENT OF ENTERPRISE AND EMPLOYMENT

EMPLOYEE'S APPLICATION FOR PAYMENT OF ARREARS OF WAGES, SICK PAY AND HOLIDAY PAY OWED BY AN INSOLVENT EMPLOYER

PROTECTION OF EMPLOYEES (EMPLOYERS' INSOLVENCY) ACTS, 1984 TO 1991

IMPORTANT   PLEASE READ THESE NOTES BEFORE COMPLETING THIS FORM

1. After completion, this form should be sent or returned to the insolvent employer's representative.

2. The insolvent employer's representative is the person appointed in connection with an employer's insolvency (e.g. receiver, liquidator, person appointed by Minister for Enterprise and Employment).

3. Deductions for income tax, pay-related social insurance and occupational pension scheme contributions, etc., will be made by the employer's representative from payments due to the employees where appropriate.

4. (A separate) Form 1P2 should be completed where payment is being claimed in respect of minimum notice and Form 1P4 should be used for claims in respect of arrears of statutory minimum wages or entitlements arising under the Unfair Dismissals Act, 1977, the Anti-Discrimination (Pay) Act, 1974 or the Employment Equality Act, 1977.

5. The maximum period for which arrears are payable for each individual item is eight weeks. In the case of sick pay, payment will not exceed the difference between any social welfare benefit payable and normal pay.

6. The amount of the gross weekly wage to be inserted in Part 2 (a) should include an average of regular overtime and any other regular commission/bonus, etc. calculated in accordance with the Redundancy Payments Acts. If rates given in Part 2 and Part 4 differ, please explain. Date of commencement of employment, number of hours normally expected to be worked per week, are required to establish entitlement and status of employees under the worker Protection (Regular Part-Time Employees) Act, 1991. For the purposes of calculating arrears a statutory ceiling on gross weekly wages is applied. The current ceiling is £250 per week.

7. Deductions for union dues, V.H.I. etc. which were made from gross wages and not paid over to the relevant authority should be inserted in Part 2 (b).

PART 1	COMPLETE THIS FORM IN BLOCK CAPITALS

EMPLOYEE'S SURNAME

EMPLOYEE'S FIRST NAME

ADDRESS OF EMPLOYEE

OCCUPATION
(If you are a Director or Shareholder please indicate)

DATE OF COMMENCEMENT OF EMPLOYMENT
Day   Month   Year

DATE OF TERMINATION OF EMPLOYMENT
Day   Month   Year

EMPLOYEE'S REVENUE AND SOCIAL INSURANCE (R.S.I.) NUMBER
Figures   Letters   Class of Ins Letter No

IF OVER 66 YEARS OF AGE OR UNDER 16 YEARS OF AGE, PLEASE GIVE DATE OF BIRTH
Day   Month   Year

BUSINESS NAME AND ADDRESS OF INSOLVENT EMPLOYER

PART 2	ARREARS OF WAGES

Number of days normally expected to be worked per week [ ]

(a)
From   Day Month Year   To   Day Month Year   **Total Number of Weeks Due**

From   Day Month Year   To   Day Month Year

Gross Weekly Pay
(See Note 6)   £

Number of Hours Normally Expected to be worked per week

Total Arrears of Wages Claimed
(See Note 5)   £

(b) Deductions from Wages: i.e. Union Dues, V.H.I. etc.

	WEEKLY AMOUNT DEDUCTED IN EACH CASE	RELEVANT PERIOD		TOTAL NO. OF WEEKS DUE IN EACH CASEE	TOTAL AMOUNT DEDUCTED IN EACH CASE
(i) Union Dues	£	From	Day Month Year		£
		To	Day Month Year		
(ii) V.H.I.	£	From	Day Month Year		£
		To	Day Month Year		
(iii) Any other Deductions (Specify)	£	From	Day Month Year		£
		To	Day Month Year		

Total Arrears of Deductions Due   £

PART 3	ARREARS DUE UNDER A COMPANY SICK PAY SCHEME

Total Number of Weeks Due

From Day Month Year To Day Month Year

Total Amount of Social Welfare Benefit Payable during the period £

Weekly Payment by Employer under Sick Pay Scheme
(Exclusive of Social Welfare Payments) £

Gross Weekly Pay *(See Note 6)* £

Total Arrears of Sick Pay Claimed *(See Note 5)* £

PART 4	ARREARS OF HOLIDAY PAY

(State only your gross basic wage)

Total Number of Weeks Due

From Day Month Year To Day Month Year

(This refers to period in which holiday entitlement arose)

Annual Leave Entitlement No of Days

Gross Weekly Pay *(See Note 6]* £

Total Arrears of Holiday Pay Claimed (See Note 5) £

I apply for paymrnt due to me under the Protection of Employees (Employers' Insolvency) Acts, 1984 to 1991 and declare that I have made no other applications in respect of the amounts shown above. I am aware that my rights and remedies against my employer in respect of this amount will be transferred to the Minister for Enterprise and Employment when payment has been made.

Signature . . . . Date. . . . .

WARNING	LEGAL PROCEEDINGS MAY BE TAKEN AGAINST ANYONE MAKING A FALSE STATEMENT ON THIS FORM

FORM IP 2

EMPLOYEE'S APPLICATION FOR PAYMENT OF AN EMPLOYMENT APPEALS TRIBUNAL AWARD UNDER THE MINIMUM NOTICE AND TERMS OF EMPLOYMENT ACT, 1973

An Rionn Fiontar, Trádála agus Fostaíochta - Department of Enterprise, Trade and Employment

Protection of Employees (Employers' Insolvency) Act, 1984

IMPORTANT: PLEASE READ THESE NOTES BEFORE COMPLETING THIS FORM

1. After completion, this form should be sent or returned to the insolvent employer's representative.

2. The insolvent employer's representative is the person appointed in connection with an employer's insolvency (e.g. receiver, liquidator, person appointed by the Minister for Enterprise, Trade and Employment).

3. This form should be used only for a claim in respect of an unpaid minimum notice award.   A separate form IP1 should be completed where payment is being claimed in respect of unpaid wages, sick pay entitlements or holiday pay and form IP4 should be used for claims in respect of arrears of statutory minimum wages or entitlements arising under the Unfair Dismissals Act, 1977, the Anti Discrimination (Pay) Act, 1974 or the Employment Equality Act, 1977.

4. There is a ceiling on gross wages for the purpose of making payments from the Fund.   You should refer to the explanatory booklet for the ceiling applicable.

PART 1	COMPLETE THIS FORM IN BLOCK CAPITALS	
Employee's Surname:	Employee's Revenue and Social Insurance (R.S.I.) Number:	
Employee's First name:	Figures Letters	
Address of Employee	Business name and address of insolvent Employer:-	
Occupation	Date of Termination of employment	Address of place of employment
	Day Month Year	

PART 2: AWARD BY THE EMPLOYMENT APPEALS TRIBUNAL UNDER SECTION 12 OF THE MINIMUM NOTICE AND TERMS OF EMPLOYMENT ACT, 1973

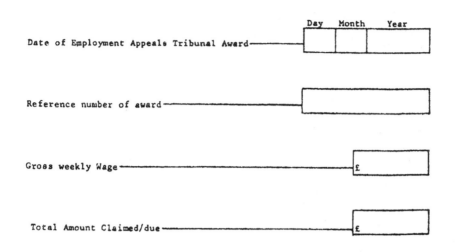

	Day	Month	Year

Date of Employment Appeals Tribunal Award

Reference number of award

Gross weekly Wage ——— £

Total Amount Claimed/due ——— £

PLEASE ATTACH A COPY OF THE TRIBUNAL AWARD

I apply for payment due to me under the Protection of Employees (Employers' Insolvency) Act, 1984 and declare that I have made no other applications in respect of the amount shown above. I am aware that my rights and remedies against my employer in respect of this amount will be transferred to the Minister for Enterprise, Trade and Employment when payment can be made.

Signature _____ Date _____

WARNING: Legal proceedings may be taken against anyone making a false statement on this form.

FORM IP 3

APPLICATION BY AN EMPLOYER'S REPRESENTATIVE FOR FUNDS IN RESPECT OF WAGES, SICK PAY, HOLIDAY PAY AND MINIMUM NOTICE AWARDS .

An Roinn Saothair - Department of Labour
Protection of Employees (Employers' Insolvency) Act, 1984

PLEASE COMPLETE THIS FORM IN BLOCK CAPITALS

Figures   Letter

EMPLOYER'S PAYE REGISTERED NUMBER

BUSINESS NAME OF
INSOLVENT EMPLOYER

BUSINESS ADDRESS

NATURE OF BUSINESS

FOR OFFICIAL USE

NACE

Date of Insolvency	Day	Month	Year	TYPE OF INSOLVENCY
(e.g. date of appointment of liquidator receiver etc.)				(e.g. liquidation, receivership, bankruptcy etc.)

To: Minister for Labour, Davitt House, Mespil Road, Dublin 4.

In connection with the provisions of the Protection of Employees (Employers' Insolvency) Act, 1984, I have accepted, based on the best information available to me, the entitlement of the employees as shown overleaf.   No other notification has been made by me in respect of these entitlements.   I understand that it may be necessary for you to refer information on the entitlements to the Revenue Commissioners and Government Departments. I hereby give my consent to the disclosure of such information as may be necessary.   I also agree to make available to you such records as may be required for examination. I undertake to distribute the appropriate amounts to the employees concerned from the funds received pursuant to this application.
Copies of forms IP1 and IP2 as appropriate signed by the employees involved are attached.

The Instrument of payment
should be drawn in favour of ———

Address ———

Signature of Employer's Representative _____

Date _____   Telephone _____

(1) Employee's Name	(2) Revenue & Social Insurance Number	(3) Total arrears of Wages £	(4) Net Total Arrears of Sick Pay	(5) Total Arrears of Holiday Pay £	(6) Amount of Minimum Notice Award by EAT £	(7) Total of Columns (3), (4), (5) & (6) £
						GRAND TOTAL £

FORM IP 4

EMPLOYEE'S APPLICATION FOR PAYMENT OF ARREARS OF STATUTORY MINIMUM WAGES, ENTITLEMENTS UNDER THE ANTI - DISCRIMINATION (PAY) ACT, 1974, EMPLOYMENT EQUALITY ACT, 1977, UNFAIR DISMISSALS ACT, 1977 OR COURT AWARDS IN RESPECT OF UNFAIR DISMISSAL.

AN ROINN FIONTAR AGUS FOSTAIOCHTA - DEPARTMENT OF ENTERPRISE AND EMPLOYMENT

Protection of Employees (Employers' Insolvency) Act, 1984

IMPORTANT: Please read these notes before completing this form.

1.   After completion, this form should be sent or returned to the insolvent employer's representative.

2.   The insolvent employer's representative is the person appointed in connection with an employer's insolvency (e.g. receiver, liquidator, person appointed by Minister for Enterprise and Employment).

3.   A separate form IP1 should be completed where payment is being claimed in respect of arrears of wages, sick pay and holiday pay and form IP2 should be used for claims in respect of Minimum Notice awards by the Employment Appeals Tribunal.

4.   Claims in respect of statutory minimum wages can only be made in respect of employments covered by an Employment Regulation Order. In case of doubt, about the application of an Employment Regulation Order, claimants should contact the Labour Inspectorate Section of this Department.

5.   Please attach a copy of the Recommendation, determination or order as appropriate, if available.

6.   Warning: Legal proceedings may be taken against anyone making a false statement on this form.

PART 1   COMPLETE THIS FORM IN BLOCK CAPITALS

Employee's Surname :	Employee's Revenue and Social Insurance (R.S.I.) Number:
Employee's First Name:	
Address of Employee:	Figures Letters
———————————————	Business Name and Address of Insolvent Employer:
———————————————	———————————————
———————————————	———————————————
Occupation: Date of Termination of Employment Day Month Year	———————————————
	Address of Place of Employment:
Gross Weekly Pay £	

PART 2 : ANTI-DISCRIMINATION (PAY) ACT, 1974

(1) Equality Officer Recommendation (Note: attach copy of recommendation).

Date of Recommendation: Day Month Year   Reference Number:

Amount of Recommendation _____ £

Has an appeal been lodged with the Labour Court? — Yes / No   tick ✓ appropriate box

(Note: If an appeal has been lodged, no payment can be made unless it is withdrawn, or is determined by the Labour Court. If it has been determined by the Labour Court, please complete section 2 following).

(2) Labour Court Determination (Note: attach copy of determination).

Date of Determination — Day Month Year   Reference Number:

Amount of Award _____ £

Has an appeal been lodged with the High Court? — Yes / No   tick ✓ appropriate box

(3) Fine arising out of Civil Court decision (note: attach copy of decision if available).

Date of Decision — Day Month Year   Amount of Award: £

Location of Sitting —

(4) Compensation awarded by Labour Court or Civil Court (note: attach copy of award).

Who awarded the compensation — Labour Court / Civil Court   tick ✓ appropriate box

Date of Decision — Day Month Year   Amount of Award: £

Reference Number (if any) — Location of Sitting — (if heard in Civil Court)

(5) High Court Judgement (note: attach copy of judgement).

Date of Judgement — Day Month Year   Amount of Award: £

PART 3 : EMPLOYMENT EQUALITY ACT, 1977

(1)   Equality Officer Recommendation (Note: attach copy of recommendation).

                            Day Month   Year

Date of Recommendation—[| |]   Reference Number: [   ]

Amount of Recommendation _____ [£   ]

Has an appeal been lodged with the Labour Court?—[Yes |]   tick ✓
                                                 [No |]   appropriate box

(Note: If an appeal has been lodged, no payment can be made unless it is withdrawn
       or is determined by the Labour Court. If it has been determined by the
       Labour Court, please complete section 2 following).

(2)   Labour Court Determination (Note: attach copy of determination).

                          Day Month   Year

Date of Determination—[| |]   Reference Number: [   ]

Amount of Award _____ [£   ]

Has an appeal been lodged with the High Court?—[Yes |]   tick ✓
                                               [No |]   appropriate box

(3)   Damages/Fine awarded by the Civil Court (Note: attach copy of fine/award, if
      available).

What did the Civil Court award?—[Damages |]   tick ✓
                                [Fine |]   appropriate box

                     Day Month Year

Date of Award —[| |]   Amount of Award: [£   ]

Location of Sitting—[   ]

(4)   Compensation awarded by Labour Court (Note: attach copy of award).

                         Day Month   Year

Date of award of
compensation—[| |]   Reference Number: [   ]

Amount of Award _____ [£   ]

Has an appeal been lodged with the High Court?—[Yes |]   tick ✓
                                               [No |]   as appropriate

(5)   High court Judgement (Note: attach copy of judgement, if available).

                        Day Month   Year

Date of Judgement —[| |]   Amount of Award: [£   ]

PART 4: STATUTORY MINIMUM WAGES UNDER AN
EMPLOYMENT REGULATION ORDER

Note: A claim under this part is not payable unless proceedings against the employer, under section 45(1) of the Industrial Relations Act, 1946, for the amount involved have been instituted.

State title of Employment
Regulation Order

Have proceedings been instituted against the employer — | Yes | / No | tick ✓ appropriate box

If yes, by whom

In which Court (if applicable)

State period in respect of which the claim is being made:

From: | Day | Month | Year | To: | Day | Month | Year | Total number of weeks

Total Arrears Claimed — £

PART 5 : UNFAIR DISMISSALS ACT, 1977

(1) Rights Commissioner Recommendation (Note: Attach copy of Recommendation).

Date of Recommendation — | Day | Month | Year | Amount of Award — £

Has an appeal been lodged with the Employment Appeals Tribunal? — | Yes | No | tick ✓ appropriate box

(2) Employment Appeals Tribunal Determination (Note: Attach copy of determination).

Date of Determination — | Day | Month | Year | Reference Number:

Amount of Award — £

Has an appeal been lodged with the Circuit Court? — | Yes | No | tick ✓ appropriate box

(3) Court Order (See note below)

Date of Order — | Day | Month | Year | Amount of Award — £

I apply for apply for payment due to me under the Protection of Employees (Employers' Insolvency) Act, 1984 and declare that I have made no other applications in respect of the amounts shown above. I am aware that my rights and remedies against my employer in respect of this amount will be transferred to the Minister for Enterprise and Employment when payment has been made. I also declare in respect of the amounts claimed above that I have made no appeal in respect of these amounts and I am not aware, to the best of my knowledge, that these amounts are the subject of appeal by anyone else.

Signature: _____   Date: _____

Note: This part should also be used to claim payment of court awards for damages at common law for wrongful dismissal.

APPLICATION BY AN EMPLOYER'S REPRESENTATIVE FOR FUNDS TO PAY ENTITLEMENTS UNDER AN EMPLOYMENT REGULATION ORDER, UNFAIR DISMISSALS ACT, 1977 , ANTI-DISCRIMINATION (PAY) ACT,1974 AND EMPLOYMENT EQUALITY ACT,1977.

An Roinn Saothair - Department of Labour
Protection of Employees (Employers' Insolvency) Act, 1984.

PLEASE COMPLETE THIS FORM IN BLOCK CAPITALS

Business Name of Insolvent Employer	Employer's P.A.Y.E Registered Number
	Figures Letter
Business address of Insolvent Employer	
	Date of Insolvency Day Month Year
	(eg date of appointment of Liquidator, Receiver etc.)
Nature of Business For Office Use Nace	Type of Insolvency (e.g. liquidation, receivership, bankruptcy, etc)

To: Minister for Labour, Davitt House, Mespil Road, Dublin 4.

In connection with the provisions of the Protection of Employees (Employers' Insolvency) Act, 1984, I have accepted, to the best of my knowledge, the entitlement of the employees as shown in, this form. No other notification has been made by me in respect of these entitlements. I understand that it may be necessary for you to refer information on the entitlements to the Revenue Commissioners and Government Departments. I hereby give my consent to the disclosure of such information as may be necessary. I also agree to make available to you such records as may be required for examination. I undertake to distribute the appropriate amounts to the employees concerned from the funds received pursuant to this application

I declare in respect of the amounts shown on this form for the employees concerned that I have made no appeal in relation to the amounts shown and I am not aware, to the best of my knowledge, that these amounts are the subject of appeal by the employees concerned or anybody else.

The instrument of payment should be drawn in favour of _____

Address _____

Signature of Employer's Representative _____

Date: _____   Telephone: _____

1	2	3	4	5	6	7
Employer's Name	Revenue and Social Insurance Number	Amount under the Anti-Discrimination(Pay) Act, 1974. £	Amount under the Employment Equality Act, 1977. £	Amount under Unfair Dismissals Act, 1977 or Court Order for wrongful dismissal £	Amount under the Industrial Relations Act, 1946 (Employment Regulation Order)	Total of columns (3), (4), (5) and (6). £

GRAND TOTAL £

FORM IP 6

AN ROINN FIONTAR AGUS FOSTAÍOCHTA	DEPARTMENT OF ENTERPRISE & EMPLOYMENT

APPLICATION FOR PAYMENT OF UNPAID OCCUPATIONAL PENSION SCHEME CONTRIBUTIONS

PROTECTION OF EMPLOYEES (EMPLOYERS' INSOLVENCY) ACTS, 1984 TO 1991

IMPORTANT	PLEASE READ THESE NOTES BEFORE COMPLETING THIS FORM

1. Part 1 of this form and the schedule should be completed by a trustee, administrator or other person competent to act on behalf of the occupational pension scheme.

2. After completion of Part 1 and the schedule, this form should be sent or returned to the insolvent employer's representative.

3. The insolvent employer's representative is the person appointed in connection with an employer's insolvency (e.g., receiver, liquidator or a person appointed by the Minister for Enterprise and Employment under Section 5 of the Protection of Employees (Employers' Insolvency) Act, 1984).

4. Part 2 of this form should be completed by the insolvent employer's representative.

5. Where a claim is being made for unpaid contributions payable by an employer on his own account, a completed actuarial certificate, Form IP 7, must be obtained by the insolvent employer's representative and attached to the claim.

6. A copy of the terms of the occupational pension scheme should be attached to this application, if not already furnished to the Department of Enterprise and Employment.

7. Documentation confirming the existence of the occupational pension scheme should accompany this application, e.g., a Trust Deed and a Deed of Adherence in the case of an industry-wide scheme and a Trust Deed in the case of an individual scheme.

8. The annual subscription rate together with a breakdown of the unpaid contributions in respect of the 12 months prior to the date of insolvency should be attached.

9. The date of insolvency for the purpose of payments under the above Act is defined in Section 4 of the Protection of Employees (Employers' Insolvency) Act, 1984.

2

PART 1	TO BE COMPLETED BY A PERSON COMPETENT TO ACT FOR THE OCCUPATIONAL PENSION SCHEME (See Note 1)

To   ...   .

NAME OF INSOLVENT EMPLOYER'S REPRESENTATIVE

I am/We are authorised to act on behalf of   ...

NAME OF OCCUPATIONAL PENSION SCHEME

In respect of employee(s) of   ...   .

NAME OF INSOLVENT EMPLOYER

TYPE OF OCCUPATIONAL PENSION SCHEME
(e.g. Contributory, Non-contributory)

I/We certify that the provisions of the occupational pension scheme, which was in operation for the 12 months prior to the date of the insolvency, provided for contributions as follows:-

Total amount of contributions payable on the employer's own account for the 12 months prior to date of insolvency   ...   .   £

Total amount of contributions payable by the employee(s) for the 12 months prior to the date of insolvency   ...   .   £

I/We apply for payment from the Social Insurance Fund, in accordance with the terms of the Protection of Employees (Employers' Insolvency) Acts, 1984 to 1991, of relevant unpaid contributions to the occupational pension scheme.

I/We declare that any money received by me/us as a result of this application will be paid into the resources of the occupational pension scheme.

I/We understand that where payment is made from the Fund in respect of pension contributions, any rights and remedies in respect of those contributions belonging to the persons competent to act in respect of the scheme shall become rights and remedies of the Minister for Enterprise and Employment.

Signature(s) _____

_____

_____   Date _____

Designation (Trustee/Administrator, etc.) _____

Name(s)

Address

3

PART 2	TO BE COMPLETED BY THE INSOLVENT EMPLOYER'S REPRESENTATIVE

Employer's PAYE Registered Number

Business Name of Insolvent Employer

Business Address

Name of Business

For Official Use

RACE

DATE OF INSOLVENCY
(As defined in Section 4 of the Protection of Employees (Employers' Insolvency) Act, 1984)

DAY   MONTH   YEAR

DATE OF INSOLVENCY
(e.g., Liquidation, Receivership, Bankruptcy, etc.)

I have examined the claim set out in Part 1 of this form and in the attached schedule, I certify, based on the best information available to me, that the amount of contributions which were not paid into the occupational pension scheme in respect of the 12 months prior to the date of insolvency are:-

Amount unpaid by the insolvent employer on his own account   ..   ..   £

Amount deducted from the employees' wages in respect of contributions to the occupational pension scheme but which was not paid into the said scheme   ..   £

Did sickness/disability form part of the scheme ☐ YES ☐ NO

If "yes" state element of contribution _____

Did Life Assurance form part of the scheme ☐ YES ☐ NO

If "yes" state element of contribution _____

An Actuarial Certificate (Form IP 7) (See Note 5):   Is attached ☐   Is not attached ☐   (Tick appropriate box)

To: Minister for Enterprise and Employment, Davitt House, 65A Adelaide Road, Dublin 2.

In accordance with the provisions of the Protection of Employees (Employers' Insolvency) Acts, 1984 and 1991. I have accepted, based on the best information available to me, the amounts outstanding to the occupational pension scheme as shown in this application. I confirm that all employees in the scheme were insurable at the date of termination of employment for all benefits under the Social Welfare Acts 1981 to 1991 in accordance with Section 3 of the Protection of Employees (Employers' Insolvency) Act, 1984. I understand that it may be necessary for you to verify information on the application with other Government Departments. I hereby give my consent to the disclosure of such information as may be necessary. I also agree to make available to you such records as may be required for examination. I undertake to pay to the applicant for payment into the occupational pension scheme concerned any funds received pursuant to this application.

Name of Employer's Representative

Address

Signature of Employer's Representative _____

Date _____   **Telephone Number** _____

WARNING	LEGAL PROCEEDINGS MAY BE TAKEN AGAINST ANYONE MAKING A FALSE STATEMENT ON THIS FORM

4
SCHEDULE

Schedule of deductions made from employees' wages (Contributory Pension Scheme) and on behalf of employees (Non-contributory Pension Scheme) In respect of contributions to the Occupational Pension Scheme which were not paid into the Scheme.

NAME OF OCCUPATIONAL PENSION SCHEME

(Attach continuation sheets to this schedule if necessary)

NAME OF EMPLOYEE *	R SI NUMBER	PERIOD OF DEBT FROM	TO	AMOUNT DEDUCTED BUT NOT PAID INTO SCHEME #
				£

	GRAND TOTAL	£

*State if any of the employees were directors of the company by placing "D" after the name above.
Contributions are payable only in respect of periods of paid employment during the period of debt.

Form IP7

AN ROINN FIONTAR AGUS FOSTAÍOCHTA   DEPARTMENT OF ENTERPRISE AND EMPLOYMENT

ACTUARIAL CERTIFICATE

UNPAID OCCUPATIONAL PENSION SCHEME CONTRIBUTIONS

PROTECTION OF EMPLOYEES (EMPLOYERS' INSOLVENCY) ACTS, 1984

IMPORTANT: PLEASE READ THESE NOTES BEFORE COMPLETING THIS CERTIFICATE

1   This certificate should be completed by an actuary.

2   This certificate must accompany Form IP6 when a claim in respect of unpaid pension scheme contributions, payable by an employer on his own account, is being made.

NAME OF OCCUPATIONAL PENSION SCHEME

BUSINESS NAME OF INSOLVENT EMPLOYER

DATE OF INSOLVENCY

(As defined in Section 4 of the Act)

Day   Month   Year

(a)   The dissolution provisions of the above occupational pension scheme are as set out in the attached copy of the terms of the occupational pension scheme.

(b)   I certify, in accordance with Section 7(3)(b) of the Protection of Employees (Employers' Insolvency) Act, 1984, that the amount necessary for the purposes of meeting the liability of the scheme on dissolution to pay the benefits provided by the scheme to or in respect of the employees of the employer is ... ...   £

SIGNATURE OF ACTUARY   **DATE**

PROFESSIONAL QUALIFICATION

BUSINESS NAME AND ADDRESS OF ACTUARY

LAST NAME   FIRST NAME

SECTION FOUR

INDUSTRIAL RELATIONS AND ADJUDICATING BODIES

This section explains the operation of the various industrial relations and adjudicating bodies, namely the Labour Relations Commission and its various services — in particular, rights commissioners and equality officers. The Director of Equality Investigations, equality officers and the new office of equality mediation officer, when operating under the Employment Equality Act, 1998, will operate independently of the Labour Relations Commission under the Department of Justice, Equality and Law Reform. The Labour Court in its role of hearing both industrial relations and equality claims is considered, as is the operation of the Employment Appeals Tribunal.

The practice and procedure for bringing claims and appeals under each piece of employment legislation is considered with the use of the relevant statutory forms (which are printed at the end of each chapter) and the actual procedure of the bodies at hearing. Irish legislation has a battery of forms and different bodies to whom claims are brought and this section aims to explain and simplify these procedures.

Chapter Twenty-two

THE LABOUR RELATIONS COMMISSION AND THE LABOUR COURT

The Industrial Relations Act, 1990, established the Labour Relations Commission, which formally came into operation on 21 January 1991. The purpose of the Labour Relations Commission is to promote better industrial relations. One of the main reasons for its establishment was to enhance the appellate function of the Labour Court, which was hearing too many matters that could and should have been resolved at a lower level or between the parties themselves.

The Labour Relations Commission comprises:

1. A chairperson, who is appointed by the Minister for Enterprise, Trade and Employment after consultation with both employer and employee organisations, namely, the Irish Business and Employers' Confederation (formerly the Federation of Irish Employers) and the Irish Congress of Trade Unions; and

2. Two employee and two employer members who are nominated by the Minister following consultation with their relevant organisations (as under (1) above); and

3. Two independent members also nominated by the Minister.

The Labour Relations Commission also has a chief executive. The first chief executive was appointed by the then Minister for Labour and each subsequent chief executive will be appointed by the Minister, after consultation with the Commission.

FUNCTIONS OF THE COMMISSION

The Commission has general responsibility for promoting the improvement of industrial relations, including the following functions:

1. To provide a conciliation service;

2. To provide an industrial relations advisory service;

3. To prepare codes of practice relevant to industrial relations, after consultation with unions and employer organisations;

4. To offer guidance and help to resolve disputes concerning their implementation;

5. To appoint equality officers of the Commission and provide staff and facilities for the equality officer service (this will be changed under the Employment Equality Act, 1998, before that legislation is fully put into effect);

6. To nominate persons for appointment as rights commissioners and provide staff and facilities for the rights commissioner service;

7. To conduct or commission research into matters relevant to industrial relations;

8. To review and monitor developments in the area of industrial relations;

9. To assist joint labour committees and joint industrial councils in the exercise of their functions.

INDUSTRIAL RELATIONS

The primary purpose of the Labour Relations Commission is to resolve trade disputes through conciliation without reference to the Labour Court. The Labour Relations Commission investigates each dispute and the Labour Court only becomes involved once the Commission reports that no further efforts will advance resolution, or if it waives its conciliation function. Of course, if there are "exceptional circumstances", the Labour Court may intervene in a dispute, provided it has first consulted the Labour Relations Commission.

The Commission may, at the request of one or more parties to a trade dispute or on its own initiative, offer its appropriate services with a view to bringing about a settlement.

Unless there is provision within a procedure for direct reference to the Labour Court, trade disputes shall be first referred to the Commission, generally to the conciliation service. Previously, industrial relations officers (more usually called conciliation officers) were part of the Labour Court, but they are now incorporated within the Labour Relations Commission.

The Labour Relations Commission has assisted in the drawing up of Codes of Practice under the Industrial Relations Act, namely the Code of Practice on Dispute Procedures, 1992 (SI No. 1 of 1992), the Code of Practice on Employee Representatives, 1993 (SI No. 169 of 1993) (see Chapter 8, "Trade Disputes") and the Code of Practice on Disciplinary Procedures, 1996 (SI No. 117 of 1996) (see Chapter 17, "Unfair Dismissal"). It has also been involved in the resolution of the many disputes since its establishment.

The Organisation of Working Time Act, 1997 (section 35), provides that the Labour Relations Commission may prepare codes of practice under this Act. The Minister for State at the Department of Enterprise, Trade and Employment may request the Labour Relations Commission to prepare a specific code of practice. A code of practice is defined in this Act as ". . . a code that provides practical guidance as to the steps that may be taken for the purposes of complying with the section". The Commission shall prepare a code of practice for the purposes of section 6(2), which deals with rest periods and breaks, but must first consult with the National Authority for Occupational Safety and Health. The Code of Practice on Compensatory Rest Periods (SI No. 44 of 1998) was made in February 1998. It was designed to assist employees and their representatives in observing the Organisation of Working Time Act as regards compensatory rest (see Chapter 13, "Organisation of Working Time").

When preparing a code of practice, the Commission must invite employer, employee and all other relevant organisations to make oral or written submissions in relation to the proposed code of practice and shall have regard to any submissions made by such bodies. The Commission shall submit a copy of the code of practice to the Minister who may declare the code to be a code of practice or may amend the code as considered appropriate. The Minister may at the request of the Commission or of their own volition amend or revoke a code of practice by order. A failure by any person to observe a code of practice shall not of itself render them liable to any civil or criminal proceedings.

A code of practice under the Organisation of Working Time Act is admissible in evidence before any court, the Labour Court or the rights commissioner. Any provision of a code relevant to any question rising in any proceedings before them shall be taken into account by the court, the Labour Court or a rights commissioner.

REFERENCE OF A DISPUTE BY MINISTER

Where the Minister for Enterprise, Trade and Employment is of the opinion that a trade dispute has either occurred or may occur in the future, and if it affects the public interest, the Minister may refer the matter to the Commission or the Court, which shall endeavour to resolve the dispute.

If the Minister is of the opinion that the trade dispute is of special importance, the Commission or the Court or others may be requested to conduct an inquiry into the dispute and to furnish a report to the Minister on the findings.

EQUALITY SERVICE

The equality service, which comprises equality officers who hear claims under the equality legislation, was originally part of the Labour Court and is now part of the Labour Relations Commission. Equality officers are independent in their function and a person who is dissatisfied with a recommendation may appeal to the Labour Court. When the Employment Equality Act, 1998, comes into operation, it will function under the Department of Justice, Equality and Law Reform, with the office of Director of Equality Investigations, who shall appoint equality officers and equality mediation officers (see Chapter 24, "Equality Claims").

RIGHTS COMMISSIONER SERVICE

A rights commissioner can hear individual grievances/disputes under the Industrial Relations Act, 1969, the Payment of Wages Act, 1991, the Unfair Dismissals Acts, 1977 to 1993, the Maternity Protection Act, 1994, the Terms of Employment (Information) Act, 1994, the Adoptive Leave Act, 1995, the Protection of Young Persons (Employment) Act, 1996, the Organisation of Working Time Act, 1997, and the Parental Leave Act, 1998. Rights commissioners are independent in the performance of their functions.

Industrial Relations Acts, 1946–1990

A rights commissioner can hear individual grievances/disputes under the Industrial Relations Acts, 1946–1990 (see section 13 of the Industrial Relations Acts, 1969). The person bringing the individual grievance/dispute may put it in writing (see form at p. 534). Applicants are reminded that a copy of this form is sent to their employer.

With respect to an individual grievance, a party to a trade dispute may object to a rights commissioner hearing the matter, but must do so within three weeks after notice has been sent by post to that party. Otherwise, the objection shall have no effect. An appeal of a rights commissioner's recommendation to the Labour Court must be notified in writing to the Court within six weeks after the recommendation. A rights commissioner must notify the Court, the Minister for Enterprise, Trade and Employment and the Commission of every recommendation made by the rights commissioner.

Rights commissioner hearings are heard in private and are relatively informal. Usually, both parties have a short written submission setting out the facts of the matter with their respective arguments. The rights commissioner commences proceedings by confirming the Act under which the claim is brought and then hears the respective arguments. At this stage the rights commissioner may wish to see each party on its own to find out further information and to see if there is a basis for a resolution to the dispute. If the rights commissioner does not see a resolution, the parties will be called back together, asked if there are further arguments and then advise that a written recommendation will be issued in due course. If there is a resolution to the dispute, the rights commissioner will act as a mediator to try to effect a settlement. When a settlement is reached, the rights commissioner may draft the settlement agreement and have it signed by both parties. This settlement agreement may then be issued in the form of a recommendation. All recommendations are private to the parties.

If there is no settlement of the dispute, the recommendation may be appealed to the Labour Court.

There are no specific forms to appeal a recommendation to the Labour Court.

Unfair Dismissals Acts, 1977 to 1993

An individual who considers that they were unfairly dismissed may refer their claim under the Unfair Dismissals Acts to a rights commissioner. The claim (in writing) must be served on the rights commissioner within six months of the date of dismissal (see page 535). The form requires details of the name and address of the applicant and the employer; name and address of the representative; date on which employment began; date of dismissal; details of gross and net remuneration; redress sought (i.e. reinstatement, re-engagement or compensation); details as to whether the employee has taken up new employment since dismissal and if so at what rate of pay; written details of the grounds of the claim; signature and date of the claim. The Unfair Dismissals (Amendment) Act, 1993, provides that, in exceptional circumstances, the claim may be served within 12 months of the date of dismissal (see Chapter 23, "Unfair Dismissal"). The employer may within 21 days of receipt of the notice object to a rights commissioner hearing the case. The objection must be in writing to the rights commissioner's office. If there is an objection, the employee may refer the matter to the Employment Appeals Tribunal. Once the unfair dismissals claim has been properly served on the rights commissioner, there is no problem on time limits. It is recommended that the employee also serve the employer with the form within the six-month period. Thus, where there is an objection to the rights commissioner hearing, the claim does not have to be referred to the Employment Appeals Tribunal within the six-month time limit (*The State (Hywel J. John)* v *The Employment Appeals Tribunal, Inbucon Management Consultants Ltd., and Inbucon Management Consultants (Ireland) Ltd.* (1984) 3 JISLL 143).

If the matter goes to hearing by a rights commissioner and is not settled, the recommendation may be appealed to the Employment Appeals Tribunal within six weeks of receipt of the recommendation. The appeal must be served on the Employment Appeals Tribunal and advisedly on the other party within the six-week time limit. The appeal must be in writing and the new T1-B Form (see Chapter 23) is used. This form is also used for appeals from a rights commissioner to the Employment Appeals Tribunal under the following Acts: Payment of Wages Act, 1991; Terms of Employment (Information) Act, 1994; Maternity Protection Act, 1994; Adoptive Leave Act, 1995; Protection of Young Persons (Employment) Act, 1996; and may also be used for appeals under the Parental Leave Act, 1998.

Aside from the usual details concerning the parties, the name of the rights commissioner, the date and reference number of the decision to which the appeal applies is extremely important because of the strict statutory time limits applicable under each Act. There is no legislative provision allowing for a time extension. Section 9(2) of the Unfair Dismissals Act, 1977 (as amended by the 1993 Act), provides:

> An appeal under this section shall be initiated by a party giving, within six weeks of the date on which the recommendation to which it relates was given to the parties concerned, a notice in writing . . . to the Tribunal and stating the intention of the party concerned to appeal against the recommendation and a copy of the notice shall be given to the other party concerned by the Tribunal as soon as may be after the receipt by it of the notice.

Form T1-B also requires the appellant to set out the grounds of appeal; for example, it could be a full appeal based on apparent misunderstanding of facts or misinterpretation of the law by the rights commissioner. The appellant could, for example, appeal the redress only.

Enforcement

If the recommendation of the rights commissioner is in favour of the employee and if it has not been appealed, then it must be carried out (i.e. reinstatement or re-engagement put into place or compensation paid). The employee may then refer the recommendation to the Employment Appeals Tribunal (after the appeal period) who, without hearing the employer's evidence, shall issue a determination the same as the recommendation.

Payment of Wages Act, 1991

Complaints Procedure

An employee may complain to a rights commissioner in writing (see form on page 536) that their employer has made an unlawful deduction or required an unlawful payment from their wages. A complaint must be made within six months of the date of the alleged breach of the Act. However, the rights commissioner has discretion if they are satisfied that exceptional circumstances prevented the making of the complaint in time. Thus, the six-month period can be extended by a further six months as is considered reasonable.

The rights commissioner will send a copy of the Notice of Complaint to the employer. The Notice requires details of deduction or non-payment (e.g. wages/pay, minimum notice, holiday pay or any other payment of the total amount allegedly due). The parties will then be given an opportunity to be heard and to present any evidence relating to the complaint. After the hearing, the rights commissioner will give a decision in writing (unless the matter is settled). Proceedings before the rights commissioner will be in public unless a party makes a successful application to the rights commissioner to have the matter heard in private.

Compensation for Illegal Deductions

If a rights commissioner considers a complaint to be well founded, the employer will be ordered to pay the employee compensation. The rights commissioner may award twice the amount of deduction or payment (by the employee) or else one week's net wages — whichever is the greater.

A rights commissioner cannot issue a decision at any time after the employee has commenced proceedings in the civil courts for the recovery of the deduction or payment. Equally, an employee cannot recover monies for the payment or deduction if the rights commissioner has given a decision.

The rights commissioner must send a copy of the decision to the Employment Appeals Tribunal.

Appeal to Employment Appeals Tribunal

Either party may appeal the decision of the rights commissioner in writing to the Employment Appeals Tribunal. Such an appeal must be made within six weeks of the date of the communication of the rights commissioner's recommendation. A copy must go to the other party within the six-week statutory time limit. The Payment of Wages (Appeals) Regulations, 1991 (SI 351 of 1991) governs appeals to the Tribunal. An appeal shall contain a brief outline of the grounds of appeal and the T1-B form may be used.

The RP51A Form (see Chapter 23) may be used for the appeal.

Time Limits for Implementation

A rights commissioner's decision or a Tribunal determination may give a date by which the decision or determination will be implemented; in other words, the date by which the monies must be paid to the employee. If no such date is given, the implementation (payment) date is deemed to be six weeks from the date on which the decision/determination was communicated to the parties concerned.

Enforcement of Decisions and Determinations

A rights commissioner's decision or a Tribunal determination may be enforced as if it were an order of the Circuit Court made by a judge of that Court.

Terms of Employment (Information) Act, 1994

An employee may claim in writing that an employer has failed to comply with the requirement to give them a written statement or that the employer made changes to the written statement without notification. This complaint must be referred to the rights commissioner within six months of the employer failing to provide the written statement or making the change to the statement. The rights commissioner may extend this time limit up to one year in exceptional circumstances. Such complaints may be made on the form entitled Notice of Complaint to rights commissioner under the Terms of Employment (Information) Act, 1994 (see page 537), and the Terms of Employment (Information) (Appeals and Complaints) Regulations, 1994 (SI No. 244 of 1994) apply. The notice must include the date on which the statement was requested and in what way the employer failed to comply with the requirement; or details where the employer changed the written statement. This form should be sent to the rights commissioner at the Labour Relations Commission. Applicants are advised that a copy of this application will be sent to their employer.

On hearing the case the rights commissioner may:

1. Declare that the claim was or was not well founded;

2. Confirm the particulars in the statement or alter or add to the statement;

3. Require the employer to give the employee a written statement containing the particulars as specified by the rights commissioner;

4. Order the employer to pay the employee compensation of up to four weeks' remuneration.

The rights commissioner's recommendation may be appealed to the Employment Appeals Tribunal within six weeks of the date of communication. The T1-B form may be used for the appeal (see Chapter 23). It is recommended that the Notice of Appeal be served on the employer also. The Tribunal may also enforce the recommendation.

Maternity Protection Act, 1994

A dispute between an employee and their employer may be referred under the Maternity Protection Act, 1994, to the rights commissioner (Section 30). Employees who are members of the Defence Forces may not refer such a dispute to a rights commissioner (s. 30). Disputes relating to a dismissal or the termination of employment or where the dispute should have been referred to the Health and Safety Authority do not fall under this reference. The more usual disputes concern the non-notification of an employee to their employer that they wish to return to work even though they have not complied with the necessary notification procedure, and are thus requesting an extension of time for the notification purposes, or for time off for pre- or post-natal care; or disputes concerning remuneration under the Act.

The matter may be referred by a notice in writing to the rights commissioner with details of the name and address of the employee and employer and of the employee's representative; date of commencement of employment and date of termination of employment (where applicable); gross and net pay; and finally written details of the dispute. This claim must be made within six months from the date on which the employer is informed of the initial circumstances relevant to the dispute; that is to say, the employee is pregnant, has recently given birth or is breastfeeding or, in the case of an employee who is the father of the child, the death of the child's mother. If there are exceptional circumstances, the rights commissioner may extend the time limit to 12 months from the date the employer was informed. On receipt of the notice of dispute from the rights commissioner, the other party must indicate to the rights commissioner that they intend defending the dispute and the facts and contentions that they will put forward at the hearing. Failure to provide such a response or defence will be treated as giving notice that they do not intend to respond or to contest the dispute.

Hearings before a rights commissioner shall be heard in private and shall hear the evidence of the parties to the dispute. The rights commissioner shall send a copy of each decision to the Employment Appeals Tribunal. The Maternity Protection (Disputes and Appeals) Regulations, 1995 (SI No. 17 of 1995) shall apply.

The rights commissioner may order such redress as is considered appropriate and grant either or both of the following:

1. The granting of leave for such period as may be so specified;

2. An award for compensation in favour of the employee to be paid by the relevant employer (Maternity Protection (Maximum Compensation) Regulation, 1999 (SI No. 134 of 1999)).

Compensation shall be up to a maximum of 20 weeks' remuneration as is just and equitable under the circumstances.

A decision of a rights commissioner may be appealed in writing to the Employment Appeals Tribunal within four weeks of the date of the decision. Form T1-B should be used. The decision of a rights commissioner may provide that the decision must be carried out before a certain date. If there is no such detail, then it shall be deemed to have to be carried out within four weeks of the date of the decision. If a party fails to carry out such a decision, the decision may be referred to the Circuit Court by the employee or the Minister for an order directing the other party to carry out the decision. The Circuit Court may direct the employer to pay interest on the compensation in respect of a period from four weeks from the date of the decision. Circuit Court proceedings shall be heard in the county where the employer ordinarily resides or carries on any profession, business or occupation.

Adoptive Leave Act, 1995

A dispute between an adopting parent and their employer may be referred under the Adoptive Leave Act, 1995, to the rights commissioner (Section 32). Adopting parents employed as members of the

Defence Forces may not refer a dispute to a rights commissioner. Disputes relating to a dismissal or the termination of employment or redundancy notice and minimum notice claims where an adopting parent is not allowed return to work (even though they have complied with the notification requirements) may not be referred to a rights commissioner.

The rights commissioner will hear the parties to a claim and make a decision in relation to the dispute and give the parties concerned such directions as the rights commissioner considers necessary or expedient for the resolution of the dispute. The rights commissioner may award compensation in favour of the adopting parent to be paid by the relevant employer. Compensation may be up to 20 weeks remuneration calculated in accordance with the Adoptive Leave (Calculation of Weekly Remuneration) Regulations (SI No. 196 of 1995).

Complaints Procedure

The employee must give notice in writing to a rights commissioner not later than six months from the day of placement or, in circumstances where no placement has taken place, within the period of six months from the date on which the employer receives the first notification of the adopting parents' intention to take leave under this Act, or in the case of an adopting father, not later than six months from the date on which the adopting mother dies. If a claim has not been lodged within the six months, the time period may be extended to 12 months if the rights commissioner is satisfied that exceptional circumstances prevented the giving of the notice.

The form used is the Notice of Complaint to a rights commissioner under the Adoptive Leave Act, 1995 (see p. 539) and the Adoptive Leave (Referral of Disputes and Appeals) (Part V) Regulations (SI No. 195 of 1995) provides that a notice must contain the following particulars: the nature of the dispute, i.e. whether it is a dispute relating to adoptive leave (e.g. entitlement to leave) or to the contract of employment (e.g. protection of employment rights whilst on leave); the date of placement and, where there was no placement, the date the employer received the first notification of the adopting parent's intention to take leave; the date on which the adopting mother died (where applicable).

The rights commissioner may request the parties to provide further details of the dispute to include oral or written submissions. The rights commissioner may commence an oral hearing, question the parties to the dispute and request the production of documents. If either party does not attend a hearing, the rights commissioner may proceed in their absence and may draw such inference as appears proper from a failure or refusal by a party to comply with a request.

The rights commissioner's recommendation may be appealed to the Employment Appeals Tribunal within four weeks of the date of the recommendation. Form T1-B should set out the grounds of appeal with the name of the rights commissioner. The Tribunal shall copy the appeal to the employer within five weeks. The decision of a rights commissioner (section 39) must be carried out by a specified date. If there is no specified date it must be carried out within four weeks from the date it was communicated to the parties. If the decision is not carried out, the employee or Minister (where appropriate) may make application to the Circuit Court for an order directing the party in default to carry out the terms of the decision. Where compensation was due to be paid, under the Courts Act, 1981, interest shall be paid for a period dating from four weeks from the date of the decision.

If there was a dismissal arising from adoptive leave, a claim should be brought under the unfair dismissals legislation.

Protection of Young Persons (Employment) Act, 1996

The parent or guardian of a child or a young person may present a complaint to a rights commissioner that the employer has used the commencement of the 1996 Act to reduce the terms and conditions of employment for an employee (section 13; i.e., where there is a reduction in hours following the repeal of the Protection of Young Persons (Employment) Act, 1977) or that an employer has penalised a child or young person for not co-operating with their employer in breaching the Act (section 17). The application to the rights commissioner must be in writing and contain the names and addresses of the employee and employer and the name of the employee's representative. It should also set out the specific details of the above complaints as alleged. The claim must be brought within six months of the date of alleged contravention of the Act or, where the rights commissioner is satisfied that there are exceptional circumstances, this time limit may be extended by a further six months. Hearings shall be in private. A rights commissioner's recommendation shall

1. Declare that the complaint was or was not well founded;

2. Order the employer to take a specific form of action;

3. Order the employer to pay the employee compensation of such amount (if any) as is just and equitable having regard to all the circumstances.

These sections also apply to the new owner of a business where the contravention took place prior to the change of ownership of the business. The rights commissioner shall furnish the Employment Appeals Tribunal with a copy of any recommendation.

A recommendation of a rights commissioner may be appealed to the Employment Appeals Tribunal within six weeks of the date of communication of the recommendation to the parties concerned. Form T1-B may be used.

Where a recommendation of a rights commissioner has not been carried out in accordance with its terms and where the time limit for bringing an appeal has expired, the matter may be referred to the Tribunal and a determination issued in the same terms as the recommendation. The Tribunal will not hear the evidence of the employer other than in relation to the non-implementation of the rights commissioner's recommendation.

Organisation of Working Time Act, 1997

An employee or trade union on behalf of its member may present a complaint to a rights commissioner that the employer has contravened one of the relevant provisions of the Act. The "relevant provisions" are the provision of compensatory rest periods (under section 6(2)); daily rest periods (section 11); rests and intervals at work (section 12); weekly rest periods (section 13); compensation for Sunday work (section 14); weekly working hours (section 15); nightly working hours (section 16); provision of information in relation to working time (section 17); provisions in relation to zero hours working practices (section 18); entitlement to annual leave (section 19); times and pay for annual leave (section 20); entitlement in respect of public holidays (sections 21 and 22); compensation for holidays on cesser of employment (section 23); a refusal by an employee to co-operate with the employer in breaching the Act (section 26); compensatory rest periods as provided for in any regulations, collective agreement, registered employment agreement or employment regulation order in respect of any exempted activity (section 6(1)); or an employee's request for a health assessment where the employee is expected to work an average of 48 hours in any period of seven days (paragraph 9 of the Fifth Schedule).

Notices of complaint must be in writing and contain the names and addresses of the employee and employer. The claim must be referred to the rights commissioner within six months of the date of the alleged contravention of the Act. The rights commissioner may extend this time limit to 12 months if there is reasonable cause for the delay in the reference of the complaint. The employee must first refer the matter to the employer before reference to a rights commissioner. The employee shall state the claim and under what heading it falls:

1. Rest periods and Sunday work;

2. Minimum and maximum working hours;

3. Holidays;

4. Refusal by an employee to co-operate with employer in breaching the Act.

The rights commissioner shall hear the parties to include any trade union of which the employee is a member. Hearings are private and the rights commissioner shall give the Labour Court a copy of each decision.

The Minister may present these same complaints to a rights commissioner where the matter had not been referred to a rights commissioner by the employee or their trade union and where it appears to the Minister that the employer is not complying with any of the relevant provisions. Such references occur where it would be unreasonable to expect the employee or their trade union to make the reference (section 31).

A decision of a rights commissioner shall do one or more of the following:

1. Declare that the complaint was or was not well founded;

2. Require the employer to comply with the relevant provisions;

3. Require the employer to pay the employee compensation as is just and equitable having regard to all the circumstances but not ex-

ceeding two years' remuneration in respect of the employee's employment.

These sections also apply to the new owner of a business where the contravention took place prior to the change of ownership of the business.

A decision of a rights commissioner may be appealed to the Labour Court within six weeks of the date of communication of the decision to the parties.

Parental Leave Act, 1998

A dispute or difference between an employer and employee relating to a dispute concerning entitlements under the Act shall be referred to a rights commissioner. Employees who are members of the Defence Forces may not refer such a dispute to a rights commissioner. Disputes relating to a dismissal or redundancy notice and minimum notice claims may not be referred to a rights commissioner (s. 18).

The rights commissioner will hear the parties to a claim and will make a decision concerning redress as follows:

a) The grant of parental leave of such length to be taken at such time or times and in such manner as may be so specified. A rights commissioner may direct that parental leave may take place when a child is older if the employee has been ill or incapacitated; may alter the timing of parental leave if there would be a substantial adverse impact in the employment or if there is a serious change in the circumstances of the employee.

b) An award of compensation in favour of the employee to be paid by the employer up to a maximum of 20 week remuneration calculated in accordance with the Parental Leave (Maximum Compensation) Regulations, 1999 (SI No. 34 of 1999).

Complaints Procedure

The employee must give notice in writing to the rights commissioner not later than six months after the occurrence of the dispute.

The form used is the Notice of Complaint to a rights commissioner under the Parental Leave Act, 1998 (see page 542); the Parental Leave (Disputes and Appeals) Regulations, 1999 (SI No. 6 of 1999) provides that this notice shall specify the nature of the dispute. If the dispute refers to parental leave, details must be provided in respect of date of commencement of employment, date of child's birth or adoption order, details of parental leave sought or granted and details of notices given and confirmed.

If the dispute refers to *force majeure* leave, details must be provided in respect of the name and address of the injured/ill person, relationship with the employee, the nature of the illness and period of *force majeure* leave to be taken.

The rights commissioner may request further oral or written submissions and request the production of documents. If either party does not attend the hearing, the rights commissioner may proceed in their absence and may draw such inference as appears prior from a failure or refusal by a party to comply with such request.

When a party to a dispute (usually the employer) receives a notice of the Notice in writing of the dispute, they shall within 14 days of receipt of the notice indicate whether they intend contesting the dispute and the grounds of defence to the rights commissioner who shall copy it to the claimant.

The rights commission's decision may be appealed to the Employment Appeals Tribunal within four weeks of the date of receipt of the decision. Form T1-B may be used for this purpose, but at the time of going to print, the Form has not been amended for appeals under this Act. It should be stated it is an appeal under the Parental Leave Act, 1998. If the decision of a rights commissioner has not been carried out and if the time period for the bringing of an appeal has expired, then the employer/employee or the Minister (where appropriate) may make application to the Circuit Court for an Order directing the party in default to carry out the terms of the decision. Where compensation was due to be paid, under the Courts Act, 1981, interest shall be paid for a period dating from four weeks from the date of the decision.

If there was a dismissal arising from adoptive leave, a claim should be brought under the Unfair Dismissals legislation.

Protections for Persons Reporting Child Abuse Act, 1998

This Act confers protection from civil liability on persons who report child abuse (see Chapter 17, "Unfair Dismissal"). An employer shall not penalise an employee for forming an opinion in relation to alleged child abuse and for having communicated it to an appropriate person, provided that the employee has acted reasonably and in good faith. If an employee is penalised by dismissal, they may have relief under this Act or under the Unfair Dismissals Acts, 1977–1993. An employee may present a complaint to a rights commissioner that their employer has contravened the Protections for Persons Reporting Child Abuse Act, 1998. The rights commissioner shall hear the complaint and give a decision. The rights commissioner can declare that the complaint was or was not well founded; may require the employer to take appropriate steps (e.g. reinstatement of the employee) and may require the employer to pay up to 104 weeks' compensation based on calculation in accordance with the Unfair Dismissals Acts, 1977–1993 (see above). A complaint must be presented within 12 months beginning on the date of the contravention of this Act, unless exceptional circumstances apply where the period may be extended by a further six months. The Terms of Employment (Information) (Appeals and Complaints) Regulations, 1994 (SI No. 244 of 1994), apply. The same rules apply as under the 1994 Act except that a hearing before the Employment Appeals Tribunal shall be in private. A Notice of Complaint and Notice of Appeal may be used as under the 1994 Act, suitably amended.

LABOUR COURT

The Labour Court was established under the Industrial Relations Act, 1946, to assist in the resolution of industrial disputes and to uphold good standards in industrial relations.

The Court consists of a chairperson and, currently, two deputy chairpersons. There are six members of the Court who are appointed by the Minister for Trade, Enterprise and Employment on the nomination of the Irish Business and Employers' Confederation and the Irish Congress of Trade Unions. These are known as employer or employee members and are experienced union and employer organisation officials or industrial relations specialists. The Court works in divisions with each division comprising the chairperson, or vice chairperson, and an employer and employee member. The members of the Court are not lawyers but the court has a legally qualified registrar who advises on legal issues. The Court can appoint technical assessors (usually specialist advisors) if it so wishes, as long as the advice is put to the parties to the dispute for their comment (see *The State (Cole)* v *The Labour Court* (1984) 3 JISLL 128).

Industrial relations matters are first referred to the Labour Relations Commission and, if matters are not settled at this stage and if the Commission is satisfied that no further efforts on its part will advance the resolution of the dispute, then the matter may be referred to the Labour Court. Both sides must agree to the Labour Court hearing the dispute. The Court will then hear the matter and issue a non-binding recommendation, which may not be appealed to a court of law. If either party to a dispute does not agree to go to conciliation, one party may refer the matter to the Court for adjudication (section 20 of the Industrial Relations Act, 1969). The Court's recommendation is binding on the parties.

A rights commissioner's recommendation (individual grievances under the Industrial Relations Act, 1969) may be appealed to the Court and the Court's recommendation is binding on the parties.

Labour Court hearings are normally held in private but either side may make application to have the hearing held in public. The Labour Court hears cases in its premises in Dublin (Beggars Bush, Haddington Road) and sits around the country as is convenient to the parties. Both parties provide written submissions to the Court; evidence is not heard by the Court as it is in a court of law. The Court also has power to summon witnesses who may be obliged to bring documents to a hearing. An application must be made personally to the Court. The Court can also hear evidence on oath, but this is unusual.

Under the equality legislation, the Court acts as a quasi-judicial body, akin to the Employment Appeals Tribunal (see Chapter 24, "Equal Pay and Equal Treatment Claims").

Organisation of Working Time Act, 1997

The Court has a new jurisdiction under the Organisation of Working Time Act, 1997, where a person may appeal a decision of a rights commissioner. The Labour Court shall have procedures concerning appeals under this Act, which appeal must be submitted in writing within six weeks of the date of the rights commissioner's decision. The written appeal must state the intention of the party to appeal against the decision. The Minister may at the request of the Labour Court refer a question of law arising in proceedings before it to the High Court for determination by the High Court, which determination shall be final and conclusive.

A Labour Court determination may be appealed to the High Court on a point of law; that determination shall be final and conclusive.

Section 39(17) of the Redundancy Payments Act, 1967, shall apply to proceedings before the Labour Court (see Chapter 23, "The Employment Appeals Tribunal"). This section provides that the Labour Court may hear evidence on oath; any person who upon examination on oath wilfully and corruptly gives false evidence or wilfully and corruptly swears anything that is false shall on conviction be liable for penalties for wilful and corrupt perjury. The Labour Court may also issue subpoenas to any person to attend and give evidence or to produce any documents in his possession, custody or control, which relate to any matter before the Court. If a person fails to attend or to produce such documents, they shall be guilty of an offence and liable on summary conviction to a fine of £1,500. Where a person is being prosecuted in respect of their failure to attend a Labour Court hearing where they have been required to attend by the Court or where they attended and refused to give evidence or where they failed to produce a requested document, then a document signed by the chairman or registrar of the Labour Court shall be evidence of the failure without further proof.

The Labour Court shall publish its determinations in such a manner as it thinks fit.

Enforcement

Where a decision of a rights commissioner has not been carried out in accordance with its terms and the time period for bringing an appeal (six weeks) has expired and no appeal has been brought, the employee may bring the complaint, in writing, to the Labour Court. The Court shall only hear evidence about the non-implementation of the rights commissioner's decision and shall make a determination the same as the decision. The Court shall not hear any evidence on behalf of the employer.

If an employer fails to implement a Labour Court determination within six weeks of the date of communication to the parties, application may be made to the Circuit Court by

1. The employee concerned

2. Any trade union of which the employee is a member (with the consent of the employee), or

3. The Minister, if the Minister considers it appropriate to make the application having regard to all the circumstances.

The Labour Court can, without hearing the employee or any evidence (other than in relation to the non-implementation of the determination), make an order directing the employer to carry out the determination in accordance with its terms.

This of course only applies where the time limit has expired for the bringing of an appeal in respect of the Labour Court determination or where the appeal has been abandoned. The Circuit Court shall, where it considers appropriate, award interest under the Courts Act, 1981, in respect of compensation for a period dating from six weeks from the date of the determination of the Labour Court. Application is made to the judge of the Circuit Court where the employer ordinarily resides or carries on any profession, business or occupation.

POWER OF "RELEVANT AUTHORITIES"

Any party may make application to a rights commissioner, the Employment Appeals Tribunal or the Labour Court (the "relevant authorities") to amend the name of the employer where it is incorrect or where there is any other material particular to be amended. This may apply to any decision under the following Acts:

1. Adoptive Leave Act, 1995

2. Maternity Protection Act, 1994

3. Minimum Notice and Terms of Employment Acts, 1973 to 1991

4. Organisation of Working Time Act, 1997

5. Payment of Wages Act, 1991

6. Protection of Employees (Employer's Insolvency) Acts, 1984 to 1991

7. Protection of Young Persons (Employment) Act, 1996

8. Redundancy Payments Acts, 1967 to 1991

9. Terms of Employment (Information) Act, 1994

10. Unfair Dismissals Acts, 1977 to 1993

11. Worker Protection (Regular Part-Time Employees) Act, 1991.

This power shall not be exercised if it would result in a person being denied an opportunity to be heard in the proceedings; for example, where the employer became the subject of any requirement or direction contained in the decision. If an employee wishes to claim for relief under any of these Acts (having already issued proceedings) and the employee was not given an opportunity to be heard where this was due to the incorrect statement in the notice of the name of the employer or any other particular necessary to identify the employer, and where the misstatement was due to a mistake, the employee may apply to the relevant authority for leave to institute proceedings against the correct person. The authority may grant leave to institute the proceedings even though the employee may be out of time,

> provided that the relevant authority shall not grant such leave to that employee if it is of the opinion that to do so would result in an injustice being done to the proposed respondent.

This is a particularly useful addition to the above legislation, as it may happen that the employee issues proceedings against the wrong employer (e.g., against a company that is not technically the employer or where the correct name of the employer may not be actually known). It may happen that this deficiency only becomes known to the employee at the hearing and outside the statutory limit for bringing a fresh claim. Hence this amendment may rectify such a situation. It is also particularly useful where employees are representing themselves.

(This power is contained in section 39 of the Organisation of Working Time Act, 1997.)

THE LABOUR RELATIONS COMMISSION
An Coimisiún um Chaidreamh Oibreachais

TOM JOHNSON HOUSE, HADDINGTON ROAD, DUBLIN 4. TEL: 01-660 9662 FAX: 01-668 5069
Teach Thomás Mac Seáin, Bóthar Haddington, Baile Átha Cliath 4. Tel: 01-660 9662 Fax: 01-668 5069
E-mail: lrc@indigo.ie   LoCall (outside 01 area) 1890 220 227

Please read carefully:
All completed forms to be returned to: Rights Commissioner Service, Labour Relations Commission, Tom Johnson House, Haddington Road, Dublin 4.

Have you completed the correct form. If you are in doubt seek information from the Information Unit at the Department of Enterprise, Trade and Employment, Davitt House, Adelaide Road, Dublin 2:Tel: 01 - 6312121

The Rights Commissioners deal with matters (disputes, complaints and claims) arising under the:

Industrial Relations Acts, 1969 and 1990
Unfair Dismissal Acts, 1977 to 1993
Payment of Wages Act, 1991
Maternity Protection Act, 1994
Terms of Employment (Information) Act, 1994
Adoptive Leave Act, 1995
Protection of Young Persons (Employment) Act, 1996
Organisation of Working Time Act, 1997
Parental Leave Act, 1998

You may bring a representative at your own expense to a hearing (a relation, friend, colleague, union official, solicitor). Be sure to bring all documentation regarding your employment to the hearing.

If you decide not to proceed with your dispute please notify us in writing quoting the reference number.

This office will not offer any advice to you regarding your entitlements. It will **only** deal with matters concerning the processing of any claim you make.

Be sure that you have processed as far as possible any issue you have with your employer before you make an official reference to this office.

If you require information, you may contact Information Unit at the Department of Enterprise, Trade and Employment on 01-6614444.

Once a dispute or complaint has been lodged then it will be processed and a date set. Unless the case is withdrawn then the hearing will proceed.

Rights commissioners hearings take place with you and your employer (and representatives, if any) present, together with the commissioner.

The hearings are formal but can take place in a relaxed manner.

The rights commissioner can only consider matters which you state in front of everybody present when issuing a decision or recommendation.

After the recommendation (decision) is issued to you in writing, this office has no further role to play. Appeals should be made as directed to you by the rights commissioner, within the specified time limits.

If you have any change of address (or telephone number) after submitting your application, please inform this office immediately.

If your employer is going into liquidation or receivership please obtain any details you can before the hearing.

THE LABOUR RELATIONS COMMISSION
An Coimisiún um Chaidreamh Oibreachais

TOM JOHNSON HOUSE, HADDINGTON ROAD, DUBLIN 4.
Teach Thomás Mac Seáin, Bóthar Haddington, Baile Átha Cliath 4.

TEL: 01-613 6700   FAX: 01-613 6701

E-mail: lrc@indigo.ie   Website: http://www.lrc.ie   LoCall (outside 01 area) 1890 220 227

APPLICATION TO RIGHTS COMMISSIONER

INDUSTRIAL RELATIONS ACTS 1969 AND 1990

(PLEASE USE BLOCK CAPITALS)

NAME: _____   NAME OF COMPANY/
                                 EMPLOYER: _____

ADDRESS: _____   ADDRESS: _____

_____   _____

_____   _____

TEL NO: _____   TEL NO: _____

NAME AND ADDRESS OF YOUR REPRESENTATIVE (IF ANY): _____
_____

DATE ON WHICH EMPLOYMENT BEGAN: _____

DATE ON WHICH EMPLOYMENT ENDED *(IF APPLICABLE)* : _____

PAY (INCLUDING BENEFITS AND REGULAR OVERTIME) PER WEEK £_____GROSS
                                                        £_____TAKE HOME

MY DISPUTE IS THAT:

_____

_____

_____

_____

_____

EMPLOYEE'S SIGNATURE: _____   DATE: _____

**PLEASE NOTE THAT A COPY OF THIS FORM WILL BE FORWARDED TO YOUR
EMPLOYER.**

Commission Members: Catherine Forde (Chairperson), Liam Downey, Prof. Joyce O'Connor, Turlough O'Sullivan, Dr. Mary Redmond, Jimmy Somers, Tom Wall.

Chief Executive: Kieran Mulvey

THE LABOUR RELATIONS COMMISSION
An Coimisiún um Chaidreamh Oibreachais

TOM JOHNSON HOUSE, HADDINGTON ROAD, DUBLIN 4. TEL: 01-660 9662 FAX: 01-668 5069
Teach Thomás Mac Seáin, Bóthar Haddington, Baile Átha Cliath 4. Tel: 01-660 9662 Fax: 01-668 5069
E-mail: lrc@indigo.ie   LoCall (outside 01 area) 1890 220 227

APPLICATION TO RIGHTS COMMISSIONER

UNFAIR DISMISSALS ACTS 1977 - 1993

(PLEASE USE BLOCK CAPITALS)

NAME: _____   **NAME OF COMPANY/**
                                              EMPLOYER: _____

ADDRESS: _____   **ADDRESS:** _____

                _____   _____

                _____   _____

TEL NO: _____   **TEL NO:** _____

NAME & ADDRESS OF YOUR REPRESENTATIVES (IF ANY) _____
_____

DATE ON WHICH EMPLOYMENT BEGAN: / /

DATE OF DISMISSAL: / /

PAY (INCLUDING BENEFITS AND REGULAR OVERTIME) PER WEEK: £ _____GROSS
                                                        £ _____TAKE HOME
REDRESS SOUGHT (RE-INSTATEMENT, RE-ENGAGEMENT, OR COMPENSATION)____
_____

HAVE YOU TAKEN UP NEW EMPLOYMENT SINCE YOUR DISMISSAL:

IF YES, WHEN: _____

AT WHAT RATE OF PAY: _____
THE GROUNDS OF MY CLAIM ARE AS FOLLOWS:

_____
_____
_____
_____

EMPLOYEE'S SIGNATURE: _____   **DATE:** _____

PLEASE NOTE THAT A COPY OF THIS FORM WILL BE FORWARDED TO YOUR EMPLOYER.

Commission Members: Catherine Forde (Chairperson), Liam Downey, Prof. Joyce O'Connor, Turlough O'Sullivan, Dr. Mary Redmond, Jimmy Somers, Tom Wall.

Chief Executive: Kieran Mulvey

THE LABOUR RELATIONS COMMISSION
An Coimisiún um Chaidreamh Oibreachais

TOM JOHNSON HOUSE, HADDINGTON ROAD, DUBLIN 4.
Teach Thomás Mac Seáin, Bóthar Haddington, Baile Átha Cliath 4.
TEL: 01-613 6700   FAX: 01-613 6701
E-mail: lrc@indigo.ie   Website: http://www.lrc.ie   LoCall (outside 01 area) 1890 220 227

> **NOTICE OF COMPLAINT TO RIGHTS COMMISSIONER**
> **PAYMENT OF WAGES ACT 1991**

NAME: _____   NAME OF COMPANY OR EMPLOYER:_____
                         FULL LEGAL NAME, IF IN DOUBT
                         CONSULT YOUR P60 OR P45)

ADDRESS:_____   ADDRESS: _____

                                                     _____

                                                     _____

TEL NO: _____   TEL NO: _____

I wish to present a complaint to a Rights Commissioner that my employer contravened
the above Act in relation to A OR B below.
(Please complete appropriate section).

N.B.: Your employer should be made aware of the claim prior to making this complaint
          to a Rights Commissioner.

(A)   DEDUCTION FROM PAY   DATE OF DEDUCTION _____

        AMOUNT OF DEDUCTION £_____   DID YOU RECEIVE NOTICE
                                                          INTENT TO MAKE THE DEDUCTION

        WHAT WAS THE REASON FOR THE   YES   NO
        DEDUCTION? please specify
        _____   IF YES HOW MUCH NOTICE?
        _____   _____

                                  OR

(B)   ARE YOU MAKING A CLAIM FOR   DATE PAYMENT SHOULD
        NON PAYMENT OF   HAVE BEEN RECEIVED

        (Please calculate monies due)   _____ / _____ / _____

        1.   WAGES/PAY   AMOUNT £ _____
        2.   MINIMUM NOTICE   AMOUNT £ _____
        3.   HOLIDAY PAY   AMOUNT £ _____
        4.   OTHER   AMOUNT £ _____
        If 4 please specify _____

        TOTAL AMOUNT £ _____

SIGNATURE: _____

DATE: _____

THE LABOUR RELATIONS COMMISSION
An Coimisiún um Chaidreamh Oibreachais

TOM JOHNSON HOUSE, HADDINGTON ROAD, DUBLIN 4. **TEL: 01-660 9662 FAX: 01-668 5069**
Teach Thomás Mac Seáin, Bóthar Haddington, Baile Átha Cliath 4. Tel: 01-660 9662 Fax: 01-668 5069
E-mail: lrc@indigo.ie   LoCall (outside 01 area) 1890 220 227

NOTICE OF COMPLAINT TO A RIGHTS COMMISSIONER UNDER

THE TERMS OF EMPLOYMENT (INFORMATION) ACT, 1994

(PLEASE USE BLOCK CAPITALS)

NAME: _____

NAME OF COMPANY/
EMPLOYER _____
(FULL LEGAL NAME IF IN DOUBT CONSULT YOUR
P45 OR P60)

ADDRESS: _____

ADDRESS: _____

_____

_____

_____

_____

TEL NO: _____

TEL NO: _____

NAME AND ADDRESS OF REPRESENTATIVE (IF ANY) _____

DATE ON WHICH EMPLOYMENT BEGAN: _/_/_

DATE ON WHICH YOU REQUESTED STATEMENT: _/_/_

(A)   HOW HAS YOUR EMPLOYER FAILED TO COMPLY WITH THE REQUIREMENT
TO GIVE YOU A WRITTEN STATEMENT? _____
_____
_____
_____

(B)   MY COMPLAINT IS THAT CHANGES WERE MADE TO MY WRITTEN
STATEMENT WITHOUT NOTIFICATION (SECTION 5). PLEASE DESCRIBE YOUR
COMPLAINT. _____
_____
_____
_____

SIGNATURE: _____   DATE: _____

PLEASE NOTE THAT A COPY OF THIS FORM WILL BE FORWARDED TO YOUR
EMPLOYER.

THE LABOUR RELATIONS COMMISSION
An Coimisiún um Chaidreamh Oibreachais

TOM JOHNSON HOUSE, HADDINGTON ROAD, DUBLIN 4
Teach Thomás Mac Seáin, Bóthar Haddington, Baile Átha Cliath 4.
TEL: 01-613 6700   FAX: 01-613 6701
E-mail: lrc@indigo.ie   Website: http://www.lrc.ie   LoCall (outside 01 area) 1890 220 227

APPLICATION TO RIGHTS COMMISSIONER

MATERNITY PROTECTION ACT 1994

(PLEASE USE BLOCK CAPITALS)

NAME:_____   NAME OF COMPANY/
                                 EMPLOYER: _____

ADDRESS: _____   ADDRESS: _____

         _____   _____

         _____   _____

TEL NO: _____   TEL NO: _____

NAME AND ADDRESS OF YOUR REPRESENTATIVE (IF ANY) _____
_____

EMPLOYMENT DETAILS

EMPLOYMENT BEGAN: _/_/_

EMPLOYMENT ENDED: _/_/_   [if applicable]

Pay (including benefits and regular overtime) per week:£_____GROSS
                                       £_____TAKE HOME

MY DISPUTE IS THAT:

_____

_____

_____

_____

_____

SIGNATURE:_____   DATE:_____

PLEASE NOTE THAT A COPY OF THIS FORM WILL BE FORWARDED TO YOUR EMPLOYER.

Commission Members: Catherine Forde (Chairperson), Liam Downey, Prof. Joyce O'Connor, Turlough O'Sullivan, Dr. Mary Redmond, Jimmy Somers, Tom Wall.

Chief Executive: Kieran Mulvey

THE LABOUR RELATIONS COMMISSION
An Coimisiún um Chaidreamh Oibreachais

TOM JOHNSON HOUSE, HADDINGTON ROAD, DUBLIN 4. TEL: 01-660 9662 FAX: 01-668 5069
Teach Thomds Mac Sedin, Bóthar Haddington, Baile Átha Cliath 4. Tel: 01-660 9662 Fax: 01-668 5069
E-mail: lrc@indigo.ie

NOTICE OF COMPLAINT TO A RIGHTS COMMISSIONER UNDER
ADOPTIVE LEAVE ACT, 1995

(PLEASE USE BLOCK CAPITALS)

NAME: _____

NAME OF COMPANY/
EMPLOYER _____
(FULL LEGAL NAME IF IN DOUBT CONSULT YOUR
P45 OR P60)

ADDRESS:_____

ADDRESS: _____

_____

_____

_____

_____

TEL NO: _____

TEL NO: _____

NAME AND ADDRESS OF REPRESENTATIVE (IF ANY)_____

_____

DATE ON WHICH EMPLOYMENT BEGAN: _/_/_

(A) MY DISPUTE RELATES TO ADOPTIVE LEAVE (PART II OF THE ACT) AND IS AS
FOLLOWS:_____

_____

_____

_____

_____

(B) MY DISPUTE RELATES TO THE PROVISIONS OF MY EMPLOYMENT CONTRACT
(PART III OF THE ACT) AND IS AS FOLLOWS:_____

_____

_____

_____

_____

SIGNATURE: _____   DATE: _____

PLEASE NOTE THAT A COPY OF THIS FORM WILL BE FORWARDED TO YOUR
EMPLOYER.

Commission Members: Catherine Foyle (Chairperson), Liam Downey, Kevin Duffy, Prof. Joyce O'Connor, Turlough O'Sullivan, Dr. Mary Redmond, Jimmy Somers

Chief Executive: Kieran Mulvey

THE LABOUR RELATIONS COMMISSION
An Coimisiún um Chaidreamh Oibreachais

TOM JOHNSON HOUSE, HADDINGTON ROAD, DUBLIN 4. TEL: 01-660 9662 FAX: 01-668 5069
Teach Thomás Mac Seáin, Bóthar Haddington, Baile Átha Cliath 4. Tel: 01-660 9662 Fax: 01-668 5069
E-mail: lrc@indigo.ie

APPLICATION TO RIGHTS COMMISSIONER

THE PROTECTION OF YOUNG PERSONS (EMPLOYMENT) ACT, 1996

(PLEASE USE BLOCK CAPITALS)

NAME: _____

NAME OF COMPANY
OR EMPLOYER: _____
(FULL LEGAL NAME, IF IN DOUBT CONSULT
YOUR P60 OR P45)

ADDRESS: _____   ADDRESS: _____

_____   _____

_____   _____

TEL NO: _____   TEL NO: _____

NAME AND ADDRESS OF YOUR REPRESENTATIVE (IF ANY) _____

I WISH TO MAKE A COMPLAINT TO A RIGHTS COMMISSIONER THAT MY EMPLOYER
CONTRAVENED THE ABOVE ACT IN RELATION TO A OR B BELOW.

(PLEASE COMPLETE APPROPRIATE SECTION)

(A)   SECTION 13 (PRESERVATION OF EXISTING RATES OF PAY AND CONDITIONS)

       IN WHAT WAY HAS YOUR EMPLOYER BEEN IN BREACH OF THIS SECTION?
       _____
       _____
       _____
       _____

(B)   SECTION 17 (REFUSAL TO CO-OPERATE WITH THE EMPLOYER IN BREACHING
       THE ACT)

       IN WHAT WAY HAS YOUR EMPLOYER BEEN IN BREACH OF THIS SECTION?
       _____
       _____
       _____
       _____

EMPLOYEES SIGNATURE:_____   DATE:_____

PLEASE NOTE THAT A COPY OF THIS FORM WILL BE FORWARDED TO YOUR
EMPLOYER.

Commission Members: Catherine Forde (Chairperson), Liam Downey, Kevin Duffy, Prof. Joyce O'Connor, Turlough O'Sullivan, Dr. Mary Redmond, Jimmy Somers

Chief Executive: Kieran Mulvey

THE LABOUR RELATIONS COMMISSION
An Coimisiún um Chaidreamh Oibreachais

TOM JOHNSON HOUSE, HADDINGTON ROAD, DUBLIN 4.
Teach Thomás Mac Seáin, Bóthar Haddington, Baile Átha Cliath 4.

TEL: 01-613 6700   FAX: 01-613 6701

E-mail: lrc@indigo.ie   Website: http://www.lrc.ie   LoCall (outside 01 area) 1890 220 227

NOTICE OF COMPLAINT TO RIGHTS COMMISSIONER

ORGANISATION OF WORKING TIME ACT, 1997

(PLEASE USE BLOCK CAPITALS)

NAME: _____

NAME OF COMPANY/
EMPLOYER: _____

ADDRESS: _____

ADDRESS: _____

_____   _____

_____   _____

TEL NO: _____

TEL NO: _____

I WISH TO PRESENT A COMPLAINT TO A RIGHTS COMMISSIONER THAT MY EMPLOYER CONTRAVENED THE ABOVE ACT IN RELATION TO A OR B OR C BELOW. (PLEASE COMPLETE APPROPRIATE SECTION).

N.B. YOUR EMPLOYER SHOULD BE MADE AWARE OF THE CLAIM PRIOR TO MAKING THIS COMPLAINT TO A RIGHTS COMMISSIONER.

(A)   REST PERIODS AND SUNDAY WORK (SECTIONS 6(1) and 6(2) and 11 TO 14 OF THE ACT)
MY COMPLAINT IS THAT: _____
_____
_____

(B)   MINIMUM AND MAXIMUM WORKING HOURS (SECTIONS 15 TO 18 OF THE ACT)
MY COMPLAINT IS THAT: _____
_____
_____

(C)   HOLIDAYS (SECTIONS 19 TO 23 OF THE ACT)
MY COMPLAINT IS THAT: _____
_____
_____

(D)   OTHER (FOR EXAMPLE, SECTION 26 ON PARAGRAPH 1 OF THE FIFTH SCHEDULE OF THE ACT)
MY COMPLAINT IS THAT: _____
_____
_____

SIGNATURE: _____   DATE: _____

PLEASE NOTE A COPY OF THIS FORM WILL BE FORWARDED TO YOUR EMPLOYER

Commission Members: Catherine Forde (Chairperson), Liam Downey, Prof. Joyce O'Connor, Turlough O'Sullivan, Dr. Mary Redmond, Jimmy Somers, Tom Wall.

Chief Executive: Kieran Mulvey

THE LABOUR RELATIONS COMMISSION
An Coimisiún um Chaidreamh Oibreachais

TOM JOHNSON HOUSE, HADDINGTON ROAD, DUBLIN 4.
Teach Thomás Mac Seáin, Bóthar Haddington, Baile Átha Cliath 4.
TEL: 01-613 6700   FAX: 01-613 6701
E-mail: lrc@indigo.ie   Website: http://www.lrc.ie   LoCall (outside 01 area) 1890 220 227

NOTICE OF COMPLAINT TO RIGHTS COMMISSIONER

PARENTAL LEAVE ACT, 1998

(PLEASE USE BLOCK CAPITALS)

NAME: _____   NAME OF COMPANY/
                                      EMPLOYER: _____
ADDRESS: _____   ADDRESS: _____

               _____   _____

               _____   _____

TEL NO: _____   TEL NO: _____

I WISH TO PRESENT A DISPUTE TO A RIGHTS COMMISSIONER THAT MY EMPLOYER CONTRAVENED THE ABOVE ACT.

N.B. IS YOUR EMPLOYER AWARE THAT YOU ARE BRINGING THIS DISPUTE TO A RIGHTS COMMISSIONER.?

1) WHEN DID YOU JOIN THE ORGANISATION _____

2) NAME OF THE CHILD TO WHOM THIS DISPUTE RELATES _____

3) DATE OF CHILD'S BIRTH _____(THIS ACT DOES NOT APPLY TO CHILDREN BORN BEFORE 3RD JUNE 1996, OR TO THOSE WHO HAVE NOW REACHED 5 YEARS OF AGE)

PLEASE ENCLOSE A COPY OF THE CHILD'S BIRTH CERTIFICATE

4) WHAT PERIOD OF PARENTAL LEAVE DID YOU SEEK? _____
    (SECTION 7 OF THE ACT)

5) DID YOU GIVE WRITTEN NOTICE TO YOUR EMPLOYER AND WAS IT ACCEPTED?
    (SECTION8, (1) TO (5) OF THE ACT)_____

6) DID YOU RECEIVE A "CONFIRMATION DOCUMENT" FROM YOUR EMPLOYER?
    (SECTION 9, (1) TO (3)_____

7) WAS YOUR PARENTAL LEAVE TERMINATED?_____

8) MY DISPUTE (UNDER SECTIONS 7 TO 9) IS THAT: _____
_____
_____

9) (SECTION 13, FORCE MAJEURE LEAVE)
    MY DISPUTE IS THAT:
_____
_____
_____

PLEASE ENCLOSE COPIES OF ALL THE NOTICES GIVEN TO, AND RECEIVED FROM, YOUR EMPLOYER IN RELATION TO THIS DISPUTE (DO NOT SEND THE ORIGINALS)

SIGNATURE:_____   DATE:_____

PLEASE NOTE A COPY OF THIS FORM WILL BE FORWARDED TO YOUR EMPLOYER

In accordance with Statutory Instrument No 6 of 1999, Regulations entitled "Parental Leave (Disputes and Appeals) Regulations 1999" paragraph 4, employers are obliged to provide a notice of appearance within 14 days of receipt of this notice.

Commission Members: Catherine Forde (Chairperson), Liam Downey, Prof. Joyce O'Connor, Turlough O'Sullivan, Dr. Mary Redmond, Jimmy Somers, Tom Wall.

Chief Executive: Kieran Mulvey

THE LABOUR RELATIONS COMMISSION
An Coimisiún um Chaidreamh Oibreachais

TOM JOHNSON HOUSE, HADDINGTON ROAD, DUBLIN 4. TEL: 01-660 9662 FAX: 01-668 5069
Teach Thomás Mac Seáin, Bóthar Haddington, Baile Átha Cliath 4. Tel: 01-660 9662 Fax: 01-668 5069
E-mail: lrc@indigo.ie   LoCall (outside 01 area) 1890 220 227

NOTICE OF COMPLAINT TO A RIGHTS COMMISSIONER UNDER

PROTECTIONS FOR PERSONS REPORTING CHILD ABUSE ACT, 1998

(PLEASE USE BLOCK CAPITALS)

NAME: _____

NAME OF COMPANY/
EMPLOYER _____
(FULL LEGAL NAME IF IN DOUBT CONSULT YOUR
P45 OR P60)

ADDRESS:_____

ADDRESS: _____

_____

_____

_____

_____

TEL NO: _____

TEL NO: _____

NAME AND ADDRESS OF REPRESENTATIVE (IF ANY) _____

HOW HAS YOUR EMPLOYER PENALISED YOU IN CONTRAVENTION OF THE ACT?
(SECTION 4 (1))

_____

_____

_____

_____

_____

_____

_____

SIGNATURE:_____   DATE:_____

**PLEASE NOTE THAT A COPY OF THIS FORM WILL BE FORWARDED TO YOUR
EMPLOYER**

Commission Members: Catherine Forde (Chairperson), Liam Downey, Prof. Joyce O'Connor, Turlough O'Sullivan, Dr. Mary Redmond, Jimmy Somers, Tom Wall.

Chief Executive: Kieran Mulvey

Chapter Twenty-three

EMPLOYMENT APPEALS TRIBUNAL

The Employment Appeals Tribunal (the Tribunal) was formerly known as the Redundancy Appeals Tribunal and was renamed by the Unfair Dismissals Act, 1977. The Tribunal hears claims and appeals under the following Acts:

- Redundancy Payments Acts, 1967 to 1991;

- Minimum Notice and Terms of Employment Acts, 1973 to 1991;

- Unfair Dismissals Acts, 1977 to 1993;

- Protection of Employees (Employers' Insolvency) Acts, 1984 and 1991;

- Worker Protection (Regular Part-Time Employees) Act, 1991;

- Payment of Wages Act, 1991;

- Terms of Employment (Information) Act, 1994;

- Maternity Protection Act, 1994;

- Adoptive Leave Act, 1995;

- Protection of Young Persons (Employment) Act, 1996;

- Organisation of Working Time Act, 1997;

- Parental Leave Act, 1998;

- Protections for Persons Reporting Child Abuse Act, 1998.

The Tribunal consists of:

1. A chairperson who must be a solicitor or a barrister of not less than seven years' standing;

2. Nineteen vice-chairpersons, who may be solicitors or barristers
    (but not exclusively); and

3   Sixty ordinary members who are representative in equal numbers
    of employers and employees. The employer members are nomi-
    nated by employer organisations and the employee members by
    ICTU.

All members are appointed by the Minister of State at the Department of Enterprise, Trade and Employment (Enterprise, Trade and
Employment (Delegation of Ministerial Functions) (No. 2) Order,
1997 (SI No. 330 of 1997), usually for a three-year term.

The Tribunal sits by division, each division comprising the chairperson or a vice-chairperson, an employer and an employee member.
A secretary from the Tribunal secretariat is also in attendance.

This chapter describes the operation of the Tribunal and the various requirements to bring claims or appeals under the Acts listed
above. The text is arranged in the appropriate procedural sequence,
as opposed to considering each Act separately, in order to avoid unnecessary repetition. At the end of the chapter are a number of forms
(with notes as to important points to keep in mind), which are used to
bring claims under the various Acts.

WRITTEN REASON FOR DISMISSAL

A person who has been dismissed should write to their employer and
ask for the written reasons for the dismissal, as provided for in section 14 of the Unfair Dismissals Acts. An employer must respond in
writing within 14 days of this request. An employer does not have to
go into detail but must give a statement of the principal grounds for
dismissal. The next stage is for the former employee to consider
whether to bring a claim under the Unfair Dismissals Acts. At this
stage it would be prudent for the employee to seek advice from a solicitor or trade union official.

There may be another option to bringing a statutory unfair dismissal claim; that is, the case could be brought to the civil courts for
wrongful dismissal. The Unfair Dismissals (Amendment) Act, 1993,
provides that once either a rights commissioner has issued a recommendation or the Tribunal hearing has commenced, an employee
cannot bring a claim for wrongful dismissal. Alternatively, once a

court hearing has commenced for wrongful dismissal, an employee cannot bring a claim for unfair dismissal (see Chapter 17, "Unfair Dismissal").

POWER OF "RELEVANT AUTHORITIES"

Any party may make application to a rights commissioner, the Employment Appeals Tribunal or the Labour Court (the "relevant authorities") to amend the name of the employer where it is incorrect or where there is any other material particular to be amended (s. 39 of the Organisation of Working Time Act, 1997). This may apply to any decision under the following Acts:

- Adoptive Leave Act, 1995;

- Maternity Protection Act, 1994;

- Minimum Notice and Terms of Employment Acts, 1973 to 1991;

- Organisation of Working Time Act, 1997;

- Payment of Wages Act, 1991;

- Protection of Employees (Employer's Insolvency) Acts, 1984 to 1991;

- Protection of Young Persons (Employment) Act, 1996;

- Redundancy Payments Acts, 1967 to 1991;

- Terms of Employment (Information) Act, 1994;

- Unfair Dismissals Acts, 1977 to 1993;

- Worker Protection (Regular Part-Time Employees) Act, 1991.

This power shall not be exercised if it would result in a person being denied an opportunity to be heard in the proceedings; for example, where the employer became the subject of any requirement or direction contained in the decision. If an employee wishes to claim for relief under any of these Acts (having already issued proceedings) and the employee was not given an opportunity to be heard where this was due to the name of the employer or any other particular necessary to identify the employer having been incorrectly stated in the notice, and where the misstatement was further to an inadvertence, the employee may apply to the relevant authority for leave to institute proceedings against the correct person. The authority may grant leave to institute the proceedings, even though the employee may be out of time "provided that the relevant authority shall not grant such leave to that employee if it is of the opinion that to do so would result in an injustice being done to the proposed respondent" (s. 39(4)(b) of the Organisation of Working Time Act, 1997).

This is a particularly useful addition to the above legislation, as it may happen that the employee may issue proceedings against the wrong employer (e.g. against a company that is technically not the employer or where the correct name of the employer may not be actually known). It may happen that this deficiency only becomes known to the employee at hearing and outside the statutory limit for bringing a fresh claim. Hence this amendment may rectify such a situation. It is also particularly useful where employees are representing themselves.

HOW TO BRING A CLAIM

In order to bring a claim (appeals are considered below) an employee must get a copy of the T1-A form (new forms were published in November 1998 — see pages 569–70) which is available from the Tribunal offices or from employment exchanges. As stated above, there are various Acts — as listed below — under which a claimant (an employee or a former employee) can claim.

Unfair Dismissals Acts, 1977–1993

A claimant must have the requisite service and must have worked the appropriate hours, and six months must not have elapsed since the date of dismissal (see "Service of T1-A" below). The "date of dismissal" may be summarised as:

- Where prior notice has been given under the contract of employment and the Minimum Notice and Terms of Employment Acts, the date on which the notice expires.

- Where either notice was not given or the notice did not comply with the notice as provided for in the contract of employment or the Minimum Notice and Terms of Employment Acts, then the date of dismissal is the later of the dates to comply with the notice in the contract or the Acts.

- If there is not a renewal of a fixed-term or specified-purpose contract, the date of the expiry or the cesser.

The 1993 Act provides that the time limit may be extended to 12 months from the date of dismissal if the rights commissioner or the Tribunal considers that there are exceptional circumstances which prevented the service of the claim within the six months. The Tribunal takes a very strict view of applications for extension of time, and these may only arise in matters such as illness, etc., arising during the six-month period.

In *Byrne* v *PJ Quigley Ltd.* ([1995] ELR 205) the Employment Appeals Tribunal considered that:

1. The words "exceptional circumstances" are strong words and should be contrasted with the milder words "reasonably practicable" in the claimant's written submission or "reasonable cause" which permit the extension of time for lodging a redundancy claim under section 12(2)(b) of the Redundancy Payments Act, 1971.

   "Exceptional" means something out of the ordinary. At least the circumstances must be unusual, probably quite unusual, but not necessarily highly unusual.

2. (a) In order to extend the time, the Tribunal must be satisfied that the exceptional circumstances "prevented" lodging the claim within the general time limit. It is not sufficient if the exceptional circumstances cause or triggered the lodging of the claim.

   (b) It seems to follow that the exceptional circumstances involved must arise within the first six months, "the period aforesaid". If they arose later, they could not be said to "prevent" the claim being initiated within that period.

Minimum Notice and Terms of Employment Acts, 1973–1991

A claimant must have the necessary service, have worked the appropriate hours, and six years must not have elapsed since the notice monies were due.

Redundancy Payments Acts, 1967–1991

The claimant must have the necessary service, have worked the appropriate hours, and one year must not have elapsed since the date of dismissal. However, the one-year time limit may be extended by a further year if the Tribunal considers that there is reasonable cause in the delay in bringing the claim.

Worker Protection (Regular Part-Time Employees) Act, 1991

Claims under this Act are usually in respect of a request to the Tribunal to determine whether an employee has the necessary continuous service under the Act. If there is another claim, such as unfair dismissal, redundancy, minimum notice or holidays, this claim should be made under the other appropriate Act(s) at the same time.

Protection of Employees (Employers' Insolvency) Act, 1984–1991

A person claiming under any of the above named Acts in an insolvency situation should claim under this Act as well and the appropriate forms (see Chapter 21, "Employer Insolvency") should be sent to the liquidator at the same time. Before an employee can be in receipt of minimum notice, the Tribunal has to hear the claim and issue a written determination granting such compensation.

(It should be noted that Form T1-C — see pages 582–3 — may be used in the event of an appeal in respect of the Minister's decision against a payment from the Social Insurance fund (see Chapter 20, "Employer Insolvency"). However, the necessary claims or appeals must first be made to the rights commissioner or Tribunal as appropriate under the relevant legislation, e.g., minimum notice, unfair dismissal, etc.)

Organisation of Working Time Act, 1997

Claims may be made in the first instance under this Act to the Employment Appeals Tribunal where there is a claim in respect of holidays outstanding. The procedures that apply, for example, to an unfair dismissals claim will attach to the claim under the Organisation of Working Time Act, 1997. Awards may be up to two years' remuneration, as is just and equitable. The time limit is that applying to the other Act under which the former employee is claiming (e.g., redundancy, minimum notice, unfair dismissal — each of which has different time limits) (s. 40 of the Organisation of Working Time Act, 1997).

A proposed claimant may bring a claim under each of these Acts separately or at the same time. It is important to tick off the relevant box or boxes in the claim form (T1-A).

For example, a former employee who considers that they have been unfairly dismissed may bring a claim under the Unfair Dismissals Acts, but they may also consider that they did not receive appropriate notice or did not receive all the notice monies due to them or did not receive all their holidays. Thus, it is important that the employee ticks off both these boxes on the claim form; if the boxes are not ticked off, the employee technically has not brought a claim under the Acts.

COMPLETION OF FORM T1-A

We shall now consider the completion of Form T1-A, which is the document that actually commences proceedings before the Tribunal under the various Acts. It is extremely important that the employee (prospective claimant) fills it out correctly and that the employer checks all the relevant details on receipt of this form. As an aid to filling out the form, readers should refer to the author's notes following the form (see pages 571–6).

Employees may complete this form themselves, though it is more usual to contact a solicitor or union official for assistance in completion and the subsequent service of the form. That same representative would represent the employer at the hearing of the case and deal with all the paperwork in the preparation of it.

If a former employee is unable to obtain a blank Form T1-A, their claim may be brought by way of letter to the Tribunal clearly stating under what Act(s) the claim(s) is (are) being made, and all the details as laid out in the form on pages 569–70. It should be noted that this is not recommended but in exceptional circumstances it may be allowed.

SERVICE OF T1-A

Once the T1-A has been completed, it should be sent by registered post or delivered personally to the Tribunal in Dublin. A copy of the T1-A should be sent to the employer either by registered post or by hand. For an unfair dismissals claim, service must be within the six-month limitation period. The Tribunal may subsequently extend the time limit up to 12 months, but only in "exceptional circumstances". The Unfair Dismissals (Amendment) Act, 1993, provides that a copy of the T1-A shall be given to the employer as soon as possible after receipt by the Tribunal of the claim. This new provision suggests that the employer does not have to be served within the limitation period. However, it would be prudent to ensure that both the Tribunal and the employer are served within the limitation period. The statutory time limits under the other legislation are equally applicable.

There is a form RP51B that may be used by either an employer or an employee when appealing against a decision of the Minister for Enterprise, Trade and Employment in a redundancy matter. In practice, this form is normally used by employers appealing to the Tribunal contending that the deciding officer in the redundancy section of the Department did not allow them a full redundancy rebate (see Chapter 18, "Redundancy").

APPEAL OF RIGHTS COMMISSIONER'S RECOMMENDATION

In order to appeal a rights commissioner's recommendation/decision/direction, the new Form T1-B may be used. Details of appealing such recommendation/decision with the various different time limits under the various Acts are considered in Chapter 22, "Labour Relations Commission and the Labour Court". The form should be completed and served on both the Employment Appeals Tribunal and the other side within the statutory time limits (noting that the various Acts have different appeal periods).

If an employee is claiming holiday entitlement under the Organisation of Working time Act, 1997, they may do so at the same time as bringing the appeal.

IMPLEMENTATION OF RIGHTS COMMISSIONER'S RECOMMENDATION

The Unfair Dismissals (Amendment) Act, 1993, the Terms of Employment (Information) Act, 1994, and the Protection of Young Persons (Employment) Act provide that if a recommendation has not been carried out by an employer and the time limit for an appeal has expired, then it may be referred to the Tribunal for a determination to implement it. The Tribunal will not have to rehear the case and will issue the determination.

TITLES OF THE PARTIES

Once the claim form has been served, the former employee and the employer are now party to legal proceedings. Thus, they shall be called the claimant (the former employee) and the respondent (the employer). When there is an appeal of a rights commissioner's recommendation, the party bringing the appeal is the appellant and the other party is the respondent. However, for simplicity, the parties shall be called the claimant (the employee) and the respondent (the employer).

DEFENCE — NOTICE OF APPEARANCE — FORM T2

Once the employer has been served with a T1-A, a defence must be filed with the Tribunal. The regulations (Unfair Dismissals (Claims and Appeals) Regulations, 1977 — SI No. 286 of 1977) provide that the Notice of Appearance — see page 584–5 — must be filed with the Tribunal within 14 days. The various regulations under each of the Acts where there is either a claim or an appeal to the Tribunal (e.g., Parental Leave Act, 1998) provides that a defence must be served.

When the T1-A is served on the employer by the claimant, there is no "blank" T2 form attached. Thus the practice has arisen where on receipt of the T1-A, the Tribunal copies it to the employer attaching a blank T2 and allots a reference number to the case — for example, UD 1/1999 — which is shown on the T2. The Acts under which the claimant is claiming (appealing) are also marked by the Secretariat of the Tribunal. There is no obligation on the Tribunal to send the T2 to the respondent/employer, however, and to avoid difficulties with the 14-day limit, the practice has arisen of the employer/respondent writing a letter to the Tribunal on receipt of the T1-A/T1-B, advising that it intends to defend the claim(s) and briefly stating the grounds of defence. It is acceptable to file the defence by way of such letter.

The 1977 Regulations (as amended) state that:

> a party to a claim or appeal who does not enter an appearance to the claim or appeal . . . shall not be entitled to take part in or be present or be represented at any proceedings before the Tribunal in relation to the claim or appeal unless the Tribunal at its discretion otherwise decides.

While the Tribunal has discretion in relation to the non-entry of a Notice of Appearance, the Supreme Court in *Halal Meat Packers (Ballyhaunis) Ltd.* v *Employment Appeals Tribunal* ([1990] ILRM 293) held that it was the duty of all courts and tribunals to administer justice and that justice required both parties to be heard. Thus, one may conclude that generally the Tribunal must hear both parties. Nonetheless, it is advisable to enter a Notice of Appearance in good time.

The grounds of defence may be stated very simply, for example:

1. The claimant was dismissed for consistent lateness following warnings;

2. The claimant was dismissed for absenteeism;

3. The claimant was dismissed after a full and thorough investigation for allegedly taking company products;

4. The claimant is not entitled to a statutory redundancy payment as there is no redundancy situation;

5. The claimant is not entitled to notice monies as he was dismissed for gross misconduct.

Respondents may complete this form themselves but it is recommended that they obtain advice before doing so.

The respondent should also state the name of the person who will represent them at the hearing. It is advisable to have a solicitor, an employer organisation representative or an industrial relations expert handle all the paperwork and the preparation of the case from this point on.

The Notice of Appearance should be served on the Tribunal by registered post or by hand and the Tribunal will acknowledge its receipt. It is also good practice to copy it to the claimant's representative or to the claimant if they are not represented. If the respondent considers that the hearing of the claim will take more than a half day, the Tribunal should be so advised at this time. Such a request should not be taken lightly, as the Tribunal allots specific dates and times for hearings. The Tribunal will (as with all documents) send a copy to the other side.

In the rare circumstances where the respondent is conceding the claim(s), the appropriate section of the form may just be signed by the employer.

NOTICE OF HEARING

The next stage in the process is that the Tribunal secretariat will send out a Notice of Hearing (see page 586). This is an important document as it states the date, time and place of the hearing of the claim(s). Even though neither party has to be formally represented by lawyers or by their respective trade union or employer representatives at the hearing, they may still obtain representation at this time. There is no requirement to notify the Tribunal of such change, but if there is correspondence or if there are any difficulties, the Tribunal will contact the claimant or the respondent directly if there is no stated representative on record. If there is representation, the Tribunal will notify both the parties themselves and also the representatives.

ADJOURNMENTS

If the date of hearing does not suit either party, it may, after the receipt of the Notice of Hearing, make application to the Tribunal for an adjournment. Application must be made to the Tribunal in person. It is not permissible to write a letter, send a facsimile or telephone the Tribunal. Only a sitting division of the Tribunal can grant an adjournment of a case.

As the dates of hearings are fixed and the intent is to have a hearing as soon as possible, the Tribunal is very reluctant to grant adjournments. The Tribunal is even less likely to grant adjournments when the case is listed for hearing outside a major city, as the Tribunal may not visit that particular town very often and the claimant may have to wait a few months before the case is listed for hearing again. Adjournments are only given when the person applying has a good reason. They should also notify the other side and have a letter of consent (from the other side) to the application for the adjournment. It should be remembered that, if a party to the hearing or a necessary witness will not be available, the representative (claimant or respondent) must write to the Tribunal at an early stage of the proceedings so that the Tribunal knows what dates not to hear the case.

NOTICE TO ATTEND AND GIVE EVIDENCE

If either party needs a particular witness to give evidence, it may have to make application to a sitting division of the Tribunal for a Notice to Attend and Give Evidence (see page 587–8). This is commonly called a subpoena, translated from Latin meaning "under penalty". An individual who has been served with a subpoena and fails to turn up at the Tribunal to give evidence is committing an offence and is liable to a criminal conviction and a fine. The Tribunal may refer the matter to the Director of Public Prosecutions if the individual does not attend, unless there is a very good reason, such as serious illness. The fine for not attending to give evidence is £1,000 and the chairperson or vice-chairperson of the Tribunal may issue a document to use in a prosecution to confirm that the person did not attend, failed to produce a document or attended but refused to give evidence.

This Notice is a relatively simple procedure. The representative (or each of the parties themselves) has to fill out a form which the Tribunal provides, giving the name and address of the proposed witness and an undertaking to the Tribunal that they shall undertake to discharge all costs and expenses in relation to the witnesses' travel arrangements and compensate them for the loss of a day's pay. Once this form has been completed, the representative makes application to the Tribunal and advises as to why the particular witness is required. In the majority of cases the Tribunal will accept the submission and ask the representative if they undertake to serve the subpoena, which should be served personally or by registered post.

In some cases a party to the claim may want an individual not only to attend and give evidence but to bring certain documents as well. This application can be done in the same way as an application for a subpoena by simply listing the specific documents. It is not sufficient to request unnamed documents, for example, all letters in respect of Mr X. The request must be specific and there must be a good reason for such documents to be brought to the hearing.

REPRESENTATION OF PARTIES AT HEARING

As stated previously, the claimant may represent themselves at the hearing or have legal or trade union representation. Employers may be represented by the owner or by a member of management, have legal representation or representation by their employer organisation. More usually, both parties have representation.

PREPARATION FOR THE HEARING

There is a considerable volume of work involved in preparing for the hearing. Each side should check all the Tribunal documents:

- T1-A/T1-B;

- T2 form;

- Notice for Particulars;

- Notice of Hearing;

- Any other Tribunal documents and letters, e.g. subpoenas.

In an unfair dismissals or minimum notice claim, the employer representative should send a Notice for Particulars to the employee's representative (i.e., a letter requiring information as to whether the claimant has obtained alternative employment and if they have with whom, when did they commence and what is the gross and net wage; if they have entered self-employment, details of their income/expenditure would be required). If they have no alternative employment, details of their job applications should be requested. Finally, in the event that they are asked if they have obtained social welfare, the type of social welfare is required, as is the amount. If a former employee was in receipt of disability benefit, they may not be entitled to compensation for the period, as they were not available for work.

Each side should fully prepare its case by going through the facts and then applying the relevant legislation to those facts. If there is any doubt as regards the application of the law, they should consult their solicitor.

The next stage is that all documents should be fully checked. The following is a useful checklist:

- Contract of employment or letter of appointment;

- Letter of promotion;

- Company handbook;

- Union–management agreement; grievance, disciplinary and dismissal procedures;

- All correspondence and memoranda relating to the reason for dismissal and other related employment issues (for an employer, it is a good idea to bring along the complete personnel file);

- Written warnings;

- Dismissal letter;

- Minutes of meetings, e.g. disciplinary and dismissal meetings;

- Medical certificates and medical reports;

- Sales figures, budgets, etc. (where applicable);

- Pension booklet;

- All pay details (including calculations);

- P45 form;

- Redundancy notices (where applicable);

- Details of previous redundancies and the method of selection;

- Details of all social welfare receipts, including the type of social welfare;

- Copies of letters applying for jobs/advertisements

- Details of all applications for maternity, adoptive and parental leave.

There should be at least six copies of every document to be presented before the Tribunal: three for the Tribunal, one for the secretary of the division of the Tribunal, one for the other side and one for the representative.

WITNESSES

As the Tribunal hears a case by the direct evidence of the parties, both sides need witnesses. There is usually no difficulty in deciding who the necessary witnesses are.

Under a claim for unfair dismissal, for example, the employer should have present the manager who dismissed the employee and all other relevant management and supervisory personnel; for example, the persons who gave warnings to the employee. Depending on the size of the respondent company, the employer side usually has more witnesses than the claimant/employee side.

All potential witnesses should be advised that evidence is given on oath and that they will be subject to cross-examination by the other side as well as to questions from the members of the Tribunal. They should also be advised that the evidence they give is privileged. In other words, they cannot be sued for defamation, though this does not mean that they can perjure themselves or tell untruths on oath. Since many potential witnesses have not given evidence before, it is useful to explain to them the procedure at the Tribunal.

It is important to remind witnesses that they can only give evidence as to what they know or what they saw; their opinions and what they heard from other people are not relevant. If a person is uneasy about giving evidence, a subpoena may be considered, but generally it is better if people give evidence of their own free will. People should not be harassed into giving evidence, as that serves nobody's interest.

It is important to go through the facts of the case with the potential witness and point out the flaws in the case and the type of questions that they may be asked in cross-examination. A witness should not be made to change their story, however, as they will be giving evidence on oath.

All persons should be advised that the Tribunal hearing is public and that the media are quite free to go along. It is rare that the Tribunal hearing is in private. This only happens when one side makes application that it be heard in private and the Tribunal rarely grants such application. An "in camera" hearing — from the Latin "in the chamber" — only happens when there are matters of a confidential nature involved, such as sensitive company documents or a sexual harassment case. The application to have the hearing heard in private is usually considered at the beginning of the hearing and such application is invariably made in public and a decision given in public. Sensitive details may be left out of the decision.

SETTLEMENTS

Sometimes the representatives of the parties may meet before the Tribunal hearing and have "off the record" discussions in an attempt to agree a settlement of the case. They may ask the Tribunal for a few minutes in order to settle the case — to which the Tribunal usually agrees. When the parties do reach agreement, they can advise the Tribunal that there is no necessity to hear the case. The representatives should not withdraw the actual claim(s) at once, though if they do they can re-enter within a specified period of time, usually four weeks. If the settlement does not then take place, they can re-enter the claim(s) and the case will be listed in the normal way again. Where there is a settlement, the Tribunal usually makes no order because the settlement is confidential to the parties.

A settlement can also take place some days before the hearing. If the representatives are satisfied that there is a settlement, it is advisable to notify the Tribunal some days prior to the actual listing of the case so that the Tribunal's time is not wasted and the same procedure as above can apply.

THE HEARING

The purpose of the Tribunal is to provide a speedy, inexpensive and informal method of adjudication. It should be noted that if either party is not represented, the members of the Tribunal invariably assist that person with their case.

While the hearings are relatively informal in comparison to a court of law, one must still bear in mind that there is a certain formality and procedure, as is evidenced by the usual arrangement of the parties at the hearing.

At the beginning of the hearing, the chairperson of the Tribunal checks all details on the T1-A/T1-B form, in particular, the correct names/titles of the claimant and of the respondent. If the claimant does not have the correct name of the employer, this is usually amended at the hearing. This will only cause a difficulty, for example, if there is an unfair dismissals claim and six months have expired after the date of dismissal. The employer may well argue that it is now too late to amend the claim where it is clearly out of time. Other details concerning date of birth, date of commencement, date of notice and date of dismissal are also confirmed with the parties. If there is any dispute regarding these dates, the Tribunal hears evidence and then decides on the correctness of these dates. In maternity cases, the date of confinement is also considered.

Details of pay, including gross weekly pay as well as overtime, commissions, pensions etc., are also considered. If there is disagreement between the parties on these figures, various pieces of documentary evidence will be considered, including the P45, pay slips, details of pension schemes and so forth. Especially in unfair dismissals cases, the Tribunal notes what the required redress is.

Once these formalities have been completed, the Tribunal asks the representative of either side (or the claimant and employer, as appropriate) to make brief opening statements. It must be noted that these are only opening statements and not evidence within the procedure of the Tribunal. The Tribunal in the normal course does not accept submissions (written or otherwise) on the facts of the case. It makes its decision based on the evidence of the parties, which is why it is vital that both parties have all their witnesses available at the hearing.

The next stage in the procedure is that, for example in an unfair dismissals case, the employer would acknowledge that dismissal is not in dispute and proceed with the employer's witnesses. However, if the dismissal is in dispute (i.e. the employer maintains that there was no dismissal or that the employee resigned), then the employee will have to give evidence first to show that there was a dismissal. The employer (including witnesses) may also have to give evidence. When the tribunal has heard this evidence, it may give a verbal determination immediately that there was or was not a dismissal. If there was a dismissal, the hearing then follows the normal course and the employer evidence is heard first and then the employee evidence. If there was no dismissal, this is the end of the proceedings, as the employer has no case to answer.

If the employer raises jurisdictional issues — for example, that the claim is out of time or that the employee does not have sufficient service — then the evidence is heard and the Tribunal considers whether it has jurisdiction to hear the case. If it does not, that is the end of the matter.

A witness about to give evidence must take evidence on oath, which is administered by the secretary of the Tribunal division. If a witness does not wish to take evidence on oath, they may affirm their evidence before the Tribunal.

When the oath is taken, the first employer (respondent) witness gives their direct evidence. Usually, the employer representative asks the witness various questions and if there are not many facts in dispute they may lead the witnesses to a certain extent. During the course of the employer's evidence, the employer representative may wish to submit into evidence various documents, such as the contract of employment, grievance/disciplinary/dismissal procedures, letters of warning, and final dismissal letter. It is important that all of these documents are put into evidence by the employer representative (with the appropriate witness), because if they fail to do so at this stage they may well be barred from introducing such evidence later on. It must be noted that while the Tribunal is informal, it generally complies with basic rules of evidence.

When the first employer witness has completed their evidence they are subject to cross-examination by the employee representative. The representative may cross-examine the witness on all aspects of the claimant's employment, but it is important to note that all questions that are in dispute must be put to the employer witnesses prior to the employee and the employee witnesses giving evidence. Otherwise the employee witnesses may not be allowed to give that evidence later on. The employee representative may want to introduce certain documents into evidence at this stage.

Once the formal evidence and cross-examination has been completed, the members of the Tribunal may ask the witness questions. These may be for clarification purposes or to find out further information, especially where both parties have glossed over certain issues. Questions that are asked by the Tribunal members are invariably extremely important and searching.

There is no limit to the number of witnesses that either party can have. Typically an employer may have the evidence of the supervisor, the personnel manager and any other appropriate members of management, whereas the employee usually has fewer witnesses.

The Tribunal has power to summon vital witnesses should it consider it necessary, though this procedure is adopted very rarely.

Once all the employer evidence has been completed, the employee gives evidence. However, an employee representative may ask the Tribunal for a direction in the case; that is, the employee representative may argue that the employer has not shown a sufficient case to surmount the burden of proof. The Tribunal may withdraw to consider the application, though usually it will direct that it wishes to hear the employee's evidence, unless it is clear that the dismissal has been unfair.

The employee would invariably give evidence first, which would be subject to cross-examination by the employer representative and to questioning by the Tribunal. The employee will then call the various employee witnesses, who shall also be subject to cross-examination and to questioning by the members of the Tribunal.

At the end of the claimant's evidence, they should give evidence as regards loss, which will also be subject to cross-examination. For example, the employee should advise the Tribunal what social welfare benefits they have been in receipt of, the type of social welfare benefit — for example, unemployment benefit or disability (which is important in absenteeism cases) — for tax rebate they received and whether they have been looking for work or not. If they have been seeking work, the employee should have copies of applications for various jobs and should show that they went looking for a job as soon as was reasonably practical after dismissal.

When all the evidence has been heard, the Tribunal will ask the parties if they wish to give closing statements. This does not happen in every case but is typical in the more complicated ones. In a closing statement, the representatives invariably give a brief summary of the case and request the Tribunal to hold with their side. The representatives may refer to various previous determinations of the Tribunal and to Irish dismissal cases from the Circuit Court and the High Court. Sometimes the Tribunal is referred to UK cases where there are similar facts and points of law.

The Tribunal will then ask the parties what redress they wish to have. The Tribunal has an obligation to ask this question in claims under the Unfair Dismissals Acts (following the Supreme Court judgment in *State (Irish Pharmaceutical Union) v Employment Appeals Tribunal* [1987] ILRM 36). Usually the claimant will ask for reinstatement and invariably the employer will state that redress is simply not appropriate. The Tribunal hears both representatives on this particular point.

If the employer's representative considers that the employee did not mitigate or lessen their loss, various submissions can be made. For example, if an employee waited six months before looking for a job, the employer representative may claim that they did not mitigate their loss and thus any unfair dismissals award should be reduced accordingly.

Furthermore, where compensation is requested by the employer representative as being the preferable redress (if the Tribunal holds in favour of the employee), the employer representative can request the Tribunal to hold that there was a contribution on the employee's part to the dismissal. Thus, any award can be reduced.

After the hearing, the Tribunal may state to the parties that they will make their decision at that time, providing that they can come to such a decision, or they can advise the parties that they will receive the determination in writing in approximately six to eight weeks. If the Tribunal awards redress under the unfair dismissals legislation, the Unfair Dismissals Act, 1993, provides that the reason for not awarding the two other forms of redress must be given.

The Tribunal determination is signed by the chairperson of the division who heard the case. The determination will have on it the date of its signature and shall be sent out to both parties at the same time by registered post. Attached to the determination is a dated covering letter which is considered to be the date of communication of the determination. This date is vitally important for time limits as regards appeals.

COSTS

The only costs that the Tribunal can award are travelling expenses. Costs are not awarded to any person who is appearing before the Tribunal in a representative capacity, whether it be the claimant, the respondent, solicitor, barrister, trade union official or an official of an employers' organisation.

However, a witness or a party to a case may be awarded costs if it is considered that it is a frivolous and vexatious claim. In certain other circumstances, the Tribunal may also award costs, but again they only relate to travelling and other expenses such as the loss of a day's pay. It is very rare for the Tribunal to award costs.

REGISTER OF DETERMINATIONS

The Employment Appeals Tribunal is obliged to keep registers of determinations under the various Acts and they are open for inspection free of charge during normal office hours.

APPEAL OF TRIBUNAL DETERMINATION

A person who is dissatisfied with the Tribunal determination may appeal it in whole or in part, obviously depending on the provisions of each Act. No time should be wasted in seeking legal advice at this stage, as there are strict time limits involved. The time limits are as follows:

Unfair Dismissals

A person has six weeks to appeal the determination, either in whole or in part, to the Circuit Court. The Notice of Appeal must be filed in the Circuit Court office within six weeks of the date of communication of the determination — that is, the date on the covering letter of the Tribunal determination (see page 589). The Notice of Appeal does not have to be served on the other side within the six-week period, though it is advisable to do so *(Morris* v *Power Supermarkets Ltd.* [1990] IR 296).

The Circuit Court will completely rehear the case. The Circuit Court decision may be appealed to the High Court within 10 days for a further rehearing. The High Court decision may be appealed to the Supreme Court on a point of law only.

Other Acts

The relevant Acts here are the Redundancy Payments Acts; Minimum Notice and Terms of Employment Acts; Payment of Wages Act;

Terms of Employment (Information) Act; Protection of Young Persons
(Employment) Act; Maternity Protection Act; Adoptive Leave Act;
and Parental Leave Act. The Tribunal determination may be appealed to the High Court on a point of law. It is advisable to do so
within 21 days, within which time the summons should be issued,
although application may be made for an extension of time. Also, the
Tribunal may request the Minister to refer a question of law to the
High Court.

During the course of any such proceedings before the Tribunal, the
Tribunal itself may refer a question of law arising in proceedings to
the High Court for a determination by it.

Organisation of Working Time Act

The appeal under this Act carries the same procedures as under the
other legislation under which the person is claiming. More usually
this will therefore be a claim for holidays linked into the Unfair Dismissals Acts; thus an appeal to the Circuit Court is the relevant
course of action. If it is linked to a claim for redundancy and minimum notice, then the High Court appeal applies.

ENFORCEMENT OF RECOMMENDATIONS/DETERMINATIONS

Unfair Dismissals Acts; Payment of Wages Act, 1991

The 1993 Act has attempted to reinforce considerably the implementation provisions in the 1977 Act. If an employer has failed to carry
out the terms of a Tribunal determination within six weeks of the
date of communication of the determination, and if there is no appeal,
either the employee or the Minister for Enterprise and Employment
may make application for its terms to be carried out. If reinstatement
or re-engagement were awarded by the Tribunal, the Circuit Court
may order compensation instead. The Circuit Court may also order
that interest be paid under Section 22 of the Courts Act, and where
the original determination ordered re-employment, the employee will
be entitled to loss of wages suffered by the failure to implement it. (If
a rights commissioner recommendation has not been carried out the
employee may refer the matter to the Tribunal; see above under Appeals of Tribunal Determination).

If an employer fails to comply with a Circuit Court order, the
Minister may make application to have the order enforced. The Cir-

cuit Court will then make the appropriate order (see statutory forms, page 590–2).

All costs will be borne by either the Minister or the employer (see Circuit Rules No. 2, 1994 (Unfair Dismissals Acts, 1977–1993, and Payment of Wages Act, 1991) (SI No. 279 of 1994).

If an employer fails to carry out a determination of the Tribunal within six weeks of the date it is communicated to the parties, the employee, the employee's trade union or the Minister may make application to the District Court for an Order directing the employer to carry out the determination. The Court will not hear evidence at such hearing. Such application can only be made where the time limit for bringing an appeal has expired or if an appeal was brought and it was abandoned. Interest under the Courts Act, 1981, will accumulate from six weeks from the date of the determination.

Applications brought for enforcement of a decision of a rights commissioner or a determination of the Tribunal under the Payment of Wages Act, 1991, shall be brought by way of Notice of Motion with a Grounding Affidavit sworn by the person seeking the enforcement exhibiting a copy of the decision/determination.

Terms of Employment (Information) Act, 1994; Maternity Protection Act, 1994; Adoptive Leave Act, 1995; Parental Leave Act, 1998; Protection for Persons Reporting Child Abuse Act, 1998

If either party fails to comply with a decision of a rights commissioner or a determination of the Tribunal, application may be made to the Circuit Court by the other party concerned (e.g. the employee whose award has not been implemented), or by the Minister if they believe that the person is not in a position to do it themselves. The Circuit Court may make an Order directing the party to carry out the decision or the determination This may only apply once the time limit for appealing has expired or if an appeal was brought it was abandoned. If the lapse of time makes the implementing of the decision or determination impracticable, then appropriate redress may be awarded. Interest may be payable on any compensation award.

The Circuit Court Rules (No. 2) of 1997 (Adoptive Leave Act, 1995) apply in respect of applications brought under s. 39 of the Adoptive Leave Act for the enforcement of decisions of a rights commissioner or determination of the Employment Appeals Tribunal. Application is made by way of notice of motion with a grounding affidavit sworn by the person seeking enforcement. A certified copy of the decision of the rights commissioner or Tribunal determination must be attached with an appropriate covering letter. The affidavit should set out all facts relating to the alleged failure to implement the decision/ determination.

Protection of Young Persons (Employment) Act, 1996

If an employer fails to carry out the terms of a Tribunal determination within a period of six weeks, application may be made to the District Court by the parent/guardian of the young person, the trade union or the Minister (if appropriate) for an Order directing the employer to carry out the determination. There shall be no hearing of the employer. This may only apply once the time limit for appealing has expired or if an appeal was brought it was abandoned. If the lapse of time makes the implementing of the decision or determination impracticable then appropriate redress may be awarded. Interest may be payable on any compensation award.

General References

Angel, J. (1990), "How to Prepare Yourself for an Industrial Tribunal", London: Institute of Personnel Management.

Department of Enterprise, Trade and Employment, *An Explanatory Leaflet on the Employment Appeals Tribunal*.

FORM T1-A

EMPLOYMENT APPEALS TRIBUNAL

Please read the notes supplied then complete this form in BLOCK CAPITALS and sign and date on reverse.

For Official Use:
Case No:

1. NOTICE OF CLAIM TO EMPLOYMENT APPEALS TRIBUNAL UNDER (Tick appropriate box or boxes)

(i)	Redundancy Payments Acts, 1967 to 1991	☐
(ii)	Minimun Notice and Terms of Employment Acts, 1973 to 1991	☐
(iii)	Unfair Dismissals Acts, 1977 to 1993	☐
(Iv)	Worker Protection (Regular Part-Time Employees) Act, 1991	☐
(v)	Organisation of Working Time Act, 1997	☐

2. NAME AND ADDRESS OF PERSON MAKING CLAIM

Phone No.
Occupation	Sex
R.S.I. No.

3. EMPLOYER'S FULL LEGAL NAME AND ADDRESS

Please refer to point (3) of Notes

Phone No.
Registered (PAYE) No.

4. WILL YOU HAVE A REPRESENTATIVE AT THE HEARING?

Yes ☐   No ☐

Name and Address of Representative (Union Official etc.), if any

Phone No.

5. TOWN OR NEAREST TOWN TO PLACE OF EMPLOYMENT

6. GIVE THE FOLLOWING DATES

	Day	Month	Year
Birth			
Employment began			
Dismissal notice received			
Employment ended			
Date or expected date of confinement			

7. NORMAL WEEKLY PAY   £   p

Basic Weekly Pay	
Regular Bonus or Allowances	
Average Weekly Overtime	
Any other payments including	
payments in kind – specify	
Weekly Total Gross	
Net	
Number of hours normally expected to work per week	

8. APPEALS UNDER REDUNDANCY PAYMENTS ACTS

Has your employer issued you with a Redundancy Certificate?   Yes ☐   No ☐

Have you applied to your employer or to the Department of Enterprise, Trade and Employment for your redundancy payment?   Yes ☐   No ☐

CLAIM UNDER UNFAIR DISMISSALS ACTS

If you wish a claim under the Unfair Dismissals Acts, 1977 to 1993 to be heard by the Employment Appeals Tribunal, please answer the following questions:

(N.B. The Tribunal cannot hear your claim unless there is an objection to a Rights Commissioner hearing your claim.)

Insert "Yes" or "No" in each box

Do you object to a claim for unfair dismissal being heard by a Rights Commissioner?

Has your employer objected to a claim for unfair dismissal being heard by a Rights Commissioner?

P.T.O.

THE REASONS FOR MY APPEAL ARE:
(you can attach additional sheets of information if necessary)

REMEDY SOUGHT (IF APPLICABLE):
Please refer to point (9) of Notes

_____

_____

_____

Signed: _____

Date: _____

Notes to Form T1-A

Box 1. Notice of Claim to Employment Appeals Tribunal

It is important to "tick off" the boxes indicating what Act the claims are being brought under.

Box 2. Name and Address of the person making the claim

This is straightforward. However, if the claimant changes address and/or telephone number after completing this form they should advise the Secretary of the Tribunal immediately. The claimant's occupation, sex and RSI number should also be specified.

Box 3. Employer's Full Legal Name and Address

The correct and complete title of the employer must be given, for example, ABC Limited, with the appropriate address, that is the registered office or business address. The correct name of the employer can be obtained on the contract of employment, pay slips, P45 or some other company documentation that the employee has received.

It is vital that the correct title of the employer is provided; otherwise, it may be argued before the Tribunal that, as the correct employer is not stated, there is no claim. In an unfair dismissals case, for example, if the correct name of the employer is not given and if six months have elapsed since the date of dismissal, the employee may not be able to bring a claim because technically the claim would be out of time. The claimant would then have to plead that there were exceptional circumstances that prevented the claim being served within six months, and ask for an extension of up to 12 months from the date of dismissal to serve the claim. As discussed earlier in this chapter, it is unlikely they will succeed. The correct name of the employer is important to have in the event of an appeal to the Circuit or High Court (as appropriate) or where the determination or Order of the Tribunal has to be enforced. Therefore, if an employee or their representative is in any doubt as to the true name of the employer, they should ascertain it through a search in the Companies Office in Dublin or, if there is sufficient time, write to the employer for the correct title of the company. Section 40 of the Organisation of Working Time Act, 1997, provides that if a determination or decision issues with an incorrect name, application may be made to the relevant authority for amendment so that the decision/determination can be enforced.

The form also asks for details of the employer's telephone number and the registered PAYE number of the employer. The latter can be ascertained from the pay slip.

Box 4: Will you have a Representative at the Hearing?

First the employee should state if they are going to have representation and if they are the claimant must put in the name and address of the person who will be representing them. This is important because the Tribunal will automatically send to the representative as well as to the employer all documentation regarding the claim. The representative may be a trade union official, a solicitor or some other person. It is important that the claimant not put the

name of a representative without notifying that person first and giving them
a copy of the claim form.

Box 5. Town or Nearest Town to Place of Employment

The Tribunal hears claims all around the country. However, if the employee
states a large town on the form, they might get a speedier hearing because
the Tribunal sits more frequently in large centres. Cases may be transferred
to Dublin by agreement.

All the Dublin hearings take place in the Tribunal premises in the Department of Enterprise, Trade and Employment (Adelaide Road). Country
sittings usually take place in courthouses, county council chambers or hotels.

Box 6. Dates

Date of birth

Though this is generally only relevant in redundancy claims, employees
should complete this and employers should check it.

Date employment began

Employees should have no difficulty in completing this as all they have to do
is refer to their contract of employment. If there is no written contract, however, employees may have difficulty in remembering the exact date of commencement. This frequently happens where the employee commenced
employment as a seasonal or casual employee. Usually, they will remember
the month and the year when they commenced employment. This detail is
extremely important for redundancy and minimum notices cases, less so for
unfair dismissal cases as long as the employee has over one year's service.
Employers should always check this date from their records and, if incomplete, they should provide the information for the Tribunal at the hearing.

Date dismissal notice was received by the employee

Employees usually remember this date, except in some cases where dismissal
is in dispute. Nonetheless, it should be completed. Employers should always
check this date, especially where there is a claim for minimum notice as well,
because an employee could put in a later date and they may pay more notice
monies than are actually due. Also, the employee may put in a later date
which would give them sufficient service within the relevant legislation.

Date employment ended

This may be the same date as the date notice was given by the employer
where, for example, the employee was not given notice or monies in lieu of
notice. If an employee was given one month's notice and worked the notice
period, then the date that they actually left employment should be given. If
the employee was in receipt of monies in lieu of notice then the date that employment ended should be the date that the employee was paid up to, that is,
if four weeks' notice was given on 1 March, then the date employment ended
is 29 March.

If an employee resigns and claims constructive dismissal, then the date
they left employment is the date that should be put in. Employers should

ensure that this date is correct, especially where monies in lieu of notice was paid.

Date or expected date of confinement:

This date is only necessary where there is an alleged dismissal by reason of pregnancy.

Box 7. *Normal Weekly Pay*

For the purposes of all the above-mentioned legislation, it is important to list the weekly pay as opposed to the monthly pay or yearly salary. For example, under the Unfair Dismissals Acts maximum compensation is 104 weeks' remuneration while the Redundancy Acts base statutory redundancy pay on a weekly basis, as do the Minimum Notice and Terms of Employment Acts.

An employee claiming under the Unfair Dismissals Acts should furnish details in net terms, that is, gross pay less income tax and PRSI. There are specific regulations under the Acts for the computation of weekly pay (Unfair Dismissals (Calculation of Weekly Remuneration) Regulations, 1977 — SI No. 287/1977). These regulations are complicated, and standard practice for overtime payments, commissions, shift premiums, etc., is to average pay received over the six-month period prior to the date of dismissal. If there is any dispute, however, the regulations may be strictly adhered to. These may be summarised as follows:

1. The weekly earnings of an employee paid at an hourly rate or on a fixed wage or salary shall include any regular bonuses or allowances or payment in kind. For the purposes of the Act, the earnings to be taken are those in the last week of employment prior to the date of dismissal. Overtime may be determined by taking an average of the 26 weeks worked ending 13 weeks prior to the date of dismissal. If an employee did not work one (or more) of those 26 weeks, a further week(s) prior to then shall be taken into account.

2. If an employee is paid by piece rate or commission, then the average is taken by dividing the pay in the 26 weeks (ending 13 weeks prior to the date of dismissal) by the number of hours worked by the employee, and multiplying that amount by the number of hours an employee in similar employment would have worked.

3. Where there are no normal weekly hours, the average pay shall be computed over the 52-week period to the date of dismissal.

4. If an employee has less than one year's continuous service, the Tribunal shall calculate the remuneration as near as it can to these regulations.

The Minimum Notice and Terms of Employment Act, 1973 provides details in the Second Schedule for the calculation of pay during the notice period. It may be summarised as follows:

1. An employee is entitled to be paid in respect of normal working hours when ready and willing to work, even if the employer had no work available. If the employee usually works overtime, it should be included in their term "normal working hours".

2. If an employee's pay is not calculated with reference to time, or if an employee has no normal working hours (for example, they may be paid by salary and commission or by commission only), then the rate of pay shall be calculated by averaging the pay in the 13 preceding weeks prior to the giving of the notice.

The Redundancy Payments Act, 1967 (as amended) provides rules for the calculation of normal weekly remuneration (subject to a ceiling of £300 per week). It is calculated from the date the employee was declared redundant, i.e. the date on which they received notice. It may be summarised as follows:

1. An employee on a fixed wage, or salary which does not vary in relation to work done, receives the normal weekly earnings (including any regular bonus or payment in kind) at the date of the declaration of the redundancy.
2. Overtime earnings are calculated by ascertaining the total amount of such earnings in the 26-week period which ended 13 weeks before the date on which the employee was declared redundant, and dividing that amount by 26.
3. The weekly remuneration of an employee paid by a piece rate of commission (i.e. where remuneration varies in relation to work done), is calculated by averaging remuneration paid in the 26-week period which ended 13 weeks prior to the declaration of the redundancy.
4. Any period within the 26 weeks in which the employee did not work should be disregarded and the most recent weeks in which the employee worked prior to the declaration of redundancy are the weeks to be taken into account.

For claims under the minimum notice and redundancy legislation, details should be furnished in gross terms, i.e. pay with no deductions of income tax and PRSI. However, for a claim made under the unfair dismissals or minimum notice legislation, details should be available on a gross and net basis.

The Organisation of Working Time Act, 1997, provides for pay in respect of annual leave and for public holidays and awards may be up to two years' remuneration. The Organisation of Working Time (Determination of Pay for Holidays) Regulations, 1997 (SI No. 475 of 1997) apply to the calculation of holiday pay. However, there is no definition of remuneration under the Act.

Basic Weekly Pay

This is just the basic pay before overtime, shift premia, commission payments etc. If a person is on a straight salary with no other payment, then the weekly salary should be included here.

Regular bonuses or allowances

This could include shift premia, commission payments and so forth. As these payments may be sporadic and uneven, the pay should be averaged out over 26 weeks ending 13 weeks prior to the date of dismissal or declaration of redundancy.

Average Weekly Overtime

This should be calculated in the same way as bonuses or allowances.

Any other payments including payments in kind

These would include VHI, company car (the personal element should be included, i.e. non-business mileage, using the individual's benefit-in-kind figure is useful), the employer's portion of a pension contribution (this may be found by checking the pension booklet, telephone rental (the personal element, which is usually assessed as one-third of the total).

The weekly total should then be filled in on both a gross and a net basis. Awards are made on a gross basis under the redundancy, minimum notice and organisation of working time legislation whilst under the unfair dismissal legislation the computation of loss under the Acts is on a net basis.

An employee who does not know the exact details of the above should put on this section that "details will be supplied". However, the Tribunal should be reverted to as soon as possible with such details.

Employers should check this section in great detail because otherwise compensation (under any heading) awarded by the Tribunal may cost them more than it should. Employers should always go to the Tribunal with all pay details for the employee for at least the nine months prior to dismissal and obviously longer in the case of a holiday claim.

Number of hours normally expected to work per week

This should be completed by the employee but it is not significant as long as the employee is normally expected to work the requisite eight hours per week.

Box 8. Appeals under the Redundancy Payments Acts

The employee must tick either "yes" or "no" in the boxes answering the questions:

- *Has your employer issued you with a Redundancy Certificate?* This is important to see if the employer acknowledges that a redundancy did take place or did the employer comply with the redundancy payments legislation at all.

- *Have you applied to the Department of Enterprise, Trade and Employment for your redundancy payment?* If the employee has then the file in the Department should be checked to see if payment has been made (see chapter 18, Redundancy).

Claim under Unfair Dismissals Acts

It must be noted that the Employment Appeals Tribunal cannot hear a claim under these Acts unless either party has objected to the claim being heard by a rights commissioner. Hence there are two questions

Do you object to a claim on unfair dismissal being heard by a rights commissioner? If the claim is to be heard by the Tribunal the answer to this should be "Yes" since the Tribunal cannot hear a claim unless the rights commissioner hearing has been objected to.

Has your employer objected to a claim for unfair dismissal being heard by a rights commissioner? If the initial claim was sent to a rights commissioner by the employee and the employer has objected to it being heard by the rights commissioner, then this should be so stated. The employer has 21 days within which to object to a rights commissioner hearing the claim. (Of course once there is an objection the employee must refer the claim to the Tribunal.)

The reasons for my Appeal are . . .

This is a new section in the new form which requires reasonably detailed information concerning the case. However, it is important that advice be sought on the completion of this section as in an unfair dismissals claim the former employee should not prejudice their position by admitting certain matters which may or may not be relevant. Caution should also be exercised because the burden of proving that it was a 'fair' dismissal falls on the employer. In requiring this information the Tribunal appear to be relying on Paragraph 4 of the Redundancy (Redundancy Appeals Tribunal) Regulation, 1968 (S.I. No. 24 of 1968). In redundancy, minimum notice and holiday claims, all reasonable information should be provided as well.

Employers should read this section as well because if there are any inaccuracies (even if the claim is going to be defended) the employer should be aware of them when they are completing the defence, known as the Form T2 (see below). Of course employers will now be required to give more information on the Form T2.

Remedy sought (if applicable)

This is obviously important, especially under the unfair dismissals legislation. Does the employee want their job back? If so, they should put in "reinstatement". If they want compensation they should state so on the form. The Tribunal will check as to what redress the employee wants at the end of the hearing, but nonetheless it should be accurately completed.

An employee claiming under the redundancy legislation should put in "redundancy lump sum" and/or "added years of service". If an employee is claiming under the minimum notice legislation, they should put in "monies in lieu of notice" and/or "additional notice monies based on correct length of service" in respect of holidays details should be included.

Employers should read this section to find out what redress the employee is seeking. For example, if the employee is looking for compensation for an unfair dismissals claim, the employer may decide to enter into negotiations if the employee is willing. There is no obligation on the employee or the employee's representative to enter into any discussions at any stage.

Signature and Date

The employee should sign and date the form, which should then be sent without delay to the Employment Appeals Tribunal at Davitt House, Adelaide Road, Dublin 2.

Form T1-B

<table>
<tr><td>For Official Use:</td></tr>
<tr><td>Case No:</td></tr>
</table>

EMPLOYMENT APPEALS TRIBUNAL

NOTICE OF APPEAL TO EMPLOYMENT APPEALS TRIBUNAL UNDER (tick appropriate box or boxes):

(i)   **UNFAIR DISMISSALS ACTS, 1977 TO 1993**   ☐

(ii)   **PAYMENT OF WAGES ACT, 1991**   ☐

(iii) **TERMS OF EMPLOYMENT (INFORMATION) ACT, 1994**   ☐

(iv)   **MATERNITY PROTECTION ACT, 1994**   ☐

(v)   **ADOPTIVE LEAVE ACT, 1995**   ☐

(vi)   **PROTECTION OF YOUNG PERSONS (EMPLOYMENT) ACT, 1996**   ☐

NAME AND ADDRESS OF PARTY MAKING THE APPEAL:

PLEASE STATE IF YOU ARE THE EMPLOYEE OR THE EMPLOYER:

NAME AND ADDRESS OF REPRESENTATIVE AT HEARING (IF ANY):

NAME AND ADDRESS OF PARTY AGAINST WHOM THE APPEAL IS BEING BROUGHT:

DATES (IF APPLICABLE):

GIVE THE FOLLOWING DATES	Day	Month	Year
Birth			
Employment began			
Dismissal notice received			
Employment ended			
Date or expected date of confinement			

PAY (IF APPLICABLE):

		£	p
Basic Weekly Pay			
Regular Bonus or Allowances			
Average Weekly Overtime			
Any other payments including payments in kind – specify			
Weekly Total	Gross		
	Net		
Number of hours normally expected to work per week		_____	

P.T.O.

TOWN OR NEAREST TOWN TO PLACE OF EMPLOYMENT:

NAME OF RIGHTS COMMISSIONER:

DATE AND REF. NO. OF DECISION TO WHICH THIS APPEAL APPLIES:

(Please enclose a copy of this decision with your application)

THE REASONS FOR MY APPEAL ARE:
(You can attach additional sheets of information if necessary)

REMEDY SOUGHT (IF APPLICABLE): _____

_____

_____

Signed: _____

Date: _____

Notes to Form T1-B

What Act(s) are you appealing under?

It is important to tick off in the correct box the Act(s) that you are appealing under.

Name and Address of the Party making the Appeal

This is straightforward. However, if the appellant changes address and/or telephone number after completing this form they should advise the Secretary of the Tribunal immediately.

Please state if you are the Employee or the Employer

Again, this is straightforward.

Name and Address of Representative (if any)

The appellant must put in the name and address of the person who will be representing them. More usually it will be the person who represented them before the rights commissioner. This is important because the Tribunal will automatically send to the representative as well as to the respondent all documentation regarding the appeal. The representative may be a trade union official, a solicitor or some other person. It is important that the appellant not put the name of a representative without notifying that person first and giving them a copy of the claim form.

Name and Address of Party against whom the Appeal is being brought

It is important to put in the correct name if the employer is appealing but it is important that if the respondent is the employer that the correct employer title is given (see under Form T1-A above).

This is very important because if the appeal is incorrect or flawed the party appealing may be prevented from proceeding with the appeal. There will not be time to correct it because the time period for bringing an appeal is short, so amendments may not usually be made within the strict statutory time limit.

Dates (if applicable)

Date of birth

This is generally only relevant in claims under the Protection of Young Persons (Employment) Act, 1996, and it should be very carefully checked.

Date employment began

See under T1-A above and also it may be relevant in appeals where service is important e.g. the Terms of Employment (Information) Act, 1994, the Unfair Dismissals Acts, 1977 to 1993, and the Parental Leave Act, 1998.

Date dismissal notice was received by the employee

See under T1-A above and also it would be important under some of the Acts; e.g. Unfair Dismissals Acts, 1977 to 1993, or Payment of Wages Act, 1991.

Date employment ended

See under T1-A above.

Date or expected date of confinement

This date is only necessary where there is an appeal under the Maternity Protection Act, 1994.

Pay (if applicable)

Basic weekly pay

This is just the basic pay before overtime, shift premia, commission payments etc. If a person is on a straight salary with no other payment, then the weekly salary should be included here.

Regular bonuses or allowances

This could include shift premia, commission payments and so forth. As these payments may be sporadic and uneven, the pay should be averaged out over 26 weeks ending 13 weeks prior to the date of dismissal or declaration of redundancy.

Average weekly overtime

This should be calculated in the same way as bonuses or allowances.

Any other payments including payments in kind

These would include VHI, company care (the personal element should be included, i.e. non-business mileage), the employer's portion of a pension contribution (this may be found by checking the pension booklet, telephone rental (the personal element, which is usually assessed as one-third of the total).

The weekly total should then be filled in.

An employee who does not know the exact details of the above should put on this section that "details will be supplied". However, the Tribunal should be reverted to as soon as possible with such details.

Employers should check this section in great detail because otherwise compensation (under any heading) awarded by the Tribunal may cost them more than it should. Employers should always go to the Tribunal with all pay details for the employee for at least the nine months prior to dismissal.

Normal weekly working hours

This should be completed by the employee but it is not significant if the appeal is under the Maternity Protection Act, 1994, the Adoptive Leave Act, 1995, or the Parental Leave Act, 1998, where there is no hourly requirement.

Town or Nearest Town to Place of Employment

See under T1-A above.

Name of Rights Commissioner

The name of the rights commissioner should be stated — you will find this information on the covering letter enclosing the decision and also on the decision itself.

Date and Ref. No. of Decision to which this Appeal applies

You should state the date of the decision which would be on the end of the decision and there would also be a reference number. The date is the crucial as if there was a delay in the appeal of the decision it is important to give consideration to the date on the decision and the date that the appealing party received the decision. If there is a dispute or if the appeal is apparently out of time, the Tribunal will have to hear evidence on the date of the receipt of the recommendation and also the date of postage of the decision from the Labour Relations Commission.

A copy of the decision should also be sent with the appeal.

The Reasons for my Appeal are

The Appellant should set out he grounds of the Appeal. The Tribunal are looking for as much information as they can get. Bearing in mind that they will have a copy of the rights commissioner's decision, it is important to state if there are matters of fact in the decision that the appellant disagrees with or also if there is a point of law that is incorrect. It is recommended that the appellant states that they are appealing the decision in full and stating that the rights commissioner was incorrect in making the decision as it was incorrect on grounds of fact and on law. The appellant can then raise a number of more minor points. It could be the case that the appellant decides only to appeal part of the decision (e.g. the remedy only may be appealed where it is accepted that it is an unfair dismissal and it is only the remedy that is appealed where the appellant requests compensation instead of reinstatement — such applications are unusual at this level).

Remedy Sought (if applicable)

If it is an appeal under the Unfair Dismissals Acts then this section is very important – see above under T1-A. However under the other Acts the remedy is as stated in the legislation e.g. compensation or under the Maternity Protection Act, the Adoptive Leave Act and the Parental Leave Act the rights commissioner may extend periods of notice for return to work for example.

Box 11. Signature and Date

The employee should sign and date the form.

Form T1-C

For Official Use:
Case No:

NOTICE OF APPEAL TO THE EMPLOYMENT APPEALS TRIBUNAL

UNDER THE PROTECTION OF EMPLOYEES (EMPLOYERS' INSOLVENCY) ACTS, 1984 TO 1991

(THIS FORM MUST BE COMPLETED IN BLOCK CAPITALS)   **(NOTE: Please read notes overleaf before completing this form).**

1. EMPLOYEE DETAILS:

Surname:
First Name:
Address:
Telephone No:
Occupation:
R.S.I. No.:

2. NAME AND ADDRESS OF EMPLOYER:

Telephone No.:

3. TYPE OF APPEAL:
(Tick (✓) relevant box)

Arrears of Wages	☐
Arrears of Holiday Pay	☐
Arrears of Sick Pay	☐
Pension Contributions	☐

4. APPEAL DETAILS:

PERIOD OVER WHICH CLAIM AROSE							
	Day	Month	Year		Day	Month	Year
From				To			
From				To			
Date of Birth:							
Date of termination of employment:							
Date informed of Minister's decision:							

5. TOWN OR NEAREST TOWN TO PLACE OF EMPLOYMENT:

6. NORMAL WEEKLY PAY:

	£	p
Basic Weekly Pay		
Regular Bonus or Allowance		
Average Weekly Overtime		
Any other payments including: Payments in kind – specify		
Weekly Total		

Normal weekly working hours	

7. NAME AND ADDRESS OF REPRESENTATIVE (UNION OFFICIAL ETC.) OF PERSON MAKING THE COMPLAINT

Telephone No.:

8. THE GROUNDS OF MY APPEAL ARE:
(Please attach copy of Minister's decision)

Signed
Date

Send this form to: **The Secretary**
Employment Appeals Tribunal
Davitt House,
65A, Adelaide Road, Dublin 2.
Telephone: (01) 6614444
1890 220222 Lo-Call from outside (01) area

NOTES FOR PERSONS COMPLETING THIS FORM

1.   A Guide to the Acts is available on request from the Information Unit of the Department of Enterprise, Trade and Employment.

2.   Employees and trustees, in the case of pension contributions, may only complete this form if the Minister for Enterprise, Trade and Employment has:

   (a)   refused to pay an amount applied for, or

   (b)   reduced an amount applied for

AND

   the claim was in respect of arrears of wages, arrears of sick pay, arrears of holiday pay or unpaid pension contributions.

3.   Complaints to the Tribunal must be made within six weeks from the date on which the Minister's decision on your application was communicated to you.

   The Tribunal has discretion to extend this time limit.

NOTES ON COMPLETING THIS FORM:

BOX 1:   If you change your address after lodging this form, inform the Tribunal immediately.

BOX 3:   A trustee of a pension scheme may only make a complaint to the Tribunal in respect of arrears of unpaid contributions.

BOX 4:   The period over which the claim arose is the period over which you were, for example, entitled to holidays and in respect of which you have not been paid.

BOX 6:   A guide to the calculation of normal weekly pay is set out in the Guide to the Acts. Basic pay means gross pay before deductions. Average overtime, bonuses and allowances are calculated by obtaining gross payment for the 26 week period which is immediately prior to 13 weeks before the date of termination of the employee's employment and dividing this figure by 26 to obtain the average.

BOX 7:   Only complete this box if you have consulted the representative beforehand and he/she is willing to attend the Tribunal hearing. Notification of the hearing will be sent to them also.

BOX 8:   If you do not have sufficient space to set out your grounds of appeal, continue them on a sheet of paper and attach to this form.

Caution: The Tribunal may award costs against a party who has acted frivolously or vexatiously in the matter of an appeal.

FORM T2   Case No:

EMPLOYMENT APPEALS TRIBUNAL

	(i)	**Redundancy Payments Acts, 1967 to 1991**
	(ii)	**Minimum Notice and Terms of Employment Acts, 1973 to 1991**
	(iii)	**Unfair Dismissals Acts, 1977 to 1993**
	(iv)	**Worker Protection (Regular Part-Time Employees) Act, 1991**
	(v)	**Organisation of Working Time Act, 1997**
	(vi)	**Protection of Employees (Employers' Insolvency) Acts, 1984 to 1991**

NOTICE OF APPEARANCE

By a party against whom a claim has been lodged under the legislation ticked above

by

against

N.B.   If employer's name is different from above, please give employer's correct legal name

Do you have a representative acting for you?   Yes   No

If Yes, please give name and address:

Do you dispute the claim/s being made?   Yes   No

If Yes, please state the claim/s at Nos. (I) to (v) above being disputed:

_____

P.T.O.

Please set out the reasons in the space provided below:
(Note: While you should try and set out your case as fully as possible, you will not necessarily be confined to what is given on this form at hearing)

Signed: _____

Date:

AN BINSE ACHOMAIRC FOSTAÍOCHTA
65 A BÓTHAR ADELAIDE
BAILE ATHA CLIATH 2

All communications should be
addressed to the Secretary

THE EMPLOYMENT APPEALS TRIBUNAL
65A ADELAIDE ROAD
DUBLIN 2

☎ (01) 631 2121
FAX (01) 676 4810

The Secretary

July 1999

DUBLIN

Hearing No:

-v-

Dear Secretary

Notice is hereby given that the appeal(s) under the REDUNDANCY PAYMENTS ACTS, 1967 TO 1991 & MINIMUM NOTICE AND TERMS OF EMPLOYMENT ACTS, 1973 TO 1991 & UNFAIR DISMISSALS ACTS, 1977 TO 1993 & ORGANISATION OF WORKING TIME ACT, 1997 will be heard by the Tribunal at ROOM G-14, DAVITT HOUSE, 65A ADELAIDE ROAD, DUBLIN 2 on   th August, 1999 at 2.30 P.M. (or as soon hereafter as may be).

Each party must appear at the hearing with witnesses (if any) at the above time and place and bring with him all documents on which he intends to rely. Any documents being submitted to the Tribunal at the hearing should be copied in advance and four copies should be provided to the Tribunal.

Each party is entitled to be represented by counsel or solicitor or by a representative of a trade union or of an employer's association or, with leave of the Tribunal, by any other person.

Please note that the non-attendance of a party or his representative or witnesses will not be accepted as reason for the adjournment of the proceedings except for very grave reasons. Adjournments are only granted in exceptional circumstances. A party seeking an adjournment must make a formal application to any sitting division of the Tribunal. Good cause must be shown and the consent of the other party sought before any application for an adjournment will be considered by the Tribunal, but the existence of such consent alone is never a sufficient reason for granting an adjournment. Only in the gravest circumstances will the foregoing procedure be departed from and then only at the discretion of the Tribunal.

Yours faithfully

AN BINSE ACHOMHAIRC FOSTAÍOCHTA
65A BÓTHAR ADELAIDE
BAILE ÁTHA CLIATH 2

All communications should be
addressed to the Secretary

THE EMPLOYMENT APPEALS TRIBUNAL
65A ADELAIDE ROAD
DUBLIN 2

☎ (01) 661 4444
FAX (01) 676 4810

(1)   **UNFAIR DISMISSALS ACTS, 1977 TO 1993**

Case Nos.

NOTICE TO ATTEND AND GIVE EVIDENCE

In the matter of an **appeal/claim** by   of

against

under 1 above.

Please note that you **are requested** by the above-named Tribunal to attend a

hearing of the above claim/appeal at Room   . **Davitt House**, 65a Adelaide

Road, Dublin 2 on   day of   . 19   at the hour of   .

(official time) to give evidence.

Dated this   day of .   19.

_____
Secretary

To:

Your attention is directed to the extract from Section 39 (as amended by
Section 18 of the **Unfair Dismissals Act**, 1977 and Section 17 of the Redundancy
Payments Act, 1979) **of** the Redundancy Payments Act, 1967 as set out on the back
of this Notice; Section 1 of the Minimum Notice and Terms of Employment Act.
1973 and Section 1 of the **Unfair Dismissals Act**, 1977.

13087.sub.cmd

EXTRACT FROM SECTION 39 (as amended) OF THE REDUNDANCY PAYMENTS ACT, 1967

Section 39(17)   (a)   The Tribunal shall, on the hearing of any matter
(as amended)   referred to it under this Section, have power to take evidence on oath and for that purpose may cause to be administered oaths to persons attending as witnesses at such hearing.

                               (b)   Any person who, upon examination on oath authorised under this subsection, wilfully and corruptly gives false evidence or wilfully and corruptly swears anything which is false, being convicted thereof, shall be liable to the penalties for wilful and corrupt perjury.

                               (c)   The Tribunal may, by giving notice in that behalf in writing to any person, require such person to attend at such time and place as is specified in the notice to give evidence in relation to any matter referred to the Tribunal under this section or to produce any documents in his possession, custody or control which relate to any such matter.

                               (d)   A notice under paragraph (c) may be given either by delivering it to the person to whom it relates or by sending it by post in a prepaid registered letter addressed to such person at the address at which he ordinarily resides.

                               (e)   A person to whom a notice under paragraph (c) has been given and who refused or wilfully neglects to attend in accordance with the notice or who, having so attended, refuses or wilfully fails to produce any document to which the notice relates shall be guilty of an offence and shall be liable on summary conviction thereof to a fine not exceeding one thousand pounds.

AN BINSE ACHOMHAIRC FOSTAÍOCHTA
65A BÓTHAR ADELAIDE
BAILE ÁTHA CLIATH 2

All communications should be
addressed to the Secretary

Your Ref:

THE EMPLOYMENT APPEALS TRIBUNAL
65A ADELAIDE ROAD
DUBLIN 2

☎   **(01) 661 4444**
FAX (01) 676 4810

Hearing No:

Appeal of

against the decision of

under
MINIMUM NOTICE AND TERMS OF EMPLOYMENT ACTS, 1973 TO 1991 & UNFAIR
DISMISSALS ACTS, 1977 TO 1993

Dear

I am directed by the Employment Appeals Tribunal to enclose a copy of the
decision of the Tribunal in the above case.

Yours sincerely

Form One

CIRCUIT   COUNTY OF

UNFAIR DISMISSALS ACT, 1977 s.10(1)
or
UNFAIR DISMISSALS (AMENDMENT) ACT, 1993,
S.11(2)(b) or (3)(c)
(Delete as appropriate)

BETWEEN:

THE MINISTER FOR ENTERPRISE, TRADE AND EMPLOYMENT
Applicant

AND

Respondent

TAKE NOTICE that the Minister for Enterprise, Trade and Employment having his office at   in the County of   hereby applies to the Court sitting at   in the County of   pursuant to the provisions of   *(insert appropriate Act and section)* on behalf of   *(Insert name of employee)* for redress under the Act and for the costs of the Application.

AND TAKE NOTICE that the Minister will rely upon the following matters in support of the application:

(1)   The said   *(insert name of employee)* is the employee of the Respondent for the purposes of the said Act.

(2)   The Employment Appeals Tribunal/Circuit Court on the   day of 19   has determined/ordered that the said employee be entitled to redress under the said Acts and accordingly ordered the Respondent to reinstate/re-engage/compensate *(delete as appropriate)* the said employee as by   *(insert brief details of the determination)*.

(3)   The Respondent has failed to carry out the terms of the said determination/Order, which was communicated to the parties on the   day of 19

AND TAKE NOTICE that the application will be listed for hearing by the Court on the   day of   19   or on the first available day thereafter. *(The words "or on the first available day thereafter" should be omitted where the application is made in Dublin.)*

Dated the   day of   19

SIGNED: ....
(Solicitor for the Applicant)
(Address)

To:

The above-named Respondent/Solicitor for Respondent
and
The Secretary, Employment Appeals Tribunal, Department of Enterprise, Trade and Employment, 65A Adelaide Road, Dublin 2

Form Two

CIRCUIT   COUNTY OF

UNFAIR DISMISSALS (AMENDMENT) ACT, 1993,
S.11(2)(b) or (3)(c)
(Delete as appropriate)

BETWEEN:

Applicant

AND

Respondent

TAKE NOTICE that the above-named Applicant of   in the County of
hereby applies to the Court sitting at   in the County of   pursuant to the
provisions of   *(insert appropriate Act and section)* for redress under the Act and
for the costs of the Application.

AND TAKE NOTICE that the Applicant will rely upon the following matters in
support of the application:

(1)   The said   *(insert name of Applicant)* is the employee of the Respondent
for the purposes of the said Act.

(2)   The Employment Appeals Tribunal/Circuit Court on the   day of
19   has determined/ordered that the Applicant be entitled to redress under the
said Act and accordingly ordered the Respondent to reinstate/re-engage/compensate
(delete as appropriate) the Applicant as by   *(insert brief details of the
determination)*.

(3)   The Respondent has failed to carry out the terms of the said
determination/Order, which was communicated to the parties on the   day of
       19

AND TAKE NOTICE that the application will be listed for hearing by the Court on the
       day of   19   or on the first available day thereafter. *(The words "or
on the first available day thereafter" should be omitted where the application is made
in Dublin.)*

Dated the   day of   19

SIGNED: ....
(Solicitor for the Applicant)
(Address)

To:

The above-named Respondent/Solicitor for Respondent
and
The Secretary, Employment Appeals Tribunal, Department of Enterprise, Trade
and Employment, 65A Adelaide Road, Dublin 2

Form Three

CIRCUIT   COUNTY OF

UNFAIR DISMISSALS ACT, 1977 SECTION 10(4)
or
UNFAIR DISMISSALS (AMENDMENT) ACT, 1993, S. 11 (1)
(Delete as appropriate)

BETWEEN:

Applicant

AND

Respondent

TAKE NOTICE that the above-named Applicant of   in the County of
          hereby applies to the Court sitting at   in the County of
pursuant to the provisions of   *(insert appropriate Act and section)* by way of
Appeal against the determination of the Employment Appeals Tribunal dated
the   day of   19   granting/refusing *(delete where appropriate)* for
redress under the said Act and for an Order providing for the costs of this
application. The said determination of the Employment Appeals Tribunal was
communicated to the Appellant on the   day of   19

AND TAKE NOTICE that the Applicant will rely upon the following matters in
support of his Appeal: *(Here insert the grounds relied upon. If appeal is against
part only of the determination, clearly identify that part against which an appeal is
sought.)*

AND TAKE NOTICE that the application will be listed for hearing by the
Court on the   day of   19   or on the first available day
thereafter. *(The words "or on the first available day thereafter" should be omitted
where the application is made in Dublin.)*

Dated the   day of   19

SIGNED: ....
(Appellant/Solicitor for the Applicant)
(Address)

To:

The above-named Respondent/Solicitor for Respondent
and
The Secretary, Employment Appeals Tribunal, Department of Enterprise, Trade
and Employment, 65A Adelaide Road, Dublin 2

Chapter Twenty-four

EMPLOYMENT EQUALITY CLAIMS

As of mid-August 1999, the Department of Justice, Equality and Law Reform advised that the Employment Equality Act, 1998, would come into operation on 18 October 1999. At the time of going to press, the various statutory instruments, to include a Commencement Order, an Order transferring the functions of the current Equality Service from the Labour Relations Commission and an Order in respect of the right to information, had not been published. No appointment had at that stage been made to the office of Director of Equality Investigations. However, the new Equality Authority designate had been appointed (see Chapter 25, "Equality Authority").

The Employment Equality Act, 1998, provides for radically different procedures in respect of employment equality claims compared to the present procedures. In this chapter, the current legislation is fully considered and then the new legislation is considered to include consideration of the new mediation procedures, adjudicating bodies and the option of separate procedures and higher redress in respect of gender discrimination claims.

Equality disputes in relation to pension schemes may also be referred through the equality adjudication machinery, but technically the procedures are now under the Pensions Act, 1990. However, before the procedures are considered, the adjudicating bodies, namely equality officers and the Labour Court, will be considered.

This chapter will consider first the new obligations under the Employment Equality Act, 1998, then there follows a brief review of the current procedures (at the time of going to press) under the Anti-Discrimination (Pay) Act, 1974, the Employment Equality Act, 1977, and then a brief discussion of the issue of pensions and equality.

EMPLOYMENT EQUALITY ACT, 1998

The Employment Equality Act, 1998, for which there is, as yet, no Commencement Order(s), provides for a different system of adjudication and different adjudication procedures for claims under the gender ground (i.e. claims falling within the scope of the Equal Pay Directive (75/117/EEC) and the Equal Treatment Directive (76/207/EEC) in that there will be a direct reference to the Circuit Court (if the complainant so wishes — see below)) and the other grounds of discrimination. First, the new adjudication system shall be considered.

Director of Equality Investigations

The Minister shall appoint a person to be the Director of Equality Investigations. The office of the Director shall consist of staff as appointed by the Minister. All such persons shall be deemed civil servants. Any person who before the commencement of the operation of the 1998 Act held office as an equality officer of the Labour Relations Commission shall become an equality officer and a member of the staff of the Director of Equality Investigations.

The Director may appoint members of staff as equality officers and equality mediation officers who shall issue decisions, as appropriate. This is a delegated function of the Director and will continue unless there are exceptional circumstances preventing the officer from acting or continuing to act in a case. The Director, equality mediation officers and equality officers shall be independent in the performance of their duties.

Equality officers, although not necessarily lawyers, have a specialised knowledge of equality law. They are currently officers of the Labour Relations Commission (LRC) though they act independently of it. Under the 1998 Act, they will transfer to the Office of the Director. Usually, they are recruited from the staff of the Department of Enterprise, Trade and Employment. Hearings before equality officers are informal and private. Such hearings are held throughout the country, although the majority are heard at the LRC premises in Dublin. They will be moving to new offices in Dublin, where both the offices of the new Equality Authority and the Director will be located. Equality officers investigate "disputes", which may include carrying out work inspections (see below) and listening to various witnesses.

Both parties usually provide detailed written submissions, which include all legal issues, details of the work of the claimant and comparator and the comparison of such work under the Acts. At the conclusion of the investigation, the equality officer issues a written recommendation.

During the course of an equal pay investigation, the equality officer will take evidence of the work of both the claimant(s) and the comparator(s). This work inspection is extremely important and is akin to the oral evidence that would be given at any court or Tribunal case. It is important that both parties are represented during the work inspection — in other words, that trade union officials, employer representatives and any other representatives be present.

The Director must, within the first six months of each calendar year, make a report to the Minister on the activities of the office of Director in respect of the previous year.

Time Limits

A claim for redress in respect of discrimination or victimisation must be referred to the Director of Equality Investigations, the Labour Court or the Circuit Court within six months from the date of occurrence or, as the case may require, the most recent occurrence of the act of discrimination or victimisation (s. 77(5)). If, on an application made by the complainant, the Director, the Labour Court or the Circuit Court is satisfied that exceptional circumstances prevented the complainant case being referred within the time limit, then the time limit may be extended to 12 months. This extension does not apply to an equal pay claim (s. 77(6)).

The term "exceptional circumstances" is also used in s. 7(a)(2)(b) of the Unfair Dismissals (Amendment) Act, 1993, and its interpretation is considered in Chapter 23, "Employment Appeals Tribunal".

If the complainant's claim for redress is in respect of discrimination by the Civil Service Commissioners, the Local Appointments Commissioners, the Minister for Defence, or the Commissioner of the Garda Síochána, the complainant shall, in the first instance, refer the claim for redress to the alleged offending body. If any of these bodies fails to give a decision on the claim within 28 days after its referral or if the complainant is not satisfied with the decision given, then the time limit (i.e. six months) shall commence at the end of that 28-day period (ss. 77(7) and (8)).

Where a member of the Defence Forces has a claim for redress in respect of sex discrimination, in the first instance, the claim shall be referred to an officer within the meaning of the Defence Act, 1954, who shall request the Director of Equality Investigations to investigate the matter. The Director must investigate the matter within the redress of wrongs procedure under the Defence Act, 1954, and make a written recommendation to the officer and copy it to the complainant. If either the procedures have not been completed within 12 months or the complainant is not satisfied, the matter may be referred directly to the Circuit Court or the Labour Court (s. 77(9) and (10)).

Right to Information

For the first time a proposed claimant will have a right to information (s. 76) and the Minister may, by regulation, prescribe forms, through which a proposed claimant may obtain information from a person who allegedly discriminated against them. However, a person who allegedly discriminated only has to reply to the question(s) if they so wish. This will apply where a person considers that there has been a contravention of the 1998 Act, or they may have been dismissed or otherwise penalised in circumstances amounting to victimisation. This right to information also applies in respect of an equal pay claim, i.e., where there is an allegation that there is a breach of an equal remuneration term in their contract of employment or where a claimant alleges that there has been breach of an equality clause in a contract of employment. Information sought may only be "material information" and cannot be confidential.

Such "material information" is relevant if it is:

1. Information as to the reasons for the alleged discrimination or for doing or omitting to do any relevant act and as to any practices or procedures material to any such act;

2. Information, other than confidential information, about the remuneration or treatment of other persons who are similar to any proposed claimant;

3. Other information which is not confidential information and which in the circumstances of the case it is reasonable for the potential claimant to obtain.

"Confidential information" means any information which relates to a particular individual and to the disclosure of which that individual does not agree. No person who has allegedly discriminated shall have to:

1. Furnish any reference (or any copy or extract) or any report (or copy or extract) relating to the character or the suitability for employment of any person (including the proposed claimant themselves); or

2. Disclose the contents of such reference or report.

Where a person considers that they may have been discriminated against by the Civil Service Commissioners, the Local Appointments Commissioners, the Minister for Defence or the Commissioner of the Garda Síochána in respect of any recruitment or selection process, then information shall not be regarded as "material information" if it relates to communications with external advisors. Information in relation to a recruitment or selection process is permitted if it identifies the successful and the unsuccessful candidates by reference to their sex or in terms of the other discriminatory grounds by reference to those who have the same relevant characteristic (e.g. in relation to marital status, the relevant characteristic is having the same marital status; or in respect of family status, having the same family status) (s.28(3)).

The Circuit Court, the Labour Court or the Director of Equality Investigations may draw all appropriate inferences if information was not supplied, or if it was false or misleading or was not sufficient (s. 81).

A "designated officer" is entitled to enter premises at all reasonable times and require any person to provide books, records and take copies or extracts from such documents or to view work in progress. A "designated officer" is the Director; the Chairman of the Labour Court; an equality officer; or a person authorised by the Director or Chairman. Such person is entitled to all "material information" relevant to the matter. These powers are not applicable in respect of a person's home unless the Minister or an officer of the Minister certifies in writing that there are reasonable grounds for believing that there is material information in the person's home. In such cases, on application, a judge of the District Court may issue a search warrant.

A person who has such information may be required to attend before the Director or the Labour Court and answer truthfully any questions put to them and sign a declaration of the truth of their answers. If a person does not provide information or come before the Director or the Labour Court, then any of the adjudicating bodies may make application to the Circuit Court for an order requiring that person to comply with the requirement. If a person is entitled to claim legal professional privilege, the Circuit Court shall set aside the requirement.

There is legal protection in respect of any person who discloses information. Also, no information produced under this Act may be disclosed other than for mediation or adjudication under this Act. Any person who discloses information in contravention of the Act shall be guilty of an offence.

REFERENCE TO DIRECTOR OF EQUALITY INVESTIGATIONS

A person may seek redress by referring their case to the Director of Equality Investigations (s. 79) if:

1. They have been discriminated against by another person in contravention of the Employment Equality Act, 1998; or

2. They have not been receiving remuneration in accordance with an equal remuneration term; or

3. They have not been receiving a benefit under an equality clause; or

4. They have been penalised in circumstances amounting to victimisation.

Also, the Authority may refer to the Director of Equality Investigations cases where discrimination or victimisation are being generally practised; where there are discriminatory rules in relation to conditions of employment; where there is discrimination or victimisation against a person who has not made a reference because it would not be reasonable for them to do so; where there is failure to comply with an equal remuneration or an equality clause and where it is not reasonable for the person to make the reference; where there is an advertisement in contravention of the Act (see Chapter 1, "Recruitment and Equality"); where a person is procuring another to discriminate or victimise a person; or where a person has procured or attempted to procure another to break an equal remuneration or equality clause (s. 85).

In such a case, any reference to the name of the complainant shall be to the Authority and the respondent shall be the person who in the opinion of the Authority carried out the alleged discrimination. Redress shall be awarded to the complainant and orders shall be made as appropriate. In cases where the Authority may make direct reference to the Circuit Court or the High Court, as appropriate, an injunction may be granted to prevent the person from carrying on the acts of discrimination. This would be applicable in cases of sex discrimination and in advertising.

Dismissal

If a person maintains that they were dismissed in circumstances amounting to discrimination in contravention of the Act or in circumstances amounting to victimisation, then a claim for redress for dismissal may be brought to the Labour Court and shall not be brought to the Director of Equality Investigations (s. 77(2)).

Gender

If any of these claims arise from the gender ground, i.e., specific provisions as to equality as between men and women or in any other circumstances (including circumstances amounting to victimisation) to which the Equal Pay Directive or the Equal Treatment Directive is relevant, then the person making the claim may seek redress by referring the case to the Circuit Court instead of referring it to the Director of Equality Investigations or to the Labour Court, as appropriate (s. 77(3)).

MEDIATION

If a case has been referred to the Director of Equality Investigations and if it appears to the Director that it could be a case that could be resolved by mediation, then the Director shall refer the case for mediation to an Equality Mediation Officer (s. 78). Equally, if at any time after a case has been referred to the Labour Court, it appears to the Labour Court that the case is one which could be resolved by mediation, the Labour Court shall either attempt to resolve the case in that way by itself, or shall refer the case to the Director for Mediation by an Equality Mediation Officer.

However, if the complainant or the respondent objects to a case being dealt with by way of mediation, the Director or the Labour Court shall not exercise their powers but shall deal with the claim in the normal way. Mediation either by an Equality Mediation Officer or by the Labour Court shall be conducted in private.

Where a case is resolved by mediation:

1. The Equality Mediation Officer concerned or the Labour Court shall prepare a written record of the terms of the settlement;

2. Written records of the terms of the settlement shall be signed by the complainant and the respondent;

3. The Equality Mediation Officer concerned or the Labour Court shall send a copy of the written record, as so signed, to the complainant and the respondent, and

4. A copy of the written record shall be retained by the Director or the Labour Court, as the case may require.

If a case has been referred to an Equality Mediation Officer or if the Labour Court has attempted to resolve a case and if it appears that the case cannot be resolved by mediation, then the Equality Mediation Officer or the Labour Court shall issue a notice to that effect to the parties.

Where such a notice has been issued and where the complainant makes an application to the Director or the Labour Court for a resumption of the hearing within 28 days and a copy of the notice must accompany the application, then the Director or the Labour Court shall proceed to investigate the claim, as appropriate.

LABOUR COURT

As stated previously, the Labour Court's main and original function was to resolve industrial conflict and to mediate industrial disputes. The Anti-Discrimination (Pay) Act, 1979, and the Employment Equality Act, 1977, added a quasi-judicial and appellate role for the Court, which continues under the 1998 Act. The Court sits by division with three members in each division — namely, the chairperson or deputy chairperson and an employer and employee member — and the division must both hear and investigate appeals against the equality officer's recommendations. In equality dismissal cases, the claims are referred directly to the Labour Court. The Court may implement an equality officer's recommendation (e.g. where the employer has not paid) but it must investigate the claim at the same time.

The Labour Court issues written determinations, which are binding on the parties unless appealed to the Circuit Court. A Labour Court determination may be judicially reviewed by the High Court (if, for example, unfair procedures were adopted at the Court hearing), and if quashed the matter is referred back to another division of the Labour Court (or the Director of Equality Investigations) for a new hearing or to decide on certain specific issues. Under the 1998 Act, there is provision for the Court to refer matters back to the Director of Equality Investigations.

The Labour Court's hearings are normally held in private unless it is requested that the hearing be in public. Both parties provide written submissions on the appeal and, especially in equal pay appeals, the Court may visit the employer's premises and undertake a work inspection. If there are major questions of EU law involved, the Court may refer questions to the European Court of Justice for judgment, as it did in the case of *Hill and Stapleton* v *The Revenue Commissioners* (see Chapter 3, "Temporary and Part-time Employment").

Burden of Proof

Discrimination must be proved by the person alleging it (*North Western Health Board* v *Martyn* [1987] IR 565). In practice, a claimant only has to show that they were in some way discriminated against and then the employer must substantiate their action (see Chapter 1, "Recruitment and Equality", *Nathan* v *Bailey Gibson Ltd. and the Labour Court* [1996] ELR 114).

The Directive on the burden of proof in cases based on sex discrimination (97/80/EC) should be brought into Irish law by 1 January 2001. The Preamble to the Directive states:

> . . . the Court of Justice of the European Communities has . . . held that the rules on the burden of proof must be adapted when there

is a *prima facie* case of discrimination and that, for the principle of
equal treatment to be applied effectively, the burden of proof must
shift back to the respondent when evidence of such discrimination
is brought.

This, in effect, is stating what Hamilton CJ stated in *Nathan* v *Bailey
Gibson, the Irish Print Union and the Minister for Labour* ([1996]
ELR 114), when considering indirect discrimination. In summary, he
said that the worker is not required in the first instance to prove a
causal connection between the practice complained of and the sex of
the complainant. It is sufficient for the complainant to show that the
practice complained of bears significantly more heavily on members
of the complainant's sex. At that stage, the complainant has established a *prima facie* case of discrimination and the onus of proof
shifts to the employer to show that the practice complained of is
based on objectively verifiable factors that have no relation to the
complainant's sex.

Article 1 of the Directive states that the principle of equal treatment means that there shall be no discrimination whatsoever, based
on sex, either directly or indirectly. For the purposes of the principle
of equal treatment, indirect discrimination shall exist where an apparently neutral provision, criterion or practice disadvantages a substantially higher proportion of the members of one sex unless that
provision, criterion or practice is appropriate and necessary and can
be justified by objective factors unrelated to sex.

Article 4 (1) provides:

> Member States shall take such measures as are necessary, in ac-
> cordance with their national judicial systems, to ensure that,
> when persons who consider themselves wronged because the prin-
> ciple of equal treatment has not been applied to them to establish,
> before a court or other competent authority, facts from which it
> may be presumed that there has been direct or indirect discrimi-
> nation, it shall be for the respondent to prove that there has been
> no breach of the principle of equal treatment.

Article 4(3) further provides:

> Member States need not apply paragraph 1 to proceedings in
> which it is for the court or competent body to investigate the facts
> of the case.

The Employment Equality Act, 1998, is apparently neutral concerning the burden of proof. It would appear that, as both the Director of Equality Investigations and the Labour Court are investigative bodies, such Directive may not apply. However, as they also make decisions/determinations in their adjudicating role, the provisions of the Directive should apply. It will apply of course to all court procedures (e.g. the Circuit Court and High Court). In the event of a sex discrimination case going straight to the Circuit Court, the burden of proof will apply because, when the Court refers the matter to the Director of Equality Investigations, it is to report on the matter and the application of the Act (Directives) rests with the Court.

The burden of proof in respect of all the other grounds of discrimination is neutral.

INVESTIGATION BY A DIRECTOR OF EQUALITY INVESTIGATIONS OR THE LABOUR COURT

The Director of Equality Investigations or the Labour Court, as appropriate, shall investigate the case and hear all persons who are interested and desiring to be heard (s. 79). An investigation shall be held in private unless at the request of one of the parties to an investigation by the Labour Court, in which instance the Labour Court can determine to hold the investigation (or part of it) in public.

In respect of an equal remuneration claim and where there is a question as to whether the different rates of remuneration are lawful, the Director may direct that that question shall be investigated as a preliminary issue. The Minister may by regulations specify:

1. Procedures to be followed by the Director or the Labour Court in carrying out investigations (or any description of investigation), and

2. Time limits applicable to such investigations, including procedures for extending those time limits in certain circumstances. However, before making any of these regulations, the Minister shall consult the Labour Court, the Equality Authority, and the Director of Equality Investigations. Any regulations shall only be made with the consent of the Minister for Enterprise, Trade and Employment. However, the Director of Equality Investigations or

the Labour Court may consider it necessary to have communications with external advisors.

To date (August 1999), no procedures or forms have been published.

At the conclusion of an investigation (including any preliminary issues) the Director shall issue a decision or the Labour Court shall make a determination. If this is in favour of the complainant, then it shall provide for redress and in the case of a decision on a preliminary issue, it shall be followed by an investigation of the substantive issue.

Where a case is referred to the Labour Court (e.g. dismissal) and the Court considers that an investigation by the Director would assist it in making its determination, then the Director will investigate the matter and make a report to the Court. During the course of this investigation, the Court may suspend or adjourn part of its investigation. The Director's report will be taken into account in reaching its determination.

Redress

The Director of Equality Investigations may award the following redress (s. 82(1)), as may be appropriate in the circumstances of a particular case:

1. An award of compensation in the form of arrears of remuneration (attributable to a failure to pay equal pay) in respect of so much of a period of employment as begins not more than three years before the date of referral of the claim;

2. An order for equal pay from the date referred to as set out in (1) above;

3. An order for compensation for the effects of acts of discrimination or victimisation which occurred not earlier than six years before the date of referral of the case (up to a maximum of 104 weeks remuneration — i.e. the actual remuneration or the remuneration that they would have received but for the discrimination or victimisation, whichever is the greater);

4. An order for equal treatment in whatever respect is relevant to the case;

5. An order that a person or persons specified in the order take a specified course of action.

The Labour Court may provide the following redress:

1. An order for compensation for the effects of acts of discrimination or victimisation which occurred not earlier than six years before the date of referral of the case (up to a maximum of 104 weeks remuneration — i.e. the actual remuneration or the remuneration that they would have received but for the discrimination or victimisation, whichever is the greater) ;

2. An order for equal treatment in whatever respect is relevant to the case;

3. An order that a person or persons specified in the order take a specified course of action;

4. An order for reinstatement or re-engagement with or without an order for compensation (up to a maximum of 104 weeks remuneration — i.e. the actual remuneration or the remuneration that they would have received but for the discrimination or victimisation, whichever is the greater).

The reference to the maximum amount of compensation being 104 weeks only applies where the claimant was in receipt of remuneration at the date of the reference of the claim (or the date of dismissal if earlier), but in any other case the maximum amount is £10,000 (e.g. in respect of discrimination concerning applications).

APPEALS FROM DIRECTOR TO THE LABOUR COURT

Either party may appeal a decision of the Director of Equality Investigations within 42 days of the receipt of the decision to the Labour Court. The appeal must be in writing, specifying the grounds of appeal.

Grounds of appeal could be as follows:

1. It was not within the jurisdiction of the equality officer to issue a recommendation granting equal pay, as the claimant and comparator were not working in the same "place".

2. The equality officer erred in law and in fact in granting equal
    pay, etc.

3. Such other grounds as may arise during the hearing of the ap-
    peal.

The listing of the grounds is very important because otherwise the
Labour Court will deem the appeal invalid.

The completed form should be sent to the Chairperson of the Labour Court and it is good practice to send a copy to the appellant or
their representative as well.

The Labour Court has an obligation to investigate the dispute. It
will hear the submissions of both sides and will usually also carry out
a work inspection with all the divisions of the Court present. Again,
both sides should have representation at the work inspection. If there
is job evaluation evidence, it will be heard from the job evaluation
expert. The Labour Court will then issue its determination, which is
legally binding. This is a detailed document setting out the facts of
the case and the reasoning for the determination.

The appeal shall be heard by the Labour Court in private, unless
the Court at the request of one of the parties hears the appeal in
public. The Court may treat part of a hearing as confidential. The
Labour Court may appoint technical assessors and has all the powers
to summons witnesses, documents and to hear evidence on oath.

The Labour Court may provide for any redress, which the Director
of Equality Investigations could order by substituting the Labour
Court for the Director. Hence, in addition to the redress as set out
above, the Labour Court can award compensation in the form of arrears of remuneration (attributable to a failure to pay equal pay) in
respect of so much of a period of employment as begins not more than
three years before the date of referral of the claim and an order for
equal pay to the date of the award.

If the Labour Court investigation is in respect of a preliminary issue and is in favour of the claimant, the case shall be referred back to
the Director for investigation of the substantive issue.

If, on appeal, the Labour Court considers that the Director's decision should be set aside, it may by its determination refer the matter
back to the Director for a new investigation and decision.

The Minister for Justice, Equality and Law Reform may bring in procedures as may be agreed with the Minister for Enterprise, Trade and Employment in respect of procedures to be followed by the Labour Court in respect of appeals and time limits.

Interest

If the grounds for the reference of the claim specifically refer to equality between men and women and in any other circumstances to which the Equal Pay and the Equal Treatment Directive are relevant (to include victimisation), then in addition to making an order for compensation, the Director of the Labour Court may also order the payment of interest under section 22(1) of the Courts Act, 1981:

1. In respect of the whole or any amount of the compensation, and

2. In respect of the period beginning on the relevant date and ending on the date of payment.

The "relevant date" means the first day to which the compensation is payable or, if there is no such reference, the date of the referral of the claim.

DECISIONS AND DETERMINATIONS

All decisions and determinations shall be in writing and include the reasons for the decision or determination of the Director or the Labour Court, as the case may be. Any mistake or omission may be rectified by the Director or Chairman of the Labour Court. A copy of each decision of the Director or determination of the Labour Court shall be given to the parties; each Director's decision shall be given also to the Labour Court. Every decision shall be published and available for inspection. Any of these documents that are made available shall be protected by absolute privilege (s. 88 and 89).

APPEALS FROM LABOUR COURT TO CIRCUIT COURT AND HIGH COURT

A Labour Court determination may be appealed to the Circuit Court within 42 days (or for such longer period as the Circuit Court may allow) from the date of the determination. The Circuit Court will hear the appeal and award redress. The Circuit Court decision is final subject to any appeal to the High Court on a point of law.

A determination of the Labour Court may be appealed to the High Court on a point of law. The Labour Court may also refer a point of law arising during an investigation or an appeal.

ENFORCEMENT BY THE CIRCUIT COURT

If a person fails to comply with a decision of the Director or a determination of the Labour Court then on application the Circuit Court may make an order directing the person to carry out the decision or determination (s. 91).

If a claim is settled at mediation and if the settlement is not carried out, then the Circuit Court may direct that the terms of the settlement be carried out. It should be noted that this only refers to a settlement effected through mediation, the terms of which must comply with redress under the Act.

Application may only be made to the Circuit Court following the expiry of the appeal period, 42 days after the date of the written record of the settlement. Application may be made by the complainant themselves or by the Authority (where the decision, determination or settlement will not be implemented without its intervention). Awards may be made for costs in favour of the complainant. The Circuit Court may also award interest on compensation effective from 42 days after the decision or determination or whenever the compensation was due to be paid, if later. Where reinstatement or re-engagement was awarded, the Circuit Court may order compensation in respect of the failure of the employer to comply with the determination.

Where there is an order for reinstatement or re-engagement, the Circuit Court may make an order for compensation instead, the maximum amount being 104 weeks' remuneration at the date of the reference of the case or what the complainant would have received but for the discrimination.

REFERENCES TO THE CIRCUIT COURT

If the grounds for the reference of the claim specifically refer to equality between men and women, and in any other circumstances to which the Equal Pay and the Equal Treatment Directive are relevant (to include victimisation), the claim may be brought directly to the Circuit Court. It is extremely important to note that, in particular, equal pay awards may amount to six years' arrears. The order for compensation for equal treatment refers to the effect of discrimination going back six years prior to the referral of the claim. There is no limit to the amount that can be awarded, except for a six-year limit on the backdating of the compensation. The reason for this unlimited monetary jurisdiction is to comply with the ECJ judgement in *Marshall* v *Southampton and South-West Area Health Authority* (No. 2) ([1993] IRLR), where it was held that it was contrary to the EC Equal Treatment Directive for national legislation to lay down an upper limit on the amount of compensation recoverable by a person who has been discriminated against. It might be further noted that the reason for the direct reference of sex discrimination claims to the Circuit Court was to avoid any constitutional difficulty arising from the Labour Court having unlimited jurisdiction, it not being a "court" under the Constitution of Ireland. Further, the jurisdictional limit of the Circuit Court (presently £30,000) does not apply.

The Circuit Court may request the Director of Equality Investigations to nominate an equality officer to investigate and prepare a report on any question specified by the Court. Such report shall be furnished to the claimant and the respondent and to any other relevant person; the report shall be received in evidence in such proceedings and the equality officer may be called as a witness by the Court, the claimant or the respondent.

Redress

The Circuit Court may award:

1. An order for compensation in the forms of arrears of remuneration (due to a failure to provide equal pay) in respect of so much of the period of employment as begins not more than six years prior to the date of referral;

2. An order for equal pay from the date of the referral;

3. An order for compensation for the effects of acts of discrimination or victimisation which occurred not earlier than six years before the date of referral of the case;

4. An order for equal treatment in whatever respect is relevant to the case;

5. An order that a person or persons specified in the order take a specified course of action;

6. An order for reinstatement or re-engagement with or without an order for compensation.

ALTERNATIVE AVENUES OF REDRESS

If an individual has commenced proceedings at common law in respect of a breach of an equal remuneration or equality clause and if the hearing of the case has begun, then they may not seek redress under the Employment Equality Act, 1998. Equally, if an individual has referred a claim under the Act and has reached a settlement through mediation or the Director has begun an investigation, they shall not be entitled to damages at common law. If an individual has referred a claim to the Circuit Court under the 1998 Act (i.e. in respect of equality between men and women), then they shall not be entitled to recover damages at common law.

An employee who has been dismissed shall not be entitled to seek redress under the Employment Equality Act, 1998, if they have instituted proceedings at common law for wrongful dismissal and the hearing has begun; or a rights commissioner has issued a recommendation under the Unfair Dismissals Acts, 1977–1993; or the Employment Appeals Tribunal has begun a hearing of the matter of the dismissal.

If the employee has referred a case concerning dismissal under this Act to the Labour Court and either a settlement has been reached or if the Court has begun an investigation, then the employee will not be entitled to recover damages for wrongful dismissal or to seek redress under the Unfair Dismissals Acts, 1977–1993. The Labour Court investigation shall not refer to a situation where there was mediation and it was not further pursued (s. 101).

STRIKING OUT OF CASES

If a case is referred to the Director and if the complainant is not pursuing the reference after the expiry of one year, then the Director may strike the reference. Equally, if there is a reference or an appeal to the Labour Court and if the matter is not being pursued after the expiry of one year, the Labour Court may strike out the reference or the appeal. The Director or the Labour Court shall inform the parties. Where a reference or an appeal is struck out, no further proceedings may be taken in relation to that reference or appeal, but there is nothing preventing a new reference to the same matters as long as there are no problems with time limits (s. 102).

OFFENCES

The dismissal of an employee in circumstances amounting to victimisation is an offence. If an employer is convicted of such an offence, the Court may, if it thinks fit and considers that the Labour Court would have power to do so, make an order for reinstatement or re-engagement or, in addition to imposing a fine for an offence, the employer may be ordered to pay compensation. The court will obviously hear any evidence and have the consent of the employee before it exercises its powers. The amount of compensation awarded shall not exceed either 104 weeks' remuneration, or, if the order is made by the District Court, £5,000 (or the limit of the District Court). The employer may appeal such an order to the Circuit or High Court, as appropriate. The employee concerned shall have the right to appeal limited to the amount of the compensation to the Circuit Court or the High Court, and such court's decision shall be final.

Any person who obstructs or impedes the Labour Court, the Director or an equality officer in the exercise of their powers or fails to comply with a requirement shall be guilty of an offence.

A person guilty of an offence under this Act on summary conviction (tried by a judge alone) shall be liable to a fine up to £1,500 or to imprisonment of a term of up to one year or both. On conviction on indictment (tried by a jury, directed by a judge on matters of law) they are liable to a fine not exceeding £25,000 or to imprisonment for a term up to two years or both. If the offence is continued after conviction, the person shall be guilty of a further offence for every day the offence continues and shall be liable on summary conviction to a fine not exceeding £250 and on conviction on indictment to a fine not exceeding £1,500. Summary proceedings may be instituted within 12 months from the date of the offence. Where the offence is committed

by a body corporate, any director, manager, secretary or similar officer shall be guilty of the offence and liable to be proceeded against.

CLAIMS UNDER THE ANTI-DISCRIMINATION (PAY) ACT, 1974 AND THE EMPLOYMENT EQUALITY ACT, 1977

At the time of going to press, as both the 1974 and 1977 Acts were
still in operation, the procedures under these Acts will only be briefly
considered. It should be noted that such legislation deals with sex
discrimination in respect of equal pay and sex discrimination and
discrimination based on marital status for equal treatment.

EQUAL PAY CLAIM

Dispute

The Anti-Discrimination (Pay) Act, 1974, provides that an equal pay
"dispute" between an employer and an employee may be referred to
an equality officer. The term "dispute" is not defined in the Act but it
may be considered broadly to be where an employee claims to be doing "like work" as specified by a certain section and subsection of the
Act — for example, Sections 3(a), (b) and/or (c) — with a named comparator in the same place, and the employer then rejects the claim.

The Employment Equality Agency (EEA) can also refer a pay issue to an equality officer where it feels "that an employer has failed
to comply with an equal pay clause" even though technically no dispute has arisen, or where it is not feasible for an employee to bring
such an action.

Evidence

An equality officer who considers that they are not getting all the
evidence that they require has the right of entry on to the employer's
premises to inspect employer records and to inspect work-in-progress.
Any person who obstructs or impedes an equality officer may commit
an offence and be liable to a fine of £100 on summary conviction or on
conviction on indictment to a fine of £1,000.

Prior to the hearing, the equality officer normally requests either
party to complete a document detailing the work done by both the
claimant and comparator. This completed document will be used as a
basis for the subsequent work inspection.

Costs and Legal Aid

An equality officer cannot award costs to either party and there is no provision for legal aid. However, the EEA may assist individuals who are bringing a claim where there is a point of principle involved and it is not reasonable for the claimants(s) to bring their own claim.

In many equal pay claims, the claimant(s) is represented by their trade union and thus would have no costs, as they would be incorporated in the trade union subscription. Employers in equal pay claims are usually represented by their employer organisation, so again these costs would be associated with membership.

In equal treatment claims, the representation is wider and many claimants and employers use legal representation and would thus have to carry their own costs.

Award of Equal Pay

Equal pay may be awarded retrospectively, that is, for up to three years prior to the date of reference of the dispute to the equality officer for investigation, or for such period as the claimant was performing "like work" with the comparator, if shorter. Equal pay is the difference between the claimant's rate of pay and that of the comparator.

The equality officer's recommendation is not legally binding, however. For example, if an award is being made in favour of a claimant and it is not implemented, the claimant should refer the matter to the Labour Court for a determination within the six-week appeal period. If the employer does not pay during the six-week appeal period and the employee fails to apply for implementation, however, the employee is entitled to nothing.

If there is a reference to the Labour Court under the 1974 Act to implement a recommendation, all references to the 1977 Act should be deleted. This must be delivered to the Chairperson of the Labour Court within six weeks of the date of the recommendation.

APPEAL OF EQUAL PAY RECOMMENDATION

An equal pay recommendation may be appealed to the Labour Court within six weeks of the date of the equality officer's recommendation. This time limit is very strict. The appellant must list the grounds for appeal.

Answer to an Appeal

On receiving a Notice of Appeal, the other side (usually called the respondent) should give the grounds for its rejection of the appeal.

Complaint of Non-implementation of a Labour Court Determination

An employee alleging that a Labour Court determination has not been implemented should refer the matter to the Chairperson of the Labour Court.

Answer to Complaint of Non-implementation of a Labour Court Determination

The employer may respond to a complaint of non-implementation by completing the appropriate form, deleting the references to the 1977 Act.

The Labour Court will consider the complaint and hear all the relevant parties. If the Court considers that the claim is well founded, it will issue an order that the determination is to be implemented. The determination must then be implemented by the employer within two months of the date of the order, or the employer will be guilty of an offence and shall be liable to a fine not exceeding £100, and, if the offence continues, a fine of £10 per day as long as the determination is not implemented. The court that hears the offence (e.g. the District Court) may impose on the employer a fine in the amount that is owed to the employee under the Labour Court determination. The employee may appeal the amount awarded to them to the court of appropriate jurisdiction (i.e. District Court up to £5,000; Circuit Court up to £30,000; and the High Court for greater amounts). It should be stressed that such a set of circumstances would be very unusual.

Appeal of Equal Pay Determination to High Court

Either party may appeal the determination to the High Court, though only on a point of law. It is effected by way of a Special Summons, which must be issued within six weeks of the date of receipt of the determination. There are provisions for an application to be made to the High Court for an extension of time for the issuing of the special summons, but such application must be made within six weeks of the receipt of the determination. The High Court judgment may be appealed to the Supreme Court on a point of law. If there are matters of EU law, the High Court may refer the legal issues for judgment to the European Court of Justice.

Judicial Review

If a party feels that they have not received a fair hearing, they may refer the Labour Court determination to the High Court for judicial review. This is a discretionary remedy on the part of the High Court and, unless there is a very good case, such a path is not recommended. If the High Court considers that there is a case for the Labour Court to answer, the determination will be quashed and referred back to another division of the Labour Court for a complete rehearing, or in some cases back to the equality officer.

EQUAL TREATMENT CLAIMS

An employee or a potential employee who considers that there is a dispute under the Employment Equality Act, 1977, should send the Section 28 form (Employment Equality Act, 1977 (Section 28) Regulations, 1977 — SI No. 344 of 1977) to the employer. The purpose of this form/questionnaire is for the prospective claimant (or their representative) to outline the grounds of the alleged discrimination and ask the employer to respond. The employer must respond within 21 days of the service of the form. If the prospective claimant is still dissatisfied with the information provided by the employer, the matter can then be referred to the Labour Court, outlining the alleged grounds of discrimination.

The Labour Court may refer a claim to an industrial relations officer or, more likely, to an equality officer for investigation.

Prospective claimants are advised to bring claims on the basis that they were discriminated against both directly and indirectly.

Time Limits

The issue of time limits is particularly important in this legislation, and all prospective claimants should be aware of Section 19(5), which provides:

> Save only where reasonable cause can be shown . . . a reference
> under this Section shall be lodged not later than six months from
> the date of the first occurrence of the act alleged to constitute dis-
> crimination.

An example of a case where the employees were not able to bring a
claim because of the time limit was *Braun Ireland Ltd.* v *Six Female
Employees* (DEE 8/1992), which concerned an allegation by the employees that they had been treated less favourably than male employees under the company's job evaluation scheme. The issue to be
considered was whether or not the incidents described by the claimants constituted the "first occurrence" of that act of discrimination.
The Labour Court determined that the claim was out of time and that
there was no reasonable cause for the delay, even though the union
had attempted to resolve matters by direct negotiation.

Equality Officer

Claims under the Employment Equality Act, 1977, are heard in exactly the same way by equality officers as under the 1974 Act, except
that it is less likely that they will do a work inspection. Normally
these matters are dealt with by submissions from both parties and
two to three hearings in order to hear all the evidence.

An equality officer's recommendation under this Act has exactly
the same status as under the 1974 Act and the same forms are used
in order to refer the matter to the Labour Court for implementation.

Appeal to Labour Court

The procedure for appealing and implementing the recommendation
to the Labour Court is exactly the same as under the 1974 Act.

The Labour Court may:

1. Hold that there was or was not discrimination;

2. Recommend a specified course of action;

3. Award compensation up to a maximum of 104 weeks' remunera-
    tion;

4. Hold that a person did or did not procure or attempt to procure
    discrimination or that a publication was or was not discrimina-
    tory.

Answer to an Appeal

The respondent may answer the appeal (i.e., put in grounds of defence) where, for example, the claimant has been awarded compensation but is appealing the recommendation because the award is too low. Thus, the employer may state that they are prepared so to pay the award.

Complaint of Non-implementation of a Labour Court Determination

There is exactly the same procedure as under the 1974 Act, though of course all references should be made to the 1977 Act. Arrears of pay are not appropriate to this Act, but there may be reference to a high award that the employer will not pay or, where the Labour Court has determined, a specified course of action which has not been implemented.

Answer to a Complaint of Non-implementation of a Labour Court Determination

Again, the legal procedure and consequence of not implementing a determination is the same as under the 1977 Act. The employer should complete the form and delete references to the 1974 Act.

Appeal to High Court and Judicial Review

This is exactly the same as under the 1974 Act.

DISMISSAL AND EQUALITY

All discriminatory dismissals must be referred directly to the Labour Court. Dismissals fall into two categories, namely, a straightforward discriminatory dismissal (e.g. unfair selection for redundancy simply because an employee is a woman); or victimisation or retaliatory dismissals.

Complaint concerning Victimisation or Retaliatory Dismissals

Victimisation or retaliatory dismissals shall be considered first. The same form is used for such claims under both the equal pay and equal treatment legislation. Again, it should be noted that the six-month time limit applies unless reasonable cause can be shown.

This form should then be sent to the Chairperson of the Labour Court.

Answer to Complaint concerning Victimisation or Retaliatory Dismissals

The employer should respond to the Chairperson of the Labour Court and send a copy to the claimant employee. The key issues are the employer's defence(s), e.g.:

1. The claimant has brought their claim outside the six-month time limit and no reasonable cause has been shown.

2. The claimant was not dismissed for discriminatory reasons; it was because of their conduct.

The following redress may be awarded: (a) reinstatement; or (b) re-engagement; or (c) compensation up to a maximum of 104 weeks' remuneration. The European Court of Justice judgement in *Marshall* v *Southampton and South-West Area Health Authority (No. 2)* ([1993] IRLR 445) may have an effect on this ceiling of 104 weeks' remuneration. The key principle in this case is that it is contrary to the EC Equal Treatment Directive for national legislation to lay down an upper limit on the amount of compensation recoverable by a victim in respect of loss and damage sustained (see "Employment Equality Act, 1998" below for significant changes on redress for gender claims).

A claimant cannot be in receipt of an award under these Acts as well as under the Unfair Dismissals Acts, 1977 to 1993.

Appeals

The Labour Court determination may be appealed to the High Court on a point of law. The same time limit as above applies. In cases of retaliatory dismissal, an employer may appeal the Labour Court determination to the Circuit Court in respect of an award of compensation. In the case of *Dornan Research Ltd.* v *The Labour Court and Others* ([1998] ELR 256), the High Court did not accept this limited form of appeal to be unconstitutional (see appeal provisions of Employment Equality Act, 1998, below).

Criminal Offences

An employer may be guilty of an offence if there is retaliatory dismissal of an employee for attempting to enforce their rights under the equality legislation. The employer in such instance will be liable on summary conviction to a fine not exceeding £1,000.

If the Labour Court makes an order in relation to either retaliatory or discriminatory dismissal and the employer fails to carry it out, the employer is guilty of an offence. If an order of the Labour Court (or other Court on appeal) has not been carried out within two months of the date of the order, the employer is liable on summary conviction to a maximum fine of £100 and, where there is a continuing offence, there can be a fine of up to £10 per day. Such a prosecution would be in the District Court.

The claimant may appeal the fine imposed by the District Court either to the Circuit Court or to the High Court (depending upon jurisdiction — see above). Such an appeal is final and is limited to:

1. The amount of damages awarded by the District Court when an employer is convicted of having failed to implement a Labour Court order relating to a discriminatory dismissal within the two-month period;

2. The amount of an additional fine imposed by the District Court where an employer is convicted of having failed to implement a Labour Court order relating to a retaliatory dismissal within the same two-month period.

It has to be generally stated that proceedings under these sections of the equality legislation are extremely rare.

PENSIONS AND EQUALITY

The Pensions Acts, 1990 and 1996, provides for equal treatment between men and women in occupational pension schemes (see Chapter 14, "Pensions"). Prior to the operation of this Act, all claims in respect of pension schemes were referred under the Anti-Discrimination (Pay) Act, 1974, or the Employment Equality Act, 1977. The procedures in respect of these disputes are now more complicated. The Pensions Board has a role in the resolution of disputes connected with equal treatment in pension schemes, yet there appears to be nothing prohibiting a person bringing a claim under the 1974 or 1977 Acts (as an employee) and under the 1990 Act (as a scheme member), as the 1974 and 1977 legislation has not been amended (see Lynch and Kelly, pp. 25–60).

Any person — namely, the trustees, a member or a prospective member of a pension scheme, or the Employment Equality Agency — may refer a dispute to the Pensions Board concerning, inter alia, whether the terms of the scheme comply with the equal treatment provisions. The Board considers the matter and issues a written determination, which may be appealed to the High Court on a point of law.

The 1990 Act provides that an employee or the Employment Equality Agency may refer a dispute to an equality officer who issues a recommendation, which may be appealed to the Labour Court. That determination may only be appealed to the High Court on a point of law. There are also similar procedures, as under the 1974 and 1977 Acts, for implementation of Labour Court determinations.

General References

Lynch, C. and R. Kelly (1990), *Pensions Act: Irish Law Statutes Annotated, 1989–1990*, Dublin: Sweet and Maxwell.

Second Commission on the Status of Women (1993), *Report to Government*, Dublin: Stationery Office, January.

Chapter Twenty-five

THE EMPLOYMENT EQUALITY AGENCY AND THE EQUALITY AUTHORITY

The Employment Equality Act, 1977, states that the Employment Equality Agency (EEA) has the general function of promoting equality of opportunity between men and women in relation to employment, and overseeing the operation of the equality legislation, namely the 1974 and the 1977 Acts.

The Employment Equality Act, 1998 (section 38), provides for the continuation of the Employment Equality Agency, as the Equality Authority. The Minister for Justice, Equality and Law Reform has appointed the new Equality Authority on a designate basis, pending the commencement of the 1998 Act. The designate Authority is charged with making all necessary preparations so that it can discharge its statutory functions on implementation day. The persons appointed to the new Authority reflect expertise in the new grounds of discrimination. Hence, when the necessary Commencement Order(s) are passed, all corporate responsibilities held by the Employment Equality Agency will be transferred to the new Authority. This will extend the general function of the new Authority to promoting the elimination of all nine grounds of discrimination, (gender, marital status, family status, sexual orientation, religion, age, disability, race and membership of the travelling community). The term of office of the Chairman and the Board of the EEA will terminate on that day. In this chapter, the provisions of the 1998 Act shall be considered side by side with the current legislation.

FUNCTIONS OF EQUALITY AUTHORITY

The functions of the new Authority are to:

1. Work towards the elimination of discrimination in relation to
   employment;

2. Promote equality of opportunity in respect of all areas to which
   the Act applies;

3. Provide information to the public on and keep under review the
   operation of the 1998 Act, the Maternity Protection Act, 1994, the
   Adoptive Leave Act, 1995, and the Parental Leave Act, 1998, and
   to make proposals to the Minister for the amending of any of
   these Acts;

4. Keep under review the working of the Pensions Acts, 1990–1996,
   as regards the principle of equal treatment and, whenever it
   thinks necessary, make proposals to the Minister for Social,
   Community and Family Affairs for amending that Act.

The 1998 Act also makes provision for the preparation and submission to the Minister for approval of a strategic plan which shall:

1. Comprise the key objectives, outputs and related strategies, including use of resources of the Authority;

2. Be prepared in a form and manner in accordance with any directions issued from time to time by the Minister; and

3. Have regard to the need to ensure the most beneficial, effective
   and efficient use of the resources of the Authority.

This plan should be prepared as soon as practicable after the coming
into operation of the new Authority and after that within six months
before each third anniversary of the coming into operation of the
Authority. Each plan shall be for the following three-year period. The
Minister shall approve the plan (with or without amendment) and
shall as soon as possible after approval have a copy of the plan laid
before each House of the Oireachtas.

MEMBERSHIP OF THE EEA

The Board of the EEA currently consists of a chairperson and ten
members who represent trade unions, employers' organisations,
women's organisations and other interested parties. All are appointed
by the Minister for Justice, Equality and Law Reform and are volun-

tary appointments. There is a full-time executive staff headed by a chief executive. Most of the staff are drawn from the public service, usually from the Department of Enterprise, Trade and Employment. The Agency has an annual allocation of funds from the Department of Justice, Equality and Law Reform.

MEMBERSHIP OF THE EQUALITY AUTHORITY

As stated above, presently there is an Equality Authority designate, pending the commencement date of the Act. However, it is still named the Employment Equality Authority.

Under the 1998 Act, the membership of the new Authority shall include a chairperson who shall be appointed either in a whole-time or part-time capacity and shall hold office for not more than four years on such terms and conditions as the Minister for Justice, Equality and Law Reform may determine. The Chairperson shall be paid such remuneration, allowances and expenses as may be determined. The Chairperson may resign at any time by letter addressed to the Minister. Equally, the Minister may at any time for stated reasons remove the Chairperson from office.

The Minister shall appoint one of the ordinary members to be a Vice-Chairperson of the Authority with the function of acting as Chairperson in the absence of the Chairperson and the Vice-Chairperson shall receive such remuneration and expenses as appropriate.

The membership of the new Authority shall consist of 12 members appointed by the Minister (one of whom shall be appointed the Chairperson), of whom at least five shall be male and five shall be female. However, in the first four years of the appointment of the Authority, of the 12, half shall be male and half shall be female. The Authority may act notwithstanding any vacancy or vacancies among members. A person who is a member of the Authority shall cease to be a member if they are nominated as a member of Seanad Éireann, elected as a member of either House of the Oireachtas or to the European Parliament. Further, any person shall cease office if they are adjudged bankrupt or make a composition arrangement with creditors, or on conviction on indictment by a court of competent jurisdiction and are sentenced to imprisonment or if they cease to be ordinarily resident in the State.

The composition of the new Authority shall be as follows:

1. One male and one female shall be persons appointed on the nomination by organisations representative of employees;

2. One male and one female shall be persons appointed on the nomination by organisations representative of employers; and

3. The remaining number shall be such persons as appear to the Minister to be persons who have knowledge of, or experience in:

    a) Consumer, social affairs or equality issues, including issues related to the experiences or circumstances of groups who are disadvantaged by reference to gender, marital status, family status, sexual orientation, religion, age, disability, race, colour, nationality, ethnic or national origin or membership of the travelling community;

    b) Issues related to the provision of goods or services;

    c) Such other subject matter (including law, finance, management or administration) as appears to the Minister to be relevant to the functions of the Authority.

Each ordinary member of the Authority shall be a part-time member; shall hold office for not more than four years; and shall be paid such expenses as appropriate. The Minister may at any time for stated reasons remove a member from office and, equally, a member may resign from office by way of letter addressed to the Minister. Where casual vacancy occurs among any member of the Authority nominated by either employee or employer organisations, the Minister shall invite the organisation to nominate a person (of the same sex as the former member) for appointment to fill the vacancy and then the Minister shall appoint the said nominee. Such a person shall hold office for the unexpired period of office of the person whom they are replacing.

The Chairperson and any ordinary member of the Authority whose term of office expires by the passage of time shall be eligible for re-appointment as the Chairperson or as an ordinary member.

The reference to persons having experience in the provision of goods or services specifically relates to the proposed equal status legislation which, when enacted, will provide for the elimination of discrimination on the same grounds in respect of the provision of goods and services. A new Equal Status Bill, 1999, has been published, as sections of the original Equal Status Bill, 1997, would have been repugnant to the Constitution of Ireland.

The 1998 Act also makes provisions for the holding of meetings by the Authority, and the Minister will fix or sanction the date, time and place of the first meeting of the Authority. Meetings of the Authority shall be held as often as required for the performance of its functions. A quorum for a meeting of the Authority shall be five members and the Chairperson shall take the chair unless absent. In such situations, the Vice-Chairperson shall act as Chairperson.

The 1998 Act also makes provision for advisory committees to advise on various matters.

The Authority shall also have a seal which shall be authenticated by the Chairperson or some other member of the Authority so authorised to act on its behalf. Judicial notice shall be taken of the seal of the Authority and any documents sealed with the seal shall be admissible in evidence.

The Act provides for the appointment of a Chief Executive Officer of the Authority who shall effectively manage the Authority and shall be responsible to the Authority for the performance of its functions and the implementation of Authority policies. The CEO shall be accountable to Dáil Éireann as required. There is also specific provision for the staffing of the Authority.

ANNUAL REPORT

The EEA is obliged to provide an annual report each year on such date as the Minister may direct. Copies of this report shall be laid before each House of the Oireachtas. The annual reports of the EEA have proved very useful over the last number of years. The report not only provides a useful summary of its activities, it also provides very useful legal commentary, summaries of equality officers' recommendations, Labour Court determinations and also summaries of judgments of the European Court of Justice.

Annual Report of New Authority

The new Authority will also provide an annual report to the Minister within six months of the commencement of each calendar year of its activities in the previous calendar year. The report shall provide an account of any equality review made in that previous year, information concerning the implementation of equality action plans and such other information as the Authority thinks fit or the Minister may direct.

ADVICE/ASSISTANCE TO CLAIMANTS

The Agency may provide assistance to a person who considers that there has been a breach of the 1974 and 1977 Acts, but the wording of the 1977 Act limits the assistance that the Agency can offer; it only refers to "assistance" in making a reference to the Labour Court or an equality officer. There is no reference to financial assistance.

Invariably, the Agency's assistance takes the form of advice prior to the reference of the claim; if a claim is brought, then assistance would include the drafting of submissions and subsequent representation before equality officers and the Labour Court. For many years, the Agency has had legally qualified staff who represent claimants before equality officers and the Labour Court. However, the Agency must be satisfied that the proposed claim raises an important matter of principle and that the person would not be in a position to represent themselves adequately or, alternatively, that their union would not be in a position to represent them. Typically, such claimants are pursuing alleged discriminatory practices where their trade union may have been a party to an agreement wherein the alleged discriminatory practice arose. Agency representation has been used by claimants in cases concerning the appointment of "twilight" shift workers to full-time positions on foot of a trade union/management agreement, alleged discrimination concerning the non-granting of a union card, in several cases concerning alleged discriminatory interviewing and in cases alleging sexual harassment.

Assistance by the New Authority

The 1998 Act provides that, if a person considers that there has been discrimination against them, the Authority may be requested to provide assistance in taking proceedings and in any proceedings resulting from or arising out of the reference or application where:

1. There has been a failure to comply with an equality clause or an equal remuneration term;

2. There has been a failure to implement a decision, order or determination in respect of a non-discrimination notice, etc., or a me-
   diated settlement, in respect of redress under the Act;

3. An important matter of principle is involved; or

4. It is not reasonable to expect the person making the request to
   present their case without assistance.

Any assistance shall be in such a form as the Authority at its discretion thinks fit. Furthermore, the Authority may delegate its functions
to an officer of the Authority and may specify how the delegated function is to be exercised (e.g. the appointment of lawyers to act in a
case).

CODES OF PRACTICE

The 1977 Act provides that the Agency "may draft and publish, for
the information of employers, guidelines or codes of practice relating
to discrimination in employment".

The Agency issued a Code of Practice in February 1984 in respect
of the Elimination of Discrimination in Employment. The Code is not
legally binding but it is admissible in evidence before the Labour
Court, equality officers and the courts. In practice, the use of the
Code in the hearing of discrimination cases is rare.

In 1993, the Agency published a Model Equal Opportunities Policy
which includes draft management statements for a commitment to
equal opportunities, selection, advertising, application forms, shortlisting for interviews, testing, interviewing, promotion, training,
placement, mobility, work experience, work and family responsibility,
pay and benefit-in-kind, leave and other matters. Incorporated into
this document is a guide to assist in the monitoring of an Equal Opportunities Policy.

A Model Policy has also been published that may be used by employers to recognise that sexual harassment will not be tolerated in
that particular employment. The Model provides a positive statement
that sexual harassment will not be tolerated; definitions of sexual
harassment (defined by the Agency as behaviour that includes "unre-
ciprocated and unwelcome comments, looks, jokes, suggestions or
physical contact which might threaten a person's job security or cre-

ate a stressful or intimidating working environment"), an outline of the responsibility of management and staff, and procedures should an employee consider that they have such a grievance.

Future Codes of Practice

The 1998 Act provides for further provisions in respect of Codes of Practice that may be prepared and submitted to the Minister in respect of the elimination of discrimination in employment and promotion of equality of opportunity in employment. The Equality Authority must submit any draft Code to all appropriate Ministers of Government. Furthermore, the Minister may declare, by Order, that the draft Code of Practice is an approved Code of Practice.

An approved Code of Practice shall be admissible in evidence and if any provision of a Code appears to be relevant to any question arising in any criminal or other proceedings, it should be taken into account in determining that question. Proceedings under this Act include any proceedings before a court, the Labour Court, the Labour Relations Commission, the Employment Appeals Tribunal, the Director of Equality Investigations and Rights Commissioners. Furthermore, every Order shall be laid before each House of the Oireachtas as soon as practicable after it is made. A resolution may be passed annulling the order within 21 days.

REVIEW OF THE LEGISLATION

The Agency may carry out a review of existing legislation if it considers that it is impeding the elimination of discrimination. However, the Minister must give it permission to do so. Over the years, the Agency has reviewed the 1974 and 1977 Acts, and has made detailed recommendations for their amendment. It has also submitted its views to the Pensions Board on the appropriate manner of implementation of EC Directive 86/378 on equal treatment in occupational benefit schemes.

Further Review of Legislation

The Equality Authority is charged with a review of legislation where it considers that there may be an impediment to the elimination of discrimination. The pieces of legislation and the relevant grounds of discrimination are as follows:

- *Marital status*: Maternity Protection Act, 1994, and the Adoptive Leave Act, 1995;

- *Race*: Solicitors Act, 1954 (s. 40(3) — Irish Language examination), and Finance Act, 1987 (s. 35 — relief for investment in films);

- *Age or disability*: the stated sections of the Air Navigation and Transport Act, 1946, the Merchant Shipping Act, 1947, the Transport (Miscellaneous) Provisions Act, 1971, the Merchant Shipping (Certification of Seamen) Act, 1979, or the Irish Aviation Authority Act, 1993;

- Age: Redundancy Payments Acts, 1967–1991.

Obviously, in relation to carrying out such review, the Authority shall consult such organisations of both employees (trades unions) and employers as it considers appropriate. The Authority may send a report to the Minister and the report shall include a recommendation amending any of the enactments.

RESEARCH AND INFORMATION

The EEA may undertake research and other activities relating to the dissemination of information. To date it has commissioned research on women working in the electronics sector, and has produced a video mainly directed at schoolgirls. A major report on women in the labour force was produced in June 1989. The Agency has clearly been hampered by the lack of necessary financial resources.

The Agency also publishes a quarterly newsletter, *Equality News*, which provides considerable information on recent case law and other useful information. The Agency has advanced public awareness of equality issues through regular press releases and considerable coverage in the media.

There is a similar provision in the 1998 Act.

INVESTIGATIONS AND INQUIRIES

The Agency has power to conduct investigations which may be either requested by the Minister for Justice, Equality and Law Reform or be carried out with the Minister's approval. In summary, an investigation may only be carried out if the Agency or the Minister considers that there has been discrimination in the employment concerned, or that there has been discriminatory advertising or an attempt to procure discrimination.

The Agency has certain statutory powers to obtain information and documents and to summon witnesses. A person who does not comply with such a request shall be guilty of an offence and liable to a fine.

When an investigation has been completed, the Agency prepares a report and makes recommendations. If the Agency is satisfied that there has been discrimination in the employment, it may serve a non-discrimination notice on the employer or other persons in question. The non-discrimination notice must detail the alleged discriminatory practice. The Act provides for time limits, etc., for response to such notices and also for an appeal to the Labour Court against them. If the notice has not been appealed, its contents will come into effect (discontinuation of the discriminatory practice, for example). The Labour Court has power to hear the views of both sides on the appeal.

It should be noted that these investigations are very rare, and they have only been carried out in three large employments to date.

The Agency can request the High Court to grant an injunction against such a discriminatory practice if the Agency considers that, within five years of the operation of the non-discriminatory notice, there is a likelihood of the discriminatory practice recurring.

Inquiries

The Employment Equality Act, 1998 provides that the Authority may conduct an Inquiry and shall do so where required by the Minister. An Inquiry may be conducted:

1. By a member of the Authority; and/or

2. By a member of its staff as may be delegated by the Authority; and/or

3. By a person duly employed as may be delegated by the Authority.

Any person carrying out the Inquiry shall, for the purposes of the Inquiry, have all the functions of the Authority. The Authority may with the approval of the Minister employ one or more persons having qualifications that, in the opinion of the Authority, are relevant to the conduct of the Inquiry.

The Authority shall not conduct an Inquiry until the terms of reference for the Inquiry have been drawn up. If the Inquiry is one which the Minister has required, then the Minister may draft the terms of reference after consultation with the Authority. The notice of intention to conduct the Inquiry may be given by the Authority by publication in at least one daily newspaper circulating generally in the State or, where the terms of reference refer to a specified person, by providing the person with a copy of the notice in writing (Section 58).

The Authority may, for the purposes of an Inquiry, do all or any of the following:

1. Require any person, by notice delivered to that person, to supply the Authority with such information as it specifies and requires for the Inquiry.

2. Require any person, by notice delivered to that person, to produce to the Authority or to send the Authority any document specified in the notice which is in that person's power or control.

3. Summon witnesses, by notice delivered to them, to attend before the Authority.

4. Administer oaths and affirmations to witnesses and examine witnesses attending before the Authority.

Any notice must be delivered personally or by registered post and should be signed by at least one member of the Authority. No notice shall be delivered unless the Authority has obtain the consent of the Minister, or the Authority believes that a person named in the terms of reference to which the Inquiry relates has discriminated or is discriminating, has contravened or is contravening section 8(4) (an employer who has rules or instructions in employment which could result in discrimination against an employee or a class of employees or operate a practice which results or would be likely to result in any such discrimination in relation to all conditions of employment); section 10 (advertising that relates to employment showing an intention to discriminate or reasonably be understood to be an intention to discriminate); or section 14 (a person who procures or attempts to procure another person to do anything which constitutes discrimination or victimisation); or has failed or is failing to comply with an equality clause or an equal remuneration term. The Authority may pay any subsistence or travelling expenses to any witness.

If a person is summonsed and fails to attend; or fails to bring the required documents; or attends and does not take the oath or affirmation; or refuses to answer any question; or does anything where if the Authority were a court of justice (having power to commit for contempt) constituted contempt; then that person shall be guilty of an offence.

Furthermore, any person to whom a notice has been delivered and who makes a false statement when supplying information to the Authority or alters, suppresses, conceals or destroys a document specified in the notice, shall be guilty of an offence.

After it has conducted an Inquiry, the Authority may make to any person, including the Minister, recommendations arising out of the Inquiry for the purpose of promoting the elimination of discrimination in relation to employment and the promotion of equality of opportunity in relation to matters to which the Act applies. The Authority shall prepare a report of the Inquiry which shall contain any findings. If the Minister requested the Inquiry, the report should be sent to the Minister as soon as practicable after its preparation. Furthermore, the report shall be available to the public. Confidential information which is not available to the public in respect of any organisation, person or the business they carry on shall not be included in the report without the consent of such person or organisation, unless the non-inclusion would be inconsistent with the duties of the Authority and the object of the report.

If the Authority is satisfied that, during the conduct of an Inquiry or after such Inquiry has been completed, any person has:

1. Discriminated or is discriminating;

2. Discriminatory conditions of employment, discriminatory advertising or is procuring discrimination or victimisation; or

3. Failed or is failing to comply with an equality clause or an equal remuneration term;

then the Authority may serve a non-discrimination notice on that person.

Where the Authority proposes to serve a non-discrimination notice, it shall before the notice is served notify that person in writing of its proposal to do so. Such notification of a proposal to serve a non-discrimination notice shall specify the act or omission constituting the discrimination and inform the person concerned of the right to make representations to the Authority. A person has 28 days to make representations to the Authority and the Authority shall consider such representations before serving a non-discrimination notice.

A non-discrimination notice shall:

1. Specify the act or omission constituting the discrimination;

2. Require the person on whom it is served not to commit the act or omission constituting the discrimination or, where appropriate, to comply with the equality clause or equal remuneration term;

3. Specify what steps the Authority requires to be taken in order not to commit the discrimination;

4. Require the person on whom it is served, within a period specified in the non-discrimination notice, to inform the Authority and any other person so specified of the steps taken in order to comply with the notice; and

5. Require the person on whom it is served, within a specified period, to supply the Authority with any additional information as specified.

A person may appeal a non-discrimination notice to the Labour Court within 42 days of the date of service. Where an appeal is not made, a non-discrimination notice shall come into operation on the expiry of the 42-day period. The Labour Court, on hearing an appeal, may either confirm the notice in whole or in part, with or without amendment, or allow the appeal. Where the Labour Court confirms a non-discriminatory notice, the notice shall come into operation on the date the Court shall fix. Where the Labour Court allows the appeal, the non-discrimination notice appealed against shall cease to have effect.

The Authority shall keep and maintain a register of every non-discrimination notice which has come into operation and the register shall be open to inspection by the public.

The Authority may make application to the Circuit Court or the High Court to grant an injunction to prevent discrimination by a person specified in the order of the Court. This applies to a case where, in a five-year period, commencing on the date on which a non-discrimination notice came into operation, the Authority specifies to the Circuit Court or the High Court that there is a likelihood of a further discrimination, contravention or failure by the person on whom the notice was served. A person on whom a non-discrimination notice is served and who does not comply with the notice shall be guilty of an offence.

ENFORCEMENT POWERS OF THE AUTHORITY

The Authority may refer the following matters to the Director of Equality Investigations under s. 85:

1. Discrimination or victimisation is being practised or there are discriminatory practices;

2. Discrimination or victimisation has occurred in relation to a person and they have not issued proceedings under the Act and are not in a position to do so (e.g. sexual harassment);

3. There is a failure to comply with an equal remuneration or an equality clause either generally in a business or in relation to a particular person who has not issued proceedings and is not in a position to do so;

4. The publication or display of a discriminatory advertisement;

5. Where a person has procured or attempted to procure another person to discriminate or to break an equal remuneration or an equality clause.

In such cases, the name of the complainant will be the Equality Authority. The redress will be for the complainant. The other orders will be a decision as to whether a person has or has not procured or attempted to procure discrimination or that an advertisement was or was not discriminatory. Following a decision of the Director of

Equality Investigations or the Labour Court (as appropriate), the High Court (or the Circuit Court), on the application of the Equality Authority, may grant an injunction to prevent any person from carrying out further discrimination/victimisation, further failure to comply with an equal remuneration or equality clause, the further publication or display of a discriminatory advertisement, or the further procuring of or attempting to procure a person to discriminate.

The Equality Authority may also make reference to the Director of Equality Investigations on behalf of a person who claims that a provision in such agreement is null and void. The Authority is referred to as the complainant in respect of the procedures (see Chapter 24, "Equality Claims").

EQUALITY REVIEWS AND ACTION PLANS

The Employment Equality Act, 1998, provides that the Authority may invite a particular business, group of businesses or the businesses making up a particular industry or sector to do either or both the following:

1. Carry out an equality review in relation to their business or businesses;

2. Prepare and implement an equality action plan in respect of that business or those businesses.

An equality review is defined in the new Act as:

1. An audit of the level of equality of opportunity which exists in employment in a particular business, group of businesses or the businesses making up a particular industry or sector; and

2. An examination of the practices, procedures and other relevant factors (including the work environment) of, in and material to that employment, to determine whether those practices, procedures or other factors are conducive to the promotion of equality of opportunity in that employment.

An equality action plan is a programme of actions to be undertaken in employment in a business or businesses to further the promotion of equality of opportunity in that employment.

The Authority itself may, if it thinks appropriate, carry out an equality review and prepare an equality action plan in relation to any business or group of businesses and may employ appropriate persons to do so. This power does not apply to any business of fewer than 50 employees.

An equality review and an action plan may be directed at the generality of equality of opportunity or at any particular aspect of discrimination in an employment.

A business includes an activity giving rise to employment, whether or not in the industrial or commercial field and whether or not with a view to profit, and a group of businesses may be defined by reference to geographical location, instead of or as well as by reference to control or any other factor.

If appropriate, the Authority may, for the purposes of an equality review or the preparation of an equality action plan, require any person on notice to supply the Authority with such information as is specified in the notice, and/or require any person to produce to the Authority or to send to the Authority any document which the Authority has specified in the notice and is under that person's power or control. However, this shall not entitle the Authority to require the supply of information or the production or sending of a document relating to a business of fewer than 50 employees.

If it appears to the Authority that there is a failure in any business or businesses to implement any provision of an equality action plan, the Authority may require any person by notice to take such action as is specified in the notice and is reasonably required for the implementation of the plan and it is within that person's power to take.

Before serving such a *substantive notice* on any person, the Authority shall give that person notice in writing (i.e. *advance notice*) of a proposal to serve a substantive notice and the proposed contents of that notice. Where a person has received the *advanced notice*, they have 28 days within which to make all necessary representations to the Authority and the Authority shall give consideration to the representations as to whether they shall serve the *substantive notice* on that person.

If a substantive notice has been served on a person, they may appeal such notice to the Labour Court within 42 days of service against the notice or any requirements in that notice. The Labour Court shall hear the appeal and may either confirm the notice in whole or in part or may allow the appeal. Where the Labour Court confirms a substantive notice, it shall come into operation on the date that the Court shall fix. Where the Court allows an appeal, the substantive notice shall cease to have effect.

If a person has failed to comply with a substantive notice, the Authority may make application to the Circuit Court or the High Court to request the Court to make an order directing the person to comply with the notice.

AGENCY MONITORING

The Agency continuously monitors rates of pay and equal treatment in all the industries and also in the public service. It is obviously not feasible to monitor each individual employment relationship.

SECOND COMMISSION ON THE STATUS OF WOMEN

The Commission's *Report to Government* in January 1993 recommended that there be equal status legislation providing for equal treatment between men and women in respect of the provision of goods, facilities and services. As stated above, the Equal Status Bill, 1997, has not been enacted arising from various sections that would be repugnant to the Constitution.

The Commission recommended various matters in respect of discrimination in employment and in the main the Employment Equality Act, 1998, includes such recommendations; for example, the extension of powers of the EEA to cover all equality issues and with wider representation on the Board; wider functions and more resources.

The Commission also recommended that the procedure for the enforcement of rights under the proposed legislation should include an informal conciliation procedure and, if necessary, a hearing before an equality tribunal whose awards would be legally enforceable (see Chapter 24).

General Reference

Second Commission on the Status of Women (1993), *Report to Government*, Dublin: Stationery Office, January.

SUBJECT INDEX

Note: The method of alphabetisation used is word by word.
Statutory forms are listed under "Forms".
Abbreviations: EAT: Employment Appeals Tribunal;
EO: Equality Officer

654 — Working within the Law

The
Broken
Eye

After Strap manacled his hands behind his back, Gavin looked at Captain Gunner, who was standing at the top of the stairs out of the hold. Gunner was Ilytian, with midnight black skin, a wild curly beard, a fine brocaded doublet worn open over his naked torso, loose sailor's pants. He had the handsome intensity of madmen and prophets. He talked to himself. He talked to the sea. He admitted no equal on heaven or earth – and in the firing of guns of any size, he was justified in that. Not long ago, Gunner had been jumping off a ship Gavin had lit on fire and poked full of holes. Gavin had spared Gunner's life on a whim.

The good you do is what kills you.

'Come on up, little Guile,' Captain Gunner said. 'I'm running out of reasons to keep you alive.'